WITHDRAWN

Volcanoes of the Earth

Volcanoes of the Earth

Second Revised Edition

By Fred M. Bullard

University of Texas Press, Austin

The Dan Danciger Publication Series

Revised edition of *Volcanoes: In History, in Theory, in Eruption*
Second revised edition, 1984

Requests for permission to reproduce material from this work should be sent to Permissions, University of Texas Press, Box 7819, Austin, Texas 78712.

LIBRARY OF CONGRESS CATALOGING IN PUBLICATION DATA
Bullard, Fred M. (Fred Mason), 1901–
  Volcanoes of the Earth.
  (The Dan Danciger publication series)
  Bibliography: p.
  Includes index.
  1. Volcanoes. I. Title. II. Series.
QE522.B87 1984   551.2'1   83-21738
ISBN 0-292-78706-5
ISBN 0-292-78707-3 (pbk.)

To Evelyn

Contents

Acknowledgments

The material on which this book is based was assembled from studies carried on in volcanic regions in many parts of the world over several decades. For the opportunity to visit the various volcanic regions, for time from my regular duties to make the investigations and to do the research necessary to assemble this material, I am indebted to many organizations, foundations, and individuals. Space does not permit a complete listing, but I would like to acknowledge to the following my appreciation for material aid in various phases of the work: the Geological Society of America and the Instituto de Geología of the Universidad Nacional Autónoma de México for aid in the study of Parícutin Volcano; the University of Texas Research Institute and the Geology Foundation of the University of Texas for research time, travel funds, and aid in the preparation of the manuscript; the U.S. State Department for two Fulbright grants which enabled me to study the volcanoes of Italy and Peru; the United Fruit Company for assistance in the work in Central America; the Compañía Minera de Guatemala (through Mr. Alan Probert, manager) for aid in the work in Guatemala; the Instituto Tropical de Investigaciones Científicas of the Universidad de El Salvador, and the Servicio Geológico Nacional de El Salvador for assistance in the work in El Salvador; Mr. Donald Spencer and associates of the Compañía Minera La India for help in the work in Nicaragua; and the Instituto Geográfico de Costa Rica for aid in Costa Rica. The Pan American Institute of Geography and History and the Inter-American Geodetic Survey also assisted in the work in all of the Central American countries.

I am also indebted to the National Park Service and the Craters of the Moon Natural History Association for the opportunity to carry on research studies at Craters of the Moon National Monument. Some of the results of this study are included in this second edition of the book.

I particularly indebted to the late Professor Arthur Holmes, University of Edinburgh, Scotland, who read the galley proofs of the first edition and offered many constructive suggestions and helpful criticisms. In addition, I greatly appreciate the many constructive reviews of the first edition which have been most helpful in the preparation of this revision.

To my many friends in each of the countries where I have worked, who contributed generously of their time and provided transportation, guides, and other services, I wish to express my deep appreciation; unfortunately the list is too long to print.

All of the photographs not otherwise credited are my own. Those obtained from other sources are acknowledged in each case, and I want to express my thanks to the individuals who have made such contributions.

I have drawn freely on published material both in the preparation of the text and for illustrations. In each case, however, the source is acknowledged, and I wish to express my thanks for the use of this material. I am particularly grateful to the authors and publishers who have granted me permission to reproduce illustrations and to quote directly from their publications.

I wish, also, to express my thanks to the staff of the University of Texas Press for their exceptional cooperation in all aspects of the production of this book.

Volcanoes of the Earth

Prologue

Volcanoes are unquestionably one of the most spectacular and awe-inspiring features of the physical world, and they have provided humanity with the most exquisite pleasure as well as the most devastating misfortune. The loftiest mountains on the face of the earth, affording majestic scenery enjoyed by millions, are volcanic cones. On the other hand, great volcanic eruptions in historic times have wrought death and destruction to many areas. In ancient times volcanoes were surrounded by mystery and superstition, and even today, notwithstanding the tremendous advances in all sciences, people still ask many unanswered questions about volcanoes. But it is highly probable that when we have learned more about them their terrific power may be harnessed for the benefit of humanity.

This book is an effort to summarize in nontechnical language our present knowledge of volcanoes. Some of the important volcanoes and volcanic regions of the earth are described as examples of the various types of volcanoes. Volcanoes are found in those regions of the earth where mountains are growing. But, since they are but one manifestation of active mountain-building processes, it is understandable that the geologic setting must be presented in the description of a volcanic region.

My own interest in volcanoes began while I was a member of a U.S. Geological Survey expedition to Alaska in 1929. On this trip I first saw an active volcano, and I was tremendously impressed. Only the year before, I had received a Ph.D. degree in geology from the University of Michigan and had taken courses with Professor W. H. Hobbs, a distinguished scholar in the field of volcanoes, earthquakes, and mountain building. Nevertheless, when I actually saw the active volcano I realized that I knew very little about it, notwithstanding my college degrees and the fact that I had been teaching geology in a major university for several years. When I voiced my thoughts to Dr. S. R. Capps, director of our party, he remarked that if I was really interested in volcanoes I should go to Hawaii and work with Dr. Thomas A. Jaggar, director of the Hawaiian Volcano Observatory and a world-famous authority on volcanoes. He further stated that he thought such a program could be arranged. It was arranged. But a severe economic depression (during the mid-thirties) intervened before I was able to go to Hawaii as an assistant to Dr. Jaggar.

There I learned the technique of modern volcanic research and acquired some of Dr. Jaggar's enthusiasm for research on volcanoes. Back in Texas in the early forties I saw little opportunity to apply my newly acquired knowledge, except in so far as it was useful in teaching. However, on February 20, 1943, the situation suddenly changed. On that date a new volcano, Parícutin, was born in Mexico. By a fortunate combination of circumstances I was scheduled to teach a course on the volcanoes of Mexico in the 1943 summer school of the

National University of Mexico. Naturally, I lost no time in visiting Parícutin and adopting it as a laboratory for my classes. Circumstances also worked out so that I spent a part of each year for the next seven years at Parícutin and was thus able to follow from personal observations almost its entire life history. Another milestone in my quest for knowledge of volcanoes was the opportunity to spend a year as a Fulbright scholar studying the classic volcanoes of the Mediterranean area. With headquarters at the University of Naples and the Vesuvian Observatory, I studied Vesuvius, Etna, Stromboli, and other volcanoes in Italy, where the science of volcanology had actually developed. Later I had the opportunity to investigate the volcanoes of Central America, followed by a Fulbright lectureship to teach volcanology at the Universidad Nacional de San Agustín de Arequipa in southern Peru. This opportunity to study the active and recently active volcanoes of the high Andes was a rewarding experience. Continuing my quest for active volcanoes, I visited Iceland, the eastern Mediterranean area, Japan, the Rift Valley of Africa, the Canary Islands and Azores of the mid-Atlantic, the Philippines, South Pacific islands, and New Zealand.

Since the publication of the first edition of this book in 1962, there have been tremendous advances in our knowledge of volcanism, largely as a result of the United States program to land a man on the moon. It had long been known that there were many craters on the moon, but a controversy developed as to whether they were volcanic or due to the impact of meteorites. In an effort to find evidence which might help resolve the controversy, an intensive study was made of many of the earth volcanoes. We now know that both types of craters are present on the moon, but the controversy continues over the assignment of particular craters to the correct type.

The study of volcanoes was long neglected because in Europe, where the science of geology developed, the rocks are mainly sedimentary, and intrusives and volcanism were regarded as superficial phenomena. We now know that almost the entire floor of the ocean is made up of volcanic rocks, and even on land the proportion of volcanic products—basalt plateaus, ash flows, etc.—is far greater than was previously recognized. Further, we now know that gases of volcanic origin play a decisive role in providing the water of the oceans and the gases of the atmosphere, without which our planet would not be habitable. Volcanic activity has taken place to some degree over virtually the entire surface of the earth during the course of its long geologic history. In each geologic age the active volcanoes were associated with the major mountain-making movements, in much the same manner as they are now aligned with the present zones of tectonic unrest.

The advances in recent years in heat flow studies and the development of the concepts of sea-floor spreading and plate tectonics have had a profound effect, not only on volcanology, but on the entire science of geology. An effort is made in this edition to incorporate the new material and the new concepts and to present a view of volcanology consistent with our present state of knowledge.

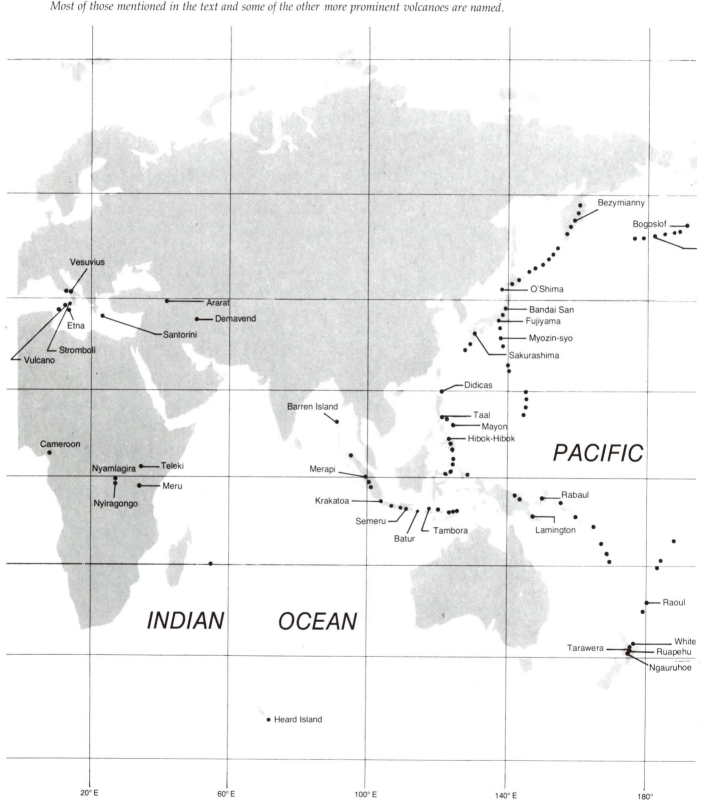

Active volcanoes of the world. It was not possible, because of the scale of the map, to locate all of the active volcanoes. Most of those mentioned in the text and some of the other more prominent volcanoes are named.

Chapter 1   What Is a Volcano?

By turns hot embers from her entrails fly,
And flakes of mountain flame that arch the
sky. —VIRGIL's Aeneid

"What is a volcano?" is a familiar question. An often-given answer is
that "a volcano is a burning mountain from the top of which issue
smoke and fire." Such a statement, although it does express the
popular idea of a volcano, held even today, contains few elements of
truth. In the first place, no "burning" in the sense of combustion,
such as the burning of wood, occurs in a volcano; moreover, volcanoes are not necessarily mountains; furthermore, the activity takes
place not always at the summit but more commonly on the sides or
flanks; and, finally, the "smoke" is not smoke but condensed steam,
mixed, frequently, with dust particles until it is dark in color, and the
"fire" is the reflection of the red-hot material on the vapor clouds
above the volcano.

The great cloud of gases, vapor, and ash particles is the most conspicuous feature of the explosive eruption of a volcano. The eruption
cloud may be luminous or dark, depending on whether the material
is incandescent and whether it contains a small or large amount of
ash particles. The "fiery" and "smoky" appearances, together with
the red glow reflected from the lava in the crater beneath, are responsible for the popular idea that volcanoes are "burning mountains."
Apparently supporting this fallacy, the materials that fall from the
eruption cloud (known to the geologist as *pyroclastics* from the Greek
pyro, meaning "fire," plus *clastic*, meaning "broken") often resemble
ash and cinders, by which names they are still known. Although
there is intense heat in a volcano, actual burning plays only a minor
role in volcanic activity and is confined to almost imperceptible
flames from certain combustible gases, such as hydrogen.

To describe what a volcano is *not* is much easier than to give a con-
cise definition of what it *is*. A volcano is a vent or chimney which connects a reservoir of molten matter known as *magma*, in the depths
of the crust of the earth, with the surface of the earth. The material
ejected through the vent frequently accumulates around the opening, building up a cone, called the *volcanic edifice*. The loftiest mountains on earth are volcanic edifices. The material ejected consists of

liquid lava and broken fragments of partially or completely solidified rock (pyroclastic debris), as well as great quantities of gases. The gases are the motivating force and the most important factor in volcanic action. Some authors have maintained that the only feature common to all volcanoes is the channel through which the molten or gaseous material reaches the surface, and therefore a volcano should be defined as "the vent through which this material is erupted." This, however, leaves us in the difficult position of trying to explain that Vesuvius is not really a volcano but merely a mountain built around one! As now used, the term *volcano* includes both the vent and the accumulation (cone) around it.

Volcanic eruptions vary between two extremes. In one, the lava rises more or less quietly to the surface and overflows the lip of the crater. The gases bubble through the lava and escape undramatically, or, in some instances, rush out with sufficient force to form lava fountains hundreds of feet in height. Nevertheless, the lava is not disrupted but flows away as a river of lava, with little resulting damage except to objects in the path of its flow. On the other extreme, tremendous explosions occur in the chimney, and as the lava rises into zones of less pressure it "froths," because of admixture with the rapidly expanding gases, and is ejected in the form of ash and pumice (pyroclastics). Thus, in these volcanoes the magma never reaches the surface as a liquid (lava) but is disrupted and ejected as pyroclastic material (ash). It was this type of material that buried Pompeii in the classic eruption of Vesuvius in A.D. 79. The explosions are sometimes so severe as to disrupt the cone, frequently blowing away large sections of it, spreading the debris over the countryside. Needless to say, such volcanoes cause extensive property damage as well as loss of life. The essential difference in the two types is in the gas content and the manner in which the gas is released when the magma reaches the surface. This is largely a function of the composition of the magma, which is discussed in Chapter 5.

The great majority of the volcanoes of the world are intermediate between the two extremes described, yielding both lavas and fragmental products.

Since it is not possible to examine the magma reservoir which feeds a volcano, our information must be obtained by studying the material ejected from the reservoir. The material, as already indicated, consists of three kinds of products: liquid (lava), fragmental (pyroclastics), and gaseous. A special problem is encountered in studying the gases, both in collecting them under hazardous—and in many instances near impossible—conditions and also in ascertaining that the gases collected are true volcanic gases and are not contaminated with atmospheric gases.

Chapter 2   Mythology and Early Speculation on Volcanoes

Science moves, but slowly, creeping on from point to point. —TENNYSON

Perhaps no other phenomenon of the physical world has been surrounded by as much mystery and as little truth as have volcanoes. Indeed, in ancient times volcanoes were regarded with suspicion and awe, and it would have been considered wicked and dangerous to attempt to investigate them. We are told by the poet Virgil that Mount Etna in Sicily, one of the large active volcanoes of the world, is the spot where the gods in their anger buried the giant Enceladus, and that the frequent earthquakes which shake the mountain are the struggles of the giant to free himself. Under such circumstances it would have been rash indeed for mere humans to meddle in the affairs of the gods.

CLASSIC MYTHS

Some of the world's most active volcanoes are near the centers of ancient civilization in the Mediterranean region: Mount Etna in Sicily and Vesuvius on the shore of the Bay of Naples. Thus it is not strange that classic literature contains many references to volcanoes and that many myths and legends are associated with them. This wealth of folklore is an important source of information on the activity of volcanoes in ancient times.

In Greek mythology Hephaestus is the god of fire, and the name, meaning "burning," "shining," or "flaming," probably originally referred to the brilliance of lightning. In Roman mythology Hephaestus was identified with Vulcan, one of the three children of Jupiter and Juno. Vulcan was the god of fire, especially terrestrial fire, volcanic eruptions, and the glow of the hearth and forge. Vulcan was the blacksmith of the gods. His forge at Olympus was equipped with anvils and all the implements of the trade. Vulcan made the arrows for Apollo and Diana, the shield of Achilles, and the invincible breast-plate of Hercules. He was toolmaker to the gods, utilizing the power of his forge for their welfare. His wife, according to the *Odyssey*, was Venus. (See Gayley 1911, p. 26.)

Poets have identified Vulcan's workshop with various active volcanoes in the belief that the smoking mountain was the chimney of Vulcan's forge. The explosions in the eruption of a volcano were believed to be Vulcan pounding on his anvil, while the fire and smoke came from the forge. It was here that Vulcan made the thunderbolts which Jove threw about so recklessly. Most frequently in ancient writings Vulcan's forge was located on the island of Vulcano, one of the Lipari or Aeolian Islands in the Tyrrhenian Sea, off the coast of Sicily (see Ch. 8). In fact, the name *volcano* is derived from the Latin name Vulcanus or Volcanus, applied to the island in ancient times because it was believed to be the location of the forge of Vulcan. From this association, the name *volcano* has been applied to all mountains which give off "smoke and fire" throughout the world.

There is a legend that, during the reign of Romulus, a temple to Vulcan was built in Rome, and a festival called Vulcanalia was held on August 23 of each year, the ceremony consisting of a sacrifice to Vulcan for the purpose of averting all mishaps that might arise from the use of fire or light.

PRIMITIVE MYTHS

Since many of the primitive peoples of the earth were fire-worshipers, it would seem reasonable that volcanoes, as a source of fire, might be a part of their mythology. In support of this idea is the fact that the earliest pyramids in Mexico, such as Cuicuilco in Mexico City, are round and similar in shape to volcanic cones. That the people were familiar with volcanoes is obvious, since this particular pyramid was partially buried by a lava flow about the beginning of the Christian era. The lava flow, known as the Pedregal, covers a large area in the southern part of Mexico City. Later pyramids are the conventional four-sided structures. Nevertheless, James B. Frazer (1930) indicates that few myths allude to volcanoes as a source of fire. An exception is the Polynesian myths, which do ascribe fire to volcanoes. The Tongan people tell of the hero Maui, who "stole fire in the nether world" and ran out of a passage and set the bushes on fire, since which time all people have had fire. A Samoan version relates that one of their ancestors struggled with the god Mafuie, and, after breaking off one of the god's hands, permitted him to go free in exchange for fire, which Mafuie had concealed in a vertical rock. The superstition today is that Mafuie is somewhere below Samoa, occasionally shaking the island with his one good hand; and the Samoans thank their gods that he has only one good hand, for with two hands he would surely shake their island into ruins.

The Legend of Pele

The legend of Pele, fire goddess of Hawaiian volcanoes, has many variations, as well as adherents, even today. The most common account relates how Madam Pele (so called by the natives in a mixture of respect and familiarity), in search of a home, visited first one island and then another looking for a suitable abode. Koko Head and Koko Crater, prominent landmarks at the eastern end of the island of Oahu, are evidences of Pele's last visit to Oahu. Pele built these craters while trying to find a home on Oahu. Finally, coming to Kilauea, an active crater on the island of Hawaii, she found a place to her liking and made this her home. In every case, the beginning of an eruption of the volcano is preceded by the appearance of Madam Pele, and many residents of the Big Island will testify that they have seen her in the form of an old woman just before an eruption. In most accounts Madam Pele is described as a revengeful goddess, taking care of her friends and destroying her enemies.

VOLCANIC ACTIVITY AND RELIGION

According to many of the early Christian teachings, hell was somewhere near the center of the earth, and volcanoes were believed to be the gateway to the infernal regions, an idea that persisted well into the nineteenth century. The fiery discharges from volcanoes were believed to come from the fires of hell in the interior of the earth, and the noise, from the shrieks and groans of the departed spirits suffering the tortures of the damned. In Dante's *Divine Comedy*, hell is described as a vast crater with Lucifer enthroned at the center. In many cultures there is a form of worship of mountain deities, such as the famous volcano Fujiyama, which is sacred to many Japanese.

VOLCANOLOGY AMONG THE ANCIENTS

A very indistinct line separates the mythologies of the early Greeks and Romans and their more scientific ideas concerning volcanoes. Although the Greeks were among the first to formulate explanations of the various physical features of the earth, including volcanoes, it should be recalled that they did not employ deductive reasoning, that is, the collection of the facts followed by the development of an explanation to interpret the facts. It was centuries later—in fact, not until the time of Charles Darwin, only about 100 years ago—that this type of reasoning came into general use.

Despite shrewd guesses of Plato, Aristotle, and Strabo and observations of Pliny the Younger, none of the early Greeks or Romans had any real concept of the true nature of volcanic activity. Aristotle (384–322 B.C.), following Plato (427–347 B.C.), referred vaguely to "pent-up" winds imprisoned in subterranean channels as being the cause of earthquakes and also of such winds' striking fire from seams of sulphur and coal as being the cause of volcanoes. Strabo (63 B.C.–A.D. 21), a learned geographer of his time, in allusion to the tradition that Sicily had been separated from Italy by a convulsion, remarked that at present the land near the sea was rarely shaken by earthquakes, since there were "now open orifices whereby fire, and ignited matter, and water escape," but that formerly, when the volcanoes Etna, the Lipari Islands, Ischia, and others had been closed up, the imprisoned fire and wind might have produced more violent movements (Strabo 1854–1857). Thus, while holding to the old Aristotelian idea of "pent-up" winds, Strabo seems to have inferred that volcanoes act as safety valves, a somewhat modern concept.

Shakespeare (1564–1616), reflecting the general idea of his time, has Hotspur reply to Glendower in *Henry IV: Part One* as follows:

> Diseased nature often times breaks forth
> In strange eruptions; oft the teeming earth
> Is with a kind of colic pinched and vex'd
> By the imprisoning of unruly wind
> Within her womb: which for enlargement striving
> Shakes the old beldame earth, and topples down
> Steeples and moss-grown towers.   (3.1.27–33)

Volcanoes, first regarded with superstition and fear, sometimes even as the abode of the gods, finally became the subject of scientific inquiry. Then investigators learned to identify the causes producing volcanoes. This knowledge made possible speculations on the prediction and control of volcanic eruptions and the development of ways and means of harnessing volcanic energy for the benefit of mankind.

Chapter 3   Volcanology Becomes a Science

Advance in science comes by laying brick upon brick, not by sudden erection of fairy palaces. —J. S. HUXLEY

Since volcanology is intimately connected with geology, it seems impossible to separate the two in tracing the development of knowledge in this field. As early as the Middle Ages, thinkers, such as Dante, recorded their speculations on the origin of the earth, and the ancients possessed considerable knowledge of minerals and metal mining. But it was not until the Italian Renaissance that geologic inquiry on modern lines was begun.

EARLY GEOLOGIC
INQUIRY

Such practical engineers as Leonardo da Vinci (1452–1519) recognized the true meaning of sea shells found in the rocks, and the interpretation of these fossils soon came into conflict with theology. Later, when all fossils were considered relics of the flood of Noah's time, the study of geology was pursued mainly for its bearing on the Mosaic account of the Creation. As a result, the early attempts at geology, such as Bishop Thomas Burnett's *Sacred History of the Earth* (1681–1689), since they were concerned with the creation of the world, were really cosmogonies. About 100 years later, methods of geologic inquiry developed facts which were inconsistent with the Mosaic account of the Creation, and a bitter controversy between geology and theology then developed. Geology deals with the earth as a whole, whereas up to that time the interest had been in the origin of the earth rather than in the later stages of its history. These thinkers were, therefore, cosmogonists rather than geologists. We have not, even to this day, developed an entirely satisfactory theory of the origin of the earth; yet geology has continued to progress. But as the modern cosmogonist, Harlow Shapley, has warned:

> . . . we should remember that the hardest problems of cosmogony would not necessarily be disposed of even if we should get a satisfactory theory of the origin of the earth. For we would ask at once concerning the origin of the sun and galaxies and eventually be driven back to deeper puzzles of the origin of matter, origin of space, of time, and of origins. Planetary genesis

is therefore only a decoy, leading to universal processes. (1945, p. 515)

Volcanology may be defined as that branch of science which deals with the eruption of magma (molten material plus its gaseous content) upon the surface of the earth or its rise into levels near the surface. It is closely related to geology and in fact may well be considered a phase of geology, but it is also intimately related to seismology, geochemistry, and geophysics. As with all other sciences, its limits are difficult to define, since all sciences are interrelated.

The beginning of volcanology as an objective account of volcanic phenomena, divorced from superstition and mythology, was the description of the eruption of Vesuvius in A.D. 79 by Pliny the Younger. It was in this eruption that his uncle, Pliny the Elder, lost his life. The description of the eruption was contained in two letters written by Pliny the Younger to the Roman historian Tacitus, at the latter's request, giving the details regarding his uncle's death. Pliny's letters are full of accurate observations and may well be regarded as the earliest contributions to the science of volcanology. These letters and a description of the A.D. 79 eruption of Vesuvius are given in Chapter 8.

For the next 1,700 years, or during the Dark Ages and well into the Renaissance, scientific subjects were completely neglected. The first noteworthy contribution after this period was a work entitled *Observations on Mt. Vesuvius, Mt. Etna, and Other Volcanoes*, by Sir William Hamilton, English ambassador to the Court of Naples, which was published in 1774. Hamilton was an enthusiastic student of volcanoes, and his firsthand accounts of the eruptions of the volcanoes of Italy still provide a valuable source of information.

The Italian naturalist Lazzaro Spallanzani (1729–1799) was one of the first to apply experimental methods to volcanic rocks. He tried to find out whether gases would escape when lava was melted and to determine the composition of these gases. His results were not conclusive, but he was obviously on the right track. Spallanzani is best known for descriptions of his travels through the volcanic regions of Italy, which far surpass in scientific accuracy and completeness all previous contributions of a similar nature (Zittel 1901, p. 98). Spallanzani's experimental researches were published in several volumes in the same series as the more popular descriptions of his travels (Spallanzani 1798).

At about the same time, the French geologist Gratet de Dolomieu (1750–1809) showed how much could be learned regarding volcanic actions by a study of the material ejected. Instead of confining his study, as his predecessors had done, to the volcanic cone and to the eruptive action, Dolomieu studied the products of eruption—the lavas and fragmental ejecta—and compared these with other rocks. He arrived at the correct conclusion that there is a complete series of transition stages between the coarsely crystalline lavas and the glassy obsidians. Dolomieu confirmed the igneous origin of basalt and recognized the similarity between the lava stream of Mount Etna and some of the "trap rocks" (dark, fine-grained igneous rocks, particularly lavas or dikes) of southern France, thus confirming their volcanic origin (Zittel 1901, p. 97). Dolomieu also called attention to the unusual composition of some of the limestones in the Alps, which he showed contained a high percentage of magnesium carbonate in addition to the usual calcium carbonate. Today such rock is known as *dolomite*. The name Dolomieu is also perpetuated in the name Dolomites given to the beautiful Tyrol section of the Alps of northern Italy.

THE NEPTUNIST-
PLUTONIST
CONTROVERSY

Unfortunately, at about this time the progress of volcanology, as well as geology in general, was delayed certainly for two or three decades because of the dispute which arose between the so-called Neptunists and the Plutonists, or Vulcanists.[1] The Neptunists, led by the renowned teacher Abraham Gottlob Werner, advocated the theory of deposition of all rocks, including lava and granite, from a universal ocean; it was for this reason that they were termed Neptunists.

Werner had a profound influence on geology. In 1775 he was named professor of mineralogy at the Freiberg School of Mines in Saxony. Mining had long been taught in France, Germany, and Hungary, and mineralogy was recognized as an important branch of mining. Werner, however, did not limit his attention to the composition and character of minerals but considered also the grouping of the rocks, their geographical position, and other relations, all of which he termed "geognosy." When Werner pointed out the application of these topics to mining, they were quickly regarded as an essential part of a professional education. In his lectures he treated all aspects of minerals, including their influence on rocks, the soil, and even the language and migration of tribes of people, which, he held, had been determined by the direction of specific strata. His charm of manner and his eloquence attracted many students and inspired many to become ardent disciples. The school at Freiberg soon became famous, and many came from distant countries to study under the great master.

Werner had not traveled far, and he had explored only a small por-

1. For a detailed account of the Neptunist-Plutonist controversy, see Adams (1938) and Geikie (1905).

tion of Germany, but he was able to convince his students that the whole surface of the earth and all the mountain chains were made after the model of his own small area. It became a passion with his students to travel to distant parts of the globe to discover his "universal formations," which, he taught, had been precipitated over the entire earth from a "chaotic fluid." The basalts of Saxony, to which his observations were confined, consisted of tabular masses capping hills and were not connected with the existing valleys, as is the case in many regions of recent volcanic activity. Strange as it may seem to us today, Werner held that basalt and all other related rocks, wherever found, had been precipitated from water.

As early as 1768, before Werner began his mineralogical studies, the true igneous nature of basalt had been established by several workers. Notable among them was the Italian scholar Giovanni Arduino (1759), who, in a study of the rocks of the region around Padua and Verona in northern Italy, divided the rocks into primary, secondary, and tertiary groups and recognized the resemblance of numerous varieties of basalt, interbedded with the rocks, to present-day lavas of Italian volcanoes.

One of the most careful studies was made by Nicolas Desmarest in the Auvergne district of southern France (Geikie 1905, pp. 140–176). He showed that the most recent craters are still intact and that their streams of lava conform in level to the present rivers. He observed that other craters are nearly destroyed and that the lavas from these are less closely associated with the present stream levels. He also noted that some volcanic rocks, still more ancient, without any visible craters, resemble in all details the rocks of Saxony, which had been attributed by Werner to precipitation from a universal ocean. Nevertheless, the dogma as expounded by Werner was accepted, and the advocates of the igneous origin of basalt were subjected to ridicule.

HUTTON AND
UNIFORMITARIANISM

James Hutton of Edinburgh, Scotland, a contemporary of Werner, was to have a leading role in the development of geology. Hutton was educated as a physician; but, instead of practicing his profession, he was content with a small inheritance from his father and gave his full time to scientific pursuits. He made frequent trips through England and Scotland and acquired considerable competence as a mineralogist, constantly striving to understand the broader concepts of geology. He finally published his observations in the *Transactions of the Royal Society of Edinburgh* in 1788 under the title "Theory of the Earth." In 1795 a more elaborate work was published. Hutton maintained that the strata which now comprise our continents were formed beneath the sea from the waste of pre-existing continents, and that the same forces are still destroying the rocks and transporting the material to the sea, where they are spread out and form strata analogous to those of more ancient date. Although loosely deposited on the sea floor they are altered and consolidated by volcanic heat and then uplifted to form new land areas: ". . . therefore, we are to examine the construction of the present earth in order to understand the natural operations of time past; to acquire principles by which we may conclude with regard to the future course of things" (Hutton 1795, 1:20). This is perhaps the most basic principle of geology and is commonly expressed as "The present is the key to the past."

This concept of Hutton's, for which he is perhaps best known, has come down to us today as the doctrine of uniformitarianism, or the uniformity of present processes in producing changes in the surface of the earth. The processes assumed in this theory require an immensity of time for the destruction of whole mountain ranges. "The immense time necessarily required for this total destruction of the land, must not be opposed to that view of future events, which is indicated by the surest facts and most approved principles. Time, which measures everything in our idea, and is often deficient to our schemes, is to nature endless" (Hutton 1788, p. 215).

When Hutton found one mountain range resting on another, and then another, he could find "no vestige of a beginning—no prospect of an end" (1788, p. 304). Such a statement, made at a time when the date of the Creation was placed at about 4000 B.C., was sensational.

Although Hutton had never visited a region of active volcanoes, he convinced himself that basalt and other similar rocks were of igneous origin and that some of them had been injected in a molten state into fissures in older strata. The absence of stratification in granite and its similarity of mineral character to that of rocks which he considered igneous led Hutton to conclude that granite was formed by solidification from a molten state. He could not fully confirm this theory unless he could find a contact of granite with other strata to see if there was any evidence of alteration by heat at the boundary, such as was common in the case of the trap rocks with which he was familiar. In 1785 he resolved to test his theory. In Perthshire (Scotland) there is a large granite mass, and Hutton surveyed the contact between the granite and the overlying strata until finally at Glen Tilt he found clear proof of his theory. Here he found not only the adjacent limestone profoundly altered but also veins of red granite branching from the main mass and traversing the limestone. On finding verification of his theory in this exposure he was filled with so much delight that the guides who accompanied him, says his biographer, were convinced that he must have discovered a vein of gold or silver (Playfair 1822, 4:75). Hutton was the leader of the Plutonists (or Vulcanists), who maintained that many rocks (even some of those now known to be of sedimentary origin) had cooled from a molten state and either had been poured out as lavas on the surface of the earth through volcanoes, or had solidified in great masses below the surface, such as granites.

The Neptunists used some arguments which were very plausible from the mineralogical standpoint against the theory of the origin of granite from a molten state. They held, of course, that all rocks, including granite, were deposits from a universal ocean. Granite is composed essentially of three common minerals: quartz, feldspar, and mica. It is obvious from the relationship of the crystals of these minerals in a granite that quartz was the last to crystallize, and since it has the highest melting point it would be expected to crystallize first; therefore, the Neptunists reasoned, granite could not have cooled from a molten state. It was many years later before it was discovered that the constituents of the granite magma form a complex solution in which the components are mutually dissolved and that the order of crystallization is governed by solubility rather than fusibility. This means that the most soluble constituents, such as quartz, crystallize last, while the least soluble crystallize first. The Plutonists, however, were as much in error in assigning to all rocks an igneous origin as the Neptunists were wrong in contending that all rocks were precipitated from water.

A NEW TOOL FOR
GEOLOGISTS

No discussion of the development of geology, however cursory, can omit the contribution of William Smith, popularly known as "Strata" Smith. An English surveyor by trade who collected fossils from the areas in which he worked, he soon came to realize that he always found the same kinds of fossils associated with the same types of rocks. This led him to conclude that he could identify the "formation" by the fossils. In 1815 he completed a map of the whole of England, based on his new-found tool, the fossil content of the various formations. The publication of his paper entitled *Strata Identified by Organized Fossils* in 1816 is one of the most important events in the development of geology. With this new tool the geologists were ready to arrange the rocks of the earth's crust in the order in which they had been deposited, even in widely separated areas, and to interpret the sequence of events of which they are the record. When geologic events could be assigned a time sequence, geology had become a historical science, an earth history.

LYELL AND MODERN
GEOLOGY

The development of geology is the result of the efforts of many individuals, but one man stands out so prominently that he may well be considered the "founder of modern geology." This man is Charles

Lyell, later knighted by the queen of England for his work in this field. Lyell was able to appreciate that many great forces had been at work in modifying the crust of the earth. He was not beset with the narrow provincialism of many of his predecessors and contemporaries, who applied to the whole world the processes at work in their own regions, neglecting or even denying the effectiveness of forces which either were dormant or had never been active in their regions. Thus Lyell, while a strong advocate of the Huttonian doctrine of uniformitarianism, was fully aware of the importance of cataclysms, such as volcanic eruptions and earthquakes, as earth processes. Lyell accomplished the monumental task of formulating an explanation of geologic processes. His *Principles of Geology*, published in 1830, was the first textbook on the subject and marked the beginning of modern geology.

THE CONTROVERSY
OVER VOLCANIC
CRATERS

Another controversy which effectively delayed the development of geology was the dispute between the adherents of the craters-of-elevation theory and the craters-of-accumulation theory.[2] Leopold von Buch, one of Werner's disciples, was the leading advocate of the craters-of-elevation theory, which held that volcanic cones are caused by molten material rising from below and arching the crust of the earth into a great blister or dome. Advocates of this theory denied that the cone is formed by the cumulative fall of material ejected by the volcano.

The Craters-of-Elevation Theory

Leopold von Buch (1774–1853) entered the School of Mines at Freiberg when he was 16 years old. He stayed 3 years, living with Werner most of the time. A man of independent means, von Buch traveled widely, always seeking to confirm Werner's teachings. However, he received a rude shock when he witnessed, in Italy, a volcanic eruption. He observed the streams of lava, the rocks hurled into the air by explosive eruptions, and the ash spread for miles around the vent. He noted the conical shape of the volcanic peak, and reasoned—incorrectly—that it could not be due to outpouring of lava, because the streams of lava were not continuous over its surface. Since many of the volcanic cones rise from the sea, he further reasoned that such a cone could not be formed from a vent on the sea floor, because the lava would immediately solidify on coming in contact with the sea water.

2. The following discussion of these theories is based on Zittel (1901), pp. 61–67.

When von Buch reached the Auvergne district in southern France and studied the Puy de Dôme and realized that here was a smooth dome-shaped mountain with no crater, he conceived his craters-of-elevation theory. He reasoned that, if the intruded mass retained its form, a mountain of the Puy de Dôme type would result; but, if the blister burst at the summit, the collapse and infalling material would form a crater such as is typical of many volcanoes. He did not realize that the Puy de Dôme is a lava plug which formed in the crater of the volcano in its last stage of activity and that the surrounding cone has since been removed by erosion. Plugs of this type, known as *tholoids*, are common throughout the world. Tholoids are now growing at Santa María (Santiaguito) Volcano, Guatemala; Mount Pelée in the Lesser Antilles; and in several of the volcanoes of Japan, notably Tarumai and Usu volcanoes. (The development of a tholoid is described in Ch. 7 on Mount Pelée.) In later years, von Buch, with great regret, relinquished the Neptunian teachings of his great master and from the accumulating evidence adopted the views of the Plutonists.

Another of Werner's students, who was to exert a profound influence, was Alexander von Humboldt. He entered the Freiberg School of Mines two years later than von Buch, and he, too, lived with Werner. He and von Buch were lifelong friends. Like von Buch, he traveled widely, devoting his life to the physical sciences. His travels took him to Central and South America, Russia, and Siberia, as well as over Europe. His life's work culminated in the publication of *The Cosmos* (1845–1862), a work aimed at presenting the whole world of nature. His main contributions were the study of volcanoes and earthquakes, and, like von Buch, he in time came to accept the truth of the Plutonists.

The Craters-of-Accumulation Theory

The craters-of-accumulation theory, supported by Lyell, Hutton, and others, is of course, the modern concept that the volcanic edifice is a result of the accumulation of ejected debris. It should be acknowledged that modern volcanology recognizes that a certain amount of swelling (or uplift of the crust) of the earth precedes the eruption of a volcano; tilt meters and other instruments have been developed to measure the swelling. Yet this feature is far different from that envisaged by the proponents of the craters-of-elevation theory. In the early editions of Lyell's *Principles of Geology* many pages of the section on volcanoes are devoted to citing evidence to disprove the craters-of-elevation theory.

Finally even the disciples of Werner were convinced that lava was molten rock which had risen to the surface from beneath the crust of the earth. Then was developed a theory that volcanoes were vents which connected the surface of the earth with a still-molten interior. This was the first explanation to be offered by modern science, and it was readily accepted for nearly a hundred years, being in vogue as recently as the beginning of the twentieth century. However, as the study of earthquakes progressed, it was found that earthquake waves are transmitted freely through the greater part of the earth; and, since some of these waves do not travel through a liquid, it followed that no considerable portion of the earth could be liquid. Accordingly, new explanations were required in order to conform with the newly discovered facts. These new explanations are in fact a description of currently held concepts. They are presented in the chapters which follow.

BEGINNINGS OF
MODERN
VOLCANOLOGY

The earliest attempt at a systematic and all-inclusive treatise on volcanoes was that by G. Paulett Scrope, entitled *Considerations on Volcanoes*, published in 1825. This work was dedicated to Lyell and was undertaken in order to point out the errors in the then popular craters-of-elevation theory. Scrope was the first (1825) to suggest that decreased atmospheric pressure accompanying stormy weather may be responsible for an increase in volcanic activity. The activity of Stromboli Volcano, in the Tyrrhenian Sea off the coast of Sicily, has long been used by the local inhabitants as a "weatherglass" to forecast the weather. Lyell was "dubious" about the connection, but the idea has adherents even today.

A contemporary of Scrope was Charles Daubeny, who in 1827 published a volume called *A Description of Active and Extinct Volcanoes*. Dr. Daubeny was trained in chemistry, and he advocated a "chemical theory of volcanic action." The second edition of his treatise, an 800-page volume published in 1848, gave information on most of the volcanic regions of the earth.

John W. Judd, a professor in the Royal School of Mines in London and an ardent student of volcanoes, made extensive studies in southern Europe, especially in the Lipari Islands in the Tyrrhenian Sea. His book, *Volcanoes: What They Are and What They Teach*, published in 1881, is a complete manual on the general characteristics of volcanoes, presenting many individual volcanoes in descriptions based on personal observations. It is really a continuation of Scrope's work, since the latter's woodcuts were turned over to Judd, and many are included in his book.

An English physician who was also an enthusiastic student of volcanoes, Dr. Tempest Anderson, contributed many valuable observations during the last quarter of the nineteenth century. His major contribution, *Volcanic Studies in Many Lands*, published in 1903, is still a storehouse of information. In the preface to that work, Dr. Anderson says:

> Very few branches of science still remain available for the amateur of limited leisure. Electricity, chemistry, bacteriology, most branches of geology and mineralogy have all led to results of highest economic value, and they are cultivated by a large body of professional men subsidized by colleges or by the government. They are in a position to give their whole time to their work, and their results are so voluminous that to keep abreast of the literature of any single branch would occupy more than the entire leisure of most men, yet this is a necessary preliminary to any attempt at original work. I was consequently led to seek some branch of science which gave no prospect of pecuniary return, and I determined on volcanology, which had the additional advantage of offering exercise in the open air and in districts often remote and picturesque. (1903, pp. ix–x)

Dr. Anderson says further "that for the last 18 years [this was in 1903] I spent the greater part of my holidays in exploring volcanic regions."

TWENTIETH-CENTURY AMERICAN VOLCANOLOGISTS

To trace adequately the development of volcanology in the twentieth century alone would require a volume. Two men in the United States, however, stand out so significantly that it seems necessary to acquaint the reader with them here. They are Frank A. Perret and Thomas A. Jaggar, who are important not only because of their actual contributions but also because of the inspiration they have afforded to other workers.

Perret

Frank A. Perret, trained in physics and chemistry, became interested in volcanology during a visit to Italy in 1903 for his health. There he became acquainted with Professor R. Matteucci, director of the Vesuvian Observatory, a man who inspired in him an intense interest in volcanoes. He was given an honorary appointment to the observatory staff as assistant to Professor Matteucci and was a witness to the great Vesuvian eruption of 1906. Perret was an expert photographer, and his training in physics and electrical engineering provided an excellent scientific background for his studies. During the next twenty years he made Naples his home and was a constant student of Vesuvius, but he also extended his studies to volcanic eruptions in other parts of the world—to Stromboli in the Lipari Islands, to Etna in

Sicily, to Tenerife in the Canary Islands, to Kilauea in Hawaii, and to Sakurashima in Japan.

In 1930 Perret established an observatory at Mount Pelée on the island of Martinique in the Lesser Antilles (West Indies). This volcano had become world famous because of the eruption of 1902, in which the entire population of the city of St. Pierre, something over 30,000 people, had been killed. A renewal of eruptive activity at Mount Pelée in 1929 convinced Perret that an observatory was needed. He maintained the observatory, which was supported largely from private gifts, until his death on January 12, 1943 (Foreword to Perret 1950, p. iii).

Jaggar

Thomas A. Jaggar, educated at Harvard University and in Germany, taught geology at Harvard from 1895 to 1906 and also worked for the U.S. Geological Survey in the Black Hills and Yellowstone regions. In 1906 he was appointed head of the Department of Geology at Massachusetts Institute of Technology, a position which he held until 1912, when he went to Hawaii to establish and direct the Hawaiian Volcano Observatory. He was one of the geologists sent in 1902 to study the results of the catastrophic eruption of Mount Pelée in the West Indies. It was this experience which guided him into volcanology as a lifetime career.

Dr. Jaggar traveled widely in his quest for knowledge of volcanoes. He visited Italy in 1906 to study the eruption of Vesuvius; in 1907 he led an expedition to the Aleutian Islands; in 1909 he visited the volcanic areas of Japan; and in 1910 he was sent to Costa Rica to study the effects of the great Cartago earthquake. Later his travels took him back to Alaska and Japan, to New Zealand, and to many of the Pacific islands.

In 1909 the trustees of the Whitney Estate gave Massachusetts Institute of Technology $25,000 to be used for research in geophysics and seismology, with a view to protecting human life and property. It was decided to use these funds to establish a laboratory at Kilauea Crater, Hawaii. The first problem selected for study was measurement of the temperature of the lava lake, and for this work special resistance thermometers were designed by Dr. Arthur L. Day and Dr. E. S. Shepherd of the Geophysical Laboratory of the Carnegie Institution of Washington. Dr. Shepherd and Dr. Jaggar were to make the measurements in the summer of 1911, but since Dr. Jaggar could not leave his work at the Massachusetts Institute of Technology at that time it was arranged for Dr. Frank A. Perret to accompany Dr. Shepherd.

Plate 1. Dr. Thomas A. Jaggar, 1939.

The people of Hawaii were eager to have the laboratory at Kilauea Crater become a permanent observatory, and through Dr. Jaggar's efforts funds were subscribed to provide for its operating expenses. In 1912 Dr. Jaggar gave up his professorship at Massachusetts Institute of Technology and became the director of the Hawaiian Volcano Observatory, a position he filled until he retired in 1940. The first few years were trying times in the operation of the observatory. Everything was new—new instruments had to be designed and built, new methods worked out, and the entire program organized. Funds were never adequate, and at times the outlook was most discouraging. However, Dr. Jaggar persisted, and in 1919 the U.S. government assumed the responsibility for the operation of the observatory, an arrangement which continues today. In the expansion of the work at the observatory, no phase of the activity of Kilauea or Mauna Loa was neglected if means could be found to include it in the program.

Dr. Jaggar was a pioneer in volcanology, and many of his methods and techniques have become standard the world over. Aside from his great contribution to the science of volcanology, he will be long remembered for his ideas on the protection of harbors and cities from lava flows. He was the first to employ aerial bombing as a means of deflecting or stopping a lava flow (see Ch. 5). He also developed detailed plans for protecting the harbor of Hilo, Hawaii, from lava flows by a system of barriers or dikes. He was an ardent advocate of the idea that many volcanic eruptions were the result of steam-blast explosions, an idea he developed during his study of the 1924 eruption of Kilauea in Hawaii. He believed that the steam explosions resulted from ground water entering the zone of highly heated rocks as the magma column receded, an idea that is now generally accepted, although there is some difference of opinion as to the immediate source of the ground water. One of his last major contributions was a special report, *Steam Blast Volcanic Eruptions* (1949), in which he presented convincing evidence that many volcanic eruptions throughout the world were steam-blast explosions. After retiring as director of the Hawaiian Volcano Observatory at the age of 70, Dr. Jaggar became research associate in geophysics at the University of Hawaii and in this capacity continued his work on volcanoes until his death on January 17, 1953.

MODERN EUROPEAN
VOLCANOLOGISTS

Several European workers made outstanding contributions during the early part of the twentieth century. Professor G. Mercalli's book *I vulcani attivi della terra* (1907) is a survey of the volcanoes of the world. Mercalli was director of the Vesuvian Observatory at Naples for many years, and he made many important contributions to volcanology from his studies of Vesuvius. Two German workers, Dr. Karl Sapper and Dr. F. von Wolff, stand out prominently. Sapper spent many years in the study of Central American volcanoes, and his work in that region is the basis, even today, for all future studies. His most important book, *Vulkankunde* (1927), is still in use. Von Wolff, in a series of publications entitled *Der Vulkanismus* (1914–1931) describes the various volcanic areas of the world.

More recent works in the field of volcanology are mentioned throughout the text. These publications are included in the bibliography.

From superstition and myth, through early objective descriptions of actual volcanic phenomena, finally to scientific attempts to understand the nature of volcanoes, volcanologists have traveled a long road and have now arrived at a point where significant knowledge indicates significant goals for man's future attainment—points further along the route to complete understanding of volcanoes and of what they can mean to the welfare of humanity.

VOLCANIC
OBSERVATORIES

Very few volcanic observatories with permanent staffs and scientific equipment are maintained throughout the world today. For the most part the study of volcanoes continues to be of an expeditionary nature, with scientists making brief trips to observe and study an eruption in progress. The actual eruption of a volcano is only one episode in the volcanic cycle, however, and continuous observations are essential if the goal of predicting eruptions is to be realized.

The Royal Vesuvian Observatory (now the Vesuvian Observatory), located on the slope of Vesuvius above the site of Herculaneum, was established in 1847. Many distinguished volcanologists have served as directors, including L. Palmieri, R. Matteucci, G. Mercalli, A. Malladra, and (as of 1973) G. Imbo. The director is traditionally a professor at the University of Naples, and at times the scientific observations have been shared with the director's duties as a professor at the university. It was here that Frank A. Perret, who was serving as honorary assistant to Professor Matteucci, director of the observatory, witnessed the great eruption of Vesuvius in 1906, and his published account of the eruption (Perret 1924) is one of the classics in volcanology.

The Hawaiian Volcano Observatory, formally established in 1912 under the directorship of Thomas A. Jaggar, has served as a model for volcanic observatories. Some of the details regarding the establishment of the Hawaiian Volcano Observatory have already been described in connection with Dr. Jaggar's contribution to volcanology.

In 1921, volcanic observations were initiated at several of the volcanoes in Indonesia, prompted by the renewal of the activity at Krakatoa.

The Japanese have long been leaders in the study of volcanoes. A permanent observatory has been in operation at Mount Asama since 1934, and in recent years others have been established at other active volcanoes.

The Institute of Volcanology under the Academy of Science of the USSR has an active program for the study of the volcanoes of the Kamchatka peninsula.

A volcanic observatory was established at Rabaul on New Britain Island by the Australian government in 1938. Temporarily abandoned during World War II when the island was occupied by the Japanese, it is now well equipped and, through a network of trained observers, is monitoring many of the volcanoes in the New Guinea area.

The Philippine Commission on Volcanology, established in 1952, maintains continuous observations at Taal and Hibok-Hibok volcanoes and intermittent studies at other volcanic centers.

New Zealand has been active in volcanological studies, largely in connection with the development of geothermal power resources in the Wairakei area of North Island. A field office has been maintained by the New Zealand Geological Survey at Rotorua since 1946.

The U.S. Geological Survey set up a temporary headquarters at Vancouver, Washington, to monitor the 1980 eruption of Mount St. Helens. Later this was made a permanent station, named the David A. Johnston Cascades Volcano Observatory, and its scope expanded to include all of the Cascade volcanoes.

The Smithsonian Institution Center for Short-Lived Phenomena at Cambridge, Massachusetts, which was established in 1968, has provided an invaluable service in reporting current volcanic eruptions. With a global network of scientists serving as correspondents, eruptions are reported to the center, and within hours the information is relayed to subscribers throughout the world.

Admittedly, much progress is being made, using modern electronic devices, in gathering information on all aspects of volcanism. However, the interpretation of the data and the application of the results to the fundamental problems of volcanology is largely still to be done.

Chapter 4   Classification of Volcanoes

*The purpose of classification is not to set forth final and indisputable truths
but rather to afford stepping stones towards better understanding.*
—L. C. GRATON

Classification, in a scientific sense, is the systematic arrangement of
all the representatives of a group, such as plants, animals, or volcanoes, based on natural relationships. It is an effort to simplify a
complex subject by grouping together those elements which have
similar characteristics. In the case of volcanoes a classification based
on the type of eruption would be useful. Although many attempts
have been made to classify volcanoes, no entirely satisfactory scheme
has yet been devised. A review of the classifications which have been
proposed will acquaint the reader with the problems involved in the
classification of volcanoes.

NINETEENTH-CENTURY
CLASSIFICATIONS

The earliest systematic treatise on volcanology was Scrope's *Considerations on Volcanoes*, published in 1825. In this work Scrope made a
distinction between (*a*) permanent, (*b*) moderate, and (*c*) paroxysmal
eruptions. The permanent type included eruptions which were of a
more quiet and regular nature, such as those of Stromboli; while the
paroxysmal eruptions were violent and irregular, such as those exhibited at times by Vesuvius. Moderate eruptions were those similar
to paroxysmal eruptions but less violent. This general distinction was
adopted by French geologists, and the terms "Strombolian stage"
and "Vesuvian stage" were used to describe the state of activity of a
volcano.

Late in the nineteenth century, volcanoes were commonly classified as (*a*) explosive, (*b*) intermediate, and (*c*) quiet (Dana 1891; Russell 1902). The explosive type, such as Krakatoa, ejects almost entirely fragmental material, which accumulates around the vent, forming
a cone with steep slopes. In the quiet type, such as the Hawaiian
volcanoes, the material is chiefly lava, which rises to the surface
without disruptive explosions and accumulates in huge, flat domes.
The great majority of volcanic eruptions belong to the intermediate
type. They begin with strong explosions accompanied by abundant
fragmental material, followed by the outpouring of lava, thus dis-

playing the characteristics of both the explosive and the quiet types. To this intermediate type the name *strato-volcano* is often applied, since the cone consists of layers of ash alternating with lava flows. This classification, although useful, is too general; its inadequacy makes necessary further divisions for a correct grouping of the various types of volcanic eruptions. Furthermore, the choice of at least one of its terms, *quiet*, seems misleading as applied to volcanoes. With all its disadvantages, however, this classification has been widely used and is still found in some texts.

LACROIX'S
CLASSIFICATION

Professor A. Stoppani (1871–1873) made an effort to devise a classification of volcanoes which would be more exact yet still based on the type of eruption. He used as type names in a general classification of volcanoes the names of Italian volcanoes which display different types of eruptions, such as Ischia, Stromboli, and Solfatara. A few years later, Professor Mercalli (1907) modified and amplified Stoppani's classification but retained the general plan. Meanwhile, the French geologist, Professor A. Lacroix (1908), who had made extensive studies at Mount Pelée following the tragic eruption in 1902, proposed a classification which, making use of terms introduced by others, recognized four types of eruptions: (*a*) Hawaiian, (*b*) Strombolian, (*c*) Vulcanian, and (*d*) Peléan. Lacroix's classification was adopted by Sapper (1927) and was later used in the National Research Council volume on volcanology (Sapper 1931, pp. 1–34). It was then widely introduced into many of the textbooks of geology. It will be of interest, at this point, to review Lacroix's types.

Hawaiian Type

The Hawaiian type, represented by the volcanoes of the Hawaiian Islands, has abundant outpourings of basaltic lava in which the gases are liberated more or less quietly. Explosive eruptions are rare, but fountains of lava, projected by jets of escaping gas, may play at heights up to 1,000 feet or more. The product is basic lava with only minor amounts of cinders and ash. The outpourings of lava develop flat lava domes, forming, as in the case of Mauna Loa (see Ch. 10), some of the largest mountains on earth.

Strombolian Type

The term *Strombolian*, introduced by the Italians in the early part of the twentieth century to indicate an eruptive type, had been used by the French to designate a type of activity at least 50 years earlier. Stromboli (see Ch. 9), a volcano in the Aeolian Islands off the coast of Sicily in the Tyrrhenian Sea, is in a constant state of activity and since ancient times has been known as the "Lighthouse of the Mediterranean." The eruptions of Stromboli consist of more or less regular explosions of moderate intensity which throw out pasty, incandescent lava (scoria), accompanied by a white vapor cloud. The lava in the crater crusts over lightly, and at intervals of about one-half hour the pent-up gases escape with mild explosions, hurling out clots of lava and fragments of the crust. Many of the fragments fall back into the crater to be blown out again, but others fall on the slope of the cone and roll into the sea.

Vulcanian Type

The term *Vulcanian*, first used by Mercalli et al. (1891), is from the Island of Vulcano, near Lipari in the Aeolian group north of Sicily. The lava from Vulcano (see Ch. 8) is more pasty and viscous than Strombolian lava, and it forms a thick, solid crust over the crater between the infrequent eruptions. Gases accumulate beneath the congealed crust, and in time the upper part of the magma column becomes thoroughly gas-saturated. Finally, with strong explosions, sometimes sufficient to partially disrupt the cone, the obstructions are blown out; and the broken fragments of the crater plug, together with some new lava in the form of "breadcrust bombs" and scoria, are ejected. Such eruptions are accompanied by a great "cauliflower-shaped" eruption cloud containing an abundance of ash. When the plug is suddenly blown out, the gas-saturated magma is disrupted into pumice and ash by the explosively expanding gases. After the clearing of the obstruction, lava flows may issue either from the crater or from fissures on the sides of the cone. Indeed, the initial explosion may split the cone from top to bottom, and lava flows may issue along the fractures.

In view of the fact that Vulcano has been inactive for the past 85 years, the latest eruption having occurred in 1889–1890, it is more appropriate to use Vesuvius as the example of the Vulcanian type of eruption. Stoppanni (1871–1873) applied the term *Plinian* (a name which had already been in use for some time) to describe an eruption of extreme violence, such as the A.D. 79 eruption of Vesuvius. The name is from Pliny, who described the A.D. 79 eruption of Vesuvius in letters to the Roman historian Tacitus (Ch. 8). Pliny described the eruption cloud as resembling the Italian stone pine tree. It was shot upward as a column by the tremendous force of the explosion and then, on reaching the height of its course, began to spread out. The

Italian word *pino*, "pine," has been adopted by volcanologists to describe explosions of unusual vigor which develop eruption clouds similar in shape to that described by Pliny. It seems useful to retain the term *Plinian* to designate a phase of the most violent Vulcanian eruptions in which *pino* clouds are developed. Most eruptions where obstructed vents must be cleared begin with Vulcanian characteristics.

Peléan Type

The only new term introduced by Lacroix is *Peléan*, all the other terms in his classification having been used previously by other writers. It is derived from Mount Pelée, on the island of Martinique in the West Indies, which erupted in 1902, destroying the city of St. Pierre with the loss of more than 30,000 lives. The Peléan type produces magma of the highest viscosity and is characterized by extreme explosiveness. The distinguishing feature of the Peléan eruption is the *nuée ardente*, or "glowing cloud." It is a highly heated gas, so charged with incandescent ash particles that it resembles a mobile emulsion, yet dense enough to maintain contact with the surface as it rushes down the slopes of the mountain with hurricane force. It was such a cloud that overwhelmed St. Pierre and resulted in the destruction of everything and everyone in its path. In Peléan eruptions the upward escape is frequently blocked by a plug of lava in the crater, and the explosions break out as horizontal blasts from beneath the plug. The magma is expelled as a highly ash-charged gas, and no lava issues except that pushed up as a viscous plug in the crater. The characteristics of this type are described in connection with the 1902 eruption of Mount Pelée, in Chapter 7.

Although Lacroix's classification has some apparent defects, as was early recognized, it is widely used and has become firmly entrenched in the literature of geology. The real difficulty, which is inherent in any classification of this kind, is that any one volcano selected as a "type" has various kinds of eruptions, so that to designate a volcano as "Strombolian" is misleading when the activity at Stromboli is variable in type. A. Rittmann (1944) has recommended, as O. De Fiore did earlier, that a new nomenclature of descriptive terms be adopted to replace Lacroix's terms based on specific volcanoes. It does not seem desirable to abandon Lacroix's classification at this time, but some modifications are introduced in this work.

In order to make Lacroix's classification more complete one new type is added, the Icelandic; and a "stage," the Solfataric, is recognized. Both of these terms have been in use for many years and inclusion of them in the classification makes possible a more comprehensive view of volcanic activity.

Icelandic Type

In the Icelandic type great volumes of lava issue from fissures, often many miles in length, and spread in sheets over the adjacent country-side. The basaltic lava is quite fluid and able to flow for long distances, building up great lava plateaus consisting of hundreds of superimposed flows covering thousands of square miles. The Columbia River Plateau, covering parts of Washington, Oregon, and Idaho, is an example of areas formed by such eruptions. The composition of the lavas in the Icelandic and the Hawaiian types is similar, but the Icelandic lavas—unlike the Hawaiian ones, which form great domelike masses—cover large areas with relatively flat-lying beds.

Historic eruptions of the Icelandic type are known only in Iceland, the most famous being the Laki fissure eruption in 1783 (see Ch. 11).

Solfataric Stage

The term *Solfataric* is applied to the final phase of a volcanic eruption, in which only gases are given off. The name is from the volcano Solfatara (Italian for "sulphur") in the Phlegraean Fields near Naples. Since its latest eruption in 1198, it has emitted only gases. A volcano may remain in the Solfataric stage for many hundreds of years after its eruptive activity has ended.

The Lacroix classification of volcanoes, as modified, is the basis for the grouping of the volcanic eruptions described in Part Two. The identification of a volcanic eruption with one of Lacroix's types, even though the classification is not entirely consistent, will enable the reader to anticipate the kind of material to be ejected as well as the general character of the eruption.

Chapter 5   What Comes Out of a Volcano

Volcanism everywhere has unity; gas is the prime mover.
—THOMAS A. JAGGAR

Gas is the active agent and the magma is its vehicle. —FRANK A. PERRET

VOLCANIC GASES   *Composition*

It has long been recognized that gas is the primary force in producing volcanic explosions. When water changes its state from a liquid to a solid (i.e., to ice) a slight expansion, equal to about one-ninth of its volume, occurs, but when water changes to the gaseous state the volume increases instantly 1,000 times! Here is the force necessary to produce a volcanic eruption. It was early recognized that the chief gas given off in a volcanic eruption was water vapor, or steam; so Scrope, Lyell, and others developed the concept that the arching (folding) of the earth's crust caused a sufficient release of pressure to permit the water in the magma to vaporize and cause an explosive eruption.

Although this is essentially the current idea, the debate as to the source of the water in the magma is still vigorously pursued. Lyell (1875, 2:226) explained the concentration of volcanoes around the ocean margin on the assumption that the sea was the source of the water. Daubeny (1827, p. 368) depended on the percolation of sea water into the deep interior, where reaction with the alkaline metals provided the heat for the "chemical theories." Others relied on meteoric (rain) water as the chief source, pointing out that, while volcanoes are concentrated on the margins of the continents, they are frequently 50–100 miles from the coast, and the percolation of sea water to depth beneath such volcanoes is highly improbable.

In the last century the proponents of seepage water, either sea water or meteoric water, have lost ground, and evidence is accumulating in favor of the theory that the water is an original constituent of the magma, that is, *juvenile water* in geologic terminology. It would appear that this problem might be resolved by simply collecting and analyzing gases from an active volcano. However, the collecting of gases from an active volcano involves some serious problems in securing the collector's safety and in protecting the samples from contamination by atmospheric gases. Early in the twentieth century several workers showed that when recent lavas were heated in a vacuum the gases given off were similar to those obtained at volcanic vents (Gautier 1906, p. 690), and it was correctly concluded that the juvenile gases were entrapped in the lava at the time of solidification. This opened up an unexpected and fruitful method of studying volcanic gases.

In 1911, Dr. A. Brun of Geneva advanced a startling theory in which he maintained that water vapor is not an abundant constituent in volcanic gases. He cited as evidence the facts that the white clouds emanating from a volcano do not dissipate in the air, as is true for steam, but drift in a streamer for many miles; that rainbows and other optical effects are absent; and finally that volcanic ash falling from such a cloud is quite dry. According to Brun, the clouds of vapor accompanying volcanic eruptions consist mainly of volatilized chlorides mixed with dust from the explosions.

This theory by a reputable scientist, challenging the long-accepted idea, proved a great stimulus to the study of volcanic gases in an effort to refute it. As is often the case, an incorrect theory does much to advance the science because it inspires other workers to pursue the subject with zeal in order to prove the theory wrong and thus to uncover entirely new evidence. The obvious way to test Brun's theory was by direct observation of gases being emitted by active volcanoes, and it was not long before such results were forthcoming.

Two capable scientists, Dr. Arthur L. Day and Dr. E. S. Shepherd, both of the Geophysical Laboratory of the Carnegie Institution of Washington, were able to collect primary volcanic (juvenile) gases at Kilauea Crater in Hawaii in 1912. Kilauea Crater, at that time, had a lake of molten lava, which provided an ideal laboratory for the study. Furthermore, the Hawaiian Volcano Observatory was at that time just being established, and its long-time director, Dr. Thomas A. Jaggar, was to repeat the experiment many times in later years and confirm the results. The problem, of course, was to collect the gases directly from the molten lake of lava without introducing atmospheric gases. Descending to the floor of the crater, equipped with gas masks, Day and Shepherd (1913) were able to thrust an iron pipe into the large gas bubbles which developed over active gas vents in the lava pool and to conduct these gases to their collecting chambers. In the course of one collection it was noticed that air coming in near the base of the bubble behaved like an air blast in a furnace, causing the gases collected at the top of the bubble to be partially burned (i.e., oxidized). Hence free hydrogen had combined with atmospheric oxygen to form water, and in a like manner sulphur had oxidized to sulphur dioxide, carbon monoxide to carbon dioxide, and so on. The interaction of these gases with the air and with each other provided an effective source of heat which actually brought the surface layers of the lava in the pool to a higher temperature than had been reached at some depth below the surface. This interesting topic is developed in a following section on the temperature of lavas.

Of 24 samples collected by Day and Shepherd, steam averaged 68.2 percent by volume. Next in abundance were carbon dioxide, nitrogen, and sulphur gases, with smaller amounts of carbon monoxide, hydrogen, and chlorine. A little argon was present in all of the samples, indicating that some contamination by air had taken place; but also the ratio of nitrogen to argon in the samples was less than in air, suggesting that some of the atmospheric nitrogen had been used up by reactions with the volcanic gases. Only small amounts of fluorine were noted.

In later collections made at Kilauea by Shepherd and Jaggar (Jaggar 1940), vacuum tubes replaced the iron pipe, which reacted to some degree with the gases. The vacuum tube was a glass container with a long, tubelike tip, which was sealed after the air had been evacuated. The tip was thrust into a jet of issuing gas and the sealed end broken, allowing the gas to be drawn into the vacuum container; then the tip was resealed by touching it to a red-hot lava surface. Although the results were better, there still remained the problem of air contamination, which could result from atmospheric gases entering the vacuum tube while the glass tip was being sealed. Further contamination might result from air entrapped in adjacent rocks or in porous crustal layers of lava which were engulfed, the released air rising with the volcanic gases. The atmosphere contains small amounts of inert gases, such as argon; and, if all the argon is assumed to be from the atmosphere, it is possible to calculate the amount of atmospheric contamination. In addition to air contamination, reactions between the gases in the collection tube while awaiting analysis introduce still another element of uncertainty.

Jaggar (1940) reported on the average of the 10 best collections of gas from Kilauea in 1917–1919 (which are still believed to be among the best made from an active volcano) as follows, in volume percentage: water (H_2O), 52.7; carbon dioxide (CO_2), 21.4; carbon monoxide (CO), 0.8; hydrogen (H_2), 0.9; sulphur dioxide (SO_2), 11.5; sulphur (S_2), 0.7; sulphur trioxide (SO_3), 1.8; chlorine (Cl_2), 0.1; nitrogen (N) plus rare gases, 10.1.

Wide variation in water content, as well as other components of volcanic gases, has been noted by many investigators. Shepherd (1938) reported a water content of 71.4 percent by volume in gases collected at Mauna Loa crater in 1926. More recently, the water content of gas samples from the Surtsey volcano, Iceland (Sigvaldason and Elisson 1968), was reported as 83.1 percent by volume. Evidence is accumulating, as will be discussed subsequently, that there is a wide variation in the composition of the gases from the same vent, even in short time intervals.

The proof that granitic magmas can contain water in solution was furnished by R. Goranson (1931) in a series of notable experiments on artificial silicate melts. These experimental studies, which unfortunately were limited to granitic rocks, are of the utmost importance in the study of volcanism as well as other aspects of geology. Geologic studies have shown that most granitic magmas have crystallized at depths of 1,220–3,650 meters and a temperature not exceeding 870° C. Under such conditions of depth and temperature, Goranson showed that a granitic magma was capable of holding from 6 percent to 9 percent water in solution. Further experiments by Goranson (1938a) using water systems containing albite or orthoclase, the most abundant minerals in granitic rocks, provided information on the tremendous pressures developed in a magma chamber by the "boiling off" of the water due to crystallization. The albite-water system at 1,100° C. and a pressure of 606 bars[1] (equal to 2.25 km. in depth) can hold up to 4.2 percent water. When the system cooled, albite began to crystallize at 960° C., and when the temperature had dropped to 819° C. more than half of the albite had crystallized, leaving a liquid that contained 9.5 percent water, and the pressure had increased to 3,000 bars. Continued crystallization must raise the pressure from 5,000 to 6,000 bars, and here, Goranson writes, "is a mechanism for developing all the pressure a volcanologist may desire" (1938b, p. 272).

The composition of the gases varies considerably from one volcanic region to another, although a high percentage of water is present in all cases. The so-called oceanic volcanoes, such as the Hawaiian volcanoes, are low in chlorine and relatively high in sulphur, while the continental volcanoes (those situated on continents) show higher chlorine and lower sulphur. Fluorine was brought forcibly to my attention when, during close observation of active fumaroles at Parícutin Volcano, Mexico, a camera lens was etched by hydrofluoric-acid gas condensing on it.

Spectrographic analyses of gases from an erupting volcano appear to be promising. At high temperatures each element gives off light radiations of a characteristic wave length which can be recorded on a photographic plate. Since this identifies only the elements present, it is not a substitute for the conventional gas analysis, but it does provide important information.

A new type of gas analysis, adapted from colorimetric methods of fume analysis in industrial plants, has been developed by I. Elskens, H. Tazieff, and F. Tonani (1964). This method, which is done in the

---

1. A *bar* is the pressure of one atmosphere at sea level (14.7 psi) and is equal to about 12 feet of rock load.

field within a few seconds of the time of collection, thus largely avoiding the reaction of the gases in the collecting tube, gives results which are believed to be accurate within a few percentage points. Analyses by this method show a wide variation in the composition of the gases from the same vent, even at intervals of only a few minutes. In eleven analyses of gases at the crater of Mount Etna in a period of 5.3 minutes, the water content varied from 3 to 36 percent, and carbon dioxide was either equal to or more abundant than water. Not only the variability but the small amount of water in the volcanic gases is contradictory to the results obtained by conventional methods of analysis.

At most volcanic vents the gases react with the lava on the walls surrounding the gas vents to form deposits of brightly colored sublimates. The most common is sulphur, of sufficient importance to provide commercial deposits in some regions, with yellow ferrous chloride and white ammonium chloride being also common. Many of the metallic oxides, such as iron, lead, zinc, and tin, also have been identified in volcanic sublimates. Although these have never been found in sufficient quantity to be of commercial importance, they do provide important clues to the way in which metals are transported through the rocks of the earth's crust and eventually concentrated in ore deposits.

Volume

The total volume of gases evolved during an eruption of a volcano is stupendous. G. B. Alfano and I. Friedlander (1928) calculated the volume of gas in the 1906 eruption of Vesuvius from the size of the conduit and the velocity of emission and concluded that not only the volume but also the weight of the gases must be many times greater than the total mass of ash and lava. Estimates of the gas content, especially water, in the eruption of other volcanoes does not support this statement; either the 1906 eruption of Vesuvius was not typical or the figures are in error.

The amount of water liberated as steam in the eruption of Parícutin Volcano, Mexico, for the year 1945 was calculated by C. Fries, Jr. (1953) to average about 13,100 metric tons per day or approximately 1.1 percent of the total weight of erupted material. The gas content of a relatively basic magma, such as occurs at Parícutin, is usually lower than that of the acidic magmas associated with Peléan type eruptions. Unfortunately, there are few reliable estimates of the volume of gases liberated in Peléan type eruptions. One such estimate, which seems worthy of note, was for the 1929 eruption of Mount Pelée on the island of Martinique, in which the amount of water liberated was estimated to equal 2.5 percent of the total weight of the erupted material (Arsandaux 1934).

Geologic Significance

A growing mass of evidence indicates that the earth's atmosphere and the waters of the ocean may have been derived from volcanic or plutonic gases throughout geologic time rather than from a dense, primitive atmosphere which was once believed to have enveloped the earth. William Rubey (1951), in a study of the geologic history of the sea, points out that the more volatile materials, such as water, carbon dioxide, chlorine, nitrogen, and sulphur, are much too abundant in our present atmosphere, hydrosphere (ocean), and ancient sediments to be accounted for as the products of rock weathering alone. From a consideration of geologic evidence he also rules out the possibility of these "excess" volatiles being residual from a primitive atmosphere. He points out that the relative abundance of the different "excess" volatiles is similar to the relative amounts of the same materials in gases escaping from volcanoes, fumaroles, and hot springs and in gases occluded in igneous rocks. It is possible, therefore, that the atmosphere and the waters of the oceans may have come almost entirely from plutonic gases. Volcanic eruptions and lava flows have brought large quantities of these gases to the surface throughout the geologic past. However, Rubey believes that intrusive magmas are probably a more adequate source of the constituents of the atmosphere and hydrosphere and that hot springs may have been the principal channels by which the "excess" volatiles reached the surface. Igneous rocks now contain about 1 percent water. On the assumption that the original magma contained 4 percent water, this would mean that the magmas have given off 3 percent water during crystallization. On this basis Rubey concludes that the crystallization of a shell of igneous rocks 40 kilometers thick would be sufficient to account for all of the water in the oceans.

Hot Springs

The presence of a preponderance of water in volcanic gases might naturally lead one to infer that "magmatic" springs should occur in regions of recent igneous activity or recent volcanism. Perhaps the surprising thing is the rarity of such features, but the fact that they do exist is in itself of great interest. Yellowstone National Park, with its many hot springs and geysers, immediately comes to mind as an outstanding example. The problem is to prove that the water issuing as a boiling spring or a geyser and heated by a magma still buried below the surface is not simply surface (meteoric) water which has become heated by contact with the cooling magma. The proof in such cases lies in the unusual constituents which are derived from a magma in contrast to the usual constituents found in normal springs.

In springs of meteoric origin the principal constituents are those of the surrounding sediments through which the water has percolated. These commonly include calcium-magnesium carbonates from limestones and dolomites, calcium sulphate from gypsum-bearing beds, sodium sulphate from some types of shales, hydrogen sulphide from the reduction of sulphates by organic matter, and carbon dioxide from reactions between calcium carbonate and other compounds. Occasionally, sodium chloride and related compounds are derived from saline formations or from original sea water (connate water) which was entrapped in the sediments.

Hot springs in regions of recent volcanic activity carry a high percentage of sodium carbonate and considerable quantities of sodium chloride. Silica is frequently an abundant constituent of these waters. Outstanding examples are the great geyser areas of Yellowstone, Iceland, and New Zealand, where extensive deposits of siliceous sinter (geyserite) are being formed. Springs in volcanic regions also frequently contain boron, fluorine, nitrogen, and carbon dioxide in notable amounts, as well as traces of arsenic, antimony, quicksilver, cobalt, copper, nickel, and other elements. Studies at Vesuvius, Etna, and elsewhere indicate that carbon dioxide is usually associated with the declining stage of volcanic activity. The possibility that it may continue to be emitted long after volcanic activity has ceased and even after erosion has destroyed the cone is suggested by the exhalations of carbon dioxide encountered in the famous gold mines at Cripple Creek, Colorado, located in the core of a Tertiary volcano (Daly 1933, p. 510).

It is obvious that the distinction between magmatic and meteoric springs is not clear-cut. This is especially true where magmatic water passes through a thick layer of rock formations in reaching the surface, with resulting modification of its composition. In many cases water of magmatic origin mixes with ground water and the two issue together. In a study of the hot springs and geysers in Yellowstone, C. N. Fenner (1936) concluded that 10–15 percent of the water was of magmatic origin, the remainder being meteoric water. Other examples of magmatic springs include Karlsbad, Czechoslovakia; Ems and Weisbaden, Germany; and Steamboat Springs, Nevada.

THE ROLE OF WATER IN
VOLCANIC ACTIVITY
The fact that magma can contain water in solution in significant amounts and the importance of the water content in volcanic eruptions have been emphasized. It seems appropriate, before we leave this topic, to speculate on the actual role of water in a volcanic eruption. Water present in a magma will migrate by diffusion, seeking to establish a uniform pressure. This does not mean, however, that the quantity of water is the same throughout, because the amount of water which can be contained in solution in the magma is determined by the confining pressure (weight of the overlying rocks) and the temperature. Water will diffuse and distribute itself in a magma so that the water-vapor pressure is the same throughout the magma chamber. This results in a concentration of water in the magma chamber in the regions of lowest pressures and temperatures. Although the effect of temperature on the solubility of water in the magma at a constant pressure is numerically small, roughly 0.5 percent by weight for each 100° C. decrease in temperature, it is highly important. Water will tend to diffuse toward the cooler, upper portion of the magma. To illustrate the effect of pressure on the water content of a magma, George C. Kennedy, who reviews this problem in a thought-provoking article, uses the following example:

> . . . let us assume that the top of a magma column extends to within 4½ miles of the surface of the earth. The confining pressure due to the weight of the rock load is approximately 2,000 bars at this depth, and if the magma is saturated with water, the top of the column will contain about 7.4 weight percent water. The equilibrium water content of the melt diminishes very rapidly with increasing depth. At a depth where the confining pressure has increased to 3,000 bars the water content . . . will have diminished to less than 5.3 percent, and the melt will be far from saturated. At a depth where the confining pressure is approximately 4,000 bars, the water content will have decreased to about 2 percent. It appears . . . that the deeper the burial of the magma chamber, the stronger the tendency of the water to be concentrated in the upper portion. Further, a magma chamber can be saturated with water vapor only at its very top. (Kennedy 1955, p. 494)

Assuming the concentration of water in the upper portion of the magma, as outlined in the preceding paragraph, the stages in a volcanic eruption may be explained as follows: At the initial outbreak the magma will be gas-saturated, and the explosive force of the expanding gases (largely steam) will shatter the material into ash and cinders. The mobility of the material, described by Doris L. Reynolds (1954) as *fluidization*, is due to the fact that the particles are suspended in a gas. This is the period in which cone building is the most important process. Later, fluid, highly vesicular lavas rich in water but not sufficiently saturated to be disrupted by the escaping gases, will pour out. In the final phase of the eruption the lavas will have a higher viscosity (due to lower water content) and contain fewer volatiles. This pattern, observed at Parícutin Volcano, Mexico, and in other eruptions, is precisely what should be expected if the water is concentrated in the upper part of the magma column. It may also be reasoned that it is the decline in the volatiles that brings the eruption to an end. Indeed, as Kennedy (1955, p. 495) has pointed out, if the water were distributed uniformly with depth in the magma, the eruption would be more catastrophic, coming to an end only when the magma chamber had been emptied, somewhat analogous to the emptying of a geyser tube.

Following an eruption, after the "wet" upper portion of the magma has been expelled, the equilibrium will have been disturbed and the water will again diffuse into the zone of lower confining pressure and lower temperatures at the top of the magma column. In time the steadily accumulating pressure will be sufficient to blast aside the retaining rocks and renew the eruption. If the magma column is connected to a relatively large body of magma at depth, it seems possible that recurrent eruptions may occur at the same site over a long period of time, the cycle depending on the rate of diffusion of water in the magma.

It must not be overlooked that the sequence of events outlined above is based on certain assumptions as to the distribution and diffusion of water in a magma chamber. Although these assumptions cannot at this time be proved, they are based on sound scientific reasoning, and, if true, they do afford an explanation for a number of aspects of volcanic activity.

VOLCANIC SOLIDS
(PYROCLASTICS)

The ejection of solid fragments (projectiles) is one of the most spectacular phases of a volcanic eruption. I was privileged to watch at close range the eruption of Parícutin Volcano, Mexico, during its most active period. At night the spectacle was awesome. With each explosion literally thousands of red-hot fragments were blown to a height of several thousand feet above the crater rim, and then, showering the cone like a giant skyrocket, they left a trail of fire as they cascaded down the sides. So abundant were these red-hot fragments that frequently the entire cone was covered with interlacing fiery trails. The fragments of solid material ejected by a volcano range in size from huge blocks of the crustal layers, which are blown out in the initial break-through of the vent, to fine dustlike particles which are so light that they may drift completely around the earth several times. The accumulation of this debris around the vent, together with any lava which may be poured out, builds the volcanic cone. All the fragmental material ejected by a volcano is described as *pyroclastic* (*pyro*, "fire," + *clastic*, "broken") material.

Classification of Pyroclastics

A simple classification of pyroclastic material, based on size and shape, is useful. The larger fragments, consisting of pieces of the crustal layers beneath the volcano or of older lavas broken from the walls of the conduit or from the surface of the crater, are called *blocks*. *Volcanic bombs* are masses of new lava blown from the crater and solidified during flight, becoming rounded or spindle-shaped as they are hurled through the air. In size they range from small pellets up to huge masses weighing many tons. Sometimes they are still plastic when they strike the surface and are flattened or distorted as they roll down the side of the cone. Occasionally one may strike a tree and be molded around a limb. I observed a splendid example of such a tree-limb-molded bomb at Parícutin during the early stage of its activity. Thinking it would make an excellent museum specimen, I returned to camp to get a saw, in order to collect it undisturbed. However, when I returned, some tourist had already broken off the limb as a souvenir! Another type, known as a "bread-crust bomb," resembles a loaf of French bread with large gaping cracks in the crust. This cracking of the crust results from the continued expansion of the internal gases.

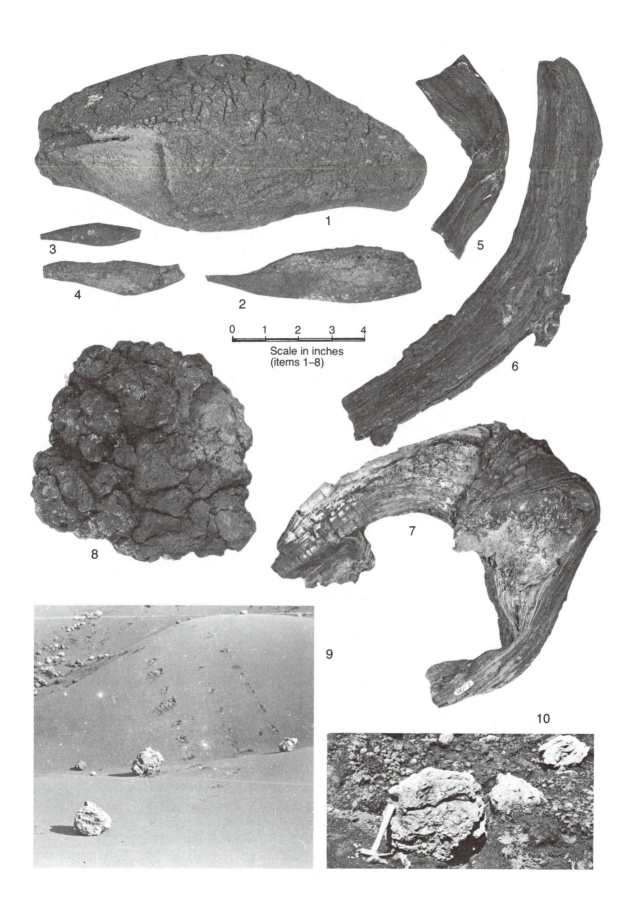

Scale in inches
(items 1–8)

Many fragments of lava and scoria, solidified in flight, fall back into the crater and are intermixed with fluid lava and again erupted. Generally rounded in shape, they frequently contain enough fluid or plastic lava to flatten somewhat on impact. Such agglomerate bombs are the most common type of bomb in many volcanic eruptions.

In contrast to bombs, smaller broken fragments are *lapilli* (from Italian, meaning "little stones"), about the size of walnuts; then, in decreasing size, *cinders*, *ash*, and *dust*. Frequently no distinction is made between ash and dust, but cinders are sand-size particles, intermediate in size between lapilli and ash. Originally the terms *cinders* and *ash* were applied because the material resembled the cinders and ashes from grates of the fires in the home, and, since volcanoes were then believed to be due to the burning of underground coal seams, the names seemed appropriate. The cinders and ash are, of course, pulverized lava, broken up by the force of the rapidly expanding gases contained in it or by the grinding together of the fragments in the crater, like a huge mill, as they are repeatedly blown out and fall back into the crater after each explosion.

Pumice is a type of pyroclastic produced by acidic lavas in which the gas content is so great as to cause the magma to "froth" as it rises in the chimney of the volcano and, with approach to the surface, into zones of decreasing pressure. When the explosion occurs, the rock froth is expelled as pumice. Much of the material is shattered into dust-size particles, but pieces varying from the size of marbles up to a foot or more in diameter are abundant. Pumice will float in water because of the many air spaces formed by the expanding gases. It should be remembered that this material is as truly magma as any lava flow, but, because of its high gas content, it is expelled as pumice and ash rather than as a liquid. The debris which buried Pompeii in A.D. 79 was pumice from the eruption of Vesuvius. It was nearly a thousand years later before any liquid lava issued from Vesuvius. Volcanoes which eject chiefly pumice are the most highly explosive volcanoes known. The volcanoes of Central America, in general, eject chiefly pumiceous material, which, over the ages, has blanketed most of the country to a thickness of hundreds or even thousands of feet (Pl. 2). Volcanic eruptions on the floor of the sea often discharge huge quantities of pumice. It was reported that in 1878 masses of floating pumice covered the sea in the vicinity of the Solomon Islands to such an extent that it took ships three days to force their way through them. At other times the pumice may drift with the currents and accumulate in such quantity in favorable bays that one can walk on the floating raft of pumice, unable to tell the exact position of the shoreline. Pieces of pumice can be found on most of the beaches of the world, having drifted throughout all the oceans.

Volcanic ash results when the rapidly expanding gases (explo-

Plate 2. Pumice layers in road cut near Antigua, Guatemala. Each layer represents an eruption. Note earlier topography (sloping surface at lower right) buried by pumice from later eruptions.

sions) shatter the rock froth. The fragments consist of sharply angular glass particles, which under the microscope are easily identified by their "shard" structure (Fig. 2). Such material is widely used as a scouring powder, just as it is found, as in Old Dutch Cleanser, or mixed with soap powder to form the "new improved foaming" type.

Lava fountains in which steam jets blow the lava into the air sometimes produce a material resembling spun glass, known as "Pele's hair," after the Hawaiian goddess of volcanoes. Pele's hair is identical to varieties of "rock wool" which are manufactured by blowing a jet of steam into a stream of molten rock. Rock wool is widely used for all types of insulation.

The coarse, angular fragments (blocks) which fill the crater of a volcano become cemented to form a rock known as *volcanic breccia*. Indeed the presence of such material is frequently the only evidence to show the location of the actual throat of the volcano after erosion has completely destroyed the cone. The finer material, such as cinders and ash, forms thick deposits, even many miles removed from the volcano. Such material becomes consolidated through the percola-

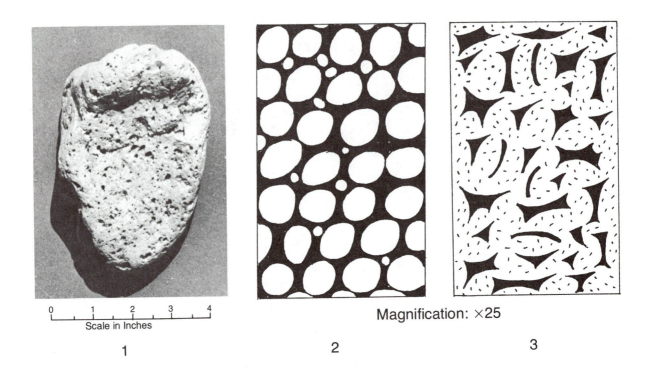

Magnification: ×25

1   2   3

Figure 2. The origin of "shards" by the explosive disruption of pumice. In diagram (2) the open cavities (gas vesicules) are shown in cross section. The "shards" (3) are fragments of the walls of the gas vesicules.

tion of ground water and is known as *tuff*. The common building stone in the volcanic regions of Italy is tuff. Soft enough to be easily quarried and shaped by hand, it has sufficient strength to be set into walls with mortar. The outer surface, as well as the inner, is plastered to keep water out of the porous material. In Italy the tuff which is removed in digging a basement or foundation for a building is chopped (with an ax) into blocks and used for the walls.

Distribution of Pyroclastic Material

The eruption of Krakatoa in 1883 provided an opportunity to study the distribution of volcanic ash in an eruption. Krakatoa is located on a small island between Java and Sumatra in Indonesia. As it was one of the great volcanic eruptions of historic time—perhaps the greatest of all—the distribution of its ash was more extensive than is usually the case. It is estimated that in the eruption one cubic mile of material was blown to a height of 17 miles and that the dust was carried completely around the earth several times by air currents. Dust fell in quantity on the decks of vessels 1,600 miles away three days after the eruption. Measurements of the sun's rays reaching the earth's surface for the year following the eruption were only 87 percent of normal, attesting to the effect of the dust in the atmosphere. The brilliant glow of the skies before sunrise and after sunset due to the reflection of the sunlight from the dust particles in the upper atmosphere attracted world-wide attention. The phenomenon suddenly appeared in a belt 15° on either side of the equator in the week following the eruption. It then gradually spread until it covered the entire earth.

In England, particularly, this phenomenon was the subject of a heated controversy which was debated in the daily newspapers as well as in the scientific journals. One group held it to be due to the "volcanic ashes" ejected into the atmosphere by the eruption of Krakatoa; others held that it was due to the earth's passing through a cosmic cloud, the tail of a comet, or a shower of meteors, or to gases foreign to our atmosphere, possibly derived from the eruption of Krakatoa or from outer space. In the United States, scientists soon took sides in the controversy and articles on the subject appeared in the leading scientific journals. The facts, as set forth in one of these articles on the "sun glows" (Hazen 1884), as well as the basis for objections to the "volcanic-ashes" theory, will be of interest. The glows were first seen in the United States at Yuma, Arizona, on October 19 (the eruption of Krakatoa was August 26), and in the eastern United States on October 30. On this night the spectacle was unusually brilliant and "fire engines were summoned at Poughkeepsie [New York] and New Haven [Connecticut] to quench the burning skies" (Hazen 1884, p. 202). The phenomenon continued, with varying degrees of brilliance, for months. It was noticeably more marked during dry periods. Two of the objections to the volcanic-ashes theory were as follows:

1. The situation required the ejection of sufficient material to cover more than 135,000,000 square miles (45° on either side of the equator). The attempt to account for this from an isolated volcano thousands of miles away "can only be regarded as an endeavor to support a weak cause" (Hazen 1884, p. 210).

2. Such distribution of volcanic ash would have required upper-air currents of sufficient velocity to carry ashes a distance of 12,000 miles in 150 hours, a velocity of 80 miles per hour, to the west. "We know little of velocities of air currents at great height but they are probably slight" (Hazen 1884, p. 210).

The advocates of the "volcanic-ashes" theory, notably Mr. Norman Locker in the December 10 issue of the London *Daily Mail*, pointed out that ash had fallen in Spain and in Holland and that analysis of this material showed that it was identical with the Krakatoa ash. Yet this was not convincing to the opponents of the theory.

The world-wide distribution of ash in the eruption of Krakatoa in 1883 provided important information on the circulation of matter in the upper layers of the atmosphere.

Although the eruption of Parícutin Volcano, Mexico, from 1943 to 1952 must be recognized as a minor eruption as compared to that of Krakatoa in 1883, the fact that it was studied in detail makes it important for purposes of comparison. The greater part of the ash from Parícutin was ejected during the first year of its activity, its more violent outbursts ejecting enough ash to cause considerable inconvenience in the streets of Uruapan, 48 kilometers away, with slight ash falls on Mexico City, 320 kilometers distant. The east-west elongate shape of the area covered by ash from Parícutin reflects the influence of the prevailing winds. It extends a greater distance to the west of the cone, indicating that the east winds of the rainy season are the stronger. Kenneth Segerstrom (1950), in connection with erosion studies at Parícutin, prepared a map showing the thickness of ash deposits around Parícutin Volcano. The one-meter line, representing the limit of a thickness of one meter or more, extends 3.8 kilometers to the east and 6.6 kilometers to the west of the cone. The one-fourth–meter (about 10 inches) line extends 7 kilometers to the east and 11.5 kilometers to the west of the cone. The one-millimeter line passes through Guadalajara, 190 kilometers to the west, and includes an area of 60,000 square kilometers.

LAVA

Meaning of the Term

The molten rock material, before reaching the surface, is one component of magma. Magma differs essentially from molten rock in being charged with varying amounts of gases. While the magma is confined under sufficient pressure, the gaseous constituents remain in solution, but, as the magma rises toward the surface and the overlying pressure is reduced, the gases escape, sometimes with explosive violence. Indeed, it is the expansive force of the pent-up gases which supplies most of the energy released in a volcanic eruption. The expansive force of a gas-charged liquid is familiar to anyone who has opened a bottle of soda water or, on a more elegant level, uncorked a bottle of champagne. The frothing of the liquid and the overflowing of the bottle are analogous, on a small scale, to the flashing of the magma into pumice (rock froth) when the pressure is suddenly relieved by the blowing out (uncorking) of the plug filling the crater of the volcano.

The term *lava*, from the Italian *lavare*, meaning "to wash," was used to denote anything which "washes away." Samuel Johnson's dictionary defines it as an Italian term meaning "a running gullet, streame or gutter, södainly caused by raine." In early Italian usage it was applied to a flood of water or mud; so they speak of "water lava" or "mud lava," or even *lava di gente*, meaning a hurrying crowd of people. It was first applied in Neapolitan dialect to lava streams from Vesuvius, and then adopted into Italian literature, from which it has developed its present meaning. The root of the verb *lavare*, common to Latin, French, Spanish, and Italian, is found in the English language in such words as *lavatory*, a place for washing. Many current misconceptions have been introduced through the misinterpretation of the meaning attached to the term *lava* in accounts of early volcanic eruptions in the Italian region. For instance, the mud flow which buried the city of Herculaneum in A.D. 79 following the eruption of Vesuvius was described as a lava flow. *Lava*, as now used, however, refers to the liquid product, or molten rock, which issues from a volcano.

Composition of Lavas

Lavas in their chemical composition are a mixture of several oxides, with SiO_2 (silicon dioxide) greatly in excess over the others. The ingredients are virtually the same in all types of lavas but vary considerably in their relative proportions. The range in SiO_2 content, which varies from as little as 35 percent up to 75 percent by weight in typical volcanic rocks, is the basis for grouping the lavas (and, in fact, all igneous rocks) into three categories. Those which contain 66 percent or more of SiO_2 are the *acidic* rocks, because SiO_2 acts as an acid, combining with the remaining oxides to form silicate compounds. The lavas with SiO_2 content between 52 percent and 66 percent are *intermediate*, and those with SiO_2 content under 52 percent are termed *basic* lavas. The composition affects the viscosity, thereby influencing the ease with which the gases are liberated, and as a consequence determines the type of eruption, the rate of flow, and other characteristics. In general, the acidic lavas, more stiff and viscous, even at high temperatures, thus causing the gases to escape with difficulty, result in explosive types of eruptions. Such lavas, known as *rhyolites*, are generally light in color, frequently grey or pink. The basic lavas are dark-colored, and, being quite fluid, flow readily, thus allowing the gases to escape with ease. Their eruptions are of the quiet type, and they yield a lava known as *basalt*. Between the two extremes described above are the intermediate lavas, known as *andesites*, from the Andes Mountains of South America. They occur abundantly throughout the western United States.

A typical acidic lava may contain 70 percent or more SiO_2, 12–15 percent Al_2O_3 (aluminum oxide), 6–8 percent alkalies—Na_2O (sodium oxide) and K_2O (potassium oxide)—and relatively small amounts, 3 percent or less, of the oxides of iron, magnesium, and calcium. An average of many analyses of basalt, a typical basic lava, with percentages rounded off to the nearest whole number, shows 49 percent SiO_2, 16 percent Al_2O_3, 12 percent iron oxides, 9 percent CaO (calcium oxide), 6 percent MgO (magnesium oxide), and relatively small amounts, 3 percent or less, of the oxides of sodium and potassium. It will be noted that, in addition to the marked difference in SiO_2 content, the chief distinction between acidic and basic lavas is the relatively high percentages of alkalies and the low percentages of iron, magnesium, and calcium in the acidic lavas, with reverse proportions in the basic lavas. The great majority of lavas, the andesites, are intermediate between acidic and basic lavas. An average of 20 analyses, with percentages rounded off to the nearest whole number, shows 59 percent SiO_2, 16 percent Al_2O_3, 7 percent iron oxides, 6 percent CaO, 4 percent Na_2O, 3 percent MgO, and 2 percent K_2O. While all lavas have a similarity in composition, no two volcanoes erupt lavas of exactly the same composition, and in fact the composition may vary from one eruption to another in the same volcano.

Temperature Observations

The color of a heated body depends on the temperature, not the nature of the material. By observing the color with which a body glows, one can make an accurate estimate of the temperature (Table 1).

The temperature of the lava as it emerges from the volcano has been measured by various devices. One of the most useful, because of its portability, is the optical pyrometer. This instrument, based on the fact that color is a true index to temperature, is designed to measure the temperature by matching the color of the glowing lava with the same color from an electrically activated cell. Red-hot and white-hot are colors associated with definite temperatures, and these, along with many intermediate shades, can be determined with the optical pyrometer in terms of temperature. Such instruments are widely used to measure temperature in brick kilns, steel furnaces, and similar industrial plants. In measuring the temperature of a lava flow, an operator focuses this instrument, which resembles a hand telescope, on an incandescent surface of the lava and rotates a dial in the instrument until the color appearing on the gauge matches that of the lava. He then reads the temperature in degrees on a scale in the instrument. Another instrument, successfully used when it is possible to approach the lava at close range, is a thermoelectric pyrometer. The "fire end" of this instrument is thrust into the lava or gas vent, and a cable connection with the cold end, where a thermometer is provided, gives the correction to a heat-generated electric current which is read directly in degrees of heat.

Basic lavas, which are the only ones on which good temperature

TABLE 1. *Approximate color scale of temperature*

Color	Degrees Centigrade	Degrees Fahrenheit
Incipient-red heat	540	1,000
Dark-red heat	650	1,200
Bright-red heat	870	1,600
Yellowish-red heat	1,100	2,000
Incipient-white heat	1,260	2,300
White heat	1,480	2,700

measurements have been made thus far, have a temperature of around 1,100° C. The highest temperature that I measured at Parícutin was 1,135° C., and in this case a slaglike crust began to develop on the incandescent lava when the temperature dropped to around 950° C. Perret (1950) recorded temperatures for the lava of the 1910 eruption of Mount Etna in Sicily of between 900° C. and 1,000° C., and from 1,015° C. to 1,040° C. on Vesuvian lavas in 1916–1918. The hottest lavas known, with temperatures in excess of 1,200° C., are the Hawaiian lavas at Kilauea Crater. One of the most unusual temperature observations ever recorded was made by Dr. Thomas A. Jaggar at Kilauea in 1917. He inserted Seger cones (ceramic cones constructed to melt at definite temperatures) into an iron pipe which he then thrust into the lava pool at Halemaumau within Kilauea Crater. Although he was able to penetrate only 20 feet or so below the surface, his test showed conclusively that temperatures at this depth were on the order of 100° C. lower than at the surface. This somewhat anomalous situation, at first perplexing, now seems simply explained when one realizes that the greater heat at the surface is generated by the reaction of the evolving gases with one another and especially with atmospheric oxygen. Temperature measurements made by inserting a thermocouple (see glossary) into molten lava through a hole drilled through the solidified crust of the lava lake in Alae Crater (Kilauea area) recorded a maximum temperature of 1,140° C., and the temperature of the half-solidified material at the base of the crust was 1,067° C. (Peck, Moore, and Kojima 1964). Minimum temperatures observed on lavas are around 750° C.

Solidification of Lava

After being poured onto the surface, the lava spreads out as tongues or sheets which flow over the countryside, often finding their way into stream valleys, along which they may extend for many miles.

Some sheets of lava, such as those forming the great lava plateaus, cover thousands of square miles and extend tens or even hundreds of miles from their source. The thickness of an individual flow may vary from a few inches to many hundreds of feet. The average person may think that lavas are something rather rare on the earth's surface. To dispel this idea one needs only to consider, in addition to the lava flows from individual volcanoes, the great plateau basalts, such as those which make up the Columbia River Plateau of the Pacific Northwest of the United States. Here, covering most of Oregon and parts of Idaho and Washington with an area of 200,000 square miles, are basaltic lavas reaching a thickness of 3,000 feet and representing hundreds of flows superimposed one upon another. When one realizes also that this is but one of many such areas of the earth, one obtains some appreciation of the tremendous quantity of lava on the earth's surface.

The mobility of molten lava depends on its composition and temperature. The stiff, viscous acidic lavas usually congeal before they have traveled far, whereas the basic lavas, being more fluid, tend to flow freely for long distances before they come to rest. The speed of a lava flow depends on its viscosity (which depends on temperature and composition) as well as upon the slope of the surface on which it is flowing. In unusual cases, some of the basic lavas on Mauna Loa, Hawaii, have attained velocities up to 10–25 miles per hour, but this is highly exceptional. At Parícutin Volcano, Mexico, velocities up to 50 feet per minute were observed near the source, but at a distance of one mile, where the lava spread out on a more gentle slope, the velocity decreased to 50 feet per hour. At Parícutin a tongue of lava might continue to move for months, finally decreasing its forward advance to only a few feet per day in its final stage.

The upper part of a lava flow is usually made up of a porous, spongelike mass of lava known as *scoria*. The porous character is due to the escape of the contained gases or to the expansion of the gases to form bubbles just prior to the freezing of the flow. These bubbles, or voids which were occupied by gas, may become elongated or drawn out into tubelike forms, as the stiff, viscous material in which the bubbles are entrapped continues to move slowly forward. The surfaces of lava flows commonly develop into one of two contrasting types, for which the Hawaiian names of *aa* and *pahoehoe* are used. In the pahoehoe type (known as "corded" in Italy) the surface is smooth and billowy and frequently molded into forms which resemble huge coils of rope. Such lava surfaces commonly develop in the basic lava, in which a skinlike surface covers the still liquid lava below; as the flow continues to move, the smooth skin is wrinkled into ropy or billowy surfaces which are preserved when the mass finally congeals. In the aa type, the surface of the flow consists of a confused mass of angular, jagged, scoriaceous blocks, often with dangerously sharp edges and spiny projections. No continuous surface forms over this type of flow, and the confused mass of angular blocks which are being carried on the surface remain when the flow freezes. The fact that some flows issue from the vent as pahoehoe but change to aa as they proceed downslope indicates the close relationship between the two types. Gordon A. Macdonald observes that "the change of pahoehoe to aa has been shown to be a function of both viscosity of the magma and the amount of mechanical stirring to which it is subjected. . . . It is a common observation that pahoehoe flows change to aa when they go down a steep slope. . . . [This change] appears to result largely from an increase in viscosity due to cooling, loss of gas, and increasing degree of crystallization" (1972, p. 91). The change from aa back to pahoehoe does not occur.

Lava Tubes

Once a crust has formed on a pahoehoe type flow, the interior may remain liquid and mobile for long periods of time, and as long as new lava is added from the vent it continues to flow. Movement of lava is by laminar flow, and the shear planes, separating laminae, give rise to the "layered lava" common in basaltic flows. As the main body of the lava cools, active flow is restricted to a mobile cylinder in the thickest and hottest part of the flow. In response to surges of lava from the vent the mobile core may migrate in a sinuous pattern within the flow. Eventually the bulk of the flow solidifies, forming layered lava, and the still molten core drains to the margin of the advancing lava flow, leaving a void or lava tube (Greeley and Hyde 1972). Lava tubes may bifurcate to form separate networks or may form cut-off branches similar to those found in river channels. Near the flow front, the lava may issue from a series of "feeder tubes" comparable to the distributary channels of a river. As the level of lava recedes in the tube, temporary halts are marked by lava benches, or "water marks," along the side of the tube. In some cases the last lava to solidify in the tube has become so viscous that it forms aa instead of the usual pahoehoe lava. Lava dripping from the ceiling forms stalactites and related features, which are common in most lava tubes.

   The size of a lava tube is influenced by the thickness of the flow, the viscosity, the rate of cooling, and the slope of the surface on which it flows. They range in size from minute channels only inches in diameter up to huge cavities many feet in diameter. Typical of many lava tubes are those of Victoria, Australia, which are described as "about the size and shape of a railway tunnel" with most tube roofs about 20 feet below the flow surface (Ollier and Brown 1965,

Plate 3A. Pahoehoe lava sur-faces, Galápagos Islands.
Left: *Pahoehoe "toes."*
Right: *Ropy lava. Photos courtesy Tad Nichols.*

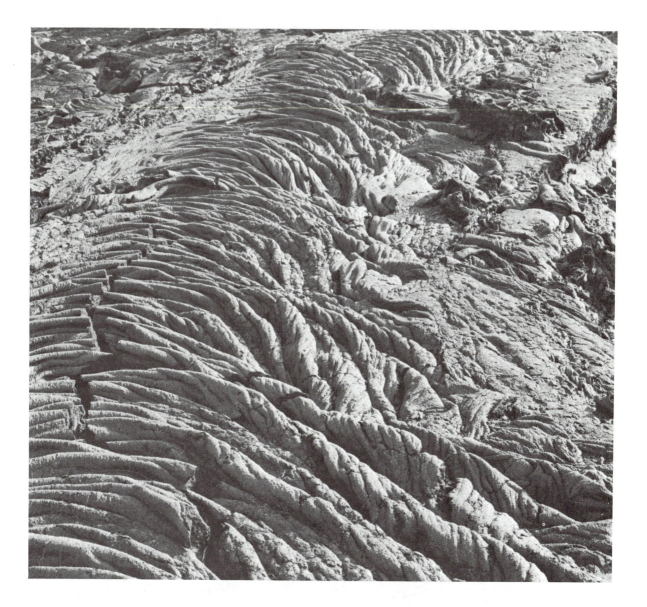

Plate 3B. Aa lava flows, Parícutin Volcano, Mexico. Above: Aa lava flow which buried the church at San Juan Parangaricutiro in June, 1944. Below: advancing aa lava flow, September 4, 1944.

p. 216). Lava tubes may extend for several miles, but commonly there are collapse areas at intervals which expose the tube and provide means of access. One of the longest tubes ever described is at Hambone, Siskiyou County, Northern California. This tube is 13.8 miles in length and has sections in which there are four distinct levels, stacked vertically for a total height of 130 feet (Greeley and Baer 1971). On the surface, lava tubes are often marked by a low ridge along their axis, because they normally follow the thickest part of the flow. Excellent examples of lava tubes are to be found in many areas. The Thurston Lava Tube in Hawaii National Park at Kilauea Volcano is one of the best known. Lava Beds National Monument in northeastern California and Craters of the Moon National Monument in southern Idaho both have many lava tubes open to visitors.

A lava tube on the outskirts of Dubois, Idaho, has been developed as a bomb and fall-out shelter which can accommodate the entire population of Dubois (about 2,500). A ramp was constructed so that the tube can be entered by automobiles, and, with a stand-by electric generator and a supply of food and water, it stands ready for any emergency.

Many lava surfaces, particularly those of the pahoehoe type, have elongate ridges resulting from the flow crust's being pushed into folds by the pressure of the moving lava flow. Such features, known as *pressure ridges*, are commonly a few feet in height and 100 feet or so in length but in exceptional cases are as much as 50 feet high and a half mile long. Similar dome-shaped features are known as *tumuli*. Molten lava rising in cracks in the crust of a flow forms *squeeze-ups*.

Tree Molds

A tree mold, or lava tree, is formed when fluid lava encases the trunk of a tree. Commonly the tree burns, but some portions may be converted to charcoal, especially the root system in the soil zone beneath the flow. In some cases the tree may be pushed over by the advancing flow, and the resulting tree mold will be more or less horizontal. When the tree remains upright, the depth of the tree-mold well is determined by the thickness of the enclosing flow. Spatter from nearby lava fountains may accumulate on and around the tree so that a whole "lava tree" is formed. The volatiles released as the trunk of the tree burns make the lava in contact with the tree more fluid, so that minute details in the structure of the bark or wood may be preserved. Tree molds are discussed further in the section on Craters of the Moon National Monument, Chapter 11.

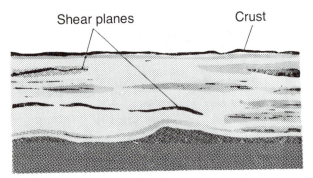

Shear planes   Crust

1. Laminar flow.

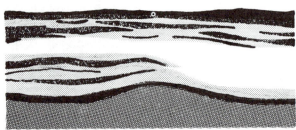

2. Mobile tube stage. The tube may migrate within the flow.

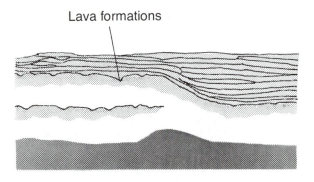

Lava formations

3. Primary tube formation. The position of the tube becomes fixed; in the sketch the left section of the tube has two levels.

Fluid lava

4. Cross-section of lava tube.

Figure 3. Lava-tube formation associated with shear planes in laminar lava flow. After Greeley and Hyde (1972).

Plate 4. Lava tubes. Above:
Spider Cave, a lava tube in
the Cave Basalt, Mount St.
Helens area, Washington.
An aa lava flow has partly
filled the lava tube. Photo
by Charles and Jo Larson,
courtesy Ronald Greeley
(from Greeley and Hyde
1972, p. 2410). Below:
Valentine Cave, a lava tube
in Lava Beds National Monu-
ment, California. Note chill
levee on either side of the lava
tube marking ''high-water''
levels of lava flows which
once occupied the lava tube.
Photo by Garrett Smathers,
courtesy National Park Serv-
ice.

Plate 5. Pressure ridges and tumulus on lava flows. Upper left: Large pressure ridge, Galápagos Islands. Photo courtesy Tad Nichols. Lower left: Aerial view of pressure ridges in Craters of the Moon National Monument, Idaho. The height is commonly on the order of 25–30 feet, with a length of 100–300 feet. Right: Tumulus on the margin of the October, 1944, lava flow at Parícutin Volcano, Mexico. The dark, still partly molten lava being ejected through the cracks is described as a "squeeze-up." The author is in the picture for scale. Photo courtesy Tad Nichols.

Crystallization of Lava

The magma is a melt in which the various constituents are, in effect, mutually dissolved. Thus the temperature may drop well below the melting point of all the constituents; yet the magma will remain liquid. Salt dissolved in water produces a similar result in that it lowers the freezing point of the water. From this it follows that the order of crystallization of the minerals from a magma is based on solubility rather than fusibility. That is, the minerals least soluble in the magma are the ones that begin to crystallize out first. The minerals which crystallize first will have well-developed crystal outlines, because they encountered no interference in development, while the last mineral to form must necessarily fill the spaces left, and its shape is determined not by its own crystal structure but by the surrounding minerals.

The early stage of crystallization of a magma doubtless begins in the magma chamber, long before the actual eruption takes place. Thus olivine, the first mineral to crystallize, may develop into fairly large crystals which are floating in the magma at the time of the eruption. When the lava is poured out on the surface the cooling is greatly accelerated, and the olivine crystals are entrapped in a groundmass of small crystals which result from the rapid cooling. If cooling is extremely rapid there may not be time for crystallization, and a glassy groundmass will form. Hence, nearly all lavas, when examined with a hand lens, will show some large, evident crystals (*phenocrysts*) embedded in a much finer-grained or even glassy groundmass. Such a texture is known as *porphyritic*, and the rock is called a *porphyry*. The lavas of Hawaii are mostly olivine basalt porphyries, and the green olivine phenocrysts are readily discernible without the aid of a hand lens. On weathering, the olivine crystals are freed from the rock and accumulate on the weathered surface of the lava flow or along the stream beds where they have been carried by water. These crystals are known locally as "Pele diamonds" and are used as a semiprecious gemstone.

Obsidian is a volcanic glass which results when viscosity is too high to permit crystallization during the period of cooling. Small amounts of obsidian are usual associates of most volcanic regions, but extensive flows of obsidian, although not common, are known in many parts of the world. Perhaps the most famous is on the island of Lipari, off the coast of Sicily, but numerous examples are also to be found in the western United States. Flow structures are an alignment of the elongate crystals in the rock, similar to that observed in a mass of logs being floated in a river to the mill. Usually such structures are best observed in thin slices of the rock viewed under a microscope.

Causes of Variation in Composition of Lavas

An interesting query in relation to lava flows is why there are so many different kinds of lavas, or for that matter, of igneous rocks in general. It was pointed out earlier in this section that different volcanoes erupt different kinds of lava and, in fact, that the same volcano may erupt lavas of different compositions in succeeding eruptions. Does this imply that separate reservoirs are tapped in different eruptions, or at different times? The answer is certainly no. The full explanation, however, would involve a topic known as *magmatic differentiation*, or the splitting of a parent magma into various components, and this subject involves a knowledge of advanced geology and physical chemistry beyond the scope of this work. Nevertheless, it is felt that the reader is entitled to at least a general idea of the types of explanations which have been proposed to account for magmatic differentiation, rather than complete avoidance of the topic. It must be admitted that it is a highly controversial subject and that perhaps generations of scientific investigations will be needed before the ultimate truth is known. An explanation which has been popular with many geologists, largely the work of N. L. Bowen (1928), will be briefly sketched.

According to this explanation the many rock types are believed to have been derived from a parent magma through a process known as *fractional crystallization*. The minerals that crystallize first from a magma are the heavier and more basic ones (olivine, pyroxene, etc.); and, as they settle, the remaining mass becomes more acidic because of the removal of the basic fraction. It is a process known to geologists as crystal differentiation by gravity and was suggested by the olivine-rich ledge in the Palisade Sill. The Palisade Sill of New Jersey, in places over 1,000 feet thick, outcrops continuously for a distance of 50 miles along the west bank of the Hudson River facing the city of New York. It was intruded into the surrounding rocks as a great molten sheet. The name refers to the huge, columnlike appearance of the outcrop, resulting from the joints which formed as the mass cooled. As olivine began to crystallize, it settled to the lower part of the mass, forming a layer about 15 feet thick. The olivine-rich bed is at the top of the lower chilled border layer about 50 feet from the base of the sill. Thus the composition of the mass was altered by the removal of the constituents making up olivine. Since the process of crystal settling, conceivably, could be halted at any point by freezing of the magma or its expulsion to the surface in a volcanic eruption, an infinite variety of rock types is possible. The process may be compared to fractional distillation, in which crude oil is split into gasoline, kerosene, and other components by heating it to different temperatures.

While many geologists regard fractional crystallization as the main factor in controlling igneous rock differentiation, a growing number hold divergent views. Other processes held to be effective in producing differentiation include assimilation of the wall rock of the magma chamber or of portions of the already crystallized magma, mingling of magmas, gaseous transfer, and thermal diffusion-convection. After reviewing the problem of magmatic differentiation, Tom F. W. Barth concluded: "Petrologists agree that differentiation cannot be attributed to any one mechanism, and for most of the igneous bodies actually studied no complete or satisfactory explanation has been proposed. Crystallization differentiation, assimilation, mingling of magmas, etc., may each have played its part, and there may be still other important processes of which we know nothing today" (1950, p. 161).

The parent magma or primary magma which has given rise, by magmatic differentiation due to crystal settling or by other processes, to the various types of igneous rocks is believed to be a world-encircling layer of basaltic composition. There is, however, a marked difference between the continental areas and the oceanic areas in crustal composition. Apart from a thin veneer of sedimentary rocks on the surface, the continents are believed to be composed to a depth of 10–35 kilometers of material known as *sial*, with much greater thicknesses (up to 60 kilometers) under mountain ranges. This material, sometimes called *granitic*, is composed of rocks rich in the oxides of *si*licon and *al*uminum, hence the name *sial*. It corresponds more or less in composition to the granitic type rocks and the acidic lavas previously mentioned.

Under the continents a basaltic layer, conforming in composition to the basic lavas and known as *sima* (*si*lica plus *ma*gnesia), underlies the sial. However, beneath the oceans the crust is sima with little or no sial present. Hence, the Hawaiian volcanoes, coming from the floor of the Pacific Ocean, erupt a primary basaltic magma, whereas, in volcanoes which occur on the continents, the primary basaltic magma must rise through the sialic crust to reach the surface. The contamination by assimilation of the sialic crust results in a more acidic type of material, yielding the andesites. The contamination (or lack of contamination) of the primary basaltic magma by assimilation as it passes through the surface layers of the earth's crust has led to the recognition of three major types of lavas:

1. The Atlantic type lavas are the primary olivine basaltic magma, believed to be world-wide in distribution, which reaches the surface without contamination. This type is necessarily found in those areas in which the sialic crust is missing. It was designated the Atlantic type because examples first cited were from islands in the Atlantic

Ocean. However, without exception, the lavas within the Pacific Ocean basin proper are Atlantic type lavas.

2. Pacific type lavas are those resulting from the contamination of an originally Atlantic type by assimilation of sialic material. The lavas erupted by volcanoes along the continental margins of the Pacific Ocean are of this type. These lavas are andesites for the most part, and the line separating Pacific and Atlantic type lavas is known as the Andesite Line. It is not exactly at the edge of the existing continents but some distance offshore (Fig. 4) and may properly be considered as the limit of the Pacific Ocean basin.

3. Mediterranean type lavas, which are produced by Italian volcanoes, do not fit into either of the other two classes, although they might be considered as a special variation of the Pacific type. In the Mediterranean region the high limestone content of the crust and the shallow depth of the magma have resulted in marked changes in the composition of the lavas because of the assimilation of large quantities of limestone by the magma in reaching the surface. Mediterranean type lavas may also be produced by the interaction of carbonate-rich basic magmas and sial and hence can occur in areas in which there is no limestone to be assimilated (Holmes 1950).

Thus, the statement made earlier that volcanoes tend to erupt basic lavas in the early stages of their history and more acidic lavas in the declining stage can now be rationalized. In the initial stage, the primary basaltic magma reaches the surface uncontaminated, but as the magma rises in the crust and has time to assimilate sialic material it becomes more and more acidic, and the lavas ejected reflect this progressive change. This statement is an oversimplification of an extremely complex and inadequately understood process. It appears that no amount of assimilation by basic magma would yield material of the composition of rhyolite, which is the end product of the eruptive cycle in many volcanic regions. The answer probably lies in the assimilation of sial by high-pressure gases, but this problem is awaiting solution.

Rate of Cooling of a Lava Flow

Lava, like all rock, is a poor conductor of heat, and it cools very slowly. The scoriaceous nature of the surface layer, with its many cavities and entrapped air spaces, provides a splendid insulation to prevent the heat of the lava from escaping. It is possible to walk over a lava stream in which only a few inches below the surface the rock is still red-hot. In my experience the gases rising from the cooling lava,

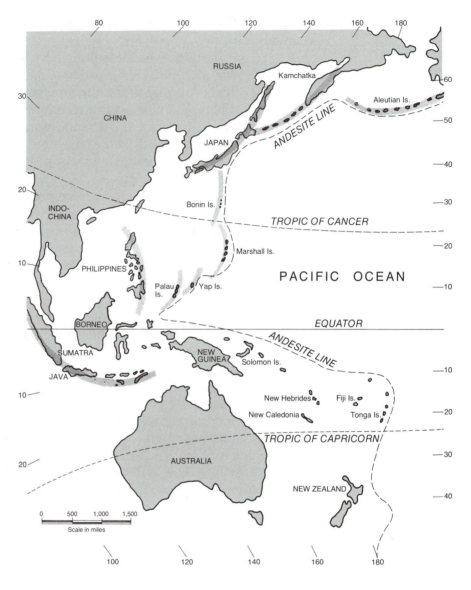

Figure 4. The Andesite Line in the Western Pacific area.

particularly from fissures, are more of a hazard than the heat of the lava surface.

How long will a lava flow remain hot? Naturally, this will depend on the size of the flow, for it will take a large mass longer to cool than a small one. The hot springs and geysers of Yellowstone National Park attest the fact that an acidic lava buried only a short distance below the surface will remain hot for thousands, even hundreds of thousands, of years. Here, the material failed to reach the surface but did come close enough to heat the ground water issuing as hot springs and geysers. Old Faithful Geyser was active during the Ice Age, as is indicated by geyser deposits interbedded with glacial deposits. Cooling at the surface, of course, would be much more rapid, but nevertheless it is a slow process in terms of our everyday concept of time. R. A. Daly (1933, p. 63) estimates that a magma at a temperature of 1,100° C., if exposed to the air on top (as a lava flow), would cool to 750° C. in accordance with this schedule:

3 feet thick	12 days
30 feet thick	3 years
300 feet thick	30 years

This, however, is down to only 750° C., and the cooling will become progressively slower as the mass approaches air temperature; so the time required for further cooling would be greatly, and disproportionately, lengthened. Many lava deposits are between 30 and 300 feet in thickness and were formed by flows in which the temperature of the lava was around 1,100° C. when it reached the surface. It is not surprising, therefore, that a lava flow will remain hot and steaming internally for years. Once a crust has formed, it serves as an insulation to prevent radiation of heat, and the cooling is a very slow process indeed.

At Parícutin Volcano, the San Juan flow of 1944, with a thickness of about 30 feet, was still steaming in 1956. The last flow to issue from Parícutin Volcano was in March, 1952. In September, 1956, it still contained some fumaroles at various points on the flow, and even small pieces of lava broken from the surface of larger blocks were too hot to hold in the hand; yet it had been cooling for four and one-half years. Judd (1881, p. 110) recorded that masses of snow, which were covered during the 1872 eruption of Vesuvius by a thick layer of scoria and afterward by a lava flow, were found three years later consolidated into ice but not melted. This attests the insulating properties of scoria.

Eleven months after an eruption of Mt. Etna, Spallanzani records that "red hot lava could still be seen at the bottom of fissures, and a stick thrust into one instantly took fire." The Vesuvian lava of 1785 was found by Breislak to be still hot and steaming internally after seven years, although lichens had already taken root on the surface. Hoffman records that the lava which flowed from Etna in 1787 was still steaming in 1830. But more remarkable is the case of Jorullo Volcano, in Mexico, which erupted lava in 1759. Twenty-one years later, it is said, a cigar could be lighted at its fissures; after forty-four years it was still visibly steaming, and even in 1846, after eighty-seven years of cooling, two vapor columns were still rising from it. (*Encyclopedia Britannica*)

In the 1959 eruption of Kilauea Iki, a crater adjacent to the caldera of Kilauea Volcano, Hawaii, a pool of lava 300 feet thick accumulated in the crater. After seven months of cooling, a diamond drill hole revealed that the crust was only 18.5 feet thick; by 1964 it had increased to 65 feet (Macdonald 1972, p. 73).

The eruption in 1963 at Alae Crater, one of the pit craters on the east rift zone of Kilauea Volcano, left a pool of lava 50 feet thick in the crater. Drilling and temperature measurements beginning six days after the eruption recorded the growth of the crust as it increased from 3.4 feet to 19 feet (at the end of 6 months). The temperature at the base of the crust was 1,067° C. The rate of cooling is, of course, faster in the initial stage and decreases as the thickening crust provides more insulation. For the first .01 month (7.3 hours) the thickness of the crust increased at the rate of 25 feet per month; at the end of 1 month it was increasing at the rate of 3.5 feet per month; and at the end of 6 months the rate had decreased to 2 feet per month.

From these and other studies it was determined that the thickness of the crust is proportional to the square root of the time elapsed since the crust began to form (Peck, Moore, and Kojima 1964; Peck, Wright, and Moore 1966). This rate, which conforms to that calculated for the conductive cooling from 1,000° C. of an extrusive sheet with latent heat of 100 calories per gram and diffusivity of 0.0071 square centimeters per second, may vary with rainfall, excessive cooling from cracks, and other factors.

Stopping a Lava Flow

In most regions the towns, either because of the accessibility of water or because of the fertility of the soil, are located in the valleys. Since lava flows seek the lowest course, the valleys are the first areas to be invaded. As a result, many towns and even cities have been destroyed by lava flows. On the thickly populated slopes of Vesuvius it would be practically impossible for a lava flow to miss all of the towns, and many of them have been destroyed repeatedly. Torre Annunziata, in the path of the 1906 lava flow from Vesuvius, had been destroyed on three previous occasions in the past 900 years but each time had been rebuilt. Torre del Greco, another important town on the slope of Vesuvius, has had a similar history, and the number could be multiplied many times over. It is reported that, in the 1669 eruption of Mount Etna in Sicily, 14 villages, with a total population of 3,000–4,000, were destroyed, and that eventually the flow swept through Catania and extended into the sea (Lyell 1875, 2:22). In the recent eruption of Parícutin Volcano in Mexico, which, compared to Italy, is sparsely populated, two towns, San Juan de Parangaricutiro, with a population of about 3,000, and Parícutin, with a population of 500, were buried by lava flows. It is only natural, then, that the problem of stopping or diverting a lava flow should have been considered since earliest times. An understanding of the structure of a lava flow is essential to the solution of this problem.

When a lava flow pours out on the surface, the edges, as well as the top, crust over, while the interior remains liquid and moves forward, carrying the surface crust along with it in the aa type flow, or flowing beneath the crust in the pahoehoe type. The cooled edges form a natural levee, or wall, which confines the lava flow in a channel. The thickness of the flow will, of course, determine the height of the levees, which in many flows will range from 10 to 50 feet.

Perhaps the first attempt—at least the first attempt on record—to alter the course of a lava flow occurred during the 1669 eruption of Mount Etna in Sicily. The flow, which originated about 10 miles above the city of Catania, was advancing toward the city and threatening to destroy it. In an effort to save the city, several dozen men covered themselves with wet cowhides for protection against the heat and with iron bars dug an opening through the side wall of the flow, in effect breaking through the natural levee. The operation was initially successful. A stream of lava escaped through the gap thus created and moved away at a high angle from the direction of the original flow, partly relieving the pressure on the tongue moving toward Catania. Unfortunately, the new flow moved in the direction of Paterno, and some 500 irate citizens of that town descended upon the men from Catania and drove them away from the newly dug lava channel. Left unattended, the gap in the wall soon clogged with cooled lava, and the main branch of the flow continued toward Catania, destroying a large section of the city as it passed on and into the sea (Rittmann 1929, pp. 95–96). Even to this day large masses of the 1669 flow block streets and cover portions of the city of Catania. Although this early effort to divert a lava flow ended in failure, it demonstrated the possibility of changing the course of a flow by artificially

Plate 6. Chill levees. Left: *Levees on the sides of lava channels, Parícutin Volcano, Mexico.* Right: *Detail of levee on the right in the photo at left.*

breaking down the retaining natural levee of the flow.

The first modern consideration given to the control of a lava flow was in Hawaii, where the city of Hilo and its harbor were in a position to be threatened from the ever active Mauna Loa Volcano. Hilo, now a city of around 50,000 inhabitants which possesses the only harbor on the island of Hawaii, was spared when the 1881 flow from Mauna Loa stopped after reaching the outskirts of the city. The harbor of Hilo is in a depression between ancient lava flows from Mauna Loa and Mauna Kea. This depression, or lowland, extending far up the mountainside, is also the course of the Wailuku River, Hilo's water supply. Being a depression (with respect to the terrain on either side), it is the natural course of the lava flows originating on the north flank of Mauna Loa. The volcanoes of Hawaii are described elsewhere in this work, but it will be useful in relation to the stoppage of lava flows to review briefly the activity of Mauna Loa at this time.

Mauna Loa, one of the world's largest volcanoes, is one of five volcanoes making up the island of Hawaii. (Mauna Loa and Kilauea, the only two active volcanoes in the Hawaiian Islands, are both located on the island of Hawaii.) Mauna Loa is a huge, shield-shaped mass, rising over 13,000 feet above sea level and consisting of innumerable

lava flows, one superimposed upon another. At the summit is a huge crater (caldera) from which lava flows frequently issue. However, most of the flows issue from a prominent fissure, or fracture zone, the Great Rift zone, which extends in a northeasterly direction through the summit crater. Dr. Jaggar, long-time director of the Hawaiian Volcano Observatory, worked out the pattern for the lava flows on Mauna Loa. He noted that from 1868 to 1926 the lava flows had been moving progressively up the mountain along the southwest rift zone (see Fig. 42). Each flow, on cooling, sealed the fissure at that point, and the next outbreak shifted to a higher point along the rift zone. In the 1933 outbreak, lava occurred in the summit crater. Summit-crater eruptions had always been followed by flank outbreaks, and Dr. Jaggar reasoned that, because of the sealing of the fissure on the south flank by successive eruptions from 1868 to 1926, the next outbreak would be on the northeast rift zone.

Firmly convinced, he issued a prediction in March, 1934, that a lava flow was to be expected within two years and that it would come from the north flank and would probably endanger Hilo. As predicted, the lava outbreak occurred on the north flank on November 21, 1935, first from a point near the summit and a week later from a point along

the rift zone, 4,000 feet lower and 10 miles from the summit. On December 22 this flow, which had pooled in the saddle between Mauna Loa and Mauna Kea, turned toward Hilo. Prior to that date a possibility had existed that it might drain westward into waste lands. When it turned eastward into the drainage of the Wailuku River it was headed for Hilo, and by December 26 it had covered 5 of the 20 miles that would put it in Hilo. Dr. Jaggar had proposed, in 1931, the possibility of controlling a lava flow by bombing. In theory the bombing could bring about the diversion of the flow by breaking the retaining walls, thereby diverting the supply of lava from the flow below the point of rupture and causing stagnation of the lower end of the flow. This could be most easily accomplished, providing the terrain was suitable, through breaking the natural levees by bombing, thus permitting the lava to feed out into other channels. This is a modern approach to the method employed by the cowhide-protected men of Catania in 1669. The new flow might move off at a high angle, as in the 1669 flow at Catania, or more likely it might simply follow the edge of the older flow, and in time reach the same destination. This, however, would be a delaying tactic, and if necessary the breaching could be repeated as many times as necessary. Further, bombs dropped directly into the flow might break the surface crust and clog the channel with solid fragments, or they might stir up the liquid lava, causing it to solidify and clog the channel, thus forcing the lava to seek a new outlet and delaying the forward advance of the lava front.

On December 23, after consultation with the military authorities, Dr. Jaggar decided that the time had come to test the bombing hypothesis. The bombing operation was carried out by a U.S. Air Corps Bombing Squadron from Honolulu. Two target areas were selected, one at an elevation of 8,500 feet, near the source of the flow, and the other about a mile below. On December 27, twenty 600-pound bombs were dropped on these two target areas from an altitude of about 3,500 feet above the lava surface. The direct hits were sufficient in number to blast open the roofed channel of the flow and also to break the levees, permitting at least one lateral flow to develop. The movement of the lava front at noon on December 27, the day of the bombing, was 800 feet per hour; by noon of the following day, it was 44 feet per hour, and by 6:00 P.M., or 30 hours after the bombing, it had stopped altogether! Such remarkable results were entirely unexpected, and the skeptics maintained that the lava stream would have stopped anyway and that the relationship to the bombing was purely coincidental. This view is also maintained by Harold T. Stearns and Gordon A. Macdonald (1946, p. 94), both experienced observers who have had many years' acquaintance with Mauna Loa and whose opinion must be respected. Dr. Jaggar, in his investigation of the effect of the bombing, concluded that the rupture of the roof of the lava channel and the resulting cooling had solidified the lava back to the source and that the remainder of the eruptive energy was expended in lava fountains at the upper end of the rift.

Another test of the bombing hypothesis was made in the same area on Mauna Loa in 1942, with comparable results. These tests show that a lava flow is in a much more delicate state of equilibrium and more sensitive to disturbance than anyone had dreamed. Dr. Jaggar had long believed that a properly designed wall would deflect a lava stream. In 1938, in conjunction with the U.S. Corps of Engineers, he prepared plans for a lava-diversion channel to protect Hilo. The plan was not to block the passage of the lava but to deflect it by means of an artificial barrier. This would force the lava stream along natural downhill grades, forcing it diagonally away from the business district, harbor, and airport of Hilo. The length of the barrier required was seven miles. Although the plan was sound from an engineering standpoint and was approved by a review board in Washington, it became involved in harbor improvements which called for a new breakwater, and in the end it was not authorized.

History records several instances where walls have deflected lava flows. Lyell, in describing the 1669 eruption of Mount Etna in Sicily says: ". . . the lava current, after overflowing 14 towns, some with a population of 3,000 to 4,000 arrived at length at the walls of Catania. These had been purposely raised to protect the city; but the burning flood accumulated till it rose to the top of the rampart, which was 60 feet in height, and then it fell in a fiery cascade and overwhelmed part of the city. The wall, however, was not thrown down, but was discovered long afterwards, by excavations made in the rock by Prince Biscardi; so that the traveler of today may now see the solid lava curling over the top of the rampart as if still in the very act of falling" (1875, 2:23).

In 1952 I attempted to verify this statement and to see if any fragments of the 1669 wall remained. However, it seems probable that the severe earthquakes during the 1669 eruption or in subsequent eruptions destroyed the wall, for no part of it could be located, and even the "arcade" of lava seems to have disappeared.

G. De Lorenzo, in reporting on the eruption of Vesuvius in 1906 says: ". . . it [the lava] reached within a few hours the cemetery of Torre Annunziata, against the walls of which it stopped, breaking into two branches" (1906, p. 476). Today a suitable plaque and shrine set in the cemetery wall commemorate the stopping of the lava at that point. I observed many actively advancing lava flows at Parícutin Volcano, Mexico. Frequently a tree or large boulder would suffice to temporarily halt the advance of the flow at some point by causing large blocks to lodge and in turn block others, until finally a considerable buttress was formed. The lava might then move ahead on other fronts, leaving the tree at the head of an indentation, or as an island. It seems probable that a properly placed barrier might have diverted the lava from the major part of the town of San Juan de Parangaricutiro, which was destroyed in 1944 (Fig. 64).

An example of the diversion of a lava flow at O'Shima Volcano, Japan, was reported by Arnold C. Mason and Helen L. Foster (1953). Miharayama is the active, central cone of O'Shima Volcano on O'Shima Island, 68 miles south of Tokyo. Active repeatedly in historic times, it experienced a major eruption in 1950–1951, when the crater filled with lava, which overflowed the rim at several points. On the northwest side of the rim was Kako Jay (Crater Teahouse), a rectangular building about 25 by 36 feet on a concrete foundation with concrete walls about 4 feet thick and 10 feet high. On March 9, 1951, as the lava began to overflow the rim of the crater, it reached the building, whose roof and wood parts burned. The lava entered the building through the windows and doors, filled the interior, and flowed out in small amounts on the opposite side. The building served as a buttress and confirms that properly placed structures will divert a lava flow.

ASH-FLOW ERUPTIONS   Covering large areas in the western United States, western Mexico, Central America, southern Peru, North Island of New Zealand, and elsewhere are thick sheets of volcanic rocks that have characteristics of lava flows and also of air-fall ash deposits. The obviously fragmental rock, with pieces of pumice and bits of other rock types, often grades downward into denser rock resembling lava. Near the base of individual sheets the pumice fragments are commonly flattened, the vesicles more or less closed, or drawn out into rods, and mixed with lenses of obsidian. It appears that the material was hot enough to soften the pumice and in extreme cases to melt it to lenses of glass (obsidian); that is, it has been "welded." The origin of such ash-flow deposits was in doubt until the 1912 eruption of Mount Katmai in Alaska produced such a deposit and scientists were able to study it firsthand (see pp. 166–170). The material in an ash flow is the product of a *nuée ardente*-type eruption from a fissure or a series of fissures, and the flows often extend for tens of kilometers from their source, leaving a deposit covering thousands of square kilometers. Ash-flow deposits range in thickness from about 1 meter up to hundreds of meters. In southwestern Utah and adjacent Nevada, individual ash-flow beds have been traced for more than 160 kilometers (Mackin 1969, p. 95). The fact that ash flows can cover such large areas and still retain temperatures high enough to produce welding of the fragments after the flow comes to rest implies very rapid extrusion of the material and spreading of the deposit with little time for loss of heat. The Valley of Ten Thousand Smokes ash flow (at Mount Katmai) was emplaced in 20 hours, and the volume of some of the ash-flow deposits of the western United States is staggering. The Bandelier tuff in the Jemez Mountains of New Mexico has a volume of about 200 cubic kilometers (Smith and Bailey 1966). Ash-flow deposits in the San Juan Mountains of Colorado had an original volume, before erosion, of nearly 21,000 cubic kilometers (Lipman and Stevens 1969). Ash flows often cover the fissure from which they are erupted, and frequently it is difficult to locate the actual source of the material. Columnar jointing is conspicuous in many ash-flow deposits, especially in the lower and middle parts. Although the columns are less well developed than in many lava flows, they are a distinctive feature and aid in the identification of an ash-flow deposit, even from a considerable distance.

There is some confusion in the terminology applied to ash-flow deposits. In describing the ones in central North Island, New Zealand, P. Marshall (1935) named *ignimbrites* (literally, glowing cloud-rocks) to indicate their similarity to the deposits of *nuées ardentes*. He pointed out that these rocks must have been formed by the welding or sticking together of still plastic bits of pumice as a result of the high temperature of the material when it came to rest. The rocks called ignimbrites by Marshall are also known as "welded tuffs." The use of the term *ignimbrite* has been criticized because it is not clear whether Marshall's original definition was based on the mode of origin of the material or on its composition and physical nature. It seems preferable to use the term *ash flow* for the eruptive mechanism and limit the term *ignimbrite* to the deposit of an ash flow, whether or not it is welded. An exhaustive study of ash flows and ash-flow deposits was made by Smith (1960) and by Ross and Smith (1961).

IN CONCLUSION

Although we have discussed the products of volcanoes under the separate headings of gasses, liquids, and solids, it must be remembered that this separation does not exist until the material approaches the surface. In the magma chamber the gases are dissolved in the magma. When the magma reaches the surface, the gases may escape more or less quietly, in which case the material will flow out as lava, or they may escape with explosive violence, disrupting the magma into fragmental material, such as ash and cinders. Thus, a study of the products ejected by a volcano will reveal the type of eruption, even though it may have occurred thousands of years ago.

Chapter 6   Cones, Craters, and Calderas

Who hath . . . comprehended the dust of the earth in a measure, and weighed the mountains in scales, and the hills in a balance?—ISAIAH 40:12

CONES

A volcanic cone is the result of the accumulation of ejected material around the vent, and its shape is determined by the proportions of lava and pyroclastic elements in the material composing it. Typically a cup-shaped depression, the crater occupies the apex of the cone. This is the surface connection of the volcanic conduit through which the ejected material reaches the surface. As the ash, cinders, and other fragmental materials shower down around the vent, a cone is formed, the slopes of which are determined by the angle of repose of the debris. Fine ash and cinders come to rest on slopes of 30°–35°, while nearer the summit coarser material may stand at 40° or more. Simple cinder-and-ash cones, with slopes of 30°–35° and a truncated summit occupied by the crater, are common features throughout all volcanic regions. Hundreds of examples are to be found in the western United States, and they are readily identified, even from a considerable distance, by the characteristic profile. Parícutin Volcano, Mexico, is an example of a cinder cone which was formed in recent years. Parícutin attained a height of 450 feet by the end of the first week and 1,000 feet by the end of the second month (Ch. 13).

Most of the larger volcanoes of the world are composite cones consisting of layers of ash and cinders alternating irregularly with tonguelike lava flows. The lava flows issue through breaches in the crater wall or through cracks on the flank or at the base of the cone. When the lava (or magma) solidifies in the fissures which serve as feeder channels for the lava flows, it forms dikes, which greatly strengthen the volcanic edifice. Mount Etna has more than 200 secondary vents dotting its surface. A volcanic cone of the composite type is known also as a *strato-volcano*.

Where the ejected material consists predominantly of lava, as in the Hawaiian volcanoes, a lava cone is formed. The successive flows of lava usually spread out in thin sheets to form a wide-spreading dome with gentle slopes, rarely more than 5°–10°.

Distinction between a Crater and a Caldera

Some volcanoes have great depressions in the truncated summit, much larger than the usual crater, giving the impression that in a violent eruption the volcano has blown away the top of the cone. Such a depression is known as a *caldera*. If a caldera was, in fact, formed by the explosive disruption of the cone, then fragments of the missing part of the cone should be prominent in the debris produced by the eruption. When, as is often the case, such fragments are rare, the only alternative explanation is that the vanished material must have collapsed into the magma chamber. Some of the greatest volcanic eruptions of historic time, such as that at Krakatoa in 1883 (described below), have produced calderas. There is considerable difference of opinion as to the origin of many calderas, even of some of those which have been formed in historic time. A working definition of a caldera is useful at this point, since the term has been applied to a variety of features.

The term *caldera*, as now used, was defined by Howel Williams (1941a) as a large depression, more or less circular in form, the diameter of which is many times greater than that of the included vent or vents. The problem then arises as to the distinction between a crater and a caldera. The crater is the vent through which cinders, ash, lava, and other ejecta are erupted to form cones. Craters may be enlarged somewhat by the force of the explosions, but rarely, if ever, do they exceed .75–1.00 mile in diameter. By contrast, many calderas with diameters of 5–10 miles, and even more, are known. Obviously, such tremendous depressions cannot be normal craters.

In the Spanish language the term *caldera* signifies a "kettle" or "cauldron," and it was originally used by the natives of the Canary Islands for all natural depressions of that shape without reference to their size or origin. The term was introduced into geological literature by Leopold von Buch early in the nineteenth century when he applied it to the summit depression of La Palma Volcano in the Canary Islands, which he considered to be a fine example of a crater of elevation. The caldera, according to von Buch, resulted from the collapse of the "blister" which had pushed up from below to form the volcanic cone (Zittel 1901, p. 262). Lyell, Scrope, and others disproved the crater-of-elevation hypothesis and proposed that calderas result from unusually violent explosions.

Ferdinand André Fouqué (1879), from a study of Santorini Volcano, Greece, in 1866, and R. D. M. Verbeek (1886), from a study of the 1883 eruption of Krakatoa, were impressed by the scarcity of fragmental debris around these calderas and concluded that they must have been formed by engulfment. Since that time many workers throughout the world have confirmed the engulfment theory of the origin of calderas. The rapid draining of magma chambers, either by flank eruptions of lava, as in the Hawaiian type volcanoes, or by the ejection of tremendous quantities of pumice and ash in the Peléan and Vulcanian types, leaves the upper part of the cone without support, and its summit collapses.

Williams's conclusion that "almost all volcanic depressions more than a mile in diameter are produced for the most part by collapse" (1941b, p. 375) may be taken as a basis for separating calderas and craters. Although such a distinction is quite arbitrary, it does work out satisfactorily in practice. It may be noted that a crater is related to cone building and is thus a positive volcanic form, while a caldera is the collapse area above an exhausted magma chamber and is thus a negative, passive form. Calderas are commonly the result of a combination of explosion and collapse. Calderas formed by explosion only are rare and relatively small. The explosion-collapse theory, although devised originally to explain the 1883 eruption of Krakatoa, has been found applicable in general to caldera-making eruptions. According to this theory, the initial stages of the eruption discharge tremendous quantities of primary magmatic material in the form of pumice. This creates an empty space in the magma chamber into which the upper part of the cone collapses. The various stages, as visualized by Williams (1941a), are shown in Figure 5. In many volcanic districts, especially among the Tertiary volcanics of Scotland, there are areas marked by a series of concentric dikes, which due to their circular plan are known as *ring dikes*. They dip steeply outward and are believed to result from the intrusion of magma along fractures formed by the subsidence of the roof of the magma chamber. Thus they may mark the site of ancient calderas in which the ring dikes and associated features (cone sheets, etc.) are exposed after erosion has removed all traces of the surface caldera. In a recent study of the mechanism of caldera formation, based on the relationships of ring dikes and related features, Reynolds (1956) concludes that rising gas streams play an important role as agents of heat transfer, magma formation, transportation, and geomorphic development in the evolution of calderas. If her conclusions are correct, caldera formation may help explain some of the funnel-shaped intrusive masses, the origin of which has long been in question. A description of three ancient caldera-making eruptions (at Crater Lake, Santorini, and Valles Caldera) and two modern ones (at Krakatoa and Coseguina) will acquaint the reader with the caldera problem. The two modern caldera-making eruptions were, perhaps, the greatest volcanic eruptions of historic time and from this standpoint alone are worthy of our attention.

Figure 5. Stages in the development of a caldera. After van Bemmelen (1929) and Williams (1941a).

1. Mild explosions of pumice. Magma stands high in conduit.

2. Explosions increase in violence. Magma level recedes into main chamber.

3. Culminating explosions. Part of the ejecta is hurled high into the air but most of it rushes down the flanks of the cone as *nuées ardentes*. Magma level is deep in chamber. Roof begins to crack.

4. Lacking support, the top of the cone collapses into the magma chamber.

5. After an interval of quiescence and erosion, new cones appear on the caldera floor, especially near the rim.

Plate 7. Crater Lake caldera, Oregon. Left: *Western end of the caldera, with Wizard Island, a cinder cone which rises about 760 feet above the lake level. Two lava flows are visible extending from the left side of the cone.* Right: *The northeastern section of the caldera. Note that Mount Thielsen, the triangular peak in the background, is also visible in the picture at left.*

Crater Lake, Oregon

One of the best-known examples of a caldera, and perhaps the most perfect, is that occupied by Crater Lake in southern Oregon. It has been exhaustively studied by experienced investigators and has been the source of much of the controversy concerning the origin of calderas. Crater Lake, one of the scenic wonders of the United States, and now a national park, is visited by thousands yearly. It is on the crest of the Cascade Range, which throughout its entire extent is surmounted by lofty volcanic cones, including Mount Rainier (14,405 ft.) and Mount Adams (12,307 ft.) in Washington, Mount Hood (11,253 ft.) in northern Oregon, and Mount Shasta (14,161 ft.) in northern California, these being only a few of the better-known volcanoes.

Crater Lake is nearly circular, stretching across its diameter about six miles, and extending in depth 2,000 feet. It is encircled by cliffs from 500 to 2,000 feet high. The deep blue waters of Crater Lake, broken only by the 780-foot symmetrical cinder cone known as Wizard Island, is an impressive sight, and few who see it fail to speculate concerning its origin. J. S. Diller (Diller and Patton 1902, pt. 1) was the first to study the problem, and he concluded that the caldera had

been formed by subsidence. He realized that if it had been produced by tremendous explosions the slopes should be covered by a vast accumulation of debris from the former top of the cone. Not finding this material, he reasoned that engulfment was the only alternative and that this implied the removal of support from beneath the summit of the cone. In Hawaii large outpourings of lava on the outer flanks of the cone frequently result in collapse at the summit caldera. Diller believed that similar flank flows had occurred at Crater Lake, and, although he was unable to locate these flows, he believed that someday they would be found.

The ancestral cone, the summit of which disappeared to form the Crater Lake caldera, has been named Mount Mazama. Like other large volcanoes in the Cascades, Mount Mazama was active during and following the Pleistocene (Ice) Age, and much glacial debris is found interbedded with volcanic ejecta. Some of the last glaciers to occupy Mount Mazama were more than 10 miles long and 1,000 feet thick, and when the top of the cone collapsed, the lower ends of the glaciers were left stranded on the slopes. Today the wide U-shaped cross sections of these glacial valleys are preserved as notches in the caldera rim. It is apparent that to support such large glaciers

Figure 6. Restoration of Mount Mazama, ancestral cone of Crater Lake. After Atwood (1935).

Mount Mazama must have risen far above its present height, probably reaching approximately 12,000 feet, or roughly the height of Mount Hood.

The first explosions of the caldera-forming eruption were probably not catastrophic, but, as at Krakatoa, they increased gradually to a climax and then diminished rapidly. After the initial activity the vents must have enlarged, and the pressure on the magma was reduced so that the gases "boiled" off with increasing rapidity. Finally, the frothy magma was expelled in such volume that it not only rose above the cone but fell back on the cone and rushed down the slope in a succession of *nuées ardentes*, spreading out on the surrounding plains for a distance of 35 miles. The temperature of the *nuées ardentes* must have been quite high, for large tree trunks embedded in the pumice as far as 30 miles from the caldera are carbonized.

Williams (1941*a*) calculated that the total volume of material blown out of Mount Mazama was between 10 and 12 cubic miles. The pumiceous material, which was obviously new magma, contained relatively small quantities of fragments from the demolished mountain. Assuming that Mount Mazama was 12,000 feet high, some 17 cubic miles disappeared when the caldera was formed, but not more than 2 cubic miles of the demolished material is mixed with the pumice. Thus, it is necessary to account for 15 cubic miles of material which disappeared from the top of the cone. The 10–12 cubic miles of inflated pumice which was blown out in the eruptions would be equivalent to only 5 cubic miles of space in the magma chamber. Assuming that the cone collapsed into this space, there would still remain about 10 cubic miles to be accounted for, and this Williams does by postulating that "collapse of the peak into the magma chamber was brought about not only by drainage resulting from the eruption but also by the drainage consequent on some form of deep seated intrusions" (1941a, p. 275). As a rule the space made available by pumice eruptions and the total volume of rock which has disappeared in forming a caldera should be equal. The discrepancy which exists at Crater Lake may be due in part to the difficulties involved in estimating volume of rock, which at best can be only an approximation.

Krakatoa Volcano, Indonesia

Location and history. A historic caldera-forming eruption and one of the greatest volcanic eruptions of all times occurred at Krakatoa in 1883. Krakatoa was an island in the Sunda Strait, between Java and Sumatra, and had long been recognized as only the stump of an old volcanic cone which had been blown to pieces by an ancient eruption. There are, at present, three main islands in the Krakatoa group (Fig. 7), of which Rakata, the largest, rises to a height of about 2,700 feet above sea level, while Lang and Verlaten do not exceed 600 feet in height. These three islands are on the rim of a caldera nearly four miles in diameter, from the floor of which rise the rocky islet of Bootsmansrots and the cinder cone of Anak Krakatoa (literally, "child of Krakatoa"), which first appeared in 1927 and has been intermittently active since that time.

The history of Krakatoa prior to the eruption of 1883, as reconstructed by B. G. Escher (1919), O. E. Stehn (1929), Williams (1941a), and others, is shown by a series of diagrams in Figure 8. The prehistoric cone which occupied the site of the present caldera is believed to have had a height of 6,000 feet (Stage 1). Following a great eruption, probably similar to that of 1883, the central part of the cone collapsed, leaving several small islands on the rim of the ancient caldera (Stage 2). A new cone, Rakata, then developed on the southeast margin of the prehistoric caldera, erupting lava and fragmental material until it reached a height of about 2,700 feet (Stage 3). Later the smaller andesitic cones, Danan and Perboewatan, 1,460 and 400 feet respectively, rose within the caldera and ultimately united with Rakata to form one large central island, which was commonly known as Krakatoa Volcano (Stage 4). The last activity prior to the eruption of 1883 was a flow of andesitic obsidian from the vent of Perboewatan in 1680.

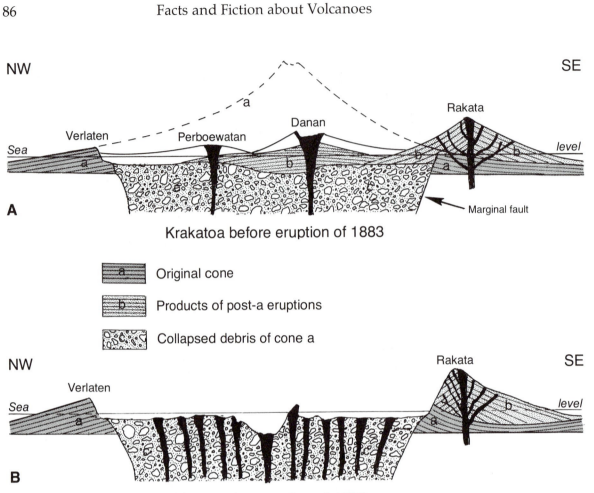

Figure 7. Krakatoa before and after the 1883 eruption. After Holmes (1965, p. 339). A represents stages 3 and 4 and B represents stage 5 in Figure 8.

Figure 8. Stages in the history of Krakatoa. Modified from Escher (1919).

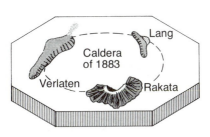

5. After the 1883 eruptions. Later eruptions have since built up the island of Anak Krakatoa within the caldera.

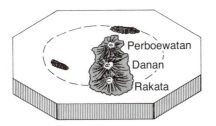

4. Krakatoa before 1883, after two later andesitic cones had coalesced with Rakata.

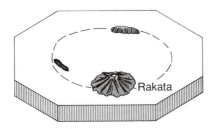

3. Growth of Rakata, a basaltic cone.

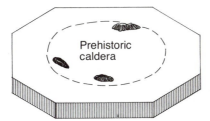

2. After explosive evisceration, probably accompanied by collapse of the superstructure, a great caldera was formed, rimmed by three small islands.

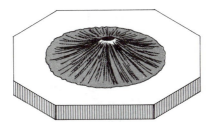

1. Original andesitic cone of Krakatoa.

The eruption of 1883.[1] The initial activity began with explosions from the vent on Perboewatan on May 20. The explosions were not particularly violent, and no one was alarmed; in fact the people of Batavia thought the display such an attraction that on May 27 a steamer was chartered to visit the island. Some of the more venturesome of the excursion party climbed to the rim of the crater, where they beheld a vast column of steam issuing with a terrific noise from an opening estimated to be about 30 yards in width. However, it was observed that Rakata and Verlaten were covered with fine ash and that the vegetation, although not burned, had been killed. Following the preliminary explosions the activity subsided, only to be resumed on June 19. A few days later a second vent opened on Danan. There is no record of activity in July, but it must be presumed that the mild explosive activity continued. When the islands were visited on August 11, the last time before the catastrophic eruption, there were three main vents, all in a state of mild activity.

At 1:00 P.M. on August 26 the first of a series of tremendous explosions occurred. At 2:00 P.M. a black cloud rose above Krakatoa to a height of 17 miles, followed by sharp explosions which increased in intensity until 5:00 P.M., when the first collapse and tidal wave occurred. The explosions continued through the night, accompanied by severe air shocks, but there were no earthquakes. The noise was heard all over Java, and at Batavia, 100 miles distant, all through the night the houses trembled and windows rattled as if heavy artillery were being fired in the streets. Because of the incessant noise, no one in all of western Java was able to sleep. Between 4:40 A.M. and 6:41 A.M. of the next day, August 27, several large tidal waves spread outward from Krakatoa, probably due to further collapse of the northern part of the main island. By 10:00 A.M. the rehearsal was over, and the real performance was to begin. The climax of the eruption was reached at this time, when the ash cloud rose to a height of 50 miles, and the noise of the detonation was heard nearly 3,000 miles away.

Westward across the Indian Ocean is the island of Rodriguez, 2,968 miles from Krakatoa, where an alert coast-guard observer carefully noted the character of the sound and the time, just four hours after the explosions, which leaves no doubt that the noise was from Krakatoa. The noise was also heard 2,250 miles to the southeast in central Australia. The intensity of the sound is better appreciated if one assumes that, were Pikes Peak to erupt as Krakatoa did, the noise would be heard all over the United States. About half an hour after the cataclysmic explosion, a tidal wave which reached a height of 120 feet in some bays swept the neighboring coasts of Java and Su-

1. Information on the 1883 eruption is based primarily on Escher (1919), Stehn (1929), and Williams (1941*a*).

matra, wholly or partially destroying 295 towns and killing 36,000 people, mostly by drowning. A Dutch warship was washed ashore and left stranded 30 feet above water level and one-half mile inland. At 10:52 A.M. a second explosion rocked the area, but it was not attended by a tidal wave. At 4:35 P.M. there was still another loud explosion, followed by a small tidal wave, and throughout the night of the twenty-seventh and the early morning hours of the next day the explosions continued, although with decreasing intensity, and then virtually ceased.

The tremendous amount of ash blown into the air plunged the surrounding region into darkness which affected areas as much as 275 miles away. At a distance of 130 miles the darkness lasted for 22 hours, and at a distance of 50 miles for 57 hours. Dust fell in quantity over a wide area (Fig. 9). Ships 1,600 miles away reported that dust began to fall on the decks three days after the eruption. The fine dust in the upper atmosphere traveled around the earth many times and remained in the atmosphere for months, causing sky glows, which were widely observed all over Europe and the United States, and which became a controversial issue, particularly in England. Tennyson records the event in verse as follows:

> Had the fierce ashes of some fiery Peak
> Been hurled so high they ranged round the globe?
> For day by day through many a blood-red eve
>
> .   .   .   .
>
> This wrathful sunset glared . . .
>
> ("St. Telemachus," lines 1–5)

This topic is discussed in more detail in the section on Distribution of Pyroclastic Material, under Volcanic Solids, in Chapter 5.

After the eruption, two-thirds of the main island had disappeared, and where the land, before the explosion, had stood 400–1,400 feet above sea level, there was now a great cavity some 900 feet below sea level. The present caldera of Krakatoa has a diameter of approximately 4.35 miles and consists of two basins, between which is a northwest-trending ridge where Bootsmansrots and the cinder cone of Anak Krakatoa are located (Fig. 7). Extending to the southwest and southeast from the caldera are elongate grabens. The southwest-trending graben is essentially parallel to the main volcanic chain of Sumatra, and the southeast-trending graben is on a tectonic line which passes through a series of volcanoes and intersects the main volcanic chain at a high angle. It seems apparent that the location of Krakatoa is determined by the intersection of these two fissure systems (Williams 1941a, p. 260).

Verbeek (1886) calculated that about five cubic miles of material

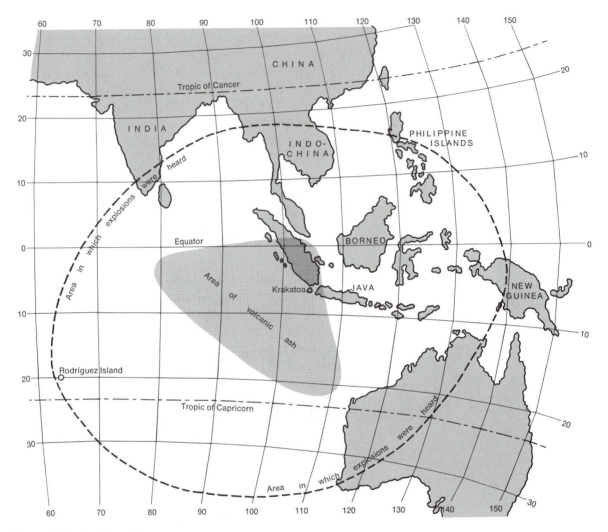

Figure 9. Limits of the volcanic ash and the noise of the explosions in the 1883 eruption of Krakatoa.

was blown out of Krakatoa in the eruption, the greater part of which fell within a radius of eight to nine miles of the volcano. The well-bedded pumice deposits of the earlier phases of the eruption were the product of a Vulcanian type eruption in which the ash was blown high into the air and drifted with the wind, while in the culminating explosions of August 27 the ash and pumice deposits were formed by *nuées ardentes* in which no sorting was possible. More significant, however, is that 95 percent of the ejecta consists of new material in the form of pumice and only 5 percent of old rock fragments from the former cones of Danan, Perboewatan, and Rakata. It follows, therefore, that these cones were not blown away but must have disappeared by collapse or engulfment into the magma chamber. Powerful support for the collapse theory comes from calculations which show that the volume of pumice erupted in 1883, when recalculated as magma, approximates closely the volume of material which disappeared. The close correlation between the volume of the erupted material and the volume of material which disappeared makes Krakatoa a splendid example of the ''collapse type'' of caldera, and in some classifications of calderas this type is designated the ''Krakatoa type.''

Eruptions since 1927. After 44 years of quiescence, Krakatoa renewed its activity in 1927, when eruptions began at the vent Anak Krakatoa on the floor of the caldera (Van Padang 1951). From the beginning of its existence until October, 1952, the eruptive center was submarine, but during a vigorous eruption on October 10–11, 1952, a cinder cone emerged, rising 72 meters above sea level. There was more activity reported in March, 1953, and again in September of the same year, when eruptions destroyed vegetation over a considerable portion of the island. At this time the cone had attained a height of 116 meters, and its crater had been enlarged by a displacement of the eruptive center (Decker 1959). Intermittent eruptions are continuing at Anak Krakatoa, enlarging the cinder cone forming in the older crater.

Coseguina Volcano, Nicaragua

The eruption of Coseguina Volcano in 1835 has been regarded as the most violent historic eruption in the Western Hemisphere and one of the great caldera-forming eruptions of all time.

Measurement of volcanic explosiveness. Coseguina is a part of a belt of active volcanoes which extends along the Pacific coast from Guatemala to the Panamanian border, one segment in the ''fire girdle of the Pacific'' (Ch. 15).

One of the greatest concentrations of volcanoes in the entire belt is

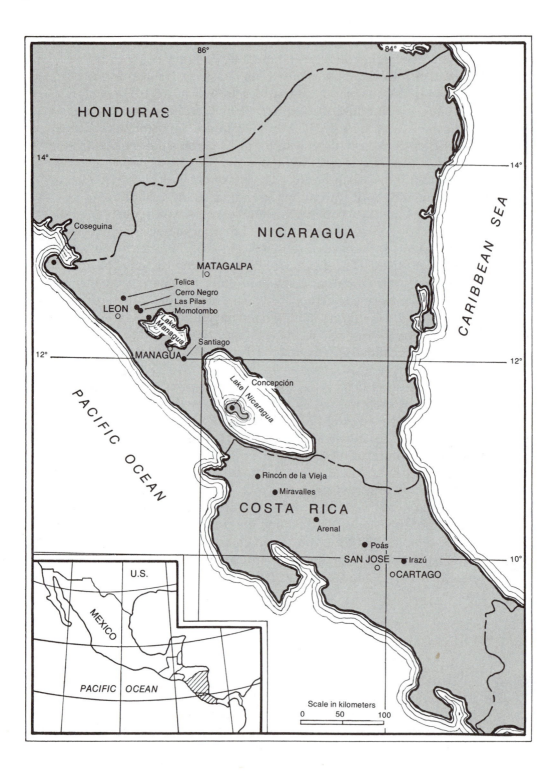

in Nicaragua, where there are six volcanoes currently in various states of activity: Concepción, Santiago, Momotombo, Las Pilas, Cerro Negro, and Telica. The activity ranges from brisk solfataric emissions to explosive discharges of ash with minor lava flows. In addition to being the center of the greatest concentration of volcanic vents, it is one of the most highly explosive volcanic regions on earth. Sapper (1927, p. 348), in an effort to compare the intensity of activity of various regions, devised an index of explosiveness:

$$\text{Index of explosiveness (E)} = \frac{\text{Quantity of fragmental material ejected}}{\text{Total ejected material}}$$

It has been shown in preceding chapters that in the most highly explosive volcanoes only ash, pumice, and other fragmental materials are ejected. This is because the stiff, viscous, acid magma is so highly charged with gases that when the pressure is released the explosive expansion of the gases shatters the magma, and it is expelled as pumice and ash, and no liquid (lava) material is ejected. This is the typical Peléan type of eruption. In the least explosive types (Hawaiian and Icelandic) the magma is more fluid, and the gases escape without disrupting the mass, so that the material is ejected as lava. Thus the ratio of fragmental material to the total ejected material is a measure of the explosiveness. If all the erupted material is fragmental the volcano is 100 percent explosive; if all the ejected material is lava the volcano is 0 percent explosive.

Sapper calculated the emission of volcanic material throughout the world in the interval from 1500 to 1914. His estimate, notwithstanding the uncertainty of the figures for some areas, does give the order of magnitude and an over-all view of recent active volcanoes. According to Sapper's calculations the two areas tying for first place, with E = 99 percent, are the Malayan Archipelago and Central America. Within a given region the distribution of volcanoes is often very irregular. In order to determine the most explosive areas, Sapper compared the ratio between quantity of fluid lava and fragmental material per 100 kilometers of distance along the volcanic belt and concluded that the most explosive zone on earth is the belt in Nicaragua, extending from Coseguina southeastward to Concepción Volcano in Lake Nicaragua. The 1835 eruption of Coseguina is the only historic example of the type of eruption which must have occurred thousands of times throughout the area in recent geologic time.

The eruption of 1835. Coseguina is a great decapitated cone with an oval-shaped crater (caldera) 1–1.5 miles in diameter occupying its summit. The crater, which is 1,500–2,000 feet deep and occupied by a clear blue lake, has precipitous walls, which reach a maximum elevation on the rim of 2,850 feet. Coseguina has an old "somma" ring (remnant of an earlier crater rim) on the northern and western flanks approximately two-thirds of the way from the base, indicating that it had been disrupted and rebuilt at least once prior to the 1835 eruption.

There are no reliable accounts of eruptions of Coseguina prior to 1835, and it was generally regarded as extinct. The details of the great eruption are based largely on the eye-witness account of Vicente Romero, then commandant of the port of La Unión in El Salvador, 30 miles away across the Bay of Fonseca. Reports from more distant points tell little about the eruption other than the fall of ash, the duration of darkness, and the noise accompanying the eruption. Col. Juan Galindo, who at the time was traveling along the Polochic River in Guatemala, has reported the most reliable information on the acoustical phenomena of the eruption. A recent description of this eruption by Williams (1952) reviews and evaluates the early accounts and adds much new information from field studies.

The inhabitants of La Unión, El Salvador, reported that about 8:00 A.M. on the morning of January 20 a white cloud, like an immense plume of feathers, rose from the top of Coseguina. It soon turned gray, then yellow, and finally crimson. Noteworthy was the absence of any preliminary earthquakes, although some rather severe shocks were felt around 4:00 P.M., about eight hours after the initial outbreak. By 11:00 A.M. the ash had so obscured the sky that lamps were lighted at La Unión. By midafternoon heavy showers of flourlike

Plate 8. Caldera of Coseguina Volcano, Nicaragua.

pumice were falling, and the darkness became complete, spreading terror and confusion among the inhabitants. At Nacaome, Honduras, 40 miles north of the volcano, the ash was three inches deep by 5:00 P.M., and at San Miguel, El Salvador, 50 miles to the northeast, there was complete darkness by 4:00 P.M., and the people "could not see their hands in front of their eyes." By nightfall the ash spread as far north as Tegucigalpa, 80 miles away, and San Salvador, 110 miles to the northeast.

On the morning of the second day conditions improved a little at San Miguel, but complete darkness, accompanied by strong earthquakes and subterranean noises, prevailed at La Unión. On Tigre Island, in the Gulf of Fonseca, 20 miles from the volcano, pumice fragments as large as hen eggs fell. Throughout the day the whole of Honduras was in darkness and some effects were observed in Guatemala City.

On the third day, January 22, the winds shifted to the southeast, and the section which had been relatively free of ash was now enveloped in it. At Chinandega, 50 miles south of the volcano, the ash fall was so thick that complete darkness prevailed. "The terror of the inhabitants at Alancho, anticipating the approach of the Judgment Day, was so great that three hundred of those living out of wedlock were married at once" (Williams 1952, p. 33). The climax of the eruption, at least according to the distance at which the noise could be heard, appears to have come on the night of the twenty-second. Colonel Galindo, who was camped on the banks of the Polochic River in eastern Guatemala, heard sounds like artillery fire, which he thought were coming from Port Izabal. To the north, in British Honduras, "the superintendent at Belize, 400 miles distant, mustered the troops of his garrison, manned the fort, under the belief that there was a naval action off the harbor" (Squier 1859, p. 756). The sounds were alarming as far away as Kingston, Jamaica, and Bogotá, Colombia. In Guatemala City the noises were so loud that the local troops, thinking it was cannon fire of an approaching enemy, hastily prepared to defend themselves. In places the roar was practically continuous for seven hours, during which time the ash fall increased and complete darkness enveloped an area with a radius of about 50 miles. Most of El Salvador was obscured, and ash fell as far north as Chiapas, Mexico, and on localities near the Costa Rican border.

On the following day, January 23, the activity began to decline, although fine ash continued to fall over El Salvador and Guatemala, and even at Jamaica, more than 800 miles to the east. At La Unión and León it started to clear, and conditions continued to improve on the twenty-fifth and twenty-sixth, although Guatemala City remained in darkness during this period. By the twenty-seventh the fall of ash had ceased, although some noises were heard in Guatemala City until the end of January. The main eruption, however, actually ceased on January 23, having lasted only four days.

For the next 35 or 40 years, visitors who climbed to the rim of the crater reported some fumes and vapor columns issuing from cracks on the crater walls, but when the crater was visited by Sapper in 1879 no fumaroles were present.

Volume of ejecta. The tremendous quantity of material ejected was one of the remarkable features of the eruption. E. G. Squier states that "the sea for 50 leagues was covered with floating masses of pumice, resembling the floe-ice of the Northern Atlantic" (1859, p. 756). Estimates of the volume of ash ejected in the eruption of Coseguina vary from 150 cubic kilometers to as little as 10 cubic kilometers. The estimate by E. Reclus (1891) of 50 cubic kilometers is the figure most often quoted and was the figure used by Sapper in his computation of the index of explosiveness. Williams, from investigations of earlier reports and from field studies, concluded that the volume of ash erupted by Coseguina "may not have been greater than 10 cubic kilometers, and possibly was even less" (1952, p. 36). How much of the mountain was destroyed in the eruption is not known, since there were no accurate descriptions of the cone before the eruption. The volume of the present crater approximates 4 cubic kilometers, and doubtless the diameter was considerably enlarged by the eruption. Williams (1952) concludes that perhaps about 5 cubic kilometers of material vanished. In his study of the ash and pumice deposits from the eruption, he calculated that not more than 7 percent of the total consisted of fragments of the old mountain top, the remainder being primary magmatic material. These figures indicate that only a small fraction of the part of the old cone which disappeared in the eruption could have been demolished by explosions. The alternative, of course, is engulfment. Thus, Coseguina followed the same pattern in developing a caldera by collapse as was the case at Krakatoa and Crater Lake. The eruption was exceptional in its violence, its brief duration, the noise, and the quantity and fineness of the ash.

Santorini (Thera) Volcano, Greece

Santorini, a medieval Italian corruption of Sant' Irene, the patron saint of Thera, is the name of a small group of volcanic islands in the Aegean Sea, roughly 210 kilometers southeast of Athens and 110 kilometers north of the island of Crete. It is one of a group of recently extinct volcanoes (Santorini being the only one still active) which lie in a convex arc facing the Mediterranean Sea. Other volcanic islands in the arc include Souski, Methana, Milos, Nisyros, and Cos. The island arc borders the sunken block of the former Aegean land mass.

The name Thera, from the Spartan leader who conquered the

Figure 11. Eastern Mediterranean area, showing the location of Santorini Volcano.

island about 1000 B.C., is the ancient name for the islands. In current usage Santorini is applied to the group of five islands, with Thera the name of the largest island in the group. Thera Island is semicircular in shape, with a length of 15 kilometers and a maximum width of 6 kilometers. On the southeast portion is the Agios Elias massif, composed of mica schist and marble and rising to a height of 658 meters. This massif is a remnant of the original land before the onset of volcanic activity. The remainder of Thera, like the other islands in the group, is entirely volcanic. The island encloses a lagoon (caldera) which is 11 kilometers from north to south and 7 kilometers from east to west, with the greatest depth of 390 meters in the northern part.

History. The history of Santorini Volcano has been described by Fouqué (1879), Williams (1941a), and G. C. Georgalas (1962); and in recent years, since the advancement of the idea that it may be the site of Plato's Lost Continent of Atlantis, it has been the subject of several books (see below).

The first volcanic eruptions, probably submarine, began in the Pleistocene, and in time the ejecta began to accumulate above the

Figure 12. Generalized geo-logic map of Santorini vol-canic complex, with hypo-thetical profile of the cone prior to collapse. After Ninkovich and Heezin (1965).

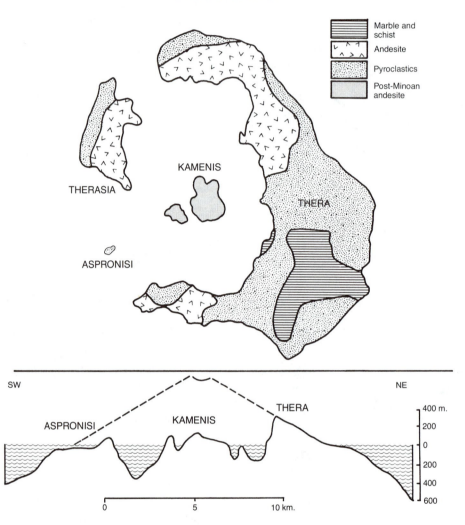

water level to form the volcanic islets of Akrotiri, Lumaravi, and Fanari. The center then shifted northward to what is now the middle of the island of Thera, and the large Thera Volcano was built, mainly by eruptions of pumice from a summit crater and lava from vents on the flanks. Eventually this great composite cone reached a height of 1,600 meters above sea level, uniting with the bedrock (massif) and the volcanic islets to the south. Before Thera became extinct, a new volcano, Peristeria, began to form to the north of Thera, and, as it continued to grow, another major cone, Simandir, formed on its western flank. These volcanoes were much less explosive than the earlier ones, erupting mainly flows of andesite and dacite. Finally, two coalescing cones, Therasia and Skaros, developed on the slopes of the earlier cones. At the close of this long period of volcanism, the area now occupied by the caldera of Santorini was a large volcanic complex made up of many overlapping cones.

A long interval of inactivity preceded the eruptions which led to the formation of the caldera. The first eruptions left up to three meters of "rose-colored" pumice over the area, and from variations in thickness and coarseness it appears that the vents were in the northern part of the present caldera area. The "rose" pumice is overlain by a thicker sequence of interbedded, well-stratified airborne and fluviatile deposits referred to as the "middle" pumice. The culminating explosions left the "upper" pumice, which has a thickness of about 30 meters on the islands. The nature of the bedding and sorting imply repeated explosions from several sources. The well-developed columnar jointing on some of the ash stranded on the inner caldera wall, as near the boat landing at Thera, indicates that some of the material was ejected as pumice flows in *nuée ardente* type eruptions.

Volume of ash. Since most of the ash from a Santorini eruption must necessarily fall into the sea, samples from the surrounding sea floor provide an important link in the story. Such samples (cores) were collected by an oceanographic research vessel of the Lamont Geological Observatory of Columbia University, New York. From a study of the samples, D. Ninkovich and Bruce C. Heezin (1965) outlined an oval-shaped area of ash surrounding Santorini which became thinner away from the volcano. Based on radiocarbon determinations the age of the ash was placed at 1410±100 B.C. This confirmed previous archeological evidence of a ca. 1400 B.C. eruption of Santorini (Marinatos 1939) and identified a volume of ash from the eruption sufficient to cause collapse of the multiple cones. The eruption is believed to have occurred in the summer, since the distribution of the ash in an elongate oval indicates northwesterly winds, which are characteristic of the summer months in that region. The two cores with the greatest thickness of ash were no. 58, 110 kilometers southeast of Santorini and 40 kilometers north of Crete, with 78 centimeters

Plate 9. Santorini Caldera. Left: Southern rim of the caldera and Kameni (Burnt Island) from the town of Thera. The multistoried building on the extreme left is the Atlantis Hotel. In the upper left, the ash from the "great" eruption (white bands extending to water level) is quarried and loaded on ships for use in cement works in Athens. Right: Interior wall of the caldera from the edge of the crater on Kameni. A small portion of the 1950 lava flow is on the extreme right. The zigzag steps from the harbor to the town of Thera on the rim of the caldera can be identified in the left central section. Note that the ash deposits on the caldera rim become thicker to the right.

(30.7 in.) and no. 50, 40 kilometers to the east of core no. 58, with 212 centimeters (83.5 in.). The ash from the eruption is estimated to have covered an area of 200,000 square kilometers, although the distribution pattern suggests that it did not reach the coast of Egypt or the eastern Mediterranean in thicknesses greater than one millimeter. However, the ash is very fine, and the initial cloud, composed of gas, vapors, and dust, may have been significantly larger than the area receiving ash deposits. The very fine nature of the ash would prolong the time for it to settle from the atmosphere and suggests that it produced an extended period of darkness over a large area.

Caldera collapse. Although the total volume of ejecta from the eruption cannot be accurately determined from the limited number of samples collected, it is clear that the volume was sufficient to remove support from the roof of the magma chamber, causing it to collapse. Santorini has been cited as an example of the Krakatoa type of caldera (Williams 1941*a*), in which the volume of collapse material approximates the volume of the material ejected. A comparison of Santorini caldera with that of Crater Lake and Krakatoa is as follows:

	Santorini	Crater Lake	Krakatoa
Collapse area	83 sq. km.	69 sq. km.	23 sq. km.
Volume of collapse	60 cu. km.	60 cu. km.	18 cu. km.

It should be noted from the preceding tabulation that the collapse area and the volume of collapse at Santorini is more than three times greater than at Krakatoa, with which Santorini is frequently compared. The volume of collapse at both Santorini and Crater Lake is based on a hypothetical restoration of the cone prior to collapse. The date of the collapse at Santorini, based on the most recent radiocarbon determinations, was 1470 B.C.

The Santorini caldera is roughly rectangular in shape, approximately 15 by 7 kilometers. The shape probably reflects structural

trends in the prevolcanic basement rocks. The shape is also controlled
by radial fractures and grabens which extend outward between the
islands of Thera and Therasia, reflecting extensions from the main
magma chamber. The scalloped margin indicates concentric fracturing and collapse of separate cones, since the centers of several concentric bays on the island of Thera coincide closely with the positions of former vents.

Renewal of activity. More than 1,000 years elapsed after the engulfment before volcanism was renewed at Santorini. Beginning in 197
B.C. and continuing in 46 A.D., domes of the Peléan type, composed
of andesite and dacite, rose from the caldera floor to form the island
of Palaea Kameni. A second island, Mikra Kameni, was formed in
1570–1573, and the third, Nea Kameni, rose in 1707–1711. Nea
Kameni was enlarged by the addition of the Georgios dome in 1866–
1870. An eruption in 1925–1926 produced the Dafni dome, and the
associated lavas united the earlier domes into what is now known as
Nea Kameni or Burnt Island. In modern Greek, the word *kameni*,
meaning "burnt," is used to denote a volcanic cone or the site of an
eruption; *nea* means "new." Other eruptions which produced domes
and lavas on Nea Kameni occurred in 1928 and in 1939–1941, when
extensive activity resulted in several domes and a large volume of
lava. The last eruption was in 1950, when a small dome and two
tongues of lava were formed. There was a severe earthquake on Santorini in 1956, but no volcanic eruption occurred. Fumarolic activity is
continuing at Nea Kameni. The lavas and domes of Kameni are classified as "dacitoides" (Georgalas 1962), that is, similar to andesites but
with a higher percentage of silica.

The legend of the lost continent of Atlantis. Santorini is considered by
some to be the site of Plato's Atlantis, and the disappearance of the
island empire "beneath the water in a single day and night" to be
the result of caldera collapse. It seems appropriate to consider briefly
some of the aspects of the Atlantis legend at this point. Plato (427–

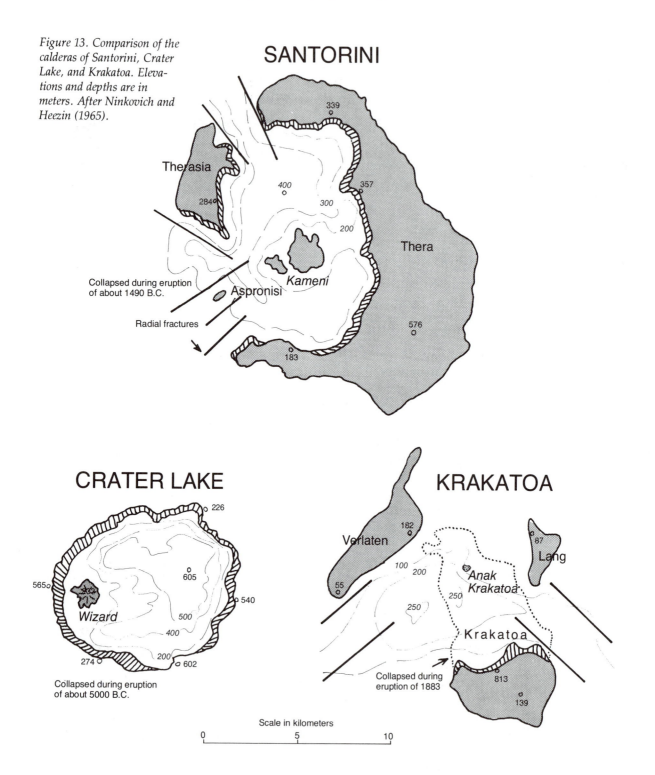

Figure 13. Comparison of the calderas of Santorini, Crater Lake, and Krakatoa. Elevations and depths are in meters. After Ninkovich and Heezin (1965).

SANTORINI

Therasia

400

Thera

Kameni

Aspronisi

Collapsed during eruption of about 1490 B.C.

Radial fractures

CRATER LAKE

Wizard

500

400

200

Collapsed during eruption of about 5000 B.C.

KRAKATOA

Verlaten

Lang

Anak Krakatoa

Krakatoa

Collapsed during eruption of 1883

Scale in kilometers

0   5   10

347 B.C.) in two of his dialogues tells a fantastic story about an island empire named Atlantis, which disappeared beneath the water in a single day and night. Was Plato recounting something that really happened, or was this pure mythology?

The story of Atlantis is told by Plato near the opening of *Timaeus* and in more detail in *Critias*. The story is credited to Critias, an Athenian political figure in the Socratic circle. He heard it when he was 10 years old from his 90-year-old grandfather, who had heard it from his father, a friend of Solon. Solon (638–559 B.C.) is best known as the founder of Athenian democracy. He was active in forming a legislative assembly, distributing land to the poor, and outlawing contracts where personal freedom was involved. It was this last reform which abolished serfdom in ancient Greece. However, Solon was apparently too progressive for his time, and he was exiled to Egypt for 10 years. While in Egypt (around 590 B.C.), he learned from the priests of Sais (one of the ancient cities of the Nile delta) the story of an island empire, larger than Libya and western Asia combined, located outside the Pillars of Hercules (Straits of Gibraltar). The Egyptian priests told Solon that, 9,000 years earlier, this island empire, under a powerful king, had sought to enslave Egypt and Greece and that the Athenians had led the defense and eventually defeated the Atlantids. Then in a single day and night Atlantis disappeared beneath the water. This is the story Solon brought back to Athens, which, after being handed down by word of mouth from father to son, was recorded in writing for the first time in two of Plato's dialogues some 200 years later (ca. 395 B.C.).

Minoan civilization. It had been known for a long time that, following the Stone Age, the first true civilization in the Mediterranean area, the Minoan civilization, developed in Crete and adjacent islands and that around 1400 B.C. this civilization suddenly disappeared, while at about the same time the Mycenaean civilization, with many Minoan traditions, appeared in southern Greece.

It had been suspected for many years that Atlantis was in the Aegean Sea and that it was the eruption of Santorini Volcano which destroyed the Minoan civilization and caused the people to migrate to Greece. One of the first to advocate such a theory was K. Y. Frost, an Irish scholar, who in 1909 published (anonymously) a newspaper article entitled "The Lost Continent." Later Frost presented his case in greater detail in an article, "The Critias and Minoan Crete" (1939). Frost's views had little impact, and it remained for S. Marinatos (1939), a Greek archeologist who had carried on excavations at the Minoan palaces of Crete, to present striking evidence in support of the idea. Marinatos was impressed by the pits full of pumice and the great rock masses which had been tilted out of position as though struck by a giant wave. Reflecting on the sudden and simultaneous destruction and abandonment of so many Minoan palaces, he became convinced that the downfall of Minoan Crete was due, not to foreign invaders, but to a natural catastrophe of unparalleled violence. The source of this cataclysm, he suggested, was Santorini Volcano, 120 kilometers to the north of Crete. The idea was not entirely new, for the French engineers who built the Suez canal in the nineteenth century had mined the thick volcanic ash layer on Thera for the manufacture of cement used in the construction of the canal. Under the ash layer they found remains of a civilization which was clearly pre-Greek but whose age was unknown.

On July 9, 1956, a severe earthquake damaged most of the houses on Thera, and 48 persons were killed. Professor George A. Galanopoulos, director of the Seismological Laboratory of the University of Athens, went to Thera to make a field study of the damage (Galanopoulos and Bacon 1969). While there he visited pits where volcanic ash is obtained for use in the cement plants at Athens. At the bottom of a mine shaft he came upon the ruins of a stone house in which he found two small pieces of wood and some human teeth. Radiocarbon dating gave an age of 1410±100 B.C. for the pieces of wood. In a paper on the tsunami of antiquity presented at the 1960 meeting of the International Union of Geodesy and Geophysics, Galanopoulos proposed that the 1400 B.C. eruption of Santorini and the tsunami which accompanied the collapse of the composite cone were responsible for the destruction of the Minoan civilization. In addition, he maintained that Santorini was in fact Plato's Atlantis and that the caldera collapse of the composite cone explained its "disappearance beneath the water in a single day and night." The 9,000 years which Plato gives as the interval between the disappearance of Atlantis and Solon's Egyptian visit seems to be an insurmountable hurdle. However, Galanopoulos clears it easily by assuming a mistake in translation or a misplaced decimal, so that the impossible 9,000-year span was actually only 900 years, making the date of the Minoan eruption of Santorini around 1400 B.C. Further, when the dimensions of the island empire (as well as other dimensions cited by Plato) are divided by ten, the whole fits quite neatly.

Since a date of around 1450 B.C. is usually assigned by Biblical scholars as the time of the exodus of the Children of Israel from Egypt, Galanopoulos invokes the eruption of Santorini to account for the plague of darkness brought by the Lord to compel the Pharaoh to let the Israelites leave (Galanopoulos and Bacon 1969). We read in Exodus 10:21–22: "And the Lord said unto Moses, stretch out thine hand toward heaven, that there may be darkness over the land of Egypt, even darkness which may be felt. And Moses stretched forth his hand towards heaven; and there was a thick darkness in all the land of Egypt for three days." An eruption of the type of Santorini would eject enormous quantities of ash into the atmosphere and plunge the surrounding region into darkness. In the eruption of Krakatoa in 1883 there was total darkness for 22 hours at a distance of 130 miles and for 57 hours at a distance of 50 miles from the volcano. Historic eruptions resulting in caldera collapse, such as those of Coseguina and Krakatoa, have lasted for three to four days. The eruption of Santorini is believed to have been substantially larger than the 1883 eruption of Krakatoa, and the three days of total darkness do not appear to be out of line. Further, a ''darkness which can be felt'' certainly would apply to a darkness caused by large quantities of ash in the atmosphere.

The collapse of the multiple cones of Santorini would, without doubt, have produced a huge tsunami, which would have swept the surrounding coasts. In the eruption of Krakatoa the tsunami reached a height of 120 feet in some of the bays. Tsunamis are not uncommon in the region. In A.D. 365, Knossus and eight other towns on Crete were destroyed by an earthquake which caused a destructive tsunami. At Alexandria, Egypt, ships were carried inland over buildings and left stranded in the streets. In 1956 a severe earthquake was centered near the southeast coast of the island of Amorgas (about 40 mi. southeast of Santorini). On the coast of Amorgas facing the epicenter, the tsunami was 24–40 meters high; on the opposite side of the island, only 2–4 meters high.

The velocity of a tsunami is dependent on the depth of the water: the deeper the water, the higher the velocity. The depth of the water around Krakatoa is shallow (50–150 m.) but between Santorini and Crete the depth is around 1,000 meters, and even close to the Cretan coast it is still 500 meters. A velocity of 350 kilometers per hour is indicated for water 1,000 meters deep—so the wave must have struck the north coast of Crete at a high velocity, and the whole northern coast was certainly inundated within 20–30 minutes after the collapse. Various estimates, ranging from 60 meters upward, have been made for the height of the tsunami generated by the collapse of Santorini. On the island of Anaphi, 24 kilometers east of Santorini, a layer of pumice 5 meters thick rests at the head of a bay 250 meters above sea level. This has been interpreted by some as the wash of a giant wave, but there is also the possibility that it is an accumulation of landfall material. J. V. Luce (1969, p. 89) states that tsunamis 200 meters in height have been observed, but he does not cite the reference. Galanopoulos, with reckless enthusiasm, invokes the tsunami accompanying the Santorini eruption to explain the parting of the waters of the Red Sea, allowing the Children of Israel to escape the pursuing forces of the Pharaoh (Galanopoulos and Bacon 1969). As a tsunami approaches a coast, the sea first withdraws, frequently exposing large areas of the sea bottom near shore, and in a half hour or so the wave returns and sweeps inland. It is this withdrawal which Galanopoulos invokes to part the waters and produce dry land; the return of the wave, he says, overwhelmed the forces of the Pharaoh as they were pursuing the children of Israel. While one may envisage a shallow submerged bar on the Mediterranean coast being exposed as "dry land" as the tsunami approached, the 20–30 minutes before the return of the wave seems wholly inadequate for the event described to have happened. In addition to the references already cited, a book by James W. Mavor (1969) will also be of interest to the reader who wishes to delve further into the Atlantis legend.

Valles Caldera, New Mexico

In the controversy over whether the craters of the moon are impact craters or volcanic craters, the much larger size of moon craters and the presence of central mountain masses in many of them have been difficult to reconcile with features of earth calderas. This discrepancy has stimulated detailed work in several areas, with the result that a new type of earth caldera, with features more compatible with those of moon calderas, has been recognized.

Studies in the Jemez Mountains in north-central New Mexico by R. L. Smith and R. A. Bailey (1962) revealed the history of the Valles Caldera and developed the concept of *resurgent calderas*. In the calderas previously described, volcanic activity commonly continues, following caldera collapse, with small basaltic cones, like Wizard Island at Crater Lake. In the Valles type caldera the renewal of activity is accompanied by the up-arching of the caldera floor, sometimes as much as several thousand feet, and calderas in which this has occurred are termed resurgent calderas. Such calderas are commonly much larger than the Krakatoa–Crater Lake type and in addition have central mountains as a result of the up-arching of the caldera floor.

Valles Caldera is a large, subcircular volcanic depression in the Jemez Mountains in north-central New Mexico, about 35 miles northwest of Santa Fe. It is 12–15 miles in diameter, with walls which rise to more than 2,000 feet above the present floor. Near the center of the caldera is a structural dome (Redondo Dome) which forms a mountain mass 8–10 miles in diameter, with a height of some 3,000 feet. In the moat between the central mountain mass and the caldera walls are more than 10 huge rhyolitic volcanic domes which range from less than 0.5 mile to more than 2 miles in diameter at the base and have 500–2,000 feet of relief. The relationship of the various features and the details of the structure are shown in a block diagram in Figure 14.

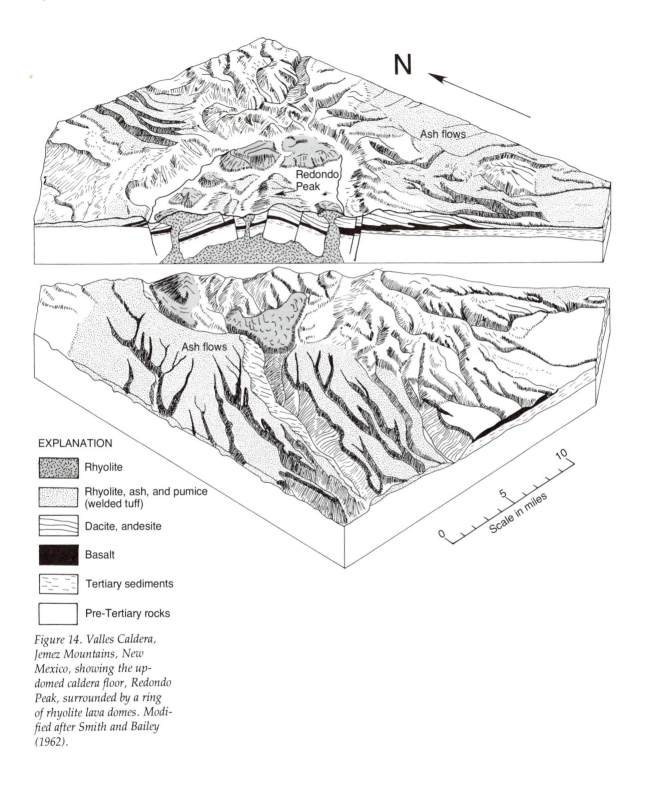

N

Ash flows

Redondo
Peak

Ash flows

EXPLANATION

Rhyolite

Rhyolite, ash, and pumice
(welded tuff)

Dacite, andesite

Basalt

Tertiary sediments

Pre-Tertiary rocks

10

5

Scale in miles

0

*Figure 14. Valles Caldera,
Jemez Mountains, New
Mexico, showing the up-
domed caldera floor, Redondo
Peak, surrounded by a ring
of rhyolite lava domes. Modified after Smith and Bailey
(1962).*

Initial volcanism began in the area of the Jemez Mountains in late Miocene or early Pliocene, about 11 million years ago, with eruptions of a variety of lavas and ash beds. It was, however, the eruption of some 50 cubic miles of rhyolitic ash flows in mid-Pleistocene, about a million years ago, which led to the first caldera collapse. These flows, known as the lower Bandelier Tuff, are related to the collapse which formed the first caldera in the region, the Toledo Caldera (Smith and Bailey 1966). After an interval of some 300,000 years another eruption of ash flows, again with a volume of about 50 cubic miles, filled the Toledo Caldera and buried the existing topography. These flows, known as the upper Bandelier Tuff, were preceded by a regional up-doming of the area which produced a series of arcuate fractures near the top of the dome. The upper Bandelier ash flows are believed to have erupted from these fractures. In the collapse of the roof of the Valles magma chamber, which followed the eruption of the huge volume of ash, a central oval block 8 by 10 miles in diameter and bounded by the inner ring fracture sank 2,000–3,000 feet as an almost intact crustal block. Surrounding it, a zone from 1 to 3 miles wide, constituting the ring-fracture zone, subsided in a series of discontinuous arcuate steps. The caldera was the site of a series of lakes, and lake deposits are intermixed with both lava and pyroclastics. These, combined with landslides from the caldera walls, completely buried the central cauldron block. In time the magma began to rise, and the central cauldron block, still largely intact, was uplifted to its present position some 3,000 feet above the caldera floor. Later, after all uplift had ceased, a series of at least 10 rhyolitic domes with associated pyroclastic cones and flows erupted in the moat area (Fig. 14). Hot springs and solfataric activity continue today in the western side of the caldera area (Smith and Bailey 1968).

Other Resurgent Calderas

Many features, the origin of which was in doubt, are now recognized as resurgent calderas. The Toba depression in north Sumatra, 60 miles long, 18 miles wide and 2,000 feet deep, is certainly among the largest volcanic depressions on earth. Although the origin of the Toba depression has long been in question, R. W. van Bemmelen (1939) correctly recognized its resurgent nature; but his work received only scant attention until the Toba depression was selected, along with Valles Caldera, as a type example of resurgent calderas by Smith and Bailey (1962). The Toba depression collapse followed the eruption of about 500 cubic miles of ash flows; and, following the collapse, magma rose under the collapsed part and, in the uplift,

Plate 10. Valles Caldera, New Mexico, from overlook on south rim, showing several of the lava domes which encircle the caldera. Redondo Peak, a portion of the up-domed caldera floor, is to the left center of the scene.

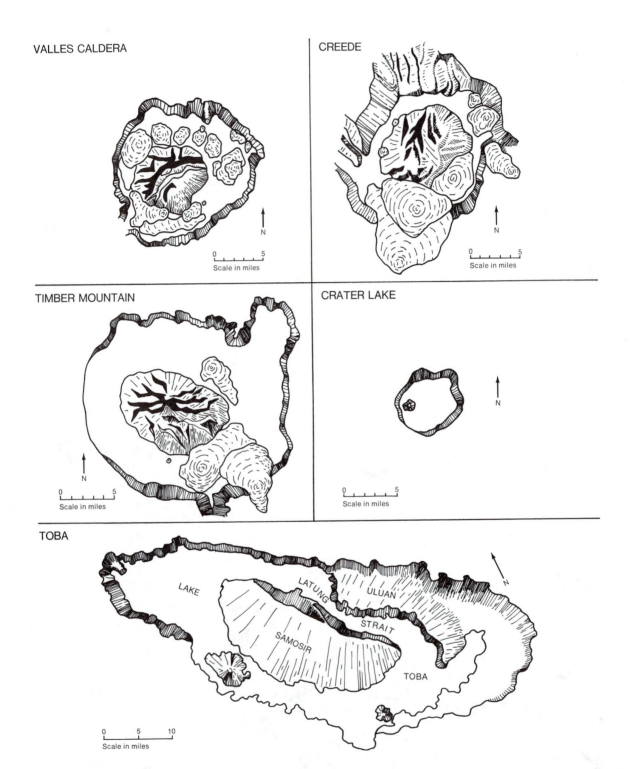

VALLES CALDERA

CREEDE

N

0   5
Scale in miles

TIMBER MOUNTAIN

CRATER LAKE

N

0   5
Scale in miles

TOBA

LAKE

LATUNG

ULUAN

STRAIT

SAMOSIR

TOBA

N

0   5   10
Scale in miles

tilted, in opposite directions, the adjacent blocks of Samosir Island and Uluan Peninsula (Fig. 15).

Creede Caldera in the central San Juan Mountains of Colorado is a basin approximately 14 miles in diameter. A central, domical mountain mass (Snowshoe Mountain) nearly 10 miles in diameter rises about 3,000 feet above the moatlike valley floor (Fig. 15).

The Timber Mountain Caldera in southern Nye County, Nevada, is a depression about 18 by 20 miles in diameter. A central mountain mass, the Timber Mountains, rises 2,000–3,000 feet above the caldera floor, which, like those of Valles and Creede, has a moatlike area between the central mountain mass and the caldera walls (Fig. 15).

BASE SURGE IN VOLCANIC ERUPTIONS

In many volcanic eruptions there is a horizontal as well as a vertical component in the eruption blast. A horizontal or lateral blast has long been recognized in *nuée ardente* type eruptions, which are described in subsequent pages, but the driving force in such eruptions is still uncertain. Base surge is defined as a ring-shaped basal cloud which sweeps outward as a density flow from the base of the vertical explosion column (see Pl. 12). Base surge was first recognized in the thermonuclear test at Bikini Atoll in the South Pacific on July 25, 1946 (Glasstone 1950, p. 41). In this test a 20-kiloton nuclear device was exploded at a depth of 27 meters below sea level. The resulting base surge continued outward for more than 4 kilometers. Its initial velocity was more than 190 kilometers per hour, but at 1.4 kilometers from the explosion center its velocity had decreased to 72 kilometers per hour.

In underground test explosions, expanding gases at the explosion center first vent vertically, pushing up and out a wall of nearly coherent roof material. This wall is pushed outward and overturned to produce the overturned synclines found not only in large explosion tests, but also at such impact craters as Meteor Crater, Arizona (Shoemaker 1960). Only after the wall is broken can expanding gases from the explosion rush over it, and carry material from it outward to feed the base surge.

It was in the study of the 1965 eruption of Taal Volcano in the Philippines that James G. Moore pointed out the significance of base surge in volcanic eruptions, and his paper, "Base Surge in Recent Volcanic Eruptions" (1967), is the basic work on the subject. The September 28–30, 1965, eruption of Taal Volcano was a phreatomagmatic eruption in which a "series of debris-laden eruption clouds moved out radially from the base of the main explosion column. These clouds carried blocks, lapilli, and ash suspended in water vapor and gases and moved outward with tremendous velocity. They shattered and obliterated all trees within one kilometer of the explosion center

Figure 15. Physiographic sketches of four resurgent calderas (after Smith and Bailey 1968) with Crater Lake, Oregon, for comparison: Valles Caldera, Jemez Mountains, New Mexico; Creede Caldera, San Juan Mountains, Colorado; Timber Mountain Caldera, Nye County, Nevada; Toba depression, northern Sumatra (note change in scale for this sketch).

and sandblasted objects up to 8 kilometers distant" (Moore 1967, p. 337). The Taal eruption began at 2:00 A.M., September 28, 1965, with the explosive ejection of incandescent blocks and cinders from a new crater on the southwest side of Volcano Island in Lake Taal. The major explosive phase, apparently the result of water gaining access to the magma conduit, began at 3:25 A.M. on the same day and continued until 9:30 A.M. During this time enormous eruption clouds rose to a height of 16–20 kilometers, and, from the base of the main cloud, flat, turbulent clouds spread laterally, transporting ejecta with hurricane velocity. These debris-laden clouds closely resembled the base surge of thermonuclear explosions. In a zone within 3 kilometers from the explosion center the base surge deposits exhibit a crude dune type of bedding. The dunes are oriented roughly at right angles to the direction of the blast, with the steeper side, frequently eroded and scoured, facing the explosion center. The largest dunes, with a wave length up to 19 meters, are adjacent to the explosion center, and the wave length decreases to 4 meters at a distance of 2.5 kilometers. Similar deposits have since been identified in other volcanic eruptions (Fisher and Waters 1970).

Base surge is common in volcanic eruptions where the ocean, a lake, or abundant ground water has access to the volcanic conduit. The resulting steam explosion commonly produces a vertical, cylindrical eruption column thousands of meters in height with a flat, collarlike, horizontally moving cloud at its base. Most examples of base surge in volcanic eruptions have come from phreatic explosions. However, explosive exsolution of magmatic gases during rapid extrusion of large volumes of oversaturated magma may produce a base surge, and *nuées ardentes* and ash flows may be the result of such base surges.

IN CONCLUSION

Thus, we have seen how prolonged volcanic eruptions from vents may construct magnificent cones, some of which are among the most lofty mountains on earth. On the other hand, prolonged eruptions may also result in the destruction of a cone by so emptying the magma chamber that the cone, left unsupported, collapses into it (caldera formation).

Part Two   Types of Volcanic Eruptions

Volcanic eruptions are one of the most awe-inspiring and terrifying phenomena of nature, having resulted in many of the great disasters of modern times. Their awesome grandeur is even more impressive when the processes of their behavior are well understood.

Volcanoes behave in varying ways and have been classified (Ch. 4) according to the nature of their eruptions. In Part Two these various types of eruptions will be explained, with a detailed description of a representative volcano for each type. A description of these types will give the reader a comprehensive view of the entire range of volcanic eruptions.

This section begins with the most explosive, or Peléan, type, and follows in succeeding chapters through the classification, ending with the least explosive, or Icelandic, type. In each case a description is given of the geologic features of the region in which the type of volcano is included. A volcano is simply one manifestation of certain geologic conditions, and by necessity the two cannot be separated. In most cases several volcanoes in each region could serve equally well as types, and in a few instances additional examples are described in order to present a more complete account of the type of eruption.

Chapter 7   The Peléan Type of Volcanic Eruption

Then the Lord rained . . . fire and brimstone . . . and, lo, the smoke of the country went up as the smoke of a furnace. —GENESIS 19:24–28

The Peléan type of eruption, which is the extreme in explosiveness, is represented by many volcanoes in Central America and the West Indies. The type was first recognized in the eruption of Mount Pelée in 1902.

STIMULUS TO
VOLCANOLOGY

On May 9, 1902, the world was shocked at the news that St. Pierre, the largest and most beautiful city of the Lesser Antilles, had been annihilated by a tremendous eruption of the nearby volcano Mount Pelée. It seemed likely that the report was grossly exaggerated. However, the confirmation of the report on the following day brought the further news that La Soufrière on the island of St. Vincent had also erupted with much loss of life and property on the day preceding the St. Pierre catastrophe. Thus there were two disasters in the same area. The United States government immediately dispatched the cruiser *Dixie* with supplies for the stricken islands. It sailed from New York on May 14 carrying scientists representing various organizations to study the eruption. Among those making the trip were Professor I. C. Russell from the University of Michigan, Dr. Thomas A. Jaggar from Harvard University, Dr. R. T. Hill and Mr. G. C. Curtis from the United States Geological Survey, and Dr. E. O. Hovey from the American Museum of Natural History. A number of correspondents from newspapers and magazines also accompanied the group. Mr. George Kennan, who is quoted later in this section, was the representative of *Outlook*, a weekly magazine. Others soon joined them, including Dr. A. Heilprin from the Geographical Society of Philadelphia, Dr. Tempest Anderson and Dr. J. S. Flett from the Royal Society of London, Dr. A. Lacroix from the French Academy of Science, and others. With such a distinguished group of scientists working in the field of volcanology, the hitherto obscure branch of science immediately became of first-order importance. In fact, the stimulus which the eruption of Mount Pelée gave to the study of volcanoes was largely responsible for the rapid development of the science. Since the eruption of Mount Pelée did not conform to the then-known types of volcanic eruptions, a new classification and new theories were required to explain its activity. A brief review of the geography and geology of the region will be helpful in understanding the eruption of Mount Pelée and that of its neighbor La Soufrière.

THE LESSER ANTILLES

The Lesser Antilles, a group of islands which stretch "like piers of a bridge" across the entrance to the Caribbean Sea, form a part of the West Indies. In the shape of an arc, bowed out toward the Atlantic Ocean, they extend for 450 miles from the Anegada Passage just east of the Virgin Islands southward almost to the coast of South America. The northern islands are sometimes referred to as the Leeward Islands and the southern ones as the Windward Islands because of their position with respect to the Trade Winds.

Geologically, the Lesser Antilles can be separated into two groups. (*a*) On the outer part of the arc to the northeast is an older, low-standing, and long-extinct series of submerged volcanoes capped by limestone deposits. This section is often called the Limestone Caribbees (Fig. 16). (*b*) A younger, western and southern series of high-standing, more or less active volcanic islands are designated as the Volcanic Caribbees. This latter group constitutes a unique and peculiar geologic province similar to the island arcs in the Pacific Ocean. It is one of only two such features occurring in the Atlantic and has given rise to much speculation that geologically it belongs to the Pacific region.

All of the Lesser Antilles are oceanic islands; that is, they have been built up by volcanic action from the floor of the ocean. They stand on a submarine ridge with a basal width at the south of 40–60 miles but with a northern range of over 200 miles. The islands are bordered on either side by deep trenches on the ocean floor. To the north and east is the Brownson Trough and its extension, the Tobago Trough, and to the south and west is the shallower, less well defined Grenada Trough. Barbados and Tobago islands, lying to the south and east, are geologically a part of South America rather than a part of the Caribbees.

All of the Volcanic Caribbees have well-preserved and still more or less active volcanic cones. Only two, however, Mount Pelée on Martinique and La Soufrière on St. Vincent, have had violent eruptions in historic time. The eruptions of these two in 1902, only 18 hours apart, with the loss of thousands of lives, are described in the following pages. Nearly all the islands have *soufrière*, or gas-and-steam, vents and boiling or hot springs attesting recent volcanic activity. Hill (1902, p. 226), after describing the islands as "pearls on a necklace," says: "Across the throat of the Caribbean extends a chain of

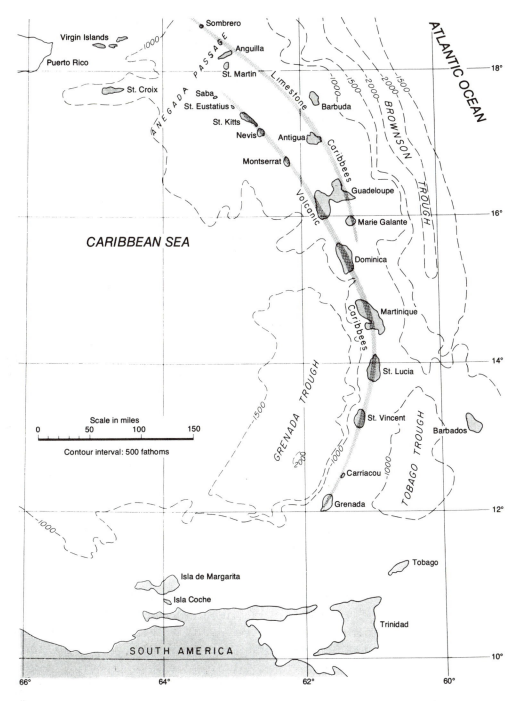

Figure 16. The Lesser Antilles, West Indies.

islands, which are really smouldering furnaces, with fires banked up, ever ready to break forth at some unexpected and inopportune moment." The northern islands of the chain, like Saba (2,820 ft.) and St. Eustatius (1,950 ft.) are simple piles of volcanic material with dominating crater cones. Likewise, St. Kitts is dominated by Mount Misery (4,314 ft.) with a summit crater 1,000 feet deep in which there is a crater lake. Montserrat consists of six adjacent mountain masses, each of which represents an old volcano modified by long-continued erosion (MacGregor 1939). The youngest and the highest volcano is Soufrière Hills (3,002 ft.), which contains a number of active fumaroles. No eruptions have occurred in historic time, and the rather considerable erosion since the last eruption indicates that possibly thousands of years have elapsed since the volcano was active. Near the center of the chain the five larger islands, Guadeloupe (4,869 ft.), Dominica (4,747 ft.), Martinique (4,800 ft.), St. Lucia (3,145 ft.), and St. Vincent (4,048 ft.), are each a complicated mass of old constructional and destructional volcanic forms. They indicate a series of eruptions in which, as the vent shifted, the cone was progressively destroyed and rebuilt.

Perret (1935, p. 114) believes that the volcanoes of the group, beginning with St. Kitts, illustrate an evolutionary sequence. Southward from St. Kitts are four great vents about equally spaced and progressively younger in the volcanic cycle. Mount Misery on St. Kitts is plugged by a massive lava dome and is probably extinct. La Soufrière on Guadeloupe is capped by a lava dome, and its only activity is the emission of steam. Mount Pelée on Martinique is still active, but it is in the process of dome formation, and at La Soufrière on St. Vincent a dome began to form in an eruption which started in November, 1971.

In the earliest period of volcanic activity in this area, extensive lava flows alternated with ash and fragmental debris. However, in recent eruptions the volcanoes have erupted only fragmental material, which formed the conspicuous cones and volcanic masses now present. The geologic history of the Lesser Antilles is not fully known, but it is apparent that the older Limestone Caribbees began on a submarine ridge and by volcanic up-piling built a string of islands. These were then submerged and covered by limestone deposits. C. Schuchert (1935, p. 728) believes that they may have started as early as late Cretaceous and were submerged by early Tertiary time. This view is based on the fact that the oldest limestone known in the islands is of Late Eocene age. The younger chain, the Volcanic Caribbees, may have existed as a submarine ridge as early as Oligocene time, but most of the islands do not contain coral reefs older than Pleistocene. Further, the chain probably developed progressively, so that it is not of the same age throughout.

Studies at Bermuda, an isolated island 580 miles east of the coast of South Carolina and about 1,000 miles north of the Lesser Antilles, have been helpful in deciphering the geologic history of this region (Pirsson 1914). Bermuda is a volcanic cone capped by limestone. A broad plain rising about 6,000 feet above the ocean floor is surmounted by a typical volcanic cone 6,000 feet in height. The cone was submerged (and doubtless eroded), and a thick layer of coral limestone was deposited on the submerged crest; this layer now forms the surface rocks at Bermuda. The history could only be surmised until a well drilled in search of water revealed the complete story. The well penetrated 380 feet of limestone before passing into weathered basaltic material, showing that it had been washed to and fro by the sea. Below this material the top of the cone was encountered. The limestone was determined, on the basis of its fossil content, to be of Oligocene age.

MOUNT PELÉE,
MARTINIQUE

Early History

Mount Pelée, or more properly Montagne Pelée, which prior to its catastrophic eruption of May 8, 1902, was scarcely known beyond its own little territory, makes up the northern end of the island of Martinique in the Lesser Antilles of the West Indies. When it was first described, about 1640, it was called Bald Mountain, from a bare spot near its summit. The name Pelée was applied much later and presumably is from the French (*pelé*, ''peeled'') for ''bald.'' However, the Hawaiian goddess of volcanoes is Pele, and one begins to wonder if there may not be some connection between the two. Definite knowledge concerning the history of Mount Pelée extends back only to the time of the first French settlement on Martinique in 1635. Prior to 1902 only two minor eruptions of Mount Pelée are recorded, neither of which was very serious or resulted in loss of life. The first was in 1792 and the other in 1851 (Robson and Tomblin 1966). The 1851 eruption, after some deep rumblings, threw out a column of ash, which settled over the southwest side of the mountain, extending as far as St. Pierre. The eruption was over in a few hours and did not cause alarm among the inhabitants.

The Cone

Mount Pelée is a roughly circular cone culminating in a single peak from which the broken surface slopes in all directions to the sea, except on the southeast, where its slope meets the ruins of the older twin cone of Carbet (3,917 ft.). The slopes of Mount Pelée are deeply

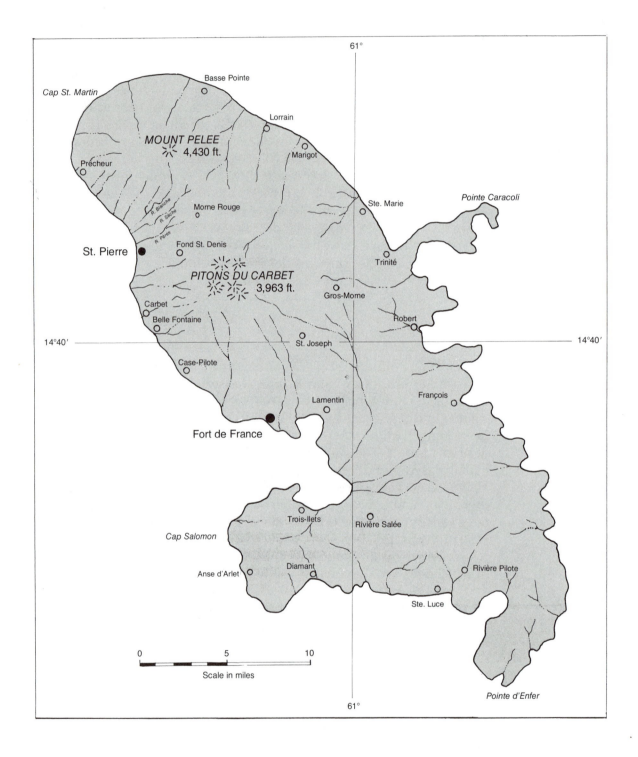

61°

Basse Pointe

Cap St. Martin

Lorrain

MOUNT PELEE
4,430 ft.

Marigot

Prêcheur

Pointe Caracoli

Ste. Marie

Morne Rouge

R. Blanche
R. Sèche
R. Pères

Fond St. Denis

St. Pierre

Trinité

PITONS DU CARBET
3,963 ft.

Gros-Morne

Carbet

Robert

Belle Fontaine

14°40'   14°40'

St. Joseph

Case-Pilote

François

Lamentin

Fort de France

Trois-Ilets

Rivière Salée

Cap Salomon

Anse d'Arlet

Diamant

Rivière Pilote

Ste. Luce

0   5   10

Scale in miles

61°

Pointe d'Enfer

Figure 17. Martinique.

cut by ravines which radiate from the summit. Nearly all of them, not more than four or five miles in length, discharge flood waters into the sea. They are the site of destructive floods during periods of heavy rain, carrying huge boulders and debris and spreading destruction in their path. The best known is the Rivière Blanche, because of its connection with the 1902 eruption. It was the flow of boiling mud down its channel on May 5 which buried the sugar mill and caused the first loss of life in the eruption. Mount Pelée appears to be a part of a complex volcanic mass which has been destroyed and rebuilt as the eruptive center shifts its location. Morne Sibérie and Piton Pierreaux, the latter nearly 2,000 feet in elevation, are prominent relics of the older mass. The volcano itself covers an area of about 50 square miles.

A description of the condition of the summit and crater of the volcano at that time will be helpful in following the events of the 1902 eruption. Of course, the crater of a volcano is usually altered rather extensively by an eruption. The summit of Mount Pelée, before the eruption, was occupied by a bowl-shaped basin, the floor of an old caldera, which had existed since prehistoric time. Around the rim of the basin was a series of peaks, of which Morne La Croix, the highest, stood about 2,000 feet above the floor. On the floor of the caldera was a lake, L'Etang de Palmistes, a popular picnic spot. The crater which gave rise to the 1902 eruption, known as L'Etang Sec, was somewhat below the summit on the south side, overlooking the city of St. Pierre. It was an oval-shaped depression about 0.5 mile in diameter at the top and surrounded on all sides, except the southwest, by precipitous cliffs. On the southwest, through a great gash cutting fully 1,000 feet below the rim, the crater drained into the canyon of the Rivière Blanche. This great cleft was an important element in the 1902 eruption because it was responsible for directing the explosions toward St. Pierre. In the 1851 eruption, the lake in L'Etang Sec dried up, but there was no other evidence of any activity in the crater. For years prior to 1902 there was a small fumarole on the floor of L'Etang Sec.

The Eruption of 1902

There are numerous descriptions of the 1902 eruption. All of the representatives of the various organizations and societies aboard the U.S. relief ship *Dixie*, mentioned previously, published accounts of the eruption, as well as other scientists and journalists who visited the area. Many of the accounts were first published in magazines, or in the journals of the organizations their authors represented, and some were published as books. A complete list of references is not feasible, but those most helpful are cited and included in the bibliography.

The first signs of activity were observed on April 2, 1902, by Professor Landes of the natural-science faculty of the St. Pierre Lycée, who noticed steaming fumaroles in the upper valley of the Rivière Blanche. On April 23, a slight fall of ash and a strong odor of sulphur were noticeable in the streets of St. Pierre, and a few minor earthquake shocks caused dishes to fall from shelves. On April 25, explosions occurred in the basin of L'Etang Sec, sending ash clouds and rocks into the air. Visitors who climbed to the rim of the crater on April 27 reported that the normally dry bed of L'Etang Sec was occupied by a lake at least 200 yards in diameter and that a small cinder cone, hardly more than 30 feet high, had formed at one side. From its summit rose a column of steam, issuing with a vigorous "boiling" noise. Light falls of ash covered the streets of St. Pierre, giving a wintry look to the city. During the days that followed, the ash falls became heavier, blocking roads and forcing business houses to close. The roar of the explosions from the volcano and the continued fall of ash caused consternation among the inhabitants. Many birds and some larger animals were smothered by the ash or asphyxiated by poisonous gases from the ash. The local newspaper, _Les Colonies_, reported in its May 3 issue: "The rain of ashes never ceases. At about half-past nine the sun shone forth timidly. The passing of carriages in the streets is no longer heard. The wheels are muffled [in the layer of ash]. Puffs of wind sweep the ashes from the roofs and awnings, and blow them into rooms of which the windows have imprudently been left open" (quoted by Heilprin 1903, p. 65). This was followed by a list of closed business houses and an announcement that the excursion planned for L'Etang de Palmistes on the day following had been canceled. Many of the inhabitants of St. Pierre were in fear and panic, and they left the city in large numbers, but they were replaced by refugees from the outlying areas who crowded into the city to swell by several thousand its normal population of 26,000. The panic reached such proportions that some action seemed necessary.

A commission appointed by the French governor at Fort de France to investigate the danger from the volcano reported the existence of no immediate danger and no reason for abandoning the city. There is some suspicion that the governor and the newspaper were anxious to keep the people in St. Pierre until after an important election scheduled for Sunday, May 10. The governor, in order to reassure the population, made a visit to St. Pierre with his wife for a personal inspection, and both were victims of the tragedy which overwhelmed St. Pierre.

Heavy rains sent floods of chocolate-colored water down all the valleys on the southwest side of Mount Pelée. Shortly after noon on

May 5, the sugar mill at the mouth of the Rivière Blanche, two miles north of St. Pierre, was destroyed by a torrent of boiling mud which swept down the stream valley with express-train speed. Thirty or more workmen (the estimates run as high as 150) were entombed in the boiling mud, which left only the chimney visible to mark the location of the mill. The mud swept into the sea, extending the coast line and creating a huge wave which overturned two boats tied at anchor and washed the adjacent coast, flooding the lower portion of St. Pierre. The tragedy at the sugar mill was the first loss of life due directly to the volcano.

A later reconstruction of events explained how this catastrophe was caused. The accumulation of ash in the basin of L'Etang Sec formed a dam, which blocked the gorge and permitted a large quantity of water to collect in the old lake basin. The water, heated by volcanic action, broke the dam shortly after noon on May 5, because of an explosion or increased pressure, and rushed from its height of nearly 3,000 feet as a deluge of mud and boulders down the Rivière Blanche. By the time it reached the lower slopes it had become an avalanche of mud, carrying huge boulders, rocks, and immense trees, and moving with precipitate speed. It swept over the sugar mill and on into the sea.

Jaggar (1949) takes exception to the view that the water causing the disastrous mudflow was from L'Etang Sec. He maintains that a fracture (rift zone) follows the gorge of Rivière Blanche from the crater to the sea and that eruptions of hot gases along this fracture converted the ground water into a flood of boiling mud. He argues that ground water must be involved, since some of the hot mudflows occurred without corresponding rainfall on the upper slope of the mountain, and further that the tremendous speed of the flows can be explained only by the migration of the eruptions along the fracture. Extension of crater blasts to lateral rift zones is a common feature in many volcanic eruptions, and it is possible that such was the case in the eruption of Mount Pelée.

On the date of the disaster at the sugar mill, *Les Colonies* reported: "A flood of humanity poured up from the low point of the Mouilage. It was a flight for safety, not knowing where to turn. The entire city was afoot. The shops and private houses are closing. Everyone is preparing to seek refuge on the heights" (quoted by Heilprin 1903, p. 70). Although the volcano was in constant eruption, the people were expecting an earthquake or a tidal wave, and the danger from the volcano was not anticipated.

On May 6 the eruption was particularly violent, explosions being heard in the neighboring islands, and the exodus from St. Pierre continued on foot and by steamer to Fort de France and the neighboring island of St. Lucia. The governor ordered soldiers to guard the roads to halt the flight. *Les Colonies* on this date declared that the alarm was not justified, and on the next day (May 7), the eve of the catastrophe, published an interview with Professor Landes of the Lycée which concluded with the statement that "Mount Pelée presents no more danger to the inhabitants of Saint Pierre than does Vesuvius to those of Naples" (quoted by Heilprin 1903, p. 75). In the same issue of *Les Colonies*, with the city in panic and many trying to flee, the editor asked why this fright and concluded a brief editorial paragraph as follows: "We confess that we cannot understand this panic. Where could one be better off than at Saint Pierre? Do those who invade Fort-de-France believe that they will be better off there than here should the earth begin to quake? This is a foolish error against which the populace should be warned. We hope that the opinion expressed by M. Landes in the interview which we published will reassure the most timid" (quoted by Heilprin 1903, pp. 76–77).

The eruptions continued on May 7, with lightning flashing through the dense cloud of ash which rose with each outburst. All of the streams on the slopes of Mount Pelée were carrying torrents of mud and water, spreading destruction in their paths. These floods were due to the heavy rains on the slope of the mountain, which converted the fine ash into a mud. Such streams of mud are able to transport huge boulders, even up to many tons in weight. On the afternoon of May 7, news of the eruption of La Soufrière on St. Vincent, 90 miles to the south, was received. This gave the eruption-weary inhabitants of Martinique some hope, for it was generally believed that the eruption on St. Vincent would relieve the pressure on Mount Pelée and thus prevent a serious outbreak. It was with some degree of reassurance that the people retired to their homes for the last fateful night in the history of St. Pierre.

The morning of May 8 dawned bright and sunny, with nothing in the appearance of Mount Pelée to excite suspicion except the immense column of vapor rising from the crater. The column was not particularly dark in color, but it did seem to be rising to an unusual height. At about 6:30 A.M. the ship *Roraima*, its decks covered with grey ashes, came into the port at St. Pierre and tied up alongside the seventeen other vessels in the roadstead. At 7:50 A.M. the volcano exploded with four deafening, gunlike reports, discharging upward from the main crater a black cloud pierced with lightning flashes. Another shot out laterally and with hurricane speed rolled down the mountain slope, keeping contact with the ground like an avalanche. In a short two minutes it had overwhelmed St. Pierre and spread fanlike out to sea. The clock on the tower of the Hôpital Militaire was stopped at 7:52 A.M.—and practically instantly the entire population of nearly 30,000 was obliterated. The lateral and vertical discharges appeared to be identical except for direction. Observers who wit-

nessed the eruption from the side as well as from boats in the roadstead described it as a black, rolling cloud, like a blast from a huge
cannon. Although some reported seeing flames in the cloud, the evidence on this is confusing, since many people associate flame with
heat and, being burned by the blast, describe it as flaming.

The blast consisted of superheated steam filled with even hotter
dust particles traveling with a velocity of around 100 miles per hour.
The dust particles gave the cloud a greater density than normal atmospheric gases have. This unusual density increased the destruc-
tiveness of the cloud by keeping it in contact with the ground and by
increasing its capacity for devastation, which was greater than that of
a West Indies hurricane of the same wind velocity. All the houses in
St. Pierre were unroofed and otherwise demolished either in part
or totally. The trees were stripped of leaves and branches down to
the bare trunks. The force of the blast is shown by the fact that walls
of cement and stone, three feet in thickness, were torn to pieces as
though made of cardboard, six-inch cannon on the Morne d'Orange
Battery were sheared from their mountings, century-old trees were
uprooted, and a statue of the Virgin Mary, weighing at least three
tons, was carried 50 feet from its base. Since the windows in most
of the houses in St. Pierre were covered only with shutters, it being a
tropical city, the highly heated gas quickly penetrated every part of
the buildings, and almost instantly the city was in flames. Those who
were not instantly killed by the initial blast were doubtless burned
in the fires that followed. Even at 11:30 A.M., three and one-half
hours after the initial blast, the heat from the burning city was so intense that a ship from Fort de France could not approach the shore.

All of the ships in the roadstead, save two, were capsized. The
British steamer *Roddam*, set free by the parting of its anchor chain,
succeeded in escaping to St. Lucia, where 12 of its men arrived dead
and 10 so severely burned that they had to be hospitalized. The other
ship to survive was the *Roraima*, which had just arrived an hour earlier. Its mast, bridge, funnel, and boats were swept away, and it took
fire fore and aft. Of the crew of 47, 28 died from shock and burns, and
only two of the passengers, a little girl and her nurse, escaped alive.
Dr. Jaggar personally interviewed the Barbados nurse of the little
girl on the *Roraima*, who gave the following account:

> We had been watching the volcano sending up smoke. The Cap-
> tain (who was killed) said to my mistress, "I am not going to stay
> any longer than I can help." I went to the cabin and was assisting
> with dressing the children for breakfast when the steward (who
> was later killed by the blast) rushed past and shouted, "Close
> the cabin door—the volcano is coming!" We closed the door and
> at the same moment came a terrible explosion which nearly burst

the eardrums. The vessel was lifted high into the air, and then seemed to be sinking down, down. We were all thrown off our feet by the shock and huddled crouching in one corner of the cabin. My mistress had the girl baby in her arms, the older girl leaned on my left arm, while I held little Eric in my right.

The explosion seemed to have blown in the skylight over our heads, and before we could raise ourselves, hot moist ashes began to pour in on us; they came in boiling splattering splashes like moist mud without any pieces of rock. In vain we tried to shield ourselves. The cabin was pitch dark—we could see nothing. . . .

A sense of suffocation came next [but] when the door burst open, air rushed in and we revived somewhat. When we could see each other's faces, they were all covered with black lava, the baby was dying, Rita, the older girl, was in great agony and every part of my body was paining me. A heap of hot mud had collected near us and as Rita put her hand down to raise herself up it was plunged up to the elbow in the scalding stuff. . . .

The first engineer came now, and hearing our moans carried us to the forward deck and there we remained on the burning ship from 8:30 A.M. until 3:00 P.M. The crew was crowded forward, many in a dying condition. The whole city was one mass of roaring flames and the saloon aft as well as the forward part of the ship were burning fiercely; but they afterwards put out the fire.

My mistress lay on the deck in a collapsed state; the little boy was already dead, and the baby dying. The lady was collected and resigned, handed me some money, told me to take Rita to her aunt, and sucked a piece of ice before she died. (Quoted by Jaggar 1945, p. 142)

Assistant Purser Thompson, one of the survivors on the *Roraima*, described the eruption as follows:

I saw St. Pierre destroyed. It was blotted out by one great flash of fire. Nearly 40,000 people were killed at once. Of 18 vessels lying in the Roads, only one, the British steamship Roddam escaped and she, I hear, lost more than half on board. It was a dying crew that took her out. Our boat arrived at St. Pierre early Thursday morning. For hours before we entered the roadstead, we could see flames and smoke rising from Mt. Pelée. No one on board had any idea of danger. Capt. G. T. Muggah was on the bridge and all hands got on deck to see the show. The spectacle was magnificent. As we approached St. Pierre, we could distinguish the rolling and leaping red flames that belched from the mountain in huge volume and gushed high in the sky. Enormous clouds of black smoke hung over the volcano. The flames were then spurting straight up in the air, now and then waving to one side or the other a moment, and again leaping suddenly higher up. There was a constant muffled roar. It was like the biggest oil refinery in the world burning up on the mountain top. There was a tremendous explosion about 7:45 soon after we got in. The mountain was blown to pieces. There was no warning. The side of the volcano was ripped out, and there hurled straight towards us a solid wall of flame. It sounded like a thousand cannon. The wave of fire was on us and over us like a lightning flash. It was like a hurricane of fire, which rolled in mass straight down on St. Pierre and the shipping. The town vanished before our eyes, and then the air grew stifling hot and we were in the thick of it. Wherever the mass of fire struck the sea, the water boiled and sent up great clouds of steam. I saved my life by running to my stateroom and burying myself in the bedding. The blast of fire from the volcano lasted only for a few minutes. It shriveled and set fire to everything it touched. Burning rum ran in streams down every street and out into the sea. Before the volcano burst, the landings at St. Pierre were crowded with people. After the explosion, not one living being was seen on land. Only 25 of those on the Roraima, out of 68, were left after the first flash. The fire swept off the ship's masts and smoke stack as if they had been cut by a knife. (Quoted by Leet 1948, p. 8)

Of the entire population of St. Pierre, only two survived the catastrophe. Auguste Ciparis, a 25-year-old Negro stevedore, was a prisoner in an underground dungeon at the time of the blast. It will be recalled that the destruction of the city occurred at 7:52 A.M. on Thursday, May 8. Because of the hot ashes, which prevented rescuers from entering the area, it was not until Sunday that the cries of the prisoner were heard and he was rescued. His cell was windowless, and the only opening was a small grated space in the upper part of the door. Auguste Ciparis was badly burned on his back and legs, but he survived and was able to give a coherent account of his experience, as reported by George Kennan (1902), who interviewed him a few days after he was rescued and before his burns had been treated.

He related that he was waiting for the usual breakfast on the eighth, when it suddenly grew dark, and simultaneously hot air and ashes entered his cell through the door grating. His flesh was immediately burned, and, though he called for help, none came. The intense heat lasted only for an instant, and during that time he almost ceased to breathe. He did not recall any noise or odor, other than his "own flesh burning." He was wearing at the time, a hat, shirt, and trousers, but no shoes. Some of the most severe burns were on his back beneath his shirt. When seen by Kennan the burns were almost too horrible to describe, and it seemed doubtful that he would survive. However, Auguste Ciparis recovered and later as "the prisoner of St. Pierre" became a side-show attraction in a circus.

Later it was discovered that Léon Compère-Léandre, a Negro about 28 years old and strongly built, had also survived. He was a shoemaker by trade. He described his experience as follows:

> On May 8, about eight o'clock in the morning, I was seated on the doorstep of my house, which was in the southeast part of the city . . . All of a sudden I felt a terrible wind blowing, the earth began to tremble, and the sky suddenly became dark. I turned to go into the house, made with great difficulty the 3 or 4 steps that separated me from my room, and felt my arms and legs burning, also my body. I dropped upon a table. At this moment four others sought refuge in my room, crying and writhing with pain, although their garments showed no sign of having been touched by flame. At the end of ten minutes one of these, the young Delavaud girl, aged 10, fell dead; the others left. I then got up and went into another room, where I found the father Delavaud, still clothed and lying on the bed, dead. He was purple and inflated, but the clothing was intact. I went out and found in the court two corpses interlocked; they were the bodies of the two young men who had been with me in the room. Re-entering the house, I came upon the bodies of two men who had been in the garden when I returned to my house at the beginning of the catastrophe. Crazed and almost overcome, I threw myself upon a bed, inert and awaiting death. My senses returned to me in perhaps an hour, when I beheld the roof burning. With sufficient strength left, my legs bleeding and covered with burns, I ran to Fonds-Saint-Denis, 6 kilometers from St. Pierre. With the exception of the persons of whom I have spoken, I heard no human cries; I experienced no degree of suffocation, and it was only the air that was lacking to me. But it was burning. There were neither ashes nor mud. The entire city was aflame. (Quoted by Heilprin 1903, p. 119)

At the time of the catastrophe St. Pierre was the most important commercial city on Martinique and one of the best known in the entire region. It was located in a crescent-shaped strip about a mile long and one-fourth mile wide, lying between the curving beach and a corresponding curving ridge or steep hill on the landward side. The main street, Rue Victor Hugo, ran from one end of the crescent to the other and was crossed at intervals by shorter streets leading

Plate 11. Ruins of St. Pierre after its destruction by a nuée ardente *on May 8, 1902. From Lacroix (1904), courtesy Académie des Sciences (France).*

from the waterfront and ending against the high, partly terraced ridge on the landward side. Although there were a number of large buildings, such as the cathedral, the town hall, and the military hospital, in the main the city consisted of two- and three-story stone buildings with red tile roofs, located on narrow, crooked streets, such as are typical of the tropics. It was a gay waterfront city sometimes called the "Paris of the West Indies."

After the catastrophe the destruction of the city was almost beyond imagination. The wrecked walls, the cover of grey ash, and the absence of signs of life made the ruins appear ancient. It was impossible to realize that only a few minutes before the blast it had been the site of a flourishing city. No building remained standing, and the destruction was so complete that the greater number of building sites were unrecognizable even to those familiar with the city. Only bare walls were left standing, most frequently those which were parallel to the direction of the blast. In most instances all that remained of the houses was their foundations, covered with a heap of rubble mixed with bedsteads, twisted iron braces, and mangled sheets of metal roofing—some of which were wrapped around posts as though they were made of cloth. Iron girders and steel bars were twisted into a mangled mass as if they were made of rope. There is no way of describing a city so completely wrecked other than to say that it was a chaotic mass of rubble, plaster, roofing tile, and shattered walls, with here and there a fire-scorched branchless trunk of a big tree.

The greater part of the destruction was the result of the highly heated, hurricanelike blast, together with the hot dust, which set fire to inflammable objects. The highly heated ash fell only in moderate amounts in comparison to the ash falls in many volcanic eruptions. Heilprin (1903) reported that in drifts it rarely exceeded 3–4 feet in depth and that over the greater part of the city it was hardly more than a foot. Compared to the 25 or more feet which buried Pompeii, this is insignificant. The death and destruction were not due to ash alone. Water, perhaps from the steam in the eruption cloud, mixed with the ash in the air to form a mud which plastered everything.

The temperature of the blast can only be estimated from its effect on objects where no conflagration took place. Glass objects were softened (650°–700° C.), green juicy fruits were carbonized, wooden decks of ships in the roadstead well offshore were set afire, but the melting point of copper (1,058° C.) was not reached. Perret (1935) concluded from his study of similar eruptions of Mount Pelée in 1929–1932 that the temperature at the point of emission at the crater was around 1,200° C. The powerful expansion incident to escape of the gas would cause much cooling, but it is apparent that it still retained a heat of several hundred degrees centigrade when it reached St. Pierre, five miles from its source.

In many cases the victims at St. Pierre were stripped of their clothing by the force of the blast. Some showed signs of momentary struggle, but the great majority gave no evidence that they had stirred after the fiery blast struck them. Death was the result of inhaling the highly heated gases or from burns, and in many cases it appeared to have been almost instantaneous. It is unfortunate that no autopsies were performed on any of the victims to determine the true cause of their deaths.

The zone of destruction covered an area of about eight square miles (Fig. 18). In the middle was a belt in which complete annihilation

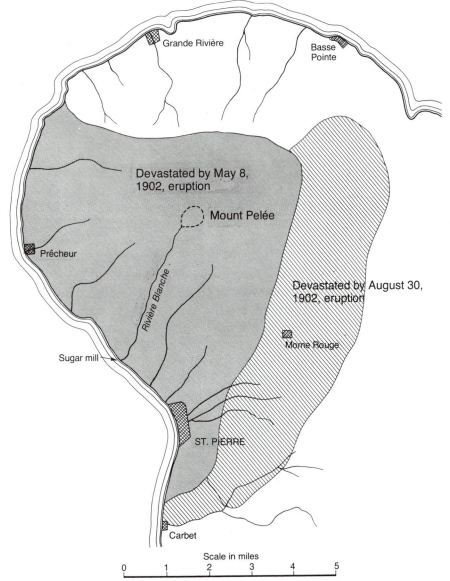

Figure 18. Areas devastated in the May 8 and August 30, 1902, eruptions of Mount Pelée. May 8 area after Hovey (1902a); August 30 area after Heilprin (1903).

occurred, gradually decreasing in intensity toward either margin, where at the extreme edge objects were only scorched. Heilprin (1903) concluded, quite correctly, that the blast consisted of super-heated steam, charged with incandescent particles of matter. Magma rising in the chimney of the volcano is highly charged with steam and under enormous pressure. As the magma rises, it reaches a point where the weight of the overlying rocks in the throat or a weak spot in the walls of the chimney is unable to contain the pressure, and it is suddenly released with a tremendous explosion. The magma is shattered into fine dust which, mixed with superheated steam, is shot out like the discharge from a colossal gun. Such blasts, unknown or un-recognized prior to the eruption of Mount Pelée, are now known to be characteristic of the gas-rich acid magmas which give rise to the most explosive types of eruptions. From his study of the 1902 erup-tion of Mount Pelée, Lacroix (1908) described such blasts as *nuées ardentes*, "glowing clouds." He believed from his study at Mount Pelée that the horizontal nature of the blast was due to explosions from the side of the dome rising in the crater. We now know that this horizontal component, known as base surge and described in Chapter 6, occurs in many volcanic eruptions. Dr. Tempest Anderson and Dr. J. S. Flett, representatives of the Royal Society of London and experienced observers of volcanoes, on the evening of July 9, 1902, were studying the effects of the great May 8 disaster. From a vessel a short distance offshore near Carbet they observed the erup-tion of a *nuée ardente* from Mount Pelée. Their description, one of the first of a *nuée ardente* by a trained observer, is as follows:

> As the darkness deepened, a dull red reflection was seen in the trade-wind cloud which covered the mountain summit. This be-came brighter and brighter, and soon we saw red-hot stones projected from the crater, bowling down the mountain slopes, and giving off glowing sparks. Suddenly the whole cloud was brightly illuminated, and the sailors cried, "The mountain bursts!" In an incredibly short span of time a red-hot avalanche swept down to the sea. We could not see the summit owing to the intervening veil of cloud, but the fissure and the lower parts of the mountain were clear, and the glowing cataract poured over them right down to the shores of the bay. It was dull red, with a billowy surface, reminding one of a snow avalanche. In it there were larger stones which stood out as streaks of bright red, tumbling down and emitting showers of sparks. In a few minutes it was over. A loud angry growl had burst from the mountain when this avalanche was launched from the crater. It is difficult to say how long an interval elapsed between the time when the great red glare shone on the summit and the incandes-

cent avalanche reached the sea. Possibly it occupied a couple of minutes. . . . Had any buildings stood in its path they would have been utterly wiped out, and no living creature could have survived that blast.

Hardly had its red light faded when a rounded black cloud began to shape itself against the star-lit sky, exactly where the avalanche had been. The pale moonlight shining on it showed us that it was globular, with a bulging surface, covered with rounded protuberant masses, which swelled and multiplied with a terrible energy. It rushed forward over the waters, directly towards us, boiling, and changing its form every instant. . . . The cloud itself was black as night, dense and solid, and the flickering lightnings gave it an indescribably venomous appearance. . . .

The cloud still travelled forward, but now was mostly steam, and rose from the surface of the sea, passing over our heads in a great tongue-shaped mass . . . Then stones, some as large as a chestnut, began to fall on the boat. They were followed by small pellets, which rattled on the deck like a shower of peas. In a minute or two fine grey ash, moist and clinging together in small globules, poured down upon us. After that for some time there was a rain of dry grey ashes. . . .

. . . There can be no doubt that the eruption we witnessed was a counterpart of that which destroyed St. Pierre. . . .

. . . a mass of incandescent lava rises and rolls over the lip of the crater in the form of an avalanche of red-hot dust. It is a lava blown to pieces by the expansion of the gases it contains. It rushes down the slopes of the hill, carrying with it a terrific blast, which mows down everything in its path. The mixture of dust and gas behaves in many ways like a fluid. . . . [The gases] apparently consist principally of steam and sulphurous acid. (Anderson and Flett 1902, pp. 442–444)

This accurate and vivid description reveals many of the characteristics of a *nuée ardente*, which have been verified by subsequent investigators. It has been clearly shown by Perret (1935) in his studies of the 1929–1932 eruption of Mount Pelée, in which many *nuées ardentes* were emitted, that it is the expansion and compression of the gases being constantly emitted by the magma fragments in their downward rush that give the *nuées ardentes* their great speed and power. In effect, the explosions (rapid expansion) of the gases in the glowing cloud continue as the mass moves forward at a tremendous velocity. Such a mass, in which the solid particles are suspended in a gas, is an example of fluidization as described by Reynolds (1954). A. G. MacGregor, in a critical review of published observations on the 1902 eruption of Mount Pelée, confirms Perret's conclusion that the mobility of the *nuées ardentes* was created by the "self-explosive (gas-generating) properties of fragments of new lava" (MacGregor 1951, p. 62).

The Peléan type of eruption is characterized by the expulsion of *nuées ardentes*. All of the magma is expelled in this type of activity as pumice and ash, and no liquid lava flows develop. In the final stage of the eruption, as is described later, a mass of viscous lava may accumulate in a domelike formation in the crater. This happens when the gas content of the magma is reduced to the point that it no longer shatters the magma on reaching the surface. Instead, it is pushed up into a dome or, as in the case of Mount Pelée, into a huge spine projecting from the crater like a giant stopper.

Following the destruction of St. Pierre on May 8, 1902, Mount Pelée continued intermittent eruptions of the same type (*nuées ardentes*) for several months (Heilprin 1903). One of these, following almost the identical path traversed by that of May 8, and equal to it in violence, on May 20 completed the destruction of St. Pierre. Any walls which had survived the first blast were leveled. Other violent eruptions occurred on May 26, June 6, July 9, and August 30. The path of the last extended somewhat to the east of the previous ones (Fig. 18) and annihilated or partially destroyed five villages, adding 2,000 victims to the death toll of Mount Pelée. Among these villages was Morne Rouge, a spot from which many had observed the initial blast of May 8. The December 16 *nuée ardente* (Pl. 12) was restricted to the area destroyed by earlier eruptions, where no further damage was possible.

The Tower of Pelée

About the middle of October a domelike mass of lava, too stiff to flow, formed in the crater of L'Etang Sec, and from its surface a spine or obelisk was protruded (Heilprin 1904). This remarkable "Tower of Pelée," with a diameter of 350–500 feet, in a few months reached a maximum height of 1,020 feet above the crater floor (5,200 ft. above sea level). There is some uncertainty as to the exact date at which the lava dome began to form in the crater. Some reports indicate that it began to appear as early as July or August, but it did not attract attention until the spine began to rise from it. The French Scientific Commission reported the spine on October 15, 1902, and by the end of November it had reached a height of 800 feet, rising like a giant stopper from the crater. Its rise was irregular, but it averaged about 30 feet per day. Huge blocks were continually breaking from the top, and its height was lowered only to be replaced by upheaval. The

Plate 12. Nuée ardente
eruption of Mount Pelée,
December 16, 1902. Height
of the eruption cloud is
13,000 feet. The "base surge"
or horizontal blast so char-
acteristic of nuée ardente
eruptions can be identified in
this scene as the tongue pro-
jecting from the base of the
eruption cloud. From Lacroix
(1904), courtesy Académie
des Sciences (France).

*Plate 13. Spine of Mount
Pelée with the ruins of St.
Pierre in the foreground,
March, 1903. From Lacroix
(1904), courtesy Académie
des Sciences (France).*

Plate 14. Spine of Mount Pelée on March 15, 1903. From Lacroix (1904), courtesy Académie des Sciences (France).

maximum height was reached on May 30, 1903, when it was 1,020 feet above the crater floor. At that time an eruption caused 180 feet of the top to crumble, and thereafter the upheaval did not keep pace with the crumbling. By the middle of August, 1903, it had been reduced to a height of about 500 feet, and the eruptions, which became more frequent during August, September, and into November, aided in the disintegration. The spine continued to disintegrate until it consisted only of a stump in the middle of a heap of rubble. Even after the spine ceased to rise, it continued to grow by swelling near the base as a result of the addition of stiff lava rising from below.

The phenomena attending the growth of the lava dome were the same as those accompanying an eruption. Great steam clouds carrying some ash rose 10,000–12,000 feet above the summit and loud detonations accompanied frequent discharges of "black clouds" of ash. Many of the "black clouds" were in fact *nuées ardentes*. Heilprin (1904) reported that the dome appeared brilliantly incandescent and at night a red glow was reflected on the clouds overhead. The dome continued to grow on a diminishing scale until October, 1905 (Robson and Tomblin 1966).

Significance of the Spine

As was true of *nuées ardentes*, the nature of such lava domes was not appreciated prior to the eruption of Mount Pelée in 1902. Since then, such features have been recognized in many volcanoes, and their significance is better understood. In volcanoes of the more acidic type, such as Mount Pelée, since the lava is very stiff and viscous, the chimney is commonly sealed after an eruption. The situation is quite different in the more basic type of volcanoes, such as Stromboli, in which the lava in contact with the air may remain liquid and the gases may continue to escape. In the Peléan type, with the chimney sealed, the gases accumulate until the upper part of the magma column becomes thoroughly gas-saturated. The initial stage of a new eruption consists of the explosive expulsion of the highly gas-charged magma, which is shattered into dust particles by the rapidly expanding gas, forming *nuées ardentes*. It must be remembered that this material is as truly primary magma as the more conventional liquid lava which flows from the more basic volcanoes. Following the expulsion of the highly gas-charged material, which in the 1902 eruption of Mount Pelée required about four months (May–August), there is a decrease in the explosive activity. The lava, now relatively gas-free and therefore highly viscous, begins to rise in the conduit and slowly accumulates in the crater as a lava dome (known as a *tholoid*). It is accompanied by *nuées ardentes* of decreasing intensity. Occasionally spines or, as in the case of Mount Pelée, giant monoliths are forced up from cracks in the surface of the lava dome. One surface of the great spine of 1903 on Mount Pelée was molded by the curving wall of the crevice through which it emerged, showing grooved and striated surfaces indicating its semirigid nature. The core of the spine is more fluid, and lava often exudes from the base.

Dome formation, like caldera collapse, signifies that a volcano is in the final stage of its eruptive history. Sometimes the initial collapse is followed by a renewal of activity and the development of a second volcanic edifice, which in turn is destroyed by collapse, and this sequence may occur several times before the volcano becomes extinct. Domes may form in craters without accompanying collapse, and conversely calderas are not always accompanied by domes. The formation of a lava dome in the crater is an indication that the eruptive force is decreasing. The dome may be disrupted or even partially destroyed and rebuilt by succeeding eruptions, but its presence is an indication that the eruptive history of the volcano is nearing its end.

Eruption of 1929

The next major eruption of Mount Pelée, following the 1902 outbreak, began on September 16, 1929, and lasted until near the close of 1932, or a little more than three years (Perret 1935). The eruption was similar to that of 1902, although of somewhat less intensity. St. Pierre, which by this time had grown to be a town with a population of about 1,000, and other villages on the western side of the volcano were evacuated; so there was no loss of life. Many *nuées ardentes* were emitted, and this phase of activity reached a maximum about the middle of December. Although of considerable violence, they did not compare in intensity with those of May 8, May 20, or August 30, 1902. Following the culmination of the *nuée ardente* phase, the explosive activity gradually declined, and a lava dome began to pile up in the crater immediately to the east of the stump of the 1903 spine. The new dome eventually covered the older one on the south and east, but it did not reach the western rim, which remained as an excellent reference point (Fig. 19). Numerous spines, some reaching heights of 150 feet, rose from the dome, but they soon crumbled. When the new lava dome began to form in the crater, Perret, who was observing the eruption, was able to assure the inhabitants that the eruption was declining and that the "worst was over" (Perret 1935).

Whether the lava dome now occupying the crater of Mount Pelée has effectively sealed the vent and the eruptive activity is ended, only time will tell. There was an interval of 27 years between the last eruptions (1902–1929), but the 1792–1851 interval was 59 years, and the

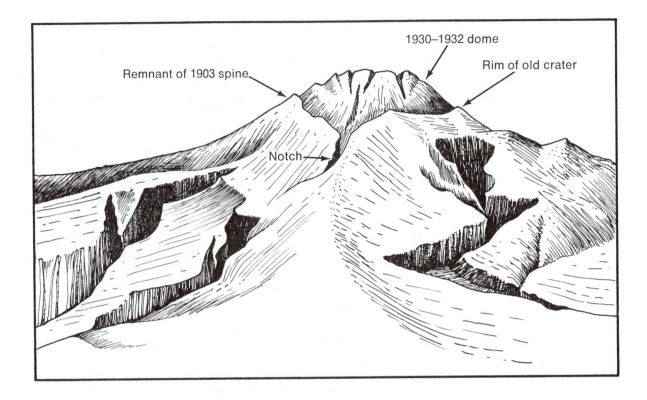

Remnant of 1903 spine

1930–1932 dome

Rim of old crater

Notch

1851–1902 interval was 51 years. Obviously this does not establish a pattern, but two of the three intervals between historic eruptions were 50–60 years.

LA SOUFRIÈRE,
ST. VINCENT

The volcano La Soufrière occupies the northern end of the island of St. Vincent, 90 miles to the south of Martinique. The island itself is a complex mass of volcanic material, similar to Martinique. The summit of La Soufrière, which rises 4,048 feet above sea level, consists of two craters, the 1812 crater and the so-called "old crater," immediately to the southwest, which was the site of the 1902 eruption. The old crater has a diameter of about 1 mile and a depth of 1,600–2,400 feet below the rim. Up to the time of the 1902 eruption it was occupied by a beautiful crater lake which stood at 1,930 feet above sea level. The 1812 crater, about 0.5 mile in diameter and 500 feet deep, is separated from the old crater by a saddle, which at its lowest point is 3,550 feet above sea level or about 500 feet below the highest point on the rim of the old crater. As on Mount Pelée, numerous valleys radiate from near the summit of La Soufrière and follow individual courses to the sea. The sides of the mountain are covered with a dense growth of tropical vegetation.

Figure 19. Lava dome in the crater of Mount Pelée, April 30, 1934. Sketched from a photograph by Perret (1935).

Early History

The only historic eruptions of La Soufrière, prior to the 1902 catastrophe, were in 1718 and 1812. These eruptions, which are summarized in some detail by Anderson and Flett (1903), were the most significant eruptions in the entire Lesser Antilles before 1902. The 1718 eruption, which began on March 26, was marked by heavy ash falls which continued for two or three days, obscuring the sun and turning day into night. The ash spread over the surrounding region, with up to nine inches reported at Martinique and four inches at St. Christopher, some 300 miles to the north. It is quite probable that in this eruption the top of a more lofty cone was destroyed, leaving the caldera which is now known as the "old crater." In the 1812 eruption, again great clouds of ash darkened the sun, and a new crater, immediately adjacent to the old crater, was formed. At Barbados, 110 miles to the east, the noise of the explosions was thought to be a naval engagement off the coast, and the garrison prepared to repel any attack. Preliminary phases of the eruption began on April 27. The climax of the eruption occurred on the morning of April 30 and continued through the morning of May 1.

Eruption of 1902

The May 7, 1902, eruption of La Soufrière preceded by less than 24 hours the climactic eruption of Mount Pelée, and several of the scientists and observers who investigated the eruption of Mount Pelée also visited St. Vincent to study the eruption of La Soufrière. The U.S. relief ship *Dixie*, previously mentioned in connection with the St. Pierre disaster, also carried relief supplies for the victims of La Soufrière's eruption. After a three-day stop to unload supplies on Martinique, the *Dixie* sailed on to St. Vincent, arriving at Georgetown, the capital of the island, on May 23. Some of the scientists, including Drs. E. O. Hovey, Thomas A. Jaggar, and I. C. Russell, who had made the trip to St. Pierre on the *Dixie*, continued on to St. Vincent. Thus, several of the early articles on the 1902 eruption of Mount Pelée include a section on the eruption of La Soufrière. Perhaps the most comprehensive report on the eruption of La Soufrière is that by Anderson and Flett (1903), but articles by Hovey (1902*a*; 1902*b*), Russell (1902*b*), and Jaggar (1902; 1949), who were among the first scientists to visit St. Vincent after the eruption, are very useful.

The first symptoms of unrest in the volcano were evident in April, 1901, slightly more than a year before the great eruption of May 7, 1902. Earthquakes were severe enough that people living on the

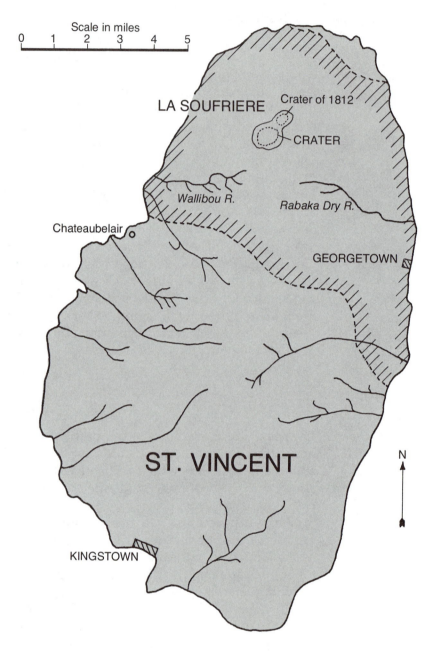

Figure 20. St. Vincent. The area devastated by the eruption of May 7, 1902, is shaded. After Hovey (1902a).

western slope of La Soufrière became alarmed, and some considered leaving the area, but the shocks ceased and the people resumed their normal activities until April, 1902, when the shocks were again felt. By the first of May the inhabitants on the leeward side of the volcano north of Chateaubelair had sought refuge elsewhere. If this had not happened, the death toll of the eruption would have been much higher. Those living on the windward side were not particularly disturbed and continued their activities as usual. It was felt that in the event of an eruption the ash and gases would be carried toward the west by the prevailing winds. When the great eruption occurred on May 7, few people were killed on the leeward side; Hovey (1902*b*, p. 445) reports only one, while on the windward side he places the loss at 1,350. However, the governor, in a letter dated May 23, reported that 1,295 bodies had been recovered, another 70 persons had died in hospitals from burns, and 200 persons were missing, giving a total of 1,565 as the number killed in the eruption (quoted by Anderson and Flett 1903, p. 414).

On May 5, fishermen crossing the mountain near the summit noticed that the water in the crater lake was discolored and agitated. The first visible outburst of steam was reported at 2:40 P.M. on May 6, and similar outbursts continued at intervals of one to two hours through the afternoon and night. By 10:30 A.M. on May 7 the eruptions had become an almost continuous roar, and the steam cloud was estimated to have reached a height of 30,000 feet. At 1:00 P.M. large stones could be distinguished in the ascending cloud. At about the same time, people who attempted to cross the Rabaka Dry River found a raging torrent of boiling mud and water more than 50 feet deep, which was rushing down the valley and out into the sea. This doubtless represented a discharge of at least a portion of the water from the crater lake into the headwaters of the stream. About 2:00 P.M. the already great activity increased markedly. A dense cloud of hot dust and steam spread down the mountainsides as a hurricane-like blast, and from it red-hot rocks fell in torrents. One observer, who described the cloud as "a terrific, huge, reddish-and-purplish cloud" advancing toward him, escaped by taking to a boat which he had in readiness (Hovey 1902*b*, p. 446). The dust-laden steam expanded with explosive violence, both horizontally and downward, following the configuration of the mountain. It was a true *nuée ardente* but of somewhat less intensity than the blasts at Mount Pelée. Observers reported that a portion of the cloud traveling eastward seemed suddenly to split and send a part back toward the volcano. Thus windows on the side away from the volcano were broken. This unexplained feature was also reported at Mount Pelée. Perhaps an inrush of air toward the crater was due to a vacuum created by the explosion.

The hot blast overturned trees, scorching them on the side facing the volcano, destroyed houses, and set fire to inflammable objects. The hot ash, which fell in great quantities, killed all vegetation and devastated an area comprising about one-third of the island (Fig. 20). Hills and ridges provided some protection for vegetation on their immediate leeward side, indicating that the blast swept past without touching the ground at these spots. A partially encircling ridge on the northeast side of the volcano accounts for the escape from destruction of a narrow fringe on the northeast edge of the island. Red-hot stones up to six inches in diameter fell in Georgetown, 5.5 miles from the crater. From the orientation of trees blown down, it was apparent that the blast had swept outward in all directions from the crater. At Mount Pelée the blast was concentrated in a relatively narrow sector, which fact may account for its greater intensity. A feature of the La Soufrière eruption not marked at Mount Pelée was the enormous amount of ash which was distributed over a wide area, even far out to sea. Ash began to fall on the *Jupiter*, a ship enroute from Africa, at 2:30 A.M. on May 8, when it was 830 miles east-southeast of Barbados. This indicated that the ash cloud had traveled at a speed of 60 miles per hour to reach the vessel at that time. The ash was spread like a gray mantle over the island, generally decreasing in thickness from the crater outward, but collecting in vast deposits in favorable valleys. In the valley of the Wallibou, deposits of more than 60 feet were formed, while in the Rabaka Dry River thicknesses up to 200 feet were reported. These huge accumulations remained hot for weeks, and violent explosions were common when surface water seeped into the heated interior. Hovey (1902a) describes one such eruption in the Wallibou Valley in which the steam column reached a height of more than a mile. Such eruptions, which were frequently believed to be new craters opening on the volcano, continued for weeks.

On the outer margin of the area the hot steam seems to have condensed to scalding water, which, mixed with the ash, formed a hot mud that adhered to everything it touched. The once dense tropical vegetation which had covered the region was replaced by dull gray ash. The greatest loss of life was on the Georgetown side near the Rabaka Dry River. The deaths were due to inhalation of the hot dust, burns from steam and dust, and contacts with falling stones. Those who escaped injury were saved by seeking refuge in cellars in which the opening was on the side away from the volcano. The most striking example of such protection was at Orange Hill, 2.5 miles north of Georgetown, where 132 persons escaped injury by seeking shelter in an empty rum cellar. The cellar, only partly underground, had one window and a door on the side away from the volcano, these openings being equipped with heavy shutters which were kept closed during the eruption. Those killed in the eruption suffered burns in exactly the same manner as did the victims at St. Pierre. The tornadic force of the blast appears to have been considerably less than the more violent of the eruptions from Mount Pelée, and the destruction was not so appalling because no large city was in its path.

Following the major outburst at 2:00 P.M. on May 7, tremendous detonations continued at such short intervals as to merge into an almost continuous roar, lasting all through May 8 and until early on the morning of May 9. Other eruptions, similar to the May 7 outburst, occurred on May 18 and September 1 and 3, but no additional loss of life was reported. The eruptions in September were equal to or even more violent than the May 7 blast, and the devastated area was extended to the southwest beyond the limits of the area affected earlier.

When the crater of La Soufrière was first visited after the May 7 and May 18 eruptions, on May 31, all that could be seen was a small lake of boiling water from which a strong column of steam rose. The level of the lake was estimated to be 1,200 feet above sea level, whereas before the eruption it had stood 730 feet higher. The 1812 crater was not disturbed in the eruption.

Eruption of 1971–1972

A pilot flying over the crater lake of La Soufrière on October 31, 1971, noted steam rising from the lake and detected a sulphurous odor. The following day government officials flew over the crater and observed areas of discoloration and turbulence of the lake surface. On the morning of November 3, a party climbed the volcano and descended the inner wall of the crater to the lake level. They found that the temperature at the lake edge was 81.5° C. (normally it is around 40° C.) and the water level was at least 15 feet above normal. The lake was calm, and steam was rising over its entire surface. The steam had a faint sulphurous odor, and the water was turbid and yellowish brown in color. The lake level, when first visited on November 3, was used as the datum for subsequent measurements (Sigurdsson, Shepherd, Tomblin, et al. 1971–1972).

It was correctly surmised that lava rising from the floor of the crater was displacing the water, causing the lake level to rise, and heating the water. Lava first appeared as an island near the center of the lake on November 20. It consisted of 10 large blocks of black lava lying within an area some 150–325 feet in diameter. These rocky protuberances were the topmost part of a dome-shaped mass of viscous lava which had been extruded through the floor of the crater lake and had just become visible. Two days later two new rocks appeared, about

820 feet northwest of the main group. The lake, about 3,200 by 4,200 feet, had a depth of 580 feet in the central part where the lava dome was forming. The lake level rose rapidly, reaching a maximum height of 92.5 feet above the November 3 datum on November 20, 1971. Thereafter the lake level dropped slowly, from six inches to a foot per day, chiefly because of evaporation. In its early stage of growth the lava dome rose about 6 feet per day, but later the rate declined as the lava spread laterally in ridges and lobes radiating from the central part of the island. The growth continued until March 22, 1972, when the dome attained its maximum height of 226 feet above the November 3 lake level, and shortly thereafter it was considered that the eruption was over. Throughout the eruption, seismic activity was limited to shocks of low magnitude which were recorded by the seismographs but were not felt by the inhabitants in the surrounding area.

The lava of the new dome is a basaltic andesite with a silica content of 55.3 percent, quite similar in composition to the earlier lavas and pyroclastics from La Soufrière.

Thus, the growth of a lava dome in the crater of La Soufrière is following the pattern observed in many volcanoes in the final stage of their activity. This does not mean that its eruptive history is necessarily over, for, as was demonstrated by Mount Pelée, subsequent eruptions may break through the lava dome or even destroy it; but it does signify that the volcano has entered the final phase of its activity.

MOUNT LAMINGTON, PAPUA NEW GUINEA

The 1951 eruption of Mount Lamington, one of the more recent examples of a Peléan-type eruption, was unusual because of the violence of the eruption and because it is one of the few such eruptions recorded by trained observers. The initial outburst was observed and photographed from a passing aircraft, and a qualified volcanologist, the late G. A. Taylor, a long-time member of the staff of the Bureau of Mineral Resources of Australia, was on the scene barely 24 hours after the initial explosion. Observations were continuous thereafter, with aircraft being used for daily inspection of developments in the crater area. Taylor's report (1958), on which the following account is based (supplemented by my notes on a visit to the area fifteen years after the eruption), is one of the most detailed and definitive reports on a Peléan type eruption.

Papua New Guinea (formerly the Territory of Papua) occupies the southeastern part of the island of New Guinea. The rugged Owen Stanley Range extends, as a backbone, throughout the narrow eastern portion of the island and rises, in places, to altitudes of more than 13,000 feet. It is composed essentially of metamorphic rocks cut by pre-Tertiary igneous intrusions. Mount Lamington lies about 25 miles inland from the northeastern coast of Papua and rises from a coastal plain of alluvial detritus, derived chiefly from the Owen Stanley Range. (See Fig. 21.)

The Lamington cone, about 5,900 feet above sea level, rises gradually from the coastal plain to a resistant summit nucleus. This resistant terminal nucleus consists of ragged peaks formed from remnants of earlier domes with a deep U-shaped crater connected to the lower slopes by Avalanche Valley, which is drained by the Ambogo River. Most of the cone is composed of unconsolidated tuffs and agglomerates deposited by *nuées ardentes* or mudflows. A sample of carbonized wood from one of the early *nuée ardente* deposits gave an age of 13,000 years.

*Figure 21. Eastern Papua
New Guinea. After G. A.
Taylor (1958).*

The Eruption of 1951

Preliminary activity. The climactic eruption occurred at 10:40 A.M. on January 21, 1951. It was generally reported that the catastrophic explosion came without warning, but such was not the case. Some six days prior to the climactic eruption there was activity in the crater, which was not generally observed or if so was not associated with an impending eruption. It seems worthwhile to describe the preliminary activities in some detail, since they provided a "warning system" which would have saved many lives had it been heeded. (Similarly, preliminary activity at Mount Pelée gave notice of an impending eruption, but there also the warning was not heeded, although Mount Pelée was known to be a volcano, whereas Mount Lamington was not recognized as one.) Landslides from the walls of the crater were observed on January 15, and, for the two days following, a thin column of vapor rose from the crater and swarms of earthquakes were widely felt in the settlements surrounding the volcano. On January 18 the gas emission rapidly increased, coming out in "belches" and loaded with ash; it rose to a height of many thousands of feet. Subterranean sounds accompanied this development, and the noise increased as the gas emission became greater. At the same time, earthquakes became so numerous that they were described as "almost incessant" at Higaturu, about six miles to the north of the crater. The early morning hours of January 19 were marked by extraordinary electric displays, described as "blue flashes," tongues of flame, sheet and chain lightning, and so on. When daylight exposed the summit of the cone, it was covered with light-colored ash. Electrical phenomena of various types are commonly associated with large Vulcanian type (ash-filled) eruption clouds in many volcanoes. On January 20, the day before the climactic eruption, a continuous ash-filled eruption cloud rose to a height of 25,000 feet or more. Had the prevailing winds carried the ash over the settled areas on the northern and western slopes of Mount Lamington, many of the inhabitants might have evacuated the area, as those on the western side of St. Vincent did in 1902, thereby greatly reducing the loss of life. The activity of Mount Lamington during the six days preceding the catastrophic eruption is fairly typical of eruptions of the Peléan type, and, for the future, it is imperative that such activity be reported, its significance appreciated, and the warning heeded.

Climactic eruption. At 10:40 A.M. on January 21, the initial catastrophic explosions produced a huge, ash-filled, mushroom-shaped cloud which within 2 minutes rose to 40,000 feet and 20 minutes later reached 50,000 feet. The base expanded rapidly, enveloping the whole countryside. Immediately preceding the explosion, the "irregular rumblings" which had characterized the activity up to this time gave way to a long, continuous roar, which was heard on the coast of New Britain, 200 miles away. A second violent eruption occurred around 8:45 P.M. For the next three days Mount Lamington was quiet, but on January 25 the explosive activity resumed. Thereafter, spasmodic outbursts, some of considerable intensity, occurred on February 6, February 18, and March 5. These were followed by milder outbursts, separated by longer periods of inactivity, and after June the extrusive or dome-building phase, which actually began a few days after the climactic eruption of January 21, became the main form of activity and continued intermittently for more than a year and a half.

It is of interest to note that the high-explosive phase of activity, which lasted less than two months, was marked by a broad periodicity with about two weeks between peak periods of energy release. Major explosive eruptions occurred on January 21, February 6, February 18, and March 5, each separated by a comparable period of about two weeks. The first two peak periods, January 21 and February 6, had the same pattern in that they represented culminating points which followed periods of increasing explosiveness. On the other hand, the outbursts of February 18 and March 5 (the last high-explosive eruption) represent the beginning of a new gas phase marked by eruptions of decreasing intensity. A pattern noted in a number of strong eruptions was a grouping of explosions in pairs separated by 12–15 hours of calm. A similar pattern has been noted in the eruptions of other volcanoes of the Peléan type. It appears that one gas phase triggers off another by changing a factor in the condition of magma equilibrium.

Nuées Ardentes

Nuées ardentes are characteristic features of the Peléan type of eruption, and they were abundantly represented at Mount Lamington. The *nuée ardente* from the climactic eruption of January 21 was distributed radially with respect to the crater and devastated an area of about 90 square miles. This area consisted of an inner zone, in which lateral velocities were high and devastation was complete, and a narrow outer zone, which was subjected more to heat than to the hurricanelike force of the *nuée ardente*. These areas are shown in Figure 22. In the zone of complete destruction, the rain forest on the slopes was flattened and in places was swept bare, not even stumps remaining as evidence of the previous forest. Buildings were carried away, and in most cases only the floors remained. In a radius of about two miles from the crater there was marked abrasive action which not only carried away the trees but scoured and grooved the ground,

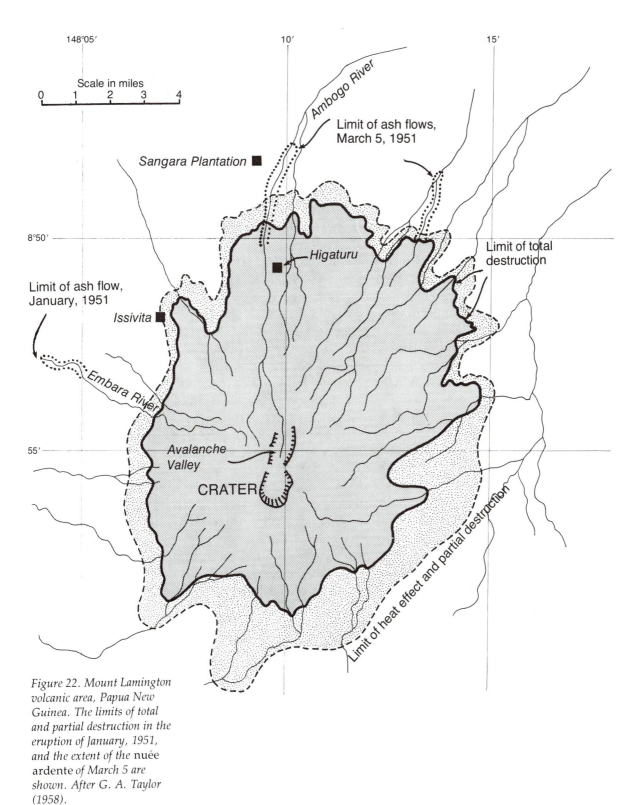

148°05'   10'   15'

Scale in miles
0   1   2   3   4

Sangara Plantation ■

Ambogo River

Limit of ash flows,
March 5, 1951

8°50'

Higaturu

Limit of total
destruction

Limit of ash flow,
January, 1951

Issivita ■

Embara River

55'

*Avalanche
Valley*

CRATER

Limit of heat effect and partial destruction

*Figure 22. Mount Lamington
volcanic area, Papua New
Guinea. The limits of total
and partial destruction in the
eruption of January, 1951,
and the extent of the* nuée
ardente *of March 5 are
shown. After G. A. Taylor
(1958).*

leaving in many places only charred root ends, cut off level with the grooved soil surface. Where a tree was left standing, the side facing the volcano was abraded and often charred.

Although the *nuée ardente* moved radially from the crater in line with the steepest slope, it was deflected by such topographic features as hills and ridges. The greater destruction to the north is due to the facts that the U-shaped crater opens in that direction and that the slopes are not interrupted by any major topographic features. Some anomalous movements, particularly near the margins, are interpreted as lateral expansions in vortexlike forms where a tongue of the *nuée* is thrust ahead of the main cloud front.

The velocities of *nuées ardentes* show a wide variation, and studies at various volcanoes have produced estimates ranging from near 300 miles per hour to 36 miles per hour. High velocities have been suspected from the destructive effects produced but they have not been accurately measured. The effect of a 75-mile-per-hour wind can be rather accurately estimated, but it is difficult to evaluate if it contains a heavy load of dust or rock fragments. At Higaturu, more than 5 miles from the crater, an automobile was left suspended on the tops of two truncated trees (Pl. 16). It is suspected that this resulted from local turbulence somewhat similar to a tornado, a situation which occurs when tongues of the *nuée* extend ahead of the main front and a vortex develops. High (i.e., tornadic) velocities in the vortex would account for some of the peculiar results, such as the stripping of the clothing from one body while another nearby was unaffected. The conclusion reached by Taylor (1958, p. 44) was that the average velocity of the *nuée ardente* was about 60 miles per hour, with local variations attaining a much higher velocity.

High temperatures are typical and in fact are an essential feature of *nuées ardentes*. In the 1902 eruption of Mount Pelée, the *nuée ardente* melted glass (650–700° C.) but did not melt copper (1,058° C.). The temperatures at Mount Lamington were very much lower, and the temperature distribution was highly erratic. The charred zone extended a little more than a mile below the end of Avalanche Valley, and at Higaturu, more than 5 miles from the crater, only plastic objects were deformed by the heat. From tests on similar plastic objects it was concluded that a temperature of 200° C. for a period of 1.5 minutes was reached. However, many of the valleys were filled with thick beds of hot ash which retained heat for months. It was not unusual to see a log which had been buried in the ash for weeks catch fire when suddenly exposed to the air, and, in places where the ash was protected from ground water and rainfall infiltration, vapor columns rising from the ash had a temperature of 96° C. two years later. Taylor (1958) obtained some unusual and dramatic pictures of the development of *nuées ardentes* at Mount Lamington, as well as

Plate 16. Truck suspended on the tops of two truncated trees after the nuée ardente *of January 21, 1953, Mount Lamington. From G. A. Taylor (1958), by permission of the director, Bureau of Mineral Resources, Canberra, Australia.*

other aspects of the 1951 eruption. A few of these remarkable photographs are reproduced here (Pls. 17–22).

Loss of Life

Although the settlements on the slopes of Mount Lamington were small and scattered, the *nuée ardente* of January 21 killed 2,942 people. The principal cause of death was believed to be steam-laden hot dust, and many who found protection from the main force of the *nuée ardente* in well-closed rooms survived. Survivors described the symptoms as pains in the mouth, throat, and eyes, followed by a burning sensation in the chest and abdomen and finally a sense of rapid suffocation. Poisonous gases were not considered to be an important cause of fatalities. Rigidity was a notable feature of many bodies and was due to the heat stiffening brought about by the coagulation of the albuminous material in the muscles. Many who survived were severely burned, but often the shielding effect of the clothing was apparent. (See Pls. 19 and 20.)

Plate 17. Development of a small nuée ardente: *as the forward movement slows, the upward expansion increases. From G. A. Taylor (1958), by permission of the director, Bureau of Mineral Resources, Canberra, Australia.*

Plate 18. Development of a nuée ardente: *the* nuée *swings to the left of the picture, following a change in direction of the valley. From G. A. Taylor (1958), by permission of the director, Bureau of Mineral Resources, Canberra, Australia.*

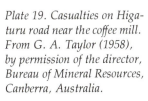

Plate 19. Casualties on Higaturu road near the coffee mill. From G. A. Taylor (1958), by permission of the director, Bureau of Mineral Resources, Canberra, Australia.

Plate 20. Scars from burns inflicted by the nuée ardente. *From G. A. Taylor (1958), by permission of the director, Bureau of Mineral Resources, Canberra, Australia.*

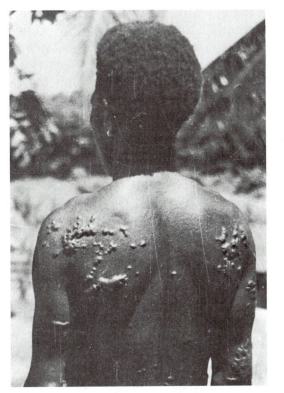

Return of Vegetation to the Area

The return of vegetation to the devastated area was surprisingly rapid. Taylor reports (1958, p. 51) that two years after the initial eruption vine-entangled thickets and tall cane grasses covered the area. When I visited the area 15 years after the eruption, the scar of the *nuée ardente* was completely healed and the devastated area was indistinguishable from the adjacent areas.

The Dome

A lava dome began to form in the crater of Mount Lamington a few days after the climactic eruption of January 21, and in about six weeks it had reached a height of more than 1,500 feet above the crater floor. The period of most rapid uplift was from February 3 to February 9, when the dome rose at the rate of 100 feet per day! The catastrophic eruption of March 5 shattered the dome, and two-thirds of it was removed in *nuées ardentes* which swept down the northern slope of the cone. However, the growth of the dome continued, first in one sector and then in another, and by mid-May the height of the dome exceeded that prior to the March 5 eruption. As early as mid-February a spine had begun to rise through a fracture in the top of the dome, but it frequently crumbled, covering the dome with rubble. In January, 1952, the spine reached its greatest height, rising nearly 400 feet above the surface of the dome. Spasmodic movements continued, and, while the mass of the dome increased, its height fluctuated around 1,800 feet above the crater floor. The dome was shaped like a truncated ellipsoid and had a volume of 0.25 cubic mile (Pls. 21 and 22).

   The lavas of the dome are all phorphyritic andesites, with hornblende the most abundant ferromagnesium mineral. The older lavas of the crater walls are very similar, except that the hornblende is altered and in some cases completely resorbed.

Lunar and Solar Tidal Influences

The fact that most of the large explosions, especially in the early phase of the eruption, occurred around the spring-tide period of full and new moon prompted Taylor (1958, p. 95) to suggest that the gravitational pull of the sun and the moon may have exerted a "triggering" effect on the activity of Mount Lamington. He notes that the eruptions of January 21, February 6, and March 5 occurred within a day or two of the maximum equilibrium tides when the attractive

Plate 21. Mount Lamington in late July, 1951, showing development of the northern sector of the dome. From G. A. Taylor (1958), by permission of the director, Bureau of Mineral Resources, Canberra, Australia.

Plate 22. Mount Lamington, November 21, 1951, showing the growth of the dome. From G. A. Taylor (1958), by permission of the director, Bureau of Mineral Resources, Canberra, Australia.

forces of the sun and moon are either in opposition or in conjunction. He further relates the peak activity of the preliminary earthquake swarms to a lunar declination maximum on January 20. The idea that the gravitational attraction of the sun and the moon influences volcanic eruptions has been advocated by many writers over the years. While the evidence at Mount Lamington appears to be too restrictive to be conclusive, it is interesting to note that the concept is still with us. For a further discussion of this topic, see the section "Volcanoes and Tides," Chapter 12.

MOUNT KATMAI,
ALASKA

The eruption of Mount Katmai on June 6, 1912, was unquestionably one of the more violent eruptions of historic times. It is also one of the landmarks in the development of volcanology, for, like the 1902 eruption of Mount Pelée, it had features that were previously unknown or at least unrecognized. It was the first eruption in which it could be demonstrated that pyroclastic flows of pumice and ash were discharged from fissures, and it led to the recognition that vast sheets of siliceous volcanic rocks, formerly regarded as lava flows, were actually products of such eruptions. Huge areas of such deposits, known as ignimbrites, welded tuffs, ash flows, pumice flows, and so on, occur in the western United States, western Mexico, and in fact in many parts of the world.

Mount Katmai is located near the eastern (continental) end of the Alaska Peninsula, opposite Kodiak Island (Fig. 23). It is in a sparsely populated and largely inaccessible area and was among the least known of the many Alaskan volcanoes. It had not been active in historic times nor were there any legends of its activity.

Before the 1912 eruption, Mount Katmai was a cone-shaped mountain, rising to an elevation of 7,500 feet, which supported numerous glaciers (Martin 1913). There were no photographs of it, but its appearance was well known, and it was but one of several cones in the immediate area (Fig. 23). The volcanoes in the Katmai group, in common with the Aleutian chain of volcanoes, rest on a platform of Upper Jurassic sediments, which for the most part are relatively flat-lying, although on the Pacific side of the Alaskan Peninsula they dip away from the range which forms the axis of the peninsula at angles of 10°–15°. Mount Katmai, as revealed in the 3,700-foot walls of the caldera which was formed in the 1912 eruption, consists of a succession of lava flows of medium to basic character mixed with fragmental material forming a great composite cone similar to the many other volcanoes of the Aleutian arc.

Although it is reported (Martin 1913) that the eruption of June 6, 1912, came without warning, earthquakes were felt at Katmai Village, 15 miles south of the volcano, on June 2, and severe shocks occurred

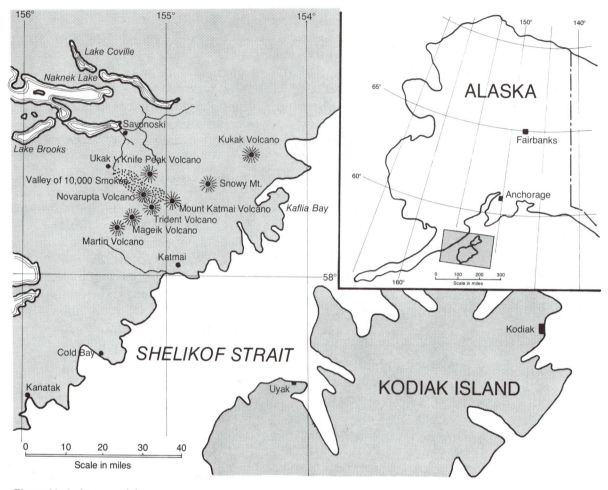

Figure 23. Index map of the Katmai area, Alaska. After R. F. Griggs (1922).

on June 4 and 5. However, earthquakes are fairly common in the region, and these did not cause alarm. The area is sparsely populated, and there were few persons in a position to actually see the volcano. The top of Mount Katmai, as well as other peaks in the region, is usually covered with clouds, so that actual observation is not possible much of the time. It is probable that some eruptive activity began on June 5, since observers at Cold Bay, 40 miles to the southwest, noticed a peculiar-looking black cloud over Mount Katmai on the evening of June 5; but the first big explosion which called attention to the volcano occurred at 1:00 P.M. on June 6. This tremendous explosion was heard at Juneau, Alaska, 750 miles to the east, and at Dawson, 650 miles to the north across the Alaska Range; but strangely it was not heard at Kodiak, 100 miles to the southwest. A second tremendous explosion occurred at 11:00 P.M. on June 6 and a third at 10:40 P.M. on June 7. Much of the ash and fragmental material discharged in the eruption is believed to have come from these three blasts. The strong explosive activity ceased on June 8, although minor eruptions continued through the summer.

Following the initial cataclysmic explosion on June 6, a dense ash cloud enveloped the area, producing total darkness, which at Kodiak lasted for 60 hours. The ash was carried eastward by the wind, and ash falls were reported from Juneau, 750 miles away, and in the Yukon Valley, 1,000 miles to the north. Fumes and rain containing enough sulphuric acid to damage washings hanging on the line were reported at Vancouver, British Columbia, 1,500 miles away. The surrounding sea was covered with floating pumice, and in Shelikof Strait, between Kodiak Island and the mainland, the accumulation was reported to be thick enough to support a man. A reddish haze from fine dust in the upper atmosphere was noted throughout much of the world, being reported from Algiers on June 19. Stories which came by wire from towns along the Alaskan coast told of an eruption of the first magnitude somewhere to the west, but the exact location was not known. The eruption had silenced the wireless communication which ordinarily connected Kodiak Island and the Aleutian Peninsula with the rest of the world. The first detailed and authentic news of the eruption came when the mail steamer *Dora* returned to Seward from its monthly trip to the Aleutian Islands and brought the news that the eruption was at Mount Katmai. The *Dora* had been in the vicinity but was unable to reach the town of Kodiak because of the darkness caused by the eruption.

Accounts of the Eruption

The U.S. Coast Guard cutter *Manning*, under the command of Captain K. W. Perry, was at Kodiak, Kodiak Island, at the time of the eruption. Captain Perry reported that at about 4:00 P.M. on June 6 he noticed a peculiar black cloud approaching from the northwest, and about an hour later coarse grey ash began to fall, followed by intense thunder and lightning (R. F. Griggs 1922). As ash continued to fall, darkness enveloped the area. The ash fall continued until about 9:00 A.M. on June 7, when five inches had accumulated. Captain Perry gave a graphic description of the eruption from his location in the harbor at Kodiak:

> At noon [June 7] ashes began to fall again, and at 12:30 were increasing until at 1:00 P.M. it was impossible to see over 50 feet. Deep concern was visible on every countenance, and the advisability of the *Manning's* getting to sea was discussed . . . At 2:00 P.M. pitch darkness had shut in; heavy static disturbances were observed, and our radio was dumb. . . . We got little sleep and the dawn of the 8th, which we anxiously awaited, failed to appear. . . . The ashes now were fine dust and flakes, and of a yellowish color. Sulphurous fumes came at times in the air, and many thought and spoke of the destruction of Pompeii. Avalanches of ashes on the neighboring hills could be heard, and these sent forth clouds of suffocating dust and ashes. . . . The crew kept constantly at work with shovels, and four streams of water from the fire mains were playing incessantly in what at times seemed a vain effort to clear the ship of its horrible burden. (Quoted by R. F. Griggs 1922, pp. 8–10)

Robert F. Griggs, who talked with many who had been aboard the *Manning*, reported: "Many have told me that it was impossible to see a lantern at arm's length, so thick was the cloud of ash which enveloped everything" (1922, p. 10).

On June 8 at 2:30 P.M. the ash fall decreased, the sky assumed a reddish color, and objects became dimly visible. The second fall of ash, about 4.5 inches in thickness, was a terra cotta color, in sharp contrast to the grey layer formed by the first fall. As soon as it became light, the population of the area, numbering about 500 persons, was taken on board the *Manning*, and at 5:45 P.M. (June 8) the ship moved to the outer harbor in order to be in a position to escape should it be necessary to do so. Soon ash began to fall again, and a third layer of fine grey ash, about 1.5 inches in thickness, was formed. On the morning of June 9, the air cleared and the people returned to their homes. However, all the streams and wells were clogged with ash, and the *Manning* furnished water for the inhabitants and stood by in order to evacuate the town should it be necessary to do so.

The monthly mail steamer *Dora*, under the command of Captain C. B. McMullen, was leaving Uyak Bay, on the northwest side of Kodiak Island, at 8:45 A.M. on June 6. There was a strong westerly breeze and fine clear weather. At 1:00 P.M., as the ship was entering the straits on the north side of Kodiak Island (almost directly to the east of Mount Katmai) a heavy cloud of "smoke" was sighted rising from the land area to the west. Captain McMullen is quoted by Dr. George C. Martin as follows: "I took a bearing on same, which I made out to be Katmai Volcano, distance about 55 miles away. The smoke rose and spread in the sky, followed the vessel, and by 3:00 P.M. was directly over us, having traveled about 20 miles per hour" (Martin 1913, p. 152). J. E. Thwaites, mail clerk on the steamer *Dora* gave a vivid description of conditions in an article published in the June 15 issue of the *Seward Gateway*. His account is as follows:

> And now began the real rain of ashes; it fell in torrents; it swirled and eddied. Gravity seemed to have nothing to do with the course of its fall. The under side of the decks seemed to catch as much ashes as the sides or the decks under our feet. Bright clusters of electric light could be seen but a few feet away, and we had to feel our way about the deck. The officers of the deck had to close the windows of the pilot-house tightly, and even then it was with the greatest difficulty that the man at the wheel could see the compass, through the thick dust that filled the room. In the meantime, lurid flashes of lightning glared continuously around the ship, while a constant boom of thunder, sometimes coinciding with the flash, increased the horror of the inferno raging about us. As far as seeing or hearing the water, or anything pertaining to earth, we might as well have been miles above the surface of the water. And still we knew the sun was more than two hours above the horizon.
>
> In the saloon everything was white with a thick layer of dust, while a thick haze filled the air. The temperature raised rapidly, and the air, what was left of it, became heavy, sultry, and stifling. Below deck conditions were unbearable, while on deck it was worse still. Dust filled our nostrils, sifted down our backs, and smote the eye like a dash of acid. Birds floundered, crying wildly, through space and fell helpless to the deck. (Quoted by Martin 1913, p. 154)

The nearest to the volcano of those within the zone of darkness were a group of natives who were in a fishing camp at Kaflia Bay, some 30 miles from Mount Katmai, at the time of the eruption. One of

them, in a letter to his wife on June 9, wrote as follows: "We are awaiting death at any moment. A mountain has burst near here, so we
are covered with ashes, in some places 10 feet and 6 feet deep. All
this began on the 6th of June. Night and day we lighted lamps. We
cannot see the daylight. In a word it is terrible, and we are expecting
death at any moment, and we have no water. All the rivers are covered with ashes. Just ashes mixed with water. Here are darkness and
hell, thunder and noise. I do not know whether it is day or night"
(quoted by Martin 1913, p. 149).

Katmai Caldera

The National Geographic Society promptly organized an expedition
to investigate the eruption. Under the direction of Dr. George C.
Martin, a geologist with the U.S. Geological Survey who had done
some work in the general region, the party arrived at Mount Katmai
just four weeks after the eruption (see Martin 1913). The National
Geographic Society sent several other expeditions to Mount Katmai
in the succeeding years under the direction of Dr. Robert F. Griggs
(see R. F. Griggs 1917; 1922; Griggs et al. 1920). It was on the 1916
expedition that Griggs and his associates discovered and named the
Valley of Ten Thousand Smokes, which he explored the following
year.

When the first National Geographic Society expedition arrived at
Mount Katmai, four weeks after the eruption, they found, just as the
natives had reported, that the top of the mountain had disappeared
and a huge basin now occupied the summit. This enormous pit, or
caldera, was nearly three miles in diameter and from 2,000 to 3,700
feet in depth (Fig. 24). In the bottom there was a lake, from the center
of which rose a small island. The walls of the caldera were nearly
vertical, and about one-third of the western rim was an ice wall,
formed by remnants of glaciers which had been beheaded by the
collapse.

Recent calculations (Curtis 1968, p. 206) of the volume of the missing top of Mount Katmai give a total of 1.45 cubic miles. If the summit
of Mount Katmai had indeed been blown away by the explosions,
then the debris should have been spread over the countryside. It
should be recalled that the cone of Mount Katmai consists chiefly of
basic andesitic lavas which would stand out prominently among the
white pumice and ash blown out in the eruption. The astonishing fact
is that little, if any, of this material can be found. The pumice which
was ejected in vast quantities represents a highly gas-charged magma which "froths" when the pressure is suddenly relieved, and it is
pulverized by the explosive expansion of the gases. If the top of the

cone was not blown away, then it must have disappeared by engulfment. Fenner (1920), Williams (1941a), and others early recognized
that the caldera of Mount Katmai was the result of collapse. However, since the ejecta consist of a mixture of rhyolitic and andesitic
materials, it was believed that a rhyolitic magma had risen in the
crater of Mount Katmai and assimilated (dissolved) the andesitic material of the cone, which was then ejected along with the pumice.
Later Williams, Curtis, and Juhle (1956) rejected the idea of assimilation and held that andesitic magma from the conduit of Mount Katmai drained to the north and mingled with the rhyolitic magma beneath Novarupta at the head of the Valley of Ten Thousand Smokes.
According to Williams, the lithostatic pressure difference of some
5,000 feet between the summit of Mount Katmai and Novarupta
forced magma from the Mount Katmai chamber out of the vent at
Novarupta. As the chamber under Mount Katmai was evacuated, the
summit collapsed. The two magmas foamed simultaneously from the
feeding fissures and were partly mingled in the process, producing
the streaky, hybrid pumice which makes up the great tuff flow of the
Valley of Ten Thousand Smokes. A detailed study of the ejecta (Curtis 1968) lends support to this view. The collapse of the summit of
Mount Katmai may have started along a concentric system of conical
fractures, which grew progressively outward from the central conduit. Thus the collapse need not have been an instantaneous event.
It is also revealed in the study that little, if any material was erupted
from the Katmai crater and that Novarupta and the associated fracture system were the major eruptive vents.

Figure 24. Mount Katmai be-
fore and after the 1912 erup-
tion. After R. F. Griggs
(1917).

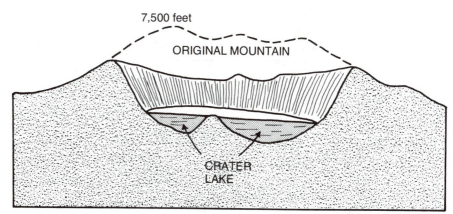

Valley of Ten Thousand Smokes

Prior to the 1912 eruption, there was a broad wooded valley which extended for some 10 miles to the northwest of Mount Katmai. In the early morning hours of June 6, 1912, before the great explosive eruption at 1:00 P.M., an ash flow issued from a series of radial and concentric fissures at the head of the valley. The emplacement of this mammoth ash flow was complete before the second great explosive eruption at 11:00 P.M., since the pumice characteristic of this eruption does not occur beneath the flow. Every detail of the former topography was covered, and the surface now forms a gently sloping plain, covering an area of about 50 square miles (Fig. 25). Thousands of fumaroles and steam jets were issuing from this deposit when it was discovered by Griggs in 1916, and these prompted him to give it the name Valley of Ten Thousand Smokes.

The material filling the valley (first called volcanic sand) consists of fragments of pumice, andesite, obsidian, and similar materials embedded in a matrix of fine ash. It fills the main valley, and tongues project into the side valleys like a flood deposit (Pls. 23 and 24). Griggs, in his first exploration of the area, recognized that this deposit was different from the widespread ash falls from the eruption and that it must be explained by some other process. It was obviously not thrown out violently into the air, for in that case it would cover all the topographic features alike; on the contrary it is limited to depressions of the former surface and must have attained its present position by some mode of flow. It was hot, probably near incandescence, because trees embedded in it are completely carbonized.

It was first described as a "hot mud flow," believed to have been derived from Mount Katmai (Griggs et al. 1920, pp. 117–142), but there are many objections to such an explanation. It was one of the first manifestations of activity in the eruption, for it is covered by all subsequent ash falls. The Katmai crater could hardly have been the source, because the slopes of the cone on this side are still covered by glaciers, which certainly would show noticeable effects of the movement of such an incandescent avalanche over their surfaces. There seems to be no other conclusion except that it originated within the valley itself and that the source was from vents in the valley floor. E. G. Zies, along with C. N. Fenner and E. T. Allen of the Geophysical Laboratory, who were with the 1919 National Geographic Society expedition with Griggs, first suggested that the deposit was formed by the extrusion of hot, dry, pumiceous sand from fissures situated in the valley (Fenner 1920, p. 577). This explanation was later confirmed and amplified by Fenner (1923). The fumarolic activity which characterized the area was doubtless localized along these fissures.

The ash flow, a typical *nuée ardente*, moved with hurricane veloc-

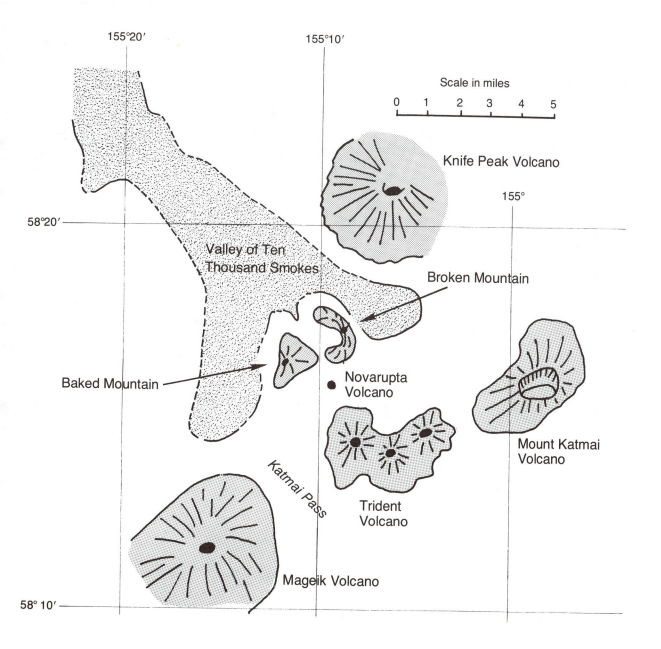

Figure 25. Valley of Ten Thousand Smokes and adjacent areas. After Fenner (1920).

Plate 23. Aerial view of the Valley of Ten Thousand Smokes, Alaska. Photo courtesy Dr. U. Clanton, NASA.

Plate 24. Astronauts on the floor of the Valley of Ten Thousand Smokes (part of their training program), July, 1967. Photo courtesy Dr. U. Clanton, NASA.

ity, as is attested by felled trees at the lower end of the valley. The velocity must be attributed to gases liberated by the ash flow and expansion of air entrapped during the turbulent advance, for, with a gradient of only slightly more than one degree in a distance of 20 kilometers, the velocity cannot be attributed to gravity. Studies by Curtis (1968, p. 187) indicate a thickness of 700–900 feet (210–270 m.) and a volume of 2.63 cubic miles (11 cu. km.). The pumiceous material is highly inflated, and when it is reduced to its solid volume or the space occupied in the magma chamber, it amounts to 1.5 cubic miles. The evidence indicates that the ash flow was erupted at an ever-increasing rate throughout the daylight hours and up to 11:00 P.M. on June 6, with an average rate of expulsion during this period of 1 billion cubic meters per hour! On the basis of seismic refraction profiles across portions of the Valley of Ten Thousand Smokes, a thickness of only 25 meters for the central branch and 50 meters for the south branch was indicated for the ash flow deposits (Gedney, Matteson, and Forbes 1970). If these thicknesses are typical for other parts of the deposit, it would of course reduce the volume drastically.

The ash flow deposit consists predominantly of pumiceous particles of sand and dust size mingled with lapilli. Some flows are wholly or partly rhyolitic ash and pumice, while others consist partly or wholly of brown andesitic material. Most of the flows, however, consist of strongly banded mixtures of the rhyolitic and andesitic materials with many small chips of andesite and sedimentary rocks. Prominent columnar jointing extends downward for 20–50 feet in the weakly indurated ash and becomes massive below. Curtis (1968, p. 183) was unable to detect any welding in the ash exposed in the walls of gorges cut into the flows, but he believes that at greater depth in the upper part of the valley the flow is welded. He bases his conclusion on fragments around the margins of explosion pits in the upper part of the Knife Creek area. These fragments show collapsed pumice fragments and flattened glass shards, and they must have come from a welded zone in the lower part of the flow. This is one of very few positive identifications of welding in historic eruptions—indeed, it may be the only one.

It is of interest in caldera-making eruptions to compare the volume of ejected material with the volume of the collapse. In the Krakatoa type of caldera these two volumes will be more or less equal. The volume of the summit of Mount Katmai which collapsed plus the volume of the caldera is 1.45 cubic miles. This closely approximates the solid volume (1.5 cu. mi.) of the ash flow in the Valley of Ten Thousand Smokes, and, since the ash flow was emplaced before 11:00 P.M. on June 6, 1912, it is tempting to speculate that the collapse of Mount Katmai was also at that time. However, Curtis (1968) discounts this as a coincidence. The volume of the ash and pumice ejected in the eruption has been calculated to be 4.75 cubic miles, which, reduced to solid volume, would equal 1.9 cubic miles. Addition of this figure to the 1.5 cubic miles for the Valley of Ten Thousand Smokes gives a total of 3.4 cubic miles for the eruption. The problem is to account for subsidence to compensate for this volume of ejected material. After deducting the 1.45 cubic miles for the collapse of Katmai Caldera, there still remain nearly 2 cubic miles unassigned. If we allow 0.5 cubic mile for subsidence around Novarupta, as suggested by Curtis (1968), then the remainder must be assigned to undetectable regional subsidence. If the thickness of the ash flow in the Valley of Ten Thousand Smokes is substantially less than that postulated by Curtis, then his figures will have to be revised accordingly.

Novarupta Volcano

Novarupta, formed at the head of the Valley of Ten Thousand Smokes in 1912, was the major vent in the 1912 eruption. The activity of Novarupta passed through three distinct (although merging) phases (Fenner 1950, p. 715). In the first phase, Novarupta and its radial—and possibly also its concentric—fissure systems were the source vents for the great ash flow of the Valley of Ten Thousand Smokes. Then explosive activity opened a crater 0.75 mile in diameter, and vast quantities of coarse pumice were spread over an area 10 miles in diameter. Finally, a viscous mass of lava welled up, forming a dome-shaped mass in the crater. Fenner describes the protrusion as a "stiff, viscous glass which as it was slowly thrust upward, broke into huge blocks. From a distance this pile of steaming lava-blocks, which is about 800 feet in diameter and 200 feet high, resembles an enormous ash heap" (1920, p. 587). Curtis (1968, p. 192) gives the height as 300 feet and the diameter as 1,300 feet (Pl. 25). The lava dome of Novarupta is quite similar to the dome now forming at Santiaguito, Santa María Volcano, Guatemala, and to the spine in the 1902 eruption of Mount Pelée. Such features, as already mentioned, are characteristic of the final phase of activity of volcanoes of the Peléan type. At Novarupta, a minor eruption in 1950 formed a small cone of fragmental material adjacent to the 1912 dome.

Fumaroles in the Valley of Ten Thousand Smokes

All volcanic activity is accompanied by fumaroles, but extra development such as occurred in the Valley of Ten Thousand Smokes is unparalleled. The thousands of steam jets which were active when Griggs (1918) explored the area in the summer of 1917 were largely

Plate 25. Lava dome in the crater of Novarupta Volcano, Katmai area. The dome is 300 feet high and 1,300 feet in diameter. Photo courtesy Dr. U. Clanton, NASA.

restricted to the valley floor, but many were on the lower slopes of the adjacent mountains, especially within a radius of about 1.5 miles of Novarupta (Pl. 26). The alignment of fumaroles along fissures extending from 0.5 to 1 mile in length doubtless reflects the location of fissures on the valley floor which contributed to the great ash flow.

Steam forms more than 98 percent by volume of the gases in the fumaroles, with hydrochloric acid, carbon dioxide, hydrogen sulphide, nitrogen, hydrofluoric acid, boric acid, and sometimes methane making up the remainder. Detailed analyses of the gases and fumarolic incrustations are contained in reports by Zies (1924; 1929). With few exceptions, the fumaroles of the Valley of Ten Thousand Smokes are believed to have been derived from the ash flow, as it continued to give off gases as it cooled. Much of the steam can be directly related to surface water, which seeped into the highly heated mass and returned as steam. The temperature range of the fumaroles in 1919 was from 100° C. to 650° C. By 1954, the only fumaroles still active were along a series of concentric fissures on the northern rim of Novarupta and well up on Broken Mountain, and temperatures were all at or under the boiling point of water for this elevation (Curtis 1968, p. 186).

Recent Activity in the Katmai Area

Since the eruption of 1912, Katmai has been quiescent, with minor explosions reported in 1920 and 1921 and weak fumarolic activity in 1931 (Coats 1950). There was a minor eruption at Novarupta in 1950, and Trident Volcano, only 5 miles to the southwest of Mount Katmai, erupted on February 15; the eruptions continued until June, 1953 (Snyder 1954). The eruptions produced a series of lava flows, and ash falls blanketed an area with a radius of about 20 miles to the southeast of the volcano. The new cone of Trident Volcano, which was formed in 1953, has been the site of explosive eruptions since the lava-erupting phase ceased in 1960. The explosive eruptions, according to H. B. Forbes (1967–1968), are caused by the cyclic extrusion and growth of an andesite dome in the vent, followed by violent vent-clearing explosions which continue until the dome is destroyed. Strong explosive eruptions, sending out highly ash-charged gas columns, were reported in June, 1962, April, 1963, May, 1964, December, 1967, February, 1968, and November, 1968. In the November, 1968, eruption, ash was spread over a fan-shaped area extending 60 miles to the northwest. The terminus of the fan had a width of 3 miles. It is apparent that the volcanic forces in the Katmai area are not exhausted, and further activity may be expected.

The Katmai area was proclaimed a National Monument in 1918.

Plate 26. The Valley of Ten Thousand Smokes in June, 1917, five years after the eruption. From R. F. Griggs (1918, p. 126). Photo by Robert F. Griggs, © National Geographic Society. Professor Griggs was director of the National Geographic Society Katmai Expeditions of 1915, 1916, and 1917. Although the Valley of Ten Thousand Smokes was discovered by the 1916 expedition, the first exploration was by the 1917 expedition, which entered the Valley of Ten Thousand Smokes in June. Professor Griggs's caption to this photograph is as follows: "A view of the first wonder of the world, from Camp 5, at the entrance to the Great Valley with its millions of steam jets always in active operation."

Originally it included the Valley of Ten Thousand Smokes, Mount Katmai, and adjacent areas. In 1931 it was enlarged in order to protect some of the great game animals of the Alaska Peninsula, especially the brown bear. In 1942 some of the islands off the coast were added in order to protect the rich marine life. Katmai National Monument now contains 2,697,590 acres and is second only to Yellowstone National Park in size of the areas administered by the National Park Service. The area is still remote, but it can be reached by air from Anchorage. A park ranger is stationed at the monument during the summer months, and two tent camps are maintained for the convenience of visitors.

BEZYMIANNY
VOLCANO,
KAMCHATKA (USSR)

The eruption of Bezymianny Volcano in 1955–1956 must rank as one of the great Peléan type eruptions in historic times. It has received little publicity because, contrary to the experience with other Peléan eruptions, such as that at Mount Pelée in 1902 and that at Krakatoa in 1883, there was no loss of life. The details of the Bezymianny eruption are well documented in a report by the Russian volcanologist G. S. Gorshkov (1959).

Bezymianny Volcano, in the central part of the Kamchatka Peninsula, is surrounded by active volcanoes frequently referred to as the Kliuchevskaia group. However, Bezymianny had no record of activity during historic times and was generally regarded as extinct. Before the eruption Bezymianny was a snow-covered cone with a height of 3,085 meters above sea level. The mountain consisted of a large lava dome, to the west of which was a younger strato-volcano with an ill-defined crater which was practically filled by a terminal cone. A deep gorge cut the rim of the crater and continued down the southeast slope to form one of the headwater branches of Dry Hapsita River.

Bezymianny apparently had a long and complex history, marked by the formation of a lava dome in the crater of a strato-volcano. Following a long period of repose the eruptive center shifted to the west, doubtless because the earlier vent was plugged by the lava dome, and a new strato-volcano formed at the margin of the old lava dome.

On September 29, 1955, earthquakes from the Bezymianny area were recorded at Kliuchi, 45 kilometers to the northeast. The earthquake frequency increased; by October 12, from 100 to 200 quakes per day were occurring, and by October 21 a total of 1,285 shocks had been recorded. The epicenters of the earthquakes were associated with Bezymianny Volcano, but since it was believed to be extinct it was felt that perhaps a new lateral vent might develop near the southern base of nearby Kliuchevsky Volcano, which had a long record of eruptions. The eruption began at 6:30 A.M. on October 22,

1955, from the exact position indicated by the seismic data. Beginning with moderate Vulcanian type eruptions which ejected ash-filled clouds, the intensity gradually increased until the end of November. The ash fall at Kliuchi was so heavy on November 17 that "lighted windows and street lanterns could not be seen at a distance of 150–200 meters" (Gorshkov 1959, p. 81). Moderate activity continued until March 29, 1956. The old lava dome was slowly uplifted more than 100 meters by the magmatic pressure from below. Gorschkov comments that observations of the eruption had to be carried on from an uninhabited region in the upper part of the Dry Hapsita River and that severe winter conditions and the heavy ash falls which hampered the use of dog-sledges—the only winter transportation possible—combined to make observations very difficult. In the spring, heavy torrents of water, due to the excessive melting of the glaciers resulting from the ash cover, also hampered the investigations.

The Paroxysmal Eruption of March 30, 1956

On March 30, 1956, at 5:11 P.M. a tremendous explosion destroyed the top of the cone, lowering the height by about 180 meters and completely changing the appearance of the volcano (Pl. 27). The initial blast was directed at an angle of about 30° from the horizon in an eastward direction. The eruption cloud quickly expanded into a fan shape with the upper part reaching a height of 35 kilometers, but succeeding explosions expanded a wedge to a height of about 45 kilometers. Gorshkov describes the initial eruption cloud as seen from Kliuchi:

Plate 27. Bezymianny Volcano after the explosion of March 30, 1956 (photo taken in April, 1956). The black line shows the outline of the volcano before the eruption. A huge semi–ring caldera now occupies the southeast portion of the volcano. From Gorshkov (1959), courtesy Dr. G. C. Gorshkov.

The cloud was curling intensely, and quickly changed its outlines. . . . It seemed to be very thick and almost tangibly heavy.
Together with the cloud came also and was growing a rumble of
local thunder accompanying incessantly flashing lightning.
About 5:40 P.M. when the cloud had already passed the zenith,
ash began to fall . . . and by 6:20 P.M. it got so impenetrably dark
that one could not see his own hand, even if brought up to the
very face. People returning from work were wandering about
the village in search of their homes. Peals of thunder were crashing with deafening loudness without any interruption. The air
was saturated with electricity, telephones were ringing spontaneously, loud speakers of the radionet were burning out . . .
There was a strong smell of sulphurous gas. (1959, pp. 86–87)

At a distance of 25 kilometers, trees a foot in diameter were leveled
by the blast. Up to 29 kilometers, trees were scorched and dead wood
set on fire. The hot ash which was deposited over an area of about
500 square kilometers melted the snow cover, and torrential mud
flows (lahars) were formed in the valley of the Dry Hapsita River and
in valleys on the flanks of adjacent volcanoes. These torrents swept
down the valleys carrying huge boulders, some weighing hundreds
of tons, which devastated everything in their path. Some of the lahars
extended as far as the Kamchatka River, a distance of 90 kilometers.
Simultaneously, a great ash flow (*nuée ardente*) swept down the
mountain slopes, particularly into the valley of the Dry Hapsita River. The ash flow (Gorschkov uses the term *agglomerate flow*) completely filled the valley and spilled onto the adjoining areas (Pl. 28).
Highly charged with gases, the ash flow had great fluidity and could
not stay on the steep flanks of the volcano. Thus, there are practically
no ash-flow deposits on the flanks of the volcano, and the flow begins, seemingly, not from the crater but from the base of the volcano.
The maximum length of the ash flow is 18 kilometers. The thickness
varies from 20–25 meters at the northern margin to probably 50
meters in the central part. With an area of 55–60 square kilometers
and an estimated average thickness of 30 meters, the volume of the
deposits amounts to 1.8 cubic kilometers. When this ash flow was
first viewed by Gorschkov, three weeks after the eruption, there
were thousands of steam fumaroles rising from its surface, and it was
immediately named the Valley of Ten Thousand Smokes of Kamchatka, after the similar feature formed in the 1912 eruption of Mount
Katmai. It was noted that the fumaroles were associated with the
southern part of the valley and were aligned in a narrow zone corresponding to the buried stream channel. The Valley of Ten Thou-

Plate 28. Bezymianny Volcano with the ash flow in the foreground in August, 1956. From Gorshkov (1959), courtesy Dr. G. C. Gorshkov.

sand Smokes is but one of several features which make the Bezymianny eruption similar to the 1912 Mount Katmai eruption.

After the gigantic explosion, Bezymianny Volcano was changed almost beyond recognition; instead of a regular, slightly truncated cone, it was now a semi–ring caldera volcano. The dome in the southeast section of the cone was completely destroyed, and a new crater, 1.5 by 2 kilometers in diameter, was formed, including not only the summit but also the entire southeast flank of the volcano. A dome soon appeared in the new crater (Pl. 29). As it continued to grow, there were weak to moderate explosions, and small glowing avalanches (*nuées ardentes*) rolled down the flank of the dome. This activity continued until August, 1956, when the dome attained its maximum height of 320 meters above the crater floor. In October a second dome grew against the southwest flank of the first dome, attaining a height of 260 meters. By late autumn the eruption was over.

About 1.0 cubic kilometer of material was ejected in the March 30 explosion, in addition to the 1.8 cubic kilometers in the ash flow previously mentioned. The ash and lavas (including the domes) are typical hornblende andesites in composition.

An unusual feature of the gigantic explosion of March 30 was that it was heard neither nearby nor at a distance, although some observers mentioned feeble muffled rumblings. This is in sharp contrast to the eruptions of Krakatoa, Coseguina, and others, in which the noise was heard for great distances—up to about 3,000 miles in the 1883

Plate 29. Dome in Bezymianny crater after the end of the eruption, May, 1957. With the exception of some parts of the summit, the dome is covered with snow, although the eruption ended only six months earlier. From Gorshkov (1959), courtesy Dr. G. C. Gorshkov.

eruption of Krakatoa. However, the air wave generated by the Bezymianny blast encircled the earth 1.5 times. It is interesting to note that V. P. Sorokin at the village of Kamaki, 65 kilometers northeast of the volcano, who first noticed the eruption, was in his house at the time, and he felt a "pressure on his ears" due to the sharp change in atmospheric pressure (Gorshkov 1959, p. 84). Running out of the house he saw the obliquely directed eruptive column rising from Bezymianny Volcano. The pronounced air wave led Gorschkov to develop a method of computing the amount of energy released in the eruption from the air wave as recorded on barographs throughout the region (see Ch. 17).

MAYON VOLCANO,
PHILIPPINES

Mayon Volcano is located on the southeastern peninsula of the Island of Luzon, Philippines, about 325 kilometers southeast of Manila. Rising 2,462 meters above sea level it is one of the most perfectly symmetrical composite volcanic cones in the world. There is a small summit crater only about 200 meters in diameter. Abundant mudflows have formed a broad apron completely around the base of the cone and have been responsible for most of the damage and loss of life during historic times (Macdonald and Alcaraz 1954). Mayon Volcano has had a long history of destructive eruptions (Van Padang 1953). The first recorded eruption occurred in 1616, and since that time about 40 eruptions, in which more than 1,500 lives were lost, have occurred. The eruptions of 1766, 1814, and 1897 were of unusual intensity.

The eruption of 1968, which has been described by Moore and Melson (1969) appears to be typical of Mayon eruptions and of moderate intensity. The eruption began with an explosion on April 21, and up to the morning of April 23 there were three more explosions; then the tempo increased, with explosions every few hours or in some cases every few minutes. The explosions reached their greatest intensity on April 25 and then continued with decreasing intensity to May 4. The explosions ejected a vertical ash-laden cloud which reached heights up to 10 kilometers. At times horizontal surges from the base of the towering eruption column (base surges) sent tongues of downward-moving hot ash clouds, or *nuées ardentes*, down the flanks of the cone, generally following the deeper ravines. It was noted by Moore and Melson (1969) that the larger *nuées ardentes* appeared to generate torrential rainstorms which eroded the loose ash and caused destructive mudflows on the lower slopes of the cone. However, it is obvious that most of the mudflows which have buried the base of Mayon Volcano have resulted from the heavy monsoon rains on the ash-covered slopes of the cone. On April 27, 1968, a large explosion breached the southwest rim of the crater, and a flow of viscous aa lava began slowly moving down the southwest flank. The flow, which attained a length of 3.5 kilometers, stopped about May 20. The largest *nuées ardentes*, which also moved down the southwest flank, extended as far as 7 kilometers, with velocities up to 63 meters per second. A preliminary estimate of 35×10^6 cubic meters for the total volume of erupted material is given by Moore and Melson (1969), with about 86 percent equally divided between the *nuée ardente* deposits and the lava flow and the remainder as airfall ash deposits.

The lava and *nuée ardente* deposits of the 1968 Mayon eruption were andesitic in composition (augite-hypersthene andesite). Peléan type eruptions usually are rhyolitic in composition, and they normally do not produce lava flows. Instead, the magma is shattered by explosions and ejected as pyroclastics, except that in the final stage of an eruption the viscous material may accumulate as a lava dome in the crater. However, the well-developed *nuées ardentes* of the Mayon eruption are so typical of the Peléan type that it seemed appropriate to include it in this section.

EL CHICHÓN
VOLCANO, MEXICO

Located about 36 miles south of Villahermosa, the capital of the state of Tabasco in southern Mexico, El Chichón is an unimpressive dome-shaped mass rising to a height of 4,430 feet above sea level. It was heavily forested with a shallow, oval-shaped crater which contained some hot springs and fumaroles. Until 1982, it had not been active in historic time (Mullerried 1932), but a series of earthquakes in the immediate area in 1930 and again in 1964 indicated that it was not extinct.

An eruption began just before midnight on March 28, 1982, and massive explosions ejected a huge ash cloud to a height of about 13 miles and 2 miles in thickness. The major activity lasted only a few hours, but the huge ash cloud drifted to the east-northeast and quickly spread over a wide area. Automobiles in Austin, Texas, roughly 1,000 miles away, were covered with a light coating of ash the second morning after the eruption. Smaller eruptions occurred on March 30 and on April 2. A strong explosion, possibly the largest of all, occurred in the early morning hours of April 4. The ash cloud from this eruption, combined with that from the earlier eruptions, spread around the earth from south of the equator to as far north as Japan. This ash cloud has been studied by atmospheric scientists throughout the world. The brilliant red sunsets which occurred for months after the eruptions attested to the presence of this layer of ash.

There were devastating ash flows (*nuées ardentes*) accompanying the eruptions, and these, combined with the heavy ash falls, resulted in hundreds of casualties and the evacuation of thousands of the inhabitants from the area around the volcano. As of June 1983 there had been no further explosive activity.

Plate 30. Mayon Volcano, Philippines. **Left:** *The volcano in October 1965.* **Right:** Nuées ardentes *in the eruption of April 24, 1968. In the lower right is the tower of the church of Cagsaua, which was destroyed by mudflows in the 1814 eruption, which killed several hundred people who had sought refuge in the church. Photo by SIX-SIS Studio, Legaspi City, Albay, Philippines, courtesy Philippine Commission on Volcanology.*

CONCLUSION

In addition to the examples of Peléan type eruptions described in this chapter, the caldera-making eruptions of Coseguina in 1835 and of Krakatoa in 1883, described in Chapter 6, are good examples of this type of activity. The Peléan type of eruption, the most violent of all volcanic eruptions, is, rather strangely, associated with the final phase of activity of a volcano. A volcano appears to react with almost human traits and, as a "last fling" before becoming extinct, stages a stupendous (Peléan type) eruption.

Chapter 8

The Vulcanian Type of Volcanic Eruption

Above the smoke and stir of this dim spot which men call Earth.—MILTON

The Vulcanian type of eruption, occupying an intermediate position in the classification scheme, includes many of the active volcanoes of the world. In a typical Vulcanian volcano, the crater crusts over solidly between infrequent eruptions. Gases accumulate beneath the congealed crust, and in time the upper part of the magma column becomes thoroughly gas-saturated. Finally, with strong explosions, sometimes sufficient to partially disrupt the cone, and accompanied by a great cauliflower-shaped eruption cloud, dark in color because of the high ash content, the obstruction is blown out. As the pressure is suddenly reduced, the gas-charged magma is disrupted by the explosively expanding gases into pumice and ash. Following the clearing of the vent, lava flows may issue from the crater or from fissures on the sides of the cone. The initial phase of a Vulcanian eruption and that of the Peléan type are markedly similar. However, the characteristic *nuée ardente* of the Peléan type is not present in a Vulcanian eruption. Vulcano, in the Lipari Islands off the coast of Sicily, was the example used by Mercalli (Mercalli et al. 1891) and later adopted by Lacroix (1908) and others for the Vulcanian type of eruption, but many consider Vesuvius to be an even better example. These volcanoes have had long, interesting histories, and I feel that it will be worthwhile to describe both of them as examples of the Vulcanian type.

MOUNT VESUVIUS

Prestige of Vesuvius among Volcanoes

Mount Vesuvius, on the shore of the Bay of Naples in central Italy, is probably the best-known volcano in the world. Located in the midst of one of the most densely populated areas of Europe, it is also in the area where the first Greek settlements were made more than 800 years before the beginning of the Christian era and from which civilization spread over Western Europe. The record of activity is, therefore, far more complete for Vesuvius than for any other volcano, and many of the ideas concerning volcanoes were developed from observations at Vesuvius. The Vesuvian Observatory, one of the few volcano observatories in the world, was dedicated in 1845. The city of Naples, which spreads out fanwise along one of the most beautiful bays in the world opposite Vesuvius, is built on a series of old craters. The steep slopes which distinguish the city, such as the Posilipo, are the inner walls of a group of intersecting crater rims.

Italy has long been a favorite recreation center, first for Western Europe and now for the entire world, and Vesuvius is one of its chief scenic attractions. Thousands of tourists have visited Vesuvius, and to many the terms *volcano* and *Vesuvius* are synonymous. Many of the leading geologists of the world have at some time visited Vesuvius, and each, of course, has written an article or a book about it. A bibliography (Johnston-Lavis 1918) of the scientific articles and books on Vesuvius, published in 1918, contains over 2,000 entries, and a great many works have been written since that time.

Detailed observations on the activity of Vesuvius extend back for several hundred years. From a close study of these records following the eruption of 1872, Professor Palmieri, then director of the Vesuvian Observatory, announced that the eruptions of Vesuvius follow a cyclic pattern which makes it possible to predict, at least to some extent, the pattern of activity of an eruption. The recognition of the cyclic behavior of Vesuvius stimulated other workers to try to establish patterns for other volcanoes, and the results of their efforts proved to be an important step in the advancement of volcanology. (A discussion of volcanic cycles, with several examples in addition to Vesuvius, is given in Ch. 12.)

Vesuvius is but one of a series of volcanoes which are located along a line, or "trend," that parallels the west coast of Italy, extending northward from Naples through Rome to the vicinity of Siena. This trend, located along a fracture which resulted from the sinking of the Tyrrhenian Sea and the uplift of the Apennine Mountains, is marked by a series of more or less evenly spaced volcanic vents. The Tyrrhenian Sea is the section of the Mediterranean lying between Italy and the islands of Sardinia, Corsica, and Sicily. The volcanic activity along this trend began at the north and shifted progressively southward until it reached the Naples area. Although the activity along this belt is of very recent age, from a geologic standpoint, the only eruptions which have occurred in historic time are in the Naples area. (See Ch. 14 for further details.)

Vesuvius is but one of many volcanoes in the Naples area. Another is Ischia, an island in the Bay of Naples, which was in vigorous eruption in ancient times long before Vesuvius was even known to be a volcano. The last eruption of Ischia was in 1302, but a severe earthquake at Casamicciola in 1883 indicates that the volcanic energy is not entirely extinct. An area called the Phlegraean Fields (Campi Phlegraei), five miles west of Naples, contains many craters, the last

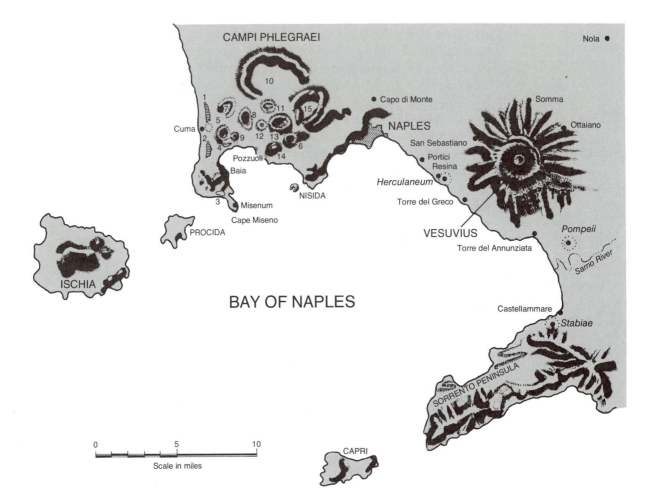

Figure 26. Bay of Naples and surrounding area. Herculaneum, Pompeii, and Stabiae, destroyed in the A.D. *79 eruption of Vesuvius, are located on the map. Index to areas in Campi Phlegraei: (1) Lago di Licola; (2) Lago di Fusaro; (3) Mare Morto; (4) Lago Lucrino; (5) Lago Averno; (6) Lago di Agnano; (7) Monte Grillo; (8) Monte Barbaro; (9) Monte Nuovo; (10) Piano di Quarto; (11) Fossa Lupara; (12) Monte Cigliano; (13) Astroni; (14) Solfatara; (15) Pianura. After Phillips (1869).*

of which, Monte Nuovo, was formed in 1538. The volcano Solfatara is one of the craters of the Phlegraean Fields. It last erupted in 1198, sending out a stream of lava which reached the sea near the harbor of Pozzuoli. Since that time it has maintained a constant emission of gases, from which the name *solfatara* (Italian for "sulphur mine") is derived. The term has been incorporated in the terminology of volcanology to indicate that any volcano which emits only gases is in the "solfataric stage."

The Phlegraean Fields

Vesuvius, the location of the present volcanic activity in the Naples area, is interestingly related to the Phlegraean Fields. The Phlegraean Fields, with 19 separate craters concentrated in an area of about 25 square miles, form a unique feature. They are the scene of many classic fables, the theme of Roman poets, and a land that excited the imagination of the ancient world. Here the gaseous emanations, deep hollows, scorched rocks, and subterranean passages might well be taken for the ruins of an older world, or imagined to be the entrance to the realm of Pluto. Indeed, it was the fumes from the Solfatara which inspired Dante's *Inferno*.

Several of the craters in the Phlegraean Fields once contained beautiful lakes. Some, such as Agnano, which is now used as a race track, have been drained in recent years for various reasons. Lake Avernus, one of the best known in ancient times, remains today (Pl. 31). It is a circular lake about one-half mile in diameter, occupying the crater of a volcano. The name, which means "without birds," was derived from the belief that gaseous emanations from the lake killed any birds flying over it. Certainly today the birds have no difficulty in flying over it at will.

Virgil (70 B.C.–A.D. 19), the great classic Roman poet, spent his last years in Naples and was, of course, familiar with the Phlegraean Fields. In his great classic poem, the *Aeneid*, he locates the entrance to the realms of Pluto (and the infernal region) on the underground road at Lake Avernus.

History of Vesuvius to A.D. 79

It is likely that Vesuvius first began as a submarine volcano in the Bay of Naples, then emerged as an island, and finally was joined to the land by the filling and upbuilding of its eruptive products. Its first eruptions are believed to have occurred after the retreat of the last Ice Sheet (Pleistocene), and if this is true its age is somewhere in the neighborhood of 10,000 years. Vesuvius is younger than the first eruptions of the volcanoes in the Phlegraean Fields, since these tuffs are found beneath Vesuvian material.

Because the ancients made no reference to Vesuvius as a volcano, it must be assumed that a long period of repose intervened between its early activity and the eruption of A.D. 79, which gave rise to the modern cone. The Greeks of the seventh century B.C. and, later, those of the fourth century B.C., who were driven from their homes on Ischia by volcanic eruptions, would hardly have settled on the slopes of Vesuvius had they recognized it as a volcano. Certainly some of the Greeks who had seen Mount Etna or Vulcano in eruption must have recognized the volcanic nature of Vesuvius, but there were no legends of any activity. Diodorus Siculus, a native of Sicily, and certainly familiar with Mount Etna, described the area as it appeared to him about 45 B.C.: "The whole region was named Phlegraean, from the culminating point, which is now called Vesuvius, bearing many indications of having emitted fires in ancient time" (bk. 4, ch. 21; quoted by Phillips 1869, p. 6). At about the same time (30 B.C.), the noted geographer Strabo observed the rich fields on the slopes of

Plate 31. Lake Avernus, Phlegraean Fields, Italy.

Vesuvius, except at the summit, which for the most part was flat and quite barren, and commented on the cindery aspect, as if it had been "eaten by fire." He speculated that in ancient times the country had been in a state of burning, being full of fiery cavities, though now extinct for want of fuel (Strabo *Geog*. bk. 5, ch. 4; quoted by Phillips 1869, p. 5). We learn from a still earlier source, which tells the story of the revolt of the Roman gladiators under Spartacus about 72 B.C., that the summit was covered with a mass of tangled vines. Spartacus, a deserter from the Roman army and later a slave placed in a training camp for gladiators at Capua, escaped from Capua with 78 fellow gladiators and sought refuge on the summit of Vesuvius. Plutarch's account of the Spartacus revolt in the *Life of Crassus* gives us one of the few descriptions of the crater of Vesuvius during this general period:

> Clodius the Praetor, with 3,000 men, besieged them in a mountain having but one narrow and difficult passage, which Clodius kept guarded; all the rest was encompassed with broken and slippery precipices, but upon the top grew a great many wild vines: they cut down as many of their boughs as they had need of, and twisted them into ladders long enough to reach from thence to the bottom, by which, without any danger, all got down save one, who stayed behind to throw them their arms, after which he saved himself with the rest. The Romans were ignorant of all this; and, therefore, coming upon them from the rear, they assaulted them unawares and took their camp. (Plutarchus 1910 [trans. Dryden], 2:279)

The barren top described by the usually accurate Strabo does not check with the description of the vine-covered summit which enabled Spartacus to escape. Nevertheless, we may conclude that Vesuvius at this time had a broadly truncated summit and that the deep crater was intact except for a narrow opening on one side. From a distance it appeared as a broad, flat-topped mountain, and the presence of the crater would not have been revealed except from the summit. It is not surprising, then, that it was not recognized as a volcano except by a few of the scholars of the time.

    The first sign of renewal of activity at Vesuvius was a severe earthquake on February 5, A.D. 63. According to Seneca, it destroyed a considerable portion of Pompeii and did much damage in Herculaneum and the surrounding area, including Naples (Lobley 1889, p. 98). In Pompeii the temple of Isis was so badly damaged that it had to be rebuilt. When a private citizen bore the expense of the reconstruction, the city in gratitude erected on the building a plaque, which was found when the area was unearthed from beneath the ejecta of the later eruption. Suetonius (A.D. 70–A.D. 160), a friend and contemporary of the younger Pliny, who for a time was the imperial secretary to Trajan and as such had access to the imperial archives, has preserved a notice of this earthquake in connection with his account of the first appearance of Nero on the stage in Naples. Nero, believing that he was a gifted singer, was giving a trial concert in Naples before he appeared in Rome: "This singular 'master of the world' loitered and amused himself much in the city of Syren, and amid the waters of Baiae. To be singing while Vesuvius thundered, and fiddling while Rome burned, was not unfitting the imperial madcap" (quoted by Phillips 1869, p. 12). The earthquakes continued intermittently for the next 16 years, finally culminating on the night of August 24, A.D. 79, in extremely violent shocks which immediately preceded the historic eruption on that date.

   In the great eruption of A.D. 79 about one-half of the cone was destroyed and a new cone, the present Vesuvius, was started. The remnant of the old cone, which now partly encircles Vesuvius, is known as Mount Somma (Fig. 27). (The term *somma* is now applied to the remnant of any cone which bears to a later cone the relationship of Mount Somma to Vesuvius.) In this eruption the cities of Pompeii and Herculaneum were completely buried, and several other cities were badly damaged, the most notable perhaps being Stabiae, where Pliny the Elder lost his life. The only eye-witness account describing the great eruption of August 24, A.D. 79, which has survived today is given by Pliny the Younger in two letters written some years afterward to his friend the historian Tacitus.

Figure 27. Vesuvius. Left: *Before the eruption of* A.D. *79.* Right: *Today.*

The younger Pliny, apparently, was born at Como in northern Italy in A.D. 61, since he states that he was 18 years old at the time of the eruption. His father died at an early age, and, as was the custom at that time, he and his mother went to live with his uncle, Caius Plinius Secundus (generally known as Pliny the Elder), who was an ardent student of natural history, making written notes on every book he read as well as on his own observations. He was an important person, a friend of the emperor, and held various offices. At the time of the eruption he was in command of the Roman fleet at Misenum. Of his numerous writings only his *Natural History* survives. He died in the eruption of Vesuvius in A.D. 79 at the age of 56. The younger Pliny, brought up in his uncle's household, studied under the best scholars of the time. He was much devoted to literature and less inclined to scientific matters than was his uncle. Ten books of Pliny's letters have survived. The majority of the letters were written for publication rather than as actual correspondence.

Pliny the Elder was at Misenum (near Baiae) at the time of the eruption. Misenum, or rather Capo Miseno, marks the northern boundary of the Bay of Naples at its westernmost point. The bay, then as now one of the most beautiful spots in the world, was crowded with villas of Roman nobility. Baiae, immediately adjacent to the Roman fleet base at Misenum, was the site of many large and elaborate baths. Puteoli (now Pozzuoli) was a busy harbor, and Neapolis (Naples) was one of the most important cities of the empire. Herculaneum, Pompeii, and Stabiae were coastal towns on the bay, behind which the flat-topped summit of Vesuvius rose to a height of 4,000 feet.

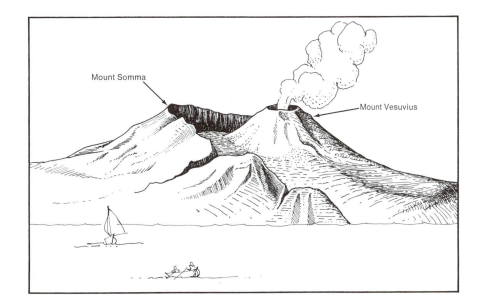

Pliny's Account of the A.D. 79 Eruption

Caius Cornelius Tacitus was the leading historian of his time. Although he was a little older than Pliny the Younger, they were intimate friends. Apparently, several years after the great eruption of A.D. 79, in which Pliny the Elder lost his life, Tacitus was compiling a history, and, since Pliny the Elder was one of the prominent men of the day, the details of his death were of importance. Accordingly, Tacitus wrote to Pliny the Younger and asked him to set down the events leading up to his uncle's death. It should be understood that Tacitus was interested in Pliny the Elder and not in an account of the eruption of Vesuvius. Pliny's letter to Tacitus is in reply to this request. Since this letter, like all of Pliny's letters, was undated, the time interval between the letter and the event he described is not known. It seems likely that the letter was written when Pliny was 24 years of age, or about 6 years after his uncle's death.

The best-known translation of Pliny's letters is the one by William Melmoth, first published in 1746. This translation, a rather free version, has been used by numerous authors, who usually have made further modifications in style. The letters reproduced here are from the Melmoth translation as revised and corrected by F. C. T. Bosanquet (1903). His alterations in the Melmoth version were made "in the direction of greater literalness in the text," and he has been quite successful in preserving the style and spirit of the original letters. The letter describing Pliny's uncle's death follows:

> Your request that I would send you an account of my uncle's death, in order to transmit a more exact relation of it to posterity, deserves my acknowledgement; for, if this accident shall be celebrated by your pen, the glory of it, I am well assured, will be rendered forever illustrious. And notwithstanding he perished by a misfortune, which, as it involved at the same time a most beautiful country in ruins, and destroyed so many populous cities, seems to promise him an everlasting remembrance; notwithstanding he has himself composed many and lasting works; yet I am persuaded, the mentioning of him in your immortal writings will greatly contribute to render his name immortal. . . . It is with extreme willingness, therefore, that I execute your commands; and should indeed have claimed the task if you had not enjoined it.
>
> He was at that time with the fleet under his command at Misenum. On the 24th of August, about one in the afternoon, my mother desired him to observe a cloud which had appeared of a very unusual size and shape. He had just taken a turn in the sun, and after bathing himself in cold water, and making a light

luncheon, gone back to his books; he immediately arose and went out upon a rising ground from whence he might get a better sight of this very uncommon appearance. A cloud, from which mountain was uncertain at this distance, was ascending, the form of which I cannot give you a more exact description of than by likening it to that of a pine tree, for it shot up to a great height in the form of a very tall trunk, which spread itself out at the top into a sort of branches; occasioned, I imagine, either by a sudden gust of air that impelled it, the force of which decreased as it advanced upwards, or the cloud itself being pressed back again by its own weight, expanded in the manner I have mentioned; it appeared sometimes bright and sometimes dark and spotted, according as it was either more or less impregnated with earth and cinders. This phenomenon seemed to a man of such learning and research as my uncle extraordinary, and worth further looking into.

He ordered a light vessel to be got ready, and gave me leave, if I liked, to accompany him. I said I would rather go on with my work; and it so happened he had himself given me something to write out. As he was coming out of the house, he received a note from Rectina, the wife of Bassus, who was in the utmost alarm at the imminent danger which threatened her; for [from] her villa lying at the foot of Mount Vesuvius, there was no way of escape except by sea; she earnestly entreated him therefore to come to her assistance. He accordingly changed his first intention, and what he had begun from a philosophical, he now carried out in a noble and generous spirit. He ordered the galleys to put to sea, and went himself on board with an intention of assisting not only Rectina, but the several other towns which lay thickly strewn along the beautiful coast. Hastening then to the place from whence others fled with the utmost terror, he steered his course direct to the point of danger, and with so much calmness and presence of mind as to be able to make and dictate his observations upon the motion and all the phenomena of that dreadful scene.

He was now so close to the mountain that the cinders, which grew thicker and hotter the nearer he approached, fell into the ships, together with pumice stones, and black pieces of burning rock; they were in danger too not only of being a-ground by the sudden retreat of the sea, but also from the vast fragments which rolled down from the mountain, and obstructed all the shore. Here he stopped to consider whether he should turn back again; to which the pilot advising him, "Fortune" he said, "favors the brave; steer to where Pomponianus is."

Pomponianus was then at Stabiae [now Castellammare],

separated by a bay, which the sea, after several insensible wind-ings, forms with the shore. He had already sent his baggage on board; for though at that time he was not in actual danger, yet being within sight of it, and indeed extremely near, if it should in the least increase, he was determined to put to sea as soon as the wind, which was blowing dead in-shore, should go down. It was favorable, however, for carrying my uncle to Pomponianus, whom he found in the greatest consternation; he embraced him tenderly, encouraging and urging him to keep up his spirits, and, the more effectually to soothe his fears by seeming uncon-cerned himself, ordered a bath to be got ready, and then, after having bathed, sat down to supper with great cheerfulness, or at least (which is just as heroic) with every appearance of it.

Meanwhile broad flames shone out in several places from Mount Vesuvius, which the darkness of the night contributed to render still brighter and clearer. But my uncle, in order to soothe the apprehensions of his friend, assured him it was only the burning of the villages, which the country people had aban-doned to the flames: after this he retired to rest, and it is most certain he was so little disquieted as to fall into a sound sleep: for his breathing which, on account of his corpulence, was rather heavy and sonorous, was heard by the attendants outside. The court which led to his apartment being now almost filled with ashes and stones, if he had continued there any time longer, it would have been impossible for him to have made his way out. So he was awoke and got up, and went to Pomponianus and the rest of his company, who were feeling too anxious to think of going to bed. They consulted together whether it would be most prudent to trust to the houses, which now rocked from side to side with frequent and violent concussions as though shaken from their very foundations; or fly to the open fields, where the calcined stones and cinders, though light indeed, yet fell in large showers and threatened destruction. In this choice of dangers they resolved for the fields: a resolution which, while the rest of the company were hurried into by their fears, my uncle em-braced upon cool and deliberate consideration. They went out then, having pillows tied upon their heads with napkins; and this was their whole defense against the storm of stones that fell round them.

It was now day everywhere else, but there a deeper darkness prevailed than in the thickest night; which however was in some degree alleviated by torches and other lights of various kinds. They thought proper to go farther down upon the shore to see if they might safely put out to sea, but found the waves still run-ning extremely high, and boisterous. There my uncle, laying himself down upon a sail cloth, which was spread for him, called twice for some cold water, which he drank, when immediately the flames, preceded by a strong whiff of sulphur, dispersed the rest of the party, and obliged him to rise. He raised himself up with the assistance of two of his servants, and instantly fell down dead; suffocated, as I conjecture, by some gross and noxious vapor, having always had a weak throat, which was often inflamed. As soon as it was light again, which was not till the third day after this melancholy accident, his body was found entire, and without any marks of violence upon it, in the dress in which he fell, and looking more like a man asleep than dead. During all this time my mother and I, who were at Misenum—but this has no connection with your history, and you do not desire any particulars besides those of my uncle's death; so I will end here, only adding that I have faithfully related to you what I saw as an eyewitness myself or received immediately after the accident happened, and before there was time to vary the truth. You will pick out of this narrative, whatever is most important; for a letter is one thing, a history another; it is one thing writing to a friend, another thing writing to the public. Farewell. (Pliny *Ep*. bk. 6, let. 16 [Bosanquet, ed. 1903, pp. 194–198])

This account, written from the recollections of an 18-year-old student some years afterward, contains some significant facts as well as some inconsistencies. It seems likely that the author's memory, or the information given to him in regard to the final scene of his uncle's death, was, in part at least, in error. We can hardly assume that "flames" could have reached as far as Stabiae, 10 miles from the crater. Perhaps there were "noxious gases" in the eruption cloud which enveloped them and in the falling ash, which did irritate the throat, but others in the party were not stricken. It seems probable that Pliny's death was due to a heart attack rather than to the cause ascribed by his nephew in the letter to Tacitus. If this were not the case, it is difficult to explain why he did not escape with the others. Pliny's description of the eruption cloud as resembling a pine tree has become a classic, and today the scientific name for such an eruption cloud is *pino*, the Italian word for "pine tree." Eruptions displaying "pinos" and of the violence of the eruption of Vesuvius are described as "Plinian eruptions." Pliny's letter to Tacitus, Book 6, Letter 16, may quite properly be considered as the beginning of modern descriptive volcanology.

Tacitus was so interested in Pliny's account that he wrote to him and asked what happened to him and to his mother at Misenum after his uncle left. This Pliny describes in a second letter to Tacitus:

The letter which, in compliance with your request, I wrote to you concerning the death of my uncle has raised, it seems, your curiosity to know what terrors and dangers attended me while I continued at Misenum; for there, I think, my account broke off:

"Though my shock'd soul recoils, my tongue shall tell."[1]

My uncle having left us, I spent such time as was left on my studies: (it was on their account indeed that I had stopped behind), till it was time for my bath. After which I went to supper, and then fell into a short and uneasy sleep. There had been noticed for many days before, a trembling of the earth, which did not alarm us much, as this is quite an ordinary occurrence in Campania; but was so particularly violent that night that it not only shook but actually overturned, as it would seem, everything about us. My mother rushed into my chamber, where she found me rising in order to awaken her. We sat down in the open court of the house, which occupied a small space between the buildings and the sea. As I was at that time but eighteen years of age, I know not whether I should call my behavior in this dangerous juncture courage or folly; but I took up Livy, and amused myself with turning over that author and even making extracts from him as if I had been perfectly at my leisure.

Just then a friend of my uncle's, who had lately come to him from Spain,[2] joined us, and observing me sitting by my mother with a book in my hand, reproved her for her calmness, and me at the same time for my careless security; nevertheless I went on with my author. Though it was now morning, the light was exceedingly faint and doubtful; the buildings all around us tottered, and though we stood upon open ground, yet as the place was narrow and confined, there was no remaining without imminent danger; we therefore resolved to quit the town.

A panic-stricken crowd followed us, and (as to a mind distracted with terror every suggestion seems more prudent than its own) pressed on us in dense array to drive us forward as we came out. Being at a convenient distance from the house, we stood still, in the midst of a most dangerous and dreadful scene. The chariots, which we had ordered to be drawn out, were so agitated backwards and forwards, though upon the most level ground, that we could not keep them steady, even by supporting them with large stones. The sea seemed to roll back upon itself and to be driven from its banks by the convulsive motion of the earth; it is certain at least the shore was considerably enlarged, and several sea animals were left upon it.

1. From Virgil, Book 2.
2. Pliny the Elder had served as governor of Spain and had many friends there.

On the other side, a black and dreadful cloud, broken with rapid, zigzag flashes, revealed behind it variously shaped masses of flame: these last were like sheet lightning but much larger. Upon this our Spanish friend, whom I mentioned above, addressing himself to my mother and me with great energy and urgency: "If your brother," he said, "if your uncle be safe, he certainly wishes you to be so too; but if he perished, it was his desire no doubt, that you might both survive him; why therefore do you delay your escape a moment?" We could never think of our own safety, we said, while we were uncertain of his. Upon this our friend left us, and withdrew from the danger with the utmost precipitation.

Soon afterwards the cloud began to descend and cover the sea. It had already surrounded and concealed the island of Capreae [Capri] and the promontory of Misenum. My mother now besought, urged, even commanded me to make *my* escape at any rate, which, as I was young, I might easily do; as for herself, she said, her age and corpulency rendered all attempts of that sort impossible; however she would willingly meet death if she could have the satisfaction of seeing that she was not the occasion of mine. But I absolutely refused to leave her, and, taking her by the hand, compelled her to go with me. She complied with great reluctance, and not without many reproaches to herself for retarding my flight.

The ashes now began to fall upon us, though in no great quantity. I looked back; a dense dark mist seemed to be following us, spreading itself over the country like a cloud.

"Let us turn out of the high-road," I said, "while we can still see, for fear that, should we fall in the road, we should be pressed to death in the dark by the crowds that are following us."

We had scarcely sat down when night came upon us, not such as we have when the sky is cloudy, or when there is no moon, but that of a room which is shut up, and all the lights put out. You might hear the shrieks of women, the screams of children, and the shouts of men; some calling for their children, others for their parents, others for their husbands, and seeking to recognize each other by the voices that replied; one lamenting his own fate, another that of his family; some wishing to die from the very fear of dying; some lifting their hands to the gods; but the greater part convinced that there were now no gods at all, and that the final endless night of which we have heard had come upon the world. Among these there were some who augmented the real terrors by others imaginary or willfully invented. I remember some who declared that one part of Misenum had fallen, that another was on fire; it was false, but they found people to believe them.

It now grew rather lighter, which we imagined to be rather the forerunner of an approaching burst of flames (as in truth it was) than the return of day; however, the fire fell at a distance from us; then again we were immersed in thick darkness, and a heavy shower of ashes rained upon us, which we were obliged every now and then to stand up to shake off, otherwise we should have been crushed and buried in the heap. I might boast that, during all this scene of horror, not a sigh, or expression of fear, escaped me, had not my support been grounded in that miserable, though mighty consolation, that all mankind were involved in the same calamity, and that I was perishing with the world itself. At last this dreadful darkness was dissipated by degrees, like a cloud or smoke; the real day returned, and even the sun shone out, though with a lurid light, like when an eclipse is coming on. Every object that presented itself to our eyes (which were extremely weakened) seemed changed, being covered with deep ashes as if with snow.

We returned to Misenum, where we refreshed ourselves as well as we could, and passed an anxious night between hope and fear; though, indeed, with a much larger share of the latter; for the earthquake still continued, while many frenzied persons ran up and down heightening their own and their friends' calamities by terrible predictions. However, my mother and I, notwith-standing the danger we had passed, and that which still threat-ened us, had no thoughts of leaving the place, till we could re-ceive some news of my uncle.

And now, you will read this narrative without any view of inserting it in your history, of which it is not in the least worthy; and indeed you must put it down to your own request if it should appear not worth even the trouble of a letter. Farewell. (Pliny *Ep.* bk. 6, let. 20 [Bosanquet, ed. 1903, pp. 200–204])

Although this account by Pliny is vivid in its description and con-veys the feelings of the writer, along with a certain amount of youth-ful boasting, it is scarcely satisfactory as a narrative of facts. Pliny does not tell us the direction they took in their flight, although we may infer from what he says about the invisibility of the island of Capri that they were along the shore of the bay. From other positions Capri would have been hidden from view by the high land of the promontory of Misenum. Again he says nothing about the time cov-ered by his narrative. Since no mention is made of spending a night in the open, we may assume that they returned to the villa at Mi-senum on the afternoon of the same day, August 25.

The Destruction of Pompeii and Herculaneum

Pliny makes no mention of the destruction of Pompeii and Herculaneum. He may have felt that Tacitus was already familiar with this aspect of the eruption or that it was not connected with his narrative. Strangely, there is an almost total lack of reference to the fate of these two cities in the literature which has come down to us from that time. Tacitus, in the preface to his *History*, states that he will record, along with the descriptions of other events, the destruction of the towns of Campania. His account of the catastrophe must have been thorough, for his seeking information from Pliny indicated the importance he attached to firsthand reports. Unfortunately this portion of his works has been lost, and no contemporary account of the calamity exists. Indeed, other than the mention of the unfortunate cities in an epigram by V. Martial, written 12 years after the catastrophe, the first reference to them is found in the writings of Dion Cassius about A.D. 230, 150 years later. Cassius (A.D. 150–235) is the author of a history of Rome from the founding to A.D. 229. It was written in Greek, and 26 of the 80 volumes are extant. Based on legends of the great eruption which he heard while living in Campania, Cassius reconstructs a fantastic tale in which he describes huge giants leaping through the smoke and tearing the mountain asunder, day turning into night, and the general belief among the people that the earth was returning to Chaos. He further states that "an inexpressible quantity of dust was blown out, which filled land, sea and air; which did much other mischief to men, fields and cattle, . . . and besides buried two entire cities, Herculaneum and Pompeii, while the population was sitting in the theatre" (quoted by Phillips 1869, p. 27). The people were not in the theaters, but the wild rumor recorded by Cassius has nevertheless persisted.

In time knowledge of the location of these cities was lost, and a thousand years later a town (Resina) had grown up on the site of Herculaneum without the inhabitants knowing that the buried city was beneath them.

The Last Days of Pompeii, a romantic novel written by Edward Bulwer-Lytton (Lord Lytton) in 1834, reanimated the scene in a most realistic manner. The final events, including a description of the eruption of Vesuvius, are based on the letters of Pliny.

The destruction of Pompeii and Herculaneum by the great eruption of Vesuvius in A.D. 79 has been described by many writers and is a subject with which everyone is somewhat familiar. Most of the works on this subject have dealt primarily with the art, customs, or life of the people of the time rather than with the physical destruction of the cities. The only surviving account of the eruption is that in the letters of Pliny the Younger, which have already been discussed, but unfortunately, since the letters do not mention the destruction of Pompeii or Herculaneum, we are forced to reconstruct the tragedy from the nature of the debris which buried the cities and from evidence uncovered in the excavations.

Pompeii was a well-established Roman city which had existed as a center of commerce for centuries. At the time of its destruction it had a population of about 20,000. The 15–25 feet of pumice and ash which buried the city not only killed many of the inhabitants but also preserved, in a unique fashion, a record of the life and customs of the times. In all parts of the city the basal 8–10 feet of the material which buried the city consists of uniformly stratified, light-colored, pumiceous lapilli, varying from the size of a pea up to fragments two to three inches in diameter. Overlying this bed is a somewhat hardened layer of ash with a thickness of 6–7 feet, showing evidence of compaction by heavy rains either during or soon after its fall. Doubtless some material has been added by later eruptions, but this is not an important factor at Pompeii. For the most part the pumice is loose and unconsolidated, a factor which makes excavation much easier than at Herculaneum. A good topsoil has developed on the surface, and today trees and cultivated fields of corn and other grains are growing on the unexcavated part of Pompeii.

There has been much speculation as to how the people were killed at Pompeii. From experience in later eruptions it is known that the ash is hot when it falls, although not in an incandescent state. Pliny mentions the hot ashes, and Perret, in connection with his study of the 1906 eruption, states that a "bucket of fine, hot ash was too hot to touch at the end of 24 hours" (1924, p. 91). Such material, since it is primary magma converted into pumice and ash by the sudden release of pressure, would contain a considerable amount of residual gases, and these would continue to escape for some time after it had fallen.

The debris which buried Pompeii was primary pumice, with insignificant quantities of material from the old cone of Mount Somma. This lends support to the conclusion that the disappearance of a portion of Mount Somma during the eruption was largely a result of collapse rather than distribution through explosion. Williams (1941a, p. 311) uses the term *sector graben* for this type, in which a segment of the cone collapses into the magma chamber as a result of the rapid expulsion of primary pumice, as occurred in the A.D. 79 eruption of Vesuvius. The problems concerning the origin of a sector graben, which is a type of caldera, are discussed in Chapter 6. Many have speculated that the deaths in Pompeii were due to *nuées ardentes*, such as that which destroyed St. Pierre in the eruption of Mount Pelée in 1902. Although there are many similarities in the two tragedies, the evidence does not support the conclusion that a *nuée ardente* over-whelmed Pompeii.

About half the area of the city of Pompeii has been excavated, and some 2,000 skeletons have been found. Many were discovered with their hands or cloths to their mouths, apparently trying to keep out the lethal gases. We may conclude that these persons died of asphyxi-ation. Others were killed by falling roofs, or were trapped in build-ings in which they sought refuge. In one wine cellar alone, 18 bodies were found. Many of the skeletons are found about 2 feet above the base of the pumice layer, indicating that they endured the eruption for a time before succumbing. During an excavation in the presence of Queen Carolina Murat, in 1812, several bodies were uncovered 10 feet above the base of the pumice layer and separated from the upper surface by only a thin bed of ash and lapilli. One of the dead was holding a bag, which had decomposed, spilling its contents of 360 silver coins, 42 bronze pieces, and 8 bright imperial gold medallions (Corti 1951, p. 171). The presence of these bodies near the top of the pumice layer indicates that they survived most of the eruption before perishing. The discovery of a great many bodies near the sea indicates that the victims were fleeing, often with some of their most precious belongings. It is possible that suffocation from the great quantity of fine dust in the air was a cause of the death of many of the inhabi-tants, or it may have been a contributing factor along with asphyxi-ation by the gases in the ash. (See Alfano and Friedlander 1928 for further information on causes of death.)

The great loss of life at Pompeii must have occurred in the initial hours of the eruption when the ash fall was at its maximum. Pliny tells us that it was the morning of the third day before the wind began to remove the black cloud which had cast darkness over the entire area. Since the darkness was due to the dense ash cloud, we can infer that the heavy ash falls continued during this period.

The situation at Herculaneum was entirely different. Although Herculaneum is nearer to the cone of Vesuvius than Pompeii, it ap-parently was not in the direct path of the heavy and destructive ash falls. Instead, the city was covered by a mudflow which in places exceeded 65 feet in thickness. The material shows no stratification but consists of a confused mass of fine ash, lava fragments, and pumice, which penetrated every nook and crevice. Breaking through open-ings, it filled the buildings, but in some instances the roofs, because of the support from the inside, did not collapse. The mudflow which destroyed Herculaneum is similar in all respects to those which have devastated numerous towns on the slopes of Vesuvius in almost all of the violent eruptions. A mudflow, on drying, becomes hardened and is frequently called a *volcanic tuff*, a term applied to any consolidated ash which breaks into lumps. Such is the material which entombed Herculaneum. The consolidated nature of the material, as well as the depth to which Herculaneum is buried, makes the excavations difficult; thus only a small section of the city has been uncovered. Only a few skeletons, probably not more than 30, have been found. This fact indicates that most of the inhabitants were able to escape.

Although many accounts state that Pompeii and Herculaneum were destroyed on the same day, this seems unlikely. The mudflow would have been more likely to occur after the eruption had progressed long enough to cover the upper slopes of Vesuvius with a thick layer of ash. Then heavy rains, which almost invariably accompany an eruption, would convert the ash into an avalanching mass of mud. The mudflow which destroyed Herculaneum may have occurred a day or two after Pompeii was buried. At least sufficient time elapsed after the eruption began for those who wished to seek refuge elsewhere to do so. After the avalanche of mud passed over Herculaneum, it was so completely sealed that its site was forgotten and it became a "lost" city. At Pompeii it was quite different. After the eruption, the tops of many of the buildings projected above the debris, and doubtless many of the former inhabitants returned to see if they could recover any of their belongings. Without much effort they were able to dig away some of the ashes and enter a room. When one room had been cleared, the next room was reached by breaking a hole in the wall. However, when the most accessible places had been emptied, the search became so difficult that it was abandoned. Relatively few houses in Pompeii, however, were untouched by either former inhabitants or plunderers. Some of the stone in the walls was quarried for use elsewhere. However, weeds soon began to grow over the buried city, and later ash falls helped to conceal it. In time, the last vestiges of the buried city were gone and all memory of its exact location was lost.

The Rediscovery of Pompeii and Herculaneum

The rediscovery of the buried cities is a fascinating bit of history which is worth recounting. There are numerous and extensive works dealing with the discovery and excavations at Pompeii and Herculaneum. One which I found interesting and which I used freely in the preparation of this section is *The Destruction and Resurrection of Pompeii and Herculaneum* by E. C. C. Corti, published in 1940 in German and in 1951 in an English translation by K. and R. Gregor Smith. A brief but interesting chapter on Pompeii is included in *Gods, Graves and Scholars* by C. W. Ceram, published in 1949 in German and in 1951 in an English translation by E. B. Garside. Two numbers in the series

Plate 32. Excavations in progress at Pompeii, Italy, in 1952.

of Guide-Books to Museums and Monuments in Italy, issued through the Minister of Public Instruction, Rome, are of special interest: no. 3, *Pompeii* (5th ed., 1951), and no. 53, *Herculaneum* (3d ed., 1945). Both were written by Professor Amedeo Maiuri, with English translations by V. Priestley.

For nearly 1,500 years following the catastrophe the buried cities were seldom mentioned, and they seem to have been almost completely forgotten. In the fifteenth and sixteenth centuries, speculation as to the location of Pompeii occurred, a vine-clad hill known as Civita being frequently mentioned as the probable site. However, no investigations were made and little notice was taken of such suggestions. About 1592 a canal was constructed to carry water from the River Sarno to Torre Annunziata, which lacked a suitable water supply. The canal crossed the site of Pompeii, and, during excavation for it, marble fragments and even some coins of the time of Emperor Nero were discovered, but these latter quickly disappeared into the pockets of workmen and no immediate conclusions were drawn from the other discoveries. By 1607, however, from excavations made dur-

ing the construction of the water-supply system, it was established
that the site of some ancient place lay beneath the Civita. But even
this seems to have been forgotten, especially after the violent eruption of Vesuvius in 1631, which again spread ash over the entire
countryside.

In 1689, excavations were undertaken at some distance from
Naples in search for water. The workers noticed several distinct
layers of different kinds of ash and found in the deepest layers some
stones which contained inscriptions, including one on which was
the name Pompeii. Although some felt that it was the site of the ancient city of Pompeii, others maintained that it was simply a Pom-
peian country house which they had encountered. Apparently stimulated by these reports as well as by the earlier bits of information,
Giusèppe Macrini, an explorer of Vesuvius, examined the hill called
Civita and in his book, *De Vesuvio*, published in 1699, announced
that Pompeii was in fact in the Civita area. His claims were not taken
seriously, and no excavations were undertaken.

The chronologic sequence of the story now shifts to Herculaneum.
The actual discovery of the ruins at Herculaneum is generally credited to the Prince d'Elboeuf, an Austrian army officer who in 1710 was
in command of the guard at the court of Naples, which at that time
was under Austrian rule. D'Elboeuf had spent a summer in the villa
of a friend near Resina (actually at Portici), which, it will be remembered, was built over the site of Herculaneum, though its inhabitants
did not know of the existence of a city beneath them. Becoming engaged to a Neapolitan princess, d'Elboeuf bought a tract of land on
the sea near Resina, intending to build a house on it. He was interested in decorative stone for his proposed house and upon inquiry
learned that a peasant, while digging a well at Resina, had found
some unusual stones. The peasant, in order to increase the supply of
water in his well, had deepened it. In so doing he found some white
and yellow marble and other "costly" stones, which appeared to be
parts of ancient pillars. The peasant was not particularly impressed
and sold the best pieces to a marble dealer. D'Elboeuf was much interested, and he subsequently purchased the land from the peasant
and began to carry on excavations of his own. Numerous statues
were discovered, and three of the best were smuggled out of the
country as a present to Prince Eugene at Vienna. After the initial
success, few statues were found, and, since the digging was difficult
because of the hard nature of the material, interest in the project
lagged. There was no indication that anyone realized that the ancient
city of Herculaneum was the source of the material. When the Prince
d'Elboeuf was transferred to France he sold his villa, which subsequently was again resold.

The political fortunes of Italy now changed, and in 1735 Naples

Plate 33. Excavations at Herculaneum, Italy. Note the mudflow at right, on top of which the present city of Resina is located.

and Sicily came under Spanish rule. The eldest son of the King of Spain, 19-year-old Charles of Bourbon, became the absolute monarch of the Two Sicilies. The royal youth, much interested in fishing and hunting, acquired for his pastime the house that had formerly belonged to the Prince d'Elboeuf. Still in the house were many of the statues which d'Elboeuf had recovered from his diggings. In 1738, young King Charles married Maria Amalia Christini, whose father, Augustus III of Saxony, was a great patron of the arts. It should be mentioned here that Augustus had purchased the three statues smuggled out to Prince Eugene at Vienna, and hence these were known by his daughter. When the king brought his young queen to Naples, she was fascinated by the ancient statuary, especially that found by d'Elboeuf, and she begged her husband for more pieces. He organized a digging force, and work was started at the original well which d'Elboeuf had taken over from the peasant. The first discovery consisted of three pieces of a statue of a huge bronze horse. Next they found the torsos of three marble figures in Roman togas and another bronze horse. As work progressed, a flight of stairs was discovered,

and on December 11, 1738, a plaque bearing the inscription Theatrum Herculanensem was unearthed. Thus, by sheer luck, it appears that d'Elboeuf had unwittingly hit upon the front of the stage of a theater, on which had collapsed, under the impact of the mudflow, the wall which served as wings and background, with its marble facing and numerous statues. This was one of the few spots, perhaps the only one, where sculpture was literally piled one piece upon the other. Thus Herculaneum was discovered.

King Charles and his queen, keenly interested in the excavations, over a period of years made a splendid collection of statues and other articles and assembled them in a museum which they established at Portici. The king, at first, tried to keep his discovery a secret, but in time the news leaked out. In March, 1748, when they were having little success at Herculaneum, it was suggested to the king that the work be suspended and a serious attempt be made to explore the Civita area. Some held this to be the ancient city of Pompeii while others maintained that it was Stabiae, which had also been buried by ash in the A.D. 79 eruption of Vesuvius. Its location was by this time long forgotten. (Castellammare now stands, at least in part, upon the ruins of Stabiae.)

The king agreed, and on April 1, 1748, 12 workers began digging at Civita, at what turned out to be a lucky spot. However, in spite of the uncovered remains of numerous houses, no one seemed to realize that they were in the middle of a town; it was still thought that this was a part of an isolated villa. On April 6 the first painted frescos were uncovered. On April 19 the first of the dead was found, a skeleton lying on the ground, that of a man from whose hands had fallen a number of gold and silver coins of the time of Nero and Vespasian. The excavations went on with redoubled vigor, but, since they were motivated by curiosity and greed rather than historical or archeological interest, the search was not systematically conducted. In November, work was shifted to an oval-shaped depressed area, which turned out to be the amphitheater. It was called the Stabian Theater, under the delusion that the town was Stabiae. The death of King Ferdinand VI of Spain, on August 10, 1759, was a serious blow to the excavations. King Charles of the Two Sicilies, being his stepbrother and heir to the Spanish throne, was obliged to give the kingdom of the Two Sicilies to his son and to ascend the Spanish throne. Unfortunately, his son, then only 18 years of age, was a very backward boy, and the affairs of the country were run largely by his ministers. King Charles and his queen had for more than 20 years enthusiastically carried on the excavations, and, while the ministers continued the work, many complications which it is not possible to detail here hampered progress. That the diggings at Civita were actually Pompeii was definitely established for the first time on August 16, 1763, when the workers unearthed a statue of white marble and a nearby pedestal bearing the following inscription: "In the name of the Emperor and Caesar Vespasian Augustus, the tribune T. Svedius Clemens has restored . . . to the public possession of the Pompeians those places which belong to them and had been taken into private possession."

The progress of the excavations at Pompeii and Herculaneum were largely dependent on the interest of the royal family. By good fortune it so happened that usually some member of the ruling family, most often the queen, was interested in the excavations, and the work was continued. One of the most enthusiastic supporters was Queen Carolina, daughter of the Empress of Austria (House of Hapsburg), who married King Ferdinand of Bourbon in 1768. She became intensely interested in the excavations and was largely responsible for having the work continued during the long reign of her husband. The Bourbon rule of Naples was interrupted during the period of the French Revolution and the Napoleonic Wars by a brief period of French occupation. During this time King Ferdinand and Queen Carolina sought refuge in Sicily. Even the French rulers, however, were patrons of the excavations, and so the work was not interrupted.

In 1808, the French Marshal Joachin Murat and his wife, another Carolina, the 26-year-old sister of Napoleon, were placed on the Naples throne. Queen Carolina Murat was even more enthusiastic about the excavations than was her Bourbon predecessor. She was a frequent visitor at the excavations and took an active part in organizing the work. It was a common practice for the workmen to place skeletons and statues back in their original positions, cover them lightly, and "find" them when the queen was present. The queen's consistent rewarding of the workers for unusual discoveries greatly stimulated the work. Many royal visitors were entertained at the excavations, and prepared "finds" were staged for them.

With the defeat of Napoleon in 1815, the French rule in Naples ended, and the Bourbons returned from their exile in Sicily to the Naples throne. King Ferdinand, who died in 1825, after 66 years on the throne, was succeeded by his son, who died in 1859 as a result of wounds inflicted in a plot on his life about 2 years earlier. After a short interval, through the leadership of Giusèppe Garibaldi, the Bourbons were displaced and Italy was united under King Victor Emmanuel II of the House of Savoy. The new king regarded it as his patriotic duty to resume the excavations at Pompeii and Herculaneum, which in recent years had been neglected by the Bourbons.

An archeologist, G. Fiorelli, who was placed in charge, carried on the work vigorously. Following a systematic plan, he had the results published in a "Journal of the excavations at Pompeii" (1861–1865).

Figure 28. Lava flows of Vesuvius. Compiled from Alfano and Friedlander (1928) and Imbo (1965b).

Thus for the first time the work was placed on a scientific rather than a treasure-seeking basis.

During Italy's participation in World War I, the excavations were halted, but, after Mussolini's ascent to power, a renewal of national pride gave fresh impetus to the work. It was at about this time that Professor A. Maiuri, who for many years was to be in charge of the excavations, became connected with the work. During World War II, work was again suspended, but following the war, with Marshall Plan funds, the work has been continued under Professor Maiuri's direction on an even larger scale.

The great care with which the work is now done, with reconstruction being carried out as the excavations are made, insures accurate restorations. But the progress is slow. About two-fifths of the area within the walls of Pompeii remains to be excavated, and the area outside the walls is limitless. At Herculaneum the work is even slower, although electric boring machines and mechanical shovels are used. The town of Resina, a thickly populated community, is a serious obstacle to expansion of the project, since it sits above Herculaneum. Fortunately, the lava flow of 1631, which is prominent along the streets in Resina, flowed on either side of the site but did not actually overflow Herculaneum. Apparently the mudflow which buried Herculaneum raised the level of the surface sufficiently to divert the lava flow to the sides of the mudflow.

Vesuvius since A.D. 79

Many writers have reported the eruptive activity of Vesuvius. The following sources, which are in English and readily accessible, are worthy of note. Sir William Hamilton (1730–1803), who compiled a list of the eruptions of Vesuvius up to 1779, was the British ambassador to the Court of Naples from 1764 to 1800. He was a keen student of volcanoes and made many significant observations which provide one of the best records of the activity of the period. In a series of letters written between June 10, 1766, and May 1, 1776, and published in the *Philosophical Transactions of the Royal Society of London*, Hamilton described in detail several of the eruptions of Vesuvius. Most of this material was incorporated in books which are listed in the bibliography. The first, a small volume containing seven letters (the last dated November 5, 1771), was published in 1774 under the title *Observations on Mt. Vesuvius, Mt. Etna, and Other Volcanoes*. The second, a more elaborate volume under the title of *Campi Phlegraei*, was published in 1776, and with a supplement Hamilton completed the record to 1779. The second edition of *A Description of Active and Extinct Volcanoes* by Daubeny, published in 1848, contains a record of the eruptive history of Vesuvius which is summarized in the several editions of Lyell's *Principles of Geology* with additional notes from Lyell's own observations. John Phillips's book *Vesuvius*, published in 1869, contains a rather detailed account of all the eruptions up to 1868, and Alfano and Friedlander in *La storia del Vesuvio* complete the record to 1928. All of the above sources have been used freely in the preparation of this section, but the last two have been the most useful, since they usually summarize the earlier reports. Perret (1924), Imbo (1951), and contemporary news accounts of twentieth-century eruptions have also been used.

For many hundreds of years following A.D. 79, only passing references to the eruptions of Vesuvius were made. It is probable that only the eruptions which resulted in loss of life or widespread damage were described in the literature, and many of the writings have not survived. Dion Cassius, to whom reference has been made in connection with the legends of the destruction of Pompeii, describes an eruption which occurred in A.D. 203, from which the following is a brief excerpt: "and the summits are clothed with trees and vines, but the interior circle is abandoned to fire, and throws up smoke by day and flame by night as if many and various kinds of incense were rising. And it is always so with more or less intensity, and often ashes are projected and fall in great quantity, and stones thrown up and under the influence of the wind. And the mountain echoes and bellows, because it has not wide but narrow secret air passages" (quoted by Phillips 1869, p. 41). Cassius is here expressing Aristotle's view that volcanoes were caused by "pent-up" winds.

An eruption occurring in A.D. 472 is reported to have spread ashes over all Europe and caused alarm as far away as Constantinople. During the next 600 years only four eruptions are recorded, in 512, 685, 993, and 1036. The eruption of 1036 is of particular significance because it was during this eruption that the first lava flows of the historic period occurred. The accounts relate that the eruption occurred not only at the top but also on the sides and that its burning products ran into the sea.

Vesuvius, in its early history as a submarine volcano and later as an island in the Bay of Naples, had given rise to lava flows, as is typical of the early history of all volcanoes. Then for a thousand years or more before the beginning of the Christian era and until 1036, it produced only fragmental materials, building the cones now known as Mounts Somma and Vesuvius. These cones were superimposed on the older lava and ash beds formed by its early activity. There is evidence that Mount Somma had been disrupted and rebuilt at least once before the eruption of A.D. 79, in which it was again destroyed, in part, and the present cone of Vesuvius was formed. Thus Vesuvius was following a pattern repeated in many volcanoes, in which the final stage is marked by cone-disrupting explosions and the ejection of only fragmental material. As the magma becomes more acid and, as a result, more viscous, the explosive release of the gases shatters it into pumice and ash, and no lava is emitted. Such eruptions, at Mount Pelée and elsewhere, have already been described as characteristic of the Peléan type of volcanic activity. Normally, they indicate that the volcano is in its final phase of activity and that, from the geologic viewpoint, the end is in sight. We may well inquire, then, why Vesuvius seems to have had a "rejuvenation" and started an entirely new cycle. The first indications of the "new life" were the lava flows in 1036. Other flows followed, but the great eruption of 1631, with its flood of lava, left no doubt that Vesuvius had embarked upon a new type of activity. This new activity resulted from a change in the composition of the Vesuvian magma, which will be described in a later section.

There are records of eruptions in 1049, 1138, and 1139, the latter two, according to Alfano and Friedlander (1928), being the most important eruptions prior to that of 1631. Sir William Hamilton, who compiled a list of the eruptions of Vesuvius and Etna (1774), stated that no eruptions occurred at Vesuvius from the year 1139 to the great eruption of 1631. However, Phillips (1869) and Lobley (1889) list eruptions in 1306 and 1500, the latter being only an eruption of ash. It would seem apparent that many small eruptions must have passed unnoticed or at least unrecorded and that only the more disastrous ones are preserved in the records. Hamilton commented that the list of eruptions which he gave could not have been compiled but for the curious fact that sacred images and vestments of the church had been used by the priests to stop the fury of the volcanoes—the veil of Saint Agatha in Sicily and the relics of Saint Januarius in Naples—and that the record of the triumphant interference of the saints had been carefully recorded by the priests.

The eruption of 1631, occurring after about 500 years of repose, is one of the great historic eruptions of Vesuvius. It also marks a turning point in the pattern of activity of Vesuvius, for prior to this eruption it had been relatively inactive with long periods of repose, but since 1631 it has been in a more or less constant state of activity. The eruption began on December 16, 1631, with strong explosions and a great ash-filled pino cloud rising from the crater. It soon spread nightlike darkness over the area, and cinders and ash began to fall. As the eruption continued, thousands of the inhabitants from villages on the slopes of Vesuvius fled to Naples. On the morning of the seventeenth, at an elevation of about 915 meters, two fissures opened on the southwest side of the cone. From them floods of lava issued and, breaking into numerous streams, rushed down the slope with great speed, invading San Giorgio a Cremano, Portici, Pugliano, La Scala, and the western part of Torre del Greco. The flows reached the sea in numerous tongues, covering the six kilometers from the source to the sea in about two hours.

On the evening of the seventeenth it began raining mud in Naples, while great mudflows invaded villages on the slopes of Vesuvius, as well as on the north slope of Mount Somma. Mudflows invaded San Giorgio a Cremano, Portici, and Resina (site of ancient Herculaneum) and formed a long peninsula of land extending into the sea. Another lava flow developed, issuing from a fissure on the south side. Dividing into three streams, it passed between Camaldoli del Torre and Torre Annunziata. Strong explosions accompanied by pino clouds continued through the eighteenth, but thereafter the violence decreased, although the eruption continued with some periods of calm into January, 1632.

The destruction by mud, lava, and ash in the densely populated and intensely cultivated area was of tremendous proportions. Six towns were destroyed by lava, nine were wrecked by mudflows, and the entire region suffered from ash falls. About 30 centimeters of ash and cinders fell in Naples. To add to the damage, tremendous deluges of rain fell during the last week in December, particularly on the north slope of Vesuvius, where the ash fall was the heaviest. The death toll was placed at 4,000 people and 6,000 domestic animals. In the eruption the cone lost 168 meters in height, and the crater was enlarged to more than twice its diameter before the eruption.

Since the grand eruption of 1631, Vesuvius has followed a pattern in which a cyclic repetition of the eruptive activity can be recognized. This pattern, or the Vesuvian cycle, is described in some detail in Chapter 12. However, a brief résumé of the cycle at this point will enable the reader to follow more intelligently the eruptions of Vesuvius which are described in the following paragraphs. The eruptive cycles vary in length, but the two latest cycles ran 34 and 38 years respectively. The cycle begins with a repose period, averaging about 7 years, in which only gases issue from the crater. The renewal of explosive activity begins with the building of small cinder and scoria cones on the crater floor. Outpourings of lava may also occur in the crater until the crater is gradually filled. Sometimes the lava flows spill over the top or issue from fissures in the crater rim, but such flows are of small volume and cause little damage. This type of moderate activity may continue for years (perhaps 20–30 years). When the cinder cones and the lava flows have filled the crater, the stage is set for the culminating eruption of the cycle. The column of lava now stands high in the throat of the volcano, and it is under tremendous pressure and saturated with gases. Finally, when the pressure becomes too great to be contained by the surrounding material, the eruption begins. Accompanied by sharp earthquakes and strong explosions, which give rise to great ash clouds (pinos), the cone splits. From the fractures, which frequently extend from the crater rim to the base, floods of lava pour out and flow rapidly down the side of the cone. These actions constitute the paroxysmal eruption which marks the end of a cycle. Such eruptions usually last for two or three weeks and are followed by a repose period which is the beginning of a new cycle.

Sir William Hamilton (1774), whose work on Vesuvius has already been mentioned, gives a detailed account of an eruption which began on October 17, 1767. This paroxysmal eruption was typical of those which mark the end of a cycle. After strong explosions which lasted for two days and were felt in Naples, fissures opened on the north-west and south sides of the cone on October 19, and streams of lava poured out. One was directed toward the town of Salvatore, while the other flowed in the direction of Torre Annunziata. Padre Torre, an ardent observer of Vesuvius, was on the mountain near the point where one of the fissures opened and his vivid account of his experience, as well as the events which followed, is worth repeating here:

> I was making observations upon the lava, which had already, from the spot where it first broke out, reached the valley, when, on a sudden, about noon, I heard a violent noise within the mountain, and about a quarter of a mile from the place where I stood, the mountain split; and with much noise from this new mouth a fountain of liquid fire shot up many feet high and then like a torrent rolled on directly towards us; in an instant clouds of black smoke and ashes caused total darkness; the explosions were much louder than any thunder I ever heard, and the smell of sulphur was offensive. My guide, alarmed, took to his heels . . . [and] I followed close and we ran nearly three miles without stopping as the earth continued to shake beneath our feet. I was apprehensive of the opening of a fresh mouth which might cut off our retreat. . . . besides the pumice stones, falling upon us like hail, were of such a size as to cause a disagreeable sensation upon the part where they fell.
>
> I observed on my way to Naples, which was in less than two hours after I left the mountain, that the lava had actually covered 3 miles of the very road through which we retreated. . . . Portici and Naples were in the extremity of alarm; the churches were filled; the streets were thronged with processions of saints, and various ceremonies were performed to quell the fury of the mountain. In the night of the 20th [October] the situation became critical, the prisoners in the public jails attempted to escape and the mob set fire to the gates [of the house] of Cardinal Archbishop because he refused to bring out the relics of St. Januarius.

The 21st was quieter but on the 22nd, at 10:00 A.M. [there was] the same thundering noise but more violent and alarming. Ashes fell in abundance in Naples, covering houses and balconies to an inch in depth. In the midst of these horrors, the mob growing tumultuous and impatient, obliged the Cardinal to bring out the head of St. Januarius and go with it in the procession . . . and it is well attested here that the eruption ceased the moment the Saint came in sight of the mountain; it is true the noise ceased about that time after having lasted five hours, as it had done the preceding day. . . . on the 27th the eruption came to an end. (Quoted by Phillips 1869, pp. 73–75)

In the latter part of the eighteenth century Vesuvius appears to have been particularly active, with much shorter cycles than during the nineteenth and twentieth centuries. After a repose of only three years following the 1767 eruption, Vesuvius renewed its activity, and after nine years of moderate activity, the paroxysmal eruption which ended the brief cycle began in May, 1779. A fissure opened on the north-northeast side, and lava flowed from this opening throughout the month of June. On August 8, according to Hamilton (1779), terrific explosions, accompanied by a liquid fountain of fire, began to rise from the crater to a height of about two miles. This blazing column was directed toward Ottaiano, and as it fell it covered the side of the cone with a band of red-hot scoria more than a mile in width. The inhabitants of Ottaiano, unable to see the crater because of the rim of Somma and unaware that they were in the path of the fiery blast, were suddenly enveloped by a deluge of red-hot scoria and cinders. Hamilton writes:

The sight of the place [Ottaiano] was dismal, half buried under black scoria and dust, all windows towards the mountain broken, some of the houses burnt, the street choked with ashes— in some narrow streets to a depth of four feet, so that roads had to be cut by people to reach their own doors. During the tempestuous fall of ashes, scoria, and stones, so large as to weigh a hundred pounds, the inhabitants dared not stir out—even with vain protection of pillows, tables, wine casks, etc. on their heads. Driven back wounded or terrified, they retreated to cellars and arches, half stifled with heat and dust and sulphur, and blinded by volcanic lightning—through 25 minutes this horror lasted; then suddenly ceased, and the people took the opportunity of quitting the country, after leaving the sick and bedridden in the churches. One more hour of this frightful visitation and Ottaiano would have been a buried city like Pompeii. (Hamilton 1779, p. 19)

After the 1779 eruption Vesuvius was in repose for five years, followed by moderate activity until the great paroxysmal eruption of 1793, which ended the cycle. This eruption began on June 15, 1793, after strong explosions and earthquakes opened a fissure between Resina and Torre del Greco low on the southwest side of the old Somma cone. Along this fracture, said to have been one-half mile in length, lava poured from six *bocas*. The flows soon united in a single stream and in a matter of six hours (from 10:00 P.M. to 4:00 A.M.) invaded Torre del Greco, flowing down the main street with a front 1,200–1,500 feet wide, and extended 362 feet into the sea on a front 1,127 feet wide and 15 feet in height. It was the third time, but unfortunately not the last, that Torre del Greco was invaded by lava. At the same time a lava flow of about half the volume of the Torre del Greco flow poured from a fissure almost directly opposite on the northeast side of the cone.

From the 1793 eruption to the middle of the nineteenth century paroxysmal eruptions, each ending a cycle, occurred in 1822, 1838, and 1850. There is some difference of opinion regarding the assignment of cycles from 1850 to 1872, but all agree that the eruption of 1872 was one of the all-time great eruptions of Vesuvius and without doubt marks the end of a cycle.

In the eruption of 1872 the cone split from top to bottom on the north flank, and the lava from this fissure poured into the Atrio del Cavallo and through the observatory gap, inundating the villages of Massa and San Sebastiano. From the main crater, strong explosions with large pinos spread both fine and coarse ash over a wide area. The explosions, heard in Naples, were particularly strong on April 28, 29, and 30, the last three days of the eruption.

One of the best-known eruptive cycles of Vesuvius extended from 1872 to 1906. The repose period was interrupted briefly in 1874, when a small cone formed on the crater floor, but the main renewal of activity began in 1877. Cone building and lava flows inside the crater followed the usual pattern of crater filling until the outbreak of the external flow of 1881. This flow issued from a fracture on the southeast side of the cone, above Torre Annunziata, but the lava was so sluggish that it accumulated around the opening, forming a cupola or dome-shaped mass of lava. Colle Margherita, a lava dome of the same type located in the Atrio de Cavallo, was formed in 1891–1894, and Colle Umberto, near the Vesuvian Observatory, was formed in 1895–1899. Colle Umberto rises 480 feet above the Atrio floor, and, while it obscures the view from the observatory into the Atrio, it does serve as a barrier to protect the observatory from future flows.

By April, 1906, the intercrater cone completely filled the crater and was, in fact, a continuation of the main cone. At this time Vesuvius reached its greatest height, having an elevation of 4,338 feet above sea level. The great eruption of 1906 began early on the morning of April 4, when a fissure opened on the south-southwestern side of the cone and a small lava flow issued from the upper end of the break at an elevation of 3,630 feet. Toward midnight another flow started from the same break but at a point 1,200 feet lower. During this time the activity in the crater increased in violence, and enormous blocks of old lava, incandescent scoria, and cinders were constantly being ejected, rising hundreds of feet above the crater rim and falling on the sides of the cone or back into the crater. Dense pinos, in which lightning flashes were seen for the first time in this eruption, rose from the crater and spread ash over the countryside. On the morning of April 6, the third *boca* opened still lower, at an elevation of about 1,800 feet and on the same zone of fractures but somewhat to the east of the previous vents. From it came the most imposing lava flow of the entire eruption, which covered a portion of Torre Annunziata. On April 7, still another flow issued from a point slightly east of the Torre Annunziata vent, and a tongue of lava flowed toward Terzigno. In the early hours of April 8, enormous quantities of fresh scoria and rocks were thrown from the crater, a portion of which described a great arch over Mount Somma in the direction of Ottaiano and San Giusèppe.

This phenomenon was a repetition of what had occurred in the eruption of 1779, previously described. About three feet of scoria and debris fell in Ottaiano, and the roofs in many houses collapsed under the weight of the debris. In San Giusèppe 105 persons were killed when the roof of a church in which they had sought refuge collapsed. The culmination of the eruption was reached with a great "gas blow-off," which began at 3:30 A.M. on April 8 and continued for 12–15 hours. This tremendous outrush of gas, which by its force enlarged the crater and carried away the upper part of the cone, was an awesome spectacle. Perret (1924, p. 45), who was an eyewitness of the eruption, gives a scale drawing of the "blow-off," which is similar to that in Figure 62, Phase 5. The gas eruption, with abundant ash, continued, but with decreasing intensity, for two days, and intermittently until the end of the eruption on April 22. The accumulation of hot ash on the upper slopes of Vesuvius gave rise to many "hot avalanches," which were a serious hazard to trips on the volcano during the closing days of the eruption. These masses of ash were very unstable, and an earthquake or even a huge boulder falling on an accumulation might be sufficient to send it cascading down the slope like an avalanche of snow. Heavy rains toward the end of April, especially in the Ottaiano area, caused mudflows which did extensive damage. The cone lost 325 feet of height in the eruption, largely because of the "gas blow-off."

Plate 34. Vesuvius and the Bay of Naples. Photo with infrared film.

The next and most recent full cycle at Vesuvius extended from 1906 to 1944. After April 22, 1906, Vesuvius was in a state of repose until May, 1913, although minor eruptions of cinders occurred in the bottom of the crater in May, 1910, and again in June, 1911. The typical pattern of cone building and lava flows in the crater began in May, 1913, and continued with varying intensity until the paroxysmal eruption of March, 1944, brought the cycle to a close. During this interval of 31 years the crater was filled, and by 1944 the cinder cone, built up from the crater floor, could be seen from Naples projecting above the rim of the crater. The initial phase of the 1944 eruption began on March 12, when a section of the summit cone collapsed, obstructing the conduit. Another collapse on March 14 further blocked the conduit. By March 18 the conduit had been reopened by explosive activity, and lava began to overflow the crater rim at a break on the east side. Moving rapidly, it reached the walls of Somma in one-half hour and then moved westward in the Atrio de Cavallo and through the observatory gap toward the towns of Massa and San Sebastiano. The lava reached these towns on March 21, and, moving at the rate of 50–100 meters per hour, it passed through the towns, leaving only a smoking lava field with the ruins of some of the

houses to mark the site. Other lava streams poured from the west side of the cone, cutting and blocking the railway and the Funicolare Vesuviana. Accompanying the outpouring of lava, explosive activity in the crater increased in violence, throwing out great quantities of ash and scoria.

On March 21, when the outflow of lava from the fissures on the side had ceased, a new phase began. It was marked by the violent overflowing of the lava column and the ejection of fountains of lava to a height of not less than one-half mile. A large amount of the ejected lava fell on the east side of the cone, forming a "pseudo-lava flow." These violent lava fountains, lasting about an hour, occurred at intervals throughout the day and into the night. (A similar type of activity had occurred in the 1779 and 1906 eruptions, devastating Ottaiano both times.) The "gas blow-off," similar to that described in the 1906 eruption, began on March 22 and in its most violent phase lasted about 10 hours. The eruption continued with the ejection of quantities of ash and cinders until March 29.

As in the 1906 eruption, marked changes occurred in the crater as a result of the 1944 eruption. These changes are believed to be due in a large measure to the "gas blow-off," which literally blew away the upper portion of the cone. At the close of the eruption the crater was an irregular, elliptical basin with a depth of about 900 feet and a long axis of about 1,800 feet in an east-west direction. Since the 1944 eruption the crater has been gradually filling by avalanching from the sides. When observed in 1952, the crater was about 700 feet deep, and the huge dust clouds which rose when an avalanche from the sides crashed into the crater were frequently reported as new eruptions. Profiles of the crater at several periods since the 1906 eruption are shown in Figure 29. Following the 1944 eruption, Vesuvius lapsed into a repose period in which it remains today. For the past 300 years the repose periods have averaged about 7 years. It is apparent that a renewal of activity at Vesuvius is long overdue.

Depth of the Magma Reservoir at Vesuvius

The depth of the magma reservoir in a volcano can be determined only by indirect evidence. In most cases the depth of earthquakes which are associated with a volcanic eruption gives a clue to the probable depth of the magma chamber. This is, of course, based on the assumption that the earthquakes originate in the magma reservoir. The depth of many such earthquakes has been recorded, and, surprisingly, a depth of around 20 miles is indicated in many cases.

Vesuvius is unique in that the geologic structure surrounding the volcano provides a means of establishing the depth of certain formations beneath Vesuvius, and from this information the depth of the magma can be determined. Since this, in the case of Vesuvius at least, answers the often-asked question, "How deep is a volcano?" it will be worthwhile to explain how the information is obtained.

The Bay of Naples is a faulted synclinal basin, with the Sorrento Peninsula (Amalfi) and the island of Capri forming one of the uptilted edges, while a similar projection on the north, known as Mount Massico, forms the northern limb of the syncline (Fig. 30). Vesuvius and the other volcanic centers in this area, such as the Phlegraean Fields and Ischia, are located near the center of this synclinal basin. The rocks of the Sorrento Peninsula consist of Triassic and Cretaceous limestones and dolomites which dip to the northwest, that is, toward Vesuvius. From the dip, the depth of these layers below Mount Vesuvius can be estimated. The conduit which connects the magma reservoir with the crater must, of course, pass through these layers of limestone. During an eruption, blocks of these limestones

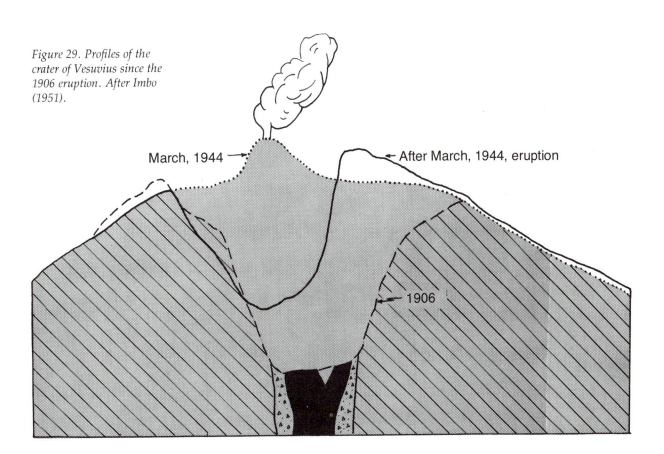

Figure 29. Profiles of the crater of Vesuvius since the 1906 eruption. After Imbo (1951).

March, 1944 →

← After March, 1944, eruption

← 1906

Plate 35. Vesuvius and the harbor of Naples.

are broken from the walls of the conduit or from the roof of the magma chamber and ejected, along with ash and pumice. Great numbers of such blocks are found among the tuffs of Mount Somma, and they can be identified on the basis of the contained fossils and lithologic characteristics.

Fragments of Tertiary rocks show little or no magmatic influence. Blocks of Cretaceous limestone are usually unaltered, or at most only recrystallized, indicating only a brief contact with the magma during their ascent in the conduit. In strong contrast, blocks of Triassic limestone are thoroughly altered, and frequently the entire rock has been metamorphosed to a silicate rock in which new minerals, largely lime silicates such as vesuvianite, have been developed. These rocks must have had a long-enduring contact with the magma, such as could take place only if they formed the roof of the magma chamber. Thus we can assume that the magma reservoir has reached the level of the Triassic rocks but has not reached the level of the overlying Cretaceous rocks (Fig. 31). Since the Triassic rocks crop out on the

Figure 30. Structure section of the Bay of Naples. After De Lorenzo (1906) and Signore (1937).

Sorrento Peninsula and their thickness and angle of dip are known, it is possible to estimate accurately their depth beneath Vesuvius. Rittmann (1933), who was among the first to work out this relationship, estimated that the top of the magma reservoir of Vesuvius is approximately 5 kilometers below sea level.

It was mentioned earlier that Vesuvius, after reaching a stage in which its eruptive history should have been approaching an end, was rejuvenated and began a new cycle. The reason for this change can now be made clear from the preceding discussion. It will be recalled that, in the initial stage of volcanic activity, basic lavas are usually erupted, and that these form plateaulike basements which underlie most volcanic areas, including Vesuvius. In time, due to magmatic differentiation, the magma progressively becomes more acidic, and in the final stage the eruptions consist mainly of ash and pumice. It is in this final stage that the cinder cone, surmounting the lava plateau, is built. Such was the condition of Vesuvius prior to A.D. 1036, when it began to pour out new flows of lava. Although for the next

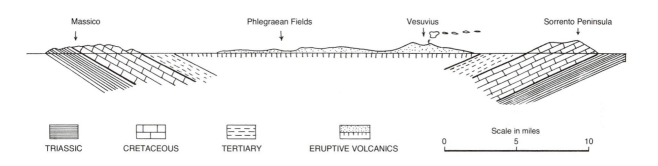

500 years the status of Vesuvius may have been open to question, the great floods of lava in the eruption of 1631 left no doubt that Vesuvius had embarked on a new type of activity.

The absorption of large quantities of limestone by the magma as it rose into the zone of the Triassic limestone would certainly have an effect on its composition. The added calcium would make the magma more basic, and this is doubtless the explanation for its "rejuvenation." This change in composition of a magma by the absorption of limestone has been described by Rittmann (1933) as "magmatic-sclerosis." Many of the volcanoes in the Mediterranean area, in addition to Vesuvius, have erupted lavas (and other products) which indicate that the magmas have absorbed large quantities of limestone. These lavas, with a composition distinct from the usual Pacific or Atlantic types, are placed in a special category known as the "Mediterranean" type.

The classic limestone-assimilation hypothesis, described above, to account for alkalic lavas has been a point of controversy for a number

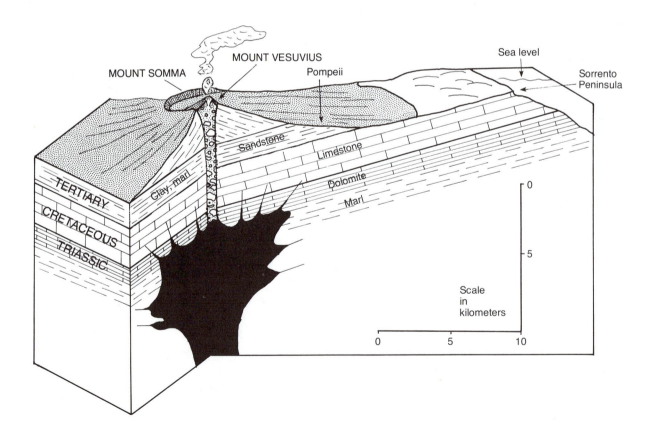

of years. It is particularly unsatisfactory in areas in which no significant amount of limestone exists in the bedrock to be assimilated. Arthur Holmes (1950), with good evidence, proposed that rocks of this type were formed by reaction between carbonatite magma (magma rich in carbonates) and granitic rocks of the sial. Thus Holmes has turned the limestone-assimilation hypothesis upside down. Instead of a silicate magma assimilating limestone to produce alkalic magma, he suggests that a carbonatite magma assimilates granite.

The well-documented record of the activity of Vesuvius through the ages has provided much information on which some of the basic concepts of volcanism are founded. Its future activity will be watched closely by scientists in order to verify some of the current theories concerning volcanic activity and to obtain possible clues to the problems of volcanology.

VULCANO

The Vulcanian type of eruption was named for the volcano Vulcano, which from ancient times until late in the nineteenth century was one of the most active volcanoes in the Mediterranean region. Its most recent eruption was in 1888–1890. However, under existing conditions, Mount Vesuvius is perhaps a better example of the Vulcanian type of eruption. But even though other volcanoes may now be better examples of this kind of eruption, the type is still called after Vulcano. Vulcano is one of two volcanoes in the Aeolian Islands which have given their names to types of volcanic eruption, the second one being Stromboli. A description of these islands, noted for their volcanic activity, will assist in the understanding of Vulcano as an example of the Vulcanian type of eruption, as well as of other volcanoes.

The Aeolian Islands

The Aeolian Islands lie in the Tyrrhenian Sea between the toe of Italy and Sicily. About 25 miles off the northern coast of Sicily, for governmental purposes they fall within the province of Messina, Sicily. The islands are known also as the Lipari Islands, from the largest island in the group. However, the Italian name Isole Eolie, or the English equivalent, Aeolian, is a name which has been used since ancient times.

The islands were frequently mentioned in classical mythology as the home of Eoius, God of Wind, and they were twice visited by Ulysses in his wanderings. According to one version, Eolus was a Greek prince ruling a colony on the islands. Being a shrewd man, he acquired some fame by his success in predicting the weather from the nature of the vapor cloud over an active volcano, believed to have

*Figure 32. Larderello steam
area, Italian volcanoes, and
major structural trends.*

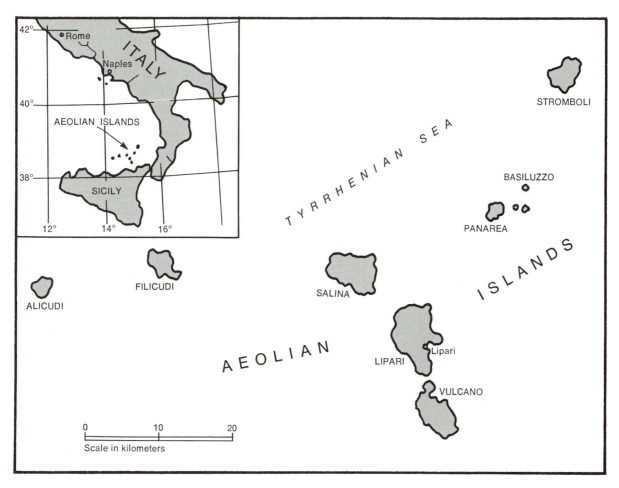

Figure 33. Aeolian Islands.

been Stromboli. The people were fishermen, and the weather was an important element in their daily lives. The power of forecasting events is often confused with that of bringing them to pass; and the prophets of one generation frequently become the gods of the next. Hence, it is not surprising to find Eolus in later mythologies referred to as the god of wind. Stromboli is still believed by the inhabitants, not without some justification, to respond like a barometer to changes in atmospheric pressure, and the density of the vapor column rising from the crater faithfully reflects the moisture content of the air. A native of Stromboli will look up at the vapor column rising from the crater and confidently predict the weather for the next day! In any case, after experiencing some of the sudden and fierce storms which sweep the surrounding sea and being stranded on Stromboli for two weeks by a storm, it is understandable to me that in Greek mythology the area is the home of Eolus, God of Wind.

The Aeolian Islands consist of seven inhabited islands and a number of uninhabited rocks, all of volcanic origin. The largest and most populous island is Lipari, with an area of 14.5 square miles. The highest peak on Lipari is 1,975 feet above sea level. The other inhabited islands, with the area and the highest point of each, are Stromboli—area 5 square miles, elevation 3,040 feet; Panarea—area 1.24 square miles, elevation 1,381 feet; Salina—area 10.25 square miles, elevation 3,155 feet; Vulcano—area 8 square miles, elevation 1,637 feet; Filicudi—area 3.75 square miles, elevation 2,542 feet; and Alicudi—area 2 square miles, elevation 2,185 feet. The islands rise from a depth of around 7,000 feet below sea level to a maximum height on Salina of 3,155 feet above sea level. Thus, only the top third of Salina is exposed above the sea, and on some of the other islands the ratio of exposed height to submerged depth is even less.

The volcanoes of Italy, in general, are located along a trend which parallels the Apennine Mountains and the Tyrrhenian coast. The uplift of the Apennines in mid-Tertiary time, in common with that of the Alps, was accompanied by a subsidence of the Tyrrhenian basin, and the volcanoes of Italy, with the exception of Mount Vulture and Mount Etna, are at the juncture of the depressed area and the upstanding block. Beginning in the vicinity of Siena, in northern Italy, and extending southward through Rome and on to Naples, volcanic centers are more or less evenly spaced along this trend. The Apennine Mountains, which make up the backbone of Italy, extend the length of Italy, through Sicily, and are continued in the Atlas Mountains of North Africa. This trend of folding, the general position of the major fracture lines, and the volcanic centers are shown on Figure 32. It will be observed that the Aeolian Islands are located in the sharply curved portion of the belt. The arrangement of the islands in a three-prong, starlike pattern (see Fig. 33) has prompted several writers to propose radiating fractures, with activity beginning at the center and progressing outward along radii. It is true that the only active vents, Stromboli and Vulcano, are at the opposite ends of two of the radii, but this relationship may be more apparent than real. Reference has already been made to the subsidence of the Tyrrhenian basin, which doubtless was broken into a series of blocks parallel to the edge of the basin, conforming with the trend of the Apennines. In many volcanic regions the location of vents is determined by fractures which intersect subsiding blocks at almost right angles. This is probably the case in the Aeolians. If so, the various islands may be not on a continuous fracture but on separate fractures, each of which intersects a subsiding block of the earth's crust.

With the exception of Panarea, which is probably only the remnant of a former cone, all the islands contain cones with well-marked craters. Filicudi, Alicudi, and Stromboli are each single cones, while Salina consists of twin cones. Lipari and Vulcano are more complex, each consisting of the ruins of several intersecting cones. Only Vulcano and Stromboli have erupted during recorded history, and these two are still active today.

Vulcano lies directly to the south of Lipari, a channel less than a mile in width separating the two islands (Fig. 34). However, the trip from the town of Lipari, where boats are obtained, to the landing point on Vulcano, Porto di Levante, is about 4 miles. Good views of Vulcano can be obtained from almost any high point on Lipari. A favorite spot of mine is that from Quattr'ochi, about 1.8 miles to the northwest of the town of Lipari, where the view of Vulcano is unobstructed and where on a clear day Mount Etna, a hundred miles distant on Sicily, can be seen in the background.

The central part of the island of Lipari is occupied by Mont Sant' Angelo (1,952 feet), with a great axial crater and several small cones on its western flank. Judd (1875) considered Mont Sant'Angelo to be the product of what he termed the second period of volcanic activity in the history of the islands. This period, during which most of the now exposed cones in the Aeolian Islands were formed, was characterized by lavas (trachytic type) and volcanic tuffs. The cones of Alicudi, Filicudi, and Salina and the central cone of Stromboli belong to this period. The first period of volcanic activity was, of course, largely submarine. Monte Pelato, better known as Campo Bianco (White Field), a volcanic cone composed entirely of pure white pumice, makes up the northeastern part of the island of Lipari. It is in part surrounded by the relic of a large cone (a somma ring) which culminates in Monte Chirica (1,975 feet), the highest point on the island. The steep walls of the crater of Campo Bianco are 400–600 feet high on all sides except the northeast, where it was breached by a stream of volcanic glass (obsidian) emerging from the crater in the

Figure 34. Lipari and Vul-
cano, Aeolian Islands.

final phase of activity. This half-mile-wide stream of glassy lava, extending as a cascade down the side of the cone and into the sea, is a striking sight. The flow, now covered with a reddish brown coating of iron oxide as a result of weathering, is known as Rocche Rosse (Red Rock). The regular inter-island steamers pass near the sea front of the obsidian flow, affording splendid views of this unique feature. (Pl. 37).

The pumice and ash deposits at Campo Bianco have long been famous and, before World War II, were the world's chief source of high-grade pumice and ash. Pumice is used as an abrasive, and ash is the chief constituent in many scouring powders. As a result of the interruption of shipping routes during the war, which made Lipari pumice unavailable, deposits in other parts of the world were developed, and Lipari has not been able to regain its former position in world markets. The ash and pumice which form the cone of Campo Bianco belong to the third and last period of volcanic activity in the Lipari area. Thus Campo Bianco conforms to the usual pattern, previously described, with lavas of basaltic or intermediate composition in the early stages (first and second periods of activity) and with ash and pumice eruptions and a dome of acidic lava filling the crater in the final stage. In the case of Campo Bianco, the obsidian flow represents the lava dome. The obsidian flow of Campo Bianco is well known to geologists because the material had been described as a separate rock type under the name of *liparite*.

The contrast of the blue waters of the Mediterranean and the snow-white cones of pumice, such as Campo Bianco, presents a most impressive view. Judd, in an outburst of almost poetic extravagance, describes the scene as follows: "Lofty cinder cones of snowy white pumice, their vast craters breached by lava streams of solid glass, seemingly fresh as when the fiery flood leaped from the volcano's throat, and poured with slow and tortuous current down its flanks; wide-spreading lava-fields, their horrid bristling surfaces coated by a reddish-brown crust, but exposing in grand cliff-sections the most marvellous combinations of variegated rocks;—these seen rising amidst the bright blue waters of the Mediterranean, and displayed in that clearness of outline and that vividness of colouring which only the brilliancy of an almost tropical sky can impart, constitute scenery of startling novelty and wondrous beauty—the impressions produced by which it is as hopeless to convey as it is impossible to forget" (1875, pp. 56–57).

Plate 36. Vulcano from Quattr'ochi on Lipari Island. See Plate 38 for the location of Quattr'ochi.

Vulcano in Mythology

In ancient mythologies Vulcano is identified as the location of the forge of Vulcan, the Roman god of fire. It was Herodotus (475 B.C.) who first mentioned Vulcano under the name Hiera, as the vent of the forge of Hepaestus, the Greek god of fire. Vulcan, the Latin equivalent, was the blacksmith of the gods, maker of the finest armor, the breastplate of Hercules, the shield of Achilles, as well as the arrows of Apollo and Diana. Vulcan's wife, according to the *Odyssey*, was Venus. The fire and smoke which came out of a volcano were believed to come from the forge. Later historians and geographers gave a more exact description of the phenomena displayed at Vulcano, and in time the name came to be applied to all mountains where similar activity occurred—thus it is the prototype of all volcanoes. It should be recalled that prior to A.D. 79, Vesuvius was inactive and in fact was not generally recognized as a volcano. However, Vulcano and Stromboli were frequently in eruption, and, since they were the only active volcanoes (other than Etna) with which the ancient Greeks and Romans were familiar, it is not surprising to find many myths and legends surrounding these islands.

Plate 37. Obsidian flow from the crater of Campo Bianco, Lipari Island.

Early History of Vulcano

Early accounts of the activity of Vulcano lead us to conclude that it was in a much more violent state of activity than has been the case in recent centuries. Its eruptions were also more explosive than those of either Stromboli or Etna. Judd (1875), in an article on Vulcano, which is one of a series on the Lipari Islands, traces the history of Vulcano from the earliest accounts to the eruption of 1873–1874. Judd acknowledges at the outset that, because of the association of Vulcano with mythology, it would be a hopeless task to separate fact from the legendary stories of the oldest classical writers. Nevertheless, the traditions associated with Vulcano offer proof that since ancient times Vulcano has had frequent and violent eruptions. The following account of the early and modern history of Vulcano, except as otherwise noted, is based on Judd (1875, pp. 99–115).

Thucydides, one of the most prominent of the early Greek historians, writing in the fifth century B.C., spoke of Vulcano as throwing out considerable smoke by day and flame by night. Aristotle (384–322 B.C.), writing about an eruption of Vulcano which was apparently in progress at the time, mentioned that a new hill was formed and

the quantity of ashes thrown out was so great as to cover the city of
Lipari, six miles away, and to extend to several of the towns of Italy.
Aristotle advocated "pent-up" winds imprisoned in subterranean
channels as a cause of earthquakes and volcanoes, an idea which
persisted for many centuries; it is discussed in Chapter 2. In the third
century B.C., Callias described Vulcano as having two craters, one of
which was 200 feet in circumference and threw out great stones with
a noise which could be heard for a distance of 50 miles. Pliny recorded that an island emerged from the sea among the Lipari Islands
early in the second century B.C., and later Grosius gave the date as
182 B.C. Apparently on the strength of these references and on the
assumption that the island was Vulcanello (once a separate island but
now part of Vulcano; see Fig. 35), the British Admiralty's Geographical Handbook gives the date for the birth of Vulcanello as about
183 B.C. (Great Britain, Naval Intelligence Division, 1945, p. 701).
Judd (1875), De Fiore (1922), and others have accepted this date for
the birth of Vulcanello. It is the one commonly found in the literature.

Recent studies attempting to trace the wanderings of Odysseus
(Ulysses) as narrated by Homer throw some doubt as to the accuracy
of 183 B.C. as the date of the birth of Vulcanello. The reader will recall
that in the *Odyssey* Homer describes the adventures of Odysseus,
King of Ithaca, in his journey home following the fall of Troy and the
end of the Trojan War. Classical scholars have long been divided as
to whether the places described are actual localities known to Homer
or whether they are entirely mythical. It is beyond the scope of this
volume to review this interesting topic. However, we are dependent
on the classics, especially the writings of Homer and Virgil, for much
of our information on the activity of the Mediterranean volcanoes in
ancient times, and the source of such information cannot be entirely
ignored. On the assumption that Homer was describing a region with
which he was familiar, it should be possible by a careful analysis of
his descriptions to detect clues which would identify the various
areas visited by Odysseus. One of the best-known as well as most
controversial works in this field is that by Samuel Butler (1897), who
concluded that the *Odyssey* had its origin at Trapani, Sicily, and was
written by a woman. A study by Professor L. G. Pocock of Canter-
bury University College, Christchurch, New Zealand, confirms in
part and rejects in part the conclusions reached by Butler as to the
route of Odysseus. A preliminary statement of Professor Pocock's
conclusions has been released in a 15-page pamphlet entitled *The
Landfalls of Odysseus* (1955) and later amplified and expanded in publications issued in 1957 and 1959. Professor Pocock makes a good case
for the argument that the islands described as Charybdis, Scylla, and
Planctae are Vulcanello (at that time still not joined to Vulcano), Vulcano, and Lipari, respectively. Charybdis is described by Homer as

not far from Planctae and within bow-shot of Scylla. If the *Odyssey* was written around 650 B.C., as Pocock (1959) maintains, and if Charybdis is Vulcanello, then the island described by Pliny as appearing in 183 B.C. must be some other island of the Aeolian group.

Regardless of the exact date at which Vulcanello appeared as an island, considerable volume was added by an eruption in 126 B.C., and by 91 B.C. sufficient debris had accumulated to form a platform surrounding it (De Fiore 1922). Confusion as to the date of its birth may arise from the fact that new volcanic cones which appear in the sea are frequently destroyed by wave action in a short time, only to reappear when a new eruption occurs. This may have happened several times before the cone attained enough volume to maintain itself against the attack of the waves, giving rise to conflicting dates as to its birth.

With the passing of the classical writers, the history of Vulcano again becomes nebulous. The inhabitants of the Lipari Islands suffered from the invasions of pirates and slave hunters and acquired a reputation for ferocity which caused the islands to be bypassed by mariners. The long period of obscurity during the Dark Ages is marked by a brief reference to Vulcano by Orosius in the fifth century, and another, perhaps legendary, account which appears in the biography of Saint Willebald, who is believed to have lived from A.D. 701 to A.D. 786. In his biography the following passage refers to Vulcano: "The Saint, [wished] to obtain a view of the boiling crater, called the inferno of Theodoric, but they could not climb the mountain from the depth of ashes and scoria, so they contented themselves with a view of the flames, as they rose with a roaring like thunder, and the vast column of smoke ascended from the pit" (quoted by Judd 1875, p. 101).

Modern History of Vulcano

The modern history of Vulcano, as reported by Judd (1875), begins with accounts by Frazello, a native of Sicily, who described the great eruption of February 4, 1444, which shook all of Sicily and was felt as far away as Naples. Judd attributes to Frazello the statement that the sea "boiled" all around the island and that vast rocks were discharged into it. Submarine eruptions were indicated by reports that smoke was rising from the waves at a number of points. Following the eruption, navigation around the island was totally changed because of the presence of many new rocks. Frazello later visited Vulcano and reported that Vulcanello was still a separate island, with a narrow channel between it and Vulcano. In 1727, M. d'Orville, after a visit to Vulcano, reported that it had two active vents and that the noise of the almost continuous explosions was so loud at Lipari, six miles away, that he could not sleep the whole night. At the time of Spallanzani's first visit to Vulcano, some 60 years later, only one crater existed. When and how the two craters were destroyed and a single cone formed is not recorded, although from the diary of Abbe Ignacio, published in 1761 by Signor Don Salvatore, we learn that between 1730 and 1740 Vulcano was in an almost constant state of eruption. In 1768, Sir William Hamilton, in passing near Vulcano by ship, observed the gas column rising from the crater and compared the activity to that of the Solfatara at Naples. Other travelers in the area in 1770 reported no "glow" over Vulcano at night; so it appears that this was a period of quiet. The repose was of short duration, for an eruption was reported in 1771 and another in 1775. The latter, according to Dolomieu, produced a large flow of obsidian on the north side of the cone. In 1786 a violent eruption, accompanied by subterranean roaring which could be heard over all the islands, threw out enormous quantities of cinders and incandescent rocks. The eruption lasted 15 days. When Spallanzani visited Vulcano two years after this eruption the terror among the inhabitants was so great that he could not induce any of them to accompany him to the crater. From Spallanzani's description, Judd concludes that no essential change in the crater took place until the eruption of 1873–1874.

The southern part of the island had been inhabited and under cultivation since ancient times, but the severe eruptions of the eighteenth century appear to have driven the inhabitants away, leaving it totally uninhabited. Following the great eruption of 1786, Vulcano was in a state of repose to such an extent that some writers, until activity was renewed in September, 1873, referred to it as extinct. During the 1873 eruption, which lasted intermittently for about 18 months, rumblings were heard in Lipari, several fissures opened on the floor of the crater, and dense columns of vapor, accompanied by some stones, were discharged. Needless to say, the sulphur-mining operation which was under way in the crater was seriously hampered.

The next eruption of Vulcano, and the most recent, began on August 3, 1888, and continued until May 17, 1890. An account of the eruption is given in English by Johnston-Lavis (1888–1890), but the report by an Italian commission provides the most complete record (Mercalli et al. 1891). The commission, as originally established, consisted of Professor O. Silvestri (Catania) as president, Professor G. Mercalli (Milan), Professor Grablovitz (Seismological Observatory of Ischia), and V. Clerici (Messina) as engineer, with A. Cerati, Professor Ponte, and A. Silvestri as assistants. Professor Silvestri died before the publication of the report but not until some months after the eruptions ceased. After his death, Professor Mercalli, the largest contributor to the report, completed it.

During the eruption strong explosions were accompanied by a dense eruption cloud which spread ash and cinders over a wide area. Most observers commented on the whiteness of the ash, comparing it to snow. Masses of pumice, breadcrust bombs, and incandescent rocks were scattered over the cone and the immediate surroundings. The explosions, which broke windows in the town of Lipari six miles away, occurred at intervals of a few minutes during the most violent periods. The strongest explosions usually followed a period of repose. Especially strong explosions were reported on August 4, 1888; December 26, 1889; and March 15, 1890. Some of the bombs were unusually large. One believed to have been ejected on March 15, 1890, in one of the last outbursts of the eruption, measured nine feet by six feet by six feet. It was a mass of older lava coated with a four-inch crust of new obsidian. Many of the bombs ejected in this eruption contained cores of older lava. No lava flows were produced, but bright "glows" over the crater following explosions indicated the presence of incandescent material. Analysis of the material ejected indicated a silica content of 62–67 percent.

A submarine cable connects Lipari with Milazzo in Sicily. This cable runs about three miles to the east of Vulcano, where the water is 2,300–3,280 feet in depth. During the eruption the cable was broken five times. The first break occurred on November 22, 1888, and the last on December 14, 1892, nearly 18 months after activity had ceased in the crater of Vulcano. At the point of the break, usually, a violent boiling of the sea occurred, and pumice or scoria appeared either on the bottom or floating near the location of the break. Without doubt the breaks marked points of eruption on the submerged flank of Vulcano. The positions of the breaks, which followed a definite alignment, are shown in Figure 34. After the eruption of 1888–1890, Vulcano lapsed into a state of mild solfataric activity which, with some fluctuations in volume, has continued to the present time.

The Cones of Vulcano

During historic times, with the exception of the eruptions which formed Vulcanello, the activity has occurred in the crater of a broadly truncated, symmetrical cone which stands more or less isolated in the northern part of the island. The cone, frequently called Gran Cone, rises to a height of 1,266 feet. Gran Cone is encircled on the south and to some extent on the west by remnants (sommas) of earlier cones. All investigators, even from the earliest times, have recognized at least

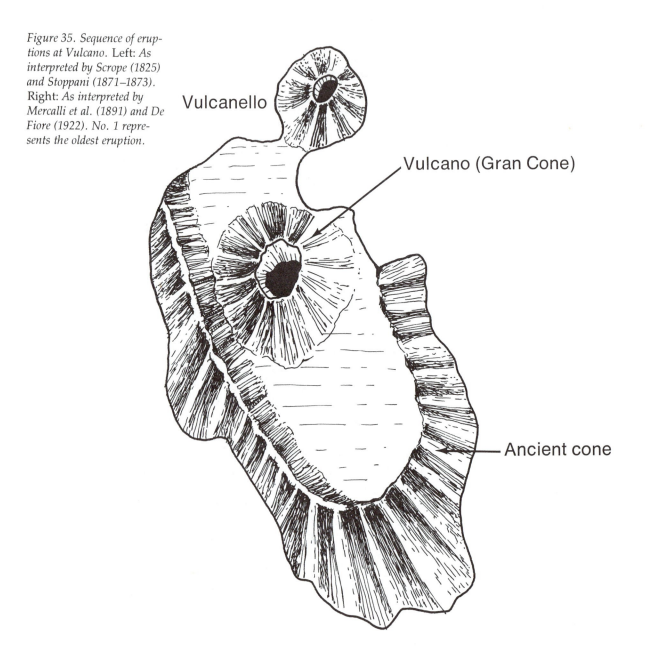

Figure 35. Sequence of eruptions at Vulcano. Left: *As interpreted by Scrope (1825) and Stoppani (1871–1873).* Right: *As interpreted by Mercalli et al. (1891) and De Fiore (1922). No. 1 represents the oldest eruption.*

Vulcanello

Vulcano (Gran Cone)

Ancient cone

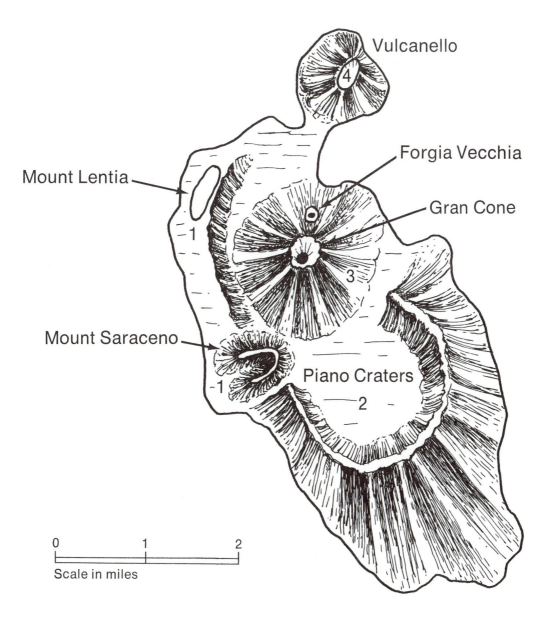

Vulcanello

Forgia Vecchia

Gran Cone

Mount Lentia

Mount Saraceno

Piano Craters

0   1   2

Scale in miles

three stages in the history of Vulcano, marked by the progressive migration of the eruptive centers northward (Fig. 35, left side). Mercalli (1891) and De Fiore (1922) believed that four stages can be identified (Fig. 35, right side). The oldest part is a rocky mass directly to the west of Gran Cone known as Mount Lentia. The cone of which Mount Lentia is the western edge may have had its center near that of the present active cone. The second center of activity was to the south of Gran Cone. Here were many eruptive centers, referred to collectively as the Piano Craters. (*Piano* is an Italian word meaning a "level plain" or "floor." Here it means that the craters rise from a relatively flat surface.) The area then collapsed, leaving a huge caldera, of which the south rim was formed by remnants of several of the Piano Craters and the west rim by Mount Lentia. Mount Saraceno, the most recent of the Piano Craters, remained active for a brief time after the subsidence. The sea doubtless flooded the collapsed area and washed against the steep sides of the surrounding rim, until the formation of Gran Cone, which has been in essentially its present condition throughout historic time.

The main crater, which occupies an eccentric position, is roughly circular, with a diameter of about one-fourth mile at the top and about one-half that at the bottom. The walls of the crater, which rise from 400 to 600 feet, are vertical in the lower part but open out into a funnel shape in the upper part. It appears that the bottom of the crater has subsided since the last eruption. When I visited Vulcano in December, 1952, many fumaroles were active on the north side of the crater walls, but none were present on the crater floor. Abundant deposits of sulphur were being formed around the more active vents. The composition of the gases from the main crater, as reported by L. Sicardi (1940), is as follows:

CO_2	55.0–69.0 percent
SO_2	6.0–21.0 percent
H_2S	11.0–20.0 percent
HCl	1.5– 1.7 percent
N	1.9– 2.7 percent

The reported range in temperature was from 99° C. to 480° C. Along the shore at Porto di Levante were several spots, both on the beach and a short distance offshore, where, because of vigorous agitation due to the escape of carbon dioxide, the water appeared to be "boiling."

Sicardi showed that a marked increase in fumarolic activity, both in the temperature as well as in the number of fumaroles, developed around 1924. Maximum temperatures in excess of 600° C. were reported from vents in the main crater, where previously the temperature had been only slightly in excess of 100° C. Although no eruptive activity occurred at this time, such a marked rise in temperature indicated the possibility of an outbreak. Sulphur had been obtained from the crater in small quantities since ancient times. Shortly after the middle of the nineteenth century a Scottish firm obtained a concession on the crater and installed a fairly extensive chemical works, which was, of course, destroyed in the eruption of 1873. Sulphur has also been obtained from the ruins of an old crater near the shore at Porto di Levante. But all sulphur operations at Vulcano were abandoned many years ago.

About halfway down the slope on the north side of Gran Cone is the small compound crater known as Forgia Vecchia, which De Fiore believed was formed early in the eighteenth century.

At the extreme north tip of the island is the cone of Vulcanello, the date of origin of which has already been discussed. It was a separate

Quattr'ochi   City of Lipari   Vulcanello

island for many centuries and was joined to Vulcano in 1550 by an accumulation of ash. Three small craters occupy the summit of Vulcanello. Waves have cut into the east side of Vulcanello, opening one of the craters into the sea and affording a striking cross section of the cone.

Vulcano's Contributions to Volcanology

Vulcano was the source of the name *volcano*, as has been already pointed out, and this in itself is sufficient to give it a leading place in volcanology. However, its chief contribution has been in serving as one of the types in the classification of volcanoes. It was in 1891, in the report of the commission appointed by the Italian government to study the 1888–1890 eruption of Vulcano, that Mercalli first defined the *Vulcanian type* of eruption. The terms *Plinian* and *Vesuvian*, as well as *Strombolian*, had previously been applied descriptively to types of eruptions, but since Vulcano did not fit the pattern of any of these, a new category was needed. As originally defined by Mercalli, the Vulcanian type was characterized only by the explosive removal of the crater plug and the discharge of bombs and scoria, accompanied by a dark, ash-filled eruption cloud. In this respect it resembled the initial outburst of the Vesuvian (Plinian) type. No lava streams were produced, and only minor earthquakes accompanied the eruption. The characteristics of the Vulcanian type, as set forth by Mercalli, were based, of course, on the 1888–1890 eruption of Vulcano. In this eruption the material discharged during the first 3 days consisted mainly of the old material blocking the crater. After an interval of 13 days the second main period of eruption began, and thereafter the products of the eruption consisted chiefly of new material in the form of ash, breadcrust bombs, and scoria. The term *Vulcanian* was later used by other Italian writers and was incorporated into the classification of volcanoes as one of the major types. However, as the term is now used, Vesuvius is a better example of the Vulcanian type than Vulcano. As originally used by Mercalli, the term *Vulcanian* was restricted to those eruptions in which the crater obstruction was removed but no lava flows developed. A typical eruption at Vesuvius begins, like those at Vulcano, with the explosive removal of the crater plug, but then, unlike Vulcano, there are extensive outpourings of lava. In the explosive removal of the crater obstruction, huge quantities of ash are produced, as the material is shattered by repeated explosions. This produces a dark eruption cloud heavily charged with ash, which is one of the characteristics of the Vulcanian type of eruption. If there is no outflow of lava, the eruption is of the Vulcanian type as originally defined by Mercalli. However, since lava flows commonly occur, the Vulcanian type has been expanded to include such eruptions. It is perhaps unfortunate that Mercalli's original use of *Vulcanian* was not preserved and another type and term introduced to include the eruptions exhibited by Vesuvius. In its broader application, Vulcanian type eruptions are perhaps the most common type among the volcanoes of the world. An example of a recent eruption is Parícutin Volcano, Mexico, which is described in detail in Chapter 13. Eruptions which fall within Mercalli's original usage of the term are less common, but Lassen Peak, California, is an example (see Chapter 19).

Chapter 9 The Strombolian Type of Volcanic Eruption

One might have thought that Nature lived hard by and was brewing on a large scale.—DICKENS

The Strombolian type of eruption was introduced into the literature by Mercalli and subsequently adopted as one of the major types in the classification of volcanoes. The essential characteristics of a Strombolian eruption are the throwing out of incandescent fragments of lava accompanied by a white eruption cloud. The white color indicates that, in contrast to the Vulcanian eruption cloud, which is heavily charged with ash and hence dark in color, the Strombolian cloud contains little ash. The lava column crusts over lightly, and at frequent intervals mild explosions break the crust, hurling the pasty, incandescent fragments into the air.

Significance of Stromboli

Stromboli occupies an important place in the study of volcanoes. It is one of the few volcanoes in the world which is in a state of permanent moderate activity. Records indicate that it has been essentially in its present condition since earliest times. Because of its convenient location and constant state of activity, Stromboli has been visited by many persons interested in volcanoes, and there are many reports on its activity. Further, it was the "observations made by Spallanzani at Stromboli in 1788 which first exhibited the true nature of volcanic action" (Scrope 1872, p. 31). In addition Stromboli was selected as the type example of one of the major divisions in the classification of volcanoes, to which it has given its name. It is apparent, therefore, that there are several reasons for including a description of Stromboli in this volume.

Appearance of Stromboli

Stromboli, the most northerly of the Aeolian Islands, is an almost perfect cone-shaped mass, with twin peaks, emerging directly out of the sea to a height of 3,040 feet (about 927 m.). Rising from the floor of the Mediterranean in water 6,660 feet (2,030 m.) in depth, Stromboli stands above its submarine base at a total height of 9,700 feet (2,957 m.), which exceeds the 9,425-foot (2,873 m.) elevation of Mount Etna above its sedimentary plaform (which is some 1,200 ft. above sea level). Thus Stromboli may well be, as Professor Ponte has maintained, the "highest active volcano in Europe" (1952, p. 3). Near sea level on the eastern and western sides of the island, on rocky benches formed by lava flows, are the villages of San Vincenzo and Ginostra, where most of the 800 inhabitants of the island live. The twin peaks forming the summit of Stromboli are remnants of the rim of an ancient crater. On a terrace about 600 feet below the most northerly of the two peaks is the active crater of Stromboli. Thus, from the summit one has an unobstructed view into the active crater below. Although it requires a strenuous climb of about three hours to reach this favorable spot, the view into the crater is well worth the effort. Scrope, who visited Stromboli in the early half of the nineteenth century, in commenting on the view from this position says: "We are there, indeed admitted almost into the recesses of Nature's laboratory, comparatively open to near inspection at all seasons, without risk, since the explosions which characterize this phase rarely exceed an average ratio, and the crater can consequently be approached and its interior viewed at leisure with complete impunity" (1872, p. 31). The crater, which is described more fully in a later paragraph, is an oval-shaped basin, filled in part with lava and blocks which have avalanched from the sides. On the mountain side, the

Plate 39. Stromboli Volcano.

crater is bordered by vertical walls, but on the seaward side it merges into a long, smooth slope called the Sciara del Fuoco (Ski of Fire), which extends from the crater to the sea (Pl. 40). Practically all the material ejected from the crater, other than that which falls back into it, rolls down the Sciara del Fuoco. Lava flows also emerge from the crater from time to time and cascade down the Sciara and into the sea.

The Sciara del Fuoco is a unique feature, and many observers have speculated upon its origin. One of the first as well as one of the simplest explanations was advanced by Scrope (1872), who held that an explosion blew away a large segment of the cone and the resulting depression was gradually filled with debris in the nature of a talus slope, forming the Sciara del Fuoco. The eccentric position of the present crater, at the head of the Sciara, would seem to support this explanation. However, this idea was discarded by later workers, notwithstanding its simplicity, largely because of the fact that on the sea floor along the northwest side of the Aeolian Islands is a sharp, almost clifflike slope which becomes steeper near the Sciara del Fuoco than elsewhere. It does not appear to me that this necessarily precludes the possibility that the cone of Stromboli was ruptured by an

Figure 36. Relative sizes of Vesuvius, Stromboli, and Etna.

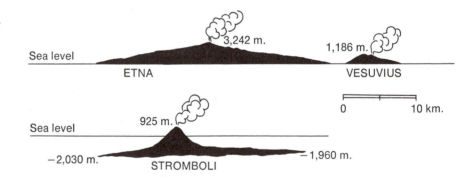

Plate 40. Stromboli and Sciara del Fuoco.

explosion, but it does offer the alternative of rupture by faulting or by avalanching from the precipitous slope. Williams (1941a) accounts for the Sciara del Fuoco by collapse and uses it as an example of what he terms a "sector graben."

Eruptive Activity of Stromboli

Although Stromboli is mentioned less frequently by ancient writers than Vulcano, it is referred to in the writings of Aristotle, Diodorus Siculus, Strabo, and others. Most remarkable, perhaps, is the description in the first century of the Christian era by Pliny the Elder, who described it in terms still applicable today (*Nat. Hist.*, bk. 3, sec. 9). The ancient name for the island was Strongyle, a name which is still used by some of the local inhabitants and which referred to the circular form. Stromboli has been known since ancient times as the "Lighthouse of the Mediterranean" because of the red glow which flashes from its summit after each explosion. The red glow, reflected on the clouds above the crater, quickly fades, only to reappear in

Plate 40. Stromboli and Sciara del Fuoco.

15–30 minutes, when the next explosion occurs. The often-described activity of Stromboli, while differing from day to day, follows the same general pattern. Spallanzani, one of the early Italian scientists interested in volcanoes, visited Stromboli in 1788 and described the eruption as follows:

> On the western side a large number of fumaroles were discharging steam, while deposits of yellow salts were forming around the openings; on the eastern side one large orifice poured out a continuous column of vapor about 12 feet in diameter. In the center there was a funnel-shaped tube which contained liquid lava. This incandescent mass was agitated, rising and falling in the tube—the vertical motion a maximum of 20 feet, sometimes slow, other times fast. On reaching a certain height, large bubbles were seen to collect and these bursting with a sharp report carried innumerable fragments in a fiery shower into the air. The lava would then sink in the tube and begin to rise again. (Quoted by Judd 1875, p. 148)

Spallanzani mentioned that the explosions were at intervals of 2–3 minutes, but with varying degrees of intensity.

In 1831 and early 1832, Friedrich Hoffman spent several weeks at Stromboli. He described the eruptions as follows:

> The largest opening occupied the center of the crater floor and gave forth vapors only, which produced yellow crusts on its sides. To the southwest, nearly under the crater wall, another mouth about 20 feet in diameter was seen. In the glowing red throat of this chimney, a fluid column of lava could be seen rising and falling, perhaps 20 to 30 feet. Through this column of lava bubbles of steam burst, the puffs taking place regularly at intervals of about a second giving rise to globes of vapor, which carried up bladders of lava. This action continued for more than 15 minutes, then suddenly a louder explosion followed by the violent escape of steam from the opening carrying thousands of fragments of glowing lava to great height. Where the crater joins the steep slope of the Sciara, a third and much smaller opening was seen, from which a small stream of lava, like a perennial fountain, flowed down the Sciara towards the sea, which, however, it did not reach, becoming solid before it arrived at the bottom; some portions of the congealed mass were becoming detached and rolling down into the water. (Quoted by Judd 1875, p. 151)

The aspect of the crater, as observed on three separate visits in 1952, is shown in the accompanying sketch (Fig. 37). The left end, in the sketch, was so deep and the walls so steep that it was not possible to see the bottom of the crater from the observation point on the summit. The floor of the crater, which had a diameter of about 400 feet, was covered with recent lava, doubtless partly the product of the June, 1952, lava flow. The two most active vents were at the east and west ends of the crater terrace with a smaller vent nearer the center. The east vent, near the edge of the Sciara del Fuoco, was an oval-shaped opening about 30–40 feet in diameter from which a grayish gas issued. At intervals, a dense white, cauliflower-shaped cloud of steam poured from this vent. There was no noise accompanying the emissions. The west vent was the most active of the three, sending out a vapor cloud, with a distinct chlorine odor, which frequently filled the entire crater. It was accompanied by a continuous roar, which may be compared to the sound of the steam exhaust from a locomotive, but with an irregular rhythm. Then at intervals of 15–20 minutes a tremendous outrush of gas (not an explosion but a "rushing" sound like that of many rockets being discharged simultaneously) carried incandescent fragments of lava to a height of 500–1,000 feet above the crater floor. Following a discharge, the crater would clear momentarily of steam, permitting a view which otherwise was obscured by the steam column. The central vent could not be seen from the observation point, but a gas column rising at irregular intervals from this point was proof of its existence. With the excep-

Figure 37. Crater of Stromboli on June 21, 1952. Sketched from a photograph (Bullard 1954c).

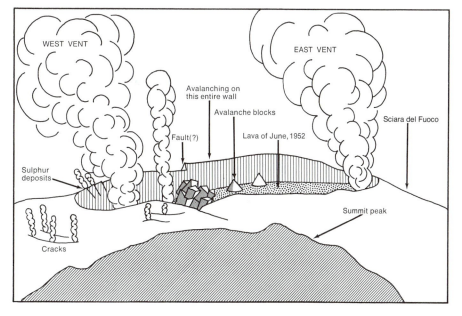

tion that the lava column was not visible, the eruption was essentially the same as that described by Hoffman 125 years earlier. A stream of lava had issued from the crater and poured down the Sciara del Fuoco and into the sea shortly before my first visit to Stromboli. It is probable that this outpouring of lava reduced the lava level in the crater to the extent that it was no longer visible from the observation point. The fact that lava was present is indicated by the incandescent slag which was thrown up with each explosion.

The persistence of the three vents within the crater of Stromboli is one of the puzzling features of this volcano. The normal pattern is for vents to shift from time to time rather than to maintain their positions. Sir William Hamilton, in 1768, reviewed all earlier reports and concluded that the three vents then present had persisted for at least 150 years (see Hamilton 1776). In relation to this repeatedly discussed problem, it is of interest to note that my observations show that three vents are still active today, in much the same position as described by previous investigators. Perret (1907) thought that they represented diverging outlets from a single conduit, but the lack of synchronous activity in the vents invalidates this explanation. Since the vents have persisted for a considerable period of time, it must be concluded that they are deep-seated channelways along which the gases from the underlying magma are reaching the surface. H. S. Washington (1917) reviewed the problem and concluded that the persistence of the vents is to be explained by Daly's "gas-fluxing" hypothesis. It is not possible to go into this controversial topic further than to say that it is based on the idea that gases rising from the magma would collect in pockets (cupolas) at the top of the chamber. The highly heated gas would react with the wall rock and, in a process described as "gas-fluxing," would melt ("blowpipe") its way to the surface, forming the vents now present in the crater.

In recent years more detailed studies of Stromboli have shown that the so-called "normal" Strombolian activity is interrupted at intervals by more vigorous eruptions, which are comparable to those of the Vulcanian type. It is also becoming more apparent that lava flows are far more common at Stromboli than was formerly believed to be the case. These eruptions are accompanied by violent explosions which shake the entire island and during which a dark eruption cloud, a pino, rises over the crater and spreads red-hot scoria, lapilli, and cinders over the island, forcing the inhabitants to seek shelter indoors to escape the falling debris. Fortunately, the rim of the old crater, which now forms the observation point on the summit, serves as a shield to protect the two villages on the island from the full fury of the eruptions. Nevertheless, the eruptions cause considerable damage, and occasionally lives are lost. Lava flows usually develop on the Sciara del Fuoco, and frequently one or more streams will reach the sea. Infrequent observations of Stromboli, particularly prior to the present century, make it impossible even to catalog the violent eruptions. In a tabulation of the violent eruptions of Stromboli by Imbo (1965b, pp. 29–30), an increase in the frequency of outpourings of lava in recent years is apparent. In the period from 1558 to 1900, outpourings of lava are listed for only 3 years, namely 1768, 1882, and 1889. In contrast, outpouring of lava, accompanied by violent eruptions, occurred in 1907, 1930, 1936, 1941, 1943, 1949, 1950, and 1952. In addition, lava flows without strong explosive activity occurred in 1954 and 1956. Although Imbo acknowledges that the record of eruptions for the early years is doubtless incomplete, it does appear that the frequency of lava flows from Stromboli has increased markedly in recent years.

The lava from Stromboli is basic in character (50–51% silica) and is classified as a basalt. As long as the lava column is kept open by frequent explosions, normal activity prevails. If the vent becomes clogged, then more vigorous explosions are required to remove the obstruction. Such explosions pulverize the material and therefore result in a dark, ash-filled cloud. Eruptions of this kind, even though they occur at Stromboli, are properly classified as Vulcanian in type.

Small but well-formed augite crystals are exceedingly abundant in the ash and cinders making up the cone of Stromboli. Augite is one of the early minerals to crystallize from a basaltic magma, and apparently the augite stage has been reached at Stromboli. As the lava is shattered by the explosions the augite crystals are deposited along with the resulting ash and cinders.

Varying theories as to Stromboli's continuing state of activity have been advanced. Some geologists believe that this peculiarity is related to the Sciara del Fuoco, the position of which causes most of the ejected material to roll into the sea, rather than falling back into the crater and clogging the conduit. Without this accumulation of debris, which would stop activity until enough pressure develops to remove the obstruction, Stromboli continues its more or less regular eruptions. It may be argued that volcanic orifices become clogged *because* the eruptive force is exhausted or "peters out" and that this is the result rather than the cause of the end of an eruption. Whatever the explanation, Stromboli is almost unique among the volcanoes of the world in that it has been in an almost constant state of activity for more than 2,500 years.

In most volcanoes, eruptions, particularly lava flows, frequently develop on the flanks of the main cone. This is strikingly shown on Mount Etna, where more than 200 eruptive centers occur on the flanks of the mountain. At Stromboli two-thirds of the cone is submerged, and it is not known how many eruptions or lava flows have occurred on the submerged flanks, or even when one is in progress.

One of the problems posed by the classification of volcanoes is well illustrated by Stromboli. It is apparent from the foregoing description that the eruptions of Stromboli show considerable variation and that they do not always conform to the so-called Strombolian type. Rather, Stromboli has a Strombolian phase, a Vulcanian phase, and sometimes, when no activity is in progress, a solfataric phase. Similarly, many volcanoes may exhibit characteristics of more than one type, even in a single eruption. For many years, because of the selection of Stromboli as a type in the classification of volcanoes, it was believed that it had a constant, uninterrupted activity consisting of a series of rhythmic explosions in which pasty material was ejected and that it did not have outpourings of lava. This, of course, is far from true, but the idea is still widely held because of the terminology of the classification.

A Visit to Stromboli

Soon after my return from Stromboli, I prepared an article describing the visit for the *Alcalde*, a local magazine. Entitled "Stromboli, Lighthouse of the Mediterranean" (Bullard 1954*d*), it presents some of the details of the trip as well as conditions on the island. It is reproduced below with a few excisions and small editorial changes in the text:

> On my first of three trips to Stromboli, my wife and I boarded the steamer *Eolo* at Naples at 6:30 P.M. on Friday, June 20, 1952. . . .
>
> About daybreak of the next morning, the perfect cone-shaped outline of Stromboli appeared on the horizon. No "red" glare could be seen, but a prominent column of white vapor was rising from the crater, and at infrequent intervals a denser cloud of yellowish brown gas was emitted. As the boat steamed around the edge of Stromboli, the big "scar" on the slope, known as Sciara del Fuoco, stood out prominently. This remarkable feature, with a slope of 35° and a width of about three-quarters of a mile, is like a tremendous talus slope and extends from the crater to the sea, a distance of about 4,000 feet. Much of the material, including lava flows ejected from the crater, lands on the Sciara del Fuoco and rolls directly into the sea. The origin of the Sciara del Fuoco is uncertain, but it appears to represent a great depression formed by an eruption which destroyed one side of the cone. The accumulation of debris in the depression has built up the present talus-like slope. The crater of Stromboli is on a terrace at the top of the Sciara del Fuoco, about 600 feet below the summit peak.

As Stromboli has no harbor facilities, the steamer anchored some distance from shore, and small boats came out to pick up the passengers and freight. The landing was made at the little village of San Vincenzo on the east side of Stromboli. Its white-washed houses stand out in sharp contrast against the black sand beach and the deep blue water of the Mediterranean. As our rowboat landed on the beach, a group of small boys scrambled for the baggage and endeavored to take us to the hotel of their choice.

On Stromboli are no automobiles, no electricity, no radios, no donkeys, in fact, not even a dog. With several small boys carrying our baggage, we picked our way across a beach strewn with boulders of lava, and followed a narrow winding street to the hotel, Locando Miramare. The Locando is built of thick blocks of lava, and even the roof is of stone. The thick stone walls keep out the sun, making the inside pleasantly cool. The hotel room was primitive, with pitcher and bowl and an oil lamp, but the sheets were clean and the air pleasant. There is no water on Stromboli, except rain water which is caught from the roofs of the buildings and stored in cisterns. Thus, during the dry summer months, water is at a premium. . . .

After we were settled in our quarters, I arranged with a local guide, Signor Salvatore Di Lose, to climb with me to the summit the next morning. In the summer the midday sun is quite hot; so we decided to leave at 4:00 A.M. in order to reach the summit while it was still cool. When Salvatore knocked on my door the next morning the sky was already showing some color in the east, and it was light enough to walk without difficulty. The barefooted guide carried my pack, which contained three cameras (movie, color, and black-and-white), notebook, water, and some lunch. As we walked through the town over the narrow cobblestone streets and the ancient lava flows, we passed many two-storied houses built of lava rock, plastered white and adorned with the vines of grape and bougainvillea. Many of these homes had a well or cistern at the front, with an oven of rock and a garden enclosed by a rock wall.

In about 45 minutes we arrived at the ruins of the abandoned Observatory pavilion, Semafor di Labronzo, which had been destroyed by the earthquake and eruption of 1930. The real climb begins at this point. The first thousand feet is over a well-established trail which winds with numerous switchbacks through a zone with some vegetation. Leaving this zone behind, the trail then enters barren slopes covered with ash, cinders, and lava flows. The trail is often indistinct, and the loose cinders make upward progress tedious and tiring. Numerous vantage points permit a view of the Sciara del Fuoco, where the recent lava flow stands out prominently. After three hours of wearisome climbing, we reach the summit of the north peak, where we were able to look down into the crater.

From an oval-shaped depression about a thousand feet in its longest diameter, and so deep that the bottom is not visible from our position on the summit peak, two prominent columns of vapor boil out like smoke from a ship's funnel. The one on the right, adjacent to Sciara del Fuoco, has a well-defined cone, and the large steam column is noiseless as it pours out. The one on the left, the larger of the two, is accompanied by peculiar sounds. The noise is more of a "sloshing," or like the sound of quickly escaping steam as a locomotive slides its wheels to start. This exhaustlike noise was interrupted at intervals of 15 to 20 minutes by a more violent outburst—not like an explosion but with a tremendous outrush of gas which hurled rocks and debris to the level of our position 600 feet above the crater floor. The crater floor and the sides of the cone are covered with yellow sulphur and greenish yellow ferrous chloride; the presence of these gases was readily detected when the wind shifted slightly toward us.

We remained on the summit peak overlooking the crater until midday, checking the intervals between explosions and studying the nature of the outbursts. I was disappointed that no liquid lava was visible in the crater, and none of the fragments ejected appeared to be red-hot. The guide had seemed disturbed for some time and had tried to tell me, in Italian, that the cinders were hot. This, I thought, was reference to the fact that the cinders were hot when they were blown out of the craters. However, on the way down, I realized that he was referring to the cinders' getting hot from the noonday sun, and, since he was barefooted, they were hot enough to burn his feet. We took a short cut on the return trip down, taking giant strides as we almost cascaded down the slope of loose cinders. Salvatore stopped frequently on a rock to let his feet "cool." In an hour and a half, we were back at the Locando, the return trip having taken only half the time required for the ascent.

My second trip to Stromboli was made in early December, on my return from a study of Vulcano. I was unable, however, to make the climb to the summit this time because of the density of the fog and the onset of a heavy rain. Weather conditions being what they were, I decided to leave Stromboli and sail to Naples on the *Eolo*. It was already dark as the *Eolo* left Stromboli, and a light mist was falling. I remained on deck to watch Stromboli disappear in the distance, thinking perhaps it was my last sight of the volcano. As I watched Stromboli grow smaller, I detected a red glow at its summit showing even through the fog which still covered the summit. Watching with renewed interest, I saw the red glow fade and reappear. Suddenly, I saw a brilliant flare, and then heard the sound of a tremendous explosion. Even at several miles' distance I could distinguish red-hot fragments hurled into the air. Two such explosions occurred during the hour I stood on the deck and watched this "Lighthouse of the Mediterranean." This was certainly the time to observe activity in the crater, and I regretted that I had not stayed at Stromboli. However, I resolved to return on the very next boat.

One week later, at 6:00 P.M. on December 12, I boarded the *Eolo* in Naples for my third trip to Stromboli. Going on deck just before daylight the next morning, I was fortunate in seeing two bursts which gave a red glow to the steam column over the crater. I was, therefore, very hopeful that my trip would be rewarded, and I resolved to climb Stromboli that very day, if at all possible.

A stiff breeze was blowing from the northwest, and the steam-and-gas column was drifting across the summit peak, which is the only point from which one can see into the crater. My guide, Salvatore, and I agreed that if the wind did not change, the trip would be useless. The wind held during the day; so we postponed the climb until the following morning. When Salvatore knocked on my door at 7 A.M. the next day the weather was not much better; low clouds were drifting over the peak, and Salvatore did not think it advisable to make the climb, but I was afraid the weather might get worse. So we decided to go. At the summit overlooking the crater terrace the wind was blowing a gale so strong that it was difficult to stand against it. The wind brought the steam and crater gases directly into our faces so that we could see little of the crater floor.

We sought shelter from the cold by crouching below the rim and digging "foxholes" in the soft ash. To my great surprise, the ash was very hot a few inches below the surface, too hot to hold our hands against, and any small hole soon became an active steam fumarole! Digging a large foxhole, I tried to warm myself, but soon the steam condensed on my clothes, and I began to get damp, which made me still colder. Then I was alarmed to discover that the whole top of the cone was hot! Activity in the crater was much the same as on my previous visit in June except that the steam column was denser, because of increased condensation due to the colder air temperature. There were frequent strong explosions, and while I could hear rocks falling on the crater walls and rolling back into the crater after each explosion, the dense steam column obscured the view. Occasionally, after an explosion, the crater would be free of steam for a few seconds, permitting a glimpse of the crater floor. I realized that it would be useless to try to observe activity in the crater, even if the day was clear, unless the wind was from the south and the steam column was drifting away from the observation point on the summit peak. We descended on the south talus slope, and I arranged with Salvatore that if the wind changed directions we would make that climb again.

For the next two days, the weather developed into storm proportions and life on Stromboli came to a complete standstill—as did our plans to climb the volcano. After the storms abated, Salvatore came to my room at seven one morning and reminded me that I had asked him to come if the wind direction shifted. He asked me to take a look at the summit peak. Certainly the wind had changed, and the gas "flume" was now drifting to the north, away from the observation point. The sky was overcast, but there was no rain; so in less than an hour we were on the trail.

The wind was cold, but even so, the exertion of climbing caused one to perspire. We maintained a steady pace, and in two hours we reached the summit. A gale was blowing at the top, even stronger than on the previous trip, but this time the steam column was blowing away from our position, and we could see the crater floor clearly. I got out the movie camera, but the wind was so strong I was afraid it would blow over. Digging a small bench on which to stand below the edge of the crater rim, I set up my cameras and crouched below the rim to escape the fury of the wind. While I was getting ready, an explosion sent up a shower of red-hot scoria from the west vent. I was so startled that I forgot to turn on the movie camera, but, having learned where to expect the outbursts, I trained my camera on this spot and waited for the next explosion. In approximately 20 minutes it occurred, and I was successful in recording it with the movie camera.

During the three hours we were on the summit, there were seven explosions at intervals of 20 to 30 minutes. Each explosion threw quantities of red-hot scoria to a height of 600 to 1,000 feet above the crater floor—our position being 600 feet above. All the red-hot fragments came from the west vent and all fell back into the crater. The east vent continued to emit large quantities of steam accompanied at irregular intervals by a shrill whistling-like noise, like the violent exhaust of a locomotive.

About 1:00 P.M. the wind began to shift, and the last two explosions, which I was waiting to photograph, occurred while the crater was obscured by steam. However, the thud of the falling fragments made it evident that the outbursts were the same as the earlier ones. Soon the wind definitely shifted to the north, and we were enveloped in a cloud of steam and volcanic gases. Hastily gathering up our equipment, we started down the talus slope on the south side. Our descent was made in a drizzling rain, and, when I returned to my hotel, I had to dry my clothes over Signor Costa's charcoal burner. (Bullard 1954d)

Current Activity

No change in the long-established eruptive pattern of Stromboli Volcano can be detected. The persistent, moderate explosive activity continues with periodic outpourings of lava on the Sciara del Fuoco, some of which reach the sea. Lava flows reaching the sea along the Sciara del Fuoco were reported in March, 1966, and April, 1971.

Chapter 10   The Hawaiian Type of Volcanic Eruption

*And the mountain burned with fire unto the midst of heaven, with darkness,
clouds, and thick darkness.*—DEUTERONOMY 4:11

Fifteen hundred miles across the central Pacific stretches the line of
islands, reefs, and shoals which make up the Hawaiian Archipelago
(Fig. 38). Beginning with Ocean (Kure) Island at the northwest, they
include Midway and Gardner islands, French Frigate Shoal, Necker,
Nihoa, and Kaula islands, all of which are small, low islands; then the
eight major islands of the Hawaiian group proper, which in order
southeastward are Niihau, Kauai, Oahu, Molokai, Lanai, Kahoolawe, Maui, and Hawaii.

The Hawaiian Islands, the most important Polynesian group in the
North Pacific, were discovered by Captain Cook in 1778 and named
the Sandwich Islands in honor of the Earl of Sandwich, first lord of
the British Admiralty at the time of the discovery. Captain Cook was
welcomed by the inhabitants and treated as a god, although in the following year he was killed by a native when he landed in Kealakekua
Bay on Hawaii. The natives, who numbered about 200,000 in the
islands when Cook arrived, are closely allied, ethnologically, to the
Maoris of New Zealand. At the time of Cook's visit each island had its
chief, but later the chief of the island of Hawaii, Kamehameha, conquered the other islands and united them under his rule. The death
of Kamehameha V in 1872 ended the long line of Kamehamehas. Following a short reign by two chiefs who followed Kamehameha, Princess Liliuokalani succeeded to the throne in 1891. At constant vari-
ance with her legislature and advisors, the Queen was deposed in
1894, and the new government promptly sent a commission to
Washington to invite annexation to the United States. The annexation question was a lively political issue for several years, but finally
after vigorous opposition the annexation resolution was passed by
Congress and signed by President McKinley on July 7, 1898.

Only tiny dots on the map of the Pacific, the Hawaiian Islands are in
reality the tops of a range of volcanic mountains, one of the greatest
mountain ranges on earth, built up from the sea floor by thousands
upon thousands of lava flows. The Hawaiian Islands rise in water

which averages about 15,000 feet in depth; thus even the lowest of the islands are mountains over 15,000 feet in height (above their base), while the highest rise nearly 30,000 feet above the ocean-floor base. The volcanic peaks rise along two main trends, N 70° W and N 55° W. Shorter trends crossing the main axis at approximately right angles have probably determined the location of the vents, which are spaced at about 25-mile intervals. Outpourings of lava formed great dome-like piles of basaltic lava, which in time accumulated to a sufficient thickness to reach the surface of the sea. Since the volcanoes began to rise above the sea, they have been subjected to the destructive attack of the waves and other erosive agents which seek to destroy them. As long as a volcano is active, the island continues to grow, but when volcanic activity dies out the power of erosion is unchallenged. In time great canyons are carved into the slopes by streams, and waves continually batter away at the shores, cutting them back into high cliffs with a broad bench of shallow water (wave-cut terrace) on the seaward side. Finally, in some instances, the whole mass is worn away, leaving a shoal a few fathoms below sea level cutting across the volcanic cone.

Before the final stage of erosion is reached, coral reefs begin to form in the shallow water offshore. In an early stage the reefs surrounding a volcanic island are attached to the shore and are known as *fringing reefs*, such as are now found on the island of Oahu, especially off Waikiki Beach at Honolulu. In later stages, perhaps because of submergence, the fringing reef becomes separated from the shore by a lagoon and is known as a *barrier reef*. If the island disappears entirely, either by wave erosion or submergence, the barrier reef forms an *atoll*, a ring-shaped coral island enclosing a lagoon.

Volcanic activity appears to have started at the northwest end of the great fissure on which the Hawaiian Islands are located and to have shifted progressively to the southeast. The accumulation of great piles of volcanic debris over the fissure eventually sealed the opening at the first point, and the activity shifted to the southeast. This pattern was repeated for each of the islands, until today the only active volcanoes in the entire Hawaiian Archipelago are on the island of Hawaii, the southeasternmost island. The relative age of the islands in the archipelago is indicated by the extent to which they have been destroyed by erosion. Thus, the exposed parts of Ocean and Midway islands, at the northwest end of the archipelago, are composed entirely of coral limestone, but it seems quite certain that at a comparatively shallow depth the limestone rests on the truncated summits of great volcanic mountains. At French Frigate Shoal a tiny pinnacle of volcanic rocks projects through the limy reefs. Necker and Nihoa islands are remains of once much larger volcanic islands, and Niihau has lost a great slice of its eastern slope by wave erosion.

*Figure 38. Hawaiian Archi-
pelago.*

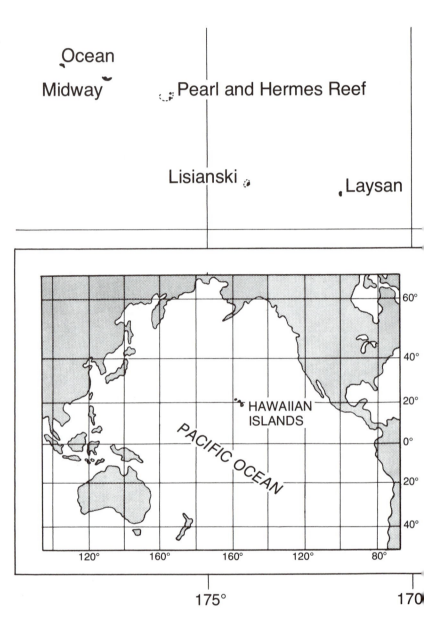

Figure 38. Hawaiian Archipelago.

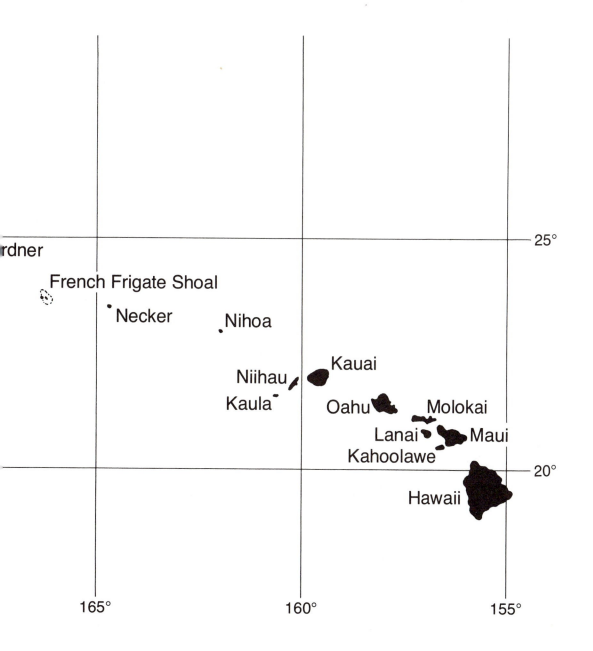

rdner

French Frigate Shoal

Necker

Nihoa

Kauai

Niihau

Kaula

Oahu

Molokai

Lanai

Maui

Kahoolawe

Hawaii

25°

20°

165°

160°

155°

On Kauai sufficient time has elapsed since volcanic activity became extinct for weathering to decompose the rocks, and a mature
topography with wide, soil-covered valleys has developed. Kauai is
often called the "garden island" because of its beautiful green valleys and excellent soil. This is in contrast to the other islands to the
southeast, which because of their younger age are more rocky and
have developed less soil.

Oahu, on which the city of Honolulu is located, is the most populous and the best known of the islands. As described by Harold T.
Stearns (1946), Oahu consists of two major lava domes, Waianae and
Koolau volcanoes, which formed along parallel fissures. Eventually
the two masses joined to form a single island. Erosion and fluctuations of sea level, the last being a submergence, have determined its
present outline (Fig. 39).

The island of Hawaii, known as the "Big Island," has an area of
4,030 square miles, which is slightly less than the area of Connecticut
but more than twice the combined area of all the other islands of the
archipelago. Hawaii consists of five volcanoes (lava domes) which
have combined to form the island (Fig. 40). Of the five, Mauna Loa
and Kilauea (described in detail in a later section) are still active, while
Hualalai, the only other to erupt in historic time, poured out a large
lava flow in 1800–1801 but has shown no signs of activity since that
time.

Crustal Drifting versus Sea Floor Fracture

Although acknowledging the long-established fact that the extinc-
tion of the volcanoes which form the Hawaiian chain progressed
from northwest to southeast, J. T. Wilson (1963a) concluded that
evidence was lacking for the fault zone on which they were believed
to be located. Accepting H. W. Menard's (1960) hypothesis that a
convection current ascends beneath the East Pacific rise and flows
laterally away from it, Wilson proposed that the Hawaiian chain of
volcanoes owed its origin to the Pacific plate moving over a fixed
"hot spot" in the mantle. According to his theory, active volcanism
occurs over the hot spot, and, as the movement of the plate carries
the area away from the hot spot, the volcanoes become extinct. To be
acceptable such a hypothesis must establish a relationship between
the rate of sea-floor spreading and the rate of migration of volcanism
along the island chain. Based on potassium-argon (K-Ar) dating of
the lavas in the volcanoes on the several islands and using the distance of each of the volcanoes from the still active Mauna Loa on
Hawaii, Ian McDougall (1964) calculated the rate of movement to be
10–15 centimeters per year, which is far in excess of the rate of

Figure 39. Stages in the development of Oahu Island, Hawaii. After Stearns (1946).

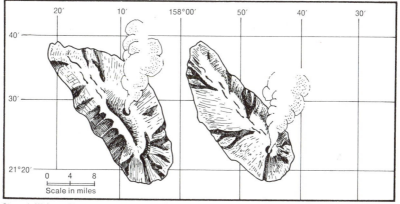

Stage 1. Waianae Volcano *(left)* is in the old-age phase with the caldera practically filled. Koolau Volcano *(right)* is actively building, chiefly along the northwest rift zone.

Stage 2. Koolau Volcano *(right)* is in the collapse phase with a large caldera at its summit. Koolau and Waianae Volcanoes are joined to form a single island (Oahu).

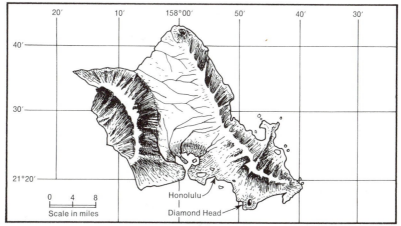

Stage 3. Submergence of Oahu to its present condition. Diamond Head, a secondary cone, is related to the last phase of volcanic activity.

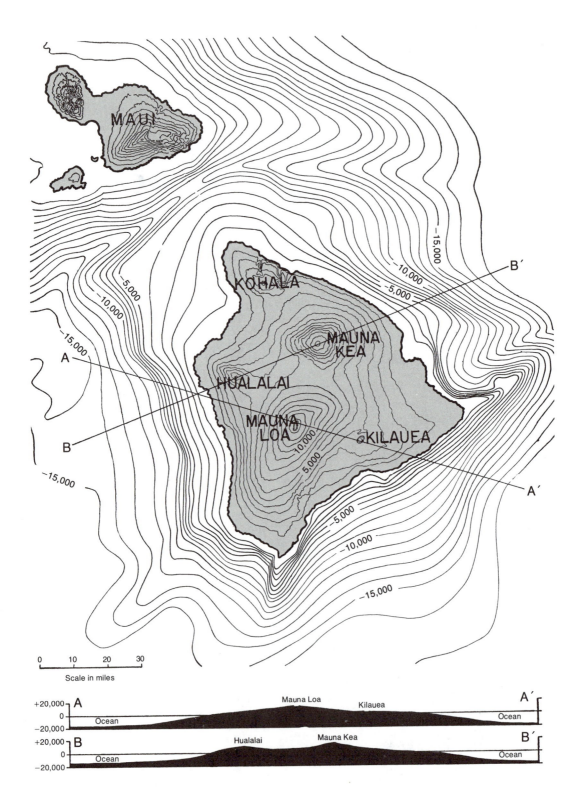

Figure 40. Hawaii, including the submerged area. Contours are in feet. After Stearns and Macdonald (1946).

movement usually assigned to convection currents in the upper mantle. It would, of course, be desirable to know the date of inception of each volcano, but the only reasonable and practical alternative is to assume that the oldest K-Ar date is the approximate age of each shield volcano. In doing so, it is necessary to assume that the volcanic shields are built fast enough that the oldest date provides a reasonable approximation for the birth of the volcano. Existing evidence suggests that this assumption may not be unwarranted. McDougall (1964) found that the main mass of the exposed parts of the shields of the principal Hawaiian volcanoes formed in 0.5 million years or less. Gordon A. Macdonald and A. T. Abbott (1970) estimated that the entire mass of Mauna Loa, from the sea floor up, could have formed within the last 1.5 million years if the volcano had erupted at its historic rate throughout its lifetime. E. D. Jackson, E. A. Silver, and G. B. Dalrymple (1972) not only accept Wilson's hot-spot hypothesis but are able to define the hot spot as being roughly 300 kilometers in diameter and now centered 40–50 kilometers north of the island of Hawaii. With faith in the validity of their conclusions, they "predict that a new locus of centers will begin about 40 to 50 km. north or east of Kilauea, perhaps coincidentally on its currently active east rift, in the near future" (Jackson, Silver, and Dalrymple 1972, p. 609).

CHARACTERISTICS OF THE HAWAIIAN TYPE OF ERUPTION

In the Hawaiian type of eruption, of which Mauna Loa and Kilauea volcanoes are examples, basaltic lava issues more or less quietly from a fissure which may extend for a number of miles. A series of earthquakes usually precedes the eruption, as the fissure opens to allow the magma to reach the surface. The lava is quite fluid, and the gases escape readily without the disruption of the lava into ash or cinders which occurs in the Peléan type of eruption. Less than 0.5 percent of the portion of the Hawaiian Islands exposed above sea level consists of fragmental material, thus attesting to the great predominance of the outpourings of lava at these vents.

In the initial stage of an eruption, spectacular lava fountains play at many points along the fissure, hurling streams of lava hundreds of feet into the air. The lava fountains, known as "curtains of fire," are caused by the frothing of the top of the lava column when the pressure is suddenly reduced by the opening of the fissure and the contained gases explosively expand. Great floods of lava issue from the fissure and flow in rivers down the mountainside. Sometimes the lava flows reach the sea, and as the red-hot material strikes the water it disrupts violently, forming cones of fragmental material or providing the black sand which forms beaches along the coast, as at Kalapana. Historic eruptions have lasted from a few days to ten months.

The vents from which the lava is issued open from time to time at different points along the fissure, so that eventually an elongate dome-shaped mass of lava is built over the fissure by the accumulation of successive lava flows. These large, flat lava domes, known as *shield volcanoes*, are characteristic of the Hawaiian type of eruption. The absence of soil layers between successive flows or, at best, the presence of very thin soil beds indicates rapid accumulation of the flows.

All of the Hawaiian volcanoes have passed through or probably will pass through more or less similar stages in the course of their development. Some of the latter stages have already been mentioned in discussing the development of coral reefs on the eroded stumps of the volcanic masses, and the earlier stages, now exhibited by the still active volcanoes of Mauna Loa and Kilauea, will be described presently. The stages as outlined by Stearns (1946) are as follows:

Stage 1

The volcano is built up from the ocean floor to sea level. Large quantities of ash are produced as the lava comes in contact with sea water in the eruption. When the cone first rises above sea level, it is composed of weakly consolidated ash and is rapidly eroded by the waves. Soon, however, new lava flows veneer the cone, and the erosive effect of wave action is greatly reduced.

Stage 2

The dome-shaped mass is formed by thin sheets of highly fluid primitive type olivine basalt, which flows from major rift zones.

Stage 3

The volcano collapses over the vent area to form a caldera on the summit and shallow grabens along the rift zone. This is the stage now represented by Kilauea and Mauna Loa.

Stage 4

When the amount of lava poured out exceeds the amount of the collapse, the caldera and grabens are partly or entirely obliterated. High lava fountains now characterize most eruptions, and large cinder cones and some bulbous lava domes are formed. Ash beds increase in number and thickness, and the profile of the dome steepens. Hualalai, Mauna Kea, and Kohala on Hawaii are in this stage.

Stage 5

Erosion partly destroys the volcanic dome.

Stage 6

Extensive submergence partly drowns the island, and extensive fringing reefs develop.

Stage 7

Volcanic activity is renewed, with the new vents showing little or no relationship to the ancient rift system of the volcano on which they form. Eruptions of this stage commonly began in middle and late Pleistocene and Recent times on such volcanoes as Haleakala, West Maui, Koolau, Waianae, and others. Following submergence, the fringing reef becomes a barrier reef.

Stage 8

If submergence continues or if the island is planed off by wave erosion during the fluctuations of sea level of the Pleistocene, an atoll may develop on the eroded and submerged volcanic mass.

The stages described above are shown graphically in Figure 41.

The island of Hawaii, or the Big Island, as stated previously, consists of five great lava domes or shield volcanoes which have coalesced to form the island. Two of the volcanoes, Mauna Loa and Kilauea, are still active and are continuing to add to the bulk of the island. These two volcanoes, the craters of which are included in the area of the Hawaii National Park, are among the most active volcanoes in the world, and they attract thousands of visitors each year. Further, they are the type examples of the Hawaiian type of eruption as described in the classification of volcanoes. A rather detailed de-

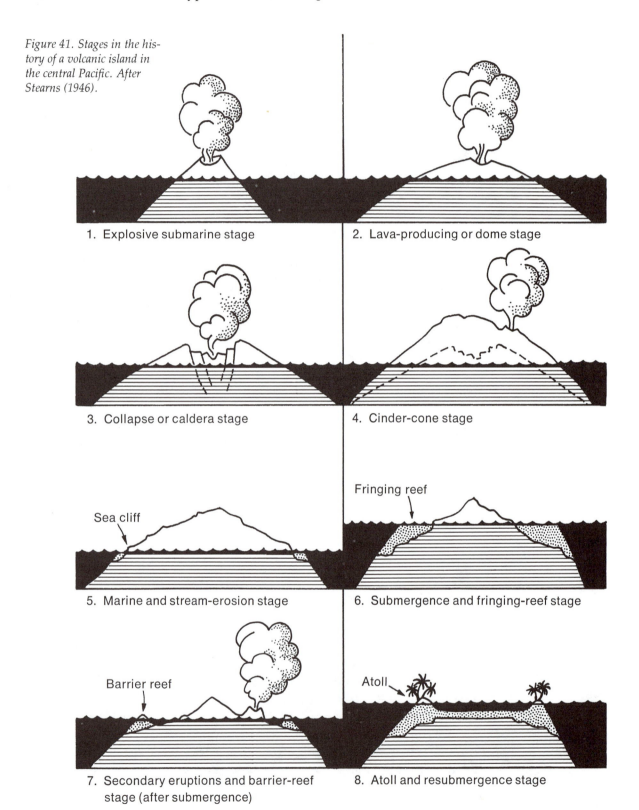

Figure 41. Stages in the history of a volcanic island in the central Pacific. After Stearns (1946).

1. Explosive submarine stage

2. Lava-producing or dome stage

3. Collapse or caldera stage

4. Cinder-cone stage

Sea cliff

5. Marine and stream-erosion stage

Fringing reef

6. Submergence and fringing-reef stage

Barrier reef

7. Secondary eruptions and barrier-reef stage (after submergence)

Atoll

8. Atoll and resubmergence stage

Figure 42. The island of Hawaii, showing the principal volcanic mountains and the general pattern of lava flows.

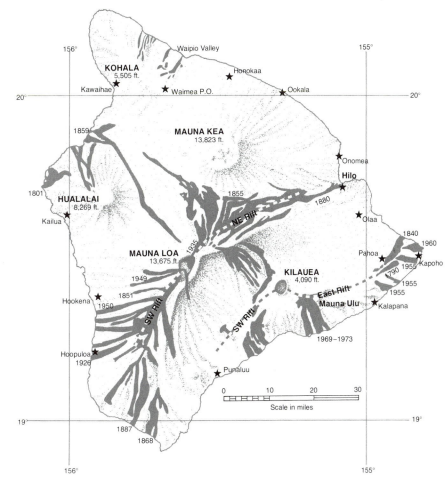

scription of these two volcanoes seems justified because of the importance of this type of eruption and in view of the fact that many people have an opportunity to visit the Hawaiian volcanoes.

MAUNA LOA VOLCANO   *Size, General Appearance, and Location*

Mauna Loa is an oval-shaped lava dome (Fig. 40) about 60 miles long and 30 miles wide, rising from a base 15,000 feet below sea level to 13,680 feet above sea level, making it truly the "monarch of mountains." It is the world's largest active volcano and probably the largest single mountain of any sort on earth. Its volume is of the order of 10,000 cubic miles, as compared to 80 cubic miles for the big cone of Mount Shasta in California. This huge bulk has been formed almost entirely by the accumulation of thousands of thin flows of lava, the separate flows averaging only about 10 feet in thickness. The broad, flat dome shape, which has given rise to the name *shield volcano* for this type, nowhere has slopes steeper than 12°, and near the top the slope is as little as 4°. Similar slopes extend outward beneath the water to the sea floor.

At the summit of Mauna Loa is an oval-shaped depression, called Mokuaweoweo, 3 miles long, 1.5 miles wide, and as much as 600 feet deep. This depression, commonly called a crater but more properly termed a caldera, was formed by collapse of the summit of the mountain. At the northern and southern ends Mokuaweoweo coalesces with adjacent pit craters formed in a similar manner. The depth of the caldera at any particular time is dependent on the ratio between subsidence and filling by outpourings of lava. In the hundred years prior to 1942, lava accumulated on the floor in excess of subsidence to the amount of 192 feet, which in effect reduced the depth of the caldera by that amount.

Mauna Loa is located on a well-defined rift zone which trends in a northeast-southwest direction (Fig. 42). This rift zone is approximately at right angles to the main fissure over which the Hawaiian Archipelago is located, and, as suggested previously, the intersection of the two zones may be responsible for the location of the volcanic vent. (The alternative hypothesis of a "fixed hot spot" instead of a fissure has been discussed above.) The rift zone on Mauna Loa is identified at the surface by many open fissures and an alignment of cinder and spatter cones formed by lava fountains along the fissure.

A Typical Eruption

A typical eruption of Mauna Loa is signaled by a series of earth-

Plate 41. Mauna Loa (shield volcano) in profile with Kilauea caldera in foreground.

quakes, which accompany the splitting of the mountain or the opening of a new fracture along the rift zone. The eruptions usually begin in Mokuaweoweo as lava fountains on the floor of the caldera and then extend down one of the rift zones. The summit activity is usually short-lived, but several days may elapse before the flank outbreak occurs. Sometimes eruptions occur in the summit caldera without any accompanying flank outbreak.

The eruption begins with a great eruption cloud rising from the crater and with lava fountains from many points along the fissure playing to heights of 500 feet or more, producing a veritable "curtain of fire." Great volumes of lava are poured out during the first few days. The rivers of lava, only 2–3 feet thick at the source, flow with high velocities which reach 10–25 miles per hour, slowing down and becoming thicker on the lower slopes. Generally the bulk of the gas is released in a few days and the lava fountains die down, building a chain of spatter and cinder cones along the fissure. During the prolonged eruptions the rivers of pahoehoe lava crust over to form

Volcano Observatory

Mauna Loa

Kilauea Caldera

Plate 42. Summit caldera (Mokuaweoweo) of Mauna Loa in 1939. The eruption shown in Plate 44 was along the line of steam vents on the far side of the caldera floor.

Plate 43. Detail of the floor of Mokuaweoweo showing pahoehoe (center left) *and aa* (center right) *lava of the 1935 eruption.*

Plate 44. The 1940 eruption ("curtain of fire") within the caldera of Mauna Loa. From a Kodachrome, courtesy Gunnar Fagerlund.

tubes, and thus insulated beneath the crust the flow may continue with only slight loss of heat for many miles down the mountainside. Division of a lava flow occurs frequently as a result of irregularities on the surface, leaving small "islands" surrounded but not covered by the new lava. In Hawaii such islands are known as *kipukas*. On the lower slopes of Mauna Loa the *kipukas* are marked by clumps of large trees, such as Kipuka Puaula, where Bird Park in Hawaii National Park is located. The longest flow in historic times was that of 1859, which continued for 10 months, reached the coast 33 miles away, and continued its flow an unknown distance under the sea. The 1881 flow stopped on the outskirts of Hilo after flowing 29 miles. Submarine flows sometimes issue from the seaward extension of the southwest rift zone.

Plate 45. The 1940 eruption of Mauna Loa from the Hawaiian Volcano Observatory, 25 miles away. The outline of the "shield volcano" is silhouetted against the "curtain of fire." From a Kodachrome, courtesy Merel Sager.

Volume of Lava Flows

Historic eruptions have produced from 1 to 5 million tons of lava per hour during their earlier phases. Since 1831, flank flows have added three-fifths of a cubic mile to the mass of Mauna Loa. At this rate the portion of Mauna Loa above sea level would have required 270,000 years to accumulate. This figure should not be taken too seriously, but it is an indication of the magnitude of the age of Mauna Loa. Also, it does point up the fact that Mauna Loa is one of the most prolific lava producers on earth.

Periodicity in Eruptions of Mauna Loa

During the period from the first recorded eruption in 1832 to the end of 1950, Mauna Loa has averaged an eruption every 3.6 years and has been active approximately 6.2 percent of the time. To some extent

there is an alternation of summit and flank eruptions, but it should be remembered that even flank eruptions usually begin with a few hours of activity at the summit. Most of the eruptions last less than a month, but a few have lasted two months, and one continued for more than a year. A summit eruption followed in two or three years by a flank eruption is the typical short-term cycle on Mauna Loa, but variations from this pattern are common. (A further discussion of this topic is included in Ch. 12.)

Eruption of January, 1949

The January, 1949, eruption of Mauna Loa is typical of the summit eruptions. After a period of repose lasting six years and eight months, Mauna Loa resumed eruptive activity on January 6, 1949. The eruption, described by Macdonald and Finch (1949), was confined to the summit caldera, Mokuaweoweo, and to the uppermost part of the southwest rift zone. Following the flank eruption of 1942 on the northeast rift zone, it thus continued the alternation of summit and flank eruptions which has existed since 1926. Heavy rumblings were heard at the Hawaiian Volcano Observatory, 20 miles from the summit of Mauna Loa, at 4:15 P.M. on January 6, and it is believed that lava reached the surface at that time. The lava broke out along a fissure which extended south-southwesterly across the floor of Mokuaweoweo Caldera from a point north of its center over the rim of the caldera, and on about 1.7 miles down the southwest side of the mountain (Fig. 43). In the initial stage, lava fountaining was nearly, if not completely, continuous along this crack, a distance of about 3 miles. Activity on the southwest side outside the caldera lasted only a few hours, and thereafter the activity was confined to the caldera area. Some very copious outpourings of lava came from the vents outside the caldera during the first few hours of the eruption. One flow, which moved westward, covered a distance of 6 miles in 24 hours. By the afternoon of January 7, after less than 24 hours of activity, more than two-thirds of the caldera floor had been flooded with pahoehoe lava. The chain of lava fountains along the fissure on the caldera floor continued for about 10 days, although they were variable in size and shifted position frequently. On January 19, two lava fountains near the caldera wall became extremely vigorous, sending up sprays of lava in which some bursts reached heights of 800 feet. The high fountains produced an exceptionally large amount of pumice, building a cone which was banked against the caldera wall and eventually projected approximately 100 feet above the rim and rested partly on the outer slope of the mountain. By January 25,

South Pit, which had been filled by lava from the caldera, began to overflow on its southeastern rim.

The lava stream moved southeasterly, and by the evening of January 26 it was two miles below South Pit, or three miles from its source at the lava fountains in the caldera. Later, new branches of lava broke out near South Pit and advanced downslope alongside the earlier flow, finally reaching some four miles beyond South Pit. The eruption ceased on February 5, having lasted just 30 days.

Eruption of June, 1950

The June, 1950, eruption of Mauna Loa is typical of the flank eruptions. A notable lack of westward tilting of the ground at Kilauea Crater after the 1949 summit eruption of Mauna Loa suggested that the magmatic pressure under Mauna Loa remained high. This, together with continued light fuming in Mokuaweoweo Caldera, indicated that the column of molten magma was standing at a high level in the conduit. On the basis of past history it was expected that the summit eruption would be followed by a flank eruption, probably within two years, but that with the magma column in such a high position the interval might be shorter. Strong earthquakes on Mauna Loa in May, 1950, indicated that the eruption might be soon, and the location of the earthquakes indicated an outbreak on the southwest rift.

The eruption began on the evening of June 1, 1950 (Macdonald and Finch 1950). Tremors started recording on the volcano observatory seismograph at 9:04 P.M., indicating that lava probably reached the surface at that time. A red glow was first observed from Volcano House at 9:25 P.M. Deep rumblings, probably emanating from the lava fountains, were heard at Naalehu, 23 miles from the point of the outbreak, at 9:10 P.M. The outbreak occurred along the upper portion of the southwest rift zone. A fissure 2.5 miles long opened from about 12,600 feet to 11,250 feet altitude, and from this fissure poured great volumes of fumes, rising in relatively narrow columns to a height of about 2 miles, then spreading laterally to form mushroom-shaped clouds brightly illuminated by the glare of the incandescent lava below. A flood of very fluid lava poured from the fissure and down the mountainside, most of it going westward toward the Kona District. The longest of these flows extended downslope about 5 miles to an altitude of 9,000 feet.

The outbreak at the upper source lasted only a few hours, and by 1:30 A.M. on June 2 the activity was greatly diminished and may have already ceased. However, as the activity at the vent diminished, a

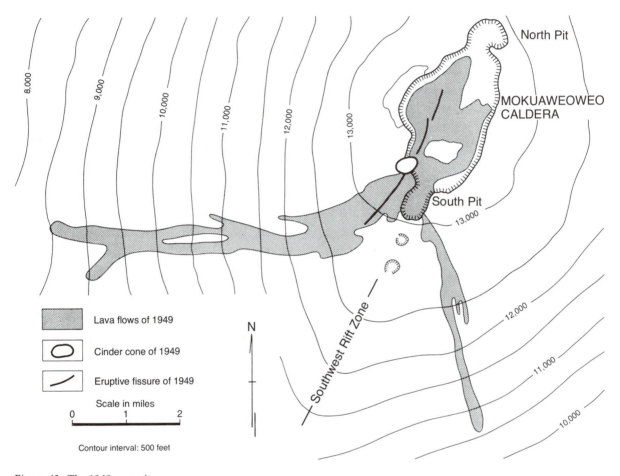

North Pit

MOKUAWEOWEO
CALDERA

South Pit

Southwest Rift Zone

■ Lava flows of 1949

◯ Cinder cone of 1949

／ Eruptive fissure of 1949

Scale in miles

0   1   2

Contour interval: 500 feet

N

8,000
9,000
10,000
11,000
12,000
13,000
13,000
12,000
11,000
10,000

*Figure 43. The 1949 summit
eruption of Mauna Loa. After
Macdonald and Finch (1949).*

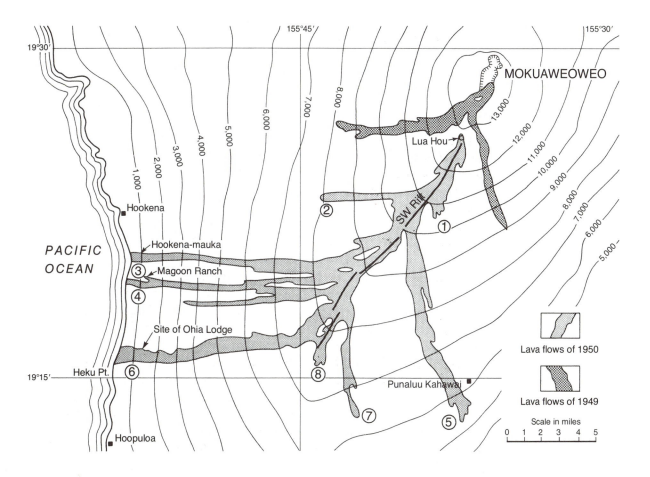

Figure 44. A portion of the southwest rift of Mauna Loa, showing the 1949 and 1950 lava flows. After Macdonald and Finch (1950).

new outbreak occurred with the opening of a fissure about 7 miles long which extended from the 10,500-foot level down to the 8,000-foot level. Floods of lava, accompanied by many lava fountains, poured from this fissure. During the first few hours of the eruption, two very rapid flows poured from the fissure near the 10,000-foot level. One of these (Fig. 44, no. 5) advanced south-southeastward in the general direction of Punaluu, and by the morning of June 2 it had covered a distance of 10 miles, reaching an altitude of 5,500 feet. The other flow (Fig. 44, no. 3) moved westward into the Kona District. This flow crossed the highway at 12:30 A.M., destroyed Hookena Post Office, several houses, and a filling station, and reached the sea at 1:05 A.M., having covered its 15-mile course down the mountain at an average rate of 5.8 miles per hour. Early on June 2, another flow (Fig. 44, no. 4) poured westward from the fissure between the 8,500- and 9,000-foot levels, and it reached the sea at 12:04 A.M. Some movement continued in this flow until the afternoon of June 3.

What proved to be the principal flow of the eruption originated at the lower end of the fissure between the 7,800- and 8,800-foot levels late on June 1 or early on June 2. This flow (Fig. 44, no. 6), known as the Kaapuna Flow, plunged into the ocean at 3:30 P.M. on June 2 over a sea cliff 50–75 feet high, sending up a great billowing cloud of steam but without violent explosions. Close to shore and directly over the flow the water was boiling, and a semicircular area of hot, turbulent water extended for a mile offshore. The cloud of steam which formed as the flow entered the sea blew inland, and condensation caused heavy rains beneath it. The flow continued until June 13.

The initial outpouring of lava from the entire length of the fissure ended on the morning of June 2, and thereafter the outpourings of lava were largely concentrated in a zone about 2.5 miles long between the 8,100- and 8,800-foot levels. Most of the lava moved westward, feeding the Kaapuna Flow. The eruption ended on June 23.

The total volume of lava erupted is estimated at about 600 million cubic yards, of which 100 million cubic yards flowed into the ocean and are not now visible. This ranks as the largest volume of lava produced in a historic eruption, being comparable to that of the eruption of 1859, which was the largest previous historic eruption. An interesting observation on this eruption was that between one-half and two-thirds of the total volume of lava poured out during the first 36 hours of the eruption.

Eruption of July 5–6, 1975

Mauna Loa, which had been in repose since the 1950 eruption, began to show signs of unrest in April, 1974, with increased seismic activity

*Lava fountain near Ka-
poho, east rift zone eruption of Kilauea Volcano,
Hawaii, January 28, 1960.
The fountain of lava is
reaching heights of about
1,000 feet. Photo courtesy
Willard H. Parsons.*

Above: *Lava fountain at Iilewa Crater (vent T, Fig. 47), four miles south of Pahoa, east rift zone eruption of Kilauea Volcano, Hawaii, March 22, 1955. The lava fountains reached heights up to 750 feet, and the lava flow encroached on nearby plantations. U.S. Geological Survey photo by Gordon A. Macdonald.* Below: *Lava from Kilauea entering the sea near Apua Point, March 23, 1973. Note that the sea water is boiling at the margin of the flow. Photo courtesy Willard H. Parsons.*

Opposite.
Upper left: *Pahoehoe lava at vent Y (Fig. 47), four miles south of Pahoa, east rift zone eruption of Kilauea, April 30, 1955. U.S. Geological Survey photo by Gordon A. Macdonald.* Upper right: *Development of pahoehoe lava surface, Kilauea, November, 1972. A thin, skin-like plastic crust forms on the flow, and, as the latter continues to move forward, friction along the sides causes a series of arcuate folds to form in the crust. Photo courtesy Willard H. Parsons.* Below: *Double fountain of lava forming a spatter cone near vent T (Fig. 47), east rift zone eruption of Kilauea, March 30, 1955. U.S. Geological Survey photo by Gordon A. Macdonald.*

Mauna Ulu eruption, Kilauea Volcano, Hawaii, 1973. Above: Lava flowing in a tunnel, January, 1973. The pahoehoe lava roof of the tunnel has collapsed in several places, exposing the tunnel flow. The fume-cloud from Mauna Ulu is in the background. Below: Window exposing lava flow in tunnel, April 18, 1973. Note lighter color at margin indicating lower temperature and banding indicative of laminar flow. Photos courtesy Willard H. Parsons.

Above: *Aa lava flow, east rift zone eruption of Kilauea Volcano, Hawaii, invading the Yamada coffee plantation, March 28, 1955. The flow issued from a vent which opened on March 26 (vent W, Fig. 47). Advancing seaward, it spread across the Yamada coffee plantation on March 28 and on the same day entered the sea, about 3.5 miles from its source. U.S. Geological Survey photo by Gordon A. Macdonald. Below: "Curtain of fire" on the first day of the eruption of Helgafell Volcano, Heimaey, Iceland, January 23, 1973. Lava fountains which reached heights of up to 375 feet were erupting from a mile-long fissure on the eastern slope of the volcano. Photo courtesy S. Thorarinsson.*

Upper left: *Parícutin Volcano, Mexico, from the observation cabin, about 0.5 mile from the base of the cone, October, 1944. The cone rises about 1,500 feet above its base. The rounded hills at the base of the cone are the first lava flows, covered with a thick layer of cinders. A portion of the parasitic cone Sapichu is on the extreme left.* Upper right: *Parícutin about three years later, on September 6, 1947. Outpourings of lava have buried the base of the cone and form a plateau above which the cone now rises about 1,000 feet. Collapse due to the outpourings of lava has resulted in the troughlike depression on the side of the cone.* Below: *Lava cascade, Parícutin, October 19, 1944. The lava, moving about 50 feet per minute, is plunging into a ravine 75 feet deep. Note a small portion of the cone in the background and a boulder of old lava, which has been rafted on the flow, perched at the edge of the falls. The boca for this flow is shown at the bottom of the page after the next.*

Eruption of Parícutin Volcano on the night of June 28, 1945 (time exposure). The bombs form a network of fiery trails as they cascade down the side of the cone.

Above: *Eruption column at Paricutin Volcano, August, 1943, six months after the birth of the volcano. Note the rain of ash from the upper part of the eruption cloud. The top of the cone (base of the eruption column) is largely obscured by steam.* Below: Lava *boca at Paricutin, October 19, 1944, about 75 feet wide. The lava, issuing from a fissure on the left, is moving about 50 feet per minute. Compare with Plates 58 and 59.*

Lava boca *at Parícutin Volcano, July 4, 1946. A series of spatter cones marks the line of a fissure which extends from the base of the cone (on the left) to the active* boca *on the far right where the lava is issuing. The spatter cones are 25–30 feet high.*

Above: *Lassen Peak, California, showing the devastated area which resulted from the lateral blast and mudflow in the eruption of May 19, 1915. The decayed trunks of large trees, pointing in the direction of the blast, are visible in the foreground. Photographed in August 1967.* **Below:** *Aerial view of Lassen Peak from the southwest. The massive plug-dome of Lassen Peak is buried by huge talus slopes, leaving only the largest bedrock spines exposed. The dacite lava flow which issued from the crater in the May 1915 eruption and extended about 300 meters down-slope is clearly visible (see pp. 565–570). Photo courtesy Phillip Kane.*

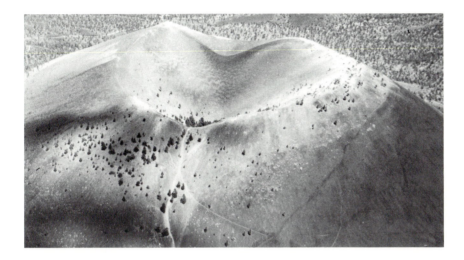

Sunset Crater, Sunset Crater National Monument, near Flagstaff, Arizona. Above: *The elongate summit crater is 2,250 feet by 1,700 feet, with a depth of 400 feet. Solfataric activity has altered the cinders at the rim of the crater to a brick-red color which gives the crater its name.*

Below: *The cinder cone rises 1,000 feet above a circular base one mile in diameter. Tree-ring studies place the date of the eruption in the fall or winter of A.D. 1064.*

Volcano Fuego (3,835 m.), Guatemala. Above: *Two views of the crater in June, 1955, showing a scoria-covered lava flow issuing from the central vent.* Below: *View from Alotenango, July, 1955. The 1953 lava flows from a notch in the crater extend about half-way down the northeast side of the cone. (A significant eruption with both lava flows and* nuées ardentes *occurred in 1973.)*

Mount St. Helens, one of the Cascade volcanoes in the state of Washington, with reflection in Spirit Lake. This photograph was taken May 19, 1982, two years after the initial cataclysmic eruption. A minor ash eruption is in progress from the lava dome in the crater. The composite dome is continuing to enlarge (see p. 558). Photo by Lyn Topinka, courtesy United States Geological Survey, David A. Johnston Cascades Volcano Observatory.

Volcano El Misti (5,825 m.), Peru. This beautiful cone, of recent origin, has not erupted in historic time, but there is some fumarolic activity in the crater. Above: *View of El Misti from Arequipa.* Below: *The summit crater consists of an older, outer rim about 900 meters in diameter and 100 meters in depth, inside which there is a black cinder cone formed by the last eruption. On the floor of the inner cone is a slaglike crust of lava from which gases rise at numerous places.*

Opposite.
Volcano Momotombo (1,258 m.), Nicaragua —a symmetrical cone with fresh cinders covering the upper portion. Upper left: *Detail of the crater. Some fumarolic activity, which is usually present, is visible on the left.* Upper right: *The upper, ash-covered portion of the cone and crater.* Below: *The crater is breached toward the north, and a lava channel with prominent chill levees leads to the 1905 lava flow, a product of the last eruption. Many older flows, covered in part by vegetation, can be identified on the lower slopes of the cone. Photo December 1972, courtesy NASA.*

Mount Erebus (3,794 m.), Ross Island, Antarctica. This is the most active volcano in Antarctica, with Strombolian type eruptions from molten lava pools in the inner crater. When observed over a two-week period from December 24, 1972, to January 6, 1973, the average interval between eruptions was 6 hours during the first week, 16 hours during the second week. Eruptions eject red-hot scoria and bombs, which normally fall back into the inner crater; infrequent eruptions of the inner crater send ash and debris to the floor of the main crater. Steam rises continuously from spots on the walls of the main crater. Above: *The summit of Mount Erebus, above a cloud layer. The summit cone fills an older crater or caldera, the rim of which is clearly defined. The main crater has a diameter of 500–600 meters, with a depth of about 150 meters. On the floor of the main crater is the cylindrical pit of the inner crater, 200 meters in diameter and about 100 meters in depth. The high-temperature activity is limited to the northern half of the inner crater; only a few weak fumaroles are scattered over the snow-covered southern half.* Below: *View of Mount Erebus from sea. Official U.S. Navy photos. Caption based on Giggenbach, Kyle, and Lyon (1973).*

and measurable inflation at the summit (Koyanagi, Endo, and Ebisu in press). While all the evidence seemed to indicate that an eruption might be expected, there was little unusual activity immediately preceding the outbreak. The eruption began just before midnight on July 5, 1975, from a fissure system which extended the length of the summit caldera, Mokuaweoweo, and partly into the southwest rift zone (see Fig. 43). Lava from the "curtain of fire" along this fissure flooded about two-thirds of the caldera floor and cascaded into South Pit. The fissure system extended both to the northeast and to the southwest. Shortly after 2:00 P.M. on the morning of July 6, a series of *en échelon* fissures opened across North Pit, and, in less than an hour, the northeast-trending fissures had extended beyond North Pit. Lava from these fissures began to flow down the northeast flank along the rift zone. There were several tongues of lava, the largest of which left the rift zone about 3 kilometers from the summit and advanced along a northerly course for about 6 kilometers before stopping. The eruption ended sometime between 4:30 P.M. and 7:30 P.M. on July 6, having lasted between 17 and 20 hours. In this space of time approximately 13.5 square kilometers of land were covered by new lava, representing a volume preliminarily estimated to be about 27 million cubic meters (Tilling et al. 1975; Hawaiian Volcano Observatory, unpublished data).

As mentioned earlier, summit eruptions of Mauna Loa are frequently followed in two or three years by a flank eruption. It will be interesting to watch for this development.

KILAUEA VOLCANO   *Location and General Appearance*

Kilauea Volcano is located on the southeast slope of Mauna Loa about 10,000 feet below the summit. It creates the impression of being a crater on the side of the higher mountain, although in reality it is a separate lava dome (shield volcano) approximately 50 miles long and 14 miles wide, built against the side of Mauna Loa. Although small compared to Mauna Loa, its summit (elevation 4,090 ft.) rises nearly 20,000 feet above the surrounding ocean floor.

Kilauea has been built largely by eruptions from two rift zones, extending eastward and southwestward from the summit caldera. The row of pit craters along the Chain of Craters road is on the east rift. Noteworthy among the fissures on the southwest rift is the Great Crack, continuous for more than 10 miles, from which issued the 1823 lava flow of Kilauea. During most of the nineteenth century and the first quarter of the twentieth, Kilauea was famous among volcanoes because of the presence of a lake of liquid lava in its crater. This unique feature was doubtless one of the reasons for the selection

Figure 45. Kilauea Caldera (crater) area. After Stearns and Macdonald (1946), modified. Note: By mid-July, 1974, when the activity at Mauna Ulu appeared to be over, the Mauna Ulu shield covered the site of the Aloi Crater.

of Kilauea as the site for the Hawaiian Volcano Observatory, established in 1912. Later the Hawaii National Park was established to include the crater areas of both Kilauea and Mauna Loa. Connected by paved road with the port of Hilo, Kilauea is the headquarters of the Hawaii National Park and offers hotel facilities and many recreational opportunities as well as the view of an active volcano.

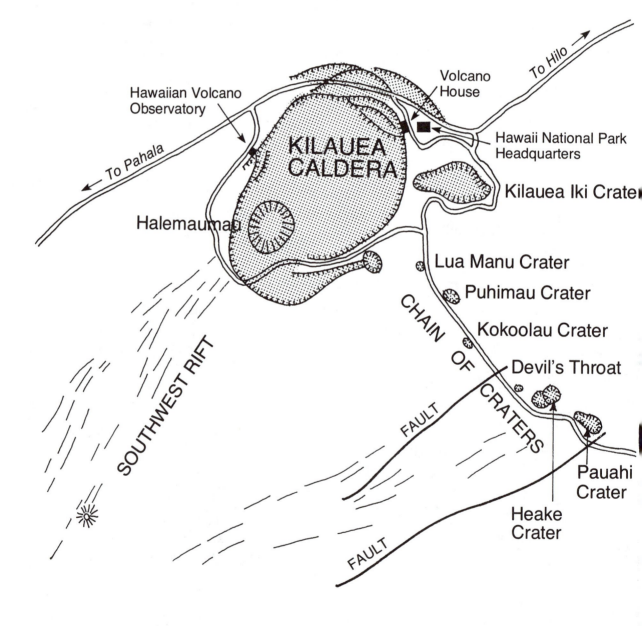

The Caldera

The summit caldera (crater) of Kilauea is an oval-shaped depression 2.5 miles long by 2 miles wide, the lava-covered floor of which is about 400 feet below the vertical cliffs which nearly encircle it. At its northern edge, below Volcano House (a hotel), and its western edge below the observatory, the walls of the caldera consist of steplike fault blocks (Fig. 45). On the floor of the caldera, near the southwestern edge, is the "fire pit," known as Halemaumau (House of Everlasting Fire), which from time to time has contained a lake of boiling

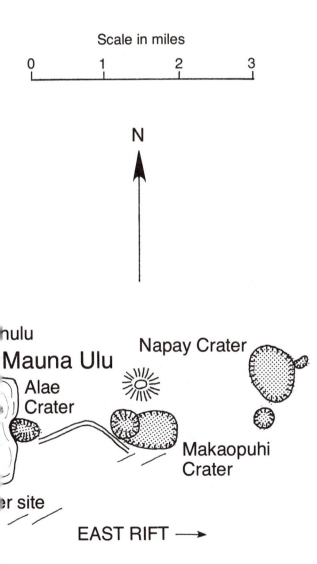

Scale in miles

0   1   2   3

N

hulu

Mauna Ulu

Napay Crater

Alae
Crater

Makaopuhi
Crater

r site

EAST RIFT →

lava. Halemaumau is a circular, pitlike depression which has varied from 2,000 to 3,500 feet or more in diameter and up to 1,300 feet in depth. Its dimensions vary from time to time, since lava flows fill it from the bottom, and since the diameter is enlarged by avalanching from the walls. Halemaumau is the focus of Kilauea's eruptive activity and the traditional home of Madam Pele, the Hawaiian goddess of volcanoes. According to tradition, Madam Pele, taking the form of a poor old woman, always appears before an eruption.

The Lava Lake in Halemaumau

For a hundred years preceding 1924 the most spectacular feature of Kilauea was the lava lake in Halemaumau. The surface of the lake rises and falls, much like a column of mercury in a barometer, sometimes overflowing and spreading lava over the floor of the caldera. Again, as in 1924, the lake may disappear altogether, and occasionally Halemaumau may be enlarged by the collapse of its walls into the pit. Halemaumau appears to be the point where the principal lava conduit of Kilauea reaches the surface. A true lava lake, such as Halemaumau, is distinguished from a pond of lava in a depression by a convectionlike circulation which connects the lake magma with the magma column at depth. During much of the period prior to 1924, the upper end of the conduit contained a plug of semisolid lava known as *epimagma*. Liquid lava, rising from below through fissures in the plug, formed a surface pool of lava about 50 feet deep on top of the epimagma. This thin, freely flowing lava, termed *pyromagma*, congealed to form typical pahoehoe lava. A constant circulation was set up by the rise of the pyromagma through source wells and its descent, convectionlike, through sinkholes. Crusts which formed continuously on the surface of the lake were dragged into heaps resembling piles of rope, or broken into cakes which tilted on edge and sank in the lava. Both the epimagma and the pyromagma were free to move up or down in the conduit, either independently or together. Because of its greater fluidity the pyromagma generally sank or rose more rapidly than the epimagma, and sometimes pieces of epimagma would project through the pyromagma as islandlike masses which gave the false appearance of islands floating on the lake. At times the pyromagma drained away, leaving exposed the glowing epimagma at the bottom of the lake; at other times both pyromagma and epimagma sank, sometimes as much as several hundred feet in a single day.

There has been much speculation regarding the means by which the high temperature is maintained for long periods of time in the lava lake. Temperature measurements at the lake showed that the surface is substantially hotter than the lava at a depth of 3 feet, suggesting that the heat, in part at least, is due to reaction of the volcanic gases with atmospheric gases (i.e., exothermic reactions). A temperature of 1,175° C. was measured at a depth of 40 feet, with a decrease to 860° C. at a depth of 3 feet, followed by a rise to 1,000° C. at the lake surface. Higher temperatures, up to 1,350° C., were recorded in the blasts of blowing cones where the gases had free access to atmospheric oxygen. Temperatures at depth were measured by means of Seger cones, bits of ceramic material constructed to melt at various temperatures, which were placed in pipes inserted to various levels in the lava lake.

The Typical Kilauea Eruption

Typical eruptions of Kilauea consist of lava flows forming lava lakes in Halemaumau or of short-lived lava flows within the crater and flank flows from fissures along the rift zones on which Kilauea is situated. Paroxysmal eruptions, due to the entrance of ground water into the zone of heated rocks, are rare, but explosions of this type occurred in 1790 and again in 1924. Eruptions of this type are known as *phreatic* eruptions. The explosive eruption of 1924 was preceded by the abrupt disappearance of the lava lake in Halemaumau and strong fissuring of the rocks both around the lava lake and in the Puna area to the southeast. The walls of Halemaumau began to collapse on April 28, 1924, with great avalanches from the sides, each sending up a tremendous cloud of dust. These avalanches continued, and on May 11, 1924, the first steam blasts began to throw rocks up through the dust cloud. The steam blasts came in pulsations every few hours like geyser eruptions, reaching a climax on May 18, when the explosion cloud reached a height of four miles. Tremendous blocks of lava from the debris avalanching into the pit were blown out and scattered over the surrounding area. One boulder weighing eight tons was blown nearly three-quarters of a mile from the pit. The steam blasts continued for 16 days, and the pit of Halemaumau was enlarged from 2,000 feet to 3,500 feet in diameter and was left 1,300 feet in depth. Red-hot walls were revealed near the base, but no molten lava was visible.

Flank lava flows, which issue from the rift zones to the east and the southwest of the crater, yield the greatest volume of lava. The flank eruptions are frequently far removed from the central crater and sometimes even occur as submarine eruptions. Flank flows have always followed increased activity and a rising stage in the lava lake in Halemaumau. After a flank outbreak the lava lake subsides rapidly and commonly disappears entirely, and the pit is enlarged by engulfment. The subsidence of the magma column, which is followed by engulfment, may result from lava discharges on the flanks, either above or below sea level; intrusion of magma into the underground area as sills or dikes; or possibly a recession of the magma into the magma reservoir. Whether an explosive eruption accompanies the collapse is purely a matter of accident, depending on whether the magma column recedes sufficiently to permit ground water to gain access to the zone of heated rocks.

For several decades following a collapse, lava flows may enter the pit through cracks in the floor or from cracks high on the walls, and slowly the pit fills. A lava lake may form and be kept hot and in motion for months, or years, by convection circulation and exothermic chemical reactions at the surface. The lake may be present only a few months during a 10-year interval, as between 1895 and 1905, or it may be nearly constantly present, as between 1851 and 1894, when it was absent only a few months in a 43-year period. The level of the lake may rise and fall within the pit, or it may slowly fill the pit and overflow onto the caldera floor, as it did in 1921 and at other times in the past. All of these features are characteristic of rising magma beneath Kilauea, which causes the mountain to actually "swell up" by an amount of increase (described as "tumescence") which can be measured by special instruments known as "tilt meters." The Hawaiian Volcano Observatory is located nearly north of Halemaumau, the volcanic center of Kilauea, and nearly east of Mauna Loa. Hence, as measured at the observatory, tumescence of Kilauea produces a northward tilt, while tumescence of Mauna Loa gives an eastward tilt (Fig. 46).

An eruption of either volcano is accompanied by a reversal of the direction of tilt, indicating a shrinkage of the mountain. During the period of gradually rising magma levels at Kilauea between 1912 and 1921, a point near the observatory was elevated about 2 feet, and by 1927, following the collapse and explosive eruption of 1924, the same point had subsided 3.5 feet. Measurements of this type appear to be one of the most promising methods of predicting eruptions.

The eruptive cycle at Kilauea Volcano develops through two stages: (a) a period of increasing pressure accompanied by rising of the magma column with lava flows in the crater and on the flanks and (b) a collapse, indicating decreasing pressure as the magma column recedes. After collapse the lava slowly returns to the crater, gradually building it up again for another eruption and subsequent collapse.

In the 11 years following the explosive eruption of 1924, seven small eruptions of short duration began the process of refilling the enlarged crater. The last of these, in 1934, marked the beginning of a 17-year period of inactivity, the longest in Kilauea's observational

Figure 46. Diagrammatic illustration of the significance of tilt, using a carpenter's spirit level to indicate direction of movement.

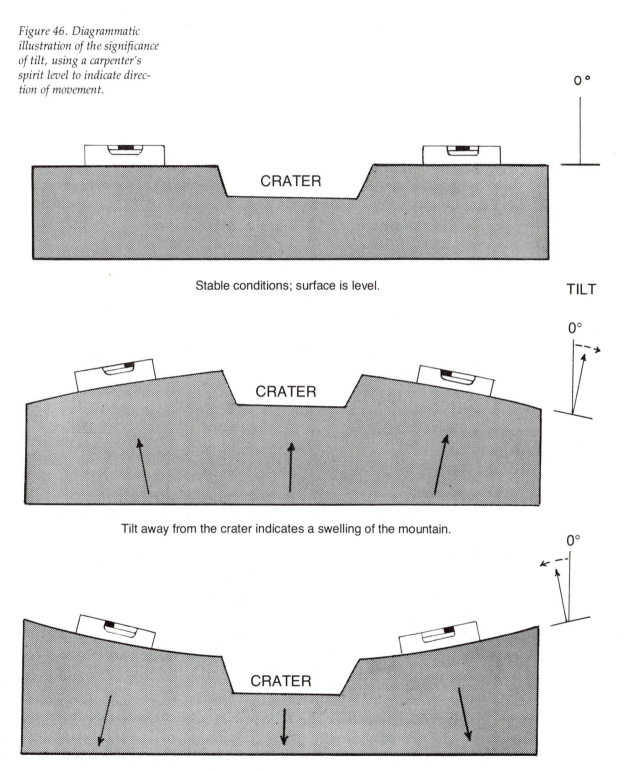

Stable conditions; surface is level.

Tilt away from the crater indicates a swelling of the mountain.

Tilt toward the crater indicates a shrinkage of the mountain.

history. Activity resumed in 1952 with an eruption in Halemaumau, followed by another in Halemaumau and on the caldera floor in 1954 and by the eruption of Kilauea Iki in 1959 (Richter et al. 1970). Prior to the 1961 eruption, every flank eruption of Kilauea Volcano (and Mauna Loa as well) was followed by at least one summit eruption. With increased activity along the east rift since 1961, this pattern has not been maintained, although summit eruptions are still interspersed with flank eruptions. The east rift zone adjacent to Mauna Ulu (which is described in the following pages) has had an almost constant outflow of lava since July, 1970, and is dilated and uplifted in response to the injection of magma. There is at least the suggestion that a shallow magma reservoir is developing along the east rift zone, apart from the one in the summit area of Kilauea. This would account for the lack of close correlation of summit and flank eruptions which had previously existed.

Some Recent Eruptions

A brief description of some recent eruptions of Kilauea will serve as examples of the type of activity. The eruption of Kilauea on June 27, 1952, ended a quiescence which had lasted since October, 1934, nearly 18 years. Prior to 1924 the longest inactive period was only 11 months. The 1952 eruption (Macdonald 1952) began with huge lava fountains on the floor of Halemaumau, which at that time was 800 feet deep. When the eruption ended on November 10, 1952, the lava filling had reduced the depth of the pit to 460 feet.

The eruption of 1954. No reversal in tilt, suggesting a release of pressure beneath the volcano, followed the eruption of 1952. On the contrary, during 1953, 12 seconds of northward tilt accumulated on the northeastern rim of Kilauea Caldera, suggesting an actual increase in pressure due to tumescence of Kilauea Volcano. Although there was no basis for predicting an outbreak at a specific time, the conditions were such that an eruption was imminent. The eruption (Macdonald and Eaton 1954) began shortly after 4:00 A.M. on May 31, 1954, after a dormancy of about 18 months. A giant lava fountain, partly obscured by a dense column of fume, played to a height of about 100 feet above the rim of Halemaumau. Rising from 460 feet below the rim, its height was between 550 and 600 feet. Lava quickly flooded the floor of the pit. One spectacular feature of the eruption was a cascade of brilliant, orange-yellow lava that poured from a fissure 300 feet above the floor, on the northeastern wall of the pit. Plunging down the wall, this incandescent stream joined the turbulent lava on the floor. The first rapid outflow of lava, during the first eight hours of the eruption, filled the pit of Halemaumau with about 63 feet of new lava, most of which was extruded during the first two hours. About noon on May 31, eight hours after the eruption started, a rapid sinking of the lava level began over the entire floor of the pit, leaving a band of congealed lava on the wall marking the former level. By the end of the eruption the level had dropped 32 feet, resulting in a net gain of 31 feet in the floor level. Ponded lava commonly shrinks as much as 20 percent in volume as a result of gas escape and of shrinkage from cooling. However, the decrease in volume of the new lava in Halemaumau was approximately 52 percent. Since this proportion appears to be far too great to have resulted from shrinkage due to cooling and loss of gases, it appears that some of the new lava must have drained back into the fissure through which it had previously risen. The eruption lasted three and one-half days.

The eruption of 1955. The 1955 eruption on the east rift zone of Kilauea in the eastern part of the Puna District was the first flank eruption since 1923 and the first eruption in eastern Puna since 1840. It was unusual in that the opening of the eruptive fissures progressed in part upslope toward the central crater of Kilauea, whereas normally they begin high on the slope and progress away from the central vent. Also unusual was the irregular manner in which activity shifted from one vent to another.

The first indications of the eruption (Macdonald and Eaton 1955) were two strong earthquakes centered in eastern Puna on March 30, 1954. The earthquakes came from a focus 12 miles deep and nearly south of Pahoa, between the surface trace of the east rift zone and the coast. Throughout the year many earthquakes originated at centers along the east rift zone and in the caldera area. At the same time, tilting of the surface at Kilauea Caldera indicated a swelling of the mountain, apparently from an increase of volcanic pressure beneath it. Further, the brief eruption on May 31, 1954, which has been described, had scarcely any effect on the tilting of the surface or the sequence of earthquakes, for both continued uninterrupted through the remainder of the year. Finally, in late February, earthquake activity increased greatly, and since it was centered in Puna it was thought that the outbreak would occur in that area.

The initial outbreak occurred just before 8:00 A.M. on February 28 in the area where the strongest earthquakes had been felt the preceding days (Fig. 47, Vent A). Small lava fountains played from a number of fissures which were arranged *en échelon*, with the most easterly fissure offset slightly to the north. The lava fountains were 50–150 feet high, and from them a rather sluggish lava flow spread southward. By noon of March 1, activity at Vents A, B, and C (Fig. 47) had ceased. However, new vents opened to the northeast in the direction of Kapoho. These vents (J, G, and E) were longer-lived than some of the other vents, and they fed a very active lava flow, the Kii Flow.

TABLE 2. *Summary of activity at Kilauea Volcano from May, 1924, to December, 1974*

Date	Type of Activity	Collapse Volume (10^6 cu. m.)	Eruption Volume (10^6 cu. m.)
1924	Phreatic explosions	203	
1924–1934	Seven short eruptions in Halemaumau		28
1952–1954	Two short eruptions in Halemaumau and caldera floor		55
1955	East-rift eruption	92	
1959	Summit eruption at Kilauea Iki Crater		39
1960	East-rift eruption	118	
1961	Three short eruptions at Halemaumau and one on east rift	16	
1962–1965	Five short east-rift eruptions	27	
1967–1968	Halemaumau eruption		84
1969–1974	Mauna Ulu eruption on east rift; began May 24, 1969, and continued, with periods of inactivity, until July, 1974		350

By 9:30 P.M. on March 3 the activity had reached the outskirts of the village of Kapoho, and lava fountains issued from a line of fissures in the outskirts of the town. However, a low ridge turned the lava flow northward, away from the main part of the village. A few houses were destroyed, but the main part of the village was unharmed. As a precaution, the village had been evacuated the previous day. By 8:00 A.M. on March 4 the activity at the Kapoho vents was over. After a lull of nearly a week, during which time it appeared that the eruption might be over, a new vent (Q) opened on March 12 to the southwest of the original outbreak. It was here that volcanologists from the Hawaiian Volcano Observatory observed the actual development of a new volcanic vent, which they described as follows:

First, hairline cracks opened in the ground, gradually widening to 2 or 3 inches. Then from the crack there poured out a cloud of white choking sulfur dioxide fume. This was followed a few

TABLE 2. continued

Date	Type of Activity	Collapse Volume (10^6 cu. m.)	Eruption Volume (10^6 cu. m.)
1971	Eruption in Kilauea Caldera, August 14		10
	Eruption in Halemaumau and on southwest rift, September 24–29		8
1973	Eruption at Pauahi Crater and Hiiaka Crater (adjacent to Mauna Ulu), May 5		1
1974	Eruption from fissures in southern part of Kilauea summit area, July 19; lava flooded southeastern part of caldera floor and adjoining pit craters		10
	Eruption within Halemaumau and nearby caldera floor, September 19		11
	Eruption of southwest rift, December 31		11

Sources: Adapted from Kinoshita et al. 1969; Peterson et al. in press; Tilling et al. 1975.

minutes later by the ejection of scattered tiny fragments of red hot lava, and then the appearance at the surface of a small bulb of viscous molten lava. The bulb gradually swelled to a diameter of 1 to 1.5 feet, and started to spread laterally to form a lava flow. From the top of the bulb there developed a fountain of molten lava which gradually built around itself a cone of solidified spatter. The same general sequence was observed at three separate points during the day. (Macdonald and Eaton 1955, p. 6)

During the remainder of March, as activity ceased at one vent a new one developed elsewhere. The activity in general migrated to the southwest along the rift zone, although there were some exceptions to this pattern, as is shown on Figure 47.

One of the most active vents was Vent T (Fig. 47), where on March 20 the lava fountains reached a height of 600–750 feet. A spatter cone

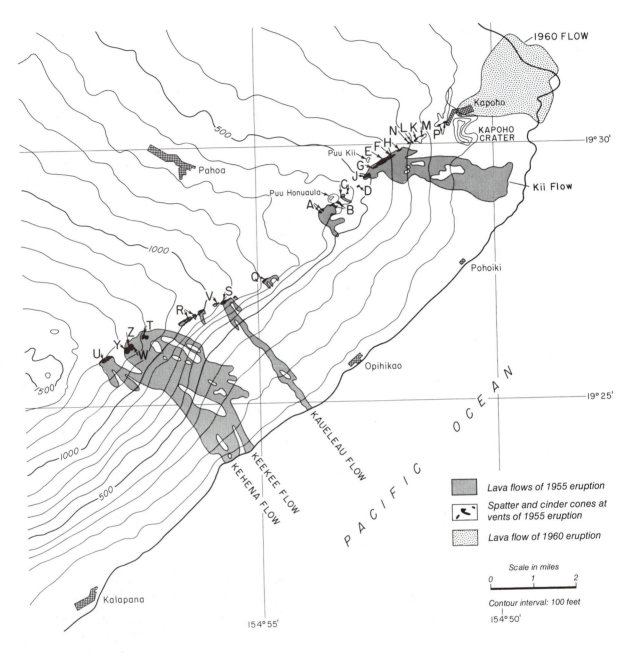

Figure 47. The southeastern part of the island of Hawaii, showing the lava flows of the 1955 and 1960 eruptions of Kilauea. Letters indicate the location of the 1955 vents mentioned in the text in the order of their outbreak. After Macdonald and Eaton (1955) and Parsons (1960).

1,000 feet across and 100 feet high was built around the larger of the fountains. The extensive lava flow from Vent T entered the head of a small valley that led directly to a small plantation camp. With a bulldozer the owner hurriedly threw up an earthen dam 1,000 feet long and about 10 feet high in an effort to protect the camp. During the afternoon the flow reached the barrier and was deflected by it but advanced along it only about 50 feet before this particular eruption ceased and the flow stopped! Activity continued in this general area, and on April 2 a tongue of lava (Kehena Flow) entered the ocean. On April 7 all lava activity ceased, and for more than two weeks no sign of activity appeared except clouds of white sulphurous fume and steam rising from the vents.

On April 24 moderate lava fountaining was resumed at Vent T, but in a few days the activity shifted to Vents Y and Z, and here it continued with renewed vigor until the end of the eruption. Large volumes of lava poured out. As it ponded in depressions and began to spill over into adjacent valleys, some spectacular lava cascades were formed. Velocities up to 30 miles per hour were attained by the lava in some of the cascades. On May 26, lava fountaining ceased, and by the morning of May 27 all movement in the lava flows had stopped. The eruption was over.

The total volume of material extruded was about 120 million cubic yards. This is about twice the volume of material extruded in the 1952 eruption in Kilauea Caldera, but only about one-fifth that extruded in the 1950 eruption of Mauna Loa.

The statement was made in a previous paragraph that "the eruption was over." It will be of interest to inquire into the basis for this conclusion. The answer lies in the action of the tilt meters and seismographs. During the eruption the inclination of the earth's surface (tilt) was recorded at Pahoa, about 2.5 miles northwest of the initial outbreak, and at Kilauea Caldera. Northward tilt at the Pahoa station, resulting from a swelling of the rift zone to the southeast, was recorded for a week preceding the initial outbreak. Swarms of earthquakes occur when new fissures are being opened, but while the eruption is in progress and lava is flowing freely at the surface very few earthquakes are recorded. As long as new vents were being opened, seismic activity continued to be high, but after the last new section of the rift was opened on March 26, seismic activity in Puna dropped to a low level, where it remained for the duration of the eruption. A southward tilt (i.e., a subsidence of the rift zone) was underway at Pahoa by March 7; however, this was temporarily reversed on March 8, and for the next two weeks there was an oscillation of swelling and sinking. At Kilauea Caldera, subsidence began on March 7 and continued, with two brief interruptions, until the end of the year. The amount of the sinking in the area of Kilauea Caldera between February 20 and April 10 has been calculated to be equivalent to about 216 million cubic yards, which interestingly is of the same order of magnitude as the volume of lava extruded in the Puna District during the same interval. Thus, with a collapse due to a decrease in pressure under the volcano, it could be confidently stated that "the eruption was over."

The eruption of 1959–1960. The 1959–1960 eruption (Parsons 1960) began on November 14, 1959, in Kilauea Iki Crater, which is immediately adjacent to Kilauea Caldera (Fig. 45). In the initial stage, lava fountains erupted from a fissure about one-half mile long on the south wall of Kilauea Iki, but within 24 hours the activity was restricted to a single fountain at the west end of the crater. This phase of the eruption continued intermittently through December 19. At one time Kilauea Iki Crater contained a lava lake 414 feet deep, but part of this lava drained back into the vent after the eruption ceased; so the crater filling was reduced to 382 feet above the previous floor.

Although the eruptions at Kilauea Iki ceased on December 19, seismic activity continued, suggesting that the lava was moving underground. In early January numerous small earthquakes were felt in the Puna District, 28 miles east of Kilauea Caldera. These became progressively more severe, and on January 13 some fairly strong shocks were felt at Kapoho and several cracks opened in the ground in the central part of the town. At 7:41 P.M. that evening, lava began flowing from an east-west fissure about one-third mile north of Kapoho. At first lava fountains played from the entire five-eighths–mile–long fracture, but they were soon restricted to the central section of the fracture, which became the main vent. In two days the lava flow reached the sea, three miles away, and as it poured into the sea great billowing clouds of steam rose thousands of feet into the air. When the eruption ended the shore line had been extended, in places up to one-half mile (Fig. 47). As the eruption continued and the valley became filled with lava, the flow widened and presented a real threat to the village of Kapoho as well as to the Kapoho School, the lighthouse, and other developments in the area. Earthen embankments were hastily constructed in a vain effort to protect some of the structures from the lava. They were ineffective, and in the end the village of Kapoho, the school, and other developments in the area were destroyed. The outflow of lava ceased on February 19. The eruption was over, having lasted 97 days, including the eruptions at Kilauea Iki and the interval between the end of the eruptions at Kilauea Iki and the outbreak at Kapoho.

The typical pattern or cycle of Kilauea is well illustrated by the 1959–1960 eruption. Tilt-meter and seismograph studies by the staff of the Hawaiian Volcano Observatory indicated that a swelling of the entire summit area of Kilauea began in 1957 and continued until the outbreak of lava in Kilauea Iki and Kapoho eruptions. Seismograph records indicated that during the swelling period the lava was rising from depths of around 25 miles. After the eruption the entire summit area of Kilauea settled, and in a few months it was back to its 1957 level.

Mauna Ulu eruption, 1969–1974. As shown in Table 2, Kilauea was quite active in the years preceding the Mauna Ulu outbreak, with eruptions more or less alternating between Halemaumau and the east rift zone. The first year of the Mauna Ulu eruption is summarized by D. W. Peterson as follows:

> The eruption began on May 24, 1969, along segments of a new fissure about 2 miles long in the vicinity of Aloi and Alea Craters on Kilauea's east rift zone. The central part of the fissure was about 6 miles east-southeast of Halemaumau, Kilauea's main summit vent. Between May and December 12, strong eruptive episodes that included lava fountains as high as 1,800 feet alternated with quiet periods when lava either sloshed within the vents or quietly overflowed onto the surface. By November, Alae Crater was completely filled with new lava. The last episode of high fountaining was on December 30, 1969.
>
> During the first half of 1970, overflows of lava from the main eruptive vent gradually built a new shield-shaped cone. When it developed as a distinct landform, it was officially named "Mauna Ulu" (Hawaiian for "Growing Mountain"), and henceforth, the eruption has been known as the Mauna Ulu eruption. By June, 1970, Mauna Ulu reached its present height of about 300 feet, and represents the largest new volcanic landform to be produced in the United States in many centuries. An unusual aspect of the Mauna Ulu eruption was the build-up of networks of lava "tubes" through which lava traveled ever increasing distances— sometimes as far as the ocean about 8 miles to the south. (Peterson 1973, p. 2)

The activity of Mauna Ulu from mid-1970 to the end of its eruptive period in mid-1974 is based on a summary prepared by the Hawaiian Volcano Observatory staff for the Hawaiian Planetology Conference (Greeley, ed. 1974). Through late 1970 and early 1971 a lava lake continuously filled the crater, but in May, 1971, the eruptive activity began to decline, the level of the lava lake steadily dropped, and by mid-October it had disappeared. On February 4, 1972, lava again appeared in the crater. It soon filled the crater, and repeated overflows covered new areas and added to the Mauna Ulu shield on the northeast slope. In mid-March, 1972, the lava lake in

*Plate 46. Floor of Halemau-
mau (Firepit) at Kilauea Volcano in the 1967–1968 eruption. Photo courtesy U.S.
Department of the Interior,
Geological Survey.*

*Plate 47. Lava fountains on
the floor of Halemaumau,
Kilauea Volcano, at the end
of the first month of the 1967
eruption. Photo courtesy
U.S. Department of the Interior, Geological Survey.*

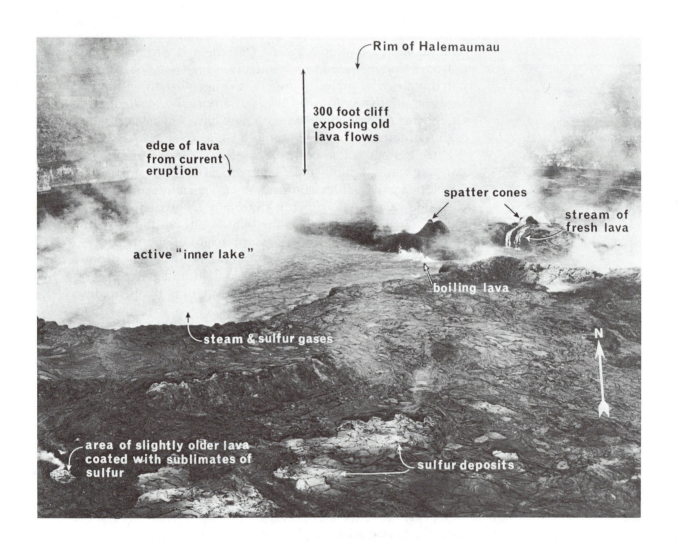

the crater of Mauna Ulu suddenly drained and new vents opened both to the east and the west. All but one of these vents were short-lived, but this vent, within the northern part of the former Alae Crater, was active for more than a year. The Alae vent was connected to the main vent at Mauna Ulu by a lava tube which sustained the lava lake. Lava flowing southward from the Alae vent developed new systems of tubes through which lava entered the sea during August–October, 1972, and February–May, 1973. This pattern of activity of Mauna Ulu, which is marked by periodic disappearance of the lava lake, an interval of inactivity, and the return of lava to the crater with overflows adding to the Mauna Ulu shield, continued until June 2, 1974, when the last overflow of lava occurred. The lava lake remained until July 22, 1974, when it drained, coincident with the activity at Kilauea Caldera and along Chain of Craters Road. In August, 1975, dense white fumes continued to issue from the crater, but it appeared that the eruptive history of Mauna Ulu was over—or was having an unusually long interval of inactivity! Mauna Ulu now rises 121 meters above the pre-1969 ground level.

The Mauna Ulu eruption was the longest and most voluminous eruption in the recorded history of Kilauea. It produced more than 350 million cubic meters of lava (not including lava which drained back into vents), which, in addition to that which poured into the sea, added 210 acres of new land to Hawaii and buried 67–77 square kilometers of ranch and forest land.

Depth of Magma Reservoir

As previously mentioned, the summit of Kilauea Volcano gradually swells as magma accumulates within the central reservoir area. This accumulation continues until a point of failure is reached, and magma then travels laterally into the east rift zone, where it either is erupted to the surface or remains underground in the form of dikes or other intrusive bodies (Fiske and Koyanagi 1968, p. 18). In an effort to determine the depth of the central magma reservoir which caused the inflation, R. S. Fiske and W. T. Kinoshita (1969) made a detailed study of the horizontal deformation of the ground near the summit of Kilauea Volcano. The ground on either side of the active area of uplift should elongate, just as points on an inflating balloon move apart as the balloon grows larger. The conclusion reached was that the inflation of Kilauea's summit can be explained in terms of a reservoir system at a depth of 2–3 kilometers, or within the upper

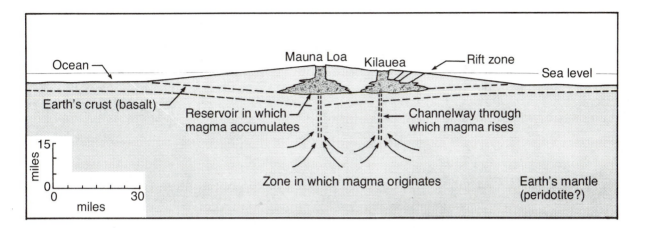

Figure 48. Schematic cross section showing possible substructure of Kilauea and Mauna Loa volcanoes, Hawaii. After Macdonald and Hubbard (1970).

half of the volcanic mass. Earlier studies by J. P. Eaton and K. J. Murata (1960) located the shallow reservoir at a depth of around 5 kilometers. The primary source of the magma is believed to be in the upper mantle at a depth of around 60 kilometers, while the shallow reservoir is a storage area where the magma accumulates awaiting eruption.

Chapter 11   The Icelandic Type of Volcanic Eruption

Fires that shook me once, but now to silent ashes fall'n away.
Cold upon the dead volcano sleeps the gleam of dying day.—TENNYSON

FISSURE ERUPTIONS   The great lava plateaus of the world, such as the Columbia River Plateau of the northwestern United States, are believed to have been derived from outpourings of lava from fissures. The Columbia River Plateau and the adjacent Snake River Plain were built up by innumerable lava flows which spread over parts of Washington, Oregon, and Idaho, covering an area of over 200,000 square miles. The combined thickness of the flows reaches a maximum of over 3,000 feet; yet individual flows rarely exceed 30–100 feet in thickness. The volume of the Columbia and Snake River plateau flows is estimated to be 60,000 cubic miles. Similar areas, perhaps even larger, are the Deccan Plateau in India and the Paraná region of South America. Other vast areas which have been flooded by basalt occur in Mongolia, in Siberia, in many parts of Africa, and in Australia. In a fissure eruption the flows spread out from the fissure, and when the eruption is over the sheet of lava conceals the eruptive vent (Fig. 50). The individual lava flows are relatively flat-lying, and the vents from which the lava issued must have shifted location widely from time to time to permit the lava to cover such an extensive area.

A fissure eruption differs from the usual volcanic eruption in that the material issues from a long crack, or fissure, rather than from a central vent. Most volcanic eruptions are, in a limited sense, fissure eruptions in that the lava issues from a crack or fissure and the cone is built over a fissure. What distinguishes the type of eruption which is called a *fissure eruption* is the extended length of the fissure through which the magma issues. In the fissure eruptions of Iceland, lava rises from a fissure or a zone of fissures several miles in length and flows as great sheets for long distances to either side of the fissure. Sometimes the outpouring is in the form of numerous tongues of lava, issuing at many points along the fissure. Small spatter cones may be formed by mild explosive activity along the fissure, but in general no main cone is formed. Indeed, in some of the prehistoric fissure eruptions the upwelling lava has sealed the fissure, leaving no indication of the location from which the lava issued.

The Icelandic type of eruption has many features in common with the Hawaiian type. The lava in both cases is primary basalt (i.e., not differentiated), and the eruptions are quite similar. In the Hawaiian type the lava piles up in great dome-shaped masses (shield volcanoes), while in the Icelandic type the lava flows form plateaus with nearly flat-lying layers. The volume of lava involved in individual plateau building and in dome making is not greatly different. In dome making, the system of fissures that supplies magma, under the domes, remains open in the same place for long periods of time, whereas in plateau building the activity shifts frequently from one fissure system to another.

The only modern examples of fissure eruptions such as are believed to have produced the great lava plateaus have been in Iceland, and eruptions of this type may appropriately be termed the Icelandic type. A description of these eruptions will be helpful in understanding this type of activity.

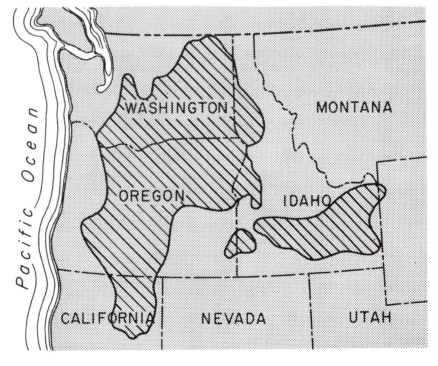

Figure 49. Columbia River and Snake River lava areas.

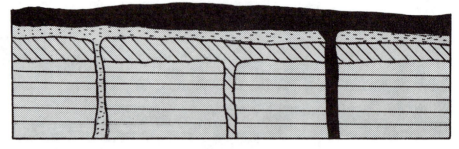

Figure 50. Icelandic type of eruption. Shifts in location of fissure vent result in a series of superimposed lava flows, forming a lava plateau.

SIGNIFICANCE OF THE LOCATION OF ICELAND

The island of Iceland, with an area of 39,758 square miles, is roughly the size of the state of Georgia. It is the exposed part of the northernmost extension of the Mid-Atlantic Ridge. Only a few of the peaks on the Mid-Atlantic Ridge, all of which are volcanic, emerge to form islands. Among these are the Azores, Ascension, and Tristan da Cunha, the latter in the far South Atlantic (Fig. 51). Iceland is 500 miles west of Norway and 200 miles east of Greenland, and its northern shore touches the Arctic Circle. Lying in the Mid-Atlantic, Iceland has long served as a stepping stone between Europe and America. The Norse Viking, Eric the Red, sailed from Iceland to Greenland in A.D. 982 and was thus the first white man to set foot on North America. His son, Leiv Eriksson, sailed from Iceland to the American continent in A.D. 1000, and settlements were established in Vinland (New England) and in Greenland, with regular trade between the colonies and Iceland. Since Iceland was a treeless country, regular trips were made to Labrador for timber. The settlements in New England were all abandoned many years before the arrival of Columbus.

Iceland is a mountainous country with its highest peak, Oraefa Jökull (glacier), rising to 6,952 feet above sea level. About 13 percent of the total area of Iceland is now covered by glaciers, shrunken remnants of the great continental ice sheets which covered much of the Northern Hemisphere during the Ice Age. The glaciers, the largest of which is about twice the size of Rhode Island, are known as "ice caps." Broad, low plains border the southern coast.

Iceland consists entirely of volcanic material, largely successive outpourings of basaltic lava, which rises from the ocean floor along the Mid-Atlantic Ridge, here between 3,000 and 5,000 feet below sea level, to nearly 7,000 feet above sea level. Depths on either side of the Mid-Atlantic Ridge in the North Atlantic range from 9,000 to 10,000 feet.

The trough, or graben, which is a significant part of the Mid-Atlantic Ridge crosses Iceland as a prominent surface feature (Fig. 52). The sea-floor-spreading hypothesis maintains that the trough at the crest of the Mid-Atlantic Ridge represents the zone where the crust

Figure 51. Iceland and the Mid-Atlantic Ridge.

is pulling apart. In Iceland this highly fissured zone of the Mid-Atlantic Ridge is on dry land and available for close study. To the north of Vatnajökull, where the belt is 30 miles wide, the trend of the fracture zone is N-S, but in south and southwest Iceland the trend shifts to NE-SW. The active volcanoes are restricted to this belt, which covers about one-third of the area of Iceland, and it ranks as one of the most active volcanic belts in the world. Since 1100 A.D., eruptions have occurred, on an average, at five-year intervals. The eruptions are predominantly effusive, pouring out basaltic lava from fissures and shield volcanoes. It has been estimated that nearly one-third of the lava produced on earth since 1500 A.D. is to be found in Iceland (Thorarinsson 1967*a*, p. 9).

EARLY VOLCANIC
HISTORY OF ICELAND

The volcanic history of Iceland began in Early Tertiary (Eocene) time with the outpouring of great floods of basalt which piled up to thicknesses in excess of 10,000 feet. Upbuilding to such heights in the latitude of Iceland would certainly result in glaciers, and since no evidence of glaciation is found during this period it is assumed that the area was sinking to compensate for the upbuilding. The Early Tertiary volcanism in Iceland was related to the enormous flood basalts that were spread from Ireland and Scotland on the south to Greenland on the north. At that time volcanism in Iceland was not unique as it is today. This early and widespread volcanism was from great fissure eruptions, but today Iceland is the only place where such eruptions are still continuing. Following a long period of repose, lasting many millions of years (Middle and Late Tertiary), modern volcanism began in Iceland in Pleistocene time (Ice Age) and has continued uninterrupted to the present. The modern volcanism is much more restricted than the earlier volcanism, being limited to a zone crossing the island in a NE-SW direction (Fig. 52).

During the geologically recent Great Ice Age, Iceland was completely covered by a continental ice sheet; consequently the volcanic eruptions during this period took place under a covering of thousands of feet of ice. The deposits of volcanic material under such conditions are of a peculiar type, similar to deposits from eruptions under water. In Iceland such deposits are known as *palagonite*. Since subglacial eruptions have occurred in Iceland in modern times, it has been possible to observe the manner in which palagonite deposits are formed.

SUBGLACIAL
ERUPTIONS

The two most famous subglacial eruptions are from Volcano Katla in the Mýrdalsjökull (*jökull*, "glacier"; cf. Eng. *jokul*) and Volcano Grimsvötn in the Vatnajökull, both in southern Iceland (Fig. 52). When a subglacial volcano erupts, the surrounding ice melts, and large quantities of water form. If the heat is not sufficient to melt the entire thickness of ice above the volcano, the trapped water will seep out along the base, and the surface of the glacier will collapse into large sinks, often several miles in diameter. If the entire ice cap around the volcano melts, a lake will form. In time the huge accumulation of water will break through the ice dam which confines it, and water and icebergs in unbelievable volume will sweep over the countryside, destroying everything in their path. Such floods are known in Iceland as *jökulhlaups*, which translated literally means "glacier runs." No words can express the violence of a *jökulhlaup*. The maximum discharge of water during the eruptions of Volcano Grimsvötn in Vatnajökull in 1934 and again in 1938, each of which lasted about one week, was about 50,000 cubic meters per second. (In recent years *jökulhlaups* have occurred from the Vatnajökull about every five years. The last reported was in March, 1972.) In 1918 Katla Volcano, in an eruption which lasted only two days, discharged 200,000 cubic meters of water per second. The magnitude of these floods can be appreciated when they are compared to the 10,000-cubic-meters-per-second discharge of the Amazon, the world's largest river. Tremendous amounts of mud, stones, sand, and debris are carried by the floods and washed into the sea. In fact, the entire contour of the south-coastal section of Iceland has been altered by these deposits since the early settlements in Iceland, about a thousand years ago. While features similar to the Icelandic *jökulhlaup* are known in other parts of the world, especially in the high Andes of South America, where volcanoes and glaciers are associated, nothing on a comparable scale is known.

Table Mountains

Subglacial eruptions in Iceland have produced a special type of land form known as a *table mountain* or a *móberg mountain*. Typically they are plateaus with steep sides or in some cases elongate ridges (Fig. 53). The steep sides consist of palagonite (or *móberg*, i.e., vitreous pyroclastic rocks) and pillow-lavas. As explained above, a volcano erupting beneath a glacier melts the ice and forms a large subglacial pocket of steam and water. A lava flow under water takes on a characteristic shape known as *pillow-lava*. The surface of the lava is also chilled and granulated by coming in contact with the water, and the glassy granules are altered to palagonite, so that a mixture of pillow-lava and palagonite results. In time the ice above the eruptive center may melt, forming a lake. In the final stage the accumulation of pillow-lava and palagonite may reach the lake level, or the lake may be drained and a normal subaerial lava flow may form a protective cap. Later, when the ice of the enclosing glacier melts, the flat-topped table mountain is left (Kjartansson 1967).

    The origin of Iceland's table mountains may provide a clue to the origin of the relief on the crest of the Mid-Atlantic Ridge as well as other submarine volcanic forms.

HISTORIC VOLCANIC ERUPTIONS IN ICELAND

While Iceland is best known for fissure type eruptions, it should be noted that Hawaiian type eruptions with accompanying shield volcanoes are also common. It has also been recognized in recent years that the Snake River Plain of southern Idaho, a typical product of a fissure type eruption, is dotted with low, broad "shields." Thus, the association of the two types may be the rule rather than the ex-

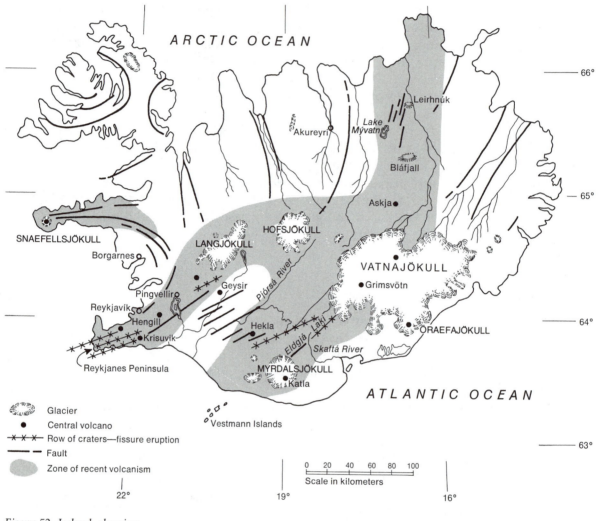

Figure 52. Iceland, showing
glaciers and major volcanic
features. After Barth (1950).

Figure 53. Hlöðufell table mountain as viewed from the south side of Langjökull, Iceland. On either side are móberg *ridges and in the background, on the right, a postglacial shield volcano. After Kjartansson (1967).*

ception. A brief description of some of the significant volcanic eruptions in Iceland in historic times follows.

The Bláfjall-Leirhnúk Fissure System

The Bláfjall-Leirhnúk area, in the northern part of Iceland (Fig. 52), was the site of a series of fissure eruptions during the five-year period from 1724 to 1729. The fissure zone extended about 35 kilometers and consisted of individual fissures 1–2 kilometers in length arranged *en échelon*. In some cases open fissures more than 180 meters in depth were formed without producing any lava. Severe earthquakes accompanied the opening of fissures, and the lava flows were generally accompanied by explosions which threw out ash, lapilli, and bombs, building cones and spatter craters aligned along the fissure. This area is unique in the great concentration of small craters or explosion vents. The shores of Lake Mývatn are thickly studded with craters, and it is doubtful that any other place on earth has such a concentration of craters in so small an area.

The total volume of lava (10^9 cu. m.)[1] extruded in the Bláfjall-Leirhnúk fissure eruptions was small compared to that from the great Laki eruption described below. The sequence of events in a fissure eruption has been studied in this area by a number of investigators, including Rittmann (1939) and Barth (1950). All agree on the general sequence of events, although they differ concerning some details. The fissure eruption is preceded by severe earthquakes which accompany the opening of the fissures. The decrease in pressure as the magma rises in the fissures causes it to "foam" and boil over and then to pour out in floods of liquid lava. Explosive activity accompanying the outpouring may build a row of spatter or ash cones along the line of the fissure. As the lava continues to flow from the fissure, the newly formed cones may be destroyed, in part, by floods of lava breaching them. When the outpouring lava ceases, the surface frequently collapses over large areas.

Laki Fissure Eruption of 1783

The Laki eruption of 1783 is regarded as the greatest lava eruption of historic times. It is the only historic example of a fissure eruption

---

1. For describing large volumes, distances, etc., it is convenient to use the *powers of ten*. Thus, 10^1 (10 with an exponent of 1) is equal to 10. The exponent indicates the number of zeroes following 1, so that 10^3 is 1 with 3 zeroes, or 1,000; 10^6 is 1,000,000; and 10^9 is 1,000,000,000.

(of the Icelandic type) such as must have been common in the past geologic ages to have produced the great lava plateaus of the world.

The location of the Laki fissure in southern Iceland is shown in Figure 52. The eruption, preceded by eight days of severe earthquakes, began at about 9:00 A.M. on June 8, 1783 (Thorarinsson 1970a). During the first days of the eruption enormous lava fountains (of the Hawaiian type) produced large quantities of Pele's hair, which formed vast clouds that rained ash over a wide area. The Laki fissure, which extends for about 25 kilometers, is divided into two nearly equal parts by the *móberg* mountain Laki, which rises some 200–240 meters above the surroundings (Fig. 54). From June 8 until July 29, the section of the fissure southwest of Mount Laki was active. Floods of lava issued from as many as 22 vents along a 16-kilometer-long fissure and flowed in a southwesterly direction. On reaching the glacial river Skaftá, the lava filled the stream bed and overflowed onto the surrounding countryside as it continued to move rapidly down the valley; in one day the lava advanced 14.5 kilometers! In the coastal area the lava spread out like a great fan 19–24 kilometers wide. The total length of the flow was about 80 kilometers. On July 29, the section of the fissure to the northeast of Mount Laki opened, and great volumes of lava poured down the bed of the glacial river Hverfisfljot, a stream parallel to the Skaftá River (Fig. 54). Thereafter, to the end of the eruption in early November, activity was confined almost exclusively to this area.

The lava produced in the section southwest of Mount Laki during the first 50 days of the eruption covered an area of about 370 square kilometers with a volume of nearly 10 cubic kilometers. Thus the average production of solidified lava (specific gravity 2.4) during these 50 days was about 2,200 cubic meters per second, corresponding to a discharge of 5,000 cubic meters per second of fluid lava from the fissure, or about double the discharge of the Rhine River near its mouth! The maximum production was certainly many times the average; a conservative estimate would be on the order of 10 times (Thorarinsson 1970a).

The total area covered by lava in the eruption was 565 square kilometers. Thorarinsson (1970a) calculates that the ash from the eruption was equal to 0.85 cubic kilometers of freshly fallen ash, or about the equivalent of 0.3 cubic kilometers of solidified lava. The total volume of lava and ash calculated as lava produced in the eruption is around 12.5 cubic kilometers. Thorarinsson (1970a) also makes an interesting calculation of the volume of gases released in the eruption, particularly the amount of CO_2. Some reliable samples of volcanic gases, believed to be free of atmospheric contamination, were collected during the eruption of Surtsey Volcano (described in subsequent pages) in 1965. Assuming that the H_2O content of the Laki

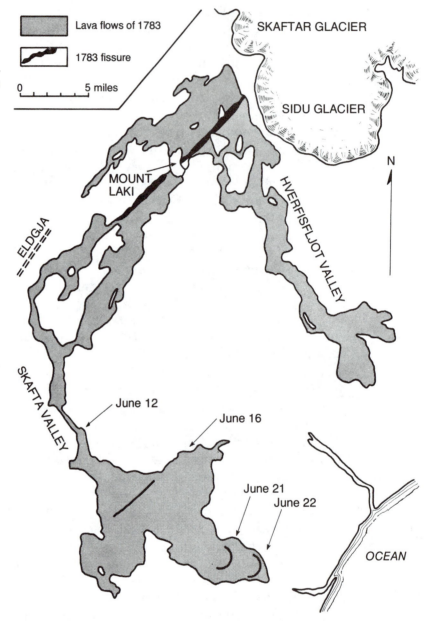

Figure 54. Lava flows from the Laki fissure eruption of 1783. The dates indicate the progress of the lava flows down the Skaftá River valley. Simplified after Thorarinsson (1970a).

magma was 0.5 percent by weight and that 0.1 percent remained in the lava, and assuming further that the percentage distribution of gases was the same as in the Surtsey magma, the CO_2 released in the Laki eruption weighed nearly 20 million tons. This is about 5 percent of the CO_2 content of the atmosphere above Iceland. If this figure is applied to the entire pile of basaltic lavas which have built up Iceland during the last 20 million years, the CO_2 content released from that pile amounts to about 60 percent of the present CO_2 content of the atmosphere above Iceland. These figures are important in considering the effect of volcanism on climate, a topic which is treated in Chapter 18.

The Laki fissure is marked by a line of cinder and spatter cones, many of which are 40–70 meters high. Of the 115 vents which can be recognized on aerial photographs, most are composed of lava spatter, but at least 2 are made up of well-stratified ash and cinders (Fig. 55).

In the 1783 eruption, rivers flooded by the melting of the glaciers and the damming of the lava-blocked streams destroyed many farms and much livestock. Although the lava flows caused great damage, even more serious was the bluish haze (probably containing SO_2) that lay over the country during the summer of 1783. It stunted the grass growth, causing a disastrous famine, still referred to as the Haze Famine. Hunger and disease following the catastrophe took their toll of human life. As a result of the eruption, Iceland lost one-fifth of its population, about three-fourths of its sheep and horses, and one-half of its cattle (230,000 head). It was a national disaster from which it took years for the country to recover.

The Eldgjá Fissure Eruption of A.D. 950

The Eldgjá fissure, in the same area as and a short distance to the southwest of the Laki fissure, erupted in the early days of the settlement of Iceland in 950. From an open fissure about 30 kilometers long, some 9×10^9 cubic meters of lava flooded an area of about 700 square kilometers (Barth 1950). Judging from the amount of fragmentary material ejected, the eruption must have been much more explosive than the Laki fissure eruption. The volume of lava, although somewhat smaller than the 12×10^9 cubic meters from the Laki eruption, is nevertheless tremendous. It is interesting to note that Surtsey, which erupted in 1963 and is described in the following pages, is on an extension of the Eldgjá fissure.

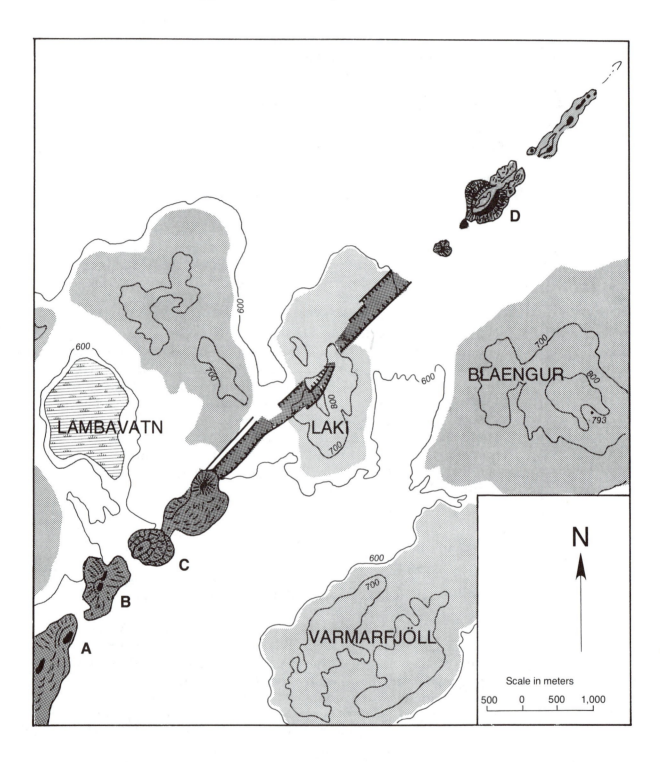

Mount Hekla

Mount Hekla is the most famous volcano in Iceland. It is located in the southern part of the country, 110 kilometers east of Reykjavík and 55 kilometers from the southern coast. It is an elongate ridge 27 kilometers long and 2–5 kilometers wide, fissured in the direction of its length with a row of craters along the fissure. It is built of successive sheets of lava and ash with a maximum height of 1,500 meters above sea level and 1,000 meters above the lava plateau on which it is situated. It is regarded by some as a strato-volcano, but to others it seems more closely related to the shield volcanoes of the Hawaiian type, although Hekla produces more ash than is generally true for typical shield volcanoes. The activity at Hekla is a modification of the typical fissure eruption of Iceland, in which successive outpourings of lava and ash-forming explosions have occurred along a fissure but in a restricted area, piling up the present mass of Hekla.

The first historic eruption of Hekla was in 1104, about 200 years after the settlement of the country. Since that time, Thorarinsson (1970b) lists 15 major eruptions with an average interval of about 60 years between eruptions, ranging from a minimum of 16 years to a maximum of 121 years. In recent centuries the intervals between eruptions have been longer than the earlier ones, with the 22-year interval between the 1947–1948 and the 1970 eruptions being an exception. The average duration of the eruptions has been about a year. An exception was the 1766–1768 eruption, believed to have been the longest in Hekla's history, which lasted for more than 2 years. Eruptions occurred in the following years:

1104	1222	1389	1636	1845[3]
1158	1300	1510	1693[2]	1947–1948[4]
1206	1341	1597	1766–1768	1970

Most of the damage from an eruption of Hekla is due to the heavy ash falls. Ash from the great eruption of 1300 is conspicuous in the soil profiles on Iceland. The 1947–1948 eruption of Hekla, which was typical, has been well described by Thorarinsson (1950; 1956). A brief résumé of this eruption, based on his account, will be of interest.

The 1947–1948 eruption. On the morning of March 30, 1947, at about 6:00 A.M. a farmer near Mount Hekla was looking at the mountain, which at that time was covered with snow. He observed a yellow-brown cloud growing rapidly in size to a height of 100–200 meters.

2. One of the most violent eruptions on record.
3. After 77 years of quiescence, this eruption produced a large volume of lava.
4. After 102 years of quiescence, this eruption produced a large volume of lava.

Several severe earthquakes were felt at about this same time. Shortly later the Hekla Ridge was split lengthwise by a fissure 5 kilometers in length, from which issued throughout its entire length clouds of ash-laden gases and outpourings of lava. As the snow melted, huge volumes of water flooded the Ytri Rangá River. By 7:00 A.M. the ash-laden cloud had reached the astonishing height of 27,450 meters! The surrounding area was enveloped in darkness and covered by pumice and ash which, 30 kilometers south of Reykjavík, reached a thickness of 10 centimeters. Forty hours after the eruption began, ash falls occurred in Finland. The main ash discharge took place during the first two hours of the eruption, and this initial phase might properly be termed a Plinian phase, but it was soon replaced by outpourings of lava. Activity decreased markedly after the first day. During the first day lava flowed from the whole length of the fissure; on the second day activity was concentrated at the summit crater and at points on either side; and on the third day lava flowed mainly from the ends of the rift at an elevation of about 830 meters. After that the activity occurred almost exclusively at the Lava Crater at the southwest end of the fissure. Here the flow continued until April 25, 1948, ending a period of almost 13 months. The lava at the vent had a temperature of 1,020°–1,040° C. In the initial phase the silica content of the lava (as well as of the ash) was 59.6 percent, but later this dropped to 57–58 percent. Thus, as has been true of previous eruptions of Hekla, the lavas are more acidic than typical flood basalts. The total volume of lava from the eruption is estimated at 1 cubic kilometer (1 billion cu. m.), while the volume of clastic ejectamenta is estimated at 220 million cubic meters. This lava output is the greatest in Iceland since the Laki eruption of 1783 and ranks among the greatest in the world for the present century.

When lava stopped flowing in late April, 1948, escaping CO_2, on calm quiet nights, accumulated up to nearly two meters in depth in surface depressions. About 20 sheep and numerous other animals were killed when they wandered into these depressions. Although the reasons for the gas are not clear, it appears that when the CO_2 emerged it had the same temperature as the ground water, and it was taken into solution under pressure and then escaped as the pressure decreased on reaching the surface. In addition to the animals killed by CO_2 poisoning, some animals were killed by fluorine poisoning. This phase of activity lasted only a few weeks, but the streams originating on the slope of Hekla still contain dissolved CO_2 and precipitate calcium carbonate when they issue at the surface. On the whole, little damage was caused by the eruption.

The 1970 eruption. After a quiescence of only 22 years, Mount Hekla again erupted in 1970. The eruption, as described by Thorarinsson (1971), began on May 5 and ended on July 5, having lasted exactly two months. The eruption was not from the main Hekla fissure which splits the mountain lengthwise but from fissures at the south-south-west and northeast bases of the Hekla Ridge. As is typical, the first phase of the eruption was a huge ash-filled cloud which attained a height of 15,000 meters. The main ash eruption lasted only about two hours, and during this time the ash production averaged 10,000 cubic meters per second. The total volume of ash, which covered an area of about 40,000 square kilometers, was estimated to be 70 million cubic meters. The ash, which had a silica content of 54–55 percent, was high in fluorine (800–2,000 ppm), and 7,500 sheep were killed by fluorine poisoning. The lava from the 1970 eruption covered an area of 18.5 square kilometers on the slopes of Mount Hekla and added a volume of 0.2 cubic kilometers.

Surtsey

A new island off the south coast of Iceland and four miles west of the southernmost Vestmann Islands (Fig. 56), was born on November 15, 1963 (Thorarinsson 1967*a*). The submarine eruption must have started several days earlier, since the water depth in this area was 425 feet and it would have required several days to build up a ridge high enough to reach the surface. The eruption was first observed on November 14, about 24 hours before the ash accumulation projected above sea level (Pl. 48). By November 16 the island had attained a height of 140 feet with a length of 1,800 feet; by November 19 it was 200 feet high and 2,000 feet long.

The island was an oblong ridge, split from one end to the other by a fissure which was flooded by the sea. During the early days of the eruption there were rarely any distinctly separate vents in the fissure. Eruptions occurred in several places, usually at both ends and near the middle, but the vents shifted from one part of the fissure to the other. With each of the explosions, which were occurring at intervals of a few seconds, great ash-filled clouds rose thousands of feet into the air.

During the first few months the eruption displayed two types of activity. (*a*) When the sea had easy access to one or more vents, either by direct flooding or by seepage through the scoria walls, the activity was typical of submarine eruptions. With each explosion, in such eruptions, a black ash-filled cloud erupts and out of it shoot numerous liquid or plastic lava bombs, each with a black, cometlike tail of ash. Within a few seconds these black tails turn greyish white and fume as the superheated vapor, which is the driving force of the bombs, cools and condenses (Thorarinsson 1967*a*). If the explosions occur at a considerable depth in the vent, the eruption column rises

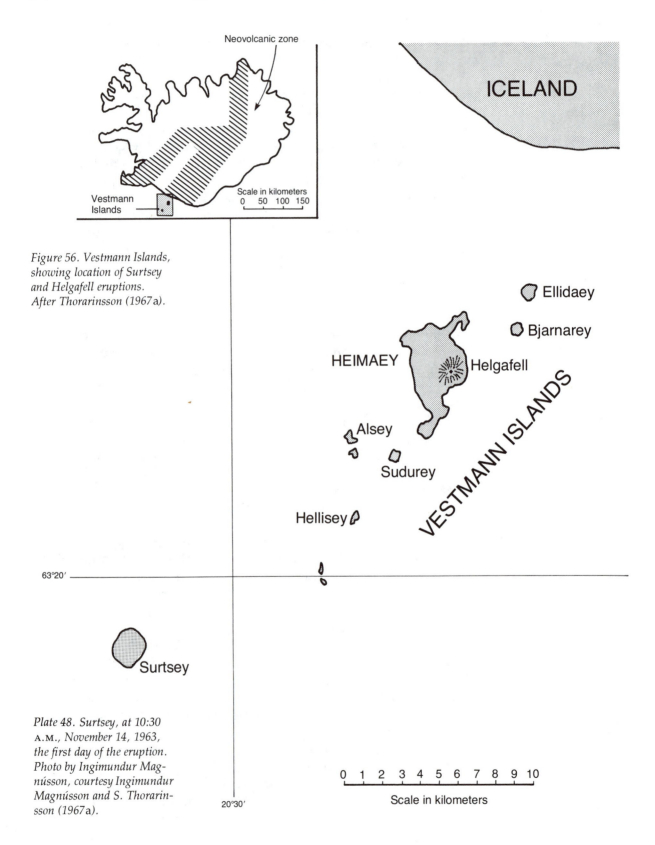

Neovolcanic zone

ICELAND

Scale in kilometers
0 50 100 150

Vestmann
Islands

*Figure 56. Vestmann Islands,
showing location of Surtsey
and Helgafell eruptions.
After Thorarinsson (1967a).*

Ellidaey

Bjarnarey

HEIMAEY   Helgafell

Alsey

Sudurey

VESTMANN ISLANDS

Hellisey

63°20'

Surtsey

*Plate 48. Surtsey, at 10:30
A.M., November 14, 1963,
the first day of the eruption.
Photo by Ingimundur Mag-
nússon, courtesy Ingimundur
Magnússon and S. Thorarinsson (1967a).*

20°30'

0 1 2 3 4 5 6 7 8 9 10

Scale in kilometers

more or less vertically. However, if the explosions occur near the top
of the vent, where the diameter is larger, the black tails of the bomb
describe a trajectory, so that the eruption cloud resembles an
enormous cock's tail (Pl. 49). Such cock's-tail patterns, one of the
more distinctive characteristics of submarine eruptions, were well
displayed in the eruption of Myozin-syo Volcano off the coast of
Japan (Pl. 62). In general, at Surtsey, the explosions were silent, the
steam muffling the noise, but sharp reports were heard as the bombs
crashed into the sea, sending up huge fountains of water. (b) If access
of sea water to the vent was wholly or partially blocked, the eruption
pattern changed. Instead of coming in intermittent explosions, the
ejection of ash and vapor was continuous. At the base of the column
the velocity of the uprush was about 400 feet per second, while at
a height of four miles it had dropped to 40 feet per second. These
more or less continuous outbursts were accompanied by a heavy,
rumbling noise.

By the end of December, approximately six weeks after the initial
eruption of Surtsey, the cone had reached a height of 415 feet. At this
time a new episode occurred in the eruptive history, one that was to
be repeated several times in the months to follow. On December 28
a new submarine eruption began about 1.5 miles from Surtsey. There
were three vents on an 820-foot fissure roughly parallel to the Surtsey
fissure but slightly to the east of it. The activity from these vents,
named Surtla, continued for about 10 days, but no island emerged.
Depth measurements a few weeks after the eruption ceased revealed
a precipitous ridge only 75 feet below sea level; a considerable portion
of the top had probably already been removed by wave erosion.

By the end of March, 1964, after 4.5 months of activity, Surtsey had
built an island 5,600 feet long and more than 500 feet above sea level,
with an area in excess of one-third of a square mile. The total volume
of ash produced up to this time was estimated to be 600 million cubic
yards, or an average ash production of 50 cubic yards per second.
However, notwithstanding the considerable volume of the island, its
permanency was by no means certain. The vigorous wave action
could have readily destroyed the loose ash and cinder cone, especially if the sea had continued to have access to the active vent with
the accompanying phreatic eruptions.

Surtsey's future is assured. On April 4, 1964, a glowing lake of lava
filled the crater of Surtsey, and shortly the lava began to overflow the
rim and streams of lava crossed the sand beach and entered the sea.
Where the lava streams entered the sea, the water was steaming hot,
and a lukewarm-to-hot surface layer of sea water averaging about
30 inches in thickness extended for hundreds of yards out in front of
the lava. The Icelanders found this pleasant for swimming, an activity
rarely enjoyed in the 7° C. (45° F.) waters on the Icelandic coast. Al-

though the lava continued to overflow the rim of the vent, a lava dome, which gradually increased in size, began to form in the crater. With some pauses, lava continued to flow until April 29, when it ceased to overflow the rim but a lava lake remained in the crater. On July 9, new flows began. Thorarinsson comments as follows: "The moon was new at the time but even before then the eruption had tended to undergo changes with a full or new moon" (1967a, p. 26). This is an interesting observation which indicates that the long-held idea that the gravitational forces of the moon and the sun influence volcanic eruptions is not entirely obsolete. As the volume of the flow increased, it carried away parts of lava-crater walls, and the entire area within the walls of the old ash crater was flooded with lava. The lava dome continued to grow until, on October 15, 1964, it was 380 feet above sea level. Although lava continued to flow until May 17, 1965, there was no further increase in the height of the lava dome. Surtsey now had an area of nearly one square mile, more than half of which was covered by lava. It was the lava cover, able to withstand the attack of the waves, which made Surtsey's future assured.

A second satellite submarine eruption. On May 22, 1965, shortly after lava ceased to flow from Surtsey, a submarine eruption started 0.6 kilometers east-northeast of Surtsey and on the same trend as the Surtla eruption of December, 1963. The eruption continued until mid-October, and an island, named Syrtlinger, rose to a height of 70 meters with an area of 0.2 square kilometers, but by October 24 Syrtlinger had disappeared, losing its battle with the sea for survival.

A third satellite submarine eruption. On December 26, 1965, a submarine eruption began 0.8 kilometers southwest of Surtsey, and an island, named Jolnir (originally called Christmas Island), rose to a height of 70 meters with an area of 0.3 square kilometers. Activity ceased on August 10, 1966, and in the following weeks the island was washed away.

Activity returns to Surtsey. With the satellite vents closed, the activity resumed at the original vent on Surtsey. On August 19 (9 days after activity stopped at Jolnir), lava eruptions began from a 220-meter fissure in the old Surtsey crater. Later the fissure was extended some 400 meters, passing through the north side of the scoria wall of the old Surtsey crater. During this period the lava issued at an average rate of 4–5 cubic meters per second. The lava flows continued with minor interruptions and at a diminishing rate until May 5, 1967. At this time the eruptive history of Surtsey, which attained an area of 2.8 square kilometers, ended, after an active life of 3.5 years. The total volume of ash and lava produced in the eruption was estimated to be 1.1 cubic kilometers (Thorarinsson 1967b, p. 10).

Helgafell Eruption, 1973

Helgafell, a well-developed cone on Heimaey, the largest of the Vestmann Islands (Fig. 56), had not erupted in the past 5,000–6,000 years,
although before the birth of Surtsey it was considered to be the
youngest of the volcanoes in the Vestmann group (Thorarinsson
1967a, p. 13). Helgafell overlooks the harbor of Vestmannaeyjar,
Iceland's most important fishing port. It is about 12 kilometers from
the mainland, and Surtsey, on the same zone of fissures, is about
20 kilometers to the southwest.

The 1973 eruption began in the early morning hours of January 23
from a fissure about 1.5 kilometers long on the eastern slope of Helgafell (Thorarinsson 1973). The fissure lengthened rapidly to nearly
2 kilometers, cutting across the island from one shore to the other.
A continuous "curtain of fire" played along the fissure in the initial
stage of the eruption, but soon fountaining became restricted to an
area about 0.8 kilometer northeast of Helgafell, and in two days a
cinder-spatter cone grew to more than 100 meters above sea level (by
the end of February it was more than 200 meters). In the first few days
of the eruption the heavy ash fall caused much damage to houses in
Vestmannaeyjar. By early February the ash fall had slackened, but
lava continued to flow unabated, and the important fishing harbor
was endangered. Efforts to stop the flow from entering the harbor
are described below.

The outpouring of lava, which at the outset reached an output
of 100 cubic meters per second, dropped to 60 cubic meters per second by February 8; to 10 cubic meters per second by mid-March; and
to 5 cubic meters per second by mid-April. By early June the eruption
had virtually ceased (Thorarinsson 1973).

The fact that two eruptions (Surtsey and Helgafell) occurred in this
area within a 10-year period after at least 6,000 years of inactivity is
in itself noteworthy. With an active life of only five months, the Helgafell eruption was unusually short, even for a fissure type eruption.

Chilling with water to restrict the lava flow. The harbor at Heimaey is
the best along the south coast of Iceland and provides access to some
of the best fishing areas in the North Atlantic, and the loss of the harbor would be a serious blow to the economy of Iceland. In early February, 1973, when the lava began to flow into the harbor, a determined effort was begun to restrict the flow of the lava by building
barriers and by pumping large amounts of sea water to cool the flow.
An experiment using city water in late February indicated that spraying water on the flow slowed its advance, causing the flow front to
thicken and solidify. In early March a pump ship was moved into the
harbor to spray water on the advancing lava front, but it soon became

apparent that a much larger operation would be required to achieve the desired results. This operation, which is described by Richard S. Williams, Jr., and James G. Moore (1973), became the most ambitious program ever attempted to control volcanic activity and to minimize the damage caused by a volcanic eruption. Since immediate action was required, the full resources of the Icelandic government were focused on the project, and by late April 47 pumps, mounted on barges in the harbor, were delivering a total of one cubic meter per second of sea water to various parts of the lava flow. The water was pumped directly on the lava front at sea level and was also pumped through three main 12-inch plastic pipes as far as one kilometer south to the surface of the flow. Each 12-inch pipe fed several 5-inch lines which spread the water over the surface of the flow. The most difficult part of the operation was to deliver large volumes of water to the surface of the flow some distance behind the lava front. It was found that the most effective results were obtained when the water was delivered about 50 meters back from the lava front or margin, resulting in a zone of cool, rubbly lava. The cooling of the margin was used in conjunction with diversion barriers of scoria which were thrown up with bulldozers adjacent to the flow margin. The cooled lava tended to pile up against the barriers rather than push under them as it would have if the lava had been more fluid. Water delivered to the surface of the flow some distance from the front had little effect for about a day; then the flow began to slow in that area. It required about two weeks to cool an area to below 100° C. The cooling apparently formed ramp structures which caused the more plastic interior of the flow to break upward and ride over itself. The fact that the harbor was saved is in itself testimony to the success of the operation, but whether the lava flow would have closed the harbor had control measures not been undertaken will, of course, never be known. It should be noted that the conditions were especially suitable for the methods used to control the lava flow because the main flow was viscous and slow-moving, so that there was time to plan and carry out the control program, and sea water was readily available.

CRATERS OF THE MOON NATIONAL MONUMENT, IDAHO

Craters of the Moon National Monument is located in the eastern part of the Snake River Plain in southern Idaho (Fig. 57). It is an area of recent lava flows and cinder and spatter cones associated with a fissure type eruption from the Great Rift, a southeast-trending fracture zone, extending from the Pioneer Mountains on the north and across the Snake River Pleistocene lava plain to Crystal Ice Cave, a distance of about 48 miles. Craters of the Moon National Monument was established in 1924 and so named because of the resemblance of the area to the craters of the moon.

Figure 57. The Great Rift and Craters of the Moon National Monument, south-central Idaho.

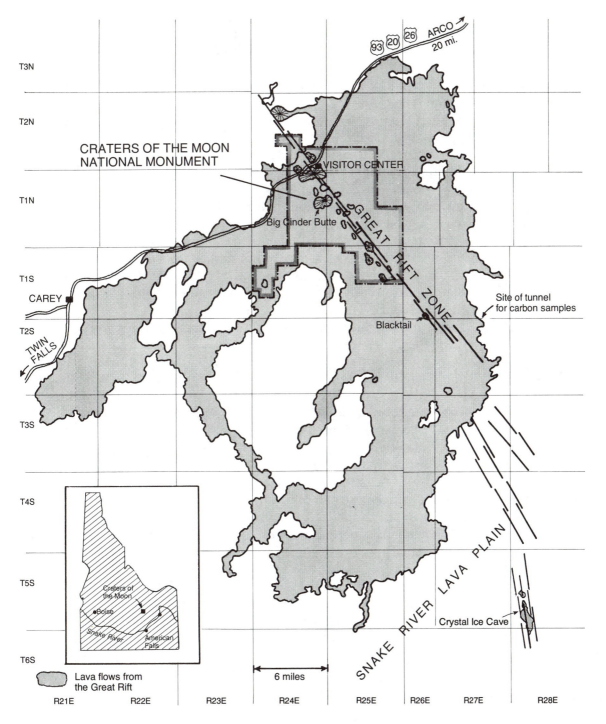

The Snake River Plain is commonly described as an eastward extension of the Columbia River Plateau of Oregon and Washington (Fig. 49), but structurally it is different from the Columbia River Plateau and, in addition to being younger (mainly Quaternary), the lavas are chemically distinct (Powers 1960). This huge lava plain was formed by lava issuing from innumerable fissures in typical Icelandic type eruptions over a time span of a million or more years. The significance of the Craters of the Moon area is that it was the location of the last eruptions in this region (near the beginning of the Christian era) and is an example of a fissure type eruption which is intact and available for study. It is comparable in many respects to the 1783 Laki eruption in Iceland.

The Great Rift is a series of *en échelon* fissures in a zone up to two miles in width (Fig. 57). At the north end of the Great Rift, in the Craters of the Moon area, prominent cinder and spatter cones were formed by explosive eruptions in the early stages of the activity. The largest of these cones is Big Cinder Butte, which rises 800 feet above its base and is a prominent landmark in Craters of the Moon National Monument (Pls. 50, 51). Other prominent cinder cones along the Great Rift, which rise in excess of 400 feet above their base, include Sunset Cone, Grassy Cone, North Crater Butte, Silent Cone, Crescent Butte, and Fissure Butte (Stearns 1963).

Following the initial explosive eruptions which formed the cinder and spatter cones, rivers of basaltic lava issued from fissures and flowed to the northeast and to the southwest of the Great Rift. There were several volcanic episodes, each resulting in a series of cinder cones and accompanying lava flows. In the end, dozens of cinder cones were formed along the eruptive fissures, and the combined lava flows covered an area of about 600 square miles with an estimated volume of about 9 cubic miles. Tongues and sheets of lava spread up to 28 miles to the southwest and up to 13 miles to the northeast of the Great Rift.

Eruptions from the extreme southern end of the Great Rift, in an area known as Crystal Ice Cave, produced flows which covered an area of about 1.1 square miles with an average thickness of about 25 feet (Pl. 52). The fissure which produced the lava is about 6 feet in width and has been explored to a depth of 800 feet. At a depth of around 150 feet in the fissure, magnificent ice stalactites and stalagmites make up Crystal Ice Cave, which has been ingeniously developed and is open to the public (Papadakis 1968). A prominent feature at Crystal Ice Cave is King's Bowl, a vertical-walled depression 250 feet long, 100 feet wide, and 150 feet deep. It was formed by a phreatic explosion (steam blast) caused by ground water entering the rift zone while the rocks were still highly heated.

Plate 50. Craters of the Moon National Monument, Idaho: view from Big Cinder Butte showing lava fields and spatter and cinder cones along the Great Rift. Big Cinder Butte is the largest cinder cone on the Great Rift. Pioneer Mountains form the background.

Cinder and Spatter Cones on Great Rift

Plate 51. Aerial view of the Great Rift from Blacktail cinder cone. The lava fields and Big Cinder Butte, Craters of the Moon National Monument, and the Pioneer Mountains form the background.

Plate 52. Aerial view of the Great Rift at Crystal Ice Cave, Southeastern Idaho. Here the open rift is about 6 feet wide and has been explored to a depth of 800 feet. King's Bowl, the oval-shaped pit in the upper center, is the result of a steam-blast explosion caused by the lava's coming in contact with ground water. It is about 300 feet by 80 feet in diameter and more than 150 feet deep. An ice cave with magnificent ice formations occurs in the Great Rift at a depth of around 150 feet. It has been ingeniously developed and is open to the public. The top of the photograph is south.

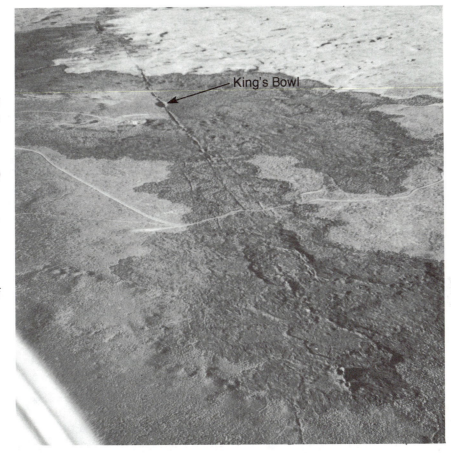

Age of Volcanic Activity

The freshness and barrenness of the lavas at Craters of the Moon National Monument impress all who view it. Indeed, for many the first impression is that it cannot be very old and might still be hot! The typical conclusion as to its age is similar to that stated by I. C. Russell in 1902: "Although it is impossible to make a well founded estimate of the time that has elapsed since the last eruption, it seems probable that it is no more than 100 or possibly 150 years" (1902, p. 105). It soon became apparent to scientists, however, that Russell had missed the age by a wide margin, since tree-ring counts showed that trees growing in the cracks of the lava were several hundred years old. Stearns (1963) reported that a core from one such tree, removed in 1954, had 1,350 years of growth as determined by a count of the annual rings by the Laboratory of the Tree Ring Research at the University of Arizona. It was estimated that the tree was 1,500 years old, allowing for some of the heartwood which had decayed.

The area seemed particularly suitable for age determination by radiocarbon methods, provided samples of charcoal could be obtained. Lava flows quite likely had buried trees and shrubs, and fragments of charcoal might still remain. The fact that numerous tree molds were present was ample evidence that trees had been growing in the area at the time of the eruptions, but a careful search of the tree molds did not yield any charcoal fragments. Apparently all charcoal which was exposed to weathering had been destroyed in the several hundred years since the last eruption. The solution was to locate

Figure 58. Cross section showing tunnel to obtain carbonized rootlets of plants buried by the advancing lava.

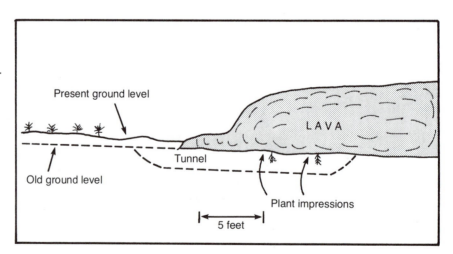

vegetation which had been burned by the advancing lava and was still protected from weathering. This might be done by tunneling beneath the flow, where the carbonized roots of shrubs killed by the advancing lava were, hopefully, still intact. The site selected for this test was on the eastern margin of the Craters of the Moon lava field, 13 miles south of Arco (Fig. 57). The details of the "dig," which was made by graduate student Don Rylander (Bullard and Rylander 1970), are shown in Figure 58.

The flow beneath which the charcoal was obtained is a well-developed pahoehoe type flow which issued from the Great Rift in the vicinity of Blacktail, a cinder cone some three miles to the west of the tunnel site. (A pahoehoe flow, which advances with a fluid layer at the base, will cover the existing vegetation and form a smooth, impervious layer which protects the carbonized roots from weathering. These conditions are not present in an aa flow, which advances over the surface as a rubbly mass.) A tunnel was extended beneath the flow for about 20 feet. The lower surface of the lava was smooth and reflected the surface over which it flowed, and the imprints of shrubs (probably sagebrush) were clearly visible on the basal surface of the lava flow. The soil from beneath the "bush impressions" contained tiny carbonized rootlets, and, with careful collecting, enough material was obtained for two samples for radiocarbon age determinations. Age determinations were made by the Radiocarbon Laboratory of the University of Texas, and the average of the two samples gave an age of 2,080 ± 85 years (Bullard and Rylander 1970). The date is valid for the particular flow involved, which may not have been the last activity in the area but certainly was a part of the final phase of activity.

At Trench Mortar Flat, about 3.5 miles southeast of the Visitor's Center at Craters of the Moon National Monument, there is a concentration of tree molds in an area bordering the Great Rift. Although no charcoal was found in a careful search of the tree molds in this area, it seemed probable that some charcoal might be preserved in the root systems of the trees, where it would have been protected from weathering. In the Trench Mortar Flat area the west trace of the Great Rift is a trench up to 15 feet deep and 10–20 feet wide, with the sides bordered by ramparts of spatter. Prior to the last eruption, Trench Mortar Flat was dotted with limber pine trees. In the last eruption, fountains of lava erupted from the Great Rift, forming a lava flow which covered Trench Mortar Flat. The bases of the trees were buried by lava, and the trunks and lower branches were plastered with spatter, forming tree molds, which are locally known as "lava trees" (Fig. 59). The upper part of the tree and the portion of the trunk encased in lava doubtless burned quickly. However, the roots in the soil beneath the flow were carbonized, and excavations at five

Figure 59. Tree mold, Trench Mortar Flat, Craters of the Moon National Monument, south-central Idaho, with explanatory sketch.

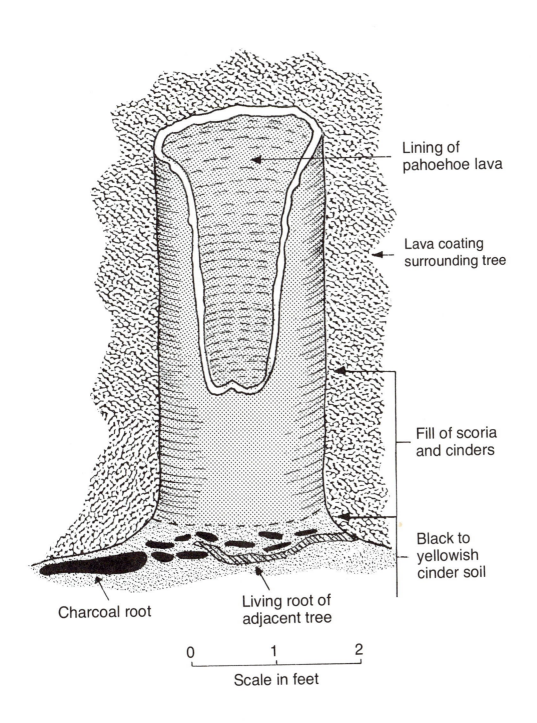

Lining of
pahoehoe lava

Lava coating
surrounding tree

Fill of scoria
and cinders

Black to
yellowish
cinder soil

Charcoal root

Living root of
adjacent tree

0   1   2

Scale in feet

of the tree molds yielded a significant amount of charcoal. In some cases the amount of charcoal was large (i.e., measured in gallons), with root sections up to three inches in diameter. Age determinations by the Radiocarbon Laboratory of the University of Texas gave ages ranging from 2,130 to 2,310 ± 80 years (Bullard 1971). With all the radiocarbon age determinations in relatively close agreement, it can be concluded that the last activity from the Great Rift was approximately 2,100–2,300 years ago.

No date for the initial activity from the Great Rift has been obtained. Efforts to find charcoal associated with the early flows were fruitless, and other methods of age determination will have to be used.

Eruptions of the Icelandic type have occurred throughout geologic time in many parts of the world, although the only historic eruptions of this type have been in Iceland. We are indeed fortunate that eyewitness accounts of these eruptions are available, for they make it possible to better understand the eruptive history of the Great Rift in the Craters of the Moon area and also to explain how the great lava plateaus of the world were formed.

Part Three   Theory, Cycles, Utilization, and
Environmental Effects of Volcanoes

Chapter 12   Volcanic Cycles

A theory is a tool—not a creed.—J. J. THOMSON

As a consequence of the earth's yearly trip around the sun and its daily spinning on its axis, there are the seasons, day and night, tides, and other features which reoccur with mathematical regularity. Orderliness prevails in the physical universe, from the atom with its nucleus, about which the electrons revolve, to the sun, about which the planets revolve, and finally to the great galaxies of stars all fitting into their respective orbits, the whole going we know not where, but perfectly adjusted and intermeshing like the delicate mechanism of a watch. The rhythmic or cyclic recurrence of many earth phenomena is well established and a basic principle in geology.

Although it is accepted as commonplace today, we have achieved the ability to accomplish what would once have seemed a miracle—the prediction of the occurrence of the different seasons at any point on the earth—because the laws which govern the seasons are known. There is a clear relationship of cause and effect, and there is the possibility, even the probability, that all recurring aspects of the earth are governed by definite laws of causal relationships. It is the province of science to discover these laws and then to predict the occurrence of phenomena which they govern. Once the pattern of activity is established, the possibility of control can be considered.

The weather may be taken as an example to illustrate this point. After long years of careful observation and scientific study, the weather can be predicted from day to day, or even for longer periods. The factors which control the weather are known, at least in part, and their effect at any given place can be predicted. Knowing these factors, the next logical step is control of the weather, and attempts are being made in this direction. The climate as a whole, however, appears to follow a cyclic pattern in which at intervals there are excessively dry years followed by wet years. Many believe that the weather and, in fact, almost all earth activities are related to sunspot cycles. Sunspots are great eruptive areas on the sun, and they may well be considered the "volcanoes of the sun." These solar disturbances, actual atomic explosions, send out a stream of electrified particles which so heavily ionize (make capable of conducting an electrical charge) the upper atmosphere as to cause discharges in the rarefied air, producing the glow of the familiar Northern Lights. This change in the electron density of the upper atmosphere also alters the intensity of the earth's magnetism, causing so-called magnetic storms, which interfere seriously with radio communication. Sunspots vary in size, number, and position on the sun from time to time, as was noted even before 1612, when Galileo trained his telescope on the sun and was able to observe them in detail. Since 1750, sunspots have been observed on a regular basis, and today the sunspot "number" is determined daily by observatories throughout the world. From the daily number is obtained a yearly average, which is an index to sunspot activity. Over the years there has been a regular repetition of sunspot activity, the individual cycle varying from 9 to 13 years, with an over-all average of 11.2 years between successive maxima. Sunspot maxima have occurred recently in 1928, 1937, 1947, and 1958.

Volcanic cycles are said to coincide with sunspot cycles, although there is wide disagreement on this subject. The causal relationship, if it exists, is obscure. Some of the evidence used to support the relationship between sunspots and volcanic cycles will be presented in the following pages.

Volcanic cycles are even less firmly established than sunspot cycles and are certainly as controversial. Most investigators will agree that volcanic activity is cyclic, but only in a few cases can they give even an approximation as to the nature and the length of the eruptive cycle. A volcanic cycle is likely to span a great many years, in some cases hundreds, and there are records for only a few volcanoes for a sufficient length of time to detect in the activity the repetition which must be observed before a cycle can be recognized. Each volcano has its own individual pattern of activity. Therefore it is impossible to formulate a cycle pattern which will apply to all volcanoes. In order to reduce the eruptive activity of each volcano to a cycle it is necessary to have detailed records for each volcano for many years. Such records are available for Vesuvius and Mount Etna in Italy, and, to a limited extent, for the Hawaiian volcanoes. The eruptive cycle for each of these volcanoes will be described in order to show the nature of a cycle and to acquaint the reader with the type of information revealed by such studies.

CYCLE OF KILAUEA

The two active volcanoes of the Hawaiian Islands, Kilauea and Mauna Loa, have been described in some detail in Chapter 10, and at this point only the cyclic pattern of the eruptions of Kilauea will be considered.

Summary of the Eruptive Cycle

The eruptive cycle at Kilauea begins with an explosion which forms a pit (Halemaumau) on the floor of the crater. Concurrent and subsequent collapse widens the pit, as happened after the explosive eruptions in 1790 and 1924. Then for several decades eruptions separated by quiescent intervals of several months or several years break out in the floor or wall of the pit and slowly fill it up. These eruptions produce cinder and spatter cones and lava lakes. Slowly the pit fills, and finally it may overflow the rim and flood the crater floor. All of these features are characteristics of rising magma beneath Kilauea, which causes the mountain to actually "swell up" by an amount which can be measured by special instruments known as tilt meters. Flank flows may occur, causing the level of the lava lake to sink to the level of the flank outflow. Flank outflows are usually of brief duration, often lasting only a few days and in most cases less than a month. The phase of upbuilding is finally terminated by another collapse, which may engulf most of the crater floor and which marks the end of the cycle.

The subsidence of the magma column, which results in engulfment, may result from lava discharges on the flanks, either above or below sea level; from intrusions of magma into the underground area as sills or dikes; or possibly from a recession of the magma into the magma reservoir. Whether an explosive eruption accompanies the collapse is purely a matter of accident, depending on whether the magma column recedes sufficiently to permit ground water to gain access to the zone of heated rocks. In summary, then, there are essentially two stages in the cycle: (*a*) a period of increasing pressure, accompanied by rising of the lava column with lava flows in the crater and on the flanks, and (*b*) a collapse, indicating decreasing pressure as the magma column recedes. Following collapse, the lava slowly returns to the crater, gradually building it up again for another collapse.

Periodicity of the Eruptive Cycle

Dr. Thomas A. Jaggar, who spent a lifetime studying Kilauea and Mauna Loa, was firmly convinced that the activity was rhythmic, with its basis an 11-year cycle. He further believed that the 11-year cycles were superimposed on a 132-year supercycle, made up of two parts of 66 years each. In considering what constitutes a cycle, Dr. Jaggar concluded, in common with most students of volcanoes, that the most distinctive feature of a volcanic cycle is the short repose period. It is only in volcanoes where the magma is visible most of the time, such as Kilauea, that the repose period is striking. His adoption of an 11-year cycle was first based on the repose periods of 1913 and 1924. Then, when this theory was applied to the entire period of 1790–1924, he found that no figure fits the repose periods as well as an 11-year interval. Further, he observed that if the entire period of 1790–1924 is divided into 12 cycles, the average length of each cycle is 11.1 years, or the same as the sunspot cycle. The supercycle of 132 years was approximately the period between the two paroxysmal eruptions of Kilauea, in 1790 and in 1924. In justifying his 11-year cycle, Dr. Jaggar pointed out that in the 1902–1913 interval both Mauna Loa and Kilauea were in complete repose at the beginning and end of the cycle and that both erupted lava during the cycle.

In his tabulation of the 11-year cycle, the repose (low-pressure) periods correspond with sunspot minima, while the periods of active discharge of lavas (high-pressure periods) correlate with sunspot maxima. Dr. Jaggar was unable to account for this relationship between sunspots and the volcanic cycle, but he felt that, "If the earth magnetism and electricity are in some way associated with gravity, volcanism may be affected. If heat by earth's radioactivity affects volcanism, the sun may in turn affect the earth's radiations. Finally, if volcanic emanations on the earth are a last remnant of solar processes here, these processes by unknown means may be sympathetic with the sun" (1931, p. 3).

Stearns and Macdonald (1946) evaluated the data on cycles in the eruptions of Kilauea and concluded that the evidence does not warrant the conclusions drawn by Dr. Jaggar. They pointed out that the 1790 explosive eruption, a key point in Dr. Jaggar's supercycle, was a "volcanic accident" and is not significant in the cyclic behavior of the volcano. The important feature is the subsidence of the magma column, and the explosion is more or less accidental. Likewise they were unable to relate the activity of Kilauea to an 11-year cycle or to see any close correlation between its activity and the sunspot cycle. The closest correlation between sunspots and eruptive periods was with Mauna Loa, which erupted during 6 of the 9 years of sunspot minima and whose eruptions for 2 of the remaining 3 years were only 1 year removed from sunspot minima.

Such conflicting conclusions point up the fact that 150 years of reliable observations is far too brief a period of observation for establishing an eruptive pattern for the volcano. Nevertheless, the facts do indicate that a cyclic repetition in the type of activity exists and that past performance is a reliable guide to future activity. It seems reasonable to conclude that this activity will fit into some rhythmic sequence, but whether it is Dr. Jaggar's 11-year cycle or some other pattern remains to be determined.

CYCLE OF MOUNT ETNA   *Eruptional History*

Mount Etna, on the island of Sicily, is one of the large volcanoes of the world and the highest in Europe, rising 10,625 feet above sea level. Its enormous cone, made up of many superimposed lava flows, is surmounted by literally hundreds of minor (parasitic) cinder cones which dot its flanks. More than 200 of these secondary cones occur within a radius of 20 miles from the summit crater. Some of these cones, such as Mount Rossi, 450 feet above its base and 2 miles in circumference, are quite prominent volcanoes in their own right.

Mount Etna has had a long eruptional history, and, unlike Vesuvius, was known from the earliest times to be volcanic in nature. Lyell in his *Principles of Geology* has a chapter on Mount Etna, based largely on observations made on frequent visits to the volcano. In a review of the early history of Mount Etna, Lyell (1875, 2:19–20) notes that it must have been active from the earliest times because Diodorus Siculus mentions an eruption which caused a district to be deserted by the Sicani before the Trojan War. Also, Thucydides (Book 3) records that in the sixth year of the Peloponnesian War, or in the spring of 425 B.C., a lava stream ravaged the environs of Catania, and that it was the third eruption since the colonization of that island by the Greeks. The second of the three eruptions took place in 475 B.C. and was vividly described by Pindar two years afterward in his Pythian Ode. The graphic description, such as it appeared five centuries before the Christian era, is comparable to that of a modern eruption. The poet is only making a passing allusion to Mount Etna, as the mountain under which Typhaeus lay buried, yet all the characteristic features are faithfully portrayed, such as "the snowy Etna, the pillar of heaven—the nurse of everlasting frost, in whose caverns lie concealed the fountains of the inapproachable fire—a stream of eddy smoke by day—a bright and ruddy flame by night; and burning rocks rolled down with loud uproar into the sea" (*Pyth*.1.20, as quoted by Lyell 1875, 2:20–21). According to Diodorus Siculus, a lava flow from Mount Etna in 396 B.C., 24 miles long and 2 miles wide, stopped the advance of the Carthaginian army. The absence of records during the Dark Ages makes it impossible to compile a complete list of the eruptions of Mount Etna. Disastrous eruptions are known to have occurred in 1169, 1329, 1536, and 1669. The eruption of 1669, which is well described, was the most violent on record. The summit cone was practically destroyed, and an enormous lava flow, 10 miles long, destroyed the city of Catania and flowed into the sea, blocking the harbor. The eruption of 1669 initiated for Mount Etna a new phase of activity which has continued to the present time.

Professor G. Imbo (1928), currently director of the Vesuvian Observatory but previously stationed at Catania, made a study of the

Plate 53. Mount Etna, Sicily,
from Taormina.

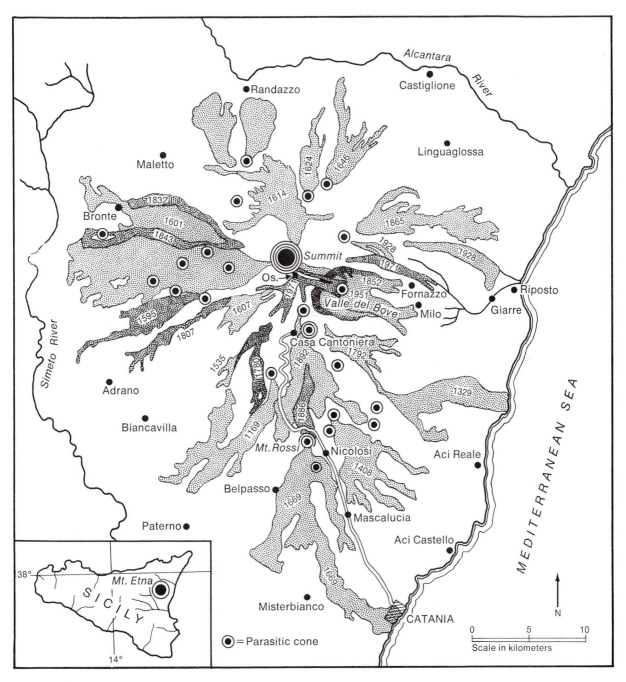

Figure 60. Mount Etna,
showing principal lava flows
and parasitic cones. Os.:
observatory.

cyclic nature of the eruptions of Mount Etna from 1669 to 1928. In this period 33 eruptions occurred, with an average interval of slightly over 8 years between eruptions. The period from 1669 to 1755 is open to some question because of poor records. During the period from 1755 to 1928, in which eruptions occurred at intervals of about 6.5 years, Imbo recognizes three major cycles:

    1755 to 1809—54-year cycle; 9-year interval between eruptions
    1809 to 1865—56-year cycle; 6-year interval between eruptions
    1865 to 1928—63-year cycle; 7-year interval between eruptions

Pattern of the Cycle

A typical eruption on Mount Etna is a "lateral eruption" in which lava issues from a fracture on the side of the cone. Generally, the lava issues from the lower part of the fracture, while explosive eruptions build cinder cones along the upper part of the fissure. In succeeding eruptions, lava issues from higher points along the fracture until its entire extent is sealed. The formation of a fracture and the outflow of lava from progressively higher points along the fracture until it is sealed constitute a cycle. Occasionally the lava flows begin at the top and proceed downward, but this is the exception. Terminal activity, which indicates that the magma is standing at a high level in the conduit, is usually the forerunner of a lateral eruption (Imbo 1965*b*). Such activity may persist for months or even years before a lateral eruption develops.

Normally the interval between an eruption closing a cycle and that initiating a new cycle is longer than the interval between eruptions within a single cycle. It requires more pressure (and time for it to accumulate) to split the cone to initiate a new cycle than to force lava out along an already existing break. The initiation of a new cycle is usually accompanied by vigorous earthquakes.

Recent Activity and the End of a Cycle

The 1950–1951 lateral eruption, which produced extensive lava flows from an elevation of around 2,700 meters, was from fissures associated with the 1928 eruptive zone. Although there were significant terminal eruptions in 1956–1957 and in 1964 (Silvestri 1964), each accompanied by lava flows which extended for three to four kilometers down the slopes of Mount Etna, they were not followed by typical lateral eruptions.

Beginning in January, 1967 (Rittmann 1969), more or less persistent activity began in the northeast terminal crater, with intermittent explosions ejecting lava "spatter" to heights up to 200 meters. As in 1964, subterminal lava flows, fed by underground channels from the northeast crater were common (Fig. 61). Such a flow in June, 1969, was producing lava at the rate of 10–12 cubic meters per second from a fissure on the west side of the northeast-crater cone. From a large blowhole which formed in the western part of the central crater in June, 1969, temperatures of 800°–1,100° C. and gas velocities around 60 meters per second (216 km./hr.) were measured (Tazieff 1969a). This activity was followed by a typical lateral eruption, which began on April 6, 1971, when four subterminal radial fissures opened at the southern and eastern base of the central cone at an elevation of 3,000 meters. Lava, accompanied by explosive activity, poured from these fissures and flowed for 3–4 kilometers down the south-southeast slope of Mount Etna, destroying the volcanic observatory, which was in the immediate area. Shortly, seven eruptive centers opened at increasingly lower altitudes, five of which were along an east-northeast fissure on the upper slope of Valle del Bove, the site of a large outpouring of lava in 1950–1951, as well as in line with the 1928 eruptive centers. The most extensive lava flow was from the lowest fracture, which was at an elevation of about 1,800 meters; although aligned with the 1928 rift, it was offset about 0.5 kilometer to the south. This flow, which began in mid-May and continued to the end of the eruption in mid-June, flowed to the southeast for a total length of about 6 kilometers, with the main front stopping near Fornazzo at an elevation of 800 meters, although a narrow tongue continued on for about a kilometer to an elevation of 600 meters (Fig. 60). Explosive activity (degassing) took place at a newly formed crater on the eastern slope of the central cone, which was about 5 kilometers from the most distant *boca*. The lava of the 1971 eruption covered an area of 7.5 square kilometers with an estimated volume of 75 million cubic meters, while the volume of the pyroclastics produced in the eruption was estimated to be 3 million cubic meters (Rittmann, Romano, and Sturiale 1971).

The eruption followed the pattern for lateral eruptions, although there was an unusually long period of preliminary activity at the terminal cone. Most of the activity was related to the 1928 fissure, and the eruption did conform, in general, to the 7-year interval between eruptions on this fissure (i.e., 1950–1951, 1956–1957, 1964, and 1971). On the basis of Imbo's interpretation, we may expect the present cycle to end around 1985, assuming a cycle of 57 years (the average of the last three cycles), and until that time eruptions may be expected to continue along the 1928 fracture zone. Thus, since we can predict the probable time as well as the direction along which eruptions will occur, the element of surprise in an eruption of Mount Etna is largely eliminated.

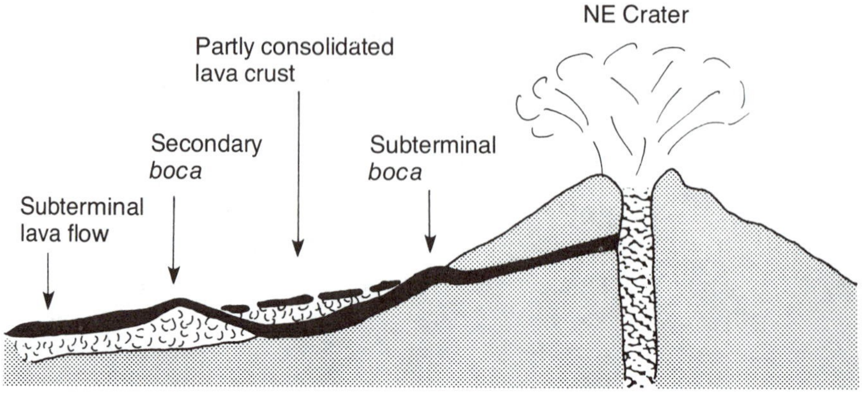

Figure 61. Subterminal and secondary bocas *and a subterminal lava flow at the northeast crater, Mount Etna. After Rittmann (1969).*

CYCLE OF VESUVIUS The geologic setting and the history of Vesuvius are described in Chapter 8. The first to recognize the cyclic nature of the eruptions of Vesuvius was Professor L. Palmieri (1873), who, following his study of the great eruption of 1872, announced that paroxysmal eruptions, such as that of 1872, always follow a long period of constructive activity and that a repose period follows the paroxysmal eruption. The eruptive cycle of Vesuvius, following the general pattern recognized by Palmieri, has been described by Mercalli (1907), Perret (1924), Alfano and Friedlander (1928), and Bullard (1954b).

Stages in the Cycle

The various stages in the Vesuvian cycle, as I interpret them, are illustrated by a series of sketches in Figure 62, to which the following explanations refer. After a grand eruption, such as those of 1872, 1906, and 1944, in which large outflows of lava occur and the upper part of the cone is destroyed and the crater enlarged, Vesuvius lapses into a period of repose which, on the average, has lasted about 7 years (Phase 1). The renewal of activity begins with explosions forming a cinder cone in the bottom of the crater. As the intracrater cone grows in size (Phase 2), outflows of lava may fill the space between it and the outer crater walls, forming a crater platform which becomes higher and higher, until it finally fills the summit crater (Phase 3). Some of the lava flows may spill over the crater rim or issue from fissures near the top of the crater, but such flows are of small volume and cause little damage. In other cases the explosive activity may throw out scoria and incandescent lava in an amount

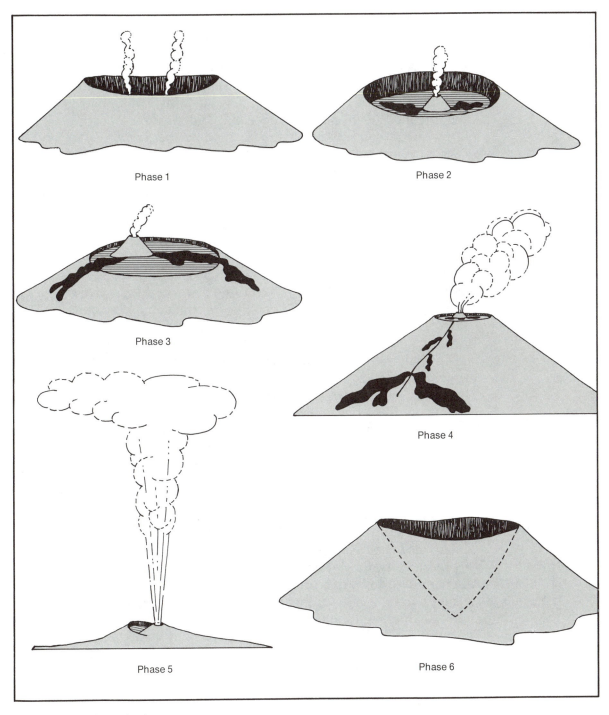

Phase 1

Phase 2

Phase 3

Phase 4

Phase 5

Phase 6

Figure 62. Eruptive cycle of Vesuvius.

equal to a lava flow. The cone building in the summit crater, or the spilling of lava over the rim, constitutes a moderate type of activity which is normal for Vesuvius and which may continue for 25–30 years. When the rebuilding of the summit cone is complete, that is, when the summit crater is filled, the stage is set for the culminating eruption. The column of lava, now standing at a high level in the throat of the volcano, is under tremendous pressure and is saturated with gas. Finally, accompanied by sharp earthquakes and strong explosions, the cone splits, frequently from the crater rim to the base (Phase 4). This fracture taps the lava in the conduit at a lower level, and, saturated with gases and under pressure of the lava column, it issues in great floods and flows rapidly down the side of the cone, destroying everything in its path. This is the grand eruption which signals the end of a cycle. Such an eruption is of short duration, lasting only a few weeks at most.

The fissures from which the lava issues usually open on the side of the main cone of Vesuvius, but three times in the last two centuries (in 1760, 1794, and 1861) the fissures opened on the outer slope of Mount Somma, indicating a deep connection with the volcanic conduit. The lava level in the conduit sinks as the lava drains out, reducing the pressure on the upper walls of the summit cone, and large-scale avalanching enlarges the crater and reduces the height of the cone. Finally, as the pressure is reduced on the lava column by the rapid outflows, a tremendous "gas blow-off" takes place, forming a gigantic eruption cloud miles in height (Phase 5). Perret (1924), who first recognized this phase in the 1906 eruption, emphasizes the continuity of the phenomenon. It is not an explosion but a continuous emission of gas under tremendous pressure, like that of a huge locomotive "blowing off" steam. This phase, in its most vigorous aspect, lasts only a matter of hours, and it marks the end of the eruption as well as the end of the cycle (Phase 6). The crater has been cleared and is now a basin-shaped depression, as represented by the dotted line on the Phase 6 diagram. The volcano then lapses into a period of repose, during which time the magma is again becoming gas-saturated and developing enough pressure to force an opening to the surface and initiate a new cycle. In summary, then, the eruptive cycle of Vesuvius may be divided into three main stages: (a) repose period, (b) moderate activity, and (c) paroxysmal eruption.

Recurrence of Cycles

Nearly all studies of the Vesuvian cycle begin with the great eruption of 1631, which initiated a new era in the activity of Vesuvius. Since that time it has been in an almost constant state of activity, and its eruptions have followed a cyclic pattern. Investigators do not agree on the number or length of the various cycles, but these differences relate to details rather than basic principles. Mercalli (1907) recognized 12 eruptive cycles since 1700, each culminating with a paroxysmal eruption followed by a repose period. The length of the cycles is variable, ranging from a minimum of 5 years (1850–1855) to a maximum, in Mercalli's list, of 25 years. However, the last two cycles, not included in Mercalli's list, 1872–1906 and 1906–1944, were 34 and 38 years respectively. Further details on the cycles of Vesuvius, including a description of several of the paroxysmal eruptions which ended cycles, is given in the section on the eruptive history of Vesuvius in Chapter 8.

Current Status

The latest grand eruption of Vesuvius, which ended a cycle, was in March, 1944, when lava flows destroyed the towns of Massa and San Sebastiano. Vesuvius then lapsed into a period of repose which marks the beginning of a new cycle. It has now been in repose for several times the average length of this period, and it is apparent that a renewal of eruptive activity is long overdue. If it follows the normal pattern, the activity will begin with explosions forming a cinder cone on the floor of the crater and will continue with cone building and outpourings of lava, which will gradually fill the crater. After some 30 years (more or less) of this type of activity, a paroxysmal eruption will end the cycle.

CYCLE OF KELUT VOLCANO

Studies by M. T. Zen and D. Hadikusumo (1965) show that the activity of Kelut Volcano, in eastern Java, Indonesia, follows a definite cyclic pattern, with an average interval of about 13 years between eruptions. The shortest period of dormancy ever recorded was 8 years, while the longest period was 18 years. Destructive mudflows, resulting from the ejection of the water of the crater lake in Kelut Volcano, have caused loss of lives and extensive property damage over the years. The efforts to control the water level in the crater lake and to prevent the destructive mudflows are described in Chapter 18.

The fact that volcanic eruptions are cyclic seems well established. However, the length and the sequence of events in a cycle, even with the best-known volcanoes, is somewhat in doubt. Volcanic observations so far, with few exceptions, have been limited to the

Plate 54. The 1805 eruption of Vesuvius. Lava is issuing from several points along a fracture which extends from the rim of the crater to the base of the cone. From an old painting.

periods of spectacular eruptions. In order to determine the eruptive cycle of a volcano, continuous observations are necessary. If such observations were carried on at all of the active vents of the earth, with use of the new equipment now available to scientists, it seems likely that a significant break-through would soon be made. With the establishment of the details of the eruptive cycle of a volcano, the next step would be prediction and control, including the possibility of utilizing the natural energy being released for the benefit of mankind. It is a goal worthy of our best efforts.

VOLCANOES AND TIDES   The gravitational pull of the moon and to a lesser extent that of the sun, resulting in the tides, are familiar to all. The tidal force varies inversely with the square of the distance; therefore the moon, although much smaller, exerts a more powerful tidal force on the earth, its force being about 2.5 times that of the sun. When the sun and the moon are aligned and their tidal forces are combined, the highest tides, known as spring tides, result. When the sun and moon are at right angles relative to the earth, lower tides, known as neap tides, result. The tidal stress is exerted on the entire earth, but only the waters of the ocean are pulled into a bulge, the rocky crust of the earth being too resistant to respond to the tidal pull. Since volcanoes and earthquakes are interrelated with pressure variations in the earth's outer shell, it is possible that they may respond to tidal stresses. Even the most ardent advocates of tidal forces as a factor in volcanic eruptions do not believe that such forces alone will cause a volcanic eruption. They feel, rather, that both volcanic eruptions and earthquakes are a release of stored energy and that tidal forces may serve as the "trigger" to release this energy. The idea is not new, for Pliny the Elder commented in his *Natural History*, published in 77 A.D., on a theory held some 1,000 years earlier by the Babylonians, according to which earthquakes are caused by the force of the stars and occur when the stars traveling with the sun are in agreement. Professor Palmieri (1873) observed, in his study of Vesuvius during the last half of the nineteenth century, that new lava flows usually occurred at the time of full moon. Although he was ridiculed at the time, the idea persisted, and others (notably Professor A. Riccò [1907]) found evidence that indicated a tidal influence in the eruptions of Mount Etna and Stromboli.

In his study of the great eruption of Vesuvius in 1906, Perret was convinced that tidal forces influenced the activity. He stated: "Midnight and midday at full moon invariably bring noticeable increase in eruptive activity—more marked during the course of an eruption or of an active period" (1924, p. 71). He arranged his trips to the crater to coincide with the lunisolar maximum (tidal) period and also took advantage of the minimum tidal period to visit the more dangerous localities. Thomas A. Jaggar, long-time director of the Hawaiian Volcano Observatory, was convinced that there was a relationship between earthquakes, volcanic eruptions, and tides, but he was uncertain of the correlation. One of my first assignments as Dr. Jaggar's assistant in 1939 was to plot the earthquakes and eruptive activity of the volcanoes in Hawaii on the tidal cycle to see if a relationship could be detected, but unfortunately the results were inconclusive.

G. A. Taylor (1958, p. 95), in his study of the eruption of Mount Lamington in 1951, noted that the eruptions were centered around the spring-tide period of full and new moon, and he speculated that the tidal stresses may have had a "triggering" effect in causing the eruptions.

Thorarinsson, in his study of the eruption of Surtsey Volcano in Iceland noted that "the moon was new at the time but even before then the eruption had tended to undergo changes with a full or new moon" (1967a, p. 26).

G. Latham et al. (1971) recognized a fortnightly and monthly cycle of seismic activity on the moon, as recorded by instruments left on the moon by the Apollo missions, and surmised that they were triggered by tidal stresses on the moon. It is not surprising that periodic tidal stresses should first be clearly detected on the moon, because the moon is free of the complicating effects of oceanic and atmospheric motion.

The eruptions of Stromboli Volcano, in the Adriatic Sea off the coast of Sicily, have long been regarded by many investigators as responding to changes in the weather (i.e., to changes in atmospheric pressure). Using the character of the steam column rising from the craters of Stromboli as a barometer, the old-time residents will confidently predict changes in the weather. If the volcano is responsive to variations in atmospheric pressure, it might also respond to tidal stresses. In an analysis of 33 of the major eruptions of Stromboli, M. J. S. Johnson and F. J. Mauk (1972) found that most of the eruptions occurred near the time of neap tides, but they were unable to detect any other correlations. The same authors (1973) extended their study to the major subaerial eruptions which have occurred between 1900 and 1971. In the 680 eruptions involved in their study, they found a concentration of eruptions around the fortnightly tidal maximum. They also found that volcanoes could be subgrouped in terms of petrology, geographic location, local crustal-deformation rates, and other geophysical factors. Andesitic and basaltic eruptions showed a significant concentration of events at the tidal maximum, but basaltic eruptions were equally concentrated at the tidal minimum. In a detailed study of the Japanese region Johnson and Mauk (1973) found that each volcano that erupted at or near the fortnightly tidal minimum is located in an area having a negative Bouguer anomaly (see glossary), a large crustal thickness, and a small rate of horizontal crustal deformation. Conversely, volcanoes in areas characterized by thinner crusts and crustal deformation rates in excess of three centimeters per year generally erupted at or near the fortnightly tidal maximum. No clear explanation for these relationships is possible until there is a better understanding of the volcanic mechanism. However, if andesitic and basaltic magma originate at different depths and have different viscosities, then a different response to tidal stresses would not be unexpected. Further, since magma migration is responsive to the direction of least compressive stress, the regional tectonic deformation must be a factor in eruptions.

A relationship between tides and volcanic eruptions was confirmed by Wayne L. Hamilton (1973) in a study which included all volcanic eruptions since 1500 A.D. In addition, he found that eruptions are favored in months when the tide is large at the latitude of the volcano. A semiannual tidal cycle results from variations in solar declination. The maximum amplitude of the semiannual component occurs on about April 22 and October 21. These are the times of maximum braking due to bodily tide torque, and they are close to the time of greatest eruption intensity. In addition, a longer tidal cycle may make certain years more favorable for volcanic eruptions. For example, every 8.85 years the moon is at perigee (i.e., nearest the earth) when the lunar declination is farthest south of the equator. This occurred in 1970. It is possible that the triggering potential may then enhance the likelihood of eruptions, especially large eruptions. Perhaps the volcanic activity in 1978–1979 will add information on this point.

Efforts to establish a relationship between tides and volcanic eruptions become unduly complicated because the time of a volcanic eruption is dependent on many factors, such as geologic structure, type of magma, geographic location, and other geophysical factors. Further, tidal stresses are a complex function, not only of the sun and moon, but also of ocean currents, the shape and size of ocean basins, and so on. Unlike the case of earthquakes, which may also respond to tidal stresses, the exact time (and even date) of a volcanic eruption is sometimes in doubt. Thus, to pinpoint the effect of tidal stress in the framework of the volcanic process is very difficult indeed. With the computer it has been possible to analyze the many factors which are involved in the relationship of tides and volcanic eruptions, and such papers as Hamilton's show the value of these studies. For more positive conclusions, more detailed information on the time and nature of individual volcanic eruptions is needed.

Chapter 13   Birth of New Volcanoes

The present is the key to the past.—SIR A. GEIKIE

The birth of a new volcano in historic times is indeed a rare event. The development of a parasitic cone on the side of an older, active volcano is a fairly common occurrence, but these should not be considered to be "new" volcanoes. Mount Etna has more than 200 parasitic cones, several of which have formed in historic time. Some of these cones are miles from the main crater and several hundred feet in height. Many of them would form impressive cones if they were on a plain where they were not dwarfed by the great mass of Mount Etna. The distinction between a new volcano and a parasitic cone is frequently difficult. Parasitic cones are related to a pre-existing vent, while a new volcano must open its own connection with the magma chamber. Thus an eruption removed from other volcanoes must be presumed to be a new vent. If, as is often the case, the eruption is near, but not a part of, an older volcano, the relationship may be uncertain. The decision is even more difficult if the older volcano has had no eruptions in historic time and appears to be extinct. In such a case the weight of evidence would favor classifying the eruption as a new volcano.

Only two new volcanoes, both in western Mexico, have been born in North America in historic times. The first was Jorullo in 1759, and the second was Parícutin in 1943; both are described in the following pages. It is quite possible that some of the submarine eruptions described as "new" volcanoes may, in fact, be parasitic cones in which the relationships cannot be determined.

PARÍCUTIN VOLCANO   *Significance of Parícutin*

Without a doubt the best-known of the "new" volcanoes is Parícutin, born in the state of Michoacán, Mexico, on February 20, 1943.

Note: The material in this section was first prepared for the Twentieth International Geologic Congress excursion to Parícutin Volcano in 1956. It was published (in Spanish) as "Resumen de la historia del Volcán Parícutin, Michoacán, México," *Twentieth International Geologic Congress Guide Book*, Excursion A-15, pp. 61–74 (Bullard 1956). It is presented here with some minor revisions.

Described as having been born in a cornfield while the owner was looking at it, it was featured in many popular magazines and has been the subject of numerous books and scientific articles. Dr. Ezequiel Ordóñez, a distinguished Mexican geologist, arrived on the scene on the third day of its activity. From that time until its activity ceased, nine years later, the volcano was under almost constant observation by a team of scientists organized as a committee of the U.S. National Research Council. As a member of that committee, I participated in its work throughout the life of the volcano. I first visited Parícutin when it was 2.5 months old, but this was only the first of many trips to observe the volcano during its nine years of activity.

In the second year of its life, which was one of its most active periods, I carried on an independent research study of Parícutin under a grant from the Geological Society of America and the University of Texas Research Institute. During the period of this study, from late July to December, 1944, I lived in a small observation cabin built by the National University of Mexico. The cabin, located about one kilometer from the base of the cone, afforded an unsurpassed view of the dramatic spectacle of a volcano in action, which may truly be called "the greatest show on earth." The cone was frequently covered with red-hot bombs of scoria ejected by tremendous explosions from the crater. Numerous lava flows poured from vents, some of which were near enough to the cabin to be observed from the doorstep. In one case a lava flow came to within 10 meters of the cabin before it stopped! When the cabin was eventually isolated by lava, I was forced to cross the still hot (but cooling) lava flows to get in and out of the area. Later the "island" on which the cabin stood was buried by lava. It had been abandoned some time before in anticipation of such a catastrophe.

It will be understandable, then, because of my personal experience with Parícutin, that more space is devoted to it than might otherwise be the case. This seems justifiable, furthermore, because, since Parícutin is one of the few volcanoes to be observed by scientists throughout its entire active cycle, it has provided much valuable information on many aspects of volcanic activity hitherto unknown or unexplained.

Named Parícutin for a small Tarascan Indian village (population 500 at the time of the eruption) 3 kilometers from the vent, the volcano is 320 kilometers due west of Mexico City. It can be reached by air, rail, or paved highway from Mexico City to Uruapan, and thence by 32 kilometers of paved and dirt road to Angahuan, 8 kilometers to the northeast of the cone.

Figure 63. Location of Parícutin and Jorullo volcanoes.

Birth of the Volcano

Parícutin Volcano was born on February 20, 1943, about 183 years after the birth of Jorullo, 72 kilometers to the southeast. Although literally hundreds of cinder cones similar to Parícutin abound in the general region, no eruptions had occurred in historic times (other than at Jorullo), and the Indians had no legends of any volcanic activity in the area.

The stories of the beginning of the volcano are varied. Fortunately, two trained scientists, Jenaro González Reyna and William F. Foshag (1947) investigated the various accounts, interviewed the eyewitnesses and many local officials, and prepared a record of the birth of Parícutin while it was still fresh in the memory of the local inhabitants.

One of the most fertile portions of this section of the state of Michoacán was the municipality of San Juan Parangaricutiro, which in-

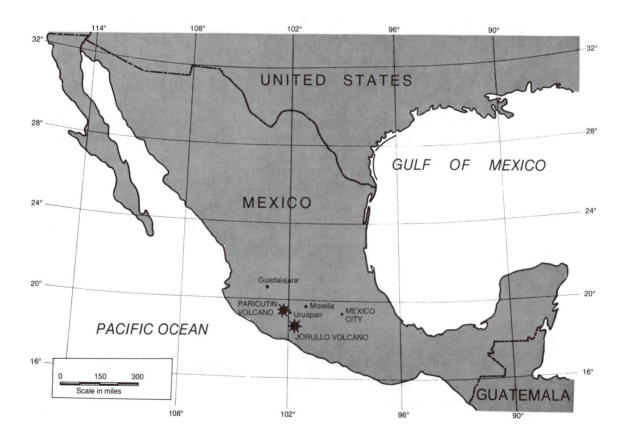

cluded also the villages of Parícutin, Anaghuan, Zirosto, Zacan, and others. The region, which consists of small, rich valleys between volcanic ridges and cones, is inhabited by the Tarascan Indians, who have maintained their own language and customs. In this section of Michoacán the tillable lands are privately owned, but the owners live in the villages and travel each day with their oxen and tools to the fields, returning to their homes in the evening. Three kilometers south of San Juan de Parangaricutiro and two kilometers southeast of Parícutin lies the valley of Rancho Tepacua. It is on the southeast slope of Cerros de Tancítaro (3,845 m.), the highest point in Michoacán.

In the valley of Rancho Tepacua a dweller in Parícutin Village, Dionisio Pulido, owned a parcel of land of about nine acres, on which a small hole had existed for many years. One of the older inhabitants recalled that as a small child, more than 50 years before, she had played about this small pit, where she frequently heard underground noises like falling rocks and felt emerging from it "a pleasant warmth."

The first indications of the eruption were a series of earthquakes, beginning on February 5, 1943. For two weeks they increased in number and intensity, and on February 19 no less than 300 were felt (Trask 1943).

On the morning of February 20, Dionisio Pulido left his village to prepare his farm for planting. He was accompanied by his wife, Paula, his son, and a neighbor, Demetrio Toral. There were, then, four eyewitnesses who saw the birth of Parícutin Volcano at close range.

As reported by González Reyna and Foshag (1947, p. 226), it was about 4:00 P.M. when Dionisio Pulido noticed a fissure which, at first only 0.5 meter in depth, extended northwest-southeast through the hole previously mentioned. Almost immediately there was thunder; the trees trembled; the ground swelled 2–2.5 meters; a smoke or fine ash-gray dust began to rise from portions of the fissure. More smoke, accompanied by a loud and continuous hissing and the odor of sulphur, followed. "Sparks" also were coming out of the fissure, and pine trees 30 meters from the opening began to burn. At this point all eyewitnesses hurriedly left the scene. By 5:00 P.M., from the plaza in San Juan de Parangaricutiro, a thin column of smoke could be seen rising, and many people gathered to discuss the phenomenon. It was decided that a group would go to investigate. Going on horseback, they soon arrived at the scene. They reported a fissure, at the southern end of which was a hole 0.5 meter across, from which issued smoke and red-hot stones. As they watched, the hole increased to 2 meters in breadth, and the volume of smoke increased.

The observers described the opening as pear-shaped. They saw this cavity erupting a fine, gray, dustlike ash, with "sparks" and stones, which were thrown out without much force to a height of 5 meters. In the opening the sand was "boiling" with a gurgling noise; a choking odor pervaded the area. Although the ash was very hot, the observers collected some, as well as two of the hot stones, to take back to San Juan de Parangaricutiro. The ground seemed to them to be "jumping up and down," but not with the swaying motion they had experienced in San Juan de Parangaricutiro (González Reyna and Foshag 1947, p. 230). In the early evening the volcano began to throw out larger stones, sufficient in size to be seen from San Juan de Parangaricutiro, although there was little noise accompanying the outbursts. Around midnight huge incandescent bombs were hurled into the air with a roar, and lightning flashes appeared in the heavy ash column. When Dionisio Pulido arrived at the scene at 8:00 A.M. on February 21, he saw a cone about 10 meters high emitting smoke and rocks with great violence. During the morning of the twenty-first the activity increased, and by midday the cone was 30–50 meters high, growing rapidly from the accumulation of great quantities of incandescent material being ejected. The amount of ash was relatively small, and the eruptive column much smaller than in later periods. The first lava issued on February 21, from the northeastern base of the new cone, spreading as a slaglike mass of black, jagged blocks about 5 meters in thickness over Sr. Pulido's farm, and moving approximately 5 meters per hour (Ordóñez 1943, p. 65). Then, on the evening of February 22, Dr. Ezequiel Ordóñez, veteran Mexican geologist, reached Parícutin. He describes the eruption, as he first observed it, as follows:

> I was witnessing a sight which few other humans had ever seen, the initial stages of the growth of a new volcano. Tremendous explosions were heard, ground tremors were felt frequently, and a thick high column of vapors with a great many incandescent rocks could be seen rising almost continuously from the center of a small conical mound then estimated to be 55 meters high. On the same night I noticed a red glow on the slope of the mound and large incandescent rocks rolled down a low rocky incline with a distinctly peculiar tinkling noise. Upon approaching this low scarp as closely as possible, it was found to be the front of a large lava flow moving from the north side of the base of the mound over a flat cornfield. (Ordóñez 1947, pp. 25–26)

The First Year

In its early stages the cone grew with startling rapidity. At the end of the first week it was 140 meters high, and its explosive activity had increased to an awesome thunderous bombardment, in which immense quantities of viscous lava were hurled continuously into the air. The noise of the explosions could be heard throughout the state of Michoacán and even in Guanajuato, 350 kilometers to the northeast (González Reyna and Foshag 1947, p. 233). Every few seconds, showers of glowing ejecta were thrown 600–1,000 meters above the crater rim, and, as they reached their zenith, they seemed to stop before beginning to fall. Then they shattered over the cone like a giant skyrocket, leaving a trail of fire as they cascaded down the sides. So abundant were these fragments that frequently the entire cone was covered with interlacing fiery trails (Bullard 1947b). Most of the bombs were from one-third meter to a meter in diameter and were smashed into fragments when they struck the ground. Occasionally they were fluid enough to flatten when they landed. Mixed with these clots of new magma were fragments of old andesite and plutonic rock torn from the wall of the conduit.

In late March the first lava flow stopped and the emission of ash greatly increased. The great ash-filled eruptive column, frequently rising to a height of 6,000 meters or more, scattered ash widely over the countryside. Heavy ash showers were frequent in Uruapan, and, on April 8, 9, and 10, fine ash falls occurred in Mexico City, 320 kilometers away.

In mid-April lava began to issue from the southwestern base of the cone, almost directly opposite the first flow. On June 10 a section of the upper part of the cone collapsed, and lava began to flow from the lower part of the break at a point 100 meters below the crater rim. Spectacular lava fountains developed, and a flow cascaded down the side of the cone, carrying huge masses of the slumped cone and fragments of earlier flows as erratics on its surface. At no other time in the history of Parícutin did lava flow from the crater; all other flows issued from *bocas* at or near the base on the northeast and southwest sides. My first visit to Parícutin, at the time of this spectacular activity, marked the beginning of an association with Parícutin which included a visit of a few weeks to several months to the volcano during each year for the next seven years.

The most violent period in the life of Parícutin was probably that of July and August of 1943, when lava stood higher in the central crater than at any subsequent period. On June 19, Parker Trask (1943, p. 504) reported lava to be only 15 meters below the rim. In general, the explosive activity at the central crater was greatest pre-

Plate 55. Parícutin Volcano, Michoacán, Mexico, on February 23, 1944. Photo courtesy Tad Nichols.

ceding the outbreak of a new lava flow. While the lava was flowing freely, the explosive activity was somewhat diminished.

On October 19, 1943, a parasitic vent named Sapichu opened at the northeastern base of the cone. It erupted with intense explosive activity, throwing out spectacular fountains of lava. Within a few weeks it attained a height of more than 100 meters, resembling in all respects the main cone. Shortly, a lava flow began to issue from Sapichu, carrying a wide section of the cone with it. This horseshoe-shaped, or "breached," cone (Pl. 56) was a familiar landmark at Parícutin until the summer of 1946, when it was finally buried by a succession of lava flows. While Sapichu was active the main cone was dormant, but as soon as Sapichu subsided the parent cone renewed its violent activity.

By the end of the first year Parícutin had reached a height of 325 meters above the cornfield where it started. It was during this period that cone building was the dominant process. Thereafter effusion of lava was the dominant process, and the growth of the cone was slight. Its height on February 21, 1950, was 397 meters, in comparison with 360 meters on the same day in 1947 and 336 meters on that day in 1944 (Fries and Gutiérrez 1951a, p. 219). When the eruptions ceased in 1952 the cone was 410 meters above the original surface of Sr. Pulido's cornfield (Fries and Gutiérrez 1954, p. 490), although it had attained greater height at various stages in its history, only to lose it by explosion or collapse.

Plate 57. Only the towers of the church project above the lava flow from Parícutin Volcano which destroyed the town of San Juan de Parangaricutiro in June, 1944. Photo by Tad Nichols, July 29, 1945.

The Second Year

In early 1944 the lava activity shifted to the southwest side of the cone, or the side opposite Sapichu, and for the next three years, or until January 19, 1947, lava emerged from closely spaced *bocas* on this side. The area of lava vents became known as the Mesa de los Hornitos (Tableland of Little Ovens), and hardly did one flow stop before another broke out from a new *boca* nearby. These flows were hotter, more fluid, and larger than the earlier flows.

It was in 1944 that the villages of Parícutin (population about 500) and San Juan de Parangaricutiro (population about 4,000) were destroyed by lava flows. Although heavy ash falls had partially buried both communities, the inhabitants had shoveled the ash from the streets and the roof tops and hoped they could survive the eruption. However, when it became apparent that they were in the path of an advancing lava flow, evacuation was the only recourse. Although

Parícutin and San Juan de Parangaricutiro were destroyed by different flows, separated by nearly three months, the evacuation pattern was the same in both cases. With the help of the Mexican army the inhabitants were hastily evacuated, many waiting until the lava was actually at their back door before they reluctantly consented to leave. One of my most vivid recollections is the confusion, bordering on chaos, in San Juan de Parangaricutiro as the soldiers of the Mexican army helped the inhabitants load their belongings in huge army trucks, with the red-hot lava front advancing on the adjoining block. In addition to their household goods, many salvaged doors, windows, lumber, and so on from their houses, material they would need in establishing a home in a new location, which in each case was provided by the Mexican government. Fortunately, there was no loss of life, only frayed tempers, in the whole operation.

The most extensive and voluminous flow from Parícutin was the flow which covered San Juan de Parangaricutiro. It began in January, 1944, from a *boca* in the Mesa de los Hornitos, and continued until August, 1944. It flowed eastward around the cone and then to the southeast until it reached a stream valley, which it followed in a northwesterly direction. The town of San Juan de Parangaricutiro, located in this valley, was largely covered during June and July, and the lava continued for about 2.5 kilometers beyond the town. The flow stopped early in August, having attained a total length of 10 kilometers.

The characteristics of the lava flows from Mesa de los Hornitos are well illustrated by the flow which covered the village of Parícutin in 1944. The flow began on September 27, 1944, while I was living in the small observation cabin about one kilometer from the south base of the cone. The following description of this flow is reprinted, with slight editorial changes, from my 1947 article in the *Geological Society of America Bulletin*:

> The first definite evidence that this *boca* was active was noted on the evening of September 27, when a strong red glow appeared on the southwest side of the cone. Since the *boca* is nearly directly back of the cone with respect to the *casita* (position of observation), some of the peculiar red glow observed about midnight on September 26 may have been associated with its development. The lava flow was first observed on the morning of September 28, when the lava front was approximately three-fourths of a mile from its source. It is perhaps worth noting that on the evening of September 27 I made the following entry: "There does not seem to be the red glow over the crater, such as has been present for several nights." This

Plate 58. Boca *of Paricutin*
lava flow of September, 1944,
photographed October 6,
1944.

Plate 59. Close view of boca
shown in Plate 58, photo-
graphed October 6, 1944.

strongly suggests that the lava in the crater drained out as the new *boca* became active.

The *boca* was located on the southwest side of the cone about 400 feet from the base and in the general vicinity of the source of the San Juan flow. The most striking feature at the *boca* was a large graben with one side at the Hornitos (actually cutting through the center of the most prominent one) and the other side about 200 yards to the northwest. The lava was issuing from a fault marking the west side of the graben. The displacement of the down-dropped block was about 30 feet.

On a trip to this area about a month before the outbreak of the flow, a large fracture cutting through the most prominent hornito was mapped and photographed. This fracture proved to be the east side of the graben. On this same trip many fractures were noted along the west side of the graben area, but their location could not be established with certainty. That these fractures were evident at least a month before the outbreak of the lava is proof that a close study of such features is essential.

The *boca* was about 75 feet in width, and the lava, rising along the fault marking the west side of the graben, was flowing at the rate of 50 feet per minute. In addition to the *boca*, there was a lake of lava, which at first appeared to be a whirlpool, but which was actually the lava welling up at either end of a circular pool and flowing to the center, where the two streams joined and disappeared together in a crevasse. The line of juncture of the two currents shifted from one side to the other, possibly in response to variations in volume and velocity of the lava streams from the two sides. Such a convection system is characteristic of lava lakes and indicates a direct connection with the underlying magma. The cooler, heavier surface lava sinks and is replaced by the hotter, lighter material from below. Convection systems of this type are common features in the fire pit of Halemaumau at Kilauea Volcano, Hawaii.

Intrusive lava was present in the southward extension of the fractures along which the lava lake and the *boca* were located. Comparatively little gas was present in the lava as it issued from the *boca*. Occasionally a blister would form, and gas would escape with a hissing noise, but there were no explosions such as were observed in the September 4 flow.

The lava flowed westward from the *boca*, carrying, in the early stages, many erratics of the San Juan flow with it. About a quarter of a mile from the *boca* the lava stream plunged into a deep ravine. This ravine was about 75 feet deep, and as the stream of lava plunged over the side it produced a most spectacular lava cascade. The flow followed the ravine, which was along the margin of the June, 1943, flow, and on reaching the end of this flow, near the village of Parícutin, it spread out, covering most of the site of the village of Parícutin, which had escaped the earlier flow. Continuing beyond the village of Parícutin, the flow reached a stream valley, which it followed to the northwest.

When the *boca* area was investigated on October 6, the lava lake was crusted over, and the surface was covered with many active gas vents. The gas vents were small chimneylike elevations, three to five feet high, and from the red-hot interior gas was escaping with a roar like the exhaust of steam from a locomotive. Dozens of these "exhausts" produced a noise that could be heard for more than half a mile. Deposits of ferrous chloride covered the entire area, and hydrochloric acid fumes made it difficult to approach the area, except under favorable wind conditions.

When the rate of advance of the flow was first measured (11:00 A.M., September 28) the lava front was due west of the *casita*, along the west margin of the June, 1943, flow. The rate of advance at this time was 60 feet per hour. Later, on September 29, the most rapid lobe was moving about 40 feet per hour. The lobe which covered the site of the village of Parícutin was advancing 20 feet per hour when it crossed the main east-west street at 5:00 P.M., on September 29. This flow joined the San Juan flow on October 17 and continued its forward movement until about November 1. (Bullard 1947a, pp. 439–441)

Activity from 1945 to 1952

The general outline of the Parícutin lava field was defined by the end of 1944 (Fig. 64). Subsequent flows, which were superimposed on earlier flows or injected sill-like into earlier flows, did not enlarge the lava area appreciably (Fig. 65). Lava continued to issue from various vents at the southwest base of the cone throughout 1945 and 1946.

On January 19, 1947, a new *boca* opened at the northeastern base of the cone not far from the former site of Sapichu and about 100 meters lower than the vents on the southwestern side. An interesting change in the surface of the cone accompanied the opening of this new vent. On December 4, 1946, two sets of steam cracks were observed on the southwestern flank of the cone. On January 15 the segment of the cone between the cracks slumped, leaving scarps 2 meters in height extending down the side of the cone, and a new lava

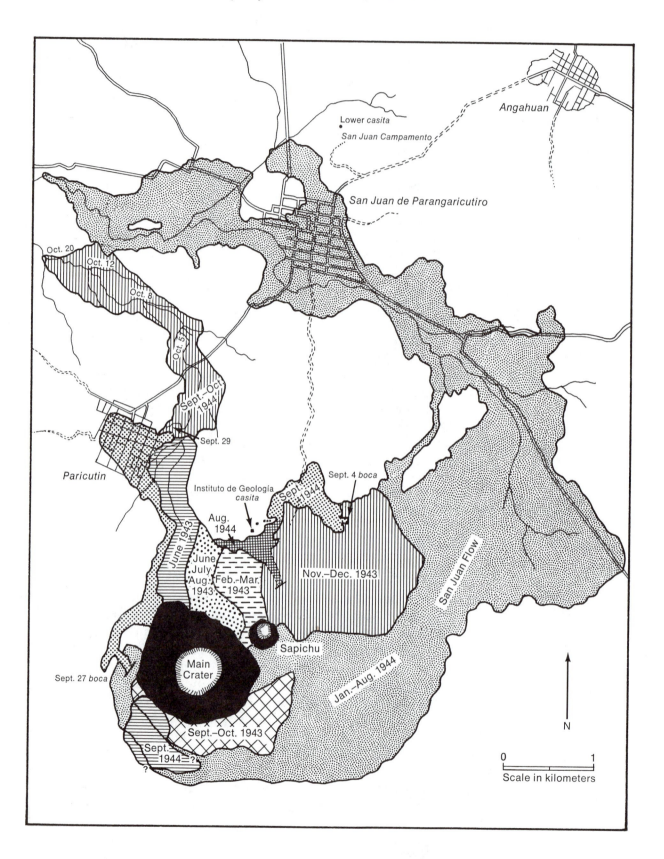

*Figure 64. Lava flows from
Parícutin during the first two
years, 1943 and 1944. From
Bullard (1947a).*

*Figure 65. Lava fields of
Parícutin at the end of the
eruption. After Fries, from
Bullard (1956).*

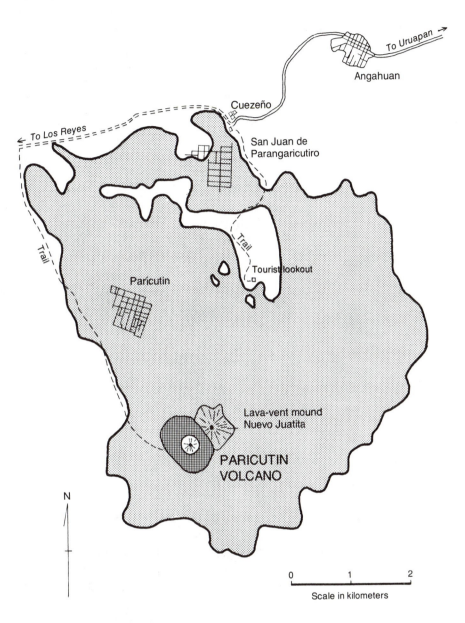

Angahuan

To Uruapan

Cuezeño

To Los Reyes

San Juan de
Parangaricutiro

Trail

Trail

Paricutin

Tourist lookout

Lava-vent mound
Nuevo Juatita

PARICUTIN
VOLCANO

N

0   1   2
Scale in kilometers

vent opened at the base of the slumped segment. Additional slumping of this segment in the ensuing weeks depressed the southwestern rim a total of about 10 meters. Diametrically opposite, a segment of the northeastern cone slumped on January 13, the fractures first appearing at the top of the cone and extending farther down the flank from day to day. On January 19 a portion of the base of the slumped segment, exactly in line with the old Sapichu vent, was pushed outward to form the new *boca*, later named the Juatito (Wilcox 1947, pp. 729–730). The development of the slumped block, or graben, directly in alignment with the fracture on which the northeastern and southwestern vents were situated, seems significant. On September 1, 1947, the old Ahuan vent on the southeastern side became active and continued to emit large quantities of lava until the end of 1947. It may be noted that the lava from the revived Ahuan vent tended to pile up around the vent and spread in lobes of much greater thickness than the previous flows. This may be due in part to the smaller gradients in the direction of flow and in part to the greater viscosity of the lava, which had by this time reached a silica content of over 58 percent (Wilcox 1954, p. 288).

On February 7, 1948, the vents at the northeastern base of the cone reopened, and shortly afterward the Ahuan vent closed. Thereafter, up to the final cessation of lava activity on February 25, 1952, lava continued to flow from the northeastern vents (Fries and Gutiérrez 1950a; 1950b; 1951a; 1951b; 1952a; 1952b; 1954).

The Final Activity

The cessation of activity came abruptly, rather than by a gradual decline, as might have been expected. As described by Fries and Gutiérrez (1954), the continued activity at the northeastern side had formed a lava-vent mound down which the lava flows cascaded from time to time. On February 8, 1952, a new cascade formed on this mound, and the lava continued to flow in large volume until February 22, when the flow became sluggish on the surface. During the evening of February 22 the emission declined abruptly, and on the morning of February 25 it ceased altogether. The cessation of lava emission also marked the cessation of continuous eruptions in the crater. Fries and Gutiérrez (1954, p. 489) reported that the strong detonations characteristic of the last two years of the eruptive history had continued to increase in frequency, some 305 detonations occurring between February 1 and February 25, 1952, when the strong eruptions ceased abruptly. This frequency compares with a total of about 400 such detonations for the last six months of 1951. Coarse pyroclastic material expelled by these intense explosions was so abundant that it frequently obscured the cone from view. Blocks of lava weighing more than 100 tons were hurled from the crater and fell beyond the base of the cone.

As reported by Fries and Gutiérrez, the final explosive activity developed as follows:

> Beginning on January 1, 1952, both crater vents were active and of nearly equal eruptive intensity. At times the eruptions were simultaneous in the two vents and at other times they showed no relationship from one vent to the other. On January 23 the eruptions alternated from white vapor to black ash-laden vapors, but at other times such an alternation was not observed. In addition to ordinary explosions every 5 to 15 seconds, intense detonations occurred at irregular intervals of 15 minutes to four hours, without exhibiting any recognizable periodicity.
>
> On February 24, the last day of strong continuous eruptive activity, the ash eruption was of the type that first began on March 18, 1943, and ash rained down over the countryside in large quantities, especially northeast of the cone, where a gray curtain extended several kilometers from the Volcano. This eruption was apparently the final spasm of activity, for during that same night continuous activity came to a halt. Except for a few intense explosions the following day, eruptions occurred only intermittently until March 4, when activity ceased entirely. (1954, p. 489)

Thus, after nine years and 12 days, the active period in the life of Parícutin Volcano came to an end.

Notes on the Eruptive Products

Volume of Ejecta. The total area covered by lava from Parícutin is 24.8 square kilometers (Fries and Gutiérrez 1954). As pointed out previously, the surface extent of the lava field did not increase a great deal after the second year, but the thickness, especially near the cone, increased markedly. On the northeastern side, where flows issued almost continuously from early 1944 to early 1947, the lava attained a thickness of about 245 meters, and a similar condition obtained on the southeastern side. As a result of the flows' burying the lower part of the cone, the height above the lava field decreased, and the cone appeared to be smaller. The total volume of rock material erupted, including both lava and pyroclastics, was computed by Fries (1953, p. 611) to be equal to 1.4 cubic kilometers in the magma chamber. Fries calculated this to be 3,596 million metric tons, or an average of 1.1 million metric tons of solids (i.e., lava and pyroclastics) per day during the entire life of the volcano. Lava constituted about 27 percent of the total, with pyroclastic material making up the remainder. The determination of the gases, including water vapor, was less satisfactory, and in the calculation made by Fries only the year of 1945 was used. During this period Fries calculated that the daily emission of water amounted to about 13,600 metric tons, and this amounted to about 1.1 percent of the total magma reaching the surface during this period.

Composition of the lava. The lavas of 1943 were olivine-bearing andesites (basic andesites) with a silica content of 55 percent. Ray E. Wilcox (1954) showed that the lava became progressively more acidic (i.e., containing a higher percentage of SiO_2) throughout the life of the volcano, with 1952 lavas containing 60 percent silica. In the first-year lavas, a few phenocrysts (crystals which can be seen with the unaided eye or a simple hand lens) of olivine and plagioclase occurred in a fine ground mass. In later flows the plagioclase phenocrysts disappeared and the olivine phenocrysts became scarce. The lavas are classified as orthopyroxene andesites.

Distribution of pyroclastics. Distribution is discussed in Chapter 5.

Geologic Setting of Parícutin Volcano

The oldest rocks exposed in the region surrounding Parícutin Volcano are volcanics which Williams (1945; 1950) named the Zumpinito formation. These rocks are exposed in deep gorges and canyons where erosion has cut through the cover of recent volcanic material. The Zumpinito formation consists of a variety of material ranging from olivine-rich basalts to rhyolites. In some areas lava predominates, while in others tuffaceous sediments are more abundant. No original volcanic forms are preserved, nor is it possible to locate any vents from which the material issued. The Zumpinito formation is usually flat-lying, except locally, as near Uruapan, where it is steeply tilted. Williams (1950) concluded that the formation must cover a considerable span of Tertiary time and that the topmost beds cannot be younger than middle Pliocene.

The oldest volcano of post-Zumpinito age in the area is the great volcanic mass of Cerros de Tancítaro, which lies immediately to the southwest of Parícutin Volcano. Rising to 3,845 meters, it is the highest peak in Michoacán and from a topographic standpoint dominates the region around Parícutin. Although Parícutin Volcano is at the base of Tancítaro, it is not a parasitic cone but belongs to a later period of activity. Williams (1950) described Tancítaro Volcano as a shield type cone which has been deeply dissected to the point that it now consists of a series of radiating, sharp-crested spurs separated by deep canyons. The lower part of the cone has been covered by ejecta from the younger volcanoes which dot the area. The eruptions which built Cerros de Tancítaro were the quiet, effusive type, consisting largely of porphyritic andesite. The age of Tancítaro is undetermined, but it was formed upon the deeply eroded surface of the Zumpinito formation, and Williams (1950) concluded that the last eruptions of Tancítaro were either in late Pliocene or early Pleistocene time.

After the growth of the large andesitic volcanoes, such as Tancítaro, the centers of volcanic activity in the Parícutin region became more numerous, and the lavas ejected were dominantly olivine basalts and olivine-bearing basaltic andesites. These younger volcanoes, of which there are literally dozens in the general area, show few effects of erosion and certainly must be postglacial (Recent) in age. Parícutin Volcano belongs in this group and is unique only in the fact that it is the last one to have formed.

JORULLO VOLCANO

The volcano Jorullo was born on September 29, 1759, in the midst of an area that was being cultivated at the time. Alexander von Humboldt (1811) visited Jorullo in 1803 and was enchanted with the notion of having found in Jorullo an example of the craters-of-elevation theory of his friend Baron von Buch. Since von Humboldt's time, nearly every geologic textbook has used Jorullo either as an example of the craters-of-elevation theory or as evidence to disprove it. It is certainly one of the best known of the volcanoes born in historic time.

Location

Jorullo is located in western Mexico in the state of Michoacán, about 150 miles west of Mexico City and some 50 miles southeast of Parícutin Volcano (Fig. 63). It is on the Pacific slope of the Mexican plateau and in an area containing a number of young basaltic cones. The general elevation is about 2,500 feet, and the climate is tropical. The region is relatively inaccessible but can be reached by a truck road south from Pátzcuaro, through Ario de Rosales to La Playa and La Huacana. The nearest settlements are La Playa, about 3 miles to the east of the cone, and La Huacana, about 7 miles to the southwest. La Playa contains the ruins of a once rather elaborate hacienda, which I was fortunate in being able to use as headquarters on two trips to Jorullo.

At the time of the eruption the Hacienda de Jorullo was one of

Figure 66. Sketch map of
Jorullo and subsidiary cones.
Lava flows are numbered
from oldest (1) to youngest
(4). After Ordóñez (1906).

three farms operated in the general area for the production of sugar
and cattle. Because of the fertility of the soil and the tropical climate,
the area was known as Jorullo, which in the language of the Tarascan Indians means "paradise."

Records of Eruptive History

Accounts of the early stages of the eruption are contained in two
diarylike reports by Manuel Román Sáyago, administrator-in-chief
of the haciendas, to the governor of Michoacán and through him to
the viceroy of New Spain. Two other brief accounts by eyewitnesses,

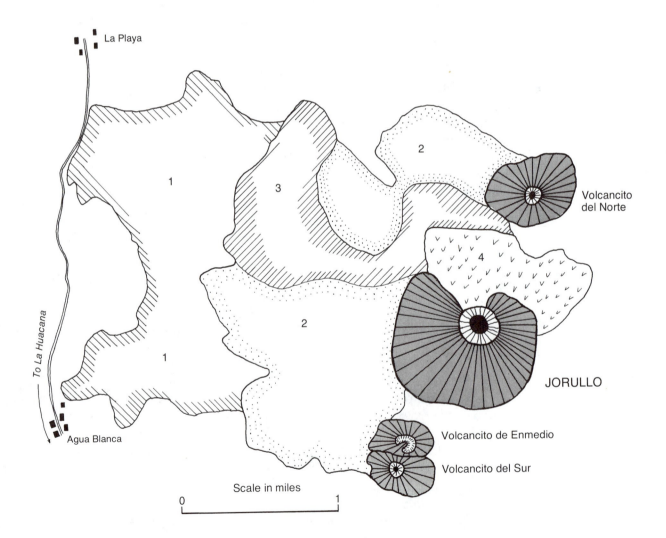

Figure 66. Sketch map of Jorullo and subsidiary cones. Lava flows are numbered from oldest (1) to youngest (4). After Ordóñez (1906).

which unfortunately add little to Sáyago's reports, are contained in letters of Joaquín de Anzagorri, priest at La Huacana, to his bishop at Morelia and to the Abbé Clavigero, the latter published in Italian but later translated into Spanish and English. Other than the accounts mentioned, which cover only the first months, no records of the eruptive history of Jorullo by eyewitnesses have been found. The next account is a report by Antonio de Riaño, governor of Michoacán, who visited Jorullo in 1789, 30 years after the initial eruption. With information he could obtain from the natives, Riaño (1789) attempted to reconstruct some of the details of the eruption. However, in the 20-odd years which had elapsed and without any written records, many of the details he obtained were hazy and uncertain. The area surrounding the volcano was abandoned, and quite likely very few, if any, of the Indians had been close enough to see what was actually going on at the volcano.

Since von Humboldt's visit in 1803, many geologists have visited Jorullo, although they have written comparatively little on it. An excursion of the Tenth International Geologic Congress, held in Mexico City in 1907, visited Jorullo. The guidebook for the excursion (Ordóñez 1906), written in French and prepared by Ezequiel Ordóñez with the help of Andrés Villafaña, is still the standard reference on Jorullo. Dr. Hans Gadow, biologist from the University of Cambridge, visited Jorullo in 1908 in order to study the reintroduction of plants and animals to the region following their destruction by the eruption. Gadow's book, published posthumously in 1930, contains, in addition to information on the plant and animal life, an excellent review of the historical material on Jorullo. Dr. Gadow, in an appendix entitled "Extracts from the Literature Concerning Jorullo" gives an English translation of Administrator Sáyago's reports and excerpts and summaries, as well as bibliographic references, for most (perhaps all) of the material on the early history of Jorullo. Dr. Gadow's scholarly work has been used freely in the preparation of this topic. I made two trips to Jorullo, one in 1945 and another in 1950.

Eruption of Jorullo

The following account of the preliminary events leading up to the eruption of Jorullo Volcano and of its early activity is based on Sáyago's reports of October 8 and November 13, 1759, as quoted by Gadow (1930, pp. 77–82).

Near the end of June, 1759, the people living at the Hacienda de Jorullo were alarmed by subterranean noises which, accompanied by mild earthquakes, continued until September 17. At this time the noises became much louder, being compared to cannon fire, and the earthquakes were strong enough to seriously damage the chapel. The frightened people fled to the surrounding hills for safety. There was a rumor that on Saint Michael's Day, September 29, Jorullo would be destroyed. The administrator sent to Pátzcuaro for a priest to celebrate Mass in order to appease the divine ire. The priest arrived on September 20, and on the twenty-first he began a nine-day Mass, during which time the noises and earthquakes continued until the twenty-seventh, when there was a brief lull. At 3:00 A.M. on September 29, about a mile to the southeast of the hacienda in a ravine known as Cuitinga Creek, a very dark and dense steam cloud rose, accompanied by sharp earth tremors and loud explosions, and soon flames burst through the cloud, which was becoming thicker and denser. The terrified people gathered in the chapel. While Mass was being heard, a rain of mud covered the roof and the ground, and, as the tremendous explosions continued, a strong odor of sulphur permeated the air. It seemed indeed that the predictions for Saint Michael's Day were coming true! For two days the volcano threw out masses of "sand [cinders], fire and thunder without one minute cessation." On October 1 a mass of "sand so hot it set fire to whatever it fell upon" rose from the outlet of the volcano, which was little more than a cleft, and flowed for nearly a mile down Cuitinga Creek. The stream bed was filled for the first half mile, and as the water underneath was converted into steam it exploded in geyserlike eruptions at many places. All of the neighboring streams became flooded, and many of the domestic animals were drowned in trying to escape. The flood of water associated with the eruption is one of the controversial points in Administrator Sáyago's account. He mentions that the floods were produced "not only by the rain from the sky, but by springs which opened from all the hills around." In fact, the volume of water was so great that he feared "that all the valleys of Jorullo, the Presentación [another one of the farms five miles to the west of Jorullo], and the village of La Huacana may be turned into one big lake."

Heavy rains accompanying volcanic eruptions have been noted in many cases, as have floods of water which do not appear to be directly related to rains. It is interesting to note that the same problem is raised at Jorullo. It may be recalled, in this connection, that the outpouring of hot gases and the tremendous quantities of steam produce what is the equivalent of a thunderstorm, but, unlike the customary thunderstorm which moves across the country, this one is stationary over the volcano.

By October 6, ash and cinders had destroyed the Presentación farm, as well as the village of La Huacana, two miles beyond, and the natives had fled to the neighboring hills. Administrator Sáyago makes special note of the fact that on October 8 began a new phase of activity, in which "the volcano threw up a great lot of stones which fell as far as half a league from its mouth, and which, as was found later on, were very soft and as if overbaked or glassy." This clearly indicates that the first scoria bombs were ejected at this time. Administrator Sáyago's first report ends with October 8, and his second and last report continues the account up to November 13.

From his second report we learn that "since this day [October 9] fell moreover great masses of rocks from the clouds, some of them as large as the body of an ox, which after having been shot up like a bullet, fell around the mouth of the volcano, and smaller pieces, thrown up higher, came down at longer distance and in such numbers that scattering in the cloud they looked in the daytime like a flock of crows and in the night like a crowd of stars" (Gadow 1930, p. 80).

On Friday, October 12, a new vent opened, 600 yards from the main crater. This is one of the three satellite cones which are aligned in a general north-south direction with the main vent at Jorullo. The dates for the origin of the others are in doubt, but it is interesting to have confirmation on at least one, although which cone is meant is in doubt, since the distance given by Sáyago does not fit any of the vents and the other information would apply equally well to all three.

The vigorous ash eruptions continued throughout the period covered by the second report, spreading destruction over a wide area in all directions from the volcano, and "the cattle could find nothing to eat, the trees and shrubs being destroyed and the leaves covered with ashes; and nothing to drink during all this time the water was rendered unfit by mud and sulphurous matter" (Gadow 1930, p. 81). Similar conditions were reported for a distance of 10–12 leagues (30–40 mi.) west of the volcano. This distance, however, seems to be somewhat exaggerated.

No lava flows were reported from the volcano during the period covered by Sáyago's first report. From his second report we learn that the governor was interested in this particular aspect and that, on November 13 (the last day covered by his report), "I went down [from the hills] for a new look at Jorullo to find out whether that pitch or lava has run, about which his Excellency has asked in particular." After which Administrator Sáyago, showing wisdom which all will envy, continued, "Please let his Excellency know in answer to his special question, that I neither have any knowledge of so-called lava, nor have I anyone to tell me what stuff it may be; but whatever it may be here does not run or flow" (Gadow 1930, p. 82).

Here Administrator Sáyago's diary ends with a note that the cone is now 300 varas (820 ft.) in height; that it began not from the top of a hill but in the deepest and most level part of the Cuitinga Valley; and finally that no lives were lost in the eruption. It is certainly regrettable that so accurate an observer as Sáyago could not have provided a complete record of the activity of Jorullo. However, since the land had been ruined for cultivation, he was ordered to move the inhabitants elsewhere, and we hear no more from him.

There are no written records covering the remainder of the active period of Jorullo. Oral tradition, compiled years later, indicates that violent eruptions continued until February, 1760, and with decreasing intensity until about 1775, making the total life of Jorullo's activity about 15 years. The outpouring of lava consisted of at least four separate flows forming a great malpais which covered nine square kilometers to depths up to 100 meters. The lava flows are believed to have appeared in 1764, considered to be the year of maximum activity. The first three flows are covered with ash and cinders, indicating that these materials were still being ejected after the outpourings of lava. However, the last flow, which issued from a breach on the north rim of the crater and flowed as a great cascade down the north side of the cone, is free of any ash or cinder cover. This "frozen" cascade of black lava is still quite "new" and "fresh" looking and is one of the striking features of Jorullo. It seems likely that this was the end of the explosive activity of the volcano and that thereafter it was in a fumarolic state. The three satellite cones, one on the north and two on the south of Jorullo, were present in 1766. It appears, therefore, that the general aspects of the eruption were completed during the first 7 years of its activity and that only minor activity continued for the next 8 years.

Posteruptive Appearance

A reliable description of Jorullo, 30 years after the eruption began, is given by Antonio de Riaño, governor of Michoacán, who visited the volcano in 1789 in company with Franz Fischer, a German mining expert, and Ramón Espelde, a local Spaniard who was living at La Playa. Espelde had made an ascent of Jorullo in 1780 and was familiar with the area. From Riaño's account it is learned that the "hill of the volcano is bare and only here and there some small trees . . . and patches of grass are beginning to take root"; also, that there were still numerous fumaroles, especially from the "hornitos" on the lava flows, and on "some spots the inner fire is strong enough to scorch the feet and one cannot hold his hand to the holes of these chimneys on account of the moist heat [steam]" (Gadow 1930, p. 87).

Riaño apparently was familiar with von Buch's craters-of-elevation theory, probably through Franz Fischer, and he pointed out that "on

Plate 60. Jorullo Volcano, Mexico. The last lava flow, which issued from the crater (no. 4, Fig. 66), is the dark mass on the left of the cone. Photo courtesy Dr. Donald Brand.

the day of the frightful event it was observed that the surface of the ground rose perpendicularly, more or less bulging up and forming huge bladders, the largest of which is today the hill of the volcano. These swellings, big bladders or cones of various sizes and shapes, burst and threw out of their mouths boiling mud . . . and stones" (Gadow 1930, p. 87).

Alexander von Humboldt (1811; 1866, bk. 4) spent two days at Jorullo on September 18 and 19, 1803, 44 years after the initial eruption. He had Riaño's description, published in 1789, and he was accompanied by Ramón Espelde, who had also accompanied Riaño. Von Humboldt was an enthusiastic supporter of von Buch's craters-of-elevation theory, and he was so eager to find support for it at Jorullo that he was unable to see any other possibility. Von Humboldt described the malpais, an area of nine square kilometers, which he did not recognize as a lava flow, as rising like a bladder: "The original limits of this elevation may still be recognized by broken strata at

Plate 60. Jorullo Volcano, Mexico. The last lava flow, which issued from the crater (no. 4, Fig. 66), is the dark mass on the left of the cone. Photo courtesy Dr. Donald Brand.

the edge . . . the convexity of the elevated area increases progressively towards the center to a height of 160 meters. . . . In the middle of the pushed up area, on a crack running NNE to SSW came six large hills, all elevated from 400 to 500 meters above the ancient plain" (1811, pp. 250–251).

Like Ordóñez and others, I was able to count only three satellite cones in addition to the main cone of Jorullo; so von Humboldt has included two additional ones. It seems incredible that von Humboldt did not recognize the true nature of the malpais as a lava flow, since its nature is so apparant. As late as 1848, after Lyell, Scrope, and others had shown conclusively that volcanic cones were the result of accumulation of ejected material, Daubeny, in an exhaustive work on volcanoes, followed von Humboldt in describing Jorullo: "A tract of ground from three to four square miles in extent rose up in the shape of a bladder" (1848, p. 480). He included a sketch (Fig. 67) to show the nature of the phenomenon. Daubeny, in a footnote, recognized that "Mr. Lyell and Mr. Paulett Scrope and others have questioned the correctness of the representation which Humboldt has given of the above phenomena, but without, as I conceive, being able to substitute a more plausible hypothesis" (ibid.).

On the surface of the malpais at Jorullo were numerous small domelike protuberances from which hot gases escaped. These are known as *hornitos* from the Spanish word for "little oven." Although somewhat of a mystery at Jorullo, they have since been observed on many active lava flows and are now a commonplace feature. At the time of von Humboldt's visit to Jorullo, many of the hornitos were still giving off hot gases to the extent that the air temperature over the malpais was somewhat higher than that of the surrounding area. However, when Hermann José Burkart visited Jorullo in 1827, he found only a few of the hornitos on the malpais giving off any heat, although there were numerous steam vents in the crater (Gadow 1930). When Emil Schleiden visited Jorullo in 1846, he noted that there were only 2 fumaroles on the malpais proper, but he counted more than 100 at other places, mostly at the southern edge of the lava flow which cascaded from the crater and from the crater rim (ibid.).

The most recent material published on Jorullo is a brief note contained in a report on erosion studies at Parícutin Volcano by Segerstrom (1950). A topographic map was made of the immediate area, and this map, which is probably the first accurate map of the volcano, is an important part of the report. The maximum height of Jorullo is 1,330 meters, although the average elevation of the crater rim is 1,300 meters. The cone rises 380 meters above its west base and 230 meters above its east base. The crater is an oval-shaped depression with a diameter at the rim of 400 meters by 500 meters. Its depth is 150 meters below the highest point, or about 120 meters below the

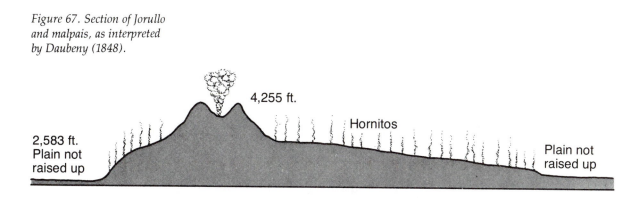

Figure 67. Section of Jorullo and malpais, as interpreted by Daubeny (1848).

average rim level. The bottom of the crater appears to have collapsed since its last eruptive activity, and the bottom is filled with rubble which has fallen from the sides. On the northwestern side of the crater, a little nearer the rim than the bottom, there is an area of perhaps one-half acre of "hot rocks." This area, which has been exposed by avalanching from the crater walls, contains a series of fissures a foot or more in width and parallel to the rim of the crater. They appear to have been caused by the collapse of the crater floor. These fissures are filled with rubble, through which the hot gases rise. The rubble is oxidized to a red color and encrusted in many places with deposits of green ferrous chloride and white ammonium chloride. Some of the vents give off steam, but others emit what appears to be only heated air. In some spots there is a disagreeable odor of chlorine. At a depth of a foot or so below the rubble the heat is too intense for the hand but not sufficient to brown a piece of paper or to make water "hiss." However, the fact that Jorullo is continuing to give off heat as well as gases after 200 years is in itself remarkable.

The cone of Jorullo is covered with trees, some of which are large enough that they have been cut for lumber. Several large trees grow in the lowest part of the crater. The malpais is also covered with vegetation, except that the last flow, which cascades from the crater, remains "new" in appearance and is barren of vegetation. In the short period of 200 years Jorullo has taken on the appearance of the other cinder cones in the surrounding area, for which there are no records of any historic activity.

MONTE NUOVO

A well-known "new volcano" of historic time was born on September 28, 1538, near Pozzuoli, a port on the Bay of Baia, about six miles west of Naples, Italy, in the Phlegraean Fields. Named Monte Nuovo (New Mountain), it is partly on the site of Lake Lucrine, a famous resort during the time of the Roman Empire.

The Phlegraean Fields

The Phlegraean Fields, a unique volcanic area (described in Chapter 8), contain 19 separate craters concentrated in an area of about 25 square miles. The craters are so closely spaced that in a number of cases they overlap, an older cone having been partly destroyed when a younger one formed. The volcanic activity in the Phlegraean Fields is older than that at Vesuvius and the area appears to have been dormant throughout historic time with the exception of an eruption of Solfatara Volcano in 1198 and the eruption of Monte Nuovo in 1538. However, gaseous emanations from several of the craters, as well as numerous hot springs, clearly indicate that the volcanic forces are not exhausted. Several of the craters in the Phlegraean Fields contain beautiful lakes, of which Lake Avernus is perhaps the best known because of its connection with classical mythology.

Birth of the Volcano

Knowledge of the 1538 eruption of Monte Nuovo is based on four separate accounts contained in letters of eyewitnesses of the event. From these letters, parts of which are reproduced below, some helpful facts have been established.

For two years prior to the outbreak the region was disturbed by earthquakes, which reached a climax in September, 1538. On September 27 and 28 the shocks were said to have been felt almost continuously day and night. About 8:00 A.M. on September 29 a depression of the ground occurred, and from this depression water began to issue, at first cold and later tepid. Four hours later the ground was seen to swell up and open, forming a gaping fissure within which incandescent matter was visible. From this fissure numerous masses of stones, some of them "as large as an ox," with vast quantities of pumice and mud, were thrown to a great height, and these, falling upon the sides of the opening, formed a mound. This violent ejection of material, continuing for two days and nights, by the third day had formed a cone of considerable size. Since some of the eyewitnesses at this time climbed the cone, we may assume that there was a lull in activity. When the eruptions continued the next day, many persons who had ventured onto the hill were injured, and several were killed by falling stones. Thereafter the eruptions decreased in violence, ceasing on the seventh or eighth day after the outbreak. Thus the greater bulk of Monte Nuovo was ejected during the first two days.

Monte Nuovo is a cone, rising 440 feet above the shore, with a cup-shaped crater, the bottom of which is only 19 feet above the level of the sea. It is composed entirely of ash, lapilli, and scoria, and differs in no way from the other cones in the Phlegraean Fields, except that it came into existence much later. The cone, which is about 1.5 miles in circumference at its base, stands partly on the site of Lake Lucrine. Lake Lucrine, occupying the breached crater of an old volcano adjoining the Bay of Baia, was a favorite resort during the period of the Roman Empire, and its shores were lined with fashionable villas, among which was one belonging to Cicero. The superior flavor of the oysters obtained from the lake was another of its attractions. At that time, as today, it was separated from the Mediterranean by a narrow bar. By means of a canal the lake was accessible as a protected anchorage for the galleys of the Roman fleet. The building of the cone of Monte Nuovo largely filled Lake Lucrine, leaving only a narrow segment of the original lake.

Significance of the Record of the Eruption

The historical record of the birth of Monte Nuovo is of more importance than the mere story of the origin of a new volcano. It will be recalled from the discussion of the development of the science of volcanology (Ch. 3) that, during the close of the eighteenth century and the early part of the nineteenth, geologists developed a heated controversy as to the manner in which volcanic cones were formed, a dispute between supporters of Baron von Buch's craters-of-elevation theory, which held that volcanic cones were formed by upheaval, like a blister on the earth's surface, and supporters of the opposing idea, ably advocated by Charles Lyell, which held that the cones were the result of the accumulation of ejected material. Today it seems strange that the craters-of-elevation theory would have been taken seriously, but it was the widely held orthodox view of the time. The controversy was centered in Western Europe, where the science of geology developed; and since Monte Nuovo was the only "new" volcano in this region, it is quite natural that each side sought to find in the origin of Monte Nuovo evidence to support its views. As a result, the records were carefully searched for any eyewitness accounts which might throw light on the problem.

Fortunately, Sir William Hamilton, English ambassador to the Court of Naples for 36 years (1764–1800), was an ardent student of volcanoes and fully aware of the controversy. Through his efforts, two narrative accounts of the birth of Monte Nuovo by contemporary witnesses of credit were discovered and preserved. These accounts, consisting of two letters written a few months after the event, were bound in a volume, with Hamilton's translation, and presented to the British Museum. The first letter was an account by Marco Antonio delli Falconi, and the second was a report by Pietro Giacomo di Toledo. Both are quoted by Phillips (1869). Two other accounts of the eruption have been preserved. One, by Simon Porzio, an eminent physician and Neapolitan scholar, is contained in a letter to the viceroy of Naples, Don Pedro di Toledo. This was published, along with other writings by Porzio, in 1551. An English translation was first published by J. L. Lobley (1889). A fourth manuscript, written immediately after the eruption by Francesco del Nero, was discovered in 1846 and published in German. An English translation (Horner 1847) was published the following year.

Because of the historical interest surrounding these letters, as well as the colorful descriptions of the eruption which they afford, several excerpts are included here.

From the letter by Marco Antonio delli Falconi:

> It is now two years that there have been frequent earthquakes at Pozzuoli, Naples, and the neighboring ports; on the day and in the night before . . . this eruption about 20 shocks, great and small, were felt at the above mentioned places. The eruption made its appearance on the 29th of September, 1538; . . . it was on a Sunday, about an hour in the night; and . . . they began to see on that spot, between the hot baths . . . and Trepergule, flames of fire . . . in a short time the fire increased to such a degree that it burst open the earth at this place, and threw up so great a quantity of ashes and pumice stone mixed with water as covered the whole country; and in Naples a shower of these ashes and water fell the greater part of the night.
>
> Next morning, which was Monday, . . . the poor inhabitants of Pozzuoli, struck with so horrible a sight, quitted their habitations . . . some with children in their arms, some with sacks full of goods; . . . others carrying quantities of birds that had fallen dead at the time the eruption began, others with fish that they had found and were to be met with in plenty upon the shore, the sea having been at that time considerably dried up. . . . The sea towards Baia had retired a considerable way, although from the quantity of ashes and broken pumice stone thrown up by the eruption it appeared almost dry. I saw likewise two springs in those lately-discovered ruins . . . Turning towards the place of the eruption, you saw mountains of smoke, part of which was very black and part very white, rising up to a great height; and in the midst of the smoke, at times, deep colored flames burst forth with huge stones and ashes, and you heard a noise like the discharge of a number of artillery. . . . After the stones and ashes, with clouds of thick smoke, had been sent up by the impulse of the fire and windy exhalations into the middle region

of the air, overcome by their own natural weight, . . . you saw them fall, . . . raining ashes with water and stones of different sizes according to the distance from the place; then by degrees with the same noise and smoke it threw out stones and ashes again, and so on by fits. This continued two days and nights, when the smoke and the force of the fire began to abate. The fourth day, which was Thursday, at 22 o'clock there was so great an eruption . . . and the quantity of ashes and stones and smoke seemed as if they would cover the whole earth and sea. . . .

Then Friday and Saturday nothing but a little smoke appeared; so many taking courage went upon the spot, and say that with the ashes and stones thrown up a mountain has been formed; . . . a thing almost incredible to those who have not seen it, that in so short a time so considerable a mountain could have been formed. On its summit there is a mouth in the form of a cup, which may be a quarter of a mile in circumference. . . .

The Sunday following which was the 6th of October, many people going to see this phenomenon, and some having ascended half the mountain, others more, about 22 o'clock there happened so great and horrid an eruption with so great a smoke, that many of the people were stifled, some of which could never be found. I have been told that the number of the dead or lost amounted to 24. . . . (Phillips 1869, pp. 220–224)

From the letter by Pietro Giacomo di Toledo:

It is now more than two years that the province of Campagna has been afflicted with earthquakes, the country about Pozzuoli much more than any other parts; but the 27th and 28th of the month of September, last, the earthquakes did not cease day or night, in the above mentioned city of Pozzuoli. . . . At last, on the 29th . . . about two hours in the night the earth opened near the lake and discovered a horrid mouth, from which was vomited, furiously, smoke, fire, stones, and mud composed of ashes; making at the time of its opening a noise like loud thunder. The fire that issued from the mouth went towards the walls of the unfortunate city; the smoke was partly black and partly white, . . . the stones that followed were by the devouring flames converted to pumice, the size of which (of some I say) were much larger than an ox.

The stones went about as high as a cross bow can carry, and then fell down, sometimes on the edge, sometimes in the mouth itself. . . . The mud was of the color of ashes, and at first very liquid, then by degrees less so; and in such quantity that in less than 12 hours, with the help of the above mentioned stones, a mountain was raised of 1000 paces height. . . .

Now this eruption lasted two days and two nights without intermission, though, it is true, not always with the same force, but more or less; when it was at its greatest height, even at Naples you heard a noise like heavy artillery when two armies are engaged. The third day the eruption ceased, so that the mountain made its appearance uncovered, to the no small astonishment of everyone who saw it. On this day I went up with many people to the top of the mountain, I saw down into its mouth, which was a round concavity about one-fourth mile in circumference [at present about one-fourth mile in diameter] in the middle of which the stones that had fallen were boiling up, just as in a great cauldron of water that boils on the fire. The fourth day it began to throw up again, and the 7th much more, but still with less violence than on the first night. It was at this time that many people who were unfortunately on the mountain were either suddenly covered with ashes, smothered with smoke, or knocked down by stones, burnt by flame, and left dead on the spot. The smoke continues to this day, and you often see in the night time fire in the midst of it. . . . (Phillips 1869, pp. 225–228)

From the letter of Francesco del Nero: Del Nero mentions the drying up of the bed of the sea near Pozzuoli, which enabled the inhabitants of the town to carry away loads of fish. He then continues:

About eight o'clock in the morning of the 29th [September], the earth sank down about two canne [13.5 feet] in that part where there is now the volcanic orifice . . . At noon on the same day, the earth began to swell up, so that the ground in the same place where it had sunk down was as high as Monte Ruosi . . . and about this time fire issued forth and formed the great gulf with such a force, noise, and shining light, that I, who was standing in my garden, was seized with great terror. Forty minutes afterwards, although unwell, I got upon a neighboring height, from which I saw all that took place, and by my troth, it was a splendid fire, that threw up for a long time much earth and stones. . . . Just so was it with the fiery gulf, from which there was shot up into the air, to a height which I estimate at a mile and a half, masses of earth and stones as large as an ox. They fell down near the gulf in a semi-circle of from one to three bow-shots in diameter, and in this way they filled up this part of the sea, and formed the above-mentioned hill. When the earth and stones fell they were quite dry. The same fire, however, threw out at the same time, a light earth and smaller stones to a much greater height, and these fell down in a soft muddy state. (Horner 1847, pp. 20–22)

Notwithstanding this overwhelming testimony in support of the craters-of-accumulation theory, Baron von Buch and others continued to hold to the craters-of-elevation explanation, even for Monte Nuovo. Lyell (1875, 1:611), in reviewing the problem, quotes von Buch, who in 1836 wrote, "It is an error to imagine that this hill was formed by eruption, or by ejection of pumice, scoria, and other incoherent matter; for the solid beds of upraised tuff are visible all around the crater, and it is merely the superficial covering of the cone which is made up of ejected scoria."

Since this natal eruption, Monte Nuovo has not renewed activity, and today, clothed with vegetation, it is indistinguishable from the prehistoric craters in the Phlegraean Fields.

Fluctuations in Ground-Level at Pozzuoli

On the shores of the Bay of Baia, six miles west of Naples, is the fishing port of Pozzuoli. Originally known as Puteoli, it was an important port in ancient Roman times and is mentioned in the Bible as the place where Saint Paul landed on his way to Rome and to martyrdom. Monte Nuovo is on the shore of the Bay of Baia, about two miles to the northeast of Pozzuoli (Fig. 26). Solfatara Volcano, which last erupted in 1198 and still emits volcanic gases, is about one mile to the northwest of Pozzuoli.

One of the classic examples of movements of the earth's crust is the history of the so-called Temple of Jupiter Serapis at Pozzuoli (Pl. 61). This ancient Roman ruin near the shore at Pozzuoli was probably a public bath and market place rather than a temple, but nevertheless the name has persisted through the centuries. Only three of the original columns and part of the floor of the building are intact. At a height of about 18 feet above the base, the columns are bored and pitted by marine boring clams, some of whose shells still remain in the holes. This "high-water mark" is a record of the level of the sea in which the marine organisms lived. It seems reasonable to assume that the "temple" was built on dry land and that a slow subsidence carried it 18 feet below sea level, after which it was uplifted to its present position. Records are not clear as to when these movements took place, but Lyell (1875, 2:173–174) refers to a paper by James D. Forbes (1829), who quotes an early Italian writer identified only as Loffredo as saying that in 1530 the sea washed the base of the hills and that "a per-

Plate 61. So-called Temple of Jupiter Serapis, Pozzuoli, Italy. The darkened area on the columns, caused by a rock-boring marine clam (Lithodomus), is about 8 feet wide, and the upper level, or "high-water mark," is 18 feet above the base of the column.

son might then have fished from the site of these ruins which are now called the stadium" (on the hills overlooking the Temple of Jupiter Serapis) (Forbes 1829, as quoted by Lyell 1875, 2:173). Although the statement quoted by Forbes is usually cited as evidence that the major uplift did not occur until after 1530, this appears to be open to some question, for there is other evidence to indicate that the uplift had begun in the early part of the sixteenth century. Lyell (1875, 2:174) cites a deed written in Italian and dated October, 1503, in which Ferdinand and Isabella granted to the University of Pozzuoli a portion of the land where the sea was drying up, and, eight years later, a document written in Latin, dated May 23, 1511, by which Ferdinand granted to the city a certain territory around Pozzuoli where the ground had dried up. Accounts of the eruption of Monte Nuovo in 1538, previously presented, record that the sea receded on the shores at Pozzuoli and Baia and exposed lately-discovered ruins

(letter of Marco Antonio delli Falconi), and that the sea abandoned a considerable section of the shores and the inhabitants were able to carry away loads of fish (letter of Francesco del Nero); so it seems likely that the main uplift was at this time. The history is complex, however, for 5 feet below the marble floor on which the columns of the "temple" rest there is a mozaic floor of an earlier structure which must have been a victim of the instability of the area.

On March 4, 1970, it was reported that the floor of the "temple" had risen about three feet and that this rise had been accompanied by very shallow foci earthquakes (Imbo 1970). This, together with reports of fissures opening in the ground, caused much alarm, and thousands of the inhabitants left their homes, anticipating a volcanic eruption. Later, a team of French scientists investigated the area and on April 21 and May 14 reported that they were unable to confirm the earlier reports of the opening of fissures and that, while there was a slow uplift, they were unable to verify the amount reported earlier. Further the fumaroles in the Solfatara showed no increase in temperature and no change in composition; so the French scientists concluded that there were no manifestations which indicated an impending eruption (Tazieff 1970). Thus, two reports by reputable scientists are not in agreement; however, it must be noted that they cover different time periods and that following the first uplift the area may have subsided to its previous level before the second observations were made. The fact that a rapid uplift may signal an impending volcanic eruption makes it essential that the area be closely observed in order to warn the inhabitants of possible danger.

SUBMARINE ERUPTIONS AND "NEW" ISLAND VOLCANOES

Extent of Submarine Volcanic Action

With three-fourths of the earth's surface beneath the sea, it is apparent that submarine eruptions must constitute an important part of the earth's volcanism. The average depth of the oceans is about 13,000 feet, and submarine eruptions of lava and fragmental products must have taken place on a stupendous scale in order to build up from the ocean depth the foundations of the numerous large volcanic islands. In the Hawaiian Islands, for example, volcanic outpourings not only reach sea level but have piled up material to a height (Mauna Loa) of more than 13,000 feet above sea level! Eruptions of this type are characterized by basaltic (basic) lavas, and the activity must continue for many thousands of years to produce such extensive archipelagoes as those of Hawaii, Samoa, and Tonga, to name only a few Pacific examples.

Unless the submarine eruption piles up enough material to form an island, the chances of a passing vessel's notice of it are remote.

Nevertheless, spots in the sea where the water was discolored and boiling violently or jets of water and steam erupting from the sea have been reported from time to time by the crews of passing vessels. Those which erupt basaltic material form cones of scoria and cinders; while those erupting more acid lavas usually have a dome-like core of lava. With both types the "new" islands are very susceptible to wave erosion and are frequently destroyed. Generally the permanency of the volcanic island is assured only when the walls of the cone are reinforced by outpourings of lava and the sea is prevented from entering the crater. The explosiveness of all types of volcanic eruptions is increased when the magma comes in contact with water, and some of the most violent eruptions on record are "steam-blast" explosions, such as the 1883 eruption of Krakatoa.

A few of the "new" island volcanoes formed by submarine eruptions are described in the following paragraphs. The eruption of Surtsey Volcano (see Ch. 11) in 1963 is a recent example of a submarine eruption which produced a permanent island.

Graham Island

The most noted of the several submarine eruptions in the Mediterranean occurred in 1831, when a new island, named Graham Island, was formed in water which, according to a survey made a few years earlier, was 600 feet deep. Graham Island was located about 30 miles southwest of Sciacca, Sicily, or about midway between the port of Sciacca and the island of Pantelleria, 60 miles to the southwest (Fig. 32). The island of Pantelleria, although of volcanic origin, has had no eruptions in historic times. A summary of published accounts of the formation of Graham Island is given by Lyell (1875, 2:58).

On June 28, 1831, about two weeks before the eruption became visible, Sir Pulteney Malcolm reported that in passing over the spot in his ship he felt the shock of an earthquake as if his ship had struck a sandbank. At the same time shocks were felt on the west coast of Sicily. On July 10 the captain of a Sicilian vessel, enroute to Agrigento, Sicily, reported that as he passed the place he saw a column of water 60 feet high and 800 yards in circumference rising from the sea like a waterspout, followed by dense steam clouds which rose to a height of 1,800 feet. On his return trip from Agrigento on July 18 he found a small island, 12 feet high, with a crater from which was being ejected volcanic debris and a huge column of vapor, the sea around being covered with floating cinders and dead fish. He reported the scoria as being of a chocolate color and the water which boiled in the circular basin as a dingy red. The eruption continued with great violence to the end of July, at which time it was visited by several persons, including the German geologist, M. Hoffmann. At this time the island was 50–90 feet high and 0.75 mile in circumference. By August 4 it had reached a height of 200 feet and was 3 miles in circumference. This was its greatest height, and thereafter it began to diminish in size. By September 3, when carefully measured by Captain Wodehouse, it was only 0.6 mile in circumference, and its greatest height was 107 feet.

During the month of August, violent agitation of the water on the southwest side of the new island emitted columns of dense white steam, indicating the existence of a second vent, which never reached the level of the sea. Near the end of October the cone had been destroyed by wave action, leaving only a small mound of scoria to mark the site. Two years later no surface vestige of the island remained, but sounding revealed that the center of the cone was marked by a large rocky mass surrounded by loose cinders some 11 feet below sea level and about 200 feet in diameter. At a distance of about 100 yards from the rocky mass, the depth of the water increased sharply. This rocky mass doubtless was composed of lava which had solidified in the throat of the volcano. If such a remnant were exposed on land it would be a "volcanic neck."

With a height of 800 feet at the peak of its growth, three-fourths of which was below sea level, Graham Island was roughly comparable in size to many of the cinder cones found in volcanic regions throughout the world. Graham Island attained its maximum height in about two months, a rate of accumulation similar to that of Parícutin Volcano, which attained a height of about 1,000 feet by the end of the second month. A remarkable feature in the record of Graham Island is the short time required for wave action to destroy the exposed portion. The material ejected at Graham Island was basaltic scoria and cinders.

The Azores

The Azores, a group of islands in the mid-Atlantic ocean about 1,200 miles due west of Lisbon, Portugal, are volcanoes superimposed on the Mid-Atlantic Ridge, as are the volcanoes of Iceland. The main structural trend of faulting in the Azores is west-northwest (Agostinho 1931, p. 124), crossing the trend of the Mid-Atlantic Ridge at a high angle. Thus, as has been noted in other volcanic areas of the world, the intersection of two lines of fissures appears to have determined the location of the volcanic vents. Each of the nine major islands making up the Azores (Fig. 68) is composed of one or more shield type cones with a caldera at the summit. An

Figure 68. The Azores.

exception is Pico Volcano, on Pico Island, which has a steep-sided, symmetrical cone.

Volcanic eruptions have occurred on five of the islands in historic time, with several additional submarine eruptions in the waters surrounding the islands. In 1638 and again in 1811, submarine eruptions near the eastern end of the group formed weak ash and cinder cones which were soon destroyed by wave erosion. The eruption of 1811 formed Sabrina Island, off the coast of São Miguel, in the eastern Azores. It consisted of loose cinders and attained a height of 300 feet above sea level with a circumference of about one mile. The eruption lasted eight days, but soon thereafter Sabrina was destroyed by wave erosion.

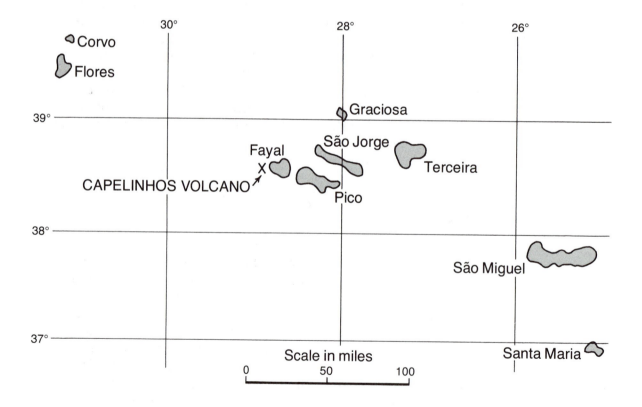

Capelinhos Volcano, Fayal Island

Fayal Island, 12 miles long by 8 miles wide, is the top of a large volcano which rises out of the sea to a height of 3,351 feet. Its slopes are gentle, as is typical of Hawaiian type volcanoes, and at the summit is a caldera about 1.5 miles in diameter and 1,000 feet deep. The volcano on Fayal is known as Caldeira (Portuguese for "kettle" or "cauldron") from the huge depression at the summit, which is an example of a caldera, as the term is used in volcanology. A line of cinder cones almost due west from the summit caldera to the sea marks the location of a fracture along which repeated volcanic eruptions have occurred in recent geologic time. In 1672 an eruption occurred near the middle of this fracture, and lava flows poured into the sea. The new volcano, Capelinhos, came up offshore at the western end of this same fracture in 1957 (Fig. 69). The events leading up to the submarine outbreak and the early stages of the eruption are described by J. E. Richey (1957) in an article in the London *Times Science Review*, on which the following account is based.

From September 16 to 27, 1957, earthquakes were felt with increasing frequency on the western end of Fayal, but they were not of great violence. On September 27 at about 8:00 A.M. the first signs of the eruption were observed on the surface of the sea. The water was boiling at the site; intermittent vapor clouds were observed near the surface of the sea; and the water was discolored or muddy for a half mile or more surrounding the area. On September 29, about 2:00 A.M., explosions began. Cinders were thrown 300 feet or more above the sea, and an eruption cloud rose to more than a mile, but the fall of cinders was not remarkable. During the next few days activity increased; on October 1, cinders were thrown to 2,000 feet, and the eruption cloud attained a height of 20,000 feet. On the following day the eruption was particularly violent, and cinders fell over a radius of a few miles out to sea. An islet now began to form around the crater. After October 3 the explosions continued to be violent but were less frequent. On October 7 the cone-shaped island was reported to be 200 feet high and 700 yards in diameter, but already its exposed side, to the northwest, was beginning to be destroyed by waves. On October 11 the island was 330 feet high and 800 yards in diameter. It was a horseshoe-shaped cone with the opening to the southwest. The sea flooded the crater through this opening, so that the actual vent of the volcano was under water, and for this reason the explosions were extremely violent and the new lava was disrupted into ash and cinders. Explosions continued through October 15, but at the same time the size of the island was being reduced by wave erosion. In the following week the island was cut into two parts, and on the morning of October 30 no por-

Figure 69. Fayal Island, Azores. Based on Scofield (1958) and Parsons and Mulford (1958).

tion of either part was visible above the level of the sea. It appeared that the waves had won in the struggle.

However, in early November explosive eruptions were renewed and a second cone was constructed. By mid-November this cone was tied to Fayal Island by a narrow bar of black ash. Explosive eruptions continued throughout the winter of 1957–1958, and by the end of March, 1958, the volcano had built a broad peninsula at the western end of Fayal Island, adding more than a square mile of land area to the island (Scofield 1958). In April a small lava flow issued from the base of the cone on the seaward side and flowed almost immediately into the sea. Other flows of this type occurred in May and June. On May 14, 1958, scores of severe earthquakes occurred along the fracture zone which connects Capelinhos Volcano with the main caldera at the summit of Fayal Island. It appeared likely that lava was moving underground along the fracture and that there might be an outbreak in the summit caldera. Actually on the floor of the caldera there did appear a small fracture, from which eruptions of ash reached a height of 1,000 feet, but no other activity resulted. In July, 1958 (Parsons and Mulford 1958), the volcano consisted of a broad horseshoe-shaped cinder-cone ring about one-half mile in diameter and, at its highest point, 500 feet above

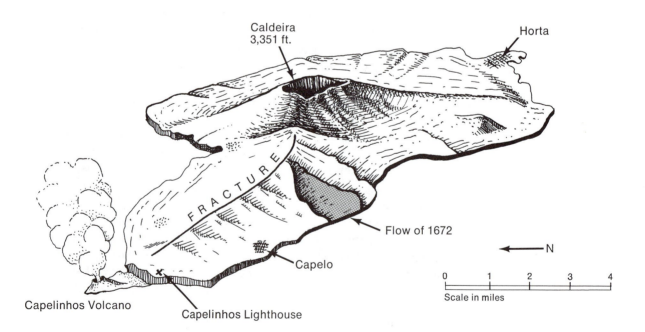

Figure 69. Fayal Island, Azores. Based on Scofield (1958) and Parsons and Mulford (1958).

sea level. A typical cinder cone formed on a land surface rises steeply, with a rather small crater at the top. However, when such eruptions rise through water, the resulting explosions, due to the meeting of the cold water and the hot lava, pile up the cinders and ash in a wide ring around a large explosion crater. Such cones are sometimes referred to as phreatic cones. Diamond Head, a well-known landmark in Honolulu, is an example of such a cone. Inside the phreatic cone of Capelinhos a steep cone of cinders and lava spatter rose 150–200 feet. With the vent protected from the sea, showers of incandescent lava were periodically thrown into the air from the inner vent. These Strombolian type eruptions continued intermittently through the summer of 1958.

Falcon Island

In 1867 a shoal was reported to have developed in the South Pacific, 30 miles to the west of Nomuka Island in the Tongas (Geikie 1903, p. 334). Ten years later smoke was observed rising from the spot, and in 1885 a volcanic island, named Falcon Island, rose from the sea during a submarine eruption which began on October 14. It was later reported by a passing steamer to be 2 miles long and 250 feet high. It steadily diminished in size until in the fall of 1892 it was only 25 feet high. By 1898 it had disappeared altogether, leaving only a shoal to mark the site. The composition of the material of Falcon Island is a basic augite-andesite.

Noyöe Volcano

In the early summer of 1783 a new island was formed by a submarine eruption 30 miles southwest from Cape Reykjanes on the west coast of Iceland (Lyell 1875, 2:49). It was reported that so much pumice was ejected that it covered the sea for a distance of 150 miles, greatly impeding the progress of ships in the area. The new island, claimed by the Danish government and named Noyöe (New), was destroyed by wave action in less than a year, leaving a submerged reef 5–30 fathoms below sea level. The disastrous eruption of the Laki fissure on Mount Skaptar (Ch. 11), located about 200 miles to the east of the submarine vent on the mainland of Iceland, began about a month after this eruption.

Bogoslof Volcano

The most famous volcano in the Aleutian Islands of Alaska is the "disappearing" island of Bogoslof, which has appeared and disappeared several times since Ship Rock, the first peak in the area, was sighted in 1768.

Bogoslof is the top of a nearly submerged volcano which rises about 6,000 feet above the ocean floor. The strange antics of this volcano are caused by eruptions which form islands that are promptly destroyed by wave erosion or shattered by explosive activity. The following description of Bogoslof's history is based on Jaggar (1945).

Bogoslof Volcano is located about midway in the Aleutian chain of islands, which extends for 1,500 miles in a broad arc westward from the mainland of Alaska (Fig. 70). About 76 major volcanoes are located in this arc, 36 of which have been active since 1760, the date of first historic records in this area. Lying to the south of the Aleutian arc is the Aleutian Trench, a deep furrow in the ocean floor with depths in excess of 20,000 feet. This typical "island-arc" structure, consisting of a deep trough on the ocean floor with an arc-shaped chain of islands surmounted by active volcanoes on the continentward side, is a feature characteristic of the margins of the Pacific Ocean. The origin of "island arcs" is discussed in Chapter 15.

About 40 miles north of Umnak Island in the Aleutians, some rocky pinnacles rise from the ocean in water that on either side drops off to around 6,000 feet in depth. These rocks are sometimes connected to form a single island, and at other times they are separated by a channel. This is Bogoslof Volcano. The rocky pinnacles are stiff lava domes which are being squeezed up in the crater of the volcano. The domes are rapidly eroded by vigorous wave action or destroyed by explosions from within the dome. However, new lava domes rise from time to time at other points within the crater. Thus the reports of the disappearance of an island and the appearance of a new one are entirely justified.

The first of the rocky spines which constitute Bogoslof Volcano was reported in 1768 by early navigators, who named it Ship Rock. In 1796 a second peak, called Castle Rock, rose to the southeast of Ship Rock, accompanied by explosions which alarmed the natives on Unalaska Island, 50 miles to the east. When surveyed in 1826, Castle Rock was 2 miles long, 0.75 mile wide, and 340 feet high. In 1883 a huge tabular mass of lava rose from the sea more than a mile to the northwest of Castle Rock. This new lava protrusion was named Grewingk, but more commonly was known as New Bogoslof. The bombs and debris from the eruption, added to the products of wave erosion, formed a bar which joined Ship Rock and

Castle Rock (or Old Bogoslof) with the new mass to form a single, elongate island (Fig. 71). A few years later wave erosion had opened a channel, again dividing the mass into two islands.

Two new domes appeared in 1906 and 1907 in the lagoon separating the two older masses. The first of these, Metcalf Cone, 400 feet high, was a conical mound of talus surrounding a spine of rock, while the other, McCulloch Peak, 500 feet high, was a typical lava dome (tholoid). However, half of Metcalf Cone was blown away by an explosion before McCulloch Peak arose (Fig. 71). Jaggar describes Bogoslof at this time as follows:

> Bogoslof was now [1907] a continuous island 2 miles long, the two active cones were 400 feet and 500 feet high, McCulloch Peak was three-fourths surrounded by steaming salt water at

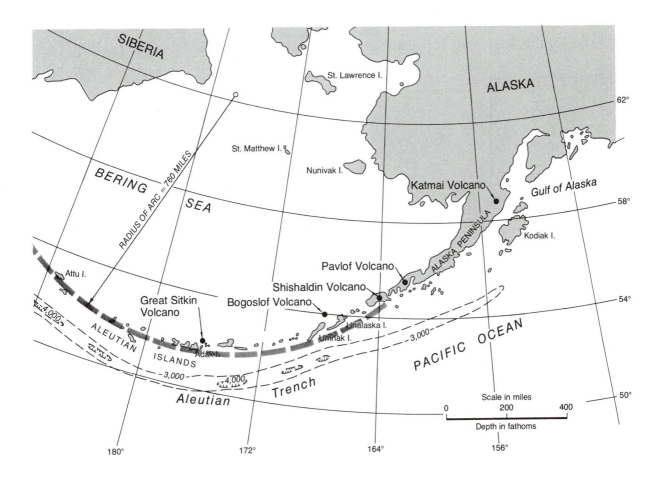

Figure 71. Successive events in the history of Bogoslof Island. Modified from Lobeck (1939). By permission from Geomorphology, *by A. K. Lobeck. Copyright, 1939. McGraw-Hill Book Company, Inc.*

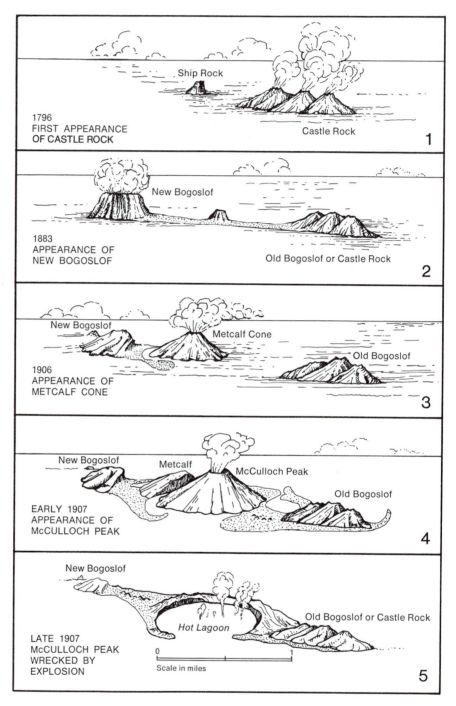

90° F; it looked like a huge lumpy potato . . . September 1, 1907, a dense black cloud rose from Bogoslof, ash fell at Unalaska mantling everything a quarter inch deep, and there were rain, lightning and distant rumblings. McCulloch Peak had blown itself up. A steaming lagoon was left in its place, the rest of the island was piled high with fallen debris . . . There appeared to be a rhythmic sequence to the events whereby Metcalf Cone built itself up 400 feet high and 2000 feet across, lived 10 months and exploded, then McCulloch Cone was built up 450 feet high and 2000 feet across, lived 10 months and was destroyed. (1945, p. 83)

Explosions, erosion, and the occasional appearance of new island lava domes in the lagoon continued to be the pattern for Bogoslof. Eruptions occurred in 1910, 1926, and 1931, but of these only the 1926 eruption gave rise to a new dome. As in previous years, explosions and wave erosion constantly altered the appearance of the islands.

The process of dome formation in the crater of a volcano may be an indication that its eruptive activity is coming to an end. Whether the life of Bogoslof is being prolonged because of its sea-level position, which permits wave erosion to destroy the domes, is, of course, unknown. This seems improbable, however, since the domes are frequently removed by explosive action quite independent of wave erosion.

Myozin-syo Volcano

On September 17, 1952, the crew of a Japanese fishing boat, the *Myozin-maru No. 11*, radioed that they had sighted a submarine volcanic eruption at a point about 420 kilometers south of Tokyo (Minakami 1956). A Maritime Safety Board boat was immediately dispatched to check the exact location. On reaching the site, the crew found that the eruptions had formed a small island, estimated to be about 150 meters in diameter and 30 meters above sea level. The volcano was erupting every few seconds, throwing out incandescent bombs and ash and a great cloud of gases. It was named the Myozin-syo, after the fishing boat which had first reported it. Shortly, however, the eruption pattern changed. The paroxysmal eruptions became more intense but spaced at greater intervals. The small cone was, of course, endangered by wave erosion. With a marked reduction in the amount of new material being ejected and the destructive effects of the strong explosions, the small island van-

Plate 62. Submarine eruption of Myozin-syo Volcano on September 23, 1952. The "cock's-tail" pattern of the eruption cloud, typical of submarine eruptions, is well displayed. Photo courtesy Dr. Takeshi Minikama and Asahi Press.

ished from sight on September 21 or 22, about one week after its birth. But violent submarine eruptions continued through September two or three times a day and thereafter at longer intervals.

The volcano was in this state of activity when a number of scientists, aboard two ships, went to investigate the eruption. One of the ships was the *Sinyo-maru*, a training ship of the Tokyo Fisheries University; the other was the *Kaiyo-maru No. 5*, from the Hydrographic Office. The *Sinyo-maru* left on September 21 and arrived at the scene in time to observe, on September 22 and 23, extraordinary submarine eruptions at close range, but still from a safe distance. The *Kaiyo-maru*, which arrived at the scene on September 24, was apparently directly over the vent when an eruption occurred, and the vessel with its crew of 22 and its 7 scientists vanished in the swirling waters. This fantastic catastrophe, although understandable, is believed to have been the first one of this nature on record. Although there were no eyewitnesses to the tragedy, it was established that a strong eruption occurred at 12:30 P.M. on September 24, at which time the vessel was at the site of the volcano. Submarine eruptions produce waves (tsunami) which are recorded on tidal gauges over a wide area, and a study of the tidal-

gauge record at the Hatizyo-sima Weather Station, 120 kilometers to the north of Myozin-syo Volcano, established that a strong eruption had occurred at that time. When the ship did not return as scheduled, an intensive search was made with planes and patrol boats, but to no avail. Later, some wrecked material from the *Kaiyo-maru* was discovered. Entrapped in the wreckage were numerous pieces of pumice similar to that ejected by Myozin-syo Volcano.

Observations by scientists aboard the *Sinyo-maru* on September 23, the day before the *Kaiyo-maru* catastrophe, reveal clearly the nature of the eruption which trapped the *Kaiyo-maru*. A series of photographs, one of which is reproduced as Plate 62, tells the story vividly. A dome of water forms on the surface of the sea over the submarine crater, and a few seconds later, with a tremendous explosion, the dome is broken, and bombs, ash, and pumice are thrown out in a dense eruption cloud of water and gases. It is obvious that no ship situated over the eruptive area would be able to survive such a blast.

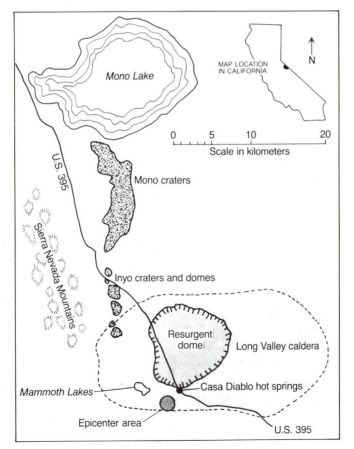

Figure 72. Index map of the Long Valley–Mono Lakes area. After Bailey, Dalrymple, and Lanphere 1976, p. 726.

The activity of Myozin-syo Volcano ceased near the end of August 1953, about one year after it started. A brief renewal of activity was reported to have occurred on November 4, 1954.

Long Valley–Mono Lakes Area

The Long Valley–Mono Lakes area, in east-central California, has been the site of volcanic eruptions for several million years. Long Valley is a caldera which formed about 700,000 years ago when explosive eruptions of huge volumes of pumice and ash (the Bishop tuff) caused the magma chamber to collapse. Subsequent eruptions resulted in the uplift of a portion of the caldera floor, forming a resurgent dome about 10 kilometers in diameter (Bailey, Dalrymple, and Lanphere 1976, p. 140). Volcanic activity in the general area within the last few thousand years formed a series of lava domes along the Inyo and Mono chain of volcanoes. The most recent eruption, north of Monument Lakes in the Inyo chain, was less than 400 years ago (Miller et al. 1982, p. 1.)

Based on geochemical studies of the initial ash falls (temperature and pressure) Bailey, Dalrymple, and Lanphere (1976, p. 731) conclude that the roof of the magma chamber was at a depth of about 6 kilometers at the time of the eruption. Seismic profiles (Hill 1976, p. 752) indicate that at present the roof of the magma chamber in the western part of the Long Valley caldera is at a depth of 7–8 kilometers.

In May 1980, a swarm of earthquakes with the epicenter about 2 miles east of Monument Lakes, near the southern edge of the Long Valley caldera, caused concern about the possibility of a volcanic eruption. Base leveling along U.S. Route 395 revealed that a broad uplift in the western part of the caldera, called a resurgent dome, had bulged upward about 10 inches since the last survey 2 years earlier. It is believed that the magma beneath the Long Valley caldera had moved upward at the time of the May 1980 swarm of earthquakes, causing the bulge (Miller et al. 1982, p. 1).

In January 1983 the most intense and prolonged swarm of earthquakes since the May 1980 swarm again occurred in the south part of the caldera, and base leveling across the resurgent dome indicated that the upward bulging was continuing.

Again this could indicate that the magma was moving toward the surface. There is no way to determine whether this magma will, in time, reach the surface and produce an eruption, or whether it will eventually cool and solidify without reaching the surface. The area is being closely monitored, and there should be advance warning of an impending eruption.

Chapter 14   Man's Use of Geothermal Energy

There are more things in heaven and earth, Horatio, than are dreamt of in our philosophy. —SHAKESPEARE

In all volcanic regions, even thousands of years after activity has ceased, the magma continues to cool slowly, and its heat is conducted to adjacent rocks beneath the surface. This high heat flow is often sufficient to affect shallow strata containing water; when the water is heated, such surface manifestations as hot springs, fumaroles, geysers, and related phenomena often occur. Such occurrences are common throughout the western third of the United States and are known throughout the world. It has been estimated that over 10 percent of the earth's surface manifests very high heat flow, and the hot springs and related features which are present in such areas have been used throughout the ages for bathing, laundry, and cooking. In many cases elaborate health spas and recreation areas have been developed around the hot-spring areas. Yellowstone National Park is an outstanding example of such an area. Although no volcanic activity has occurred in the Yellowstone area for thousands of years, the 3,000 hot springs and related phenomena clearly indicate that the magma is still cooling and that it is close enough to the surface to heat the underground aquifers. The cooling of a magma, even though it is relatively close to the surface, is such a slow process that in terms of human history it may be considered to supply a source of heat indefinitely.

Temperatures in the earth rise with increasing depth; the rate of increase, or *geothermal gradient*, varies considerably from place to place but averages about 1° F. (0.56° C.) for 100 feet of depth. Thus, if a well is drilled at a place where the average surface temperature is 60° F. (15.6° C.), a temperature of 212° F. (100° C.) would be expected at about 15,200 feet (an increase of 152° F. [66.7° C.] added to the surface temperature of 60° F.). Many wells are drilled in excess of 20,000 feet, and temperatures far above the boiling point of water are encountered. In the deep diamond mines of Africa, elaborate air-conditioning equipment has been installed to cool the mines!

Nevertheless, under normal conditions it is not practical to drill a well to produce "geothermal heat." It has been estimated (Bruce and Shorland 1932–1933) that to obtain a continuous heat yield equivalent to 4,000 horsepower it would be necessary to drill a hole 30 miles deep and 2 feet in diameter! Serious attempts to obtain heat by drilling, however, are not unknown. In the September, 1885, issue of the *Geological Magazine*, a distinguished scientific journal, J. Starkie Gardner referred to an attempt then being made to obtain a supply of heat by drilling: ". . . the deepest artesian well in the world is being bored at Pesth, already 951 meters. The work is [being done] partly at the expense of the city which has granted 40,000 pounds for the purpose, with the intention of obtaining an unlimited supply of warm water for public baths and municipal purposes. The present temperature is 161° F. and they propose to continue until water 178° F. is obtained" (1885, pp. 404–405). No further mention of this project has been found in the literature.

Most of the earth's heat is far too deeply buried to be reached by man, notwithstanding the possibility of radical developments in the technology of drilling. On the assumption that the greatest depth at which heat might be extracted economically was around 10 kilometers, D. E. White (1965) calculated that the heat available in the outer 10 kilometers of the earth's crust was more than 2,000 times the heat represented by the total coal resources of the world. However, most of this *geothermal energy* (i.e., natural heat of the earth) is far too diffuse ever to be recovered economically. Only where the heat is concentrated into restricted volumes, similar to the concentration of valuable metals into ore deposits or of oil and gas into commercial pools, will it be a potential energy resource. The thermal energy (enthalpy) is stored both in the solid rock and in water and steam filling the pore spaces and fractures. The water and steam serve to transfer the heat from the rocks to a well and then to the surface. Water in a geothermal system also serves as the medium by which heat is transferred from a deep igneous source to a geothermal reservoir at a depth shallow enough to be tapped by drilling. Geothermal reservoirs are located in the upward-flowing part of a water-convective system. Rain water percolates underground to a depth where it is heated by coming in contact with hot rocks. On heating, the water expands and moves upward in a convective system. If the upward movement is unrestricted, the water will be dissipated at the surface as hot springs; but, if the upward movement is impeded, as by being trapped by an impervious layer, the geothermal energy accumulates, forming a geothermal reservoir. Until recently, it was thought that the water in a geothermal system was derived mainly from water given off by the cooling of a magma below the surface. However, studies of hydrogen and oxygen isotopes in geothermal waters indicate that most of the water is from surface precipitation, with not more than 5 percent from the cooling magma.

Commercial utilization of geothermal energy to date has been limited, for the most part, to regions of recent volcanic activity. However, geothermal energy resources are also present in areas far removed from recent volcanism, and it will be in order to briefly outline the various types of geothermal resources:

1. Vapor-dominated convective systems.
2. Hot-water–dominated convective systems.
3. Hot dry rock systems.
4. Geopressured sands.

The varied types of geothermal resources do not permit a simple classification to be made. The four types listed above, adapted from L. J. P. Muffler and D. E. White (1972) and W. J. Hickel et al. (1972) are now generally recognized, and, though they do not provide complete coverage of geothermal energy resources, they do provide a framework for the treatment of the subject.

Vapor-Dominated Systems

Vapor-dominated geothermal systems produce superheated steam with minor amounts of other gases (CO_2, H_2S, NH_3) but little or no water. In such cases all the fluid can be piped directly to the turbines. Within the vapor-dominated reservoir, saturated steam and water coexist, with steam being the phase which controls the pressure. With decrease in pressure upon drilling and production, heat contained in the rocks dries the fluid first to saturated steam and then to superheated steam, with as much as $55°$ C. of superheat at a wellhead pressure of five to seven kilograms per square centimeter. A wellhead pressure of six kilograms per square centimeter is commonly used in geothermal installations. Vapor-dominated systems are relatively rare, and only three are commercially productive—those at Larderello, Italy; The Geysers, California; and Matsukawa, Japan. Fields of this type are in areas of recent volcanic activity and associated with large folded mountain chains or volcanic island arcs. In continental areas the reservoir rocks are often graywackes overlain by ophiolites (altered metamorphic rocks) which provide an impermeable cap for the reservoir.

Hot-Water–Dominated Systems

Hot-water–dominated geothermal systems contain water that may be far above the surface boiling point because of the effect of pressure on the boiling point of water. In major zones of upflow, coexisting steam and water may reach the surface as hot springs or

Figure 73. Model of a high-temperature hot-water geothermal system. The temperature profile from recharge at A to discharge at E is shown in the diagram on the left. Cold water enters the system at A, migrates downward because of its relatively high density to C, dissolving SiO₂ and other constituents as it is heated to 250°C. by thermal convection through rocks of high temperature gradients, assumed for simplicity to be a straight-line gradient such as dashed line GFC. If some hot fluid were escaping from the magma, gradients would be distorted, perhaps similar to GF'C. Because of the high pressure at C the water rises to D with little change in temperature. At D the hydrostatic pressure has decreased to the vapor pressure of water at 250°C. and the first steam bubbles begin to form. From D to the surface (E), hydro-

geysers (Fig. 73). The water in most hot-water geothermal systems is a dilute solution (1,000–30,000 milligrams per liter) containing mostly sodium, potassium, lithium, chloride, bicarbonate, sulphate, borate, and silica. The silica content and the ratio of potassium to sodium are dependent on temperature in the geothermal reservoir, thus enabling prediction of reservoir temperatures from chemical analysis of the hot-spring waters (Fournier and Rowe 1966). In hot-water geothermal systems a mixture of steam and water is produced, and the two must be separated before the steam is fed to the turbines. Water at 250° C. will produce only about 20 percent by weight of steam when the confining pressure is reduced to six kilograms per square centimeter, the usual wellhead pressure for geothermal installations. Wairakei, New Zealand, which has been in commercial production since 1954, and Yellowstone National Park, which because of its park status will never be developed as a commercial energy source, are examples of hot-water geothermal systems.

Another, slightly different type of hot-water geothermal system occurs in rift basins, such as the Salton Trough in California and the Central Rift Zone of Africa. The Salton Sea geothermal reser-

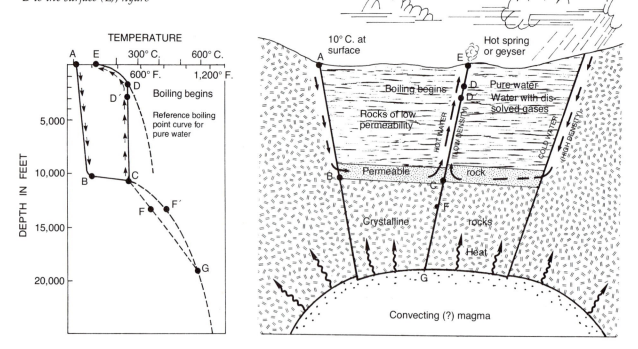

*static pressure declines con-
tinuously so that more steam
forms from the still liquid
water. After White (1973).*

voir contains a brine with more than 25 percent by weight of dissolved solids, mainly chloride, sodium, calcium, and potassium. Although temperatures reach 360° C., the highly saline waters present an operational problem.

In several hot-water geothermal systems attention is being given to using a heat-exchange system (binary system) in which the reservoir fluid is brought to the surface in a closed system and passed through a heat exchanger using a low-boiling-point fluid, such as freon or isobutane, which flashes to a vapor to provide turbine power. The original reservoir fluid is then reinjected as water into the ground. In some cases the steam flashed from hot water is so corrosive or contains so much other gas that the maintenance of a steam turbine is not practical. The fact that isobutane is noncorrosive makes the construction and maintenance of a turbine much simpler in a heat-exchange plant than in a steam plant. Further, the heat-exchange system permits the use of lower-temperature water, and the water can be returned to the ground without danger of atmospheric pollution (J. H. Anderson 1973).

Hot Dry Rock Systems

In the western United States there are abundant occurrences of late Cenozoic igneous intrusions (plutons) which failed to reach the surface and are cooling at relatively shallow depths. The masses are similar to and perhaps related to the once-molten masses of granite which form the core of the Sierra Nevada as well as to various other once-molten masses known as *batholiths*. The hot rocks are dry, of low porosity, and almost entirely impermeable. They cool very slowly, even from a geologic viewpoint, and are responsible for the high heat-flow values in many areas of the western United States. Studies indicate that it may be possible to utilize the heat energy stored in these rocks. The plan is to drill wells into the hot rocks, using standard drilling techniques, and then fracture the rocks to establish intercommunication between the wells. Fracturing, such as is contemplated, is a standard practice in oil-field development. Water would be injected at one well, heated while passing through the hot, fractured rocks, and returned to the surface through an adjacent well. After passing through a heat-exchanger, using a low-boiling-point fluid, such as isobutane, which would flash to a vapor and be fed to a turbine, the water would be recycled to continue the process. It has been estimated (Hickel et al. 1972) that the thermal energy released by cooling one cubic mile of rock from an initial temperature of 350° C. to 177° C. would be equivalent to that obtained from 300 million barrels of oil! It is believed that as the rock cools the fractures will expand, exposing more surface area for heat extraction—or the wells might be drilled deeper to expose fresh hot rocks. The system would be pollution-free, since it would be a closed water system, and if this method proved to be feasible it would supply an almost unlimited amount of energy for the western United States.

A test of the dry hot rock system is being made by the Atomic Energy Commission at Valles Caldera in New Mexico (described in Ch. 6). Preliminary reports indicate that the first well has penetrated the pluton and that it proved to be impermeable, which is a requirement if this method is to be successful. Additional wells are now being drilled.

Geopressured Sands

Unlike the previously described geothermal systems, the geopressured-sands type is not related to volcanism. It is included here in order to provide a more comprehensive outline of geothermal resources. The following discussion is based, in part, on Hickel et al. (1972).

Deep sedimentary basins filled with sand and clay of Tertiary age are generally undercompacted below depths of 1.25–2 miles, and the interstitial fluid pressure carries a part of the overburden load. Such regions are said to be *geopressured*. Such conditions exist in the northern Gulf of Mexico basin in a 750-mile belt from Mississippi Sound to the Rio Grande of Texas. Here the deposition of clays, muds, and sands as deltaic deposits by streams emptying into the Gulf of Mexico has formed thicknesses of sediments measured in miles which have accumulated in a subsiding basin (sometimes known as the Gulf Coast geosyncline). The geopressured deposits underlie the Coastal Plain inland for 60–100 miles and for a like distance beneath the Continental Shelf offshore. Geopressured aquifers are not continuous over the entire region but are in lenses and blocks bounded by faults.

The water in geopressured reservoirs is derived from the compaction and dehydration of the clays, which takes place at temperatures between 80° and 120° C. The water thus liberated is fresh water and, as a result of the compaction of the clay, is forced into the sand aquifers. In addition to being under abnormally high pressure, the water also has an abnormally high temperature, because the normal heat-flow of the earth is trapped by insulating, impermeable clay beds in a subsiding depositional basin. Pressures at depth are significantly in excess of hydrostatic levels and may approach lithostatic levels.

The top of the geopressured zone begins at depths of 8,000–10,000 feet, and temperatures usually range from 150° to 180° C., although temperatures up to 270° C. have been encountered. Wellhead pressures would range from 4,000 to 6,000 pounds per square inch. Because the high temperatures and pressures have resulted in a natural cracking of the petroleum hydrocarbons, the geopressured reservoir fluids commonly contain 10–16 standard cubic feet of natural gas per barrel of fluid, and these dissolved hydrocarbon gases would be a valuable by-product in the utilization of the hot water (Hickel et al. 1972). The energy stored in the geopressured reservoirs is of three classes: (*a*) the intrinsic heat of the water, (*b*) the dissolved gases, and (*c*) the mechanical energy available from the high pressure of the discharged water. Ideally, a portion of the water would flash to steam at surface conditions and could be used to power turbines; the natural gas dissolved in the water could be recovered and added to our decreasing supply of the valuable fuel; and finally, after the heat is extracted from it, the water (which is fresh water) would be a valuable resource.

The drilling for oil and gas has uncovered geopressured reservoirs in many countries. The only utilization I know about (as of 1974) is in Hungary, where hot water from a geopressured reservoir is being used for space heating.

Figures for the amount of energy stored in the geopressured reservoirs in the Gulf Coast area alone are staggering, and with the increasing demand for energy this source may provide at least part of the answer. Present technology in the petroleum industry is capable of bringing these waters to the surface—the need is for a research program to demonstrate the feasibility of recovering the energy which they contain.

GEOLOGIC
ENVIRONMENT OF
GEOTHERMAL SYSTEMS

The occurrence of a geothermal system, other than the geopressured type, is generally determined by a deep igneous mass (at a depth perhaps greater than 5 km.) that is the probable heat source driving the overlying meteoric convective system. Accordingly, the high-temperature regime of the upper few kilometers has been superimposed on whatever rock units happen to be there, regardless of age or mode of formation. For example, at The Geysers, California (discussed in a later section of this chapter), a Quaternary geothermal system occurs in rocks of Jurassic and Cretaceous ages. The physical characteristics, such as porosity and permeability of the reservoir rocks, strongly influence the nature of the geothermal system. Further, the structure and stratigraphy of the rocks control the convective system, since hot water will rise buoyantly up the path of least resistance; this need not be vertical, and consequently the hot water can be displaced from the heat source (Combs and Muffler 1973).

With the development of the theory of plate tectonics, it is now possible to delineate the distribution of potential geothermal areas. The relationship of plate tectonics to volcanism is treated in Chapter 16, and only brief mention of it will be made here.

High-temperature shallow geothermal reservoirs are near the margin of crustal plates, or *subduction zones*, where the crust is being either created or consumed (Muffler and White 1972). In both cases molten rock is generated and moves upward in the earth's crust to provide the heat to drive the convective system of meteoric water. Subduction zones are found throughout the circum-Pacific region and within the Mediterranean Sea and its eastward extension into Asia along the boundary of ancient Tethys, the large Mesozoic sea between Asia and Africa. Geothermal fields associated with subduction zones are found in California (The Geysers), Italy (Larderello), Japan, the Philippines, New Zealand, and elsewhere.

Another major type of geothermal reservoir occurs in areas where the crustal plates are separating or rifting. The disruption of former continental areas by rifting over rising convective cells, followed by the separating of the continental fragments as new oceanic crust rises from the mantle, is the concept known as *sea-floor spreading*. If the upwelling in the mantle is initiated beneath a continent, the continent will split apart, with the formation of a new ocean basin by lateral spreading from the original rift. Thus the continental-drift hypothesis, proposed many years ago to explain the striking parallelism of the Atlantic coasts, has new support. The Mid-Atlantic Ridge, where the rifting began, is marked by a graben along its axis and active volcanoes at a number of places (Fig. 51). The Mid-Atlantic Ridge rises above sea level in Iceland, where it is marked by a zone of active volcanism and major geothermal resources. Other areas of crustal spreading are now under investigation as potential sources of geothermal energy. The Imperial Valley of California and Mexico, where rifting in the Gulf of California has given rise to intrusive igneous masses beneath the ancient Colorado River delta, is an area of tremendous geothermal resources. One geothermal field in this area, Cerro Prieto in Mexico, began commercial production in 1973. The Red Sea–Gulf of Aden rift and the Great Rift of East Africa are being investigated as potential geothermal areas.

STATUS OF GEO-
THERMAL RESOURCE
DEVELOPMENT

Although geothermal resources are widely distributed throughout the world, commercial use of geothermal energy is limited to a few areas, as shown in Table 3.

The surge of interest to develop alternate power sources, due to the decreasing supply of petroleum and natural gas, is evident in the field of geothermal energy. Some of the new areas being developed, as well as expansion of existing fields, are shown in Table 4.

Space does not permit a description of all the geothermal developments, but some of the larger and older ones are described below.

DEVELOPMENTS IN
ITALY

The backbone of Italy is made up of the Apennine Mountains, an extension of the Alpine system of southern Europe. In relatively recent geologic time, Italy has experienced a number of uplifts and subsequent sinkings, during which the waters of the Mediterranean Sea covered much of the present area of Italy. The most recent of these disturbances was an uplift of the Apennine Mountains, accompanied by a sinking of what is now the Tyrrhenian Sea to the west. This uplift began in Pleistocene time (just prior to the Ice Age) a few hundred thousand years ago and is actually still in progress in some areas.

Distribution of Volcanoes

The volcanoes of Italy are located along a trend which parallels the Apennine Mountains and the Tyrrhenian coast, following a fracture or series of fractures which resulted from the sinking of the Tyrrhenian Sea and the uplift of the Apennines. Along this fracture, more or less evenly spaced, are located a series of volcanic centers. Beginning at the north, about midway between Florence and Rome (Fig. 32), and extending southward, these volcanic centers are (*a*) Vulsini (Lake Bolsena), (*b*) Cimini (Lake Vico), (*c*) Sabatini (Lake Bracciano), (*d*) Alban Hills, (*e*) Roccamonfina, and (*f*) the Naples area, including Vesuvius and the Phlegraean Fields. All of these volcanic centers are similar in character, belonging to a type which volcanologists have designated as the Mediterranean type. They are multiple-center volcanic masses with a series of intersecting craters or calderas forming low, flat cones rising only slightly above the surrounding countryside. They are composed essentially of pumiceous material with minor lava flows, except in the southern part of the belt, particularly Vesuvius, which has yielded abundant lava flows in recent eruptions. From the Alban Hills area northward, the cra-

TABLE 3. *Geothermal fields producing in 1973*

Country	Field	Year Production Began	1973 Capacity (in megawatts)
Italy	Larderello	1904	380
	Monte Amiata	1959	26
New Zealand	Wairakei	1958	170
United States	The Geysers	1960	400
Japan	Matsukawa	1966	20
	Otake	1967	13
Iceland	Namafjall	1969	3
USSR	Pauzhetsk	1967	29
Mexico	Cerro Prieto	1973	75

ters or calderas are occupied by lakes which lend much charm to the scenery of this part of Italy.

Activity along this belt began at the north and progressively shifted southward, until today the only activity along this line is at Vesuvius. Although the activity began in the Pleistocene, very recent from a geologic viewpoint, there is no record of any activity in historic time in the centers north of Rome. A slight eruption in the Alban Hills, just south of Rome, is reported as late as 290 B.C., but this is open to some doubt. Activity in the Naples area, of course, has continued until the present time.

Active volcanoes occur in two other areas in Italy today, at Stromboli and Vulcano in the Lipari Islands (north of Sicily) and at Mount Etna in Sicily. The relationship to the Apennines is not as apparent in these areas as it is in the volcanic centers to the north, but the trend of folding represented by the Apennines is continued through Sicily and the Atlas Mountains of North Africa.

Larderello Field

Italy has been the pioneer in the utilization of geothermal energy and has served as a laboratory for others interested in this field. Though the broad extent of recent volcanic activity in Italy provides wide distribution of hot springs and fumaroles, only in the Larde-

TABLE 4. *Geothermal fields under development in 1973*

Country	Field	Planned Capacity, 1977 (in megawatts)
El Salvador	Ahuachapan	30
Guadeloupe	La Bouillante	30
Japan	Hashimanta	10
	Hatchobaru	50
	Katsukonda	50
	Onikobe	25
Philippines	Bicol	?
Taiwan	Tatun	10
Turkey	Kizildere	30
United States	Salton Trough	50
	The Geysers[a]	600
Mexico	Cerro Prieto[a]	150

[a] Already producing (see Table 3); being expanded in 1973.

rello and nearby Monte Amiata areas, in Tuscany, south of Florence, have the natural steam resources been developed.

The natural steam vents, known as *soffioni*, and the pools of water formed by the condensation of the steam, called *lagoni*, have been known for centuries but were long regarded as evil by the peasants. In 1777, a pharmacist at the court of Leopold III, Grand Duke of Tuscany, isolated boric acid from the waters of the *lagoni*. Boric acid reacts with soda to form borax, a product which had up to this time been imported from the Orient at great cost. Some early crude attempts were made to produce boric acid, but it was not until 1827 that Count Francesco Larderel, a French exile, conceived the idea of utilizing the steam to concentrate the boric-acid solution, and a profitable industry developed (Utilization . . . 1924). The area was subsequently named in honor of Count Larderel.

Heat from the natural steam was used in various stages of the chemical industry for many years, but no attempt was made to use it for generating power until near the end of the nineteenth century. In 1897 the natural steam was used to heat boilers which provided steam to run a reciprocating engine. In 1904 Prince Piero Ginori

Figure 74. Relation of volcanic areas to Larderello and possible northwest-southeast alignment along the volcanic belt.

Conte, then general director of the Larderello works, fed steam directly from a *soffione* into a piston engine used to drive a small dynamo that provided lights for the chemical works. By this time drilling had been undertaken in order to increase the flow of the steam for the boric-acid plant, and it was found that higher pressures and steam with superheat could be obtained at depth. The first steam turbine using steam directly from a *soffione* was installed in 1913. It was connected to a 250-kilowatt electric generator. In 1916 three units of 3,000 kilowatts each were added. These did not use the natural steam directly but used steam from pure water heated in boilers by the *soffioni*, thus avoiding the difficulties from corrosion and from the high gas content (4–5 percent) of the natural steam.

This procedure was followed until about 1923, when an apparatus for removing about 90 percent of the contaminating gases was de-

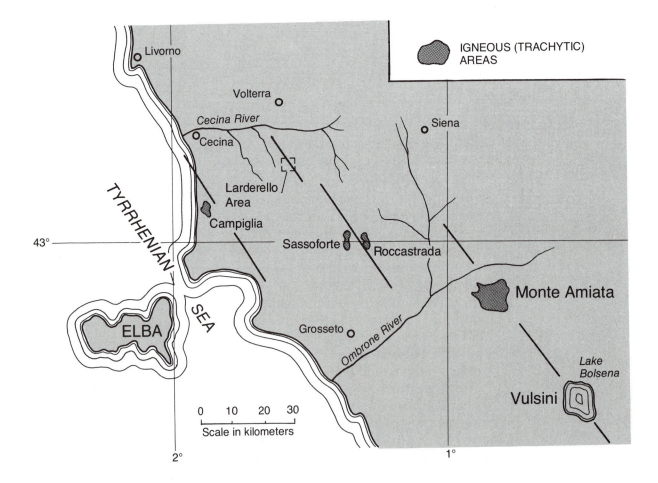

Plate 63. Larderello geo-thermal field, Italy.

Plate 64. Condensing towers of chemical plant at Larde-rello.

vised, and the steam was then fed directly to the turbogenerators, so that the intermediate stage was unnecessary. This process, known as the Bringhenti, after the man who devised the apparatus, is still being used. The wells drilled in the early twenties were usually less than 500 feet deep, and the steam issued at an average pressure of two atmospheres absolute and a temperature varying from 100° to 190° C. In 1931 deep drilling tapped steam with higher pressures and higher temperatures. The first large well, Soffionissimo No. 1, drilled in 1931 to a depth of 900 feet, yielded 440,000 pounds of steam per hour at a pressure of 52 psi and a temperature of 205° C., including 50° C. superheat. At the end of 1944, installations for electric power generation totaled 135,000 kilowatts, and the total electric output in 1943 was 908 million kilowatt hours.

During the retreat of the German Army through Italy in 1945 the installations at Larderello were wrecked and many of the wells destroyed. Since the war the area has been redeveloped, new methods have been introduced, and the output has been expanded. The output in 1952 was 1,840 million kilowatt hours, or about 6 percent of the total electric energy output of Italy for the year. In 1960 the output was 1,914 million kilowatt hours, and while this was about one-third of the thermoelectric power produced in Italy, it was only 3.88 percent of the total power production for the year (Banco di Roma 1954, 8:21; information for 1960 supplied by Banco di Roma in a personal letter).

The Larderello area, which is now producing from 13 pools in an area about 20 kilometers in diameter, covers about 250 square kilometers. With a production of over 365 megawatts, it was until recently the world's largest producer of geothermal energy, but it is now being surpassed by The Geysers in California. The steam wells at Larderello now average about 1,000 meters in depth, with a reservoir temperature of 245° C. and an average yield of about 23,000 kilograms of steam per hour. The steam at Larderello is produced from permeable, cavernous limestone, dolomite, and anhydrite of Late Triassic to Late Jurassic age. The reservoir is capped by a thrust sheet consisting of impermeable carbonates, argillites, and ophiolites (metamorphic rocks rich in serpentine, chlorite, etc.) of Jurassic to Eocene age. The *soffioni*, or natural steam vents, at the surface occur along faults which extend to the carbonate-anhydrite reservoir beneath the thrust plate. Although the closest Upper Tertiary volcanics exposed at the surface are at Roccastrada (Fig. 74), about 25 kilometers to the southeast, it is obvious that a cooling pluton must be present at a relatively shallow depth in the Larderello area to provide the source of heat. Roccastrada, where steam has also been discovered, is about halfway between Larderello and the Monte Amiata geothermal field.

The steam wells at Larderello are usually spaced about 600 feet apart and are drilled with customary rotary drilling equipment in the same manner used for drilling oil and gas wells. Surface casing is commonly 20-inch, decreasing to 12-inch, which is carried to the steam horizon. The steam is carried in insulated lines (about 12 inches in diameter) from the wellhead to the power plant and the condensing towers of the chemical plant.

Composition of the steam. The steam at Larderello contains an average of 0.06 percent boric acid, with a maximum of 0.1 percent, and from 4 to 6 percent by weight of gases, mainly carbon dioxide (over 90 percent) and small quantities of hydrogen sulphide, hydrogen, methane, oxygen, nitrogen, ammonia, argon, and helium. The composition is remarkably constant over the entire area despite the continued drilling.

The following analyses (Manelli n.d.) are typical.

One kilogram of vapor contains:

	Grams
H_2O	945.87
CO_2	51.85
H_2S	0.86
H_3BO_3	0.50
NH_3	0.10
CH_4, H_2, etc.	0.40
O_2	0.01
N_2	0.42
Rare gases . . . about 1 cc.	

After condensation of the water vapor and elimination of the boric acid and the ammonia, the gases contain, per 100 liters of gas:

	Liters
CO_2	93.0
H_2S	2.4
H_2	1.8
CH_4	1.8
N_2	1.0
He, Ar, etc. . . . about 3 cc.	

The boric acid is concentrated by evaporation in special pans to a solution of about 8 percent. This is cooled and the crude acid, up to 90 percent pure, is crystallized out. The annual pre–World War II production was around 8,000 tons of boric acid and about 4,500 tons of borax. The boric-acid recovery works, established in 1812, was shut down in 1969 because of the inability to compete with other sources of borax. Other chemicals produced at Larderello include: carbon dioxide and "dry ice," liquid ammonia, ammonium carbonate, sodium perborate, ammonium chloride, and boron carbide.

Monte Amiata

About 65 miles to the southeast of Larderello (Fig. 74) is Vulsini, a complex volcanic mass composed primarily of pumice and ash, with the main crater (caldera) occupied by Lake Bolsena, a body of water about 9 miles long and 6.5 miles wide. It is the northernmost of a group of volcanic centers which extend to the southeast beyond Rome. Lying between Larderello and Vulsini are several other volcanic areas, including Monte Amiata and Roccastrada. The volcanic activity in these areas was somewhat different from that in the crater-lake areas to the southeast, where explosive activity was the rule and ash and pumice the chief products.

Monte Amiata, the largest of the areas and typical of this group, is a craterless volcanic mass consisting chiefly of superimposed trachytic lava flows, which are believed to have issued from northwest-southeast–trending fissures, rather than from explosive centers. The activity is clearly post-Pliocene but is believed to be older than the activity represented by Vulsini and the volcanic centers to the southeast (Preller 1924, p. 141). The crudely conical mass of Monte Amiata, with slopes of about 9°, rises 1,800 feet above the surrounding area, with its summit 5,250 feet above sea level. Mines on the eastern margin have been an important source of mercury for many years.

In the Monte Amiata geothermal field, as at Larderello, the steam reservoir is beneath an impervious thrust sheet. Postvolcanic collapse is believed to have occurred, fragmenting the reservoir rocks and controlling mercury mineralization and hot-spring activity. The relationship between acidic and alkaline volcanism, postvolcanic collapse, mercury mineralization, and hot-spring activity is observed at many geothermal fields throughout the world (Koenig 1973). Commercial production of geothermal energy began at Monte Amiata in 1959, and four plants are now supplying more than 26 megawatts of electric power.

Other Areas

Exploration work is being carried on at a number of volcanic centers in the vicinity of Monte Amiata, including Roccastrada and Radicofani. Future geothermal exploration is anticipated in the volcanic belt which extends southward from Monte Amiata, including Vulsini, Cimini, Sabatini, and the Alban Hills to the southeast of Rome (Fig. 32). These volcanic centers are large calderas occupied by lakes and surrounded by low cones of ash and pumice. The region around Naples, including Pozzuoli and the Phlegraean Fields (Fig. 26) is also being investigated for possible geothermal resources.

DEVELOPMENTS IN NEW ZEALAND

New Zealand consists of a group of islands in the South Pacific east and slightly south of Australia. Twelve hundred miles from Australia, even farther from the nearest Pacific islands, and over 6,000 miles from South America, they are extremely isolated. The two important islands, called North and South, contain 44,131 and 58,120 square miles respectively. North Island is about equal to Pennsylvania in area, while South Island compares in size with Georgia.

Geologic Characteristics of New Zealand

Even though North Island is 515 miles long and up to 200 miles in width, no point is more than 65 miles from the sea. Its central physical feature is a series of unbroken mountain chains running northeast from Cook Strait to East Cape on the Bay of Plenty. The height is always in excess of 3,000 feet but does not reach 6,000 feet. To the west of the backbone range is the volcanic plateau, a great triangular area with its base along the Bay of Plenty, and its apex to the south, built up by eruptions which began in Late Tertiary time and have continued to the present. It contains the still active cones of Tarawera and Ngauruhoe, as well as a number of extinct or dormant volcanoes. This volcanic area is described in some detail in later paragraphs.

The backbone of South Island is formed by the impressive Southern Alps, which extend the full length of the island. With an average crest elevation of over 8,000 feet and with 17 peaks over 10,000 feet, they rise steeply from the plains to well above the snow line. With numerous glaciers and spectacular waterfalls, South Island is strikingly similar to many parts of Switzerland. On the west the Southern Alps plunge sheer into the sea along a coast famed for the grandeur of its fiord scenery.

Extending in a north-northeasterly direction from the central part of North Island to the Bay of Plenty is a relatively low-lying belt which includes the basins of Lake Rotorua at the north and Lake Taupo at the southern end. This troughlike belt, or graben, known as the Taupo Volcanic Zone (Fig. 75), is regarded as due to collapse as a result of the eruption of large quantities of volcanic material.

The active and recently active volcanoes of North Island are located along the eastern side of the collapse belt, along a fault, which perhaps should be called a tectonic zone. Along this tectonic zone, called the Whakatane Fault, extending from the Bay of Plenty to Mount Ruapehu, are the active volcanoes of White Island, Mount Tarawera, Mount Ruapehu, and Mount Ngauruhoe, as well as the following dormant or extinct volcanoes: Mount Tongariro, Mount Tauhara, Mount Edgecumbe, and Mount Maungakakaramea. The greatest thermal activity is also along this line. The Whakatane tectonic zone is approximately in line with the Alpine Fault, which extends south-southwesterly along the west margin of South Island. There is no volcanic activity, however, in South Island.

The alignment may be projected northward for a thousand miles through the Kermadec Islands to Tonga and Samoa (Fig. 76). All of these island groups support active or dormant volcanoes. Since 1774 (first historic records), the doubtlessly incomplete record indicates that at least 48 volcanic eruptions have occurred along this trend. To the east lies the great Tonga-Kermadec Submarine Trench, which locally attains a depth of 20,000 feet. This trench is believed to represent a major down-warping of the earth's crust due to the under-thrusting of the westward-moving Pacific plate (Ch. 16).

Volcanic eruptions have occurred along the Whakatane tectonic zone from the Late Tertiary to the present day. The extent of this activity is indicated by the widespread covering of volcanic debris which mantles much of North Island. A rhyolitic welded tuff (ignimbrite), although largely covered by recent pumice and ash deposits, is present over an area of about 5,000 square miles northward from Lake Taupo. The ignimbrite, encountered in steam wells at Wairakei at a depth of around 2,000 feet, is estimated to represent the astonishing volume of 200 cubic miles of material. It was erupted in prehistoric time as a series of incandescent blasts of ash (*nuées ardentes*), probably from longitudinal rifts or from multiple centers along such rifts.

All volcanic eruptions in historic time (i.e., since European settlement in 1839) have been in this zone. Especially noteworthy is the great eruption of Tarawera Volcano in 1886. White Island Volcano, in the Bay of Plenty, erupted in 1914, 1926, and 1971. Ngauruhoe and Ruapehu volcanoes, south of Lake Taupo in Tongariro National Park, have erupted in recent years. Eruptions of Ngauruhoe are recorded for 1869, 1949, 1954, and 1959. Ash eruptions, accompanying the rise of a stiff plug of lava in the crater of Ruapehu Volcano began in 1945 and have continued intermittently. A disastrous mud-flow (lahar) claimed 151 lives on December 24, 1953. An eruption from the dome in the crater of Ruapehu produced both lava and mudflows in 1971.

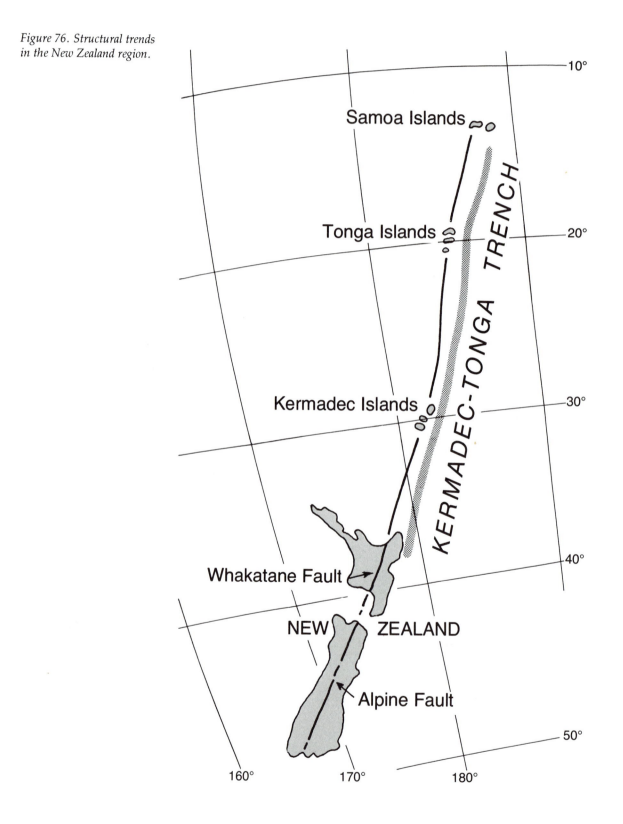

Figure 76. Structural trends in the New Zealand region.

Geothermal Resources of New Zealand

The development of geothermal energy resources in New Zealand has been confined largely to the Taupo Volcanic Zone of North Island. This zone is a major volcanic-tectonic depression that extends for 160 miles from the active volcanoes of Tongariro National Park to White Island Volcano in the Bay of Plenty (Fig. 77). From vents in and near the zone more than 4,000 cubic miles of lava, ash-flow tuffs, and air-fall tuffs, all dominantly of rhyolitic composition, have been erupted in Pliocene and Holocene time (Healy 1964). All of New Zealand's active volcanoes and thermal areas, such as boiling springs and geysers, are located in the Taupo Volcanic Zone. The most important developments for electric power are at Wairakei, near Lake Taupo, and at Kawerau, in the northern part of the zone. Steam and hot water are used extensively at Rotorua as well as at many other places throughout the zone for space heating. Prospective geothermal areas (hot-spring areas) are widespread, as is shown in Figure 76, and at least a dozen of these have been explored by drilling.

The Maori people, in the thermal region, have used the hot water for cooking and washing since ancient times. However, no other use was made of the thermal resources until very recently. At various times during the 1930's, the possibility of using natural heat from the thermal areas was suggested. J. A. Bruce and F. B. Shorland (1932–1933) in the early thirties suggested the use of water from the hot springs for heating greenhouses to grow out-of-season vegetables, for heating homes, for evaporation of sea water for salt recovery, for recovery of boric acid and other chemicals, and for power production.

W. M. Hamilton (1954) and L. I. Grange (1955) have each briefly described the history of the development of geothermal power in New Zealand. In 1940 the matter was investigated by the Council of Scientific and Industrial Research, and, while the investigation revealed that it was entirely feasible to develop power from the natural steam, because of the abundance of water power in North Island it did not seem to be worthwhile. At Rotorua, where hot ground could be encountered at a shallow depth, a number of wells were drilled, and by 1940 the municipal building, a theater, several hotels and schools, and a number of dwellings were using natural heat. By 1944, 50 wells had been drilled, and since then the number has greatly increased. The possibility of producing "heavy water," used as a moderator in atomic piles, from natural steam was proposed in 1946. This, together with the marked increase in the consumption of electric energy and the awareness that hydroelectric developments could not keep pace with the demand, again directed

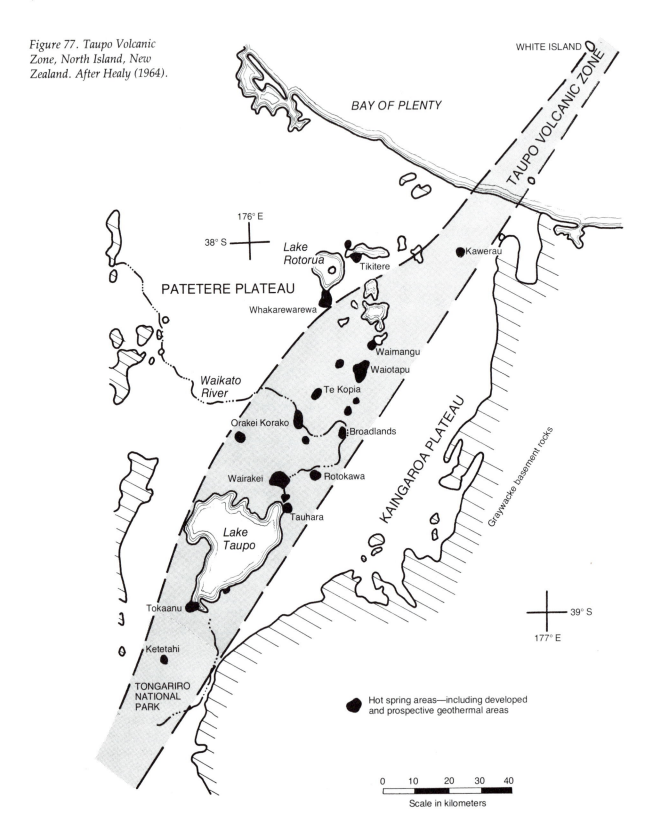

Figure 77. Taupo Volcanic Zone, North Island, New Zealand. After Healy (1964).

attention to the thermal areas. The government appointed a volcanologist (in 1945) to undertake a study of the thermal areas with the intention of setting up power plants, should it be feasible to do so. After some preliminary work, a five-year program of simultaneous exploratory drilling and investigation was approved by the government in 1949. Work was started in the Wairakei area, which was considered to be the most promising.

Wairakei geothermal field. Located about 6 miles north of Lake Taupo (Fig. 77), the Wairakei field occupies a surface area of about 10 square miles. It is situated in the south-central part of the Taupo Volcanic Zone. At the northeast and southwest extremities, the Taupo Volcanic Zone is about 10 miles across, but in the central part it widens to about 25 miles. The central part of the zone is characterized by rhyolitic volcanism, whereas at the ends of the zone the volcanoes are andesitic. The hydrothermal activity is concentrated in the central, rhyolitic region. The Taupo Volcanic Zone is flanked in the central part by plateaus of flat-lying sheets of ignimbrite, erupted from vents or fissures within the zone. The zone itself, a huge trough filled with thousands of feet of volcanic material, has been described as a volcanic-tectonic depression resulting from calderalike collapse following the eruption of huge volumes of rhyolitic ash and pumice. However, G. W. Grindley (1965) presents evidence to show that the depressions within the zone have grown progressively by differential subsidence along active faults and that the structure is not the result of a great catastrophic collapse.

The geothermal field at Wairakei is underlain by a sequence of nearly flat-lying rhyolitic volcanics, as shown in Figure 78. The stratified volcanic sequence is draped over a basement horst (an upstanding block bounded by normal faults) and thickens eastward and westward in adjoining basins. The hot-water reservoir is essentially a pumice-breccia in which hot water, with temperatures up to 265° C., has accumulated. This reservoir of hot water is tapped by drilling through a relatively impermeable mudstone (deposited when the area was temporarily a lake) which covers the reservoir at a depth of 600–1,000 feet. The mudstone forms an impermeable cap for the hot-water reservoir. The hot water is believed to enter the reservoir through the underlying ignimbrite along steeply dipping fault planes. Several of these faults are visible on the surface, but others are concealed by more recent deposits. The best-producing wells, with individual outputs ranging up to 17,000 kilowatts from an eight-inch hole, are aligned along the three prominent faults shown in Figure 78; see also Plate 65. By drilling anywhere into the porous strata, it is possible to obtain steam at shallow depths, but most of the production wells are located to intersect a fault in the ignimbrite, for these wells yield high-pressure steam.

Figure 78. Cross section of the Wairakei steam area. Modified from Grindley (1965).

The production wells are usually drilled to a depth of around 2,000 feet, with an eight-inch hole completed to the steam horizon. A typical high-pressure well yields about 500,000 pounds of steam and water per hour. About 80 percent by weight of the discharge consists of water, which is removed under pressure by separators at the wellhead, leaving dry steam to be piped to the turbines. Wells are classified as having *high pressure* at 210–220 psi and *intermediate pressure* at around 80 psi. Each group has separate transmission lines for piping the steam to the power plant. *Low-pressure* steam, obtained at the power plant as the discharge from intermediate-pressure turbines and as "flash" steam from hot water discharged at the wellhead, is also being utilized in turbines which operate with a steam pressure of 0.5 psi. The high-pressure and intermediate-pressure turbines operate at 180 and 50 psi, respectively. The problems involved in the exploitation of the Wairakei field, such as deposition

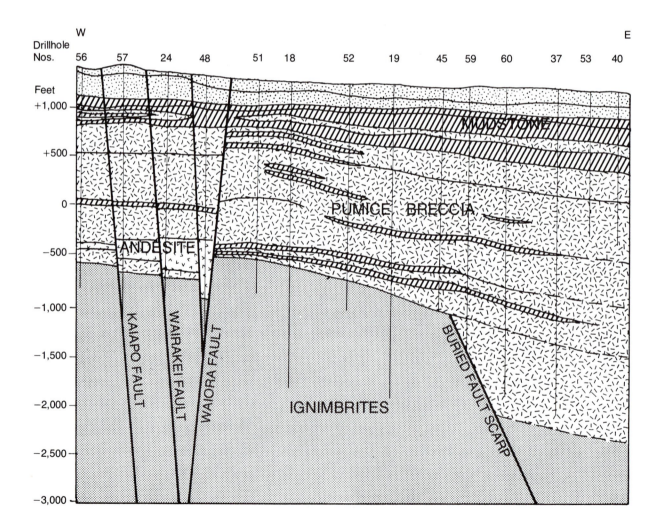

of calcite and silica in the well casing, changes in pressure and temperature in the reservoir, and others, are described by Grindley (1965) and will not be elaborated here.

Although by mid-1953 exploratory drilling had demonstrated that sufficient steam was available to warrant the installation of a power plant, it was not until 1956 that construction began, and the first turbines went into operation on November 15, 1958. The initial stage of development, which was completed in 1960, had a capacity of 69 megawatts. The current output of 160 megawatts, which was reached in 1965, was scheduled to be increased to 250 megawatts by 1976. However, the discovery of natural gas in New Zealand has changed this plan and no additional development is planned for the immediate future, although municipal and industrial utilization of the hot-water resources is encouraged.

The filling of the great trough which marks the Taupo Volcanic

Zone with volcanic ash, pumice, and other debris must have extended over a long period of time. From radiocarbon studies it is known that many volcanic eruptions have occurred in this area during the last 9,000 years. One of the most recent, about 1,700 years ago, spread five cubic miles of ash over an area of 8,800 square miles. Another eruption occurred at Tarawera about 700 years ago, and of course, the great eruption of Tarawera in 1886 is a matter of record. The thermal activity in the Wairakei-Taupo area is doubtless related to the cooling of the magmas responsible for these eruptions. As the intruded magma cools, it releases steam (with other gases) which finds its way to the surface along faults in the basement rocks. Hydrothermally altered mudflow conglomerates in the mid-Pleistocene mudstones (Huka Falls formation) which cover the reservoir rocks led Grindley to conclude that the hydrothermal activity was at least 500,000 years old.

In the thermal area around Wairakei the top 120 feet of the trough filling consists of loose gravel and pumice. This rests on a pumice breccia to about 2,000 feet, followed by an ignimbrite which is widespread and of unknown thickness (Fig. 78). In the Wairakei area the ignimbrite has been uplifted to form an elliptical block. The uplift appears to be in the form of two domes, separated by a narrow down-faulted zone. The hydrothermal activity is closely associated with these structures and especially with the faults. Geophysical evidence indicates that the basement rocks are about 8,500 feet below sea level in the deepest part of the trough east of Wairakei and about 4,000 feet below the top of the Wairakei block (Grindley 1965). The basement is believed to be graywacke, similar to the rocks exposed in the adjoining highlands.

The steam is believed to rise along fissures in the basement rocks into the permeable volcanics filling the trench. The permeable surface rocks are saturated with circulating ground water, which is heated by rising steam and gases. The hottest areas appear to be associated with northeast trending faults. If it is assumed that 2,000 feet of permeable rocks are saturated with circulating ground water, the boiling point at 2,000 feet would be raised to 265° C. by the increased pressure. At 1,000 feet it would be approximately 230° C. In most wells the temperature at the bottom is slightly less than the corresponding value on the boiling-point curve; near the surface it is considerably less. Temperatures above the boiling point, giving dry steam, are encountered in narrow zones, the result of impermeable beds impeding circulation. The temperature and average steam content at various depths are approximately as shown in Table 5.

Drilling steam wells. Drilling in hot ground and against high pressures introduces many of the problems encountered by the oil industry and requires employment of the same techniques. The wells

TABLE 5. *Temperature and steam content in Wairakei wells*

Depth in Feet	Temperature (C.)	Steam at Atmospheric Pressure (%)
0	100°	0
130	150°	9
540	200°	19
1,000	230°	25
1,500	250°	30
1,800	260°	32
2,150	270°	34

are drilled with a rotary type rig, and the pressure is controlled by circulation of drilling mud, which also keeps the drill bit cool. A column of water 2,000 feet deep would exert a pressure of about 1,000 psi at the bottom, and, since the mud used has a somewhat higher density, it would withstand a somewhat higher pressure. The circulating mud is also viscous enough to carry out the drill cuttings from the hole. Generally three strings of casing are installed in geothermal wells. Eighteen-inch casing is set from the surface to a depth of 60–200 feet. Eleven- to thirteen-inch anchor casing is set inside the surface casing to a depth of 300–600 feet, with eight-inch casing carried to the top of the steam horizon. This casing is fitted with a special valve to stop the flow of water and steam through the casing until it has been cemented into place. The casing is cemented into position by placing a precalculated amount of cement in the lower part of the casing and then forcing the cement, by water pressure, to rise around the outside. The bottom valve and any cement remaining in the bottom of the hole are removed by drilling. A master valve, in conjunction with a gate valve for reducing the size of the bore, is fitted to the top of the casing as a master control. When large steam wells are initially opened, water and steam issue in a plume rising 200–500 feet, accompanied by considerable quantities of rock fragments. After the debris is discharged, the steam and water are usually discharged horizontally into a silencer to reduce the noise.

The ratio of steam to water from a well depends on the extent to which the well is "throttled" down to give increased pressure. The quantity of steam varies inversely with the wellhead pressure. A good eight-inch well will discharge four tons of a steam-and-water mixture per minute. The noise from such a well is tremendous, and the need for a silencer is obvious. The large eight-inch wells give a shut-in pressure as high as 430 psi, but 200–350 psi is more common.

About 90 percent of the water in the steam-water mixture discharged by the wells can be removed by passing the discharge over a 180° bend centrifuge separator; the remaining 10 percent must be removed in a cyclone separator. Since most of the corrosive impurities are in the water fraction, a good separation is essential.

Composition of the steam-and-water mixture. The gas content of the steam is low, rarely exceeding 0.05 percent. The proportion of gases varies from well to well, but usually runs around 90 percent carbon dioxide, with small quantities of hydrogen, nitrogen, hydrogen sulphide, methane, and ethane. The water contains principally sodium chloride, with minor amounts of metaboric acid (HBO_2), potassium, lithium, fluoride, ammonium, and other substances. A typical analysis, as given by W. M. Hamilton (1954), is as follows:

	Parts per million
Sodium	820.00
Potassium	57.00
Lithium	3.00
Ammonium	2.30
Chloride	1254.00
Fluoride	4.00
Sulphate	9.20
Bicarbonate	35.00
Metaboric acid	71.00
Hydrogen sulphide	.01

DEVELOPMENTS IN ICELAND

A general description of Iceland has already been given in Chapter 11 in connection with the Icelandic type of eruption. It may be well, however, to point out again that Iceland consists entirely of volcanic material, chiefly successive outpourings of basaltic lava which have piled up a mass that rises from the ocean floor to nearly 7,000 feet above sea level. Following a long period of repose, the present volcanic activity, which began in the Pleistocene (Ice Age) and has continued uninterrupted to the present, is limited to a zone which crosses the central portion of the island in a northeast-southwest direction (Fig. 52).

Plate 66. Wairakei geothermal field, 1965. Pipes carry the steam from the separators, adjacent to the flash towers, to the main steam lines (left center) which service the power plant.

Hot Springs and Geysers of Iceland

As defined by Allen and Day, "Hot springs are circulating ground water of surface origin heated and augmented by steam originally in a superheated state rising from an underlying magma through deep cracks in the earth's crust" (1935, p. 32). This statement so completely fits the hot springs and geysers of Iceland that no additional comment is needed.

Hot springs and geysers are widely distributed in Iceland, but the most abundant and best known are in the southwestern part in the vicinity of Reykjavík. A geyser is a special type of hot spring which at intervals erupts a column of steam and boiling water. There are about 30 true geysers in Iceland, and they represent only 1 percent or less of the total number of hot springs. This compares with 200 geysers in Yellowstone National Park, which is about 10 percent of the number of hot springs there. New Zealand, the only other area in the world in which geysers are found, has fewer than Iceland, but its chief claim to geologic fame is based on the world's largest geyser, Waimanga, which was active from 1890 until 1904.

The most famous spouting hot spring in the world, which has given the name *geyser* to such phenomena, is Big Geysir in Iceland. The name, an Icelandic word meaning "to gush," was first applied to this particular spring in 1647 by Bishop Sveinsson (Barth 1950). Thus, in Iceland the word Geysir is a proper name and applies only to this particular boiling spring. In 1846 the German scientist R. Bunsen studied Big Geysir and proposed an explanation for its intermittent eruptions (see Bunsen 1847). Through his work the word was introduced as a technical term for all hot springs which show intermittent fountain action. For unknown reasons the English spelling was modified to *geyser*.

Big Geysir, known long before the Yellowstone or New Zealand geysers, is owned and carefully supervised by the Icelandic government. Its eruptions, which range from 100 to 200 feet in height, occur at irregular intervals varying from a few hours to a few days or even weeks. From 1915 to 1935 it was absolutely inactive, but it was reactivated by the cutting of a notch in the lip surrounding the basin, which lowered the water level about 3 feet. Immediately it became active again, and, although the gap was subsequently closed, with the return of the water level to its previous mark, the activity continued.

The Nature of Geyser Action

Geysers have much in common with volcanoes, in addition to occurrence in the same regions, in areas where recently active volcanoes exist. Geyser activity is quite similar to volcanic eruption in its intermittent nature and in the part played by steam. In fact, the eruption of Big Geysir has been compared to a volcanic eruption (Sonder 1937). Bunsen proposed the commonly accepted explanation of geyser action, a theory based on studies of Big Geysir more than 100 years ago. Bunsen's explanation takes into account the increase in the boiling point of water due to increase in pressure in the geyser tube. If the tube is too restricted to allow convection currents to operate, much of the water in the geyser tube will be heated to a temperature above the surface boiling point but will not boil because of the increased pressure. Finally, some of the water in the tube reaches its boiling point, even at the increased pressure, and some steam forms. The expanding steam pushes up the column of water sufficiently to cause some of it to overflow. This may happen several times, reducing the pressure in the tube until the water is above its boiling point and it flashes into steam. This is the eruption, which continues until the tube is emptied. The tube refills and the process is repeated, sometimes at regular intervals, as in the case of

Old Faithful geyser in Yellowstone National Park, but more often irregularly.

While the above explanation is the one still commonly given in textbooks, it has long been known that it does not fit all types of geysers. It is beyond the scope of the present work to review all the theories which have been proposed, but it is appropriate to call attention to the work of Thorkelsson (1940) on the geysers of Iceland. His theory, published in Icelandic and Danish journals, is not widely known in the United States. It is based on the entrance of "spring" gas (derived from magmatic water and from normal ground water) into the geyser tube. As the gas rises it produces a gentle ebullition (boilinglike action), which carries the heat upward in the geyser tube and also reduces the density of the water in the tube. The gases, being in contact with hot water, will become saturated with steam. Thorkelsson calculated that if the temperature is $2°$ C. below the boiling point the spring gases make up 6.9 percent by volume against 93.1 percent steam. The gases, however, in spite of their small quantity, are necessary for the existence of the "steam bubbles," which many investigators have observed rising in the geyser tube. Barth (1950, p. 60) cites an example of a geyser in Iceland which boils slowly for a period, then increases to violent boiling, which empties the basin. It then fills again with slowly boiling water, gradually becomes violently boiling, and again is emptied. This cycle takes about one hour. However, the maximum temperature in the spring is $97°$ C., showing that ebullition by rising gases rather than steam is responsible for the boiling. Such "cold"-water geysers have forced a re-examination of Bunsen's theory. Barth summarizes Thorkelsson's theory as follows: "The influx of gas will produce violent ebullition; heat will be carried rapidly upward by the gas bubbles and the ebullition will spread downward; great quantities of gas and water become engaged in the eruption. It is like opening the stopper of a bottle of soda water: gas bubbles form in the bottle and the contents erupt" (Barth 1950, p. 82). Thus the striking similarity between geysers and volcanoes, in both of which gas is the prime agent in the eruption, is apparent.

Utilization of Geothermal Heat

It has long been the custom of the Icelanders to use the hot springs near Reykjavík as a free public bath and wash-house. At one time many also cooked their food either in the hot ground or in the hot springs. For example, bread was cooked by placing it in tin molds and covering it with hot earth or lowering it into the spring. About the middle of the nineteenth century the hot water from the springs was used to evaporate sea water which had been pumped into shallow pans in order to recover salt. The average temperature of Iceland (37° F.) is too cold for many types of plants, but in the vicinity of the hot springs mild temperatures permit the growing of many plants not possible elsewhere. In some cases the warm areas are extended by carrying the hot water in pipes through the soil. Natural hot water is also used to heat extensive greenhouses in which many vegetables, flowers, and even tropical fruits, such as bananas, are grown.

Initially, in 1928, hot water from the nearby springs was pumped to Reykjavík and used to heat the hospital, a school, and a swimming pool. The results were so satisfactory that it was decided to expand the system to a city-wide basis. Since a larger source of water was needed, a spring at Reykir, 10 miles east of Reykjavík was selected for development. This spring had a flow of 1,320 gallons per minute at a temperature of 80° C. In order to increase the amount of water, wells were drilled to depths ranging from 450 to 1,200 feet. Work was begun in 1939 but was stopped by World War II before completion of the project. The wells, ranging from four to eight inches in diameter, are concentrated in an area of 160 acres. The water temperature from the wells is 87° C., as compared to 80° C. in the surface spring. Work was renewed on the project by Danish engineers, and the first houses heated by the new works were connected in December, 1943. In 1973, 90 percent of the houses in Reykjavík, a city of 55,000 population, were heated by the municipally owned water system under the supervision of the Hot Water Board. The main problem in piping the hot water is insulation, since the source is 10 miles from the city and the low winter temperatures in Iceland would soon cool the water. For the main supply pipes the insulation is lava slag and peat; for the urban system, lava slag; and for the individual houses, glass wool sealed with tar paper. The heat loss from the wells to the outlet in the homes is held to between 5° and 6° C. (Illingworth 1949). Borings within the city of Reykjavík are providing per second about 100 liters of water with a temperature of up to 138° C., while the springs and wells at Reykir furnish per second about 320 liters of water at 87° C. (Bodvärsson 1960).

The water is piped from the wells to insulated holding tanks, from which pumps deliver it through 14-inch insulated lines to the main reservoir tanks above the city. From these reservoir tanks there is gravity feed to the outlets in the city, with booster pumps helping out when the load is heavy. In the schools the water serves a double function: after it has run through the radiators it is used in swimming pools. Charges for the water, which is metered, are based on the amount used. The average cost is about 10 percent below the cost of hot-water heating which utilizes conventional fuels. The upkeep is low, and the city realizes a substantial profit on the investment.

The town of Sellfoss, Iceland, also has a municipal hot-water system similar to that at Reykjavík. The utilization of natural heat for domestic heating and for greenhouse heating is being expanded; as of 1973 about 50 percent of the population of Iceland had geothermal heating, and this is due to increase to over 60 percent by 1980 (Koenig 1973).

At Namafall, near Lake Myvatn in Northern Iceland, deposits of diatomite (a silica powder used in the manufacture of pottery glazes, etc.) are being dried with geothermal steam. Nearby, a geothermal power plant, opened in 1969, is producing 25,000 kilowatts. A district space-heating system is being designed to utilize the residual hot water from these operations.

The high-temperature geothermal areas occupy the zones of crustal rifting and active volcanism in Iceland. To the east and west of this zone are extensive sheets of Late Tertiary basalts from which many warm and hot springs issue. The high-temperature reservoirs, however, are associated with the main Quaternary rift, especially with Late Quaternary centers of dacitic and rhyolitic volcanism. The high-temperature regions now known include Myvatn in north-central Iceland and three areas in southwest Iceland (Fig. 52). The southwest areas, aligned from southwest to northeast at intervals of about 30 kilometers, are Reykjanes, Krysuvik, and Hengill, the largest, which has an area of about 70 square kilometers and includes the Hveragerdi field (Pl. 67) at its southern end. These areas have reservoir temperatures ranging from 220° to 280° C.

DEVELOPMENTS AT THE GEYSERS, SONOMA COUNTY, CALIFORNIA

The Geysers geothermal area is about 75 air miles due north of San Francisco in the northeastern corner of Sonoma County, California. Clear Lake is about 15 miles to the northeast of The Geysers (Fig. 79). The Mayacmas mountain range, one of the northern coast ranges, trends northwest across the area. The highest peak in the range is Mount St. Helena (4,344 ft.). The area called The Geysers—actually a series of hot springs and steam vents—is on the north bank of Big Sulphur Creek, about 16 miles upstream from its junction with the Russian River at Cloverdale. The area may be reached by paved, but narrow and winding, roads from Cloverdale and Healdsburg.

Plate 67. Steam well at Hveragerdi, Iceland. A natural steam power plant with a capacity of 15,000 kilowatts is planned.

Figure 79. Generalized geologic map of The Geysers area, Sonoma County, California. Modified from McNitt (1960; 1968).

General Geologic Characteristics

Like the geothermal areas already described, The Geysers is in a region of both recent volcanism and recent faulting. The rocks in the region belong to the Franciscan formation of Late Jurassic to Cretaceous age. These rocks form the "basement" in this region. They include graywacke interbedded with shale, basalt, minor beds of chert, and bodies of serpentine and diabase. The Franciscan rocks are usually highly folded, fractured, and sheared to the point where few of the original bedding features can be recognized. To the northeast of The Geysers, the Franciscan is covered by Plio-Pleistocene volcanic rocks which are very abundant in the Clear Lake area. The Clear Lake volcanic formation nearest The Geysers is the Cobb Mountain rhyolite, which caps a ridge about five miles to the northeast of Big Sulphur Creek. A prominent northwest-trending fault

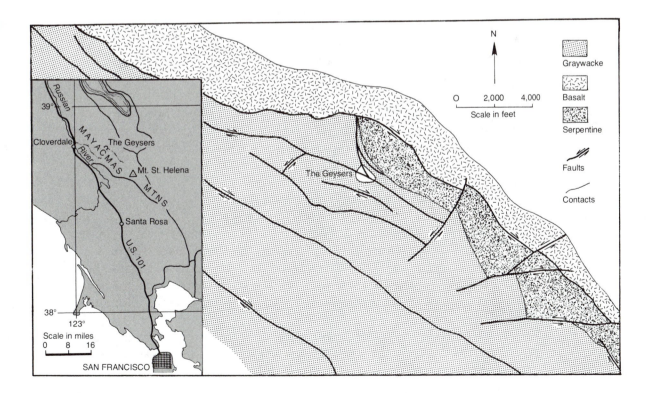

Figure 79. Generalized geologic map of The Geysers area, Sonoma County, California. Modified from McNitt (1960; 1968).

zone displaces the Franciscan rocks in the Big Sulphur Creek area; it is but one of several such faults which mark the western flank of the Mayacmas Mountains (Fig. 79). The Big Sulphur Creek fault zone has been the dominating factor in controlling the location of thermal areas in the Mayacmas Mountains as well as the location of mercury deposits which were an important source of quicksilver for many years. (Monte Amiata, Italy, is another example of the frequent association of mercury deposits with geothermal areas.)

The Big Sulphur Creek fault, as is also true for the other faults in the area, is described as "right lateral"; that is, if the observer faces the fault, the block on the far side has moved horizontally to the right with respect to the block on which the observer is standing. In this case the west side of the fault block moved to the northwest with respect to the opposite side (McNitt 1960). It may be of interest to recall that the 1906 San Francisco earthquake resulted from a "right-lateral" displacement (up to 23 feet, plus 3 feet of vertical displacement) on the San Andreas fault, which is about 20 miles to the west on the Pacific coast. Although the northwest-trending faults, which conform to the direction of bedding, dominate the area, the serpentine sills and adjacent rocks have been displaced by northeast-trending "left-lateral" faults (Fig. 79). The serpentine, which shears easily under stress, as compared to basalt and graywacke, permits the northeast faults to develop, and at these points the relief of the stress is shared equally by the two sets of faults (McNitt 1960). The large thermal areas occur at the intersection of these two fault systems. James R. McNitt (1968) interprets the Mayacmas Mountains as a horst, with the southwest boundary fault largely covered by alluvium of the Russian River, while the northeast boundary fault is concealed by lake deposits and recent volcanic material. The presence of domes and ridges of volcanic rock on the projection of this fault led McNitt to conclude that it served as the major volcanic conduit for eruptions in the Clear Lake area.

Source of Heat and Nature of the Steam Reservoir

The source of the heat in The Geysers geothermal area is believed to be the same magma which produced the Clear Lake volcanics. A pronounced gravity low, centered just to the south of Clear Lake, is the basis for the estimate that the magma underlies an area of 300–400 square kilometers and is at a depth of five to eight kilometers (Koenig 1973).

The reservoir rocks for the geothermal steam are the graywacke and associated rocks of the Franciscan formation. These rocks are practically impermeable, but the high rate of flow of the steam and

Plate 68. The Geysers geothermal area, Sonoma County, California. Steam at the right and in the middle of the photograph are from producing wells. The power plant on top of the hill, which serves this section, went into operation in 1972. Photo courtesy Pacific Gas and Electric Co.

the relatively rapid recovery of pressure after shutting in a well indicate that a large steam reservoir is present. Permeability, therefore, probably exists in fault and shear zones and zones of shattering in the graywacke.

Geothermal Development

The Geysers is said to have been discovered by a bear hunter in 1847 and became a nationally known health spa in the latter part of the nineteenth century. It seems rather surprising that the name Geysers was applied to an area devoid of geysers, especially since the term *geyser* was not well known prior to the 1870 discovery of Yellowstone, which contains the only natural geysers in North America. The resort development was near the mouth of Geyser

Creek, a small tributary which enters Big Sulphur Creek from the north. The hot springs are generally along the creek bed, while the steam vents are higher on the banks. The most active area comprises about 50 acres. The fumarole which discharges the greatest volume of steam is called the Smokestack; others are Steamboat and Safety Valve. The temperature, as recorded by Allen and Day (1927), at a depth of three feet was 101.5° C. at Steamboat Fumarole and 98° C. at Safety Valve Fumarole.

The first drilling was done in 1921 by Mr. J. D. Grant in the hope of using the steam to generate electric power (Allen and Day 1927). At a depth of 203 feet a steam pressure of 62 psi was encountered. In 1922, when a second well was drilled, using steam from the first

for power, a pressure of 61 psi was found at a depth of 318 feet. By 1925 a total of eight wells had been drilled to depths ranging from 320 to 636 feet. The pressure was greater in deeper wells but did not increase in proportion to depth. Closed-in pressures varied from 60 to 275 psi. Each well was calculated to deliver about 1,000 kilowatts. Drilling of new wells did not affect the pressure. Although an adequate supply of steam was obtained, the project failed because of the lack of demand for electric power. Renewed interest in geothermal power in 1955 resulted in the Magma Power Company's leasing the area of active steam vents near the resort and, in cooperation with Thermal Power Company, drilling six wells between 1955 and 1957, the deepest to a depth of 1,404 feet (Koenig 1969). Following flow test, which indicated a total steam flow at the wellhead of about 300,000 pounds per hour at 115 psi for four wells, Pacific Gas and Electric Company signed a contract for the purchase of steam, and construction of the first power station began. This station, with a capacity of 12,500 kilowatts, began generating electricity in June, 1960, from the steam supplied by four wells.

Since 1960 the development has proceeded rapidly. The wells, which earlier were around 2,000 feet or less in depth, now average 7,000–8,000 feet and have not shown a notable decrease in fracture permeability (Koenig 1969). Deeper drilling, which in the graywacke requires bits specifically designed for hard-rock drilling, have caused well costs to rise sharply. The probability of finding a profitable steam well diminishes rapidly with depth, because, in addition to the increased cost of drilling, the greater length of steam flow to the surface decreases the quantity of steam. For example, with all other factors held constant, a well completed at 10,000 feet delivers almost 20 percent less steam than the same well completed at 5,000 feet. There is, therefore, an important economic factor in determining the depth to which wells may be drilled in prospecting for steam.

The Geysers geothermal field has been greatly enlarged from the original 80-acre site near the resort area. As of 1972, some 110 wells had been drilled, with 85 completed as steam producers. As defined by drilling, the field is in two segments, one over 2 miles long and at least 0.5 mile wide; the other (Little Geysers), 4 miles to the southeast, covering about 200 acres. In addition, there are large areas as yet untested.

The reservoir temperature at The Geysers reaches about 250° C., and the reservoir pressure of 450–500 psig reduces to about 125 psig at the wellhead, as the steam flowing from the reservoir to the surface expands and cools; and the turbines are thus designed to operate at 80–100 psig intake pressure. Geothermal steam rapidly loses its heat energy when transported through a pipeline; so it must be utilized as close to the steam well as possible. Generating units with a capacity of 55 megawatts are being installed at The Geysers. Each unit requires about 1 million pounds per hour of superheated steam, and, since the average production per well is around 150,000 pounds per hour, seven wells are required to supply each unit. As production from these wells declines, new wells are drilled to insure a steady supply of steam to the generators. The plants being built at The Geysers as of 1973 are of 110-megawatt capacity, in pairs of 55-megawatt units. The location of each plant is determined by exploratory drilling to "block out" the steam supply for the plant (Budd 1973). By late 1972, The Geysers was producing 302 megawatts, and plans call for the annual addition of 110 megawatts through 1980, which would give a capacity of 1,180 megawatts. Currently The Geysers is the world's largest producer of geothermal energy, and the prospects are that this status will be maintained for the next decade.

WORLD-WIDE GEOTHERMAL DEVELOPMENTS

The geothermal areas currently in production and the expected developments to 1977 are listed in Tables 3 and 4. Space does not permit a description of additional geothermal fields, but fortunately a recent survey of the status of geothermal resource development on a world-wide basis is available (Koenig 1973).

The extent to which geothermal exploration and development is being carried on throughout the world is indicated by the large number of countries listed in Table 6.

THE ENERGY OUTLOOK

Not all the frontiers of the future are in outer space. The heat and power from within the earth are still largely an unexplored dimension of our universe. The developments described in the preceding pages provide examples of how the power resources from within the earth may be utilized. New and inexpensive sources of power must be developed for the future, since the conventional sources of energy—oil, gas, and coal—all have foreseeable ends of supply. Water power is necessarily limited, and nuclear power, which at one time was believed to be the answer to our energy problems, poses serious environmental problems.

The consumption of electric energy is increasing at a phenomenal rate. In many areas the consumption of power has doubled in the last decade, and this pattern may continue for some time into the future. To meet this tremendous increase, all sources of energy must be tapped. With the realization that a serious energy shortage will face the world at least for the next decade, it is imperative that we utilize all the indigenous energy resources that can be developed

TABLE 6. *Status of geothermal exploration and development, 1975*

Nation	Electric-Power Generation/ Construction	Experimental Power Stations	Significant Direct Utilization	Other Geothermal- Field Discoveries	Additional Exploration Under Way[a]
Azores (Portugal)					•[b]
Chile				•	
China					•
Costa Rica					•
Ethiopia					•
France			•		
French Somaliland					•[b]
Greece					•[b]
Guadeloupe (French West Indies)				•	
Guatemala					•
Hungary			•		
Iceland	•		•	•	
India					•
Indonesia				•	•
Italy	•			•	•
Japan	•	•[c]	•	•	•
Kenya			•	•	•

with modern and future technologies. A promising source of energy for early development in large quantities is geothermal energy. The engineering problems of utilizing geothermal steam in vapor-dominated systems (The Geysers) and hot-water–dominated systems (Wairakei) have largely been solved by the application or modification of oil-field technology. However, these types of geothermal resources are relatively scarce, and the technology to utilize other types of geothermal resources, such as hot dry rock systems and geopressured sands, must be developed. Huge reserves of energy are stored in such systems, and research is urgently needed to de-

TABLE 6. continued

Nation	Electric-Power Generation/ Construction	Experimental Power Stations	Significant Direct Utilization	Other Geothermal- Field Discoveries	Additional Exploration Under Way[a]
Mexico	●	●	●	●	●
New Zealand	●		●	●	●
Nicaragua				●	
Philippines	●d			●	
El Salvador	●			●	
Taiwan				●	
Turkey				●	
USSR	●	●	●	●	●
United States	●	●c	●	●	●
Zaire		●c			

Source: after Koenig (1973), as revised by James B. Koenig, 1975 (personal communication).
[a] Other areas of geothermal exploration/interest: Algeria, Bulgaria, Canada, Colombia, Czechoslovakia, Ecuador, Fiji Islands, Iran, Malawi, Morocco, New Britain, New Hebrides, Panama, Peru, Spain (Canary Islands), Tanzania, Uganda, Venezuela, Yugoslavia, Zambia.
[b] Recent deep drilling.
[c] Inactive.
[d] Under construction.

termine whether it is economically feasible to utilize this energy.

Italy, lacking the more conventional sources of energy, was more or less forced to utilize its natural steam resources, which now have been developed to the point where they are an important national asset. The first geothermal power installation in the United States was put into operation late in 1960, and the capacity has been increased annually, with the result that it is now the world's largest geothermal power development.

Electric power produced from geothermal steam appears to be competitive with—in many cases even cheaper than—that from fossil-fuel plants. In addition, the environmental impact of geo-thermal power development appears to be more acceptable than that of fossil- or nuclear-fuel power development.

Geothermal power is not, in itself, the full answer to our energy shortage. A recent assessment of the potential for geothermal ener-gy (Hickel et al. 1972) forecasts that the United States could be sup-plying about 13 percent of the nation's power requirement from geothermal sources by 1985, provided that recommended research and development are carried out. Even this amount could bridge the gap until other sources of energy (solar, oil-shale, etc.) are devel-oped, reduce the need for additional imports of petroleum prod-ucts, and release petroleum and natural gas for more appropriate uses.

Chapter 15

Distribution, Current Activity, and Geologic Relationships of Volcanoes, Island Arcs, and Mountains

Come wander with me, she said,
Into regions yet untrod;
And read what is still unread
In the manuscripts of God.
—LONGFELLOW

Although the number of volcanoes known in the world runs into the thousands, only about 500 have been active in historic times and are considered, therefore, to be "active volcanoes." A recent list of the active volcanoes of the world (Macdonald 1972) contains 516 entries, of which 69 are submarine eruptions. In this list any volcano which has erupted in historic times is considered to be active. Actually, this is somewhat misleading, because some of the volcanoes which are included in the list have not erupted for centuries and today appear to be extinct or dormant. A listing which included only those that show some signs of activity would be most helpful, especially to a person who wished to seek an active volcano in order to observe an eruption. However, for our immediate purpose, that is, to consider the distribution of volcanoes as a clue to their origin, the present listing is quite satisfactory. Any eruption in historic time, regardless of how remote, is certainly in the "present" if considered as a part of geologic time.

To acquaint the reader with the current status of volcanic activity, a tabulation of volcanic eruptions reported for each of the years from 1969 to 1973 is included later in this chapter.

DISTRIBUTION OF
ACTIVE VOLCANOES

General Distribution

The great majority of the active volcanoes, as well as the recently active, are concentrated in a belt bordering the Pacific Ocean (see map on end papers). So marked is the concentration of active volcanoes in this belt that it is known as the "fire girdle of the Pacific." The volcanoes in these encircling areas are associated with geologically young or still growing mountains which are arranged as a series of festoons or arcs around the margin of the Pacific Ocean. The convex side of the arc is always toward the Pacific Ocean. A second belt of recent mountain building which contains active volcanoes is the Alpine-Himalayan zone, extending from southeastern Europe through the Mediterranean and southern Asia and into the East Indies Archipelago. In addition, more or less isolated volcanoes occur within each of the three great oceanic regions of the world, the Pacific, the Atlantic, and the Indian oceans.

In the circum-Pacific belt the volcanoes are either near the margin of the bordering continent or in island arcs which lie along the continental margin. In striking contrast, the lands bordering the Atlantic Ocean are relatively free of volcanoes, earthquakes, and growing mountains. In only two places do the Pacific type island arcs encroach on the Atlantic: in the volcanic loop of the Lesser Antilles at the eastern border of the Caribbean Sea and in a similar loop, the Scotia arc of the Southern Antilles, which links Patagonia with Grahamland in the far South Atlantic. Otherwise, volcanic activity in the Atlantic is limited largely to islands on the Mid-Atlantic Ridge, such as the Azores and Iceland, and to the Canary and Cape Verde islands off the west coast of Africa.

The tabulation of the world's active volcanoes in Table 7 is based largely on the *Catalogue of the Active Volcanoes of the World, Including Solfatara Fields* (1951–1967). Additional information was compiled from various sources, including Coats (1950), Gorshkov (1970), Macdonald (1972), and reports from the Center for Short-Lived Phenomena (1969–1973) of the Smithsonian Institution.

The list of 516 active volcanoes in Table 7—the same number Macdonald (1972) included in a similar tabulation—must be considered to be only an approximation, although it is based on the most reliable information available. The known submarine eruptions are included, but there must be a far greater number that were not reported or even observed. In the first edition of this book (1962) the number of active volcanoes was listed as 454. In less than 15 years the number has increased by more than 12 percent, a fact which attests to the increased efficiency of world communications and the reporting agencies. Some, but not more than 1 percent, of the increase can be attributed to the birth of new volcanoes in that period or to the eruption of volcanoes that had been considered extinct.

TABLE 7. *Active volcanoes of the world*

Location	Number of Active Volcanoes	Totals
Circum-Pacific belt		
Kamchatka, USSR	19	
Kuril Islands	33	
Japan	31	
Ryukyu Islands	6	
China Sea	7	
Mariana and Izu islands	20	
Philippines	15	
Melanesia (New Guinea, New Britain, Admiralty Islands, Solomon Islands, Santa Cruz Islands, New Hebrides)	30	
New Zealand	5	
Tonga-Kermadec-Samoa	18	
North America		
Aleutians and Alaska	39	
Western United States	7	
Mexico	10	
Central America		
Guatemala	7	
El Salvador	7	
Nicaragua	11	
Costa Rica	7	
South America		
Colombia	7	
Ecuador	9	
Peru	4	
Chile	27	
Subtotal		319
Scotia arc and Antarctica	10	10

Location	Number Active Volcanoes	Totals
Pacific Ocean		
Hawaiian Islands	4	
Galápagos Islands	7	
Juan Fernández Islands	2	
Others (submarine)	3	
Subtotal		16
Alpine-Himalayan belt		
Mediterranean area (Italy, Sicily, Aegean Sea)	13	
Continental Asia	5	
Barren Island, Bay of Bengal	1	
Indonesia		
Sumatra	12	
Java	20	
Lesser Sunda Islands	20	
Banda Sea	8	
Celebes	5	
Sangihe Islands	5	
Moluccas	5	
Subtotal		94
Iceland and Jan Mayen Island	22	22
Atlantic Ocean		
Azores	11	
Canary Islands	3	
Cape Verde Islands	1	
Tristan de Cunha	1	
Lesser Antilles (West Indies)	9	
Others (submarine)	4	
Subtotal		29

Location	Number Active Volcanoes	Totals
Asia Minor and Red Sea	8	8
Africa		
Ethiopia	4	
East Africa	7	
Central Africa	2	
West Africa	1	
Subtotal		14
Indian Ocean	4	4
Grand total		516

Table 7 fails to give the reader any idea of the year-to-year volcanic activity. To provide such a view, the volcanoes reported as having erupted in each year of a five-year period, from 1969 through 1973, are tabulated in Table 8. The information is based chiefly on the *Bulletin of Volcanic Eruptions*, numbers 9 (1969) and 10 (1970), published by the International Association of Volcanology, reports of the Center for Short-Lived Phenomena (1969–1973), Macdonald (1972), Swanson (1973), and Christiansen (1974). While this information is the most complete and reliable available, it can be assumed that some eruptions, perhaps in remote areas, were not reported, although it is believed that the number of such unreported eruptions is small.

Perhaps the most significant fact revealed by Tables 7 and 8 is that almost two-thirds of the active volcanoes are in the Pacific region. This concentration of volcanoes in a belt surrounding the Pacific Ocean suggests that in this zone must exist some unusual conditions which have a direct relation to the origin of volcanoes. When it is discovered that most of the earthquakes of the world are also centered in this same belt and that it also includes the youngest mountains, some of which are still growing, the connection seems unmistakable. A brief survey of the two major volcanic belts will be helpful in speculating on these relationships.

TABLE 8. *Volcanic activity for 1969–1973*

Key to type of activity:
a—ash or cinders
c—central crater
d—dome
e—normal explosions
f—lava flow
l—lateral crater or fissure
m—mudflow or lahar
n—*nuée ardente* (ash flow)
p—phreatic explosion
s—submarine eruption

Year	Name and Location of Volcano	Type of Activity	Comments
1969	*Bezymianny, Kamchatka, USSR	c,e,a,d,n	Lava dome now forming
	O'Shima, Japan	c,e,a	
	Sakurajima, Japan	c,e,a	
	Kutinoerabu-zima, Ryukyu Islands	c,e,a	
	Didicas, Babuyan Islands, Philippines	c,e,a	Submarine eruptions until 1952 when permanent island formed
	Canlaon, Negros, Philippines	c,e,a,m	
	Taal, Luzon, Philippines	c,e,l,a,f	
	*Mayon, Luzon, Philippines	c,e,m	
	Farallón de Pájaros, Mariana Islands	s	
	Kovachi, Solomon Islands	s	
	Yasour, New Hebrides	c,e	Constant Strombolian activity
	Matupi, New Britain	c,e	Cone in Rabaul Caldera
	Merapi, Java, Indonesia	c,e,d,f, n,m	Destructive *nuées ardentes* and lahars; multiple lava domes
	Lokon, Celebes, Indonesia	c,e,a	
	Gunung Ija, Flores Island	c,e,a	
	Ebu Lobo, Flores Island	c,e,a	
	Amburombu, Flores Island	c,e,f,n	
	Ruapehu, New Zealand	c,e,a,m(?)	
	Deception Island, Antarctica	c,e,a,m	
	Kiska, Aleutian Islands, Alaska	c,e,a,f(?)	
	Telica, Nicaragua	c,e,a	
	Poas, Costa Rica	c,e,a	
	Rincón de la Vieja, Costa Rica	c,e,a	
	Arenal, Costa Rica	c,e,f	Erupted same day as Poas
	Ubinas, Peru	c,e,a	
	*Kilauea, Hawaii	l,f	On east rift, mainly Alae and Aloi craters
	*Etna, Sicily	c,e,l,a,f	Continuation of eruption which began in 1967

*Described in some detail elsewhere in this book.

Year	Name and Location of Volcano	Type of Activity	Comments
1970	*Bezymianny, Kamchatka, USSR	c,e,a,d,n	Extrusive dome in crater continues to grow
	Karimsky, Kamchatka, USSR	c,e,a,f	One of the most active volcanoes of Kamchatka
	Sakurajima, Japan	c,e,a	Minamidake, summit crater of Sakurajima
	Akita-Komagatake, Japan	c,e,a,f	Strombolian-type eruptions at Medake, central cone of the double volcano
	Aso, Japan	c,e,a	
	O'Shima, Japan	c,e,a	
	*Myozin-syo, Japan	s	
	Suwanosezima, Ryukyu Islands	c,e,a	
	Cablan, Negros, Philippines	c,e,a	
	Taal, Luzon, Philippines	c,e,a	
	Kovachi, Solomon Islands	s	
	Bagana, Bougainville Island	c,e,a,d,f	
	Langila, New Britain	c,e,a,n,f	
	Ulawun, New Britain	c,e,n,d	
	Tonga, South Pacific	s	
	*Kilauea, Hawaii	l,f	On east rift, largely at Mauna Ulu
	Pacaya, Guatemala	c,e	
	San Miguel, El Salvador	c,e,a	
	Cerro Negro, Nicaragua	c,e,a	
	Masaya, Nicaragua	c,e	Fluid lava appeared in crater
	Telica, Nicaragua	c,e,a	
	Rincón de la Vieja, Costa Rica	c,e,a	
	Arenal, Costa Rica	f	Lava flow from 1969 continued
	Beerenberg, Jan Mayen Island	c,e,a,l,f	In Greenland Sea
	*Hekla, Iceland	e,a,l,f	Thousands of sheep killed by fluorine poisoning
	Deception Island, Antarctica	c,e,a	

Year	Name and Location of Volcano	Type of Activity	Comments

Year	Name and Location of Volcano	Type of Activity	Comments
1971	Sakurajima, Japan	c,l,e,f	
	Akita-Komagatake, Japan	c,e	
	Karua, New Hebrides	s	Has formed an island several times which waves destroyed
	Tinakula, Santa Cruz Island, South Pacific	c,a,e,f	Intermittently active most of the time
	White Island, New Zealand	c,a,p,m	
	Ruapehu, New Zealand	c,e,d,f,m	
	*Kilauea, Hawaii	c,l,f	Continued activity at Mauna Ulu on the east rift; eruptions on the floor of Kilauea Caldera producing "fountains of lava" and lava flows in August and September
	Nyamuragira, Rwanda, Africa	c,l,e,f	
	Nyiragongo, Zaire, Africa	c,e	Lava lake in crater most of the time
	Erta'Ale, Ethiopia, Africa	c,l,e,f	Shield volcano with lava lake
	*Etna, Sicily	c,l,e,f	
	*Stromboli, Aeolian Islands, Sicily	c,e,f,n	Essentially continuously active
	Teneguila, La Palma, Canary Islands	l,e,f,n	
	*La Soufrière, St. Vincent Island, Lesser Antilles	d	Lava dome growing in crater
	Cerro Negro, Nicaragua	c,e,l,f,m	
	Fuego, Guatemala	c,e,d,f,m	Loss of lives in eruption
	Telica, Nicaragua	a,e	Lava in crater
	Villarica, Chile	c,e,a,f	
	Caldera Cerro Ventisquero, Chile	e,f,m	Melting of snow, resulting in lahars killing 30 people

Year	Name and Location of Volcano	Type of Activity	Comments
1972	Sakurajima, Japan	c,e	
	Alaid, Kuril Islands	a,f	
	*Krakatoa, Indonesia	a,e	Eruption at Anak Krakatoa, cone in Krakatoa Caldera
	Semeru, Java, Indonesia	c,f	A strato-volcano, very active in 19th century, causing much damage and loss of life
	Merapi, Java, Indonesia	c,e,a,n	
	Ritter Island, New Britain	s	
	Piton de la Fournaise, Réunion Island, Indian Ocean	a,f	
	Karthala, Comaro Island, Indian Ocean	c,e,a,f	
	*Kilauea, Hawaii	l,f	Chiefly east rift at Mauna Ulu
	Fernandina, Galápagos Islands	e,a	First activity since caldera collapse in 1968
	Erta'Ale, Ethiopia, Africa	c,e,f	Lava lake in crater
	Nyiragongo, Zaire, Africa	c,e,f	
	*La Soufrière, St. Vincent Island, Lesser Antilles	d	Eruption ceased on March 20
	Acatenango, Guatemala	c,e,a	
	Pacaya, Guatemala	e,a,l,f	
	Poas, Costa Rica	c,e,a,p	Eruption cloud with andesitic ash reached heights up to 3 km.
	Puyehue, Chile	c,e	Strato-volcano
1973	Ivan Grozny, Iturup Island, Kuriles	c,e	Somma rim, with merging extrusive domes in central cone
	Tiatia, Kunashire Island, Kuriles	l,e,a	Strato-volcano; dormant since 1812
	Sakurajima, Japan	c,e,a	
	Asama, Japan	c,e,a	Strong air-wave shocks

Key to type of activity:
  a—ash or cinders
  c—central crater
  d—dome
  e—normal explosions
  f—lava flow
  l—lateral crater or fissure
m—mudflow or lahar
  n—*nuée ardente* (ash flow)
  p—phreatic explosion
  s—submarine eruption

Year	Name and Location of Volcano	Type of Activity	Comments
1973	Nishino-shima, Bonin Islands	s,a	
	Paluweh Island, Indonesia	c,a,e	
	Long Island, near New Guinea	p,a,f	
	Langila, New Britain	c,e,a,f	
	Ulawun, New Britain	c,e,a,f,n	
	*Kilauea, Hawaii	l,f	Eruption on east rift, mainly Mauna Ulu vent
	Akutan, Aleutian Islands, Alaska	e,a	
	Pavlof, Aleutian Islands, Alaska	c,e,f	
	Curacoa Reef, Samoa	s	
	Fernandina, Galápagos Islands	f	
	Erta'Ale, Ethiopia, Africa	c,e,f	
	*Helgafell, Heimaey, Iceland	a,l,f	Huge amounts of sea water sprayed on lava to check advance
	Acatenango, Guatemala	c,e,a	
	Fuego, Guatemala	a,n	
	Pacaya, Guatemala	c,e,a,f,l	
	Santiaguito Dome (Santa María), Guatemala	a,d,n,m	More or less continuously active; first *nuées ardentes* since 1934

Volcanic Belts

Circum-Pacific volcanic belt. In a survey of the circum-Pacific volcanic belt (see map on end papers) it will be convenient to begin with the Alaska Peninsula and its continuation, the Aleutian Islands, which contain 39 volcanoes that have erupted in historic times. The Kamchatka Peninsula and the Kuril Islands, with 52 active volcanoes, are the Asiatic counterpart of the Alaskan-Aleutian arc. Farther southward the next area is the Japan arc, then through the Ryukyu Islands to the Philippines, the latter with 15 active volcanoes. The belt then continues through New Guinea, the New Hebrides, and the Solomon Islands, where numerous active volcanoes occur, and to New Zealand. From New Zealand the belt is continued to the northeast through the Kermadec Islands, the Tongas, and Samoa.

From Alaska southward down the Pacific coast of North America no active volcanoes occur until the volcanic peaks of the Cascade Mountains of the northwestern United States are reached. Although

Lassen Peak in northern California, which erupted in 1914–1917, was long considered to be the only active volcano in the 48 contiguous states, it has now been confirmed that other volcanoes in the Cascades erupted in the nineteenth century, including Mount Baker, Mount Rainier, Mount St. Helens, Mount Hood, Mount Shasta, and Cinder Cone (see Chapter 19). A wide gap exists in the volcanic belt from California to southern Mexico, where active volcanoes again are found. With some minor gaps the belt is then continuous through Central America, with 32 active volcanoes, and the Andes of South America, with 47.

Alpine-Himalayan belt. Along the Alpine-Himalayan belt—apart from Indonesia—volcanoes are distributed more sporadically. It may be noted that this belt, in contrast to the circum-Pacific belt, where an ocean plate is in contact with a continental plate, is the juncture of two continental plates. The significance of these relationships is discussed in Chapter 16. The Alpine-Himalayan belt can be traced from the Canary and Madeira islands through the Mediterranean region, where it includes Vesuvius, Stromboli, Vulcano, and Etna in Italy and Sicily, thence to the Aegean volcanoes, the best known being Santorini, and eastward to Mount Ararat on the Turkish-Armenian border and Mount Demavend in Iran, near the southern end of the Caspian Sea. Mount Ararat and Mount Demavend, although prominent volcanic cones, have not been active in historic times. (Mount Ararat, according to biblical accounts, was the resting place of Noah's ark after the flood; a remote mountain 16,000 feet high seems an unlikely site; perhaps in ancient times the name was applied to a more accessible peak.)

Beyond the Himalayas the volcanic belt reappears in Burma and continues southward through Barren Island, in the Bay of Bengal, where historic eruptions are known to have occurred. The belt then continues through Sumatra, with 12 active volcanoes, Java, with 20, and the Lesser Sunda Islands, with 20. the Indonesian section (Sumatra, Java, etc.) is a typical island arc, like those characteristic of the circum-Pacific belt, and also is the juncture of an oceanic plate and a continental plate.

With the uneven spacing of volcanoes in this belt, long gaps occur, especially in the main section of the Alps and Himalayas. It has been suggested that in these regions, where the crust has been greatly thickened by folding and overthrusting, the magma has not been able to penetrate to the surface. Volcanoes are present around the margins of such areas, but the central portions of both the Alps and the Himalayas, as well as the highly compressed cores of other fold-mountain ranges, exhibit no recent volcanic activity.

Atlantic Ocean. The volcanoes of the Atlantic Ocean are, for the most part, related to the Mid-Atlantic Ridge. This ridge, throughout its entire extent, from Iceland on the north to Tristan de Cunha in the far South Atlantic, is the site of magma rising from the mantle and spreading to either side, creating new ocean crust. This concept, known as "sea-floor spreading," is discussed in Chapter 16.

Linear Spacing of Volcanoes

A particularly striking feature of the linear arrangement of volcanoes is the tendency for the interval between members of a group to be nearly constant. For example, the volcanoes of the Galápagos Islands are roughly 20 miles apart (Fig. 80). A similar spacing is indicated in Hawaii, Fiji, and Tahiti. In the Canary Islands, as well as in the Lesser Antilles, the distance is roughly doubled; and in the northern Andes it is halved. In the Phlegraean Fields the volcanoes are situated at the corners of a triangular network in which the cones are only 1–2 miles apart. The question which naturally arises is whether the spacing is significant and what inferences, if any, can be drawn from it. It has been repeatedly stressed that volcanic vents are located at the intersection of two sets of fractures. If this is true, then the spacing may be a clue to the thickness of the earth's crust. To illustrate this point, S. J. Shand (1938, p. 83) suggests that a slab of chocolate be used to represent the earth's crust. It can be broken by bending, and the pieces, in turn, can be broken in the same way, but with greater and greater difficulty as the length and the width of the pieces approach their thickness, after which they can no longer be broken by bending. In the same way, the interval between neighboring volcanoes, assuming that they are along fractures which divide the earth's crust into blocks, should be roughly equal to the thickness of the earth's crust at each place.

Admittedly the interval is only suggestive, but it is a point worthy of consideration. One cannot fail to be impressed by the frequency of an interval of about 20 miles between the larger volcanoes and by the further coincidence that earthquakes accompanying many volcanic eruptions come from a depth of about 20 miles. The shallowness of the magma at Vesuvius (adjacent to the Phlegraean Fields), perhaps about 3 miles in depth, although not, of course, as shallow as indicated by the spacing in the Phlegraean Fields, still suggests a general area of agreement and gives support to this theory of relationship between the thickness of the earth's crust and the distance between volcanoes.

ISLAND ARCS

Location and Structure

Island arcs are a very conspicuous feature of the earth's surface, but they are not uniformly distributed. They are common features around the borders of the Pacific Ocean, especially along the eastern border of Asia (Fig. 4). They do not occur in the Atlantic Ocean, except for the Lesser Antilles and Scotia arc, as has already been mentioned. Island arcs are usually surmounted by active volcanoes, and they are also zones of strong seismic (earthquake) activity. They are so situated that a deep furrow in the ocean floor (known as a marginal deep) lies on their convex, or ocean-basin, side and a relatively shallow platform attaching the shoal to the continental mass lies on their concave, or landward, side. In some cases deep sea basins

Figure 80. Spacing of volcanoes in the Galápagos Islands. After Shand (1938).

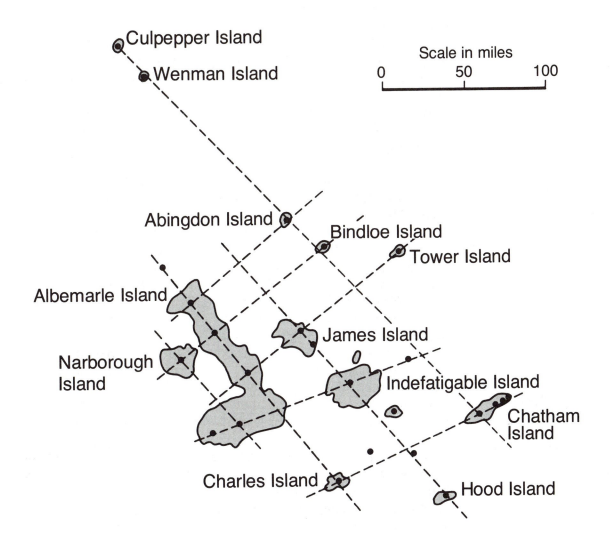

separate the island arc from the mainland, and the island arcs, such as the Mariana, Yap, and Palau arcs off the China coast, stand more or less isolated in front of the continental mass. Others continue into the continent and have counterparts on the mainland. Such are the East Indies arc, which continues into the Asiatic continent at Burma, and the Aleutian arc, which continues into the North American continent at Alaska. The Aleutian Islands, with a front of 1,450 miles, are bordered on the Pacific side by the Aleutian Trench, a long narrow trough more than 2,000 miles long and 50–100 miles wide with a maximum depth of slightly over 25,000 feet. Back of it is the Bering Sea, a relatively shallow body of water, much of which is less than 100 fathoms in depth. The Aleutian arc fits a radius of 760 miles (Fig. 70).

The main island of Japan is defined by an arc with a radius of 650 miles. Offshore from the northern part of the arc lies the Tuscarora deep, a part of the Japan Trench.

An island arc is a structural feature and must have a marginal deep on the ocean side; it must also give evidence of volcanic activity. Hence, a row of islands more or less arc-shaped, such as those off the coast of British Columbia, is not a typical island arc if the islands are not associated with deep sea troughs and are not the site of active volcanoes. The association of active volcanoes with typical island arcs is so striking that the arcs become an important factor in considering the origin of volcanoes.

It was the great Austrian geologist Eduard Suess (1904) who early in the twentieth century, in his classic work *The Face of the Earth*, focused attention on the arcuate structure of the great mountain systems of the earth. It was early noted that the arcuate belts are arranged around the ancient nucleus of each continent, spreading in an ever-widening arc; the younger the arc, the greater its distance from the nucleus. Many ancient mountain systems were the sites of active volcanoes when they were being formed. We may infer, then, that the present island arcs, with their associated volcanoes, are mountain ranges in the process of being formed.

Island arcs, to the geologist, are one of the most challenging features of the earth's surface. Many theories have been offered to explain them, but none is entirely satisfactory. However, the concept of sea-floor spreading and plate tectonics (Ch. 16), if verified, appears to provide a reasonable explanation for island arcs and associated volcanism.

Island arcs occur as single arcs and as double arcs. Where the arc is double, as in the Sumatra-Java arc of the East Indies (Fig. 86), the active volcanoes are always associated with the inner arc. Some arcs are strongly arcuate, while others have only a slight curvature. It was early pointed out that many mountains and island arcs are truly circular if traced on a large-scale globe. If one slices deeply into an orange, the trace of the slice on the peel is circular, but if the peel is flattened out, as in the case of a flat map of the earth, it becomes arcuate. Further, the radius of the arc is dependent on the angle of the slice. It appears, then, that a slice (or shear zone) at the base of each island arc would account for its shape. No other explanation is so simple or complete. If a shear zone, or *thrust plane* in geologic terminology, is present, the dip or slope can be determined because it is equal to the angle subtended at the center of the earth by the radius of the arc. This explanation of island arcs appears to hinge on evidence of a deep shear zone associated with each island arc. Such evidence is obtained from a study of earthquakes associated with island arcs.

Relationship to Earthquakes

Earthquakes, which are due primarily to the jar given the earth by slippage along a fault or shear zone, are shaking the earth constantly. The great majority of earthquakes originate in the crust of the earth at depths not exceeding 35 kilometers. In fact, it was long held that no earthquakes could originate below this depth. Such reasoning was based on the idea that because of great heat and pressure the rocks below this depth could not rupture and would yield to stresses by flowage. Thus originated the concept of a zone of fracture, the surface crust down to a depth of 10–15 miles, and below this a zone of flowage. In 1928 Harold Jeffreys, a distinguished English scientist, made an exhaustive survey of earthshocks and concluded that the great majority originated in the outer layers of the earth's crust at depths not exceeding 35 kilometers, apparently confirming the zone-of-flowage and zone-of-fracture concept. In the same year, K. Wadati (1928), in a study of the earthquakes in the Japanese region, produced clear evidence that, aside from the normal shocks with which Jeffreys was dealing, there were other earthquakes in the area around Japan with a focal depth of several hundred kilometers.

Later B. Gutenberg and C. F. Richter (1938; 1941) recognized three classes of earthquakes: (*a*) normal shocks, at depths not exceeding 60 kilometers, (*b*) intermediate shocks, at depths of 60–250 kilometers, and (*c*) deep shocks, at depths of 250–700 kilometers. No earthquakes have been positively identified with foci exceeding 700 kilometers (435 mi.) in depth. The discovery that earthquakes occur at great depths in the earth does not mean that the earlier idea of a zone of fracture and a zone of flowage is entirely erroneous. A re-examination of the effect of stresses on plastic material has revealed that such material will respond to sudden shocks of short duration, just as a piece of wax may be fashioned into a tuning fork which will respond as a brittle substance to a sudden blow, but will be deformed as a plastic when subjected to slow-acting stresses. Seismologists agree that deep-focus earthquakes are in no essential respect different from normal shocks and are caused by slippage along shear zones (Gutenberg and Richter 1938). This conclusion is basic if deep-focus earthquakes are to be used in the interpretation of island arcs.

Deep-focus earthquakes are known mostly in the island-arc areas around the margin of the Pacific Ocean. In the Japanese area deep-focus earthquakes occur at depths of 300–650 kilometers. The important feature concerning these shocks is that the foci increase in depth toward the continent and away from the ocean basin. Similar results are obtained from many other island-arc areas. In island arcs normal seismic activity is concentrated in the marginal trough lying on the convex side of the arc. Shocks with foci of intermediate depth occur continentward, followed in turn by deep-focus shocks sometimes situated well under the continental margin. This establishes the presence of a shear zone extending from the island arc under the continent, and, further, makes possible the determination of the angle of slope (or dip) of the zone. This zone is known as the Benioff zone, from Hugo Benioff, an eminent seismologist and one of the pioneers in this work.

Along the Pacific coast of South America the situation is similar. Off the coast of Peru and northern Chile is a marginal trough. In this area deep-focus earthquakes occur continentward, finally attaining a depth of more than 600 kilometers to the east of the Andes. Further, the area contains many active and recently active volcanoes. Thus, the Andean Cordillera has the basic characteristics of an island arc. It seems clear, then, that shear zones (as defined by deep-focus earthquakes) are associated with island arcs and that they dip inward beneath the continents, implying that the continents are overriding the ocean basins or that the ocean basins are underthrusting the continents. The slope of the shear zone as determined from the depth of earthquake foci varies considerably from that determined by the curvature of the arc. In most cases the curvature of the arc is rather arbitrarily established, and there is also the possibility of crustal deformation of the arc by later movements. More probable, however, is the possibility of a change in the slope of the shear plane as it extends deeper into the earth. Having established the fact that island arcs are at intersections of shear zones with the earth's surface, the geologist still must answer the problem of origin. Before we can intelligently consider this question we must give some attention to the composition of the outer part of the crust of the earth, which is basic to a solution.

THE EARTH'S CRUST   The outer shell, or *crust*, of the earth is made up of rocks in great variety, which on land areas of the globe are commonly covered by a layer of soil or loose debris. Information on the earth's crust (and the nature of the earth's interior) comes primarily from the response of the earth to earthquake waves. A Yugoslav seismologist, Dr. A. Mohorovičić (1910), in a study of an earthquake in Croatia (a province in Yugoslavia) found that the velocity of the earthquake waves increases abruptly below a depth of about 30 miles. The level at which the abrupt change in velocity occurs, indicating a change in the material, has come to be known as the Mohorovičić discontinuity and marks the base of the earth's crust. The depth to the Moho (as it is commonly known) varies, and the 30 miles reported by Mohorovičić for Croatia is more than the average but not out of line with depths reported elsewhere. From later studies of the rate of transmission of earthquake waves, which are described by Gutenberg (1959), it is known that the crustal zone has a thickness of about 25 miles, a density of under 3.0, and a structure which consists of two relatively distinct layers. Below the crust and extending to a depth of about 1,800 miles is a zone known as the *mantle* (Fig. 81). The velocity of earthquake waves in this zone indicates that it is solid and of somewhat greater density than the crust. Below the mantle and extending to the center of the earth is the *core*. The core is believed to be composed of nickel-iron alloys and to have a central density of around 15. The fact that the S-wave of an earthquake is not transmitted through the core leads to the conclusion that it is, at least in part, liquid.

Volcanoes are not related in any way to the liquid core of the earth but have their origin in the crust and upper mantle layers, at depths which may vary widely. As previously stated, the magma source at Kilauea in Hawaii is estimated to be at a depth of around 40 miles (Macdonald 1972, p. 401). In the island arcs of the circum-Pacific belt there is evidence that the andesite magmas are formed at depths ranging, in general, from 75 to 100 miles in or close to the Benioff zone (Hatherton and Dickinson 1969). It is apparent, then, that our attention must be focused on the upper-mantle and crustal layers of the earth in our consideration of volcanoes.

From thousands of analyses of the rocks of the earth's crust the average composition has been established. The remarkable fact is that eight elements make up more than 98 percent of the rocks of the earth's crust. These eight elements in the order of their abundance

Figure 81. Section of the earth showing the various zones.

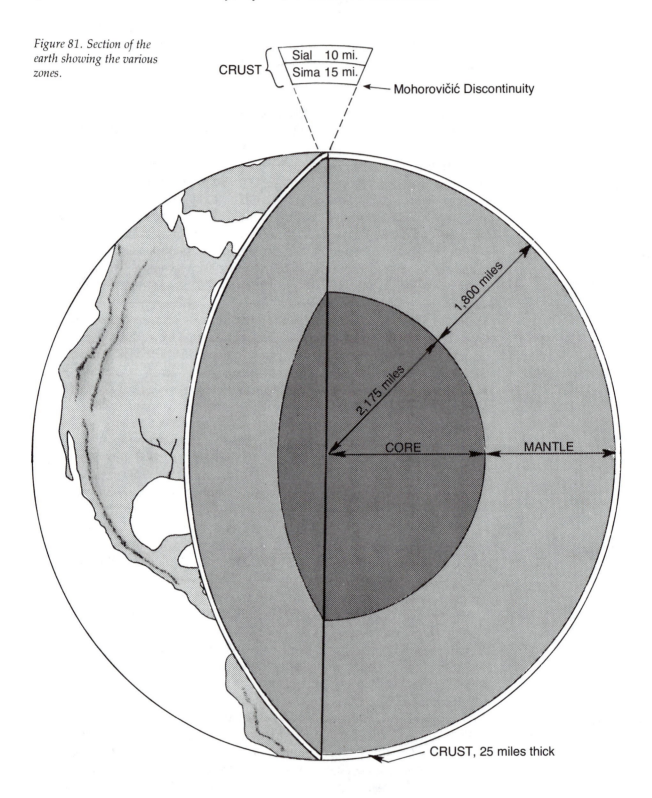

are oxygen, silicon, aluminum, iron, calcium, sodium, potassium, and magnesium. These elements rarely occur independently but are generally found in combination, usually with oxygen to form oxides. Some of these oxides are minerals, like hematite (Fe_2O_3), but more commonly several of the oxides combine to form a mineral. In this process the oxide of silica (SiO_2) is especially important because it not only forms quartz, a very common mineral, but also enters into chemical combination with the other oxides to form a group of rock minerals known as the silicates, which are important constituents of many rocks. The classification of rocks into igneous, sedimentary, and metamorphic is well known and need not be reviewed here. We are primarily concerned with the igneous rocks: those which cooled from a molten state and are regarded as primary rocks. Granitized rocks, when they reach the stage of transfusion by through-passage of hot gases, pour out on the surface as lavas (known as rhyolites) or, more commonly, as ash flows.

In general the rocks of the earth's crust fall into two contrasted groups, arranged in separate layers:

1. Light-colored rocks, including granite and related types, having an average specific gravity of about 2.7. Chemically these rocks contain a high percentage of *si*lica, up to 70 percent, while *alu*mina is the most abundant of the remaining constituents. These rocks are referred to as the *sial*.

2. Dark-colored rocks, including basalt and related types, having a specific gravity ranging from 2.9 to 3.4. In these also *si*lica (40–50 percent) is the most abundant constituent, although in considerably lower proportion than in the sialic rocks, while *ma*gnesia is the most abundant of the remaining constituents. This layer is known as the *sima*.

The sial and sima, constituting the crust of the earth, together have a thickness of 18–27 miles, although beneath some of the mountain ranges, such as the Alps, the thickness is much greater. The sial, or upper layer, varies from 5 to 15 miles in thickness; the sima, or under layer, from 10 to 20 miles. The continents consist of sial resting on sima; the ocean floors are composed of sima with little or no sialic cover.

In the plate-tectonics hypothesis, which is discussed in Chapter 16, the layers of the earth which are recognizable units in the process do not conform to those described above. Instead, three layers distinguished chiefly on the basis of strength (as defined below) are recognized: (*a*) the *lithosphere*, which generally includes the crust and the uppermost mantle, has significant strength, and is of the order of 100 kilometers in thickness; (*b*) the *asthenosphere*, which is a layer of effectively no strength extending from the base of the

Figure 82. Section of continental area and ocean basin showing the relationship of sial and sima. After Stokes (1960).

lithosphere to a depth of several hundred kilometers; and (*c*) the *mesosphere*, which may have strength and which makes up the remaining portion of the mantle. The boundaries between the layers may be gradational within the earth. The asthenosphere corresponds more or less to the low-velocity layer of seismologists, while the lithosphere and mesosphere have relatively high seismic velocities. These terms are not new, having been proposed and defined by Daly (1940) in his studies on isostasy, which anticipated many of the ideas now a part of plate tectonics.

Definition of strength. As used in geology, the strength of a body is the force (load) per unit area that is required to break it, at room temperature and pressure. Fluids, both liquids and gases, have no strength; they yield continuously under the slightest load or stress. It might appear that tar is "stronger" than water, but an iron bar will gradually sink in it and reach bottom; the tar is simply more viscous than water—it has no true strength to support the bar. Most solids, although brittle under surface conditions, will begin to deform at a load less than the rupture strength, and some will yield greatly before breaking. Whether they deform or break under a given load depends largely on the prevailing temperature and pressure. At red heat a bar of iron is solid, but it will flow (bend) under stress much smaller than that required at room temperature. Many rocks buried deep within the earth have flowed and bent (folded) in response to the heat and pressure of the earth's interior. The rocks do not melt, just as the red-hot bar of iron remains solid; yet they respond much like a plastic substance to the stress. Rocks deep in the earth become stronger because of the "confining pressure"

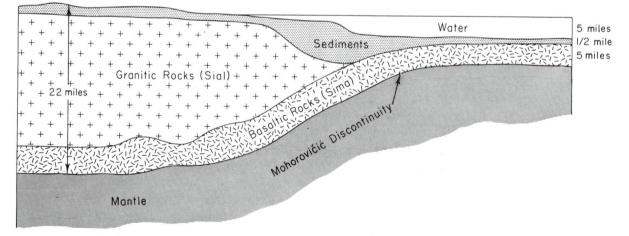

due to the weight of the overlying rocks, but at the same time they are weakened by the higher temperature. Gilluly, Waters, and Woodford conclude: "There is nothing really inconsistent in the apparent incongruity of an earth whose rocks are 'rigid and strong' enough to maintain large relief features on its surface, yet at the same time so 'weak' that, in the long course of geologic time they react plastically to loads as large as mountain chains. Our chief difficulty is in visualizing how a substance must act in very large masses and under pressures and temperatures unfamiliar to us" (1968, p. 178).

THE ORIGIN OF
MOUNTAINS

The close association of volcanoes with actively developing mountains, especially in the belts surrounding the Pacific Ocean, has been discussed. It will be useful, at this time, to inquire briefly into the history of a mountain system.

Deposition of Sediments

The great mountain systems of the earth, such as the Appalachians, the Alps, and the Rockies, invariably consist dominantly of sedimentary rocks and volcanic material, frequently highly metamorphosed by earth movements. It has taken many years and the work of many geologists to firmly establish the concept that the great mountain systems were born out of downwarps in the earth's crust in which tremendous thicknesses of sediments had accumulated. It was near the middle of the last century when the Rogers brothers discovered from their studies in the Appalachian Mountains that the folded sediments, out of which the mountains were formed, were shallow-water types, largely marine, which at places attain a thickness of 40,000 feet (Rogers and Rogers 1842). In the nonfolded region in the interior of North America, rocks of the same age are only a fraction of this thickness. Thus it came to be recognized that the great mountain systems of the earth invariably consist of thick accumulations of sediments mixed with volcanic material. It is true that these rocks have been profoundly metamorphosed by earth movements until now they may be slates, marbles, or similar rocks, but the original sedimentary nature is unmistakable.

   The sediments making up the mountain chain are usually shallow-water deposits with ripple marks, mud cracks, and other shallow-water features, in some cases coal beds, indicating that at times swampy conditions existed. Basins receiving deposits of such material, accumulating over many millions of years and reaching a thickness of 30,000–40,000 feet or more, are the birthplace of mountain chains. The evidence of shallow-water deposition indicates that such deposits do not represent the filling of ocean deeps, although they are thick enough to overflow any existing deep. Only one conclusion seems possible: the crust of the earth was slowly sinking as the sediments accumulated, and the depth of the water was never very great at any time. As the sediments were deposited the basin warped slowly downward, making possible the accumulation of tremendous thicknesses of sediments. Such a trough is known as a *geosyncline*. The Appalachian geosyncline, out of which the Appalachian Mountains were born, extends more than 1,500 miles from Newfoundland to Alabama in a belt 300–400 miles in width.

It might be inferred that the weight of the accumulated sediments would cause the trough to sink, but, while this may be a factor, it cannot account for such great thicknesses as 30,000–40,000 feet. The accumulating material is surrounded by denser rocks, and their buoyancy would set a limit to the depth to which they can sink under their own weight, a situation similar to that of an iceberg, which floats with one-ninth its volume above water. Some other factors must be involved in the origin of the sinking trough. Since volcanism and igneous activity are commonly associated with geosynclines, it is appropriate that we inquire into the problem here.

Kinds of Geosynclines

Detailed studies of geosynclines have led to the recognition of many types, but it will be sufficient to recall Marshall Kay's (1951) twofold subdivision of a geosyncline into the *miogeosyncline* on the continental-platform side and the *eugeosyncline* on the oceanic side. Miogeosynclines are characterized by relatively thin deposits of sediments belonging to the sandstone-limestone associations typical of the shallow-marine-shelf seas. Eugeosynclines are characterized by thick accumulations of graywacke type sediments mixed with abundant volcanics, derived from a volcanic island arc on the oceanic side.

The Orogenic Cycle (History of a Mountain Chain)

Following the accumulation of tens of thousands of feet of sediments over hundreds of millions of years, the trough is filled and the orogenic (Greek *oros*, "mountain"; *genic*, "origin" or "birth") stage begins. Lateral pressures fold and crumple the rocks, often breaking and overthrusting the beds, resulting in an apparent shortening of the earth's crust by tens of miles. It is as though the crustal

Figure 83. Distribution of Alpine-Cascade and circum-Pacific orogenic belts. Note that the West Indies, although in the Atlantic, appear to be a part of the circum-Pacific system. Adapted from Umbgrove (1947).

blocks of the foreland had acted as the jaws of a giant vise, irresistibly closing on the geosynclinal sediments and mashing them into folds. The actual orogeny probably extended over a few tens of millions of years and in geologic terminology is referred to as a *revolution*. Erosion, of course, begins to operate on the rocks as soon as they are uplifted above sea level. In the final stage of the orogenic cycle there is widespread, more or less vertical uplift without folding, which may raise the area thousands of feet, permitting erosion effectually to carve the rocks into the shapes which are the actual mountains as they appear today.

The last great mountain-making revolutions to disturb the earth were the Alpine orogeny of Europe and the equivalent Coast Range orogeny of western North America. Starting in Mid-Tertiary time (about 20 million years ago) in the Alps and in Late Tertiary time (about 10 million years ago) in North America, the movements are still in progress in some areas, most notably in the East and West Indies. The results of these orogenies were a fold belt of mountains

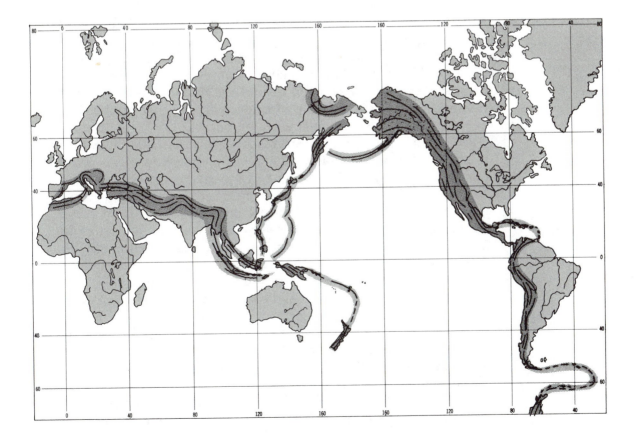

Figure 83. Distribution of Alpine-Cascade and circum-Pacific orogenic belts. Note that the West Indies, although in the Atlantic, appear to be a part of the circum-Pacific system. Adapted from Umbgrove (1947).

which encircle the Pacific Ocean and a Mediterranean belt, which is a part of the Alpine-Himalayan system. It will be noted from Figure 83 that two corresponding mountain systems appear in the Western Hemisphere, one on each side of the Caribbean Sea: a northern one, which is in effect a continuation of a fold belt from North America, and a southern one, which swings eastward from the Andes through northern Venezuela and Trinidad. The two systems are now being joined by the actively growing volcanic arc of the Lesser Antilles.

Causes of Mountain Building

The problem resolves itself into a need for explanations of several elements: (*a*) the geosyncline, (*b*) the forces which cause the folding, (*c*) the uplift following the folding, and (*d*) the association of volcanoes with geosynclines and orogeny. Here again we are facing questions on which no uniformity of opinion prevails, but it will be helpful to speculate on these problems.

Many attempts have been made to find some mechanism competent to account for forces of sufficient magnitude to buckle and crumple the rocks of the earth's crust and to explain the sequence of events in the orogenic cycle. In a body like the earth, gravity tends to maintain equilibrium and stability, and the only agency believed to be capable of disturbing this equilibrium is heat. Increase of temperature causes expansion and fusion, and decrease in temperature results in contraction and consolidation. Thermal change, then, appears to be the most fruitful line of approach.

The contraction theory. It seems reasonably certain that the earth was originally molten and that it attained its present state by cooling. A theory long held to account for mountains was the contraction hypothesis. It held that, once a crust had developed and the interior of the earth continued to cool and shrink away from it, the rigid crust must accommodate itself to a smaller core by crumpling, much as the skin of an apple wrinkles when it dries. Although the simplicity of this explanation is appealing, there are so many objections from a geological point of view that it must be discarded. One of the principal objections is that the shrinkage would shorten every great circle, resulting in a decrease in diameter with a consequent increase in speed of rotation. No evidence of any such changes can be detected in the geologic record. Further, if one is to account in this manner for all the crumpling in the mountains of the earth, the surface area involved would be fantastic. The Alps alone, if smoothed out, thus removing all the folds, would be 100 miles wider! When the Appalachian, Rocky, Sierra Nevada, and all the other mountain systems of the earth are added to this, the total is staggering. Still further, the crustal wrinkles produced by uniform shrinkage should be in an allover pattern, like those on a drying apple, rather than concentrated or localized in restricted areas, as in orogenic belts.

It is now realized that folding and faulting do not necessarily imply crustal shortening and, further, that estimates of shortening have been grossly exaggerated. Moreover, due to the concentration of heat-producing radioactive minerals in the crust, it is not even certain that the earth is actually cooling!

The convection hypothesis. An explanation for the origin of mountains based on subcrustal convection, resulting in sea-floor spreading and the consequent moving of plates of the earth's crust, is now receiving serious attention. Plate tectonics and related topics are more thoroughly discussed in Chapter 16, and only a bare outline of how the concept relates to mountain building will be included at this point.

Convection refers to mass motion in a fluid produced by gravity acting on density differences produced by unequal temperatures. In a pan of water on the stove, the water at the bottom is heated, the heat causing it to expand and rise; as it rises, colder (denser) water sinks to the bottom to take its place. Thus a convection system is set up. Convection occurs on a large scale in the atmosphere and oceans because of the unequal heating in the equatorial region and the high-latitude areas of the earth.

In order for a convection system to operate, it is necessary to have a source of heat which is continuously replenished. This heat source was found in 1906 when R. J. Strutt, later Lord Rayleigh, discovered the presence of radioactive materials in the rocks of the earth's crust. Of the hundreds of rock samples tested from all parts of the world, not one was found to be without radioactive material. In fact, the rocks contain so much radioactive material that if it were present throughout the earth in amounts comparable to that present in the earth's crust, the earth would be in a molten state or have disappeared altogether! We must conclude, therefore, that such heat-generating material is concentrated in the earth's crust, but it need not be entirely absent from the mantle. Even minute quantities would suffice to keep convection going, and there is also the possibility that the mantle may receive some heat from the still-liquid core. At any rate, the way seems open to explore some hypothesis based on subcrustal convection.

It may seem absurd, when evidence from seismic waves shows that the earth is rigid to a depth of at least 2,000 miles, to think of the subcrustal part of the earth as a liquid subject to convection overturning. However, from the folded and contorted rocks exposed in mountain ranges it is apparent that these rocks, although never molten, have been deformed as though they were in a viscous state. In addition, the sinking of the earth's crust in response to the great weight of the accumulated ice in northern Europe and northern North America during the last ice age is another proof of the yielding of the earth's crust. In fact, the rate of uplift of these regions in response to the melting of the glacial ice, a readjustment which is still in progress, has afforded a method of computing the viscosity of the mantle.

Although there is much disagreement on the viscosity of the mantle, a number of investigators report that convection could exist in the mantle, even though it is viscous enough to behave as a solid in transmission of seismic waves. A substance may respond elastically to a rapid stress but may be deformed viscously by a stress applied over a long period of time. The low-velocity zone (see above)—a zone 200–300 kilometers thick in the upper mantle with relatively low density and viscosity—is believed to be the source of any convection that may occur, and if drift results it must involve the upper mantle above that zone and the crust.

The idea of thermal convection as a possible mechanism of mountain building is not new, having been proposed more than 100 years ago, but the suggestion was largely ignored until 1928, when Arthur Holmes, a British geologist and one of the leaders in geologic thought in the twentieth century, revived and elaborated the idea of convection in the mantle as the cause of mountain building. At about the same time convection was accepted by Alfred Wegener (1966) as a possible mechanism for continental drift, an old concept he had recently revived. Experiments by D. Griggs (1939), an American geophysicist, on convection in the earth with scale models were convincing, and, until the advent of plate tectonics in the mid-1960's, convection was the most widely endorsed hypothesis to explain mountains, volcanism, island arcs, and related phenomena.

The convection hypothesis, as elaborated by Holmes (1945), postulated that cold material from the crust sinks to replace hot (lighter) substratum material. This initiates the development of a geosyncline which is slowly filled with sediment as it continues to sink. Currents moving horizontally along the under surface of the crust exert a powerful "drag" on the crust, developing tension where they diverge and compression where they converge. Thus, orogenic belts would be expected where two opposing currents meet and turn downward. The descending currents would "drag" the sial deep into the sima, resulting in a "root" of lighter material pulled into the denser sima. This, in geologic terminology, is known as *root formation*, that is, formation of the root of a mountain chain, or a *tectogene*.

At the beginning of a convection cycle the rate of flow must be extremely slow. The subcrust, not being a true liquid, has a certain resistance to flow, which must be overcome before convection can begin. As hotter and lighter materials from the base rise to become ascending currents, and heavier and denser materials from the top form descending columns, the velocity is increased (Fig. 84). It is during this accelerated stage that the drag of the descending currents pulls the sial (crust) down into a root. As the downbuckle (root) continues to grow, lateral pressure is exerted, like a vise closing, folding the geosynclinal sediments. The material at the base of the root (Fig. 84B, Stage 3) is carried to a depth at which it may melt, providing the magma for the large intrusive igneous bodies commonly associated with fold mountains. When the hotter material reaches the top and begins to spread out and the cooler material begins to flow along the bottom, the currents slow down and eventually come to rest. Thus a cycle of convection begins slowly, speeds up to a maximum, and then slows down and stops. The cooler material at the bottom is again heated by radioactive material, or by conduction from the core of the earth, until a new cycle is initiated, possibly at another location. When the "drag" of the descending currents, which is responsible for carrying the root of lighter material into the denser substratum, is no longer effective, vertical uplift occurs, as the lighter root rises in response to the difference in density (isostatic adjustment). Such vertical uplifts, frequently amounting to thousands of feet, are common in many mountain systems.

In an effort to test the convection hypothesis, D. Griggs (1939) made a very effective series of experiments with scaled-down and speeded-up models simulating earth conditions. In one model, designed so that earth processes requiring a million years could be reproduced in one minute, the crust was made of a mixture of oil and fine sawdust and the mantle of glycerine. Physical analysis showed that these substances have the same properties in relation to the scale of the model as rocks do to the earth. The currents were obtained by rotating drums (Fig. 84A). When the drums are rotated slowly the crust is gently downwarped (Fig. 84B, Stage 1). As the rotation is speeded up, the greater part of the crust is dragged downward to form a root, and the material in the depression is folded and crumpled (Stage 2). When rotation is slowed down, the currents stop and the buoyancy effect lifts the root well above its original level (Stage 3).

Island Arcs and the Convection Hypothesis

On the basis of the convection hypothesis, the island arcs and related features find a relatively simple explanation. The shear zone,

Figure 84. Diagrammatic illustration of how convection currents form mountains. The cold (heavier) surface material sinks to replace the hot (lighter) material in depth. In the resulting convection cell the descending sequence is cold-cool-warm-hot, while the ascending sequence is the reverse. Two of the intermediate stages in the sequence are shown in Stages 1 and 2. Adapted from D. Griggs (1939).

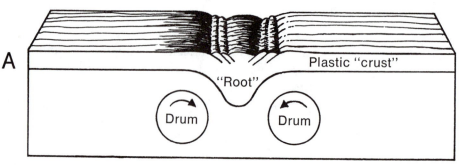

Model showing how convection currents can drag a plastic crust together and form a "root" projecting into the subcrustal layer.

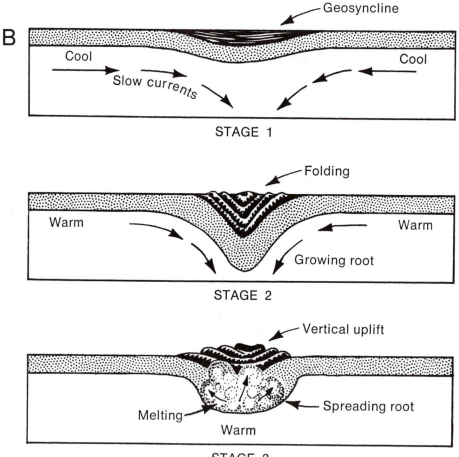

along which deep-focus earthquakes occur, is due to convection currents, although its exact location is probably controlled by the different character of the rock of the ocean floor on either side of the shear zone. On the continent side is a layer of sial, while on the ocean basin the sialic layer is absent and the ocean floor consists of sima. This boundary between the continental mass, with a cover of sial, and the ocean basin, devoid of sial, is known as the Andesite Line (see Ch. 5; Fig. 4). The marginal deep, offshore from an island arc, is the depression developed by the drag of the convection currents and the resulting root formation. The concentration of earthquakes in the present marginal deeps attests to the fact that crustal disturbances are still in progress in these zones.

A diagram of a simple island arc is shown in Figure 85. Here the sialic crust is being pulled down into a root along a shear zone. The slope of the shear zone is established by the depths of deep-focus earthquakes occurring in this zone. The diagram shows the sial playing out on the oceanward side, which would mark the position of the Andesite Line. The upward arching of the crustal section on the left is due to underthrusting by the ocean basin. The direction of relative movement is indicated by arrows. The arching also causes fractures, which provide avenues for the liquid and gaseous emanations from the magma to reach the surface, and volcanoes develop at these points. The asymmetrical nature of the trough and the conclusion that the continental segment is being arched upward and is overriding the ocean segment are based on gravity surveys which will be described in the following section.

Volcanoes and earthquakes are, then, according to the convection hypothesis, simply effects of or accompaniments to the formation of an island arc, which in turn is one stage in the history of a mountain chain.

It has been the fate of nearly all geologic hypotheses that, as new evidence is found, the hypothesis is modified and in the end replaced by one which conforms to the new body of information. The convection hypothesis is no exception, and its survival as a tenable hypothesis was longer than that of most of its predecessors. Even Holmes, who was largely responsible for the acceptance which the convection hypothesis received, comments: "But the scheme is much too simple to fit the complexities of mature orogenic belts. It does not account for the frequent occurrence of volcanic rocks, or for the part played by tension and stretching during the geosynclinal stage, or for the tendency of geosynclines to migrate laterally" (1965, p. 1171). A new hypothesis, also based on thermal convection but involving sea-floor spreading and plate tectonics, now appears to provide a satisfactory explanation for the origin of mountains, distribution of earthquakes, and associated volcanism. Plate tectonics and related topics, which have literally produced a "revolution" in geologic thinking, are discussed in Chapter 16.

GRAVITY
MEASUREMENTS AND
ISLAND ARCS

One of the most convincing lines of evidence in support of the convection hypothesis for the origin of mountains was the discovery by F. A. Vening-Meinesz in 1930 that large gravity anomalies were present over the deep-sea trenches off the coast of Java and Sumatra (see Vening-Meinesz, Umbgrove, and Kuenen 1934). This same evidence is now one of the foundations of the plate-tectonics hypothesis. A brief discussion of gravity anomalies, as well as of the contributions of Dr. Vening-Meinesz, will be helpful in presenting this evidence.

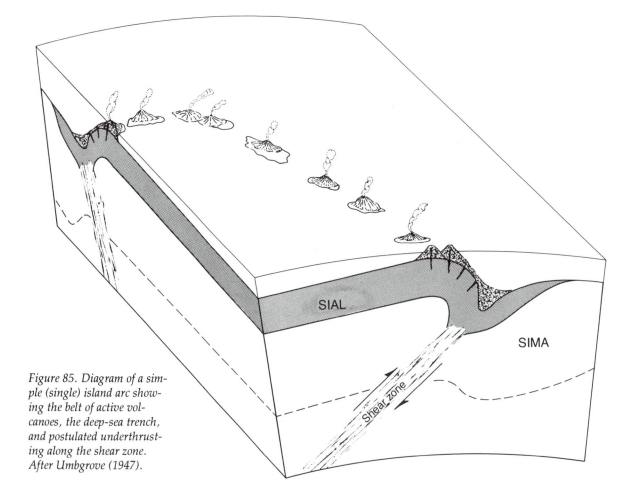

Figure 85. Diagram of a simple (single) island arc showing the belt of active volcanoes, the deep-sea trench, and postulated underthrusting along the shear zone. After Umbgrove (1947).

Every particle of the universe attracts every other particle by a force which is directly proportional to their respective masses and inversely proportional to the square of the distance between them. Thus is stated the universal Law of Gravitation, a law defining the force which draws all objects toward the center of the earth, which was first recognized by the great English scientist Sir Isaac Newton (1642–1727). On the surface of the earth, comparisons between two objects are made by weighing them, a procedure which actually compares the earth's attraction for one mass in relation to that for another. The weight of a body on the earth is a measure of the force that gravity exerts on it. The distance from the center of the earth and the density (as it determines mass) are factors affecting gravity (or weight). Weight differs numerically from mass by a constant called the *acceleration of gravity*, or *g*; thus mass × acceleration of gravity = weight ($mg = w$), where *g* equals the number of feet per second by which a body falling freely in a vacuum increases its speed during each second of fall. At 45° latitude at sea level, the value of *g* is 32.17 feet per second, which is the accepted standard.

For practical purposes the latitude and density of large rock bodies near the earth's surface affect the force of attraction (gravity). The unit of measure for differences in gravity is a *gal*, named from Galileo. By definition, a gal is an acceleration of one centimeter per second during each second of free fall. The acceleration of gravity at the earth's surface is around 980 gals, but changes as small as a ten-millionth of this may be significant. Consequently, the practical unit for expressing gravity differences is the milligal, or one-thousandth of a gal. Changes in the force of gravity will be reflected in changes in the weight of a body.

Very delicate instruments for measuring the force of gravity have been perfected to aid in the search for hidden deposits of petroleum. Such instruments are known as gravity meters. They measure the force necessary to support a suspended mass, or the force of gravity. The force of gravity at any given point is based on (*a*) distance of the point from the center of the earth, (*b*) latitude (since centrifugal force developed by the earth's rotation partially counterbalances the pull of gravity, and such forces are greatest at the equator and zero at the poles), and (*c*) density of the rocks in the immediate area. Factors *a* and *b* can be accurately computed for any point on the earth and a correction factor applied to reduce the results to a common plane or to sea level. Thus, a theoretical value for the force of gravity at any point can be obtained. If the gravity meter shows the actual reading to be different from the theoretical value, the difference must be due to factor *c*, the density of the surrounding material. Such differences are known as *gravity anomalies*.

The gravity meter was early used in the Gulf Coast area of Texas

Figure 86. Indonesia, showing gravity anomalies. Note the double arc in Sumatra (the Mentawai Islands define the outer arc), with volcanoes limited to the inner arc. After Vening-Meinesz, Umbgrove, and Kuenen (1934).

and Louisiana to locate salt domes, with which oil is commonly associated. One of the first large salt-dome oil fields was Spindletop, near Beaumont, Texas, which was discovered in 1901. A salt dome is a cylindrical mass of salt which rises like a column for thousands of feet into the overlying sediments. Some salt domes actually reach the surface or come so close to the surface that they form small hills, such as Spindletop, Barbers Hill, Damon Mounds, and others on the Texas Gulf Coast. These were easily located, but those that lie several thousand feet below the surface could not be detected. This was where the gravity meter was employed. The salt, having a lower density than the surrounding sediments, produces a gravity anomaly which can be measured. For example, a sphere of salt 2,000 feet in radius, with its center 4,000 feet below the surface and surrounded by sedimentary formations 10 percent denser than the salt, would cause the force of gravity directly above it to be about one milligal less than in the adjacent area. Thus, a gravity-meter survey of the region would detect the negative gravity anomalies, and, with

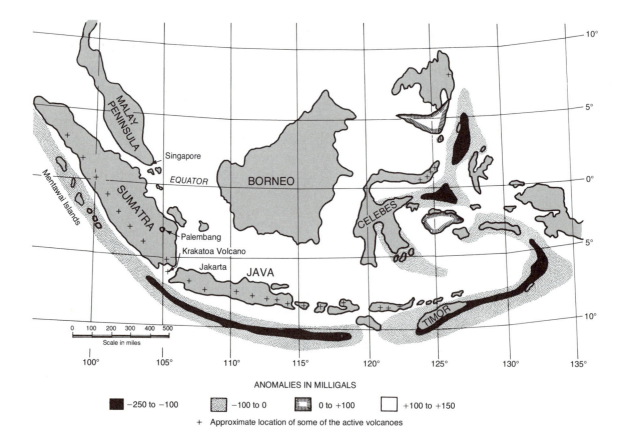

ANOMALIES IN MILLIGALS

−250 to −100   −100 to 0   0 to +100   +100 to +150

+ Approximate location of some of the active volcanoes

Figure 87. Gravity profile of Guam Island and Nero Deep. After Vening-Meinesz, Umbgrove, and Kuenen (1934).

the known presence of salt domes in the region, it would be reasonable to conclude that the anomalies are due to the presence of buried salt domes. Only the drill can definitely locate a dome and determine whether oil is associated with it.

From the above discussion it is apparent that the gravity meter offers a means of comparing the density of the earth at various points. It has been used to produce some highly significant results in connection with the problem of island arcs. The distinguished Dutch geodesist, Dr. F. A. Vening-Meinesz, using a submarine of the Royal Dutch Navy between the years 1923 and 1932, determined the value of gravity at many points on the sea floor (Vening-Meinesz, Umbgrove, and Kuenen 1934). Since that date other workers have added similar observations from many parts of the globe. Interestingly, when Dr. Vening-Meinesz crossed the island-arc areas he found an elongate belt with a width of only 60–70 miles, characterized by a surprisingly great deficiency of gravity. Even after all corrections had been applied for various factors, such as the depth of the submarine and the topography of the underlying sea floor, a strong negative anomaly still existed. The belt is so narrow and the deficiency so strong that only a deep root of light rocks would account for it. Thus, as provided in the convection hypothesis, a deep root of sial extending into and displacing the denser sima is indicated. According to the plate-tectonics hypothesis it is the lithosphere plate being thrust into the denser asthenosphere which produces the negative gravity anomaly. Many of Dr. Vening-Meinesz's studies were carried on in the East Indies, and a map showing the gravity anomalies of this region is reproduced in Figure 86. Numerous measurements were made at other points, where the results

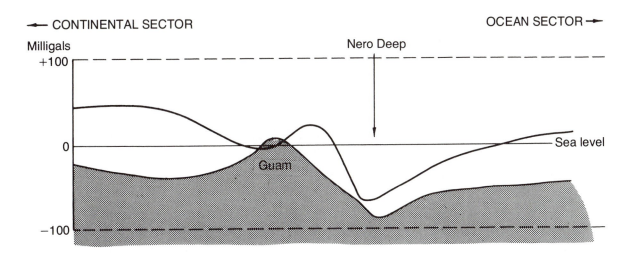

invariably indicated marked negative anomalies whenever the marginal deep of an island arc was crossed. The single-island-arc type, represented by the group of which Guam is a part, will serve as an example. Strong negative anomalies were found over the marginal deep (Nero deep), implying that the margin of the Pacific plate is being either thrust or dragged into the trench, replacing denser mantle material. The asymmetrical nature of the gravimetric profile (Fig. 87) suggests that the eastern, or oceanic, plate is under-riding the western, or continental, plate, causing this part to arch upward and fracture, thus accounting for the volcanoes associated with it.

Chapter 16   Continental Drift, Plate Tectonics, and Volcanism

He looketh on the earth and it trembles;
He toucheth the mountains and they smoke.—PSALMS 104:32

The science of geology has been shaped by a series of great controversies, each in the end serving to advance the science as the facts,
both pro and con, were marshaled to support opposing views. The
Neptunist-Plutonist controversy of the eighteenth century, in which
Werner as the advocate for the Neptunists held that all rocks, including granite and lava, were deposited in a universal ocean, has
been discussed (Ch. 3). Also in the eighteenth century was the controversy in which Hutton's doctrine of uniformitarianism was opposed by the then more generally accepted view that great cataclysms had shaped the features of the earth (Ch. 3). Indeed, the
acceptance of Hutton's doctrine of uniformitarianism was the real
beginning of the science of geology. In the nineteenth century many
bitter controversies developed, such as the one over the organic nature of fossils; the view that volcanic cones were great blisters on the
earth's crust (craters of elevation vs. craters of accumulation, Ch. 3);
and the heated debate over evolution which Darwin's *Origin of Spe-
cies* precipitated, a controversy which is still going on in some areas.

CONTINENTAL DRIFT   Foremost among the controversies of the twentieth century has
been the debate for and against continental drift. Continental drift is
an old idea. The remarkable jigsaw-puzzle fit of the Atlantic coasts
of Africa and South America was apparent from the time that the
continental outlines appeared on world maps, leading to the speculation that the continents had once been joined (Fig. 88). Late in the
nineteenth century, geologists of the Southern Hemisphere had
concluded that by reassembling Africa and South America they
could explain some puzzling features, such as mountain ranges
abruptly terminating at the Atlantic coast, only to continue with the
same trend and rock types on the opposing continent. Numerous
other features, which cannot be discussed here, such as similarities
in plant life, glacial features, and lava plateaus, fall into place if it is
assumed that the continents were once joined. At the turn of the
century the Austrian geologist Eduard Suess (1904) proposed that

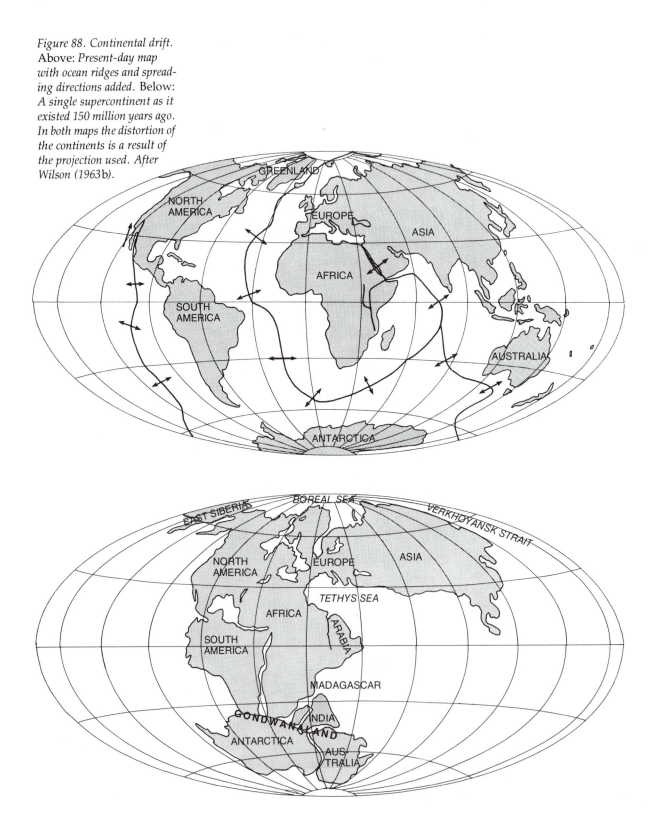

Figure 88. Continental drift. Above: Present-day map with ocean ridges and spreading directions added. Below: A single supercontinent as it existed 150 million years ago. In both maps the distortion of the continents is a result of the projection used. After Wilson (1963b).

all the continents had been at one time joined in a single giant land mass, which he called Gondwanaland (after a geological province in east-central India). Although a number of workers had developed hypotheses involving continental drift, notably Frank B. Taylor in a pamphlet printed privately in 1908 but not published until 1910 and Howard B. Baker in an article written in 1911 but published in 1912, the idea received scant attention until Alfred Wegener, a German meteorologist, presented his proposal in 1912 (see Wegener 1966). It should be noted that the concept of continental drift was in direct opposition to one of the basic tenets of geology, namely, that the continents and ocean basins were a part of the general framework of the earth and had remained essentially stable throughout geologic time. It was recognized that temporary floodings of the land by shallow seas had occurred, but the "permanency" of the continents and ocean basins had generally not been questioned. Wegener and his followers compiled an impressive list of evidences supporting the existence of a single supercontinent which he called Pangea.

The concept of continental drift was stimulated by the discovery that, under the weight of the continental glacier which covered much of northern Europe and northern North America during the last ice age, the earth's crust subsided, and, following the melting of the ice, some 10,000 years ago, the crust has been springing back into place. In Finland and Sweden there are raised beaches which show a maximum uplift of around 900 feet, and the uplift is continuing at the rate of about 3 feet per century. Similar raised beaches occur on the Great Lakes in the United States and Canada. In fact, it is the rate of postglacial uplift which has provided scientists with important information on the viscosity of the earth's mantle. Wegener reasoned that if the continents could move up and down they could also move laterally.

According to Wegener, South America and Africa began to drift apart, initially, about 180 million years ago, while the opening of the North Atlantic was much later, mainly during the last few million years. He believed that, in spite of the apparent high viscosity of subcrustal materials, small forces acting over very long periods of time could cause the material to yield and allow the continents to flow slowly through the upper mantle. Identification of the force or forces responsible for the drift was, of course, a major problem. One of the forces Wegener invoked was centrifugal force: since the continents stand higher than the oceans, they are subject to greater centrifugal force, which tends to cause them to drift toward the equator. Another force which he thought was involved is the tidal attraction of the sun and moon, which, as the earth rotates from west to east, tends to drag the continents westward. Physicists were quick to point out that, although the forces postulated by Wegener do exist, they are at least a million times too small for the task assigned. Geologists also rushed to the attack, pointing out errors in the geologic evidence (after all Wegener was a meteorologist!). Most of the geologic inconsistencies were soon cleared up by a South African geologist, A. L. DuToit, who took up the cause of continental drift in his book *Our Wandering Continents* (1937), in which he scathingly attacked the "antidrifters" (mostly Americans) for their groundless worship of the orthodox dogma of the permanency of continents and ocean basins. He also ridiculed the countless land bridges which had become popular among antidrifters to explain similarities of many land organisms, both living and fossil, on opposite sides of the Atlantic.

The source of the forces necessary to move the continents remained unanswered, but DuToit and the "drifters" accepted the inescapable deductions from the wealth of geologic evidence and left the problem of the mechanism to the physicists. As stated by R. H. Dott, Jr., and R. L. Batten, "This was another [example] of the empirical attitude that 'if something has happened, it can happen,' as distinct from the more theoretical viewpoint that 'unless we can conceive a theoretically sound mechanism, it cannot have happened'" (1971, p. 537). The argument continued until a stalemate was reached in the 1940's. Just about everything that could be argued for and against continental drift had been written many times, and the debate faded for lack of additional evidence.

Paleomagnetism

The continental-drift controversy was revived in the 1950's, when research on *paleomagnetism*, or the magnetism preserved in the rocks at the time of formation, began to reveal new evidence bearing on continental drift. Before this evidence is taken up, a few comments on the earth's magnetic field will be helpful.

The compass needle has been used for navigation for nearly a thousand years, but it was not until 1600 that Sir William Gilbert, an English physician, demonstrated that the earth behaves as a huge magnet, with its poles near the geographic poles. Since lodestone (a variety of the mineral magnetite, which is a natural magnet) was well known, it was quite naturally assumed that the permanent magnetism of material in the interior of the earth was responsible for the magnetic field. The discovery by the French scientist Pierre Curie in 1895 that magnetic substances lose their magnetism on heating above a certain temperature, appropriately named the *Curie point*, made it necessary to reconsider the problem. No mineral has a Curie point higher than 800° C., a temperature reached at a depth of only 30–35 kilometers in the earth's crust. The most common magnetic mineral is magnetite, an oxide of iron, which has a Curie point of 578° C. This seemed to eliminate any deep-seated source for the earth's magnetic field, and the magnetic properties in the thin crustal zone above the Curie-point level are wholly inadequate to produce the observed field. There was no satisfactory answer until the mid-1950's, when two English scientists, Sir Edward Bullard and H. Gellman (1954), and an American scientist, W. M. Elsasser, (1956) independently proposed an explanation which has come to be known as the *dynamo theory*. They reasoned that, with the high temperature and liquidlike state of the outer core, permanent magnetism was impossible. The magnetic field must therefore be continuously produced and maintained, and this suggests the generation of electric currents in material characterized by high electric conductivity and capable of internal movements. The outer core, which is thought to be molten iron, a conducting but nonmagnetic substance, would fulfill these requirements. When an electric conductor is moved through a magnetic field, an electric current is generated in the conductor. Current is generated in an ordinary dynamo by the rapid rotation of wire coils in a strong magnetic field. In the outer core of the earth the rotating coils are represented by thermal convection cells. Given a magnetic field to start the system working (a very weak field would suffice), convection provides the motion necessary to generate electric currents in the convecting material. The electric currents increase the intensity of the magnetic field, which in turn increases the strength of the electric currents— and so on until the magnetic field reaches an approximate state of equilibrium. Two basic problems are (*a*) the source of the original magnetic field and (*b*) the source of energy to maintain the thermal convection. Reasonably satisfactory answers have been proposed for these problems, and the theory has received wide acceptance.

Because of the earth's rotation the convection currents in the core are dragged in the direction of spin, and the magnetic field tends to be symmetrical about the geographic poles of the earth. The symmetry is by no means perfect, and it is also modified by the fact that the field constantly changes and drifts slowly westward, a drift which is believed to result from eddies in the convecting core. As a result, the magnetic poles do not coincide with the geographic poles, the north and south magnetic poles being more than 15° and 20° respectively from the geographic poles.

Remanent magnetism. The record of the magnetic field "frozen" in the rocks at the time they were formed is called *remanent magnetism*. When a lava flow cools, its magnetic minerals crystallize, and as the temperature drops below the Curie point they become magnetized parallel to the local magnetic field. The magnetism is not greatly affected by continued cooling of the lava; so the direction and inclination of the earth's magnetic field at the time the lava solidified is permanently preserved. Methods have also been perfected for measuring remanent magnetism in sedimentary rocks. The earth's magnetic field causes a compass needle to point to the magnetic poles, but, if the needle is pivoted to move in a vertical direction also, it will indicate the inclination as well. A magnetic needle points straight down at the magnetic poles, is horizontal at the magnetic equator, and occupies intermediate angles of inclination in between. Thus, from specimens properly collected, not only will the remanent magnetism reveal the direction of the magnetic poles at the time the rock was formed, but the inclination (which depends on latitude) can be used to calculate the distance from the poles as well (Fig. 89).

Remanent magnetic data for rocks of different ages have been collected from each of the continents. Analyses of these data show that the magnetic poles for each geologic period on each continent consistently fall in about the same area. However, each geologic period has a different location for the magnetic poles, and the poles for any period fall in different locations for each continent. Even if the magnetic poles had moved, they should be at the same location during a

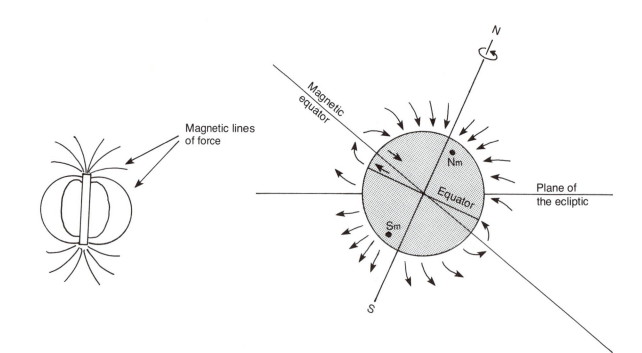

given period of time for each continent, if the continents had maintained fixed locations—but, on the contrary, each continent gives a different location for each period. The obvious conclusion is that the continents have moved in relation to one another—that in past geologic ages the continents occupied positions relative to the poles and to one another markedly different from today's familiar geography.

Reversals of the earth's magnetic field. In the early part of the twentieth century Bernard Brunhes (1906), a French physicist, accidentally discovered that the remanent magnetism of a lava flow in central France was exactly opposite to the present magnetic field; that is, the magnetic poles were reversed. At first he thought that somehow a mineral could assume a magnetic position the reverse of the encompassing field, but the phenomenon remained unexplained. Later, the Japanese geophysicist M. Matuyama (1929) found that many of the Pleistocene volcanic rocks were reversedly magnetized. Although "self-reversal" of the magnetic field is now known to be possible, there is convincing evidence that an overwhelming number of rocks showing reversed magnetism were actually formed when the earth's magnetic field was reversed in respect to its present polarity. Potassium-argon dating of the rocks reveals that there have been long epochs during which the magnetic field was the same as today, alternating with equally long epochs when the field was reversed. Thus, a time scale based on magnetic reversals can be established. The longer epochs of constant polarity have been named for the several geophysicists who made contributions to this study; for example, the Brunhes normal epoch extends from the present to about 0.7 million years ago, while the Matuyama reversed epoch extends from 0.7 to 2.5 million years ago (Fig. 90).

The cause of field reversals is not understood, but they are not necessarily in conflict with the dynamo theory of the origin of the earth's magnetic field. They do indicate that the electric currents in the core which produce the magnetic field must at times flow "backward" in relation to their present motion. Variations in the intensity of the earth's magnetic field, which are well documented, are believed to be involved in the reversal event. The intensity of the earth's magnetic field has been diminishing for the past 135 years; perhaps it will diminish to zero at some time in the future and reverse polarity. After a careful study (Cox and Dalrymple 1967) of the reversal data, the duration of polarity events was estimated to be from 70,000 to 160,000 years, and the time required for the earth's field to undergo a reversal of polarity averaged about 4,600 years. On the geologic time scale even 4,600 years is a "sudden" event. Reversals provide a world-wide time zone to which other events may be related.

Figure 90. Magnetic polarity reversal time scale. After Cox, Dalrymple, and Doell (1967).

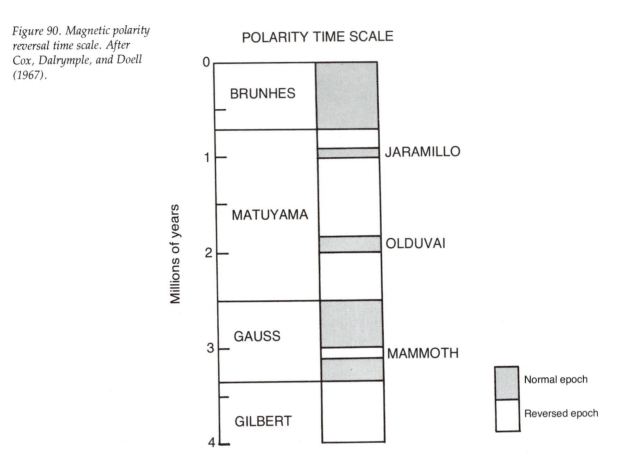

SEA-FLOOR SPREADING

With the publication of paleomagnetic evidence in the mid-1950's which seemed to substantiate continental drift and the discovery that a rift valley (a down-dropped block indicating tension) follows the crest of the Mid-Atlantic Ridge, it became increasingly important to find an explanation consistent with the mounting geologic and geophysical evidence. Interest centered on a convection type hypothesis, some elements of which had been advocated by Holmes (1928) and others many years earlier. In 1960, the late H. H. Hess, a Princeton University professor, presented a concept, which later became known as *sea-floor spreading*, that was to revolutionize geologic thinking. Hess (1962) postulated that the continents do not "plow" through the oceanic crust, as was held by the early advocates of continental drift, but are carried passively on a mantle that is overturning because of thermal convection. Convection currents bring new oceanic crust from the mantle to the crest of the mid-oceanic ridge, where it spreads laterally, carrying the older oceanic

Figure 91. Sea-floor spreading. Large plates of lithosphere containing the continents migrate away from the oceanic ridges as if on a conveyor belt. The Pacific oceanic plate (lower left) is underthrusting the continental plate (subduction zone) where it returns to the mantle and is absorbed. After Wyllie (1972).

crust as if on a conveyor belt. The sea floor is thus spread apart at the mid-oceanic ridge, and the tension gap is continually filled with new oceanic crust rising from the mantle below. Thus the continents move *with* the adjacent sea floor and not through it. Where convection cells converge (at the margin of plates, to be described below) a slab of lithosphere is carried down (or dragged down) into the mantle and eventually assimilated. These descending currents are the sites of compression characterized by mountain ranges, deep-sea trenches, and associated volcanic arcs. For this over-all process R. S. Deitz (1961) coined the term *sea-floor spreading*. The continents are a part of the lithosphere, a layer approximately 100 kilometers thick which is "floating," so to speak, on the asthenosphere, or low-velocity zone, in the upper mantle; and, as the lithosphere moves, so do the continents (Fig. 91). This startling concept postulates the disruption of the continents by rifting over rising convection currents, followed by the progressive separation of the continental fragments as new oceanic crust is formed. Thus the ocean basins, instead of being "permanent" features, are youthful and constantly changing. Sea-floor spreading also provides, for the first time, an adequate mechanism or driving force for continental drift.

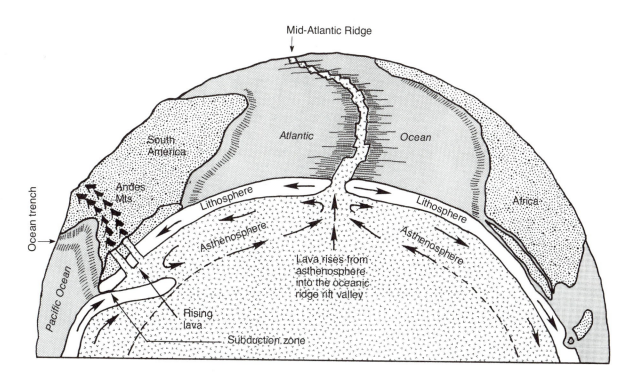

Magnetic "Stripes"

During the 1950's, ships exploring the ocean basins began routinely to measure the strength of the earth's magnetic field. This became possible with the development of self-recording magnetometers which could be towed behind the ships. Some of the early measurements were made in the eastern Pacific Ocean basin, and when the results were plotted they showed "ridges" of high magnetic intensity alternating with "valleys" of low intensity. These came to be known as magnetic "stripes," which more properly are a series of magnetic anomalies. A magnetic anomaly is the difference between the observed magnetic value and the calculated value. The anomaly is said to be positive if the observed value of the field is stronger than the predicted value and negative if the reverse is true. Similar magnetic stripes were obtained in profiles across the Mid-Atlantic Ridge and in fact in nearly all areas of the ocean basins, but the origin of the magnetic stripes remained a puzzle. In 1963, Vine and Mathews developed an explanation by combining Hess's sea-floor-spreading hypothesis and the research then being done on the time scale for magnetic reversals. They proposed that, as new oceanic crust rises along the crest of the oceanic ridge, it cools, passing through the Curie point, at which time the magnetic-field strength and polarity are "frozen" in. If the magnetic field reverses its polarity intermittently, then stripes of crust of alternate polarity will be formed as new crust rises and moves away from the axis of the ridge. This results in a series of bands of magnetic anomalies that are parallel and symmetrically distributed on either side of the crest of the ridge. The anomalies appear to record each polarity-reversal event, as new oceanic crust forms in the central-ridge rift, cools to its Curie point, and acquires and retains the polarity of the field at that time (Fig. 92). When the stripe is magnetized in the direction of the earth's present field, the effect is additive, and a strong magnetic intensity results. When the stripe is magnetized in the opposite direction (reverse polarity), it subtracts from the present magnetic intensity, leaving a low value. The stripes can be correlated with the normal- and reverse-polarity epochs which have been established from a study of lava flows on the continents. Thus, the distance of an anomaly stripe from the crest of the ridge can be used to calculate the rate of sea-floor spreading. Studies on the Reykjanes Ridge (the northern part of the Mid-Atlantic Ridge, southwest of Iceland), indicate a spreading rate of one centimeter per year for each limb of the ridge, or a separation rate (both limbs) of two centimeters per year (Fig. 93). There is considerable variation in the rates; for example, in the South Atlantic a separation rate of around four centime-

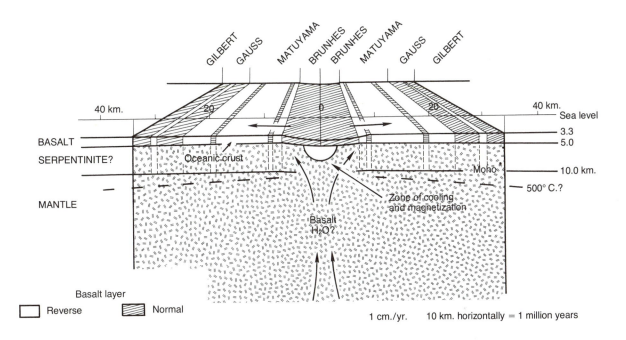

Figure 92. Diagrammatic representation of sea-floor spreading at a mid-oceanic ridge and the development of new oceanic crust. An active spreading rate of one centimeter per year has been plotted on the geomagnetic reversal time scale of Cox, Dalrymple, and Doell (1967). After Vine (1969).

ters per year is indicated, while in the Pacific rates up to nine centimeters per year have been calculated.

The time scale based on polarity reversals is valid (at this writing) only for about 4 million years, but, if it is assumed that the spreading rate remained relatively constant, the linear spacing of the magnetic anomalies can be used to extrapolate the time scale back into geologic time. Such calculations indicate that the spreading from the Mid-Atlantic Ridge began between 150 and 200 million years ago (i.e., this is the age of the Atlantic Ocean). It must be emphasized that this is only an approximation, for spreading rates may vary, and the ridge axis itself may shift laterally as spreading occurs.

The ocean floor created by sea-floor spreading in the last 65 million years (i.e., during the Cenozoic Era), based on the extrapolation of the geomagnetic polarity-reversal time scale, as discussed above, is shown in Figure 94. Since the age of the Atlantic Ocean, as well as the other oceans of the world, occupies only a small fraction of the geologic age of the earth, and since oceans existed throughout much of geologic time, we must conclude that our present oceans were preceded by a series of oceans which, in turn, were formed and destroyed.

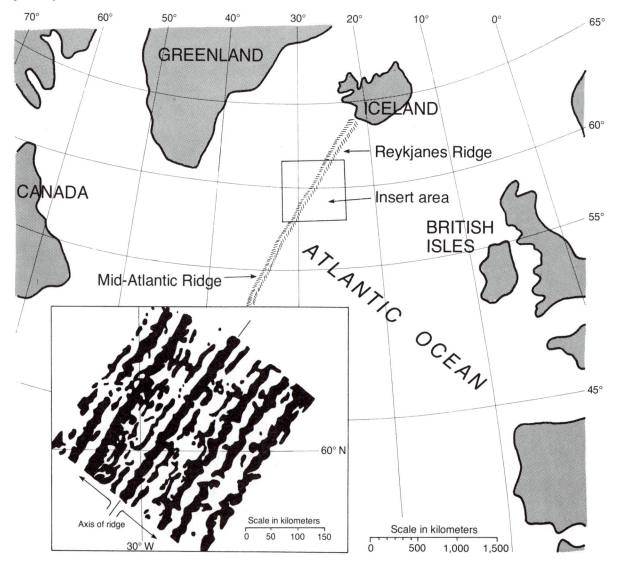

Figure 93. Magnetic stripes and the magnetic anomaly pattern across the Reykjanes Ridge (Mid-Atlantic Ridge southwest of Iceland). Areas of positive anomaly are shown in black. With a spreading rate of one centimeter per year for each flank, a 100-kilometer-wide band of new ocean floor has been formed on each side of the ridge in the past 10 million years. After Vine (1969).

With the confirmation that mid-oceanic ridges were present in all of the major oceans, it was apparent that sea-floor spreading was a global process and that a simple two-dimensional model would not suffice. Although the oceanic-ridge system appears to be a continuous feature on a large scale, the crest of the ridge is actually discontinuous in many places (Fig. 94). These offsets coincide with the intersection of major fracture zones—long linear zones with rough slopes that resemble major fault zones on the continents. In considering the problem, J. T. Wilson (1965), a Canadian geophysicist and strong advocate of continental drift, postulated the existence of *transform faults* (at that time unknown). A transform fault is a type of strike-slip fault (one with horizontal displacement) which crosses mid-oceanic ridges and along which movements are opposed on opposite sides of the ridge crest, where new sea-floor is being formed. The horizontal displacement along the fault is "transformed" (or absorbed) by sea-floor spreading, and the growing ridge is, in turn, terminated by the fault (Fig. 95).

It was the tendency of transform faults and their associated fracture zones to lie along small circles (those smaller than a circumference of the earth) that first suggested the idea of plate tectonics to W. J. Morgan (1968) and X. Le Pichon (1968). They showed that the distribution of fracture zones and observed rates of spreading on oceanic ridges, as determined by geomagnetic data, could be explained by the relative motion of a few large plates of lithosphere which move more or less independently (Fig. 96); these blocks are jostled about much like gigantic ice floes. Where two blocks move apart, an ocean ridge forms and new oceanic crust is produced; where two blocks move toward each other, either shortening or compression produces a fold mountain belt, or crust is destroyed as one block is thrust under the other. If the earth's surface is considered to consist of a number of rigid blocks, the relative displacement of any block with respect to another is a rotation on the spherical surface of the earth. In such cases the transform faults and related fractures would lie on concentric circles around the pole of rotation. Further, the velocity of one block relative to another (or the rate of spreading) would vary from zero at the pole of rotation to a maximum at the "equator." Morgan (1968) recognized that the fracture zones in the Atlantic Ocean between 30° N and 10° S are all very nearly small circles centered about a point near the southern tip of Greenland, and the spreading rates, as determined from geomagnetic data, roughly agree with the velocity required for the opening of the Atlantic Ocean about this pole. Thus the variation in the rate of spreading on the Mid-Atlantic Ridge (previously discussed) finds a logical explanation.

Figure 94. Sea-floor spreading. Shaded area indicates the ocean floor created during the past 65 million years. Within the ocean basins, trenches are indicated by thick dashed lines, ridge crests by thick solid lines, and fractures (transverse to ridge crests) by thin solid lines. Thin solid lines, parallel to the ridge crests, are linear magnetic anomalies drawn to represent 10-million-year "growth lines" suggested by Heirtzler et al. (1968). Ocean floor spreading is about three times as rapid in the South Pacific as in the Atlantic. After Vine (1969, p. 13). Note: A segment of the ridge system south of Africa appears to be inactive; off the west coast of North America less than half the magnetic anomaly pattern is preserved, indicating that North America has overridden not only the nearby ridge, but also a portion of the ocean floor that lay originally on the far side of the ridge.

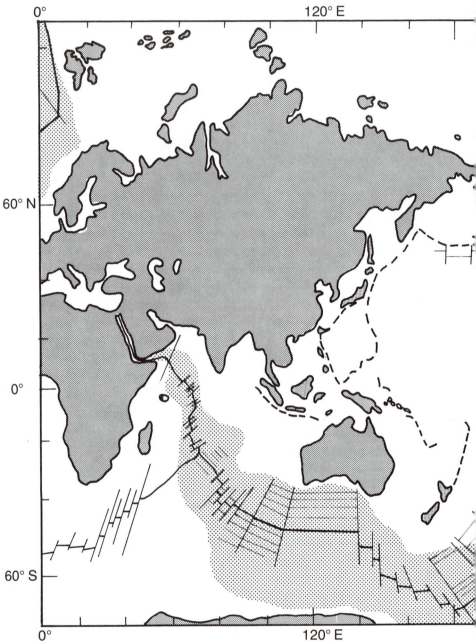

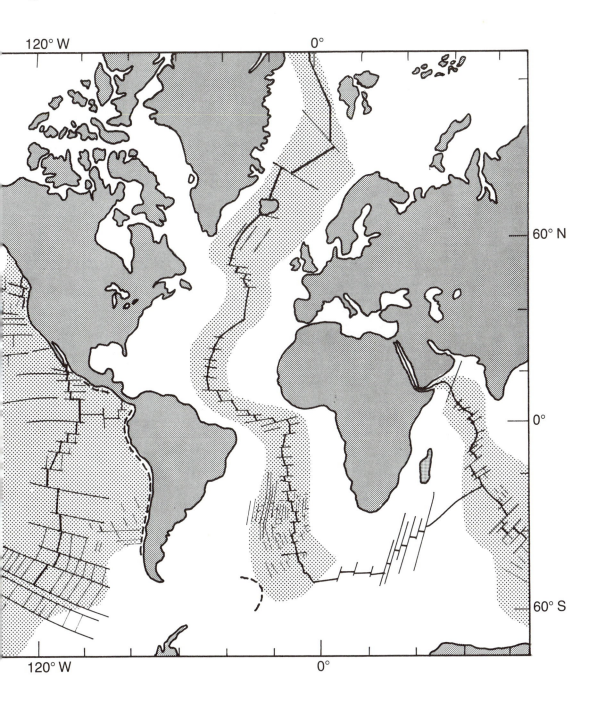

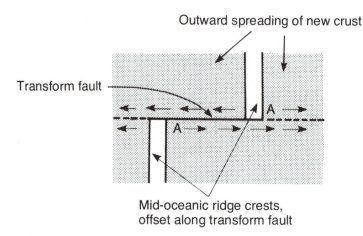

Figure 95. Transform fault. If a mid-oceanic ridge is broken, so that the two segments are offset, the spreading motion away from each segment gives rise to horizontal (strike-slip) movement along the line of offset. The relative movement occurs only between the offset segments; beyond the segments the movement on either side of the line of the offset is the same. Adapted from Krauskopf (1974).

Based on sea-floor-spreading rates for each ocean and on seismic evidence, Le Pichon (1968) divided the earth's surface into six large rigid plates which are in motion relative to one another (Fig. 96). Slightly different plate distributions have been proposed, and some smaller plates, such as the Cocos and Nazca plates, are recognized. The relatively rigid plates, which include both oceanic crust and continents, are believed to be about 100 kilometers in thickness and include the upper part of the mantle, which, together with the crustal layer of the earth, is termed the lithosphere. The lithosphere is resting on (or moving on) the asthenosphere (also known as the low-velocity zone), a relatively mobile, although still solid, zone in the mantle capable of movement by slow deformation or creep, in contrast to the lithosphere, which fractures if deformed. The plates are moving away from one another at the oceanic ridges, where new crust is being formed, and toward one another along lines of volcanic island arcs and active mountain chains. During relative motion of the lithospheric plates, the area of the earth's surface must be conserved; so the rate at which new crust is being formed at oceanic ridges must be balanced by the rate at which it is being absorbed at the plate margins. The margins of the plates, where crust is being consumed, fall into three types: (*a*) oceanic against continental, as with the Pacific and South American plates; (*b*) oceanic against oceanic, as with the western two-thirds of the Aleutian arc; and (*c*) continental against continental, as with the Himalayas at the juncture of the African and Eurasian plates. It should be noted that two plates may slide past each other, as the Pacific and American plates do on the California coast, with the San Andreas rift being the plane of slippage. Since earthquakes would be expected to occur where two plates are in contact, the active seismic belts of the earth have been used to aid in identifying plate boundaries.

ISLAND ARCS, VOL-
CANISM, AND PLATE
TECTONICS

The volcanic island arcs, which are prominent features, especially on the western margin of the Pacific plate (Fig. 96), have already been discussed. It will suffice here to recall that, not only are they the site of active volcanism, but also nearly all deep and intermediate-range earthquakes are associated with a zone (Benioff) which dips from the island arcs down under the continents at an angle of about 45°, extending to a maximum depth of around 700 kilometers. Further, island arcs (and associated deep sea trenches) are known to be areas of large gravity anomalies (Ch. 15). These facts fit the concept of the leading edge of a lithospheric plate's underthrusting the island arc as it is thrust (or pulled) into the mantle and reabsorbed. If crustal material does descend into the mantle, as postulated by plate tectonics, the island arcs are the most likely sites of the sinks, and the ocean trenches are interpreted as the surface expression of the subduction zone along which the plate is carried into the mantle.

Magmas are being formed at both ends of the moving lithospheric plates, both at the oceanic ridges where new crust is being formed and along the subduction (Benioff) zone where crust is apparently being consumed. The new crust being formed at the active oceanic ridges is largely tholeiitic basalt, although in some areas, notably Bouvet and Jan Mayen islands (north of Iceland) it is mainly alkaline basalt. Iceland, which is astride the Mid-Atlantic Ridge, is made up of huge volumes of basaltic lava. It is unique, however, in that it is the only place in the 40,000-mile extent of the oceanic ridges that any considerable volume of granite (and related rhyolite) is known. This poses a problem, since granitic type rocks are restricted to continental regions and should not be associated with new basaltic material derived from the mantle. Although it is difficult to account for sialic (continental) rocks persisting astride a spreading oceanic ridge, James Gilluly speculates, "I cannot help suspecting that one such block remains trapped beneath Iceland, there to contaminate a basaltic magma to produce granite" (1971, p. 2384). The volcanoes associated with the oceanic ridges are predominantly of the Icelandic and Hawaiian types, although the occurrence of siliceous rocks in Iceland and in smaller amounts elsewhere along the ridges indicates that there have been some episodes of explosive volcanic activity.

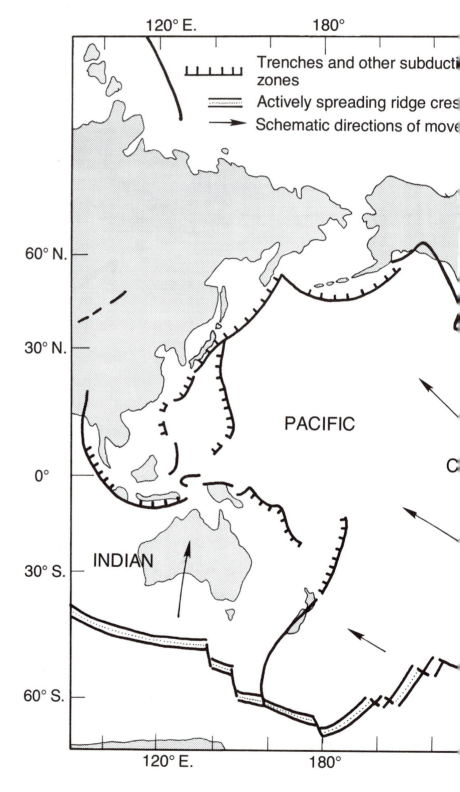

Figure 96. Major lithospheric plates. Mid-oceanic ridges, where plates move apart, are represented by double lines. Trenches and other subduction zones are shown by solid lines with teeth on one side; the teeth point in the direction of the descending slab. The subduction zone around the margin of the Pacific plate includes most of the island arcs and also most of the active volcanoes of the world. It is also the site of most of the intermediate- and deep-focus earthquakes. The subduction zone which marks the juncture of the African and Indian plates with the Eurasian plate is the site of the Himalaya Mountains. Modified from Le Pichon (1968).

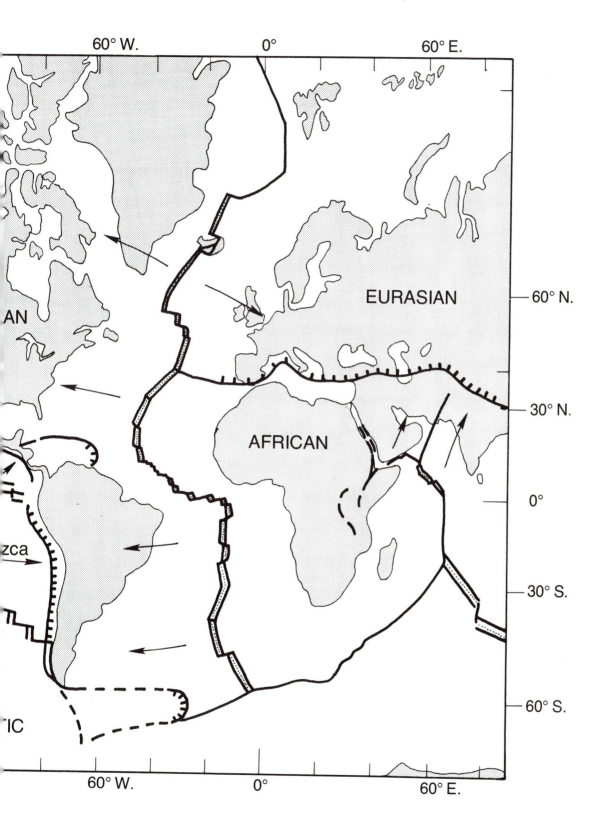

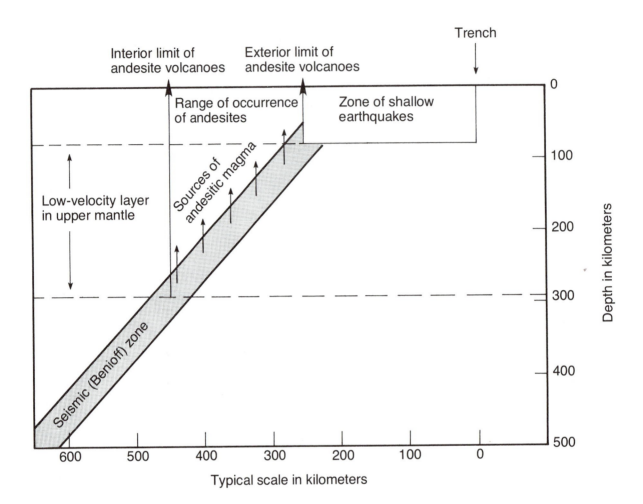

Figure 97. Schematic diagram of model proposed for andesite production and distribution in island arc zone. After Hatherton and Dickinson (1969, p. 5302).

Magma Evolution along Subduction Zones

It might appear that the introduction of a relatively cold slab of lithosphere into the mantle would hinder the development of magma, but the active volcanic belts associated with the subduction zone (and the absence of volcanoes where crust is not being consumed) prove that magma is indeed developed. It has been suggested that frictional heat, developed as the slab of lithosphere is thrust (or pulled) into the mantle, soon overcomes the original temperature difference, and, as the low-melting material is carried deeper into the mantle, magma forms. It is also maintained that, at the point of maximum bending of the slab, the slow release of energy by aftershocks of earthquakes, about half of which energy is released as heat, may contribute to the melting of the rocks and to volcanism.

Partial melting at different depths, and therefore different pressures, may produce magmas of different composition, as suggested by H. Kuno (1966). Studies have shown that the potash content of an andesitic volcano in the circum-Pacific island arcs increases with depth; that is, the deeper the Benioff zone, the higher percentage of potash (Dickinson and Hatherton 1967). Andesitic rocks were found to be related to a depth range of 80–290 kilometers, an interval corresponding approximately to the low-velocity layer of the mantle (Fig. 97). As early as 1962, Coats realized that the Aleutian arc had been formed by underthrusting of the oceanic crust, and he presented evidence to show that the magmas of andesitic volcanoes were formed by basaltic magma from the mantle mixing with sediment dragged down by the plate. A layer of sediment which averages about 1 kilometer in thickness overlies the basaltic ocean crust. At the subduction zone this sediment is either scraped off the downgoing slab and piled up along the edge of the continent or carried down into the mantle; or some of each may occur. When Gilluly was unable to find evidence of such volumes of material piled against the continent, he concluded that "a lot of rocks that went down the subduction zone were sandstone, chert, and radiolarian oozes. . . . Such a secondary derivation might account for much of the great volume of andesitic magmas of the circum-Pacific" (1971, p. 2386). The fact that the sediments were less dense than the surrounding material, at least when they started down, poses a problem. How far can you push a cork into water? Gilluly reasons that under increased pressure there would be phase changes which would increase the density and further that the sediments would probably not go all the way to the bottom of the zone. Rather they would melt and drift off to form magma pockets that seismologists think characterize the low-velocity zone—somewhere from 80–90 kilometers to around 200–300 kilometers in depth (Fig. 98).

All explosive volcanic activity—that is, activity of the Peléan and Vulcanian types, in which rhyolitic and andesitic material are the chief products—is associated with subduction zones. The source of the huge granitic batholiths and tremendous rhyolitic ash flows of the western United States has long been a problem. If they are the end products of crystal differentiation of a primary basaltic magma, then gigantic volumes of intermediate rocks would have to have been formed as a part of the process. Since such huge volumes have not been recognized, some other explanation for magmas yielding granitic and related rocks is required. The recycling of sediments and the crustal layers of the earth, as postulated by the plate-tectonics hypothesis, is an acceptable alternative.

Figure 98. Idealized cross section of the development of a cordilleran type mountain belt (such as the Andes) and associated volcanoes by the underthrusting of a continent by an ocean plate. Modified after Dewey and Bird (1970, p. 2638).

Problems with the Plate-Tectonics Concept

Although most of the currently active volcanoes are related to plate boundaries, there are numerous exceptions. Many of the volcanoes of oceanic islands, not situated on an active ridge, are not related to plate boundaries. The Hawaiian Islands, more or less centrally situated on the Pacific plate, are a prominent example. They represent a series of volcanic centers which formed in succession from northwest to southeast. Each began with eruptions of tholeitic basalt which changed to alkaline basalt in the final stages of activity, indicating that the lavas were being derived from a deeper source in the mantle. The suggestion, previously discussed (Ch. 10), that the ocean crust is drifting northwestward over a "hot spot," thus accounting for the progressively younger volcanoes which make up the group, has been questioned by Gilluly (1971). If the magma source becomes deeper near the close of the activity of one volcano

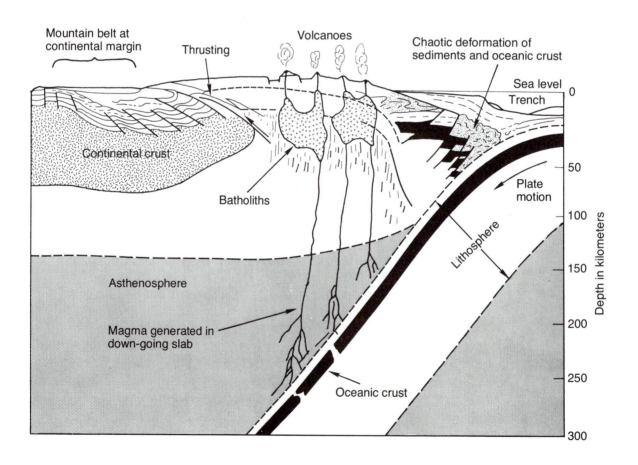

in order to provide the alkaline magma, it is difficult to explain why it would rise again as the next-to-be-born volcano drifts over the site—and especially why it would do so repeatedly. Much of the volcanism of the ocean basins, as well as some of the continental volcanism, does not relate to plate boundaries. The huge Columbia and Snake river lava plateaus and the volcanics of the German Rhineland were formed after the present pattern of plate motion had been established; yet they are far removed from plate boundaries.

There are other major problems in the plate-tectonics concept which have not been satisfactorily resolved. Not only the driving force for movement of the crustal plates but also the conditions and manner in which plate margins descend into the mantle at subduction zones are controversial, although there is compelling evidence that plates *do move* and that they *do descend* into the mantle at subduction zones.

According to the sea-floor-spreading concept, the island arcs, where oceanic crust is descending into the mantle, would appear to be areas of compression, but the presence of active volcanism indicates areas of tension. Is it possible that stresses in the downgoing slab vary with depth? Volcanoes appear to develop in areas subject to tension, and a volcano is, in fact, a magmatic diapir (see glossary) which finally reaches the surface by eruption. Tanner (1973) draws an analogy between salt domes (salt diapirs) and volcanoes, noting that where salt diapirs rise to the surface, as on the Gulf Coast of Texas, there is no spectacular display of any kind, but where a magmatic diapir reaches the surface a volcano is born. Based on seismic evidence, Isacks, Oliver, and Sykes (1968) concluded that in the Aleutian, Japanese, and Tonga arcs the slab is under compression parallel to its dip at all depths greater than 75–100 kilometers, and any extension in the slab (tension) must be at shallower depths. They do postulate tension where the slab bends sharply as it plunges beneath the trench, which correlates with the tension indicated by shallow earthquakes in this area. Tension is also postulated at the base of the lithospheric plate being underthrust (Fig. 99). Lliboutry (1969) was also concerned with this problem, and he proposed a model which, like that of previous investigators, envisages a descending plate dipping at an angle of about 45°. However, in his model, as soon as the stress on a vertical plane reaches the shear-strength value, a vertical fault is produced, originating an earthquake. Thus the descending plate is sheared into vertical fragments, although it retains, as a whole, the shape of an inclined plate (Fig. 100). According to Lliboutry, the faulting locally lessens the lithostatic pressure, thus allowing the oceanic crust, already heated in the depths, to melt. The magma pockets thus

Figure 99. Lithospheric plates sinking into mantle beneath island arc. The overriding lithosphere, in contact with the down-going slab, is bent upward by overthrusting, producing an area of tension. Tension also results where the slab bends abruptly in the deep-sea trench area. Seismic zones near the surface of the slab and in adjacent crust are indicated by the symbol S. No vertical exaggeration. After Isacks, Oliver, and Sykes (1968, p. 5869).

formed rise to the surface to produce volcanic island arcs or, if there was formerly a geosyncline at the margin of the plate, volcanism within the geosyncline. In a review of the conflicting evidence and opinions, Tanner (1973) concludes that compression is of little significance in creating and maintaining the major structures which underlie trenches and island arcs; that there is no "downgoing" slab, whether driven by pushing from the rear or by pulling from a sinking front edge; and that the only important motions to be accepted for island-arc and trench areas are horizontal tension and strike-slip. The destruction of oceanic plates in subduction zones is basic to the sea-floor-spreading and plate-tectonics concepts, and certainly more evidence is required to reconcile the divergent views on this crucial point.

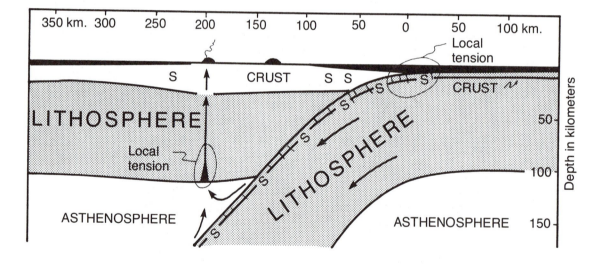

Figure 100. Lithosphere plate sinking into mantle beneath island arc, with discontinuous shearing along vertical fault planes. After Lliboutry (1969, p. 6525).

Plate tectonics, in bringing together evidence from seismology, geophysics, and oceanography, as well as geology, has had a stimulating and unifying effect on all the earth sciences. The appeal of plate tectonics is its simplicity and its ability to explain a wide range of observations about our planet. In fact, the plate-tectonics concept has enjoyed such a phenomenal success as a working hypothesis that it is being accepted as an established theory, and one tends to forget that there are still many unresolved questions. It should be recalled that the history of geology has been marked by a succession of controversies, some of which were mentioned earlier in this discussion, and in each case the concept was acclaimed as "practically proven," only to be replaced as new evidence was uncovered. Could this be the fate of plate tectonics?

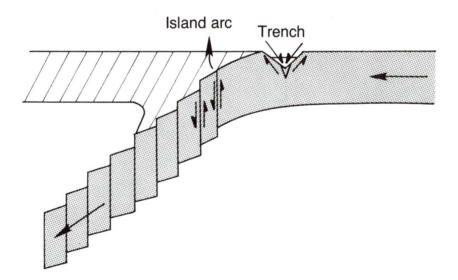

Chapter 17   Intensity and Energy of Volcanic Eruptions

Or speak to the earth and it shall teach thee . . . —JOB 12:8

The need for a means of comparing the intensity of volcanic eruptions has long been needed. A scale of intensity for earthquakes, although modified from time to time, has been in use for many years.
More recently a scale of magnitude has largely replaced the earlier
intensity scales. Frequently the scientists who study earthquakes
are also involved in the investigation of volcanoes; so it comes as no
surprise that the earthquake intensity and magnitude scales have
been a dominant influence in the development of similar scales for
volcanic eruptions.

EARTHQUAKE
INTENSITY SCALE

The effects of an earthquake are most intense near the epicenter and
gradually become less intense outward. In order to express earthquake intensities, several scales have been used. The Mercalli scale,
which is typical, recognizes degrees of intensity ranging from I to
XII. It is based on how humans react to the earthquake and on the
damage to property. For example, intensity II is felt by only a few
persons at rest; VI is felt by all, many run outdoors in fright, dishes
fall from shelves, and so on; IX damages well-constructed buildings
and cracks the ground; XI destroys nearly all masonry structures,
bends railroad tracks, and so on. Such a scale, although useful, is
far from satisfactory in determining the actual size of an earthquake.

EARTHQUAKE
MAGNITUDE SCALE

In recent years precision seismographs have made it possible to
determine the amplitude of motion of the bedrock during an earthquake. Using this type of information C. F. Richter (1935) developed
a scale of magnitude which is now routinely reported for most
earthquakes throughout the world. On the Richter scale, which is
an index of the amount of energy released at the source, property
damage begins with about magnitude 5. The largest magnitude assigned to an earthquake to date is 8.6, and four of that size have
occurred: (*a*) in Alaska, September 10, 1899; (*b*) in Colombia, January 31, 1906; (*c*) in Asia, August 15, 1950; and (*d*) in Alaska, March
27, 1964. The only earthquake in history that may have been larger,

judging from the reported effects, is the one near Lisbon, Portugal, on November 1, 1755, which may have had a magnitude of between 8.7 and 9.0. The San Francisco earthquake of 1906 had a magnitude of 8.3. The amplitude of motion of the bedrock depends on the amount of energy released; so there is a definite relationship between magnitude on the Richter scale and the energy released in the earthquake. As discussed later, a scale of magnitude for volcanic eruptions is also based on the amount of energy released.

VOLCANIC INTENSITY BASED ON VOLUME OF EJECTA

In his study of Central American volcanoes, Sapper (1927) devised an "index of explosiveness" in order to compare the intensity of volcanic activity of various regions of the world. The index of explosiveness, which has been described in some detail (Ch. 6), is based on the ratio of fragmental material to the total quantity of ejecta. Thus, if all the material erupted is fragmental, the index of explosiveness is 100 percent; if all is lava, the index is 0 percent. In order to compare the most explosive areas, Sapper calculated the ratio between the quantity of fluid lava and the quantity of fragmental material per 100 kilometers of distance along the volcanic belts of the world and concluded that the most explosive zone on earth is the belt in Nicaragua, with Java being a close second. Although it was tacitly acknowledged that the volume of material erupted was a measure of the intensity of the eruption, it remained for H. Tsuya (1955), in connection with a study of the 1707 eruption of Fujiyama, Japan, to propose a scale of intensity based on the volume of ejecta. Tsuya's intensity scale, with selected examples, is given in Table 9.

During historic times the largest eruptions have reached an intensity of VIII. Early estimates of the volume of ejecta in the 1815 eruption of Tambora were as high as 150 cubic kilometers, but more recent studies place the amount at 100 cubic kilometers to as low as 30 cubic kilometers (Van Padang 1951). Likewise, early estimates of the volume of ejecta in the 1835 eruption of Coseguina, Nicaragua, were in excess of 100 cubic kilometers, but, as noted earlier (Ch. 6), this figure has been sharply reduced.

ENERGY OF VOLCANIC ERUPTIONS

The energy released in a volcanic eruption comes from a number of sources. P. Hedervari (1963), following I. Yokoyama (1957), lists the following sources of energy:

1. Kinetic energy, represented by the velocity and mass of fragmental material ejected in the eruption.

2. Potential energy, represented by the changes in the height of the magma column.

TABLE 9. *Intensity of volcanic activity, based on volume of solid ejecta*

Intensity	Volume of Ejecta (cu. km.)	Volcano	Year of Eruption	Kind of Ejecta	Volume of Ejecta (cu. km.)
IX	More than 100	Tambora, Sumbawa	1815	B	150[a]
VIII	10–100	Krakatoa, Sunda Strait	1883	B	18
VII	1–10	Shtyubelya, Kamchatka	1907	B	3.0
		Bandai San, Japan	1888	C	1.2
VI	0.1–1	Fuji San, Japan	1707	B	0.8
		Taal, Philippines	1911	C	0.5
V	0.01–0.1	O'Shima, Japan	1950–1951	A	0.03
IV	0.001–0.01	Keleot, Java	1901	B	0.002
III	0.0001–0.001	Asuma San, Japan	1893	B	0.0005
II	0.00001–0.0001	Tokachi-dake, Japan	1926	C	0.00001
I	Less than 0.00001	Yakeyama, Niigata	1949	C	Small
0	0	Volcanoes displaying fumarolic activity only		0	0

Source: Adapted from Tsuya 1955.
A: essentially lava flows.
B: fragmentary ejecta only.
C: essentially old detritus.
[a] This is the highest estimate. See discussion in text.

3. Thermal energy, represented by the heat of the lava, pyro-clastics, and gases.

4. Energy of earthquakes and earth tremors.

5. Energy of sea waves (tsunami) and tornadoes (and air waves) associated with volcanic eruptions.

6. Energy required to fracture (open eruptive channels) or deform the earth's crust.

The most important of these is thermal energy, which generally is 10–100 or even 1,000 times greater than the others, and the order of thermal energy gives the order of magnitude of the total energy released in an eruption.

The formula for the thermal energy of a volcanic eruption used by Yokoyama (1957) and adopted by Hedervari (1963) and others is as follows:

Thermal energy, $E_{th} = V\ d(\alpha T + B)J$, where V = volume of ejecta; d = mean density; T = temperature; α = specific heat of lava (0.25 cal/gr. °C); B = latent heat of lava (50 cal/gr.); and J = joule (a unit of energy or work, = 10^7 ergs). (An erg is the amount of energy expended in moving a body one centimeter against a force of one dyne. A dyne is the force which, acting on a gram for one second, imparts to it a velocity of one centimeter per second [equal to about the force exerted by a milligram weight under the influence of gravity].)

Yokoyama developed formulae for calculating the various types of energy released in an eruption (kinetic, potential, etc.), but he concluded that, "we may take into account, for order-of-magnitude estimates, only thermal energy because energies of other kinds do not contribute much to the total sum of energies" (1957, p. 85). Yokoyama then calculated the energy released in the eruptions of a number of Japanese and Indonesian volcanoes and related these to Tsuya's scale of intensity. Since Yokoyama's calculations of released energy were based on the volume of ejecta, there is a close correlation with Tsuya's results, except where revised values for the volume of ejecta were used, as for Krakatoa (1883) and Tambora (1815), each of which is one grade lower on Yokoyama's scale than on Tsuya's. The total energy released in a number of volcanic eruptions is given in Table 10.

An examination of the figures in Table 10 shows that the amount of energy released is not necessarily a guide to the explosiveness or violence of the eruption. For example, the 1952 eruption of Kilauea, based on the amount of energy released, was certainly one of the large eruptions, although there were no great explosions. The 1950 eruption of Mauna Loa is of the same order of magnitude as the great eruption of Krakatoa in 1883, although explosive activity was practically absent in the Mauna Loa eruption. In both cases the

TABLE 10. *Total energy released in selected volcanic eruptions*

Volcano	Year	Type	Total Energy in Ergs	Comments
Santorini, Aegean Sea	ca. 1500 B.C.	B	ca. 1.0×10^{27}	Based on volume of 72 cu. km.
Laki, Iceland	1783	A(B)	8.6×10^{26}	Icelandic type
Tambora, Sumbawa	1815	B	8.4×10^{26}	Based on volume of 100 cu. km.
Coseguina, Nicaragua	1835	B	4.8×10^{26}	Based on volume of 50 cu. km.
Katmai, Alaska	1912	B	2.02×10^{26}	Peléan type
Bezymianny, Kamchatka	1955–1956	B	2.2×10^{25}	Peléan type
Krakatoa, Indonesia	1883	B	ca. 1.0×10^{25}	Peléan type
Mauna Loa, Hawaii	1950	A	1.4×10^{25}	Hawaiian type
Asama, Japan	1783	AB	8.8×10^{24}	Vulcanian type
Fuji San, Japan	1707		7.1×10^{24}	Peléan type
Agung, Bali	1963	AB	4.5×10^{24}	Peléan type
Capelinhos, Azores	1957	AB	4.0×10^{24}	Began as submarine eruption
Surtsey, Iceland	1963	A	1.9×10^{24}	Icelandic type
Kilauea, Hawaii	1952	A	1.8×10^{24}	Hawaiian type
Vesuvius, Italy	1906	AB	1.7×10^{24}	Vulcanian type
Mihara, Japan	1950–1951	A	9.4×10^{23}	Strombolian type
Komagatake, Japan	1929	B	5.6×10^{23}	Peléan type
Asama, Japan	1935	B	4.8×10^{23}	Vulcanian type
Bandai San, Japan	1888	C	ca. 1.0×10^{23}	Phreatic eruption
Taal, Philippines	1965	BC	1.0×10^{23}	Phreatic eruption
Mihara, Japan	1954	A	1.3×10^{22}	Strombolian type
Arenal, Costa Rica	1968		1.0×10^{22}	Peléan type

Sources: Compiled from Yokoyama (1957), Hedervari (1963), and Macdonald (1972). I am indebted to Dr. Hedervari for prepublication access to some of his results.
A: essentially lava flows.
B: fragmentary ejecta.
C: essentially old detritus.

eruptions were marked by outpourings of huge volumes of highly heated lava, which resulted in the release of a large amount of thermal energy. Most of the heat energy released in such eruptions is slowly lost by irradiation and conduction, and only a small part contributes to explosive activity. Clearly, when the material is chiefly lava, the amount of thermal energy released does not reflect the intensity of the eruption as the term is commonly used. However, when the erupted material is chiefly fragmental, as in the 1883 eruption of Krakatoa, there is a much closer relationship. But, even in eruptions in which the ejecta is chiefly fragmental, the physical character (especially the thermal character) of the material plays an important role in the amount of energy released. For example, the volume of ejecta in the 1888 eruption of Bandai San, Japan, was quite large; yet the total energy was comparatively low. This was due to the fact that almost all the ejecta consisted of the disrupted mass of the old cone, which was not highly heated.

In a study of eruptive energies, which had been in progress for some time, Hedervari (1963) calculated, in so far as possible, the six sources of energy released in an eruption which were listed earlier in this discussion. Like Yokoyama, he concluded that the order of magnitude of thermal energy usually determines the order of magnitude of total energy released in an eruption. Hedervari introduced an eruption-magnitude scale for volcanic eruptions, comparable to the Richter scale of magnitude for earthquakes. Both are based on the total energy released. An intensity of I on Tsuya's scale is about 5 on Hedervari's eruption-magnitude scale; the 1883 eruption of Krakatoa is rated 9.5. Hedervari also expressed the eruption magnitude in terms of atomic-bomb equivalents, using 8.4×10^{21} ergs as equal to one atomic bomb (Bikini test bomb).

Realizing the problem of relating total energy released in an eruption to explosiveness, Imbo (1965a) computed the "dynamical eruptive energy." This is the energy related to the liberation and expansion of the volatiles contained in the magma. The magmatic pressure, which must be considered, depends on the volatile content and the depth of the magma. Although reliable information is rarely available on either of these factors, Imbo was able to arrive at some worthwhile results. Information on the height of the eruptive column for the March, 1944, eruption of Vesuvius enabled Imbo to compute the velocity of the fragments erupted, and, knowing the density, he was able to determine the pressure at the eruptive vent. He reasoned that the pressure at the eruptive vent would approximate the magmatic pressure for only the highest initial velocities. Imbo's study, which is based on mathematical analyses of many aspects of eruptive energies, will be of interest to the specialist in the field but is beyond the scope of this treatment. It may be noted, however, that Imbo recognizes that the information needed for his computations is not always available, especially for eruptions of past years. In such cases he uses a method based on the volume of solids erupted, on the assumption that the "energy is assumed to be a function of the solid mass erupted, as the latter is believed to be proportional to the erupted mass of volatiles" (1965a, p. 135). In his calculations he found that about 0.011 grams of volatiles are erupted with each gram of solid mass, and that this is about one-half the volatile content of the magma. Using the eruption-magnitude scale of Hedervari (1963), Imbo relates the eruption magnitude to equivalent megatons and assigns the March, 1944, eruption of Vesuvius a magnitude of 6.6 and an equivalent in megatons of 7.8×10^{-2}. (A one-megaton nuclear device is the equivalent of 1,000,000 tons of T.N.T. and equals 4.18×10^{22} ergs. One kiloton equals 1,000 tons of T.N.T. and equals 4.18×10^{19} ergs. The atomic bombs dropped on Japan were about 20 kilotons each. By comparison, the 1883 eruption of Krakatoa has been rated as equal to 200 megatons.)

SOME CONCLUDING
COMMENTS

The comparison of the energy released in volcanic eruptions with that released in earthquakes emphasizes the relationship between volcanoes and earthquakes. The total energy of a "large" volcanic eruption is about 10^{24} to 10^{25} ergs, which is comparable to the energy released in a "large" earthquake. Although the association of volcanoes and earthquakes has long been recognized, before the advent of plate tectonics in the 1960's the conclusion stated by Yokoyama was typical: ". . . the writer is not able to say positively that volcanism is a derivative of earthquakes and prefers to say that both are equally the derivatives of the same rank from the thermal energy contained in the bottom of the crust or the mantle" (1957, p. 106). However, with the development of the concept of plate tectonics, many feel that there is an acceptable explanation for the association of volcanoes and earthquakes in the subduction zones (i.e., where the plate margin is descending into the mantle).

The various efforts to develop a scale of intensity or scale of magnitude for volcanic eruptions, which have been described in the preceding paragraphs, although stated in terms of "energy released" or "eruption magnitude," ultimately depend on the volume of material erupted, which was the basis of Tsuya's scale of intensity described above.

Perhaps a new approach to the problem of assigning intensity or magnitude to volcanic eruptions is needed. One effort in this direction was a study by Gorshkov (1959) of the 1955–1956 eruption of Bezymianny Volcano, Kamchatka (see Ch. 7). The climax of this eruption was a gigantic explosion on March 30, 1956, which destroyed the top of the volcanic cone and was followed by caldera collapse. Gorshkov calculated the energy of the air wave generated by the explosion as recorded on barographs throughout the region. Elements used in his calculations included: height of the atmospheric layer involved; air density at the surface; sound speed; distance of the explosion source in degrees; pressure; and duration of the vibrations. Stating that in a hydrogen bomb blast not more than 0.3 percent of the entire energy goes into the air wave, he concluded (without giving any evidence) that in a volcanic eruption the amount would be about 10 percent. On this basis the energy of the March 30 explosion was 4×10^{23} ergs. The thermal energy released in the Bezymianny eruption, calculated in the conventional manner, is about 2.2×10^{25} ergs. Thus the explosion energy is only about 2 percent of the total thermal energy of the eruption, a calculation which led Gorshkov to conclude: ". . . the main active agent of the eruption is the heat energy of the magma, and gas only serves to transform this energy into an explosive one" (1959, p. 108). This is contrary to the prevailing view, as stated in a quotation from Perret, that "Gas is the active agent and the magma is its vehicle" (1924, p. 59).

The determination of the energy of an air wave is a relatively simple problem, and a simple classification for the strength of volcanic explosions, based on the energy of the air wave, would make it possible to compare objectively eruptions of a wide range. Gorshkov (1960) recommends that all volcanological stations be equipped with microbarographs in order to register a wide range of explosions.

A rule of thumb used by some observers to compare the intensity of volcanic eruptions is the duration of darkness at various distances from the volcano. For example, in the 1883 eruption of Krakatoa there was total darkness for 57 hours at a distance of 50 miles and for 22 hours at a distance of 130 miles. In the 1912 eruption of Mount Katmai there was complete darkness for 60 hours at Kodiak, 100 miles to the southwest. Here again the volume of material erupted is the basic element involved, but the time factor does provide an index of the "violence" of an eruption.

It seems reasonable that any scale to measure intensity or magnitude of volcanic eruptions should relate to the classification of volcanoes, since the basis for the classification is the manner in which they erupt. Unfortunately, there is no relationship, because the scales proposed are based largely on the volume of material erupted. A Hawaiian type eruption, in which there is little or no explosive activity but a huge volume of lava, will be assigned a higher degree of intensity than one of the much more explosive Peléan type if a smaller volume of material is produced in the latter. One of the few references dealing with the energy of a volcanic eruption in which the type of volcano is even mentioned is that by Yokoyama (1956), in which he compares Volcano Asama, a typical Vulcanian type, with Volcano Mihara, a typical Strombolian type. Studies over a 20-year period of Volcano Asama showed that the energy of a violent eruption was on the order of 10^{20} ergs and that of a moderate one was 10^{18} ergs. It was further noted that the seismic energy of Mihara is comparable to that of Asama if it is considered through a period of activity, but the energy of an individual Vulcanian explosion is 100–1,000 times that of a Strombolian explosion.

Relating a volcanic eruption, on the basis of the total energy released, to atomic bombs, megaton nuclear devices, or even earthquakes seems to be of doubtful value because of the different manner in which the energy is released. A megaton nuclear device releases about the same amount of energy as an earthquake of magnitude 6. However the energy is applied quite differently—highly concentrated and released instantly in the nuclear device, while in an earthquake it is dispersed along the line of fracture, although it also is released more or less instantly as the stress in the earth's crust is relieved by slippage along the fracture. In a volcano, however, the energy is released throughout the eruption, which may last for days, weeks, or even many months. Thus, such a "large" volcanic eruption as the 1950 eruption of Mauna Loa, approximately equal to the 1883 eruption of Krakatoa which is rated as equivalent to 955 atomic bombs, did not produce any significant explosions!

Chapter 18   Volcanoes and the Environment

A part of Wisdom is to know that we don't know, and not fool ourselves with long words.—UPTON SINCLAIR

There is a tendency to view volcanoes only as agents of destruction and to overlook their beneficial contributions to our environment. Many of the destructive as well as the beneficial aspects of volcanism have been described in the preceding chapters, and a brief review will suffice to enable the reader to assess the environmental effects. However, the major environmental impact of volcanoes is in their effect on climate and on soils, topics which will now be considered.

VOLCANOES AND CLIMATE

The idea that volcanic dust in the atmosphere may have important climatic effects is not new. Benjamin Franklin wrote, in May, 1784:

> During several of the summer months of the year 1783, when the effects of the sun's rays to heat the earth in these northern regions should have been greatest, there existed a constant fog over all Europe, and parts of North America. This fog was of a permanent nature; it was dry, and the rays of the sun seemed to have little effect in dissipating it as they easily do a moist fog rising from water. They were, indeed, rendered so faint in passing through it that, when collected in the focus of a burning glass they would scarcely kindle brown paper. Of course their summer effect in heating the earth was exceedingly diminished. Hence the surface was nearly frozen. Hence the snow remained on it unmelted, and received continual additions. . . . perhaps the winter of 1783–84 was more severe than any that happened for many years.
> The cause of this universal fog is not yet ascertained. . . . whether it was the vast quantity of smoke, long continuing to issue during the summer from Hecla [volcano] in Iceland, and that other volcano [Skaptar Jökul] which rose out of the sea near the island, which smoke might be spread by various winds, is yet uncertain. (Quoted by Abbe 1906, p. 127)

Although the Icelandic volcanoes were undoubtedly contributors, the great eruption of Volcano Asama in Japan in 1783, stated to be one of the most violent eruptions on record, was possibly the main source of the ash.

"Year without a Summer"

The year of 1816, unusually cold the world over and commonly referred to as the "year without a summer," followed the eruption of Tambora Volcano on the island of Sumbawa, Indonesia (Lamb 1970; Hoyt 1958). Tambora Volcano was initially a shield volcano; later it developed a strato-volcanic cone which prior to the 1815 eruption was 4,000 meters high. In the 1815 eruption the top of the cone disappeared, leaving a caldera some 6 kilometers in diameter and 600–700 meters deep. The caldera is now partially filled with a lake. The initial explosions marking the beginning of the eruption occurred on April 5, 1815, and they were heard at distances up to 1,400 kilometers. The most intense phase of the eruption occurred on April 10–12, but some activity continued until mid-July. During the most intense phase of the eruption, dense ash clouds caused complete darkness for three days on the island of Madura, 500 kilometers away. Ten thousand people were killed in the eruption, and an estimated 82,000 died of starvation and disease in the months following the eruption, resulting in a total loss of life of 92,000 (Van Padang 1951).

The climatic effects of the huge quantity of dust ejected into the atmosphere were apparent in many parts of the world. Cyclonic activity seems to have been abnormally concentrated in a position near Newfoundland and from central Ireland across England to the Baltic, resulting in almost continual rains from May to October, 1816. The average summer temperature of the summer months in London was 2°–3° C. below normal. In New England there was widespread snow between June 6 and 11, and frosts occurred each month. Some crops did not ripen, others rotted in the fields, and in Ireland and Wales there were serious food shortages. Estimates of the volume of ash ejected into the atmosphere vary widely, but all agree that it was substantially greater than that in the 1883 eruption of Krakatoa. H. H. Lamb (1970) assigns a dust veil index (discussed in the following pages) of 3,000 for the 1815 Tambora eruption, three times that of the 1883 Krakatoa eruption.

Figure 101. Annual average pyrheliometric values. After Humphreys (1940); volcanoes added.

Solar Radiation and Volcanic Dust

Although known temperatures from various parts of the world seem to support the conclusion that 1784 was an unusually cold year and that 1816 was the year without a summer, the lack of accurate measurements of solar radiation on a world-wide basis at that time makes it impossible to verify these conclusions. However, for the past century, direct measurements of solar radiation by means of the pyrheliometer, an instrument that measures the total heat of sunshine, show marked fluctuations from year to year. Dr. H. H. Kimball of the U.S. Weather Bureau prepared a graph (reproduced by Humphreys 1940, p. 601) showing the changes over the period from 1882 to 1913 (Fig. 101). The yearly values are given in

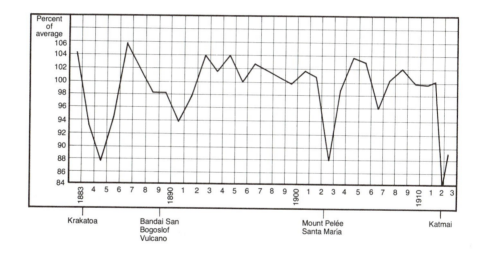

terms of the average for the entire period; so the percentages of this average do not represent the full effect of the disturbing causes, "of which volcanic dust certainly is the chief" (Humphreys 1940, p. 601). The marked decrease in solar radiation in 1884–1885 coincides with the great eruption of Krakatoa. The low in 1890–1891 corresponds to the eruptions of Bandai San in 1888, Vulcano in 1888–1890, and Bogoslof in 1890; the low in 1902–1903 was during the eruption of Mount Pelée and Santa María; and the 1912 low was at the time of the eruption of Mount Katmai. As a result of these and other studies, Humphreys concluded: "There is, then, abundant pyroheliometric evidence that volcanic dust in the upper atmosphere actually does produce the decrease in direct solar radiation. . . . [and] may be regarded as conclusive both of the existence of volcanic dust in the upper atmosphere and its efficiency in intercepting direct radiation from the sun" (1940, p. 602). It might be argued that the lows in the amount of solar radiation received by the earth are due to sunspots and that the volcanic eruptions were merely coincidental. Humphreys considered this problem and, after plotting sunspot cycles, concluded that the great drops in solar radiation received by the earth did not occur at times of sunspot changes but were simultaneous with violent volcanic eruptions.

It will be of interest to inquire into the manner in which dust in the atmosphere results in lower temperatures. Dr. Humphreys, a physicist long associated with the U.S. Weather Bureau, considered the problem, and the following discussion is based on his work. Dust particles in the atmosphere absorb some solar radiation, but they also reflect and scatter the sun's rays. The dust particles (as is true of rocks in general) have a greater coefficient of absorption for terrestrial radiations than for solar radiations. This means that the dust particles absorb more earth-radiated heat than sun-radiated heat; so the net effect of the dust, so far as absorbed heat is concerned, would be to slightly increase rather than decrease temperature. However, reflection and scattering are both important and work in different ways. The amount of reflection and scattering depends on the wave length of the rays and the size of the dust particles. If the wave lengths are small compared to the size of the particles, more reflection and scattering will result. Humphreys calculated the average diameter of the particles, from the optical effects, as 1.85 microns (.00185 mm.), which is greater than the wave length of solar radiation. On the other hand, the wave length of terrestrial radiation (cooling of the earth by radiation of absorbed heat) is six or seven times the diameter of the particles and would pass through dusty air with little loss. Thus, the dust particles act as a screen which prevents heat from reaching the surface of the earth but lets it escape freely. It may be compared to the type of window screen which permits those on the inside to see out but prevents those on the outside from seeing in. Such small particles would take, according to Humphreys's calculations, from 1 to 3 years to settle out of the atmosphere from the levels to which they are blown by volcanic eruptions. The total volume of dust necessary to reduce solar radiation by 20 percent, the figure obtained from measurements in the fall of 1912 following the eruption of Mount Katmai, is surprisingly small. Realizing that in most regions of the earth the sun's rays will pass through the dust layer at such an angle that they must encounter roughly twice as many dust particles as if they came from directly overhead, a reduction of 20 percent in solar radiation would require only 0.0027 cubic kilometers of solids. This is small compared to the 20.8 cubic kilometers contributed by Krakatoa. Even this small amount, if contributed every 2 years, would be sufficient to maintain continuously a reduction of about 5.6° C. (10° F.) in the average mean temperature and greatly extend the permanent snowfields of the earth. Humphreys reasons (incorrectly, as is pointed out later) that the location of the volcano or volcanoes would be unimportant, since the winds of the upper atmosphere would soon spread the dust more or less uniformly over the entire earth. One might think that this quantity of dust would produce a recognizable layer on the earth's surface. Calculations show that this quantity of dust yearly over a period of 100,000 years would produce a layer over the earth of 0.0508 centimeters thick!

There are other ways in which dust in the atmosphere could produce climatic effects in addition to acting as a blanket to screen out some of the sun's radiation. Dust clouds could reduce the amount of sun radiation by different amounts at different places, and, since differences in temperature between the tropics and higher latitudes are responsible for the prevailing wind system of the earth, the effects might be far-reaching. By increasing temperature differences between regions, the dust clouds might accelerate circulation currents and produce cold, stormy winters and cool, cloudy summers. It has also been discovered that dust particles can act as nuclei to form ice crystals in subfreezing air saturated with water vapor. In the upper atmosphere the dust might increase cloudiness, which would add to the effect of the dust itself in decreasing solar radiation received by the earth.

One of the most convincing studies on the effect of volcanic dust on solar radiation was that reported by C. G. Abbot and F. E. Fowle (1913), who were making solar radiation measurements at the time of the Mount Katmai eruption in 1912. As director of the Smithsonian Astrophysical Observatory, Abbot had been engaged for several years in making observations at Mount Wilson on the daily quantity of solar heat. In 1911 and 1912, simultaneous observations were made at Mount Wilson, California, and at Bassour, Algeria, to avoid any errors due to local atmospheric conditions at Mount Wilson. During the summer of 1912, Abbot in Algeria and Fowle at Mount Wilson were measuring the intensity of the radiations of the sun. On June 19 at Bassour, Algeria, Abbot noticed streaks which resembled smoke near the horizon; this phenomenon continued all summer and was especially marked before sunrise and after sunset, covering the sky nearly to the zenith. After a few days the sky became mottled, somewhat like a so-called mackerel sky, although there were no clouds. In the months of July and August and as long as the expedition remained in September, the sky was very hazy, and it was found that the intensity of the radiation of the sun was greatly reduced by the haziness. Similar features were noticed at

Mount Wilson beginning on June 21, and publications in Europe and elsewhere indicated that the haziness was world-wide.

It had been suggested that the haze in question was due to the eruption of Mount Katmai in Alaska on June 6–8, in which huge amounts of ash were ejected (see Ch. 7). Studies by S. R. Capps (1915) show that ash from the 1912 eruption of Mount Katmai covered an area roughly 250 by 150 miles, with a thickness varying from up to 50 feet near the source to 0.1 foot at the margin of the area studied. However, ash in decreasing amounts covered an area many times larger than that indicated. Significant amounts of ash were reported from Juneau, 750 miles to the southeast, and in the Yukon Valley, 1,000 miles to the north.

As noted above, the haze began to affect measurements in Algeria on June 19 and at Mount Wilson on June 21. The effect increased during July and reached its maximum for Algeria in mid-August but continued to increase at Mount Wilson to the end of August. The maximum decrease of total solar radiation attributable to the haze was around 20 percent at each station. Abbot concluded that if this decrease continued it would result in a temperature lower by about 7° C. However, other factors would affect the climate, such as a change in the general cloudiness and in the radiation of heat from the earth at night. The haze would decrease nocturnal radiation and compensate to some extent (perhaps up to one-half) for the lowering of temperature. In an effort to determine whether there was a lowering of temperature in 1912, readings were obtained from a number of stations throughout the world (including 7 in the United States), and these stations showed a lower temperature during July than normal. Since temperature may fluctuate with the 11-year sunspot cycle, Abbot considered whether the decrease in temperature which he noted might be the sunspot effect. However, 1912 was near the low point of a cycle, when a somewhat higher temperature than normal would have been expected. Abbot and Fowle concluded that effects of volcanic haze on terrestrial temperatures are worth serious consideration, and, although many local influences may mask the effect of haze, they predicted that periods of haziness, such as those produced by the great volcanic eruptions of 1883 and 1912, may well influence temperature by several degrees.

Volcanic Dust and Global Temperatures

The role of volcanic dust in temperatures on a global scale, firmly advocated by Abbot and Fowle (1913), Humphreys (1940), and others, was re-examined by J. Murray Mitchell, Jr. (1961), in an effort to account for the world-wide changes in temperature. Beginning in the 1880's, a more or less systematic world-wide warming trend set in, which reached a climax in the 1940's and since that time has reversed direction. In the 60-year period from 1880 to 1940, world annual average temperature increased by about 1° F. (0.56° C.). Since 1940 these trends have reversed so that, roughly speaking, temperatures have now returned to the levels typical of the 1910's or 1920's.

Catastrophic volcanic eruptions, such as those of Krakatoa (1883), Mount Katmai (1912), and Bezymianny (1956), depress normal incident solar radiation by 10 percent or more over intercontinental distances and for durations of several months, causing widespread lowering of temperature. Valuable information on how long the dust remains in the atmosphere (*residence time*) was provided by studies on the residence time in the stratosphere of radioactive waste debris following nuclear bomb tests. Since the bomb debris and dust from the more violent volcanic eruptions probably reached comparable heights and were comparable in size, the comparison is valid. It was concluded (Stebbins 1960) that dust from such eruptions is removed from the atmosphere after five years. Studies also revealed that debris ejected into the stratosphere of one hemisphere disperses to virtually all latitudes of that hemisphere, but very little crosses the equator into the other hemisphere. In a survey of major volcanic eruptions since 1855, Mitchell (1961) concluded that there was a consistent tendency for eruptions to be followed by a lower five-year average temperature in the eruption hemisphere. The results are consistent with the conclusion that planetary temperatures are depressed by 0.5° F. (0.28° C.) or more in the first or second year of a major eruption and lend support to the idea that the low global temperatures in the late 1880's and early 1890's were due to the eruption of Krakatoa in 1883.

Later, Mitchell (1970) considered the problem of pollution of the atmosphere by carbon dioxide and particulate loading (i.e., particles of dust, smoke, etc.), especially the long-term changes in the amount of these constituents in the atmosphere and fluctuations in the average global temperature. Since late in the nineteenth century, man has released carbon dioxide to the atmosphere at an ever-increasing rate through the combustion of fossil fuels (primarily petroleum, natural gas, and coal). Although carbon dioxide gas is a minute constituent of the atmosphere (about .03 percent by volume) it is a very efficient absorber of thermal (infrared) radiation, and an increase in the carbon dioxide content of the air would result in a rise in temperature. The concentration of carbon dioxide in the atmosphere has increased by around 10 percent since the nineteenth century, largely because of the burning of fossil fuels. Such an increase would raise the temperature by about 0.3° C., which is only

Figure 102. Estimated chronology of world-wide atmospheric particulate load by volcanic activity (stratospheric loading only, dotted curve) and by human activity (heavy solid curve). The 120-year average of loading by stratospheric volcanic dust is added for comparison (thin solid line). Estimated effect on planetary temperature is shown outside margin at right. After Mitchell (1970).

one-third of the observed world-wide warming trend between 1880 and 1940. Moreover, the increased use of fossil fuels since 1940 has resulted in a continued increase in the carbon dioxide content of the air (estimated by Mitchell [1970] to increase by 20 percent over the nineteenth-century level by 1990), but the cooling observed since 1940 has occurred in spite of further warming contributions by carbon dioxide in this period. Thus, other mechanisms are required to account for part of the warming (about two-thirds) observed between 1880 and 1940 and for the cooling observed since 1940. The answer, according to Mitchell, is to be found in changes in atmospheric dust loading, both by man and by natural forces. Mitchell's conclusions as to the relative importance of particulate loading of the atmosphere by human activities and volcanic activity are shown in Figure 102. In assigning contributions from volcanic eruptions it was assumed that 1 percent of the total ejected mass reached the stratosphere, and a residence time of 14 months was assigned to all dust which reached the stratosphere, regardless of geographic location. If the data in Figure 102 are only roughly correct, Mitchell points out that the volcanic dust load of the atmosphere after the 1963 eruption of Agung Volcano, Bali, was of the order of 10 times the human-derived particulate loading.

It is the *changes* in dust load over the years that are relevant to the abrupt world-wide climatic changes, such as the cooling after 1940. However, Mitchell observes: "It is possible to attribute a major part of the latter-day cooling [since 1940], if not all of it, to natural particulate loading changes that have accompanied a recent enhancement of world-wide volcanic activity. In this respect, it appears that man has been playing a very poor second fiddle to nature as a dust factory in recent years" (1970, pp. 110–111).

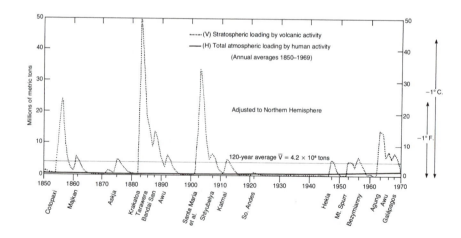

Dust Veil Index

A British meteorologist, H. H. Lamb (1970) made a rather detailed study of the effects of huge quantities of volcanic dust erupted into the atmosphere. In order to consider the climatic effects, he assembled available information on noteworthy dust veils since the year 1500 and gave each a quantitative assessment by assigning a dust veil index for each eruption. In calculating a dust veil index (d.v.i.) for an eruption, information on at least one of the following is required: (*a*) loss of incoming solar radiation, (*b*) temperature lowering in the middle latitudes, or (*c*) volume of material erupted into the atmosphere. In assessing the meteorological effects, the area of the earth covered by the volcanic dust veil at its maximum extent and how long the dust remains in the atmosphere are significant. Depending on the information available for the eruption, one of three alternative formulae is used to determine the d.v.i. Each formula includes a numerical factor designed to bring the index to 1,000 for the 1883 eruption of Krakatoa, which was selected as a basis for comparison.

In a chronology of volcanic eruptions from 1500 to 1968, Lamb lists 25 individual eruptions with a d.v.i. of 1,000 or more (i.e., equal to or greater than the 1883 eruption of Krakatoa). Most of these eruptions occurred in Indonesia or adjacent islands. A d.v.i. of 4,000, the highest assigned, was the 1835 eruption of Coseguina Volcano, Nicaragua (see Ch. 6). However, it should be noted that Lamb uses Sapper's estimate of 50 cubic kilometers for the volume of ejected material, a figure much larger than a more recent estimate by Williams (1952). Lamb reports 50 individual eruptions in which the d.v.i. ranges from 100 to 800, a figure he considers to be large enough for the eruption to have significant effects on the climate.

Because of the upper wind circulation, the location of the volcanic eruption determines the extent to which the dust is spread over the earth, as discussed earlier in this section. Volcanic eruptions in the higher latitudes of each hemisphere create dust veils dense enough to affect radiation balance over latitudes 30°–90° in that hemisphere, while eruptions near the equator produce world-wide dust veils. From studying the course of constant-height balloons, it appears that volcanic dust should take, on an average, 2–4 weeks to circuit the globe in the troposphere over temperate and higher latitudes and 3–6 weeks to do so over the equator, where winds are lighter and the circumference of the earth greater. The dust from the 1963 eruption of Agung (Bali) seems to have taken 4–5 weeks to make the first circuit. Dust from low-latitude eruptions spreads slowly over the whole earth, although the advance into the polar areas seems to take place in steps, particularly in late autumn. The size of the dust particles and their height in the atmosphere will determine the length of time they stay aloft. It is the dust concentrations in the lower stratosphere (20–27 km.) that are responsible for the most persistent and densest dust veils. Dust in the troposphere is soon washed out by rain. In the most violent eruptions, such as that of Krakatoa in 1883, dust particles reach the upper stratosphere at heights of 45–50 kilometers. Optical effects produced by intermediate-sized particles from the 1883 eruption of Krakatoa were last seen over Europe 2.8 years later and in Colorado 3.1 years later.

Lamb concludes: "Some association between great volcanic dust veils (d.v.i. of 100 in one hemisphere), weather and climate are indicated by this brief investigation. But they differ according to the latitude of the injection of the dust" (1970, p. 493). He notes that the level of statistical significance is rather low and concludes that volcanic dust is not the cause of all decade-to-decade and century-to-century climatic differences, although in many specific cases the relationship seems to be well established.

Volcanism and the Ice Age

The possibility that reductions in solar radiation due to volcanic dust in the atmosphere might lower the temperature sufficiently to produce a glacial climate has received serious consideration. During the glacial ages the snowline (level above which snow remains on the ground throughout the year) was lowered about 2,500 feet. This would require a mean annual world temperature some 5° C. (in some places as much as 8° C.) below the present mean. Probably the lowering of the snowline was due, in part, to heavier snowfall; so the mean annual temperature change may have been less than indicated. The present line of mean annual freezing temperature lies far closer to the equator than the limit of present ice-sheets, and this clearly indicates that low temperature alone is not sufficient to produce glaciation and that increased precipitation is also required.

Although climate is a complicated problem, C. E. P. Brooks (1949), in an excellent analysis of the evidence, concluded that mean temperature is dependent on four variables: (a) extent of the land area, (b) height of the land, (c) ocean currents, and (d) volcanic activity. To produce the change required for a glacial climate, Brooks felt that all four climatic factors must operate in the direction of lower temperatures. This is frequently described as the "topographic hypothesis," since the area and height of the land are essential considerations. Brooks concluded that, if all other factors were favorable, it is entirely possible that a period of violent volcanic eruptions and the resulting decrease in solar radiation in summer would permit glaciers to form. Once started, the ice sheet would perpetuate itself by increasing its height by additions of snow and in time would spread over larger areas.

It must be pointed out that other hypotheses have largely replaced the topographic hypothesis, whose basic elements have been sketched, but a discussion of the various hypotheses is not within the scope of this work. However, the role of volcanic dust continues to be an important factor in studies of changes in world climate which might lead to ice ages (Wexler 1952; Mitchell 1965). One of the more baffling problems in connection with the Ice Age is to account for the recurrence of the glacial climate. The great Ice Age (Pleistocene) began about 2 million years ago and consisted of four advances of the ice, separated by relatively long "interglacial" stages. The interglacial stages varied in length but are estimated to have been on the order of 200,000 years or more, and the climate in some cases was comparable to that of today, while in others it was somewhat warmer. From radiocarbon determinations it is known that the last maximum extent of the ice in North America and Europe was about 18,000 years ago. The shrinkage of the ice to its present position was marked by several conspicuous expansions, one of which occurred about 2,500–3,000 years ago and another only 200–300 years ago. It appears, then, that we could be in an interglacial stage of the Ice Age, a stage in which the shrunken remnant of the ice sheet is largely confined to the island of Greenland. At the maximum extent of the Ice Age, about 30 percent of the land surface of the earth was covered by ice, and 10 percent is still covered. The future holds out the prospect of one of two alternatives. Either there will be a slow restoration to a more genial climate, in which the remaining ice sheet will melt, or we are living in an interglacial stage to be followed by yet another advance of the ice, relentlessly destroying everything in its path. If the climate should get warmer and melt the existing ice sheets, the water returned to the oceans would raise the level of the sea about 100 feet. To the major cities of the world this would be a disaster as fatal to their existence as an advancing glacier. Either alternative is sufficiently alarming to justify a careful study of current climatic trends and the possible causes of ice ages.

There are so many factors which affect climate that no single cause can be singled out. Nevertheless, the fact that a single volcanic eruption (Krakatoa, 1883) can substantially reduce the amount of solar radiation reaching the earth for as long as three years clearly indicates that volcanic eruptions are an important factor in changes in world climate.

VOLCANOES AND SOILS It has long been known that in regions where there are periodic falls of volcanic ash the soil maintains its fertility. Although this is common knowledge, there are few studies which document this fact. It is beyond the scope of this discussion to go into the origin of soils, but it may be of interest to note that at least 16 elements are currently considered necessary for plant growth. Carbon, hydrogen, and oxygen are obtained from air and water. The remaining 13 elements are obtained largely from the soil. Nitrogen, phosphorous, potassium, calcium, magnesium, and sulphur are required in rather large quantities and are referred to as *major elements*. Nutrients required in much smaller amounts are called *trace elements* and include manganese, iron, boron, zinc, copper, molybdenum, and chlorine. The plant nutrients are contained in the minerals which make up igneous rocks, the primary parent of soil. However, most of the nutrients, as they exist in minerals, are insoluble or unavailable to plants. They become available through weathering, which converts these constituents to a form which plants can use. Thus, the richer the parent material of the soil is in plant food, the more fertile the soil. Intermediate-to-basic volcanic rocks (which contain the highest percentage of the essential plant nutrients) produce the very best soils; next in order are the more acid volcanic rocks; then limestones; then marls; and finally sandstone, which makes very poor soil. The more disintegrated the rock material is before being subjected to chemical weathering, the more quickly it is transformed into soil. Volcanic ash, composed of fine particles and containing varying amounts of chemically unstable glass, is especially susceptible to rapid weathering. Solid and compact rocks, such as lava flows, weather very slowly, and hundreds or even thousands of years may be required to produce a soil cover. Climate is an important factor in chemical weathering; so it is not possible to make broad generalizations. In addition to providing a parent material rich in plant food, volcanic ash serves as a mulch, enabling the soil to retain its moisture.

The soluble plant foods contained in the soil are subject to removal by leaching, and in time most soils become impoverished. This is particularly true in the tropics, where high temperatures and high rainfall combine to accelerate the process. Accordingly, most tropical soils are impoverished and of low fertility. In a study of the relation of climate and soil in Indonesia, E. C. J. Mohr (1945a) was able to assess the contribution of volcanic eruptions. In an eruption the surrounding region is buried under a blanket of volcanic ash and cinders which presents a picture of complete desolation. However, in a few years (Mohr suggests 25 or so) the new surface becomes covered with a mantle of vegetation. The new soil remains extraordinarily fertile for centuries, but in the end it will finally become impoverished as the soluble products are leached by tropical rains, unless further eruptions provide new layers of volcanic ash to rejuvenate the soil. Mohr comments that, before the 1883 eruption of Krakatoa, the Lampong District of southeastern Sumatra was a poor country with little development; after the eruption it showed remarkable signs of new life in regard to both native and European agriculture, and many new inhabitants moved into the region to share in the prosperity. In a continuation of his study Mohr (1945b) was able to show a direct relationship between the density of population in Indonesia and the location of active volcanoes. In an interesting study, based on the 1930 census, he found the population density of Java to be 316.11 per square kilometer, while the average for the whole region was only 31.89. Although various factors are obviously involved in population density, Mohr was able to show that basically it was determined by the fertility of the soil. The most fertile soils in Indonesia are in Java, which also has nearly all the currently active volcanoes. The contrast between the soils of Java and those of the other islands of Indonesia is quite marked, because in the absence of periodic eruptions of volcanic ash the soils are impoverished by leaching. Only by the application of generous amounts of fertilizers, as is the practice in many of the more developed countries, can the fertility of these soils be restored. Mohr concludes: "But these are dreams [i.e., the extensive use of fertilizers] that can only be realized in a far distant future—perhaps they are not realizable at all. For the present, then, and for many a long year to come, the fact remains that in the Netherlands Indies the population density is a function of the nature of the soil, and this is a function of the presence of active volcanoes" (1945b, p. 257).

The New Hebrides archipelago provided P. Quantin (1971) an opportunity to compare the soil just beginning to form on Ambrym and Tanna islands, which contain currently active volcanoes, with the soil on Aoba and Banks islands, where the last eruptions were about 1,000 years ago, and with the Shepherd Islands, where volcanic eruptions occurred several thousand years ago. The New Hebrides are in the tropics, more or less midway between the Solomon Islands and the Fiji Islands in the South Pacific. Quantin noted that, on Ambrym Island, 30 years was sufficient for a fertile soil to develop on a basalt flow covered with volcanic ash. The rapid and continuous release of basic elements (Ca, Mg, K, and Na) and available phosphorous accounts for the fertility of very young volcanic soils, although these elements, indeed very necessary for plant life, constitute but a very small fraction of the whole soil. Quantin also noted that in the southern part of Malekula Island and in the Shepherd Islands light falls of fine volcanic ash in recent years have restored the fertility of the soils despite the old age and high degree of weathering of the preceding soil. Both Mohr and Quantin, in their studies in Indonesia and the New Hebrides respectively, agree that 25–30 years is sufficient for soil to develop on a fresh volcanic ash deposit. However, R. L. Hay, in a 1960 study of soil formation on St. Vincent Island in the Lesser Antilles, found that the ash deposited in the 1902 eruption of La Soufrière Volcano (on St. Vincent Island) was not visibly altered. The 1902 eruption of La Soufrière Volcano was a violent Peléan type eruption in which some 1,600 people were killed (Ch. 7). Hay was investigating the development of soil on a 4,000-year-old ash deposit, and his comments on the 1902 ash were apparently only an incidental observation. He concluded that clayey soil formed from the 4,000-year-old ash deposit at an average rate of 1.5–2 feet per 1,000 years.

More studies are required, with a wider range of climatic conditions than those cited, in order to fully understand the development of soils from volcanic deposits.

IN CONCLUSION   Volcanoes are so widely considered to be agents of destruction that their contributions to the development of the earth are usually overlooked. Indeed, the word *volcano* itself is synonymous in everyday language with something explosive and violent. The destruction of property and the loss of life resulting from volcanic eruptions have been described in the preceding chapters and will not be repeated here. One needs only to recall the catastrophic explosions with accompanying bombs, cinders, ash, lava flows, *nuées ardentes*, lahars, tsunami, and so on to be reminded of the destructive effects of volcanoes. The useful aspects, or some of the important contributions of volcanoes to the environment, have also been described. However, since the beneficial aspects of volcanoes are less widely recognized than the destructive effects, it is appropriate to summarize some of the useful contributions.

1. Volcanoes have been a major contributor to the building of the continents as well as the ocean floor (Ch. 16).

2. With few exceptions, all the oceanic islands owe their existence directly or indirectly to volcanoes. The Hawaiian island chain is a good example (Ch. 10). Volcanoes are also adding new land to existing islands; for example, the eruption of Capelinhos on the island of Fayal in the Azores added an area of nearly a square mile (Ch. 13); the 1960 eruption of Kilauea added nearly half a square mile of land area to the island of Hawaii (Ch. 10); and the 1973 eruption of Helgafell on Heimaey in the Vestmann Islands off the coast of Iceland added half a square mile of land area to the island (Ch. 11).

3. Geothermal power resources are directly related, for the most part, to recent volcanic activity (Ch. 14).

4. The waters of the ocean and the gases of the atmosphere are

believed to have been derived from the cooling of magma and to have reached the surface through volcanoes and hot springs. Indeed, as was pointed out in Chapter 5, volcanoes, by providing water and the atmosphere, are responsible for the earth being a habitable planet!

5. Volcanoes have provided some of the most magnificent scenery and recreational areas not only in the United States but throughout the world. Many of the areas have been set aside as national parks, such as Crater Lake in Oregon, Lassen Peak in California, and Tongariro in New Zealand.

Although the beneficial aspects of volcanoes are substantial, the goal must be to reduce or at least to minimize the destructive effects. If volcanic eruptions could be predicted with accuracy, then the next step would be to control or minimize the effects of the eruption. The key to prediction of volcanic eruptions, as previously pointed out, is continuous observation of all the world's active volcanoes. Only with detailed observations over a long period of time can the pattern of activity be established, and knowledge of this pattern is essential to prediction of eruptions. In the meantime, the public should be made aware of the protective measures which may be taken to minimize the destructive effects of a volcanic eruption. Admittedly, the best advice is to evacuate the danger area immediately, but at times this is not feasible. Some of the protective measures have been described in previous chapters, and only brief reference will be made to them at this point.

Lava flows have been stopped or diverted by bombing (Ch. 5), by building dikes (Ch. 5), and by spraying the lava front with cold water (Ch. 11).

Mudflows are potentially more dangerous than lava flows. Lava flows, with few exceptions, do not move fast enough to entrap the inhabitants, but mudflows usually move so fast that it is difficult for the inhabitants in the path of one to escape. Further, mudflows are difficult to predict, since they may occur at the beginning of an eruption, any time during an eruption, and for weeks or months after the eruption has ended. The first loss of life in the 1902 eruption of Mount Pelée was due to a mudflow which buried a sugar mill three days before the main catastrophe (Ch. 7). By contrast, the mudflow which buried Herculaneum in the A.D. 79 eruption of Vesuvius occurred a day or two after the climax of the eruption, after most of the inhabitants had evacuated the city (Ch.8). The accumulation of a thick layer of ash on the slopes of a cone poses a threat of mudflows for weeks or even months after the eruption has ended. For many years the farmers cultivating land on the slopes of Vesuvius have built stone walls in an effort to prevent mudflows from entering their vineyards. As is the case with lava flows, the most successful tactic is to divert the mudflow by a wall rather than try to stop it with a dam.

Disastrous mudflows are also caused by the sudden discharge of the water of a crater lake, or by the sudden melting of snow, ice, or glaciers which frequently cap a volcanic cone. The following examples are typical of this type of activity.

Mount Ruapehu, New Zealand. Mount Ruapehu (9,175 ft.) is the highest peak in the Tongariro National Park, North Island, New Zealand (Fig. 75). It has, in addition to Whangaehu Glacier, permanent snow fields and is a favorite ski area of North Island. The summit of Ruapehu, as described by D. R. Gregg (1960), consists of an outer rim about one mile long and one-half mile wide, within which there is an inner volcanic cone with a central crater occupied by a lake. Permanent fields of snow and ice fill the depression between the inner cone and the outer rim on the south, west, and north, but on the east the outer slopes of the cone descend steeply and directly to Whangaehu Glacier. The lake in the crater of the inner cone, although surrounded for the most part by snow and ice fields, is usually warm. The lake water drains at the lowest point on the rim through a tunnel beneath the ice at the south-east end of the lake into the head of Whangaehu Valley. The following account of the Christmas Eve, 1953, disaster (also known as the Tangiwai disaster) and the events leading up to it is based on J. Healy (1965).

In March, 1945, a dome of black andesitic lava appeared near the center of the crater lake, and as it continued to grow the lake disappeared. By the end of August the dome had spread out on the old lake floor and almost filled the crater. Explosive eruptions of ash followed, and when they subsided at the end of the year the crater was 1,000 feet deep. The crater began to fill with water and by the summer of 1952–1953 the lake had reached its old level. However, the lava dome and debris from the explosive eruptions blocked the old outlet, and the lake level continued to rise until it reached a level approximately 26 feet higher than the old level, when it spilled over the debris to form a new outlet beneath the ice. Suddenly, about 8:00 P.M. on December 24, 1953, the barrier collapsed and the lake water swept down the Whangaehu Valley as a tremendous flood. The water, loaded with blocks of ice, trees, and boulders, reached the railway bridge at Tangiwai, destroying the bridge only minutes before the express train from Wellington to Aukland arrived. The train plunged into the raging torrent with the loss of 151 lives. The flood continued as a lahar down the Whangaehu River to its mouth. The lake level fell 26 feet to its old level, where it remains. Former floods from Crater Lake had occurred in 1861, 1887, 1895, and 1925, but all were smaller than the 1953 flood. However, such floods must have been common for the past several thousand years to have formed the plain of overlapping lahar deposits which surround Mount Ruapehu. The Crater Lake of Mount Ruapehu is now being closely watched in order to anticipate any future flood.

Mount St. Helens, Washington. Mount St. Helens is one of the Cascade Range volcanoes, and like other volcanoes in this range, is described in some detail in Chapter 19, pp. 544–559. In the catastrophic eruption of May 18, 1980, debris flow and mudflow (technically a type of lahar; see Glossary) were major products of the eruption. Two of the three river systems which head on the volcano were devastated by mudflows: the Toutle River of the north and northwest and tributaries of the Lewis River, Smith Creek, Muddy River, and Pine Creek on the south and southeast (see Fig. 106, p. 553). The main force of the eruption was to the northwest, so the Toutle River received the major part of the load, with a lesser amount moving down the tributaries of the Lewis River. The North and South forks of the Toutle River head on the slopes of Mount St. Helens and flow westerly for about 40 miles, where they join to form the Toutle River, which empties into the Cowlitz River, which flows south, emptying into the Columbia River downstream from Portland, Oregon.

The initial eruption of Mount St. Helens on May 18, 1980, was triggered when the huge bulge on the north face of the volcano gave way and crashed into the headwaters of the North Fork of the Toutle River, generating a debris flow which extended for about 12.5 miles downvalley. The mudflows* on the North Fork of the Toutle River originated in the water-saturated parts of the debris-avalanche deposit in the upper valley. It was made up of many smaller flows which took several hours to merge into one giant mudflow. In the process the mud became steaming hot from volcanic debris in the avalanche. The downvalley progress of the mudflow was interrupted by massive log jams that, when they broke, caused flood surges that were especially destructive. Due to the high density of the mudflow, which resembled fresh mortar, it carried on its surface a jumble of logs, fragments of bridges and houses, and other debris. One observer reported seeing a fully loaded logging truck being carried upright on the surface, submerged only to the lower tier of logs. The velocity of the mudflow varied greatly from place to place, depending on the channel, the gradient, and the consistency (amount of water) of the mudflow. The average peak velocity of the North Fork mudflow flow was about 4.8 miles per hour.

*This account is based largely on Foxworthy and Hill 1982, Lipman and Mullineaux 1981, and personal observations.

Only minutes after the initial eruption a mudflow, originating on the western slope of the cone, moved rapidly down the valley of the South Fork of the Toutle River. It was much smaller, less dense, and its average velocity three times that of the North Fork mudflow. The mudflows from the Toutle River continued down the Cowlitz River and into the Columbia River, having covered a path of more than 72 miles.

In the lower part of the Cowlitz River the mudflow resulted in channel filling of about 15 feet, reducing the river to only 10 percent of its former capacity, creating a serious flood hazard. The Cowlitz empties into the Columbia downstream from the port area of Portland-Vancouver. For about 2 miles downstream the channel filling reduced the depth from 40 feet to only 15 feet, stranding some 20 ships in port and an equal number seeking to enter the port. Several weeks were required to dredge a channel to open the port.

Mudflows also moved rapidly down Smith Creek, Muddy River, and Pine Creek, which drain the south and southeastern side of Mount St. Helens. The mudflows, laden with logs and other debris, swept away bridges in their path and entered the upper (eastern) end of Swift Reservoir about 30 minutes after the initial eruption. The mudflows poured about 11,000 acre-feet of mud and debris into Swift Reservoir causing an overall rise of 2.6 feet in the water level. However, Swift Reservoir, which had been drawn down about 30 feet in anticipation of such floods, held the added volume and a possible disastrous flood in the downstream section of the Lewis River was avoided. There are two reservoirs for power generation on the Lewis River, downstream from Swift Reservoir, and should a mudflow cause the water of Swift Reservoir to overtop or destroy the dam, the downstream reservoirs would doubtless be destroyed, resulting in a flood of enormous magnitude.

IN CONCLUSION

The loss of life and the destruction of property in volcanic eruptions are of such a magnitude that an all-out effort must be made to perfect techniques for predicting eruptions in order to warn the inhabitants of the impending danger. In practically all cases there are warning signals of an impending eruption, which too often are not heeded or not recognized. To receive these signals, permanent installations of seismographs, tilt meters, temperature gauges, and other instruments are needed in areas subject to dangerous eruptions. Portable equipment must also be available to extend the coverage to isolated areas. Our technology is able to provide much better protection from volcanic eruptions than is now available, except in the few areas where volcanological observatories are located.

Chapter 19

Volcanoes of the Cascade Range, Northwest United States

"Vancouver, Vancouver, this is it!"—DAVID JOHNSTON
(8:32 A.M., May 18, 1980)

GEOLOGIC SETTING

The Cascade Range, composed of volcanic products and surmounted by a chain of huge strato-volcanoes, extends from northern California through Oregon and Washington to British Columbia. It consists of two physiographic units: the Western Cascade Range and the High Cascades. The Western Cascade Range, the older of the two, consists of lava flows with intercalated pyroclastic rocks, which are for the most part Miocene in age. The rocks are mostly in the andesite to dacite range. Andesite with a silica content of around 56 percent is the most abundant, but rocks containing up to 70 percent silica are moderately abundant (Peck et al. 1964, p. 1).

In general the oldest subaerial volcanoes that retain in any degree their original constructional form are less than 10 million years old. The lavas of the Western Cascade range are from 10 to 25 million years old and deeply dissected by erosion; any vestiges of former volcanic cones have long since been destroyed by erosion. However, many old volcanic centers can be recognized by their feeding channels that have been exposed by erosion or from the structural relationship of the lavas and tuffs to the surrounding rocks. Unquestionably, many separate volcanoes were required to produce the huge volume of volcanic products which make up the Western Cascade Range. If we take the approximate volume of pre-Pliocene lavas of the entire Cascade Range and divide by the approximate volume of later individual cones of the range, some 1,500–2,000 separate volcanoes are required to build the Western Cascades (Macdonald 1972, p. 353).

Following an erosional interval which extended from Late Miocene to Early Pliocene, volcanic activity resumed in the Early Pliocene. A new series of volcanic rocks, the High Cascades, was erupted to form a ridge overlapping and parallel to the Western Cascades but slightly to the east. The early High Cascade lavas were very fluid basalts and basaltic andesites that erupted more or less quietly from fissures, building a broad ridge of overlapping, low shield volcanoes and lava flows. In time some of the lavas became more silicic and the explosive activity increased, resulting in big composite cones of interbedded lava flows and pyroclastic material. These cones, with associated domes and flows of dacite, form the nearly undissected crest of the High Cascade Range today. Some of the most magnificent and better-known volcanoes are Lassen Peak and Mount Shasta, California; Crater Lake, Mount Jefferson, and Mount Hood, Oregon; Mount St. Helens, Mount Adams, Mount Rainer—the highest of the Cascade volcanoes, with an elevation of 14,410 feet—and Mount Baker, Washington (see Fig. 103). Many of the peaks are permanently snow capped and support numerous active glaciers. The Cascades offer today's visitors a spectacularly scenic recreational area, as is attested by the fact that four national parks are within the boundaries of the range. Mount Rainier National Park was established in 1899; Crater Lake National Park in 1902; Lassen Volcanic National Park in 1916; and in 1968 one of the last true wilderness areas in the United States, north of Mount Rainier, was set aside as the North Cascades National Park. Unlike the high peaks in the Rocky Mountains which rise from a high upland, 5,000 feet or more above sea level, to elevations of more than 14,000 feet, Mount Rainier rises abruptly above the Puget Sound lowland and has a visual height nearly equal to its actual vertical height of 14,410 feet. To a slightly lesser degree the same is true of many of the High Cascade volcanoes. As a result, they completely dominate the landscape for 50–100 miles in all directions.

The successive development of belts of folding and volcanism in western North America has commonly been from the continental side toward the ocean, resulting in a seaward growth of the continent. Thus the Rockies were followed by the younger Sierra Nevadas and Coast Ranges. In the Cascades the order is reversed, with the High Cascades (the younger range) to the east of the older western Cascades.

COMPOSITION OF CASCADE LAVAS

The rocks of the Western Cascades consist of lava flows of basaltic, andesitic, and dacitic composition, with interbedded layers of pyroclastic rocks, some of which are rhyolitic. In many cases the rocks have a greenish color resulting from the alteration of the ferromagnesium minerals to chlorite and related minerals. The High Cascade rocks range from basalt to rhyolite with pyroxene andesite predominating (Macdonald and Gay 1969, p. 109).

Detailed studies indicate that, on the basis of lava composition, the volcanoes of the High Cascades can be divided into two gen-

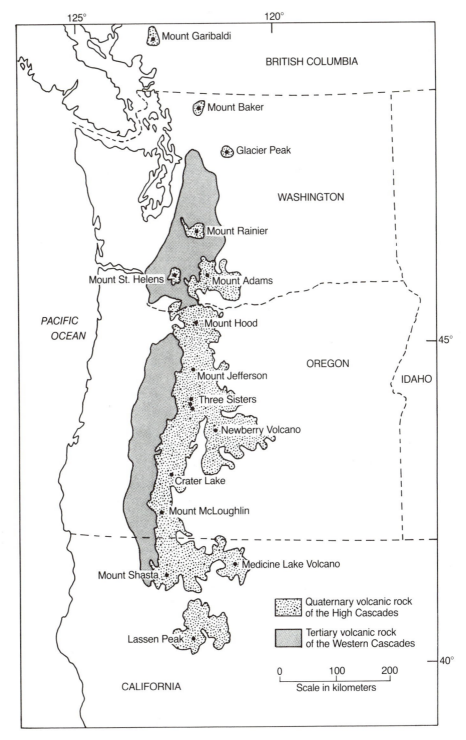

Figure 103. Index map of the Western Cascades and High Cascades, showing the location of major volcanoes of the High Cascade Range.

eral types (McBirney 1968, p. 101). In the first type the lavas form a coherent series of fairly uniform composition or, at most, a limited range of continuous variation. In the second type the rocks are more varied and become increasingly divergent with time. Most of the volcanoes of the Central High Cascades—Baker, Rainier, Hood, and Jefferson—belong to the *coherent* type. The lavas from these volcanoes are andesites or andesitic basalt of fairly uniform composition; rhyolites are usually not present and basalt, if present at all, grades into andesite.

Lavas of the second, or *divergent*, type are found at the northern end of the High Cascade Range and to the south of Mount Jefferson at the southern end of the range. In these volcanoes the most abundant rock types are siliceous andesites or dacites. These were followed, in time, by basalts of varied composition and small volumes of rhyolite obsidian or pumice, both the products of flank eruptions. While it seems logical to look for a relationship of such features to the composition of rock types which may represent the parent magma, A. R. McBirney (1968, p. 103) was reluctant to draw definite conclusions pending further study. Measurements of magnetic polarity suggest that the bulk of the lava of the High Cascades appears to be normally polarized and can thus be presumed to be younger than the last magnetic reversal, which occurred about 770,000 years ago.

THE JUAN DE FUCA
PLATE AND CASCADE
VOLCANISM

The role of plate tectonics in volcanism has been discussed in some detail in Chapter 16 and will not be repeated here. The Juan de Fuca plate is not indicated in Figure 96 (p. 494), but, like the Cocos and Nazca plates, which lie at the margin of the Pacific plate, off the coast of Central America and South America respectively, the Juan de Fuca plate is at the margin of the Pacific plate off the coast of California, Oregon, Washington, and Vancouver Island (Fig. 104).

The Pacific plate and the American plate are moving past each other, with the San Andreas fault system in California and the Queen Charlotte fault system off western Canada in the zone of contact. The continuous level of high seismicity along these strike-slip faults attests to the active movement of the plates. The recent geologic record, offshore and onshore, indicates a right-lateral movement at an average rate of 5–6 centimeters per year (Riddihough 1978, p. 837). The movement of the Juan de Fuca plate, relative to the American plate, depends on the balance between the movement of the Pacific-American plates and the spreading at the Juan de Fuca ridge. Magnetic anomalies at the Juan de Fuca ridge indicate a spreading rate of 5.8 centimeters per year (half-rate, 2.9 centimeters per year), parallel to the southeast-trending Blanco Fracture

Figure 104. Relation between the North American plate and the Juan de Fuca plate, giving rise to the volcanoes of the Cascade Range. After Riddihough (1978); volcanic segments (dashed lines) after Hughes, Stoiber, and Carr (1980); cross-section (not to scale) after Foxworthy and Hill (1982). The Juan de Fuca plate is slowly thrusting under the North American plate, resulting in the formation of magma. It also causes a zone of weakness in the American plate through which magma rises to feed the Cascade volcanoes.

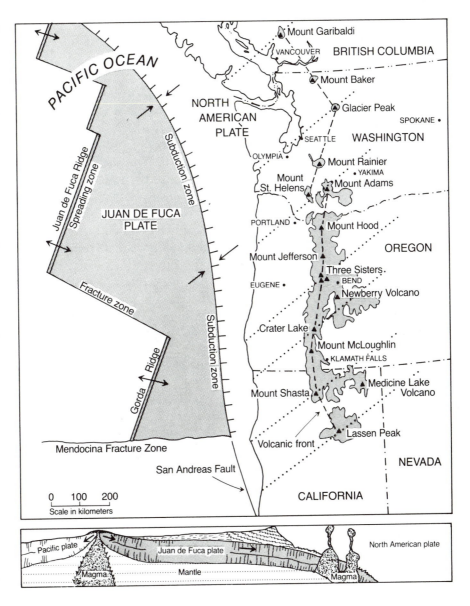

Zone. The resulting motion of the Juan de Fuca plate with the American plate is a compression in a north-northeast direction of 2.5 centimeters per year (Atwater 1970, pp. 3531–3532). If other rates of movement are assumed for the Pacific and American plates, the direction and amount of movement of the Juan de Fuca plate will vary, but all result in a convergence of the Juan de Fuca plate and the American plate.

The plate tectonic concept holds that new volcanic crust is formed at divergent plate boundaries, i.e., oceanic ridges, where plates are moving apart; crust is consumed at convergent boundaries where one plate slides beneath another along an inclined subduction zone; and crust is neither created nor consumed where plates slide horizontally past each other. Most of the world's active volcanoes are associated with plate convergence or divergence, or rifting within a plate. The andesitic volcanism which occurs in the island arcs and the continental margins of the Pacific Ocean, the "fire girdle of the Pacific," is the result of the convergence of the Pacific plate, at subduction zones, with the bordering continental plates. The frequency of volcanic activity in a given area seems to be dependent, in part, on the rate at which the thrusting plates plunge under the bordering plate at the subduction zone. In Japan and Indonesia, where the subduction rate is 6–7 centimeters per year, there is usually at least one volcanic eruption per year. In the Cascades, with a subduction rate of 2–3 centimeters per year, the eruptions are more widely spaced (Decker and Decker 1981, p. 68).

The trace of the subduction zone, defined by intermediate to deep seismic activity and known as the Benioff zone, is commonly the site of a deep sea trench (see pp. 457–459 for additional details). There is no deep-sea trench offshore from the Cascade Range, and the maximum depth of earthquakes is near 70 kilometers, barely exceeding the 60-kilometer depth for normal shocks. The absence of the trench may be due to filling by rapid sedimentation over the past million years. With the adjacent land area just emerging from the last glaciation, rapid sedimentation might be expected. The damming effect of the Juan de Fuca ridge, only a few hundred kilometers offshore, may also have contributed to the rapid accumulation of sediments (Riddinhough 1978, p. 838).

The absence of seismic activity deeper than 70 kilometers does not preclude the continuation of the subduction process according to Robin P. Riddihough (1978, p. 839). He points out that deep earthquakes occur where the downgoing material remains brittle, and the extent of the brittleness depends on the rate at which the slab heats up. He postulates that the Juan de Fuca plate, being both young and thin (probably no more than 20 kilometers thick) and subducting slowly, would probably become plastic at a shallower depth. The evidence seems to support the association of the Cascade volcanoes with the subduction zone of the Juan de Fuca plate, and on the basis of the potash content of the lavas (see p. 497), the eastward-dipping slab is present at depths of 100–150 kilometers beneath the Cascade Range.

The decline of Cascade volcanism, which seems to have been in progress for the past thousands of years, is compatible with the concept that the underthrusting plate is getting smaller and is partially coupled to the American plate (Christiansen and Lipman 1972, p. 276).

SEGMENTATION OF THE CASCADE VOLCANIC BELT

The volcanoes of the High Cascades have long been considered a simple linear chain, but to John M. Hughes, R. E. Stoiber, and Michael J. Carr (1980), the alignment of the volcanoes suggests a segmented convergent plate boundary. They propose a pattern with six linear segments that make up the volcanic front, with transverse boundaries parallel to the direction of plate convergence, which is considered to be north-northeast (Atwater 1970, p. 3521).

The major Cascade volcanoes are found in three locations: (1) along the volcanic front within a segment, (2) along the volcanic front at segment boundaries, and (3) near segment boundaries behind the volcanic front (Fig. 104). Earlier in this chapter, the "coherent" and the "divergent" types of volcanoes, proposed by McBirney (1968), were discussed. The coherent volcanoes (Mounts Baker, Rainier, Hood, Jefferson, and McLoughlin), are located within segments and on the volcanic front (group 1). The divergent volcanoes lie at or near segment boundaries and show a greater variety of volcanic activity. They can be divided between group 2—those which are on the volcanic front, Mount Garibaldi, Glacier Peak, Mount St. Helens, Three Sisters, Crater Lake, Mount Shasta, and Lassen Peak—and group 3—those that lie to the east of the volcanic front, Medicine Lake and Newberry. Although the type of activity and the composition of the eruptive products seem to be related to the position of a volcano on a segment, no adequate explanation has been developed.

ERUPTIONS OF CASCADE VOLCANOES

The northwestern part of the United States was not settled until around 1800, and there have been few eruptions of Cascade volcanoes since that time. The lack of records of earlier eruptions resulted in disregard of the possibility of eruptions and it was not generally realized that these volcanoes were only dormant, not extinct. However, with the eruption of Mount St. Helens in 1980 this situation quickly changed.

Detailed studies by the U.S. Geological Survey of the hazards from eruptions of Cascade volcanoes have been underway for a number of years, and reports on individual volcanoes are issued from time to time. These studies led to the identification of six potentially dangerous volcanoes in the Cascade Range: Mount Baker, Mount Rainier, Mount St. Helens, Mount Hood, Mount Shasta, and Lassen Peak. It should be noted that these six, plus Cinder Cone, which is included with Lassen Peak in the following pages, are listed as the active volcanoes of the Cascade Range in the *Catalogue of active volcanoes of the world* (Combs 1960). Of the potentially dangerous volcanoes in the Cascade Range, Mount St. Helens was considered the one most likely to erupt, and a report (Crandell and Mullineaux 1978) on the potential hazards of an eruption was issued in 1978. The eruption of Lassen Peak in 1914–1917 was, prior to the eruption of Mount St. Helens, the only well-documented historic eruption in the contiguous 48 states. Of the fifteen major Cascade volcanoes shown in Figures 103 and 104, only six do not exhibit some type of thermal activity. They are Mount Garibaldi, Mount Jefferson, Three Sisters, Crater Lake, Mount McLoughlin, and Medicine Lake (Foxworthy and Hill 1982, pp. 4–7; Coombs 1960). The others exhibit weak to strong fumarolic activity, usually in the summit crater. The six considered most likely to erupt are described in the following pages. Crater Lake, one of the best known of the Cascade volcanoes, is described on pages 82–85.

Mount Baker

Mount Baker is an andesitic strato-volcano located about 15 miles south of the Canadian border in the High Cascade Range in Washington. It has an elevation of 10,778 feet and rises about 5,000 feet above the general level of the High Cascade Range. It is a relatively smooth cone, and while one-fourth of its 80-square-mile area is covered by glaciers, the destruction by erosion can be measured in hundreds of feet, rather than thousands, as at Mount Rainier (Coombs 1939, p. 1499). The summit of Mount Baker consists of two peaks, separated by Sherman Crater. A stream of ice from the higher northern peak partly fills Sherman Crater, 1,150 feet lower and about one-half mile south of the summit. The rim of Sherman Crater is breached on the east by a notch nearly 500 feet deep at the head of Boulder Glacier and on the southwest by another notch about 300 feet deep at the head of Deming Glacier. Among the unusual features are the ice caves (sometimes referred to as steam caves) in Sherman Crater. They are formed by heat from the crater floor which has melted a series of passageways and chambers between the crater floor and the overlying ice that partially fills the crater. Although the size and extent of the caves alter with changes in the thermal activity, when explored in 1974 they had a total length of approximately three-quarters of a mile (Harris 1976, p. 239).

The present cone of Mount Baker was formed prior to the last major glaciation, which began in this area about 25,000 years ago, but it may be considerably older (Hyde and Crandel 1978, p. 1). An earlier eruptive center, known as Black Buttes, lies about 2 miles west of the main peak. The Buttes have been deeply eroded and now stand as irregular crags and cliffs, rising some 3,000 feet above the general level of their base. Radiometric dates from two old flows, thought to be from Black Buttes, gave an age of about 400,000 years (Easterbrook and Rahn 1970, p. 20).

Mount Baker rests on the eroded surface of sedimentary and metamorphic rocks of Paleozoic to Early Tertiary ages (Coombs 1939, p. 1496). This is in contrast to the Tertiary age of the rocks on which Mount Rainier developed. Like that at Mount Rainier, the surface on which Mount Baker formed has been carved into a series of deep canyons and intervening ridges, and the early lava flows were mainly intracanyon flows, some of which now stand out as ridges as a result of the erosion of the enclosing canyon walls.

The lavas from Mount Baker are porphyritic, medium to dark grey andesites, almost identical to those found at Mount Rainier. Pyroclastics constitute probably less than 5 percent of the total volume of Mount Baker, an amount comparable to that at Mount Rainier, but markedly different from that of the volcanoes to the south, which contain abundant pyroclastic material (Coombs 1939, p. 1499). Further, at Mount Baker there is little variation in composition from the oldest to the youngest lavas.

In a study of postglacial volcanic deposits at Mount Baker, Jack H. Hyde and Dwight R. Crandell (1978) were able to reconstruct (to the extent that recognizable deposits were left) the eruptive history of Mount Baker for the past 10,000 years. Their results are summarized in a report on the volcanic hazards of the Cascade Range (Crandell, Mullineaux, and Miller 1979), and the following account is based on that summary. The first known eruption in postglacial time was about 10,300 years ago when a small volume of black lithic ash was deposited on and beyond the east and northeast flanks of the cone. This was followed by a major eruptive period between 10,000 and 8,000 years ago, when lava flows, hot pyroclastic flows, and mudflows from Sherman Crater formed a thick valley fill on the east side of the cone. A little later, pumice erupted from a vent near the south base of the cone, and subsequently andesitic lava issued from this same vent and flowed for

more than 7 miles downvalley to the east. During the past 10,000 years large avalanches of hydrothermally altered rock debris occurred at least eight times, with mudflows extending for up to 15 miles down the valleys which drain the slopes of the cone.

Historic eruptions. The first recorded eruption of Mount Baker since the settlement of the Oregon Territory occurred in 1843 (Gibbs 1874, pp. 357–358). George Gibbs reported that officials of the Hudson Bay Company, and also the Indians, confirmed that the eruption of 1843 was the first one known, and that it broke out simultaneously with Mount St. Helens and covered the whole country with ashes. However, Hyde and Crandell (1978, p. 3), in a study of postglacial volcanic deposits at Mount Baker, were unable to identify any deposits that could be attributed to historic eruptions. This does not preclude the possibility that some ash was erupted but in amounts insufficient to leave a recognizable deposit. George Davidson (1885), who reported an eruption in 1854, was perhaps the first scientist to report an eruption based on personal observations. He also recognized Sherman Crater as the site of the eruption. H. A. Coombs (1960) in the account of Mount Baker in the *Catalogue of active volcanoes of the world*, accepts 1843, 1854, 1859, and 1870 as reasonably well confirmed dates of eruptions. The historic eruptions of Mount Baker are reviewed in considerable detail by Stephen L. Harris (1976, p. 240–249). The eruptions consisted of ash clouds rising from the crater to heights of a few hundred feet up to 2,000 feet above the crater. In the eruption of 1859, the clouds over the crater were brilliantly illuminated at night (Coombs 1960, p. 3).

Thermal activity at Sherman Crater. Fumarolic activity at Sherman Crater has been present since the earliest observations and changed very little over the years until March 1975, when there was a marked increase in activity. Prior to the March 1975 event, there were two major clusters of steam vents at Sherman Crater, one on the southwest side and the other on the east side. Many of the steam vents issued with a hissing noise, sending up impressive columns of steam. Temperatures were about 90°C., which is the boiling point of water at that altitude. Another, less well known fumarole area, known as the Dorr Fumarole Field, is located midway up the north side of the cone (Malone and Frank 1975, p. 680). The marked increase in fumarolic activity at Sherman Crater in March 1975 caused concern that an eruption might be imminent. As a result, a close monitoring of the volcano was instituted, using geophysical and geochemical techniques. Not only did new fumarole areas develop, but most of the existing areas enlarged. The results of the monitoring are reported by David Frank, Mark F. Meier, and Donald A. Swanson (1977) and by Stephen D. Malone and Frank (1975).

Even if the volcano did not erupt, it was felt that the increased thermal activity might trigger avalanches from the rim of Sherman Crater, where large areas of rocks weakened by hydrothermal alteration are present. Such an avalanche would probably descend Boulder Creek valley, and, if it reached Baker Lake, a huge water wave might be generated which could overtop the dam and cause disastrous floods downstream. Recognizing the potential hazards, scientists of the U.S. Geological Survey briefed the governmental agencies concerned. On June 25, 1975, the Baker Lake area was closed to public access and the Baker Lake reservoir level was lowered about 30 feet, in order to accommodate a possible debris flow. Although the high level of thermal activity continued, there were no other indications of an inpending eruption and on April 16, 1976, the Baker Lake area was opened to the public. For a full discussion of the hazards from an eruption and the details of the closing and later opening of the Baker Lake area see Frank, Meier, and Swanson (1977, pp. 30–43).

Mount Rainier

Mount Rainier is a large andesitic strato-volcano in the central part of the High Cascades in the state of Washington. With an elevation of 14,410 feet, it is the highest peak in the range. It rises 7,000–8,000 feet above the surrounding area, dominating the landscape for many miles in all directions. It supports the largest single glacial system in the contiguous 48 states, with 20 glaciers radiating from its summit. The Emmons Glacier on the east side of Mount Rainier, with a length of about 5 miles, is the largest in the United States, with the exception of Alaska.

The composite cone of Mount Rainier consists mainly of andesitic lava flows but also contains breccias, mudflows, and ash. The volcano developed on a mountainous landscape carved into rocks of the Tatoosh pluton (Late Miocene–Early Pliocene) and the Stevens Ridge Formation (Middle Oligocene–Early Miocene). In the initial stage of activity, lava flows filled the canyons, some of which were at least 2,000 feet deep. The original walls of these canyons have long since been removed by erosion, leaving the intracanyon flows standing as ridges. The date when volcanic activity began is not known, but based on the amount of erosion since the first intracanyon flows, an early Pleistocene age is indicated (Fiske, Hopson, and Waters 1963, p. 67).

In the early stage of its development, the activity at Mount Rainier was in the form of large lava flows, which poured out in rapid succession, filling the adjacent canyons. This activity was relatively non-explosive, since very little pyroclastic material is associated with the canyon-filling flows. The main cone of Mount Rainier rises above the intracanyon lava flows which form its base. It consists mainly of thin lava flows erupted from a central vent and breccias formed by violent steam explosions where the lava became mixed with melt water on slopes covered by snow and ice. Only minor amounts of pumice and ash are present, and throughout the history of Mount Rainier, pyroclastic eruptions have been greatly subordinate to the outpouring of lava.

Mount Rainier reached its maximum height of 15,000–15,500 feet before the end of the last Pleistocene glaciation. Earlier workers surmised that a catastrophic eruption had destroyed the top of the cone, leaving a huge crater at the 14,000-foot level. More recently, R. S. Fiske, C. A. Hopson, and A. C. Waters (1963, p. 79) suggested that the summit may have been destroyed by engulfment (caldera development) or by the rapid erosion of an extensive solfatarized area at the summit. Extensive outpourings of olivine andesitic lava from two satellite vents (Echo Rock and Observation Rock) may have contributed to the collapse of the summit, although no definite time relationship has been established. Crandell (1969,

MOUNT RAINIER   LITTLE TAHOMA PEAK

INGRAHAM GLACIER

COWLITZ GLACIER

Lateral moraine

p. 40) supports the view that one or more huge avalanches, resulting from volcanic explosions, removed the former top of the volcano. He reasons that the topmost part of Mount Rainier consisted of rocks weakened by hot volcanic fumes (solfataric action) and that the resulting clay and rock provided the material for the Osceola Mudflow (described below).

Mount Rainier has been deeply eroded, and none of the original constructional surface remains, other than the summit cone which was formed after most of the dissection had been accomplished. Little Tahoma Peak, on the east slope, appears to be a secondary cone. Instead, it is a remnant of the east slope of Mount Rainier which has been isolated by glacial erosion. Even the top of Tahoma Peak may not represent the full extent of the former surface of Mount Rainier. By restoring Mount Rainier's former constructional surface, based on profiles drawn to conform to the original slope of its lavas, Fiske, Hopson, and Waters (1963, p. 86) calculated that at least one-half of the original volume of the cone had been destroyed by erosion. Glacial erosion was largely responsible for the destruction of the cone, but streams, avalanches, rockfalls, and mudflows also made important contributions.

The lavas erupted by Mount Rainier have been of remarkably uniform composition throughout its history. They are pyroxene andesites with conspicuous phenocrysts of plagioclase feldspar and smaller pheoncrysts of pyroxene. The olivine andesite erupted from Echo Rock and Observation Rock differs from the typical andesite by the presence of large phenocrysts of olivine.

Recent activity. Although volcanic activity at Mount Rainier appears to have declined greatly since the Late Pleistocene, repeated eruptions have occurred in the past 10,000 years. Mudflows have exceeded all other products in both frequency and volume. The two most active periods in Mount Rainier's recent eruptive history were between 6,500 and 4,500 years ago and between 2,500 and 2,000 years ago (Crandell, Mullineaux, and Miller 1979, p. 205). During the earlier period several eruptions blanketed the immediate area with pumice and ash. Few of the ash falls were more than a foot thick, and most were only a few inches. During this period tremendous avalanches of altered rock from the volcano produced numerous mudflows. The largest was the Osceola Mudflow, about 5,000 years ago. It swept down the White River Valley for a distance of 45 miles and then spread out on the Puget Sound lowlands covering an area of more than 100 square miles to a depth of up to 70 feet. This enormous mudflow has a volume of about half a cubic mile. Since there is no chasm on the side of the volcano large enough to provide a source of the mudflow, Crandell (1969, p. 40) reasons that it must have come from the summit, although other views as to the source of the material have been advocated (Fiske, Hopson, and Waters 1963, p. 86). The summit cone, formed on the eastern rim of the old summit depression, rises nearly 1,000 feet above the rim of the old summit and is a mile in diameter at its base. It is composed of blocky, black, glassy lava with two small craters at the top. Its smooth slope, unscarred by glacial erosion, shows clearly that it was formed after the last Pleistocene glaciation. Crandell, Donal R. Mullineaux, and C. Dan Miller (1979, p. 205) state that the cone was formed in the depression left by the avalanche which produced the Osceola Mudflow.

The youngest large mudflow from Mount Rainier, known as the Electron Mudflow, occurred about 500 years ago. It extended for about 30 miles down the valley of the Puyallup River and, like the Osceola Mudflow, spread out on the Puget Sound lowland. Its volume was less than one-tenth that of the Osceola Mudflow. Mudflows such as these would cause untold damage if they were to occur today (see Fig. 105).

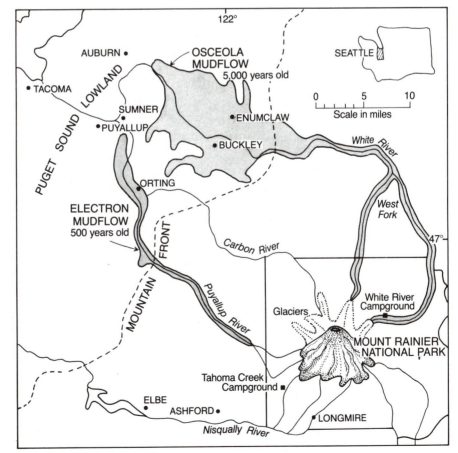

Figure 105. The Osceola Mudflow, about 5,000 years old, and the Electron Mudflow, about 500 years old, covered areas that are now the sites of a number of towns. After Crandell and Mullineaux (1967, p. 2).

Historic eruptions. It should be recalled that "historic" time in the Pacific northwest goes back only about 150 years, and prior to the Civil war the area that is now western Washington was largely unsettled. The earliest "historic" eruption supposedly occurred about 1820, and, despite the scanty population, no less than sixteen eruptions were reported by casual observers between 1820 and 1894. It should be noted, however, that rock falls and avalanches, which are common on Mount Rainier, would send up clouds of dust, which at a distance would appear to be an eruption. Harris (1976, pp. 210–214) reviews many of these reported eruptions. The only field evidence of an explosive eruption of Mount Rainier in historic time is from scattered deposits of pumice which have been dated from their relation to young glacial end moraines. The age of the end moraines has been established on the basis of tree ring counts which indicate that the pumice was erupted between 1820 and 1854 (Crandell 1969, p. 22).

Recent rockfalls and mudflows indicate that thermal activity at Mount Rainier may be increasing. One of the largest avalanches in historic time occurred on December 14, 1963, when approximately 14 million cubic yards of debris from the north face of Little Tahoma Peak fell to the surface of the Emmons Glacier, 1,700 feet below, and cascaded downvalley for 4 miles from its source (Pl. 73). The possibility that this may have been triggered by a steam explosion cannot be ruled out. In August 1967, a mudflow covered the Tahoma Creek Campground in Mount Rainier National Park, and studies showed that the mudflow resulted from melting of the Tahoma Glacier by increased thermal activity. Fortunately, the campground had been closed to the public the day before the mudflow, due to the high fire risk. During the summer of 1969, melting of the Emmons Glacier, between the 10,000- and 13,000-foot levels, resulted in openings wide enough to reveal the bare rock beneath the glacier (Harris 1976, p. 220). Infrared aerial surveys, which are made periodically, show that there are several "hot spots" in the summit crater area, and the volcano is being closely monitored. To acquaint the public with the consequences of an eruption, a special report on the volcanic hazards at Mount Rainier was issued by the U.S. Geological Survey (Crandell and Mullineaux 1967).

Mount St. Helens

Mount St. Helens is the youngest, and one of the smallest and most varied in composition of eruptive products of the major Cascade volcanoes. It is located in southern Washington (Fig. 103), about 70 kilometers northeast of the city of Portland, Oregon. Prior

Plate 73. Mount Rainier from the east. The avalanche-debris flow, which originated at Little Tahoma Peak in December 1963, covered portions of Emmons Glacier, and continued down the White River valley. The maximum distance of movement of the avalanche was a little over 4 miles. U.S. Geological Survey photo by Austin Post.

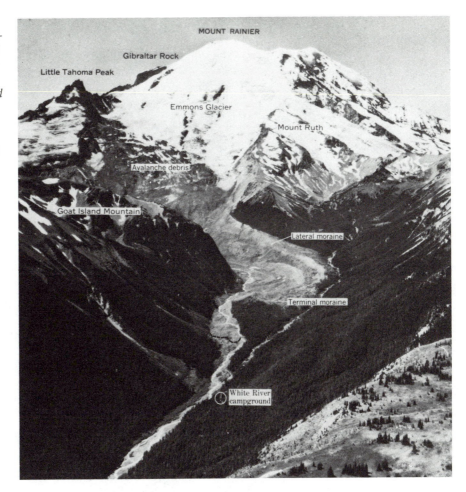

to the 1980 eruption its height above sea level was 9,677 feet. As seen from a distance it was a beautiful, symmetrical cone rising about 5,000 feet above a base 4 miles in diameter. The symmetrical shape of the cone led some to refer to it as the "Fujiyama of America" (Harris 1976, p. 167). Unlike most of the other major Cascade volcanoes, this cone was postglacial in age and had not been subjected to destructive glacial erosion.

The cone consisted of lava flows of olivine basalt and pyroxene andesite surrounding a summit plug of dacite, believed to have been emplaced only 350–400 years ago (Crandell, Mullineaux, and Miller 1979, p. 207). Deposits at the base and adjacent to the volcano include pyroclastic flows, lahars, and alluvium interbedded with tephra and glacial deposits related to an earlier eruption center. The first activity at that center occurred between 40,000 and

Plate 74. A small ash erup-
tion from the dome in the
crater of Mount St. Helens.
Photo from Harry's Ridge,
May 19, 1982. Courtesy
U.S. Geological Survey,
David A. Johnston Cascades
Volcano Observatory, Van-
couver, Washington. For a
close-up view of the lava
dome see Plate 78.

50,000 years ago, prior to the last major glacial epoch. The pre-1980 cone largely concealed the eroded remnants of the earlier volcanic center. The lavas from the earlier cone were largely hornblende hypersthene dacite and andesite; then about 2,500 years ago the composition of the lava changed rather abruptly to olivine basalt, dacite, and pyroxene andesite, which made up the greater part of the pre-1980 cone (Hyde 1975, p. B-1).

Early eruptive history. The first stratigraphic evidence of volcanic activity at Mount St. Helens consists of pyroclastic flows of dacitic composition overlying deeply weathered glacial drift from the next-to-the-last alpine glaciation of the Cascade Range. These deposits, formed about 40,000 years ago, are the oldest of nine eruptive periods, separated by long dormant intervals, recognized at Mount St. Helens (Crandell and Mullineaux, in Lipman and Mullineaux, eds. 1981, p. 8). In the volcano's early history and up to about 2,500 years ago, repeated eruptions produced dacitic domes, accompanied by pyroclastic flows, tephra, and lahars of similiar composition. The lava flows, with few exceptions, are limited to the past 2,500 years. During the past 4,500 years Mount St. Helens has been more active and more explosive than any other volcano in the Cascade Range (Crandell, Mullineaux, and Rubin 1975, p. 438). A study of the eruptive behavior of Mount St. Helens during the last 1,500 years (Hoblitt, Crandell, and Mullineaux 1980, p. 556) recognized three eruptive periods (the last three of the nine mentioned earlier), which were identified on the basis of the radiocarbon age dates of the eruptive products. A condensed version of the results is presented in Table 11.

Historic eruptions. It may be well to recall that before 1800 very little was known of the Pacific Northwest. Captain George Vancouver, a British navigator and explorer, in search of the "Northwest Passage," saw Mount St. Helens from his ship at the mouth of the Columbia River in 1792 and named it for the British ambassador in Spain, Baron St. Helens (Foxworthy and Hill 1982, p. 11). The first permanent settlement in the Oregon region, a fur-trading post, was established in 1811 (*Columbia Encyclopedia*, 1963, p. 1561). The first influx of settlers over the Oregon Trail was in 1843.

Early explorers recorded Indian accounts of eruptions before the coming of the whites. All accounts agree that there was a large eruption about 1800 which spread ash and pumice over a wide area. This marks the beginning of the Goat Rock period in Table 11. The historic eruptions are described in detail by Harris (1976, pp. 173–182), and only a few of the salient points are included here. An American missionary at Fort Vancouver, Samuel Parker, includes an account of an 1831 eruption in his *Journal*, but he did not witness it himself. The first eyewitness to publish an account of

TABLE 11. *Eruptive sequence at Mount St. Helens during the last 1,500 years*

Eruptive Period	Date	Eruptive Products
1980 eruption	1980–?	Tephra, pyroclastic flows, mudflows, avalanche-debris flow; dacite dome forming in crater
Dormant interval: 123 years		
Goat Rock period	1800–1857	Dacite pumice and lithic tephra, andesite lava flows; dacite dome (Goat Rock)
Dormant interval: about 170 years		
Kalama period	ca. 1530–1630	Dacite and andesite tephra and pyroclastic flows, lahars; dacite dome at summit
Dormant interval: about 700 years		
Sugar Bowl period	ca. 850	Dacite dome (Sugar Bowl), minor pyroclastic flows and lahars
Dormant interval: 500–600 years		

Source: Hoblitt, Crandell, and Mullineaux 1980, p. 556.

an eruption appears to have been Dr. Meredith Gairdner, a physician with the Hudson's Bay Company at Fort Vancouver. His account, in a letter to the *Edinburgh New Philosophical Journal*, appeared in January 1836. Both the 1831 and the 1835 eruptions "seem to have produced billowy, ash laden clouds which spread volcanic ejecta for miles over the countryside. All accounts agree that the 1831 activity produced a more severe plague of darkness, even to the point of necessitating candles during daylight hours" (Harris 1976, p. 177). The 1831 eruption was the beginning of a period of activity that continued intermittently until 1857. An unusually strong eruption in 1842–1843 was noteworthy for the huge eruption cloud, which spread ash over the countryside.

The last reported eruption of Mount St. Helens before 1980 was in April 1857. All accounts mention a huge eruption cloud, but it left no recognizable deposits.

The 1980 eruption[1]. On May 18,1980, at 8:32 A.M., a cataclysmic eruption of Mount St. Helens destroyed the north flank of the volcano, devastated an area of 150 square miles, and caused the death of at least 62 people as well as millions of dollars in property damage.

The first indications of a possible eruption of Mount St. Helens, after a dormant period of 123 years, was a magnitude 4 earthquake on March 20. Seismic activity continued, reaching a peak on March 27, when 47 earthquakes of magnitude 3 or greater occurred within a 12-hour period. Virtually all the earthquakes were centered about 2 kilometers directly north of the summit crater at depths ranging up to 5 kilometers with a few as deep as 10 kilometers. There were many small shocks which probably originated in or near the base of the cone. The first steam explosion occurred on March 27, generating an ash-filled eruption cloud, the ash apparently derived from explosions within the 350-year-old summit dome. These phreatic-type eruptions continued intermittently until the major eruption on May 18. In the March 27 eruption a series of large east-west trending cracks developed in the summit area. Another, somewhat less continuous system of fractures formed high on the north flank of the volcano, marking the upper edge of a block which showed a distinct bulge or uplift. Later, photogrammetric measurements showed that by April 12 the bulge involved an area nearly 2-kilometers in diameter which had moved up or out as much as 100 meters. Regular measurements which began on April 25 showed that the bulge was continuing to expand at rates up to 1.5 meters per day, with the displacement nearly horizontal to the north-northwest. The bulge was apparently due to pressure from magma rising into the throat of the volcano, and an eruption, a huge avalanche, or both appeared imminent. Anticipating that this huge bulge would break from the mountainside and avalanche down the slope, all persons in its path were ordered to leave. Harry Truman, who had a lodge on Spirit Lake, immediately below the bulge, refused to leave and was killed when his lodge was buried under the avalanche of debris. Interestingly, the authorities made Truman a deputy sheriff, thereby making it legal for him to remain.

In the violent, death-dealing eruption that began at 8:32 A.M. on Sunday, May 18, there were three distinct events, which occurred within seconds of each other: (1) the breaking away of the bulge and the resulting avalanche-debris flow and mudflows, (2) the lateral blast of hot, ash-filled gases, and (3) the vertical eruption cloud and ash fall. There had been no unusual activity at the volcano to

1. This account is based largely on Decker and Decker 1981; Christiansen 1980; and my personal observations.

indicate an impending eruption, when at 8:32 A.M. an earthquake of about 5 on the Richter scale shook the mountain, probably triggering the breaking away of the bulge. Dorothy and Keith Stoffel, both geologists, had boarded a light plane at the Yakima airport early Sunday morning to take a look at the volcano. The day was clear, and while making several overflights they did not detect any unusual activity. At 8:32 A.M. they were directly over the summit looking down into the crater from a height of about 1,100 feet. They reported that "the whole north side of the summit crater began to move as one gigantic mass. . . . The entire mass began to ripple and churn without moving laterally. Then the whole north side of the summit began sliding to the north along a deep-seated slide plane" (Stoffel 1980, p. 10). From their position the initial eruption cloud seemed to mushroom to the north, then plunge down the slope. They decided to return to the Yakima airport, but were unable to outdistance the onrushing eruption cloud and escaped by turning to the south out of its path. The enormous avalanche of more than two-thirds of a cubic mile of rock debris and glacial ice, fluidized by exploding steam and entrapped air, accelerated to velocities of up to 250 kilometers per hour. It splashed into Spirit Lake, struck a ridge beyond, and was deflected down the north fork of the Toutle River as a hummocky debris flow which continued for about 21 kilometers downvalley, filling the lake and valley with debris to depths up to 150 meters. The water from Spirit Lake, the Toutle River, and entrapped snow and ice mixed with the volcanic debris to form a huge mudflow which continued down the north fork of the Toutle, into the Cowlitz River, and on to the Columbia. (See pp. 527–528 for description of the mudflows.)

As soon as the crack at the upper edge of the bulge opened, a horizontally directed blast of hot gas issued from the crack and soon overtook the avalanche as it rushed downslope. The blast of hot gas, largely steam filled with ash and fragments of volcanic rock and with temperatures up to 300°C., moved with speeds of up to 400 kilometers per hour. The steam blast and its fluidized charge of volcanic rock fragments rolled over major ridges and valleys, extending in places up to 28 kilometers from its source. The slopes of the mountain were heavily forested with prime Douglas fir, and an area of about 550 square kilometers on the north side of the volcano was completely devastated. For the first few kilometers entire trees 1–2 meters in diameter were uprooted and swept away, leaving a bare surface. Beyond this was a blow-down zone 10–15 kilometers wide where the trees, stripped of their limbs and bark, were snapped like matchsticks and left lined up with the trunks pointing, in general, away from the direction of the blast (Pl. 75). Turbulent (tornadic-like) eddies in the onrushing blast in some cases

Plate 75. The blow-down area at Mount St. Helens, June 30, 1980. The logging roads are about 12 feet wide. U.S. Geological Survey photo by Austin Post.

left the trees in a mangled heap. There was a narrow zone at the margin of the blow-down area where the trees were left standing but scorched (see Fig. 106). The avalanche-debris flow and the lateral blast of hot ash-filled gas caused most of the loss of life and destruction of property, and, amazingly, this part of the eruption was over by 9:00 A.M.

Among the 62 known dead was David Johnston, age 30, a geologist with the U.S. Geological Survey team monitoring the volcano. At the time of the eruption he was at the observation station known as Coldwater II, about 5½ miles north of the summit. From this station, measurements on the bulge and other data were radioed to the central office at Vancouver on a regular schedule. Johnston had radioed his 7:00 A.M. report and presumably was watching the volcano when it erupted. His excited call, "Vancouver, Vancouver, this is it!" was received, then only silence. His body was never found.

Before the lateral blast had reached its full development, a huge eruption cloud, filled with ash, burst from the crater and within 10 minutes had reached a height of 63,000 feet (Pl. 76). The dark, ash-filled cloud was carried to the northwest by the prevailing winds. So great was the amount of ash in the cloud that it obscured the sun's rays, causing total darkness in many communities. At Spokane, Washington, 250 miles away, visibility was reduced to about 10 feet when the cloud reached the area in mid-afternoon. Ash falls covered a wide area, extending into Idaho and central Montana. At Yakima, 90 miles away, up to 5 inches fell, causing a problem for some residents with respiratory problems and a massive effort by the city to remove the ash. Ash falls of up to 2 inches were common in western Montana, west of the Continental Divide, but only dusting fell on the eastern slopes. Small amounts of ash were noted in Denver on May 19. The ash cloud encircled the globe in 11 days, a remarkably short time compared to the 2–3 weeks usually required for such an event. The huge Plinian column continued to erupt vigorously for about 9 hours, then gradually declined. In the eruption the volcanic conduit was reamed out, forming a central crater about 1.5 kilometers in diameter. This crater, along with the area previously occupied by the north flank of the cone, which was removed by the avalanche-debris flow and the lateral blast, formed an amphitheatre-shaped basin, 1.5 by 3 kilometers, open to the northeast (Pl. 77). In the eruption Mount St. Helens lost 1,370 feet in height.

The huge avalanche, with a volume of about two-thirds of a cubic mile (2 cubic kilometers), is the largest landslide known to have occurred in historic time, and is one of the unique features of this eruption. It was the sudden release of pressure on the underlying magma when the bulge separated from the mountain that resulted

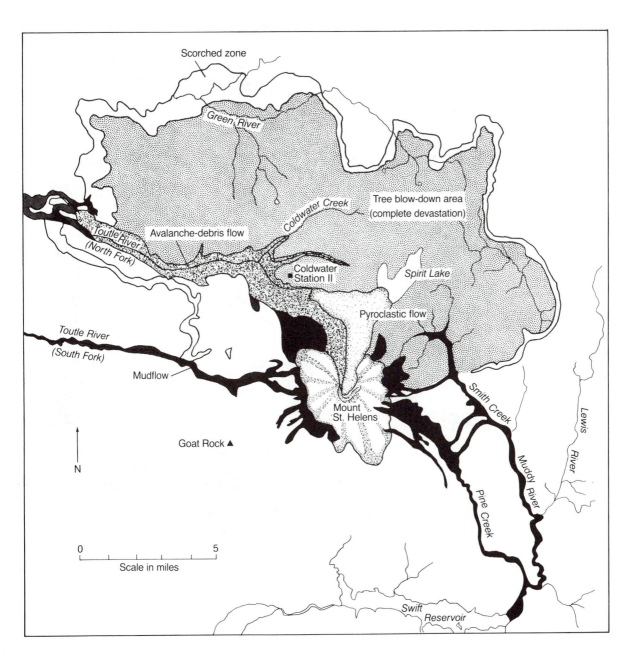

Figure 106. Features related to the May 18, 1980, eruption of Mount St. Helens. After U.S. Geological Survey Map, open file report 80-925.

*Plate 76. Eruption of Mount
St. Helens, May 18, 1980.
U.S. Geological Survey
photo by Donald A. Swanson.*

in the explosive release of the lateral blast and the vertical eruption column.

Shortly after the initial eruption, pyroclastic flows of fine ash and pumice blocks began, at intervals, pouring down the north slope of the volcano through the breach in the amphitheatre-shaped crater. These fluidized emulsions of ash and pumice moved at speeds up to 100 kilometers per hour and covered the earlier debris flow and lateral blast deposits. There were a succession of pyroclastic flows throughout the day (May 18), many reaching as far as the south edge of Spirit Lake.

On May 25 a large ash eruption, although an order of magnitude less than the May 18 eruption, spread ash over a wide area of western Washington and Oregon. Similar but smaller ash eruptions occurred on June 12, July 22, August 7, and October 16–18, and in most cases were accompanied by pyroclastic flows. Temperatures up to 705°C. were recorded on some of the pyroclastic flows.

The lava dome. The first lava produced in the eruption was a very viscous dacitic lava which began to accumulate as a dome-like mass in the crater on June 12. The dome continued to grow and by June 20 had reached a height of 65 meters. In the July 22 ash eruption this dome was blown out, and on August 8–9 a new dome began to form in the crater. The August dome was destroyed by an eruption on August 16, and a third dome began to form in the crater on October 18. This dome remained essentially intact through 1982, but new lobes of lava were added from time to time, as follows: December 1980–January 1981; February 1981; April 1981; June 1981; September 1981; October–November 1981; March–April 1982; April 1982; May 1982; and August 1982.

The eruption of new lava at the dome is commonly preceded by expansion of the dome's surface and by increased seismic activity. The expansion of the dome is measured by reflecting laser beams off fixed targets on the dome, and this information combined with the seismic record has made it possible to predict eruptions, a few days in advance, with considerable success. The explosive activity accompanying the addition of a new lobe of lava varies widely. In many cases there is little or no explosive activity, although dust clouds, which rise above the crater rim, are often generated by the avalanching of rock debris from the side of the dome. In other cases significant ash plumes are generated. For example, in the eruption of March 1982, vigorous explosions resulted in an ash plume which reached a height of 14 kilometers, and a significant amount of ash was carried up to 60 kilometers to the south-southeast of the volcano. The eruptions triggered massive snow and ice avalanches, which, mixed with pumice and rock debris, swept out of the crater and down the slope of the volcano as far as Spirit Lake.

Plate 77. Mount St. Helens after the May 18, 1980, eruption. Aerial view courtesy of David Ellison and CH₂M Hill Co., Reston, Virginia.

Toutle River

Spirit Lake
(surface covered with logs)

As a new lobe of lava is extruded, the dome usually expands to accommodate some of the new magma (endogenous growth), and some overflows portions of the older dome. A subsidence of the upper part of the dome, sometimes general and at other times more localized, is common following the addition of a new lobe. As a result the dimensions of the dome vary from time to time. At the end of 1982, the composite dome was an elongate oval with a long axis of about 2,000 feet. Due to subsidence of the crater floor, avalanching from the crater walls, and the talus slope surrounding the dome, it is more difficult to determine the height, but it was on the order of 600 feet (Pl. 78).

The significance of the formation of a lava dome in the crater of a volcano is discussed on p. 139.

The future of Mount St. Helens. Predictions of the behavior of a volcano are always hazardous. However, if Mount St. Helens follows the usual pattern, the dome will continue to grow, perhaps for a number of years, and then the volcano will become dormant.

The previous dormant period lasted for 123 years, but at present we have no basis for speculating on the length of the next one. Lateral blasts of hot, ash-filled gases (*nuées ardentes*) frequently erupt from fissures in growing domes. It is interesting to note that such a feature accompanied the emplacement of the October–November 1981 lobe at Mount St. Helens. Its effect was limited to the immediate crater area, but larger and more destructive *nuées ardentes* are possible in the future.

Mount Hood

Mount Hood, one of the major volcanoes of the High Cascade Range, is near the northern boundary of Oregon, about 45 miles east-southeast of Portland. It has an elevation of 11,245 feet. As viewed from Portland, it is a symmetrical cone terminating in a sharp peak, but, viewed from other directions, it is highly asymmetrical as a result of glacial erosion, which has stripped away large portions of its original bulk and reduced its height by at least 1,000 feet. Mount Hood is said to be the second most climbed snow peak in the world, second only to Japan's Fujiyama (Harris 1976, p. 145).

Mount Hood rises some 8,000 feet above a deeply dissected base of Pliocene andesites and basalts. Some of the early intracanyon flows now stand as ridges on the flanks of the cone. A few of these, with lengths up to 8 miles and thicknesses of over 500 feet, have volumes of nearly half a cubic mile. The oldest flows associated with Mount Hood are intracanyon flows of olivine pyroxene andesite exposed along Compass Creek, a deep canyon on the north side of the volcano. As the present cone developed, it completely buried the earlier cone which gave rise to these flows. Erosion has since uncovered parts of the earlier cone which are now exposed below the terminus of the Sandy Glacier (Wise 1968, p. 81).

William S. Wise (1969, p. 993) estimates that lava makes up 70 percent of the bulk of Mount Hood, with subordinate amounts of breccia and pyroclastic debris. This comes as somewhat of a surprise, at least to the casual visitor, because glaciation has left an extensive mantle of clastic debris over most of the lower slope, giving a false impression of the composition of the cone. Some of the structures in Mount Hood lavas are described by Wise as follows:

> Platy jointing is developed near the base of the flows. The sub-parallel arrangement of groundmass plagioclase along shear planes causes the rock to fracture into slabs. Downslope movement of the flow develops the shear planes only where solid-

ification was nearly complete, in most cases near the base. A crude columnar jointing forms in the portion of the flow that was subjected to little movement during the final cooling. . . . The piling of the lava at the base of a steep slope produces a characteristic ramp structure. After the front part of the flow stops, later surges of lava are ramped (thrust) over it. This ramping causes curved shear zones that rise over the front part of the flow. (Wise 1968, pp. 81, 84)

After Mount Hood had reached its maximum size and activity had ceased at the summit, prior to the last glaciation, lava was erupted from two satellite vents, one on the north and the other on the northeast slope of the cone. From each vent several flows of olivine andesite were produced, some extending up to 15 miles into the upper Hood River Valley. The plug of one vent forms the Pinnacles, while the other, near Cloud Cap Inn, has been eroded by Elliot Glacier and covered by a moraine.

Before the last glaciation, about 25,000 years ago, Mount Hood is believed to have been a rather symmetrical cone. However, during the last advance of Pleistocene glaciers the mountain was the center of an icecap which completely covered the volcano and extended far down adjacent valleys, especially on the north and east. During this period glacial erosion removed a thousand feet from the mountain's sides and top, changing the smooth cone into the four-faceted horn seen today. As the glacial period drew to a close, the glaciers retreated to their present high altitudes, where eleven glaciers continue to carve cirques into the mountainside (Harris 1976, p. 154).

Like other Cascade volcanoes, Mount Hood began in the Pleistocene, but there is some question whether it dates from Early, Middle, or Late Pleistocene.

Eruptive history. Since the last major glaciation, three major eruptive periods have been identified at Mount Hood (Crandell and Rubin 1977). Each period was characterized by the extrusion of one or more dacite domes, and avalanches of hot rock debris from the flanks of the domes produced mudflows and lithic pyroclastic flows. The first eruptive period began during the late stage of the last glaciation, 12,000–15,000 years ago. Dacite domes were formed at the summit of Mount Hood, and hot avalanches of debris from the domes and the resulting mudflows formed large fans on the flank of the volcano between glaciers. Mudflows formed deposits on the floors of the major valleys on all sides of Mount Hood during this period.

The second eruptive period, about 1,500–1,800 years ago (Crandell, Mullineaux, and Miller 1979, p. 209), was marked by the ex-

Plate 79. Aerial view of the southeast side of Mount Hood. White River Glacier is cutting into part of the Recent hornblende andesite debris fan, which covers the entire slope of the volcano west (left) of the glacier. Newton Clark Glacier is on the east slope of the volcano. Below the solid portion of Crater Rock is a breccia margin. The smooth slopes in the center and lower right are underlain by crudely stratified debris redistributed after Fraser Glaciation. U.S. Geological Survey photo 80 RI-41 by Robert Krimmel.

trusion of a dome of hornblende dacite (Wise 1969, p. 994) in a crater that developed high on the south slope, about 1,000 feet below the summit. As the dome pushed through the thick cover of snow and ice, the outer surface shattered, sending an avalanche of hot boulders, some up to 20 feet in diameter, crashing down the slope. The melted snow and ice generated huge mudflows which swept down the mountainside. As the lava dome continued to grow, perhaps over a period of several hundred years, wave after wave of debris swept down the slope of the cone, and a broad fan was formed on the south slope. The scars of glacial erosion were buried, and the relatively smooth surface of the fan gives the symmetrical appearance which Mount Hood presents when viewed from the south. The apex of the fan is at Crater Rock, the solid portion of the lava dome (Pl. 79).

In the third eruptive period, about 200–250 years ago, another lava dome formed on the south side of the volcano. The hot pyroclastic flows and mudflows accompanying the emplacement of the dome were limited to valleys on the south and west sides.

An eruption during the past 200 years left a widely scattered deposit of pumice on the eastern and southern flanks of the cone. This was the first pumiceous material to be erupted from Mount Hood in postglacial time, in contrast to other Cascade volcanoes in which pumice is a common product (Crandell, Mullineaux, and Miller 1979, p. 209).

Although there are reports of historic eruptions of Mount Hood, the evidence is not conclusive. Harris (1976, pp. 146–150) reviews the reports of historic eruptions and concludes that there seems to be evidence for a minor eruption between 1846 and 1865.

Mount Shasta

Mount Shasta, at the southern end of the High Cascade Range in northern California, is the largest of the High Cascade volcanoes and one of the large strato-volcanoes of the world. With an elevation of 14,162 feet, and rising some 10,000 feet above the general level of the surrounding area, its snow-capped peak can be seen for 100 miles or more in all directions.

In contrast to some of the High Cascade volcanoes to the north, Mount Shasta has not been deeply eroded. The summit area and much of the north and upper east flanks are intact, and only on the south and to a lesser extent on the east and west sides has the original surface been removed by erosion. There is much less precipitation at Mount Shasta than at Mount Rainier, and as a result of the drier climate and southerly location the snowline is much higher. Mount Shasta supports five glaciers, but they are small compared to those on Mount Rainier. The older parts of Mount Shasta suffered glacial erosion during the Pleistocene, but products from postglacial eruptions have filled most of the eroded scars (Harris 1976, p. 67).

Mount Shasta rests on a bedrock of sandstones, slates, and limestones ranging from Devonian to Jurassic in age (Williams 1932*b*, p. 418), which had been weathered to a surface of low relief prior to the beginning of volcanic activity. As a result, the thick intracanyon lava flows, common at Mount Rainier, Mount Hood, and Mount Baker, are absent at Mount Shasta. Instead the volcanic products form a massive apron at the base of the cone.

Although Howel Williams (1932*b*, p. 420) recognized that Mount Shasta was composed of at least two cones, it remained for Robert L. Christiansen and C. Dan Miller (1976) to decipher the complex history of the volcano and show that it was made up of four overlapping cones of different ages, piled atop and against one another. Each cone consists of pyroxene andesite lava flows, block and ash flows, and lahars, with dacite domes as a late or final product. A long, jagged outcrop on the south side, known as Sargents Ridge, is the remnant of the oldest cone, formed at least 100,000 years ago. The last summit eruption at the Sargents Ridge cone produced hornblende-pyroxene andesite flows and a hornblende dacite dome.

In Late Pleistocene, but before the last advance of the ice (Tioga glaciation), about 25,000 years ago, the second cone developed on the north flank of the Sargents Ridge cone. This cone is called the Misery Hill Volcano, because the upper part of its eroded surface represents the long slope which climbers find so tiring to ascend on their way to the summit (Harris 1976, p. 69). In its final stage of activity a dome of pyroxene-hornblende andesite formed at the summit. The remaining two cones of the Mount Shasta complex date from the post-Pleistocene, some 10,000–12,000 years ago. The first of the postglacial cones was Shastina, on the west slope of the Misery Hill cone. It is large enough, if it stood alone, to rank as the third highest mountain in the entire Cascade Range, with only Mount Rainier and Shasta itself exceeding its 12,330 feet above sea level. Shastina's broad summit area, which includes a circular crater about one-half mile in diameter, is composed of five domes of pyroxene-hornblende dacite. From at least four of the domes, repeated collapse possibly caused by explosions produced a series of hot pyroclastic flows which moved down Diller Canyon, a V-shaped gash which heads at a gap in the Shastina crater rim and extends down the west flank of the volcano. It is about one-quarter mile wide and up to 400 feet deep. Diller Canyon may owe its origin to lateral or downward blasts accompanying the pyroclastic flows, as first proposed by Williams (1932b, p. 427), or to collapse and erosion by pyroclastic flows. The pyroclastic flows form a fan extending westward from Diller Canyon for about 17 kilometers. It has a width of up to 6.5 kilometers and covers an area of about 65 square kilometers, including most of the town of Weed. The pyroclastic flows consist of ash and blocks of hornblende pyroxene dacite, identical in lithology to the dacite domes at the summit of Shastina. Charcoal from a log at the base of the lowest flow gave a radiocarbon date of 9,230±300 years before the present (Miller 1978, p. 617).

The last major cone, the Hotlum, named for the glacier on its north face, forms Mount Shasta's summit and undissected north and northeast flanks. It was formed by a series of blocky pyroxene andesite flows. A dome of hornblende-pyroxene andesite formed in the crater, and the Crags, which are the highest point on Mount Shasta, are the erosional remnants of the dome which marks the rim of a poorly defined summit crater (Harris 1976, p. 71). The age of the Hotlum Volcano has not been established, but it began only a few thousand years ago and is overlain by no glacial deposits older than a few centuries; further solfataric activity at the summit indicates that the dome is still cooling (Christiansen and Miller 1976, p. 361). Flank vents, particularly along a north-south zone, have produced dacite domes, andesite flows, and cinder cones. Most are of Sargents Ridge age, but some are younger (Christiansen and Miller 1976, p. 361). One of the largest of the domes is Gray Butte, which has a base about 1–2 miles in diameter and rises some 1,500 feet above the surrounding lavas.

Black Butte. At the western base of Mount Shasta, a steep-sided cone with three peaks rises about 2,500 feet above the surrounding base. Appropriately named Black Butte, it is a series of plug-domes of hornblende dacite which rose in an existing crater. The plug-domes filled the mile-wide crater and overflowed the sides, except on the south and southwest, where a depression known as the "moat" separates the plug-domes and the old crater rim (Miller 1978, p. 622). Williams, who made the first detailed study of Black Butte, describes its origin as follows: ". . . magma welled up sluggishly into the crater and built an almost vertical-sided plug or dome. As the lava rose its crust crumbled continuously so that now the only part of the solid 'core' to be seen rising through the talus are a few structureless crags at or near the summit" (1932*b*, p. 428). As interpreted by Miller (1978, p. 622), eruptions at Black Butte began with the ejection of volatile-rich dacitic magma, producing pyroclastic flows containing vesicular debris. Later eruptions produced a viscous, volatile-poor dacite, and a succession of four domes were formed. At least two pyroclastic flows, caused by dome collapse, spread mainly to the west and south, covering an area of about 44 square kilometers.

The pyroclastic flows from Black Butte can be distinguished from those from Shastina, with which they are in contact, because the former have only hornblende dacite blocks while the latter contain blocks of dacite with varying proportions of hypersthene, augite, and hornblende (Miller 1978, p. 614). Radiocarbon dates for the Black Butte pyroclastic flows indicate that they are essentially the same age as those from Shastina, that is 9,230±300 to 9,500±350 years before the present (Miller 1978, p. 621).

Recent activity. The most recent eruption of Mount Shasta which left a recognizable deposit was about 200 years ago (Crandell, Mullineaux, and Miller 1979, p. 211). In this eruption proclastic flows

Plate 80. Western side of Mount Shasta with Black Butte in the foreground. Fans composed of pyroclastic-flow deposits cover the slopes toward the communities of Mount Shasta (north edge of town shown in lower right corner) and Weed (just out of picture, lower left corner). U.S. Geological Survey photo.

extended down the southeast side for about 12 kilometers, and mudflows on the east side traveled more than 20 kilometers. There are reports of steam and smoke rising from Mount Shasta as late as the 1850's by travelers in the area and in Indian legends. However, brisk solfataric activity may have been mistaken for eruptions. At the time of the first recorded ascent of Mount Shasta in 1854, the climbers reported that there were about a dozen hot boiling sulphur springs just below the summit peak (Eichorn 1957, p. 27), but in 1982 there were only two small fumarole areas on the summit dome, one of which had a small acidic hot spring (Foxworthy and Hill 1982, p. 6).

Lassen Peak

Lassen Peak (10,457 feet) is located in northern California at the southern end of the Cascade Range. Unlike the other prominent Cascade volcanoes, it is not a strato-volcano but an unusually large dacite dome which towers conspicuously above the cluster of minor

Plate 81. Lassen Peak from the head of Little Hot Springs Valley. The massive plug-dome of Lassen Peak is covered by huge talus slopes, giving the cone the appearance of a truncated pyramid. The 300-meter-long dacite lava flow which emerged from the crater in the May 1915 eruption is faintly visible at the crater rim. Photo by Clay Peter, courtesy Lassen Volcanic National Park.

domes on its south and west sides, while on the north and east its slopes merge into the valleys of Hat and Lost creeks. Lassen Peak has the form of a truncated pyramid due to the enormous talus banks which cover its slopes (Pl. 81). The name is derived from Peter Lassen, one of the early settlers in the region. Prior to the 1980 eruption of Mount St. Helens, Lassen Peak was frequently said to be the only volcano to erupt in the contiguous 48 states in historic time. Although there had in fact been other eruptions (see p. 453 and elsewhere in this chapter), the 1914–1915 eruption of Lassen Peak certainly was the only major one on record.

Brokeoff Volcano. Immediately to the southeast of Lassen Peak lie the ruins of a great andesitic strato-volcano with a diameter of 11–15 miles at its base and an original height of around 11,000 feet. The history of Brokeoff Volcano is reviewed by Williams (1932c, pp. 217–219). Late in its history new vents opened on the northeast slope, probably close to, if not immediately beneath, the present edifice of Lassen Peak. From these vents, streams of fluid dacite lava flowed radially, but chiefly to the north, piling up a thick apron of lava which now largely encircles Lassen Peak. Williams refers to

these flows as the pre-Lassen dacites. Domes of viscous dacite, such as Bumpas Mountain, Mount Helen, Eagle Peak, Vulcan's Castle, and others, rose to the south of Lassen Peak. The outflowing of so much lava may have been a contributing factor to the subsequent collapse of Brokeoff Cone. The collapse, which occurred along a series of more or less vertical faults, resulted in a caldera approximately 2.5 miles in diameter. Williams comments, "So imposing is the great fault scarp at Brokeoff Mountain and so sharply are the strongly bedded lava cut off the cliff, that even the casual tourist will agree that the peak is well named" (1932c, p. 241).

About 11,000 years ago, long after the collapse of Brokeoff Cone, a dacite dome began to rise in the crater of the pre-Lassen dacite flows, and in a short time the huge dome of Lassen Peak was emplaced (Crandell 1972, p. 179). The volume of the solid core plus the talus which surrounds it represents about 1 cubic mile of material, making it one of the largest such domes in the world (Williams 1932, p. 219). The dome is composed of glassy dacite and is estimated to have been elevated about 2,500 feet above the original crater floor. The dome itself is largely concealed by its own talus, the result of fracturing of the outer surface of the dome during emplacement.

Activity of Lassen Peak. Very little is known of the activity of Lassen Peak prior to the eruption of 1914. R. H. Finch (1930, p. 2) identified mudflows which originated from Lassen Peak within the past 500 years, and Crandell et al. (1974, p. 58) determined that the events which resulted in Chaos Jumbles occurred about 300 years ago. Further, steam is reported to have been observed rising from the northeast flank of Lassen Peak in 1857.

The eruption of 1914–1915. A detailed account by Arthur L. Day and E. T. Allen (1925) and the photographic record by Benjamin Franklin Loomis (1926) give a comprehensive view of the 1914–

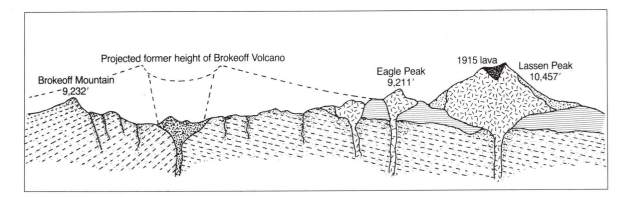

1915 eruption. In addition, the eruption has been summarized by
Williams (1932c) and by Harris (1976). The following account is
based largely on these sources, which the reader may wish to con-
sult for additional details.

The eruption began on May 30, 1914, with a brief, mild steam
explosion which opened a vent about 25 by 40 feet on the inside of
the old crater rim, about halfway up on the northwest side. The
steam-blast eruptions continued at intervals of a few days throughout the remainder of the year. Ash and small rock fragments were
carried by the prevailing winds to the northeast. In 1914 and the
spring of 1915, more than 170 explosions were recorded, enlarging the crater to about 1,000 feet in diameter. The crater was oval-
shaped, with its rim broken by V-shaped notches at the east and
west ends.

At no time during the first year were red-hot rocks erupted, and
most of the ejected material was too cold to melt the snow upon
which it fell. It is of some interest to note that the low-temperature
explosions began at the time of rapid melting of the heavy snow
cover which had accumulated in the crater area during the winter.
This led Day and Allen (1925, pp. 75–76) to conclude that the penetration of meltwater into the hot interior of the dome, where it
was converted to steam, was the cause of the explosions. While
this seems to be a reasonable explanation, abundant meltwater had
been present each spring for centuries, so some change must have
taken place in 1914 to bring about the explosions. The change may
have been the rise of the magma within the dome, bringing the
highly heated material nearer to the surface and also opening fractures which permitted the meltwater access to the heated interior
of the dome.

The eruption of May 1915. In early May 1915, lava began to fill the
crater. On May 16–18, lava was observed projecting above the level
of the notch at the west end of the crater rim, and on May 19 it
spilled over in the form of a tongue 1,000 feet long. This was the
first appearance of glowing lava since the activity began. On the
same evening a disastrous mudflow swept down the eastern flank
of the mountain and into the valleys of Hat and Lost creeks, carrying boulders, some up to a weight of 20 tons, for a distance of 5–6
miles; some damage was reported as far away as 30 miles. The origin of the mudflow has been open to controversy, but the melting
of the snow cover by a tongue of lava which spilled through the
eastern notch in the crater rim, in the same way that a tongue
spilled through the western notch, may have been an important
factor (Finch 1930, p. 2). Accompanying the mudflow, and doubtless an important factor in melting the heavy snow pack which
generated the mudflow, was a hurricane-like horizontal blast, a

Plate 82. Fifty years afterward, decayed trunks of many of the huge trees leveled in the 1915 Lassen Peak eruption were still present, lined up like matchsticks.

nuée ardente of moderate temperature, heavily charged with ash and rock fragments, which destroyed everything in its path, including a dense virgin forest of trees up to 5 feet in diameter. A triangular-shaped area, up to 4 miles from the volcano and with a maximum width of a little over 1 mile, was swept clean. The force of the blast was so violent that the area was left without stumps or roots to indicate its previous forest cover. This area is appropriately known as the "devastated area" (see color section). At the margin of the blast area, in a zone about 2 miles long, the trees were uprooted and left in rows with their tops pointing away from the volcano (Pl. 82). At the borders of the blast area, the trees were left standing but badly scorched; yet the temperature appears not to have been hot enough to set fire to the trees (only one fire was reported). While most of the trees were uprooted, some were broken off a few feet above ground. The standing stumps in such cases were sandblasted, rounded off on the side facing the volcano, while the bark was unaffected on the opposite side.

The "Great Eruption," considered to be the climax in the activity of Lassen Peak, occurred on May 22, 1915. It was accompanied by a mudflow which covered essentially the same area as the previous

Plate 83. The giant mush-room-shaped cloud in the May 22, 1915, eruption of Lassen Peak, as viewed from Anderson, 50 miles west of the volcano. Photo courtesy of the National Park Service.

one. In addition, there were minor mudflows on the north and west flanks of the volcano. As in the earlier eruption, a terrific horizontal blast swept down the eastern slope and over the area covered by the mudflow. Simultaneously a huge eruption cloud boiled out of the summit crater, reaching a height of about 5 miles (Pl. 83). As the giant mushroom-shaped eruption cloud spread over northern California, ash rained down over a wide area. The prevailing winds carried the eruption cloud to the east, and ash fell on some towns as far away as 200 miles.

Decline in activity. Following the strong eruption of May 1915, the activity gradually declined. For the next two years, mild steam and ash eruptions occurred at irregular intervals, culminating in a rather violent explosion on May 18, 1917.

In an effort to check on the possibility that melting snow in the crater was instrumental in triggering an eruption, Allen and Day (1925, p. 26) visited the crater in May 1916. They found that the new lava plug, emplaced in the May 1915 eruptions, had remained hot enough to prevent any accumulation of snow during the winter of 1915–1916. Interestingly, there were no eruptions in May 1916. However, the plug apparently cooled so that during the winter of 1916–1917 there was a normal accumulation of snow in the crater, and the eruptions which occurred in May and June 1917 essentially marked the end of the activity. However, reports of black "smoke" issuing from the crater in January and April 1919 and in October 1920 may have resulted from small ash eruptions.

Pumice and lava from the May 1915 eruption. The pumice of the 1915 eruption of Lassen Peak is banded in shades of greyish brown. There is considerable variation, and some of the bands are nearly white while others approach black. The light bands are dacitic, while the dark bands are andesitic. They represent two distinct magmas which were imperfectly mixed at the time of eruption. The material was fluid at the time of eruption and was drawn into bands by flowage (Macdonald and Katsura 1965, p. 479).

The lava that filled the crater at the top of the dome and spilled over in the May 1915 eruption is a dark grey to black glassy dacite containing about 20–40 percent white feldspar phenocrysts much like those in the dacite of the dome. The SiO_2 content is about 65 percent. The mixing of the magmas and the events leading to the climactic eruption of Lassen Peak in 1915 are summarized as follows:

> The magmas, in the process of mixing, were guided to the surface by an existing path of least resistance that has also repeatedly guided the magmas of previous eruptions. Probably in early 1914 the magma was already approaching the surface and causing a swelling and cracking of the old Lassen dome. This, in turn, allowed melt water from the thick snow accumulation in the crater to penetrate down into hotter regions within the dome (perhaps coming in contact with the new rising magma itself) where it was transformed into steam and produced the phreatic explosions of 1914 and early 1915. Further cracking and blasting out of the crater by the steam explosions opened a pathway to the surface and led to the eruption in May 1915 of the imperfectly blended magma. (Macdonald and Katsura 1965, p. 481)

Chaos Craigs and Chaos Jumbles. Chaos Craigs is a group of huge dacite domes just north of Lassen Peak. Chaos Jumbles is an avalanche-like deposit resulting from the collapse of one of the domes. Prior to the extrusion of the domes, hot pyroclastic flows issued from the same eruptive centers, some of which extended for a distance of up to 8 kilometers. Radiocarbon dates on charcoal from the pyroclastic flows range from 1,000 to 1,200 years ago (Crandell et al. 1974, p. 49). At least four domes, with a combined volume of 1 cubic kilometer, then erupted in the earlier craters. The domes are spectacular features, roughly circular in plan, about a mile in diameter, and rising 1,800 feet above the pyroclastic ash flow surface at its base. Enormous banks of talus, many more than 1,000 feet high, surround the domes. The talus banks represent the crumbling of the flanks of the dome as it was being pushed upward. Massive rock falls, caused by the disruption of one of the domes, produced high-velocity, air-cushioned avalanches of rock debris which extended up to 4.3 kilometers. This rock debris is known as Chaos Jumbles. Williams (1932c, p. 354) postulates that one of the domes was disrupted by explosions, resulting in the rock debris avalanches. Crandell et al. (1974, p. 49) considered various possibilities but were unable to come to a definite conclusion as to the cause of the disruption of the dome which gave rise to Chaos Jumbles. Based on the age of trees associated with the avalanches, it is believed that the event occurred about 300 years ago.

Cinder Cone. Cinder Cone, a perfectly preserved cone about one-half mile in diameter at the base and 600 feet high, is located about 10 miles east-northeast of Lassen Peak in the northeast corner of Lassen Volcanic National Park, in California. The last lava flow from Cinder Cone occurred in 1851, making it the most recent lava flow in the contiguous 48 states.

The initial activity at Cinder Cone consisted of pyroclastic eruptions which formed the cone and spread an apron of ash and cinders over a surrounding area about 8 miles in diameter. It is not to be inferred that Cinder Cone was formed in a single eruption, for R. H. Finch and C. A. Anderson (1930, p. 254) recognized that, in addition to the two rims of craters commonly noted, there are two older remnants on the northwest side. While these crater rim remnants may have been due, in part, to shifting wind directions, they also suggest that Cinder Cone may have been formed by several eruptive episodes, widely spaced in years. The next stage in the history of Cinder Cone was a lava flow from the south base of the cone, followed by more pyroclastic eruptions. Following a period of quiescence, the final activity was the outpouring of at least two lava flows, again from the south base of the cone. The last of these flows, which occurred in 1851, is a black, blocky basalt. It flowed to the southeast for about one-half mile, then encountered a median depression in an earlier flow and followed this depression to the northeast until it reached Butte Lake, for a total length of about 3 miles.

The lavas from Cinder Cone are unusual in that they are a quartz basalt. Quartz, a common constituent of acidic rocks such as granite and rhyolite, is rarely found in basalt. Various explanations to account for the presence of quartz have been proposed. After considering the various possibilities, Finch and Anderson concluded that "the quartz basalt is a hybrid rock in which acidic zenoliths and zenocrysts, derived from a differentiated dacitic magma, have been added to a basalt of low silica content" (1930, pp. 270–272). It is worth recalling that most of the rocks in the Lassen region show a mixture of acidic and more basic components, such as the banded pumice from the 1915 eruption of Lassen Peak. Further, the Twin Lakes andesites, lying to the south of Cinder Cone (Williams 1932c, p. 373) are rich in xenocrysts of quartz, lending support to the suggestion that this whole area may be underlain by a highly differentiated mass of dacite.

Retrospect

The reader who has reached this point may wish to take one last, fleeting backward glance over the way we have traveled—to glimpse in a parting view of broad outlines the main features of volcanoes.

The history of volcanology, like that of all our sciences, was interwoven with mythology and superstition in ancient times. With the acceptance of volcanoes as a natural phenomenon not related to the supernatural, volcanology began to be organized as a body of knowledge. No real progress was made, however, until the development of geology, from which volcanology is inseparable. In fact, the development of geology was to a large extent fostered by the controversies which surrounded volcanoes. As is true of most sciences, real progress is frequently the result of some outstanding event, a break-through in some aspect of the field, or some great catastrophe. The first artificial splitting of the atom revolutionized the field of physics and gave it a stimulus which will carry it on—perhaps indefinitely. Perhaps no single comparable event can be picked for volcanology, but the eruption of Mount Pelée in 1902, with the tragic loss of life which accompanied the destruction of St. Pierre, certainly focused attention on volcanology. This tragedy drew the wonder and sympathy of the civilized world, and scientists from many countries were dispatched to study the eruption. By common consent it was agreed that in some way information must be obtained which would prevent the reoccurrence of such a catastrophe, or at least give notice to the inhabitants so that they could escape. The impetus given the study of volcanoes at that time is still felt in volcanology today.

Another event which had a profound influence on volcanology was the U.S. program to land a man on the moon. It had long been known that there were craters on the moon, which some thought were the result of volcanic activity, while others held that they were due to the impact of meteorites on the lunar surface. Certainly if we were going to land a man on the moon it was imperative that we know the character of the lunar surface. A lively controversy developed as to whether the lunar craters were "volcanic" or "impact" craters. As a result the few recognized impact craters (such as Meteor Crater near Winslow, Arizona) and the many volcanic craters throughout the world were studied in great detail in efforts to find evidence in support of one or the other view. When the first lunar landing was made on July 20, 1969, it was confirmed that both impact and volcanic craters occur on the moon. Meanwhile, the intensive investigation of earth volcanoes has dramatically advanced our knowledge of volcanology.

After the eruption of Mount Pelée it was clear that volcanic eruptions were of different types and that with study the type of eruption might be anticipated. Accordingly, a classification of volcanoes based on the type of eruption was devised. This classification, with examples of the different types of eruptions, drawn from throughout the world, forms Part Two of this book. Only eruptions of volcanoes accepted as "types" are described, although in some cases examples could have been drawn from other volcanoes in which the eruption was more spectacular.

Developed along with the classification of volcanoes according to the type of eruption was the idea that the eruptions were often repeated at more or less regular intervals and that a volcanic cycle could be recognized. Information in sufficient detail to enable the eruptive cycle to be recognized was available for only a few volcanoes, but the idea that a cycle can be recognized has been an incentive for more detailed observations at many volcanoes. With the recognition of an eruptive cycle, the prediction of an eruption becomes a possibility; when this goal is reached the next step is to work out some means of control. This is a goal so far in the future that speculation on it at the present may be idle fancy, but some startlingly rapid advances have been made in science in recent years, and it seems unwise to relegate anything to the "impossible."

One paying asset in the study of volcanoes is the utilization of volcanic energy for the development of power. The conventional basis for developing electric power is solar heat, stored as coal and oil in the earth's crust. Even water power is based on solar heat, since the sun's evaporation of the water results in the rainfall which keeps the streams flowing. It does not seem so remote, then, to utilize volcanic heat (also solar heat in that it was inherited from the sun when the earth was born) for the development of power. This phase of volcanology, which is one of the few immediate economic applications, is capable of tremendous expansion in many of the remote areas of the world where conventional sources of power are lacking or quite limited. It should be a great factor in the future development of all areas where geothermal energy is available.

The important relationship of volcanology to geology is underscored by speculation on the causes underlying volcanic activity. Since volcanic activity is intimately associated with mountain building and, in turn, with the origin of continents, it becomes one of the most fundamental problems of geology. The sea-floor-speading and plate-tectonics concepts, described in some detail, cannot be claimed as a complete answer but are probably an important part of the answer, since they offer an attractive explanation for many of the problems involved in the origin of mountains and the causes of volcanism. The progress of science is marked by the alternate development and modification of theories—theories which explain a set of facts and which are modified when new facts are discovered. The plate-tectonic theory may be in this category.

The reawakening of Mount St. Helens in March 1980 and the catastrophic eruption of May 18, 1980, surely will rank among the most significant geologic events in the United States in the twentieth century. Although the eruption was not the most voluminous in amount of material ejected nor the greatest in amount of energy released among recent historic eruptions, it was unusual in that it occurred close to a major industrial-urban area. The loss of life in the eruption was greatly reduced by the warning, control, and evacuation programs instituted by the local, state, and federal authorities. It dramatically demonstrated the need for advance planning in areas where future eruptions might occur. The eruption was also remarkable for the high degree of national attention it received and the exceptional opportunity for detailed scientific observations. It was perhaps the most photographed and the most closely monitored with "high-technology" equipment of any volcanic eruption. It made the public aware that the Cascade volcanoes were capable of eruption and demonstrated the need for advance warning of an impending eruption. As a result, the temporary observation post established at Vancouver, Washington, by the U.S. Geological Survey to monitor the eruption of Mount St. Helens is now a permanent observatory, charged with the study of all Cascade volcanoes. It has appropriately been named the David A. Johnston Cascades Volcano Observatory, after David Johnston, a member of the observatory staff, who lost his life in the May 18 eruption.

Appendix A   Geologic Time Scale

			Approximate Age in Millions of Years before the Present (at Beginning of Unit)[a]
Cenozoic Era	Quaternary Period	Holocene (Recent) Epoch	0.01
		Pleistocene Epoch	2–3
	Tertiary Period	Pliocene Epoch	12
		Miocene Epoch	25
		Oligocene Epoch	40
		Eocene Epoch	60
		Paleocene Epoch	70
Mesozoic Era	Cretaceous Period		135
	Jurassic Period		180
	Triassic Period		225
Paleozoic Era	Permian Period		270
	Pennsylvanian Period		325
	Mississippian Period		350
	Devonian Period		400
	Silurian Period		440
	Ordovician Period		500
	Cambrian Period		600
Precambrian Era			3,500(?)[b]

[a]Cambrian to Holocene ages after Holmes (1965).
[b]The oldest rocks recognized to date are about 3.5 billion years old; the earth itself is believed to be 4–5 billion years old.

Appendix B   Units of Measure and Conversion Tables

Units of Measure

LINEAR MEASURE

1 mile (mi.)	= 5,280 feet (ft.)
1 foot (ft.)	= 12 inches (in.)
1 kilometer (km.)	= 1,000 meters (m.)
1 meter (m.)	= 100 centimeters (cm.)
1 centimeter (cm.)	= 0.01 meter
1 millimeter (mm.)	= 0.001 meter

AREA MEASURE

1 square mile	= 640 acres
1 acre	= 43,560 square feet
1 acre	= 4,840 square yards
1 square meter	= 10,000 square centimeters
1 square kilometer	= 100 hectares

VOLUME AND CUBIC MEASURE

1 cubic foot	= 1,728 cubic inches
1 cubic yard	= 27 cubic feet
1 barrel (oil)	= 42 gallons
1 liter	= 0.001 cubic meter

WEIGHTS AND MASSES

1 short ton	= 2,000 pounds
1 long ton	= 2,240 pounds
1 pound (avoirdupois)	= 7,000 grains
1 ounce (avoirdupois)	= 437.5 grains
1 gram	= 15.432 grains
1,000 grams	= 1 kilogram
1,000 kilograms	= 1 metric ton

Conversions

ENGLISH-METRIC CONVERSIONS

1 inch	= 25.4 millimeters
1 inch	= 2.54 centimeters
1 foot	= 0.3048 meter
1 yard	= 0.9144 meter
1 mile	= 1.609 kilometers
1 square inch	= 6.4516 square centimeters
1 square foot	= 0.0929 square meter
1 square yard	= 0.836 square meter
1 acre	= 0.4047 hectare
1 square mile	= 2.590 square kilometers
1 cubic inch	= 16.39 cubic centimeters
1 cubic foot	= 0.0283 cubic meter
1 cubic yard	= 0.7646 cubic meter
1 cubic mile	= 4.168 cubic kilometers
1 gallon	= 3.784 liters
1 ounce	= 28.33 grams
1 pound	= 0.4536 kilogram
1 acre-foot	= 1,233.46 cubic meters

METRIC-ENGLISH CONVERSIONS

1 millimeter	= 0.0394 inch
1 centimeter	= 0.394 inch
1 meter	= 3.281 feet
1 meter	= 1.094 yards
1 kilometer	= 0.6214 mile
1 square centimeter	= 0.155 square inch
1 square meter	= 10.764 square feet
1 square meter	= 1.196 square yards
1 hectare	= 2.471 acres
1 square kilometer	= 0.386 square mile
1 cubic centimeter	= 0.061 cubic inch
1 cubic meter	= 35.3 cubic feet
1 cubic meter	= 1.308 cubic yards
1 liter	= 1.057 quarts
1 cubic meter	= 264.2 gallons (U.S.)
1 cubic kilometer	= 0.240 cubic mile
1 gram	= 0.0353 ounce
1 kilogram	= 2.205 pounds

Temperature Scales

1° F. = 0.56° C.
1° C. = 1.8° F.
0° C. = 32° F. (freezing point of water)
100° C. = 212° F. (boiling point of water)

To change from Fahrenheit (F) to Centigrade (C): $°C = \dfrac{(°F - 32°)}{1.8}$

To change from Centigrade (C) to Fahrenheit (F): $°F = (°C \times 1.8) + 32°$

Glossary

aa: lava with a surface composed of angular, jagged blocks.

acidic: a descriptive term applied to those igneous rocks which contain more than 66 percent SiO_2, as contrasted with *intermediate* and *basic*.

agglomerate: an accumulation of angular fragments of volcanic rocks.

Al_2O_3: aluminum oxide.

amygdaloid: an igneous rock (usually basalt or andesite) which contains numerous gas cavities filled with secondary minerals.

andesite: a lava of intermediate composition, usually light grey in color.

Andesite Line: a map line designating the boundary of the Pacific Ocean basin, based on the composition of the eruptive products. Extrusive rocks on the Pacific side of the line are basaltic in composition, and those on the continental side are andesitic.

Ar: the element argon.

ash, volcanic: uncemented pyroclastic material consisting of fragments mostly under 4 mm. in diameter. Two grades are commonly distinguished: coarse ash, 0.25–4.0 mm. in diameter; fine ash, less than 0.25 mm. in diameter.

ash fall: a rain of ash from an eruption cloud.

ash flow: an avalanche consisting of volcanic ash and gases, highly heated, traveling down the flanks of a volcano. SEE ALSO *nuée ardente*.

asthenosphere: a zone within the earth, some tens of kilometers below the surface and of undefined thickness. It is a zone of weakness where plastic movements occur.

atoll: a ringlike coral island or reef encircling or nearly encircling a lagoon.

barrier reef: a coral reef which runs parallel to the coast but is separated from it by a lagoon.

basalt: a dark-colored, fine-grained lava, of basic composition.

basic: a general descriptive term for those igneous rocks that are comparatively low in SiO^2, usually containing less than 52 percent.

batholith: a large intrusive mass of igneous rocks having an exposed area of more than 100 sq. km.

Benioff zone: a seismic zone dipping beneath a continental margin and having a deep-sea trench as its surface expression. It is the zone of the foci of intermediate and deep earthquakes.

block lava: a term applied to lava flows which occur as a tumultuous mass of angular blocks.

boca: Spanish for "mouth," equivalent to Italian *bocca*. In volcanology it refers to the vent, frequently on the side or at the foot of a volcanic cone, from which lava and gases issue.

bombs, volcanic: fragments of lava which were liquid or plastic at the time of ejection but which acquired a distinctive shape or surface markings while flying through the air or at the time of landing.

Bouguer anomaly: the gravity value after the Bouguer corrections to a level datum have been made. A negative Bouguer anomaly indicates that the density of the substratum is less than the normal value.

Bouguer correction: a correction made in gravity work to take into account the altitude of the station and the rocks between the station and sea level.

breached cone: a cinder cone from which a lava flow has carried away a sector, leaving an opening on one side.

breadcrust bomb: a volcanic bomb in which the surface is cut with cracks (like a loaf of French bread).

breccia: a rock composed of angular fragments.

C: the element carbon.

Ca: the element calcium.

caldera: a large, more or less circular, more-than-a-mile-in-diameter depression formed either by collapse or by explosion, usually at the summit of a volcano.

Cambrian Period. SEE Appendix A.

CaO: calcium oxide.

Cenozoic Era. SEE Appendix A.

CH_4: methane, a gaseous hydrocarbon, commonly known as marsh gas.

cinders: a general term applied to loose, vesicular volcanic ejecta 4–32 mm. in diameter.

Cl: the element chlorine.

CO: carbon monoxide.

CO_2: carbon dioxide.

cone sheets: thin sheets of intrusive (dikelike) material dipping concentrically inward toward the source of the magma. They are usually associated with ring dikes.

connate water: water trapped in the pore spaces of a sedimentary rock at the time the sediments were deposited.

convection currents: movements of material due to differences in density, generally the result of heating.

core (of the earth): the central zone of the earth, with a radius of about 3,480 km.

cored bomb: a volcanic bomb consisting of a nucleus of older lava coated with a layer of new lava.

crater, volcanic: a steep-walled depression at the top or on the flank of a volcanic cone, out of which the volcanic materials are ejected.

Cretaceous Period. SEE Appendix A.

crust (of the earth): that part of the earth lying above the Mohorovičić discontinuity.

dacite: the extrusive equivalent, in composition, of a rock intermediate between a rhyolite and an andesite.

Devonian Period. SEE Appendix A.

diapir: the mobile core of a fold, such as salt or magma, which has injected the more brittle overlying rocks.

diastrophism: the process by which the rocks of the earth's crust are deformed, producing mountains, folds, faults, etc.

dike: a tabular body of igneous rock that cuts across the structure of the adjacent rocks.

dip: the angle at which a stratum or any tabular planar feature is inclined from the horizontal.

d.v.i.: dust veil index.

enthalpy: the heat content per unit mass.

Eocene Epoch. SEE Appendix A.

epimagma: a gas-free, vesicular residue, semisolid to pasty, formed by cooling and depletion of the gas content of liquid lava in a lava lake.

fault: a fracture or fracture zone along which there has been displacement of the sides relative to one another.

Fe_2O_3: iron oxide (hematite).

fissure eruption: an eruption in which lava or pyroclastic material issues from a narrow fissure or a group of fissures.

fluidization: a concept which accounts for the movement of some intrusive igneous bodies, tuff flows (ignimbrites), and certain types of lava flows as being composed of solid particles supported by gas.

fringing reef: a coral reef which closely encircles or forms a fringe around the land, in contrast to a barrier reef, which is separated from the shore by a lagoon.

fumarole: a vent from which fumes or vapors issue.

gal: a term used in gravity measurements, equal to an acceleration of 1 cm. per second. A milligal is 0.001 gal.

geologic time. SEE Appendix A.

geopressured: said of an underground reservoir in which the water pressure is higher than the hydrostatic pressure, suggesting that the water is carrying the weight of the overlying rocks.

geosyncline: a surface of regional extent subsiding through a long time while contained sedimentary and volcanic rocks are accumulating.

geothermal gradient: the change in temperature of the earth with depth.

geyser: a hot spring from which a column of hot water and steam is explosively discharged at intervals.

graben: a long, relatively narrow block which has been downthrown along faults relative to the rocks on either side. SEE ALSO horst.

graywacke: a variety of sandstone composed of material derived from the disintegration of basic igneous rocks of granular texture.

H: the element hydrogen.

H_3BO_3: boric acid.

He: the element helium.

H_2O: water.

Holocene Epoch. SEE Appendix A.

hornito: a small beehivelike mound formed on the surface of a lava flow by the accumulation of clots of lava ejected through an opening from below.

horst: a block of the earth's crust, generally long in relation to its width, that has been uplifted along faults relative to the rocks on either side. SEE ALSO graben.

H_2S: hydrogen sulphide.

hydrostatic pressure: the pressure exerted by the weight of water at higher levels.

igneous: a rock formed as the result of the solidification of a molten mass.

ignimbrite: a type of silicic volcanic rock formed by the eruption of dense clouds of incandescent ash. SEE ALSO *nuée ardente*; welded tuff.

intermediate lava: a lava containing between 52 and 66 percent SiO_2.

isostasy: a condition of approximate equilibrium in the outer part of the earth, so that different segments of the crust, if of equal area, also have the same mass. The blocks thus balance one another. The less the mean specific gravity of a block, the higher it will stand.

isostatic anomaly: the difference between the observed value of
gravity at a point, after the various corrections have been
applied to it, and the normal value of gravity at that point.
isotopes: elements having an identical number of protons in their
nuclei but differing in the number of their neutrons.

jökulhlaup: a destructive flood due to a volcanic eruption beneath a
large glacier.
Jurassic Period. See Appendix A.
juvenile water: water derived from the interior of the earth that has
not previously existed as atmospheric or surface water: i.e.,
water derived from magma.

K: the element potassium.
kipuka: Hawaiian term for an islandlike area surrounded by lava
flows.
K_2O: potassium oxide.

lahar: an Indonesian term which includes debris flows and
mudflows; a flow of water-saturated debris down the slope of
a volcano in response to gravity.
laminar flow: flow without turbulence, in which the fluid elements
follow paths that are relatively straight and parallel to the
channel walls.
lapilli: volcanic ejecta ranging mostly from 4 to 32 mm. in diameter,
or about the size of peas.
lava fountain: a jetlike eruption of lava issuing vertically from a
fissure or a central vent.
lava plateau: a broad, elevated tableland underlain by a thick
sucession of lava flows.
lithic tuff: an indurated deposit of volcanic ash in which the fragments are composed of previously formed rock.
lithosphere: the solid portion of the earth, as contrasted with the
atmosphere and the hydrosphere.
lithostatic pressure: the pressure in the crust of the earth due to
the weight of the overlying rocks.

maar: a relatively shallow, flat-floored explosion crater, the walls of
which consist largely of loose fragments of the country (surrounding) rock.
magma: molten rock together with its included gases as it exists
underground.
magmatic differentiation: the process by which different types of
igneous rocks are derived from a single parent magma.

magmatic stoping: a process of igneous intrusion whereby a magma gradually eats its way upward by breaking off blocks of the country (surrounding) rock.

malpais: a term applied to any rather extensive area covered by recent lava flows; literally, "bad land."

mantle (of the earth): the intermediate zone of the earth. Surrounded by the crust, it rests on the core at a depth of about 2,900 km. (1,800 mi.).

mesosphere: layer of the atmosphere above the stratosphere, extending to a height of about 80 km. (50 mi.).

Mesozoic Era. SEE Appendix A.

meteoric water: water derived from the atmosphere, i.e., rain water.

metric equivalents. SEE Appendix B.

Mg: the element magnesium.

MgO: magnesium oxide.

Miocene Epoch. SEE Appendix A.

Mississippian Period. SEE Appendix A.

móberg: an Icelandic term for vitreous pyroclastic rocks. SEE ALSO palagonite tuff.

Mohorovičić discontinuity: the seismic discontinuity that marks the base of the crust of the earth.

N: the element nitrogen.

Na: the element sodium.

Na2O: sodium oxide.

nested craters: a series of craters, one within another.

NH3: ammonia.

nuée ardente: a French term applied to a highly heated (incandescent) mass of gas-charged ash which is expelled with explosive force and rushes down the mountainside with hurricane speed.

obsidian: a volcanic glass.

Oligocene Epoch. SEE Appendix A.

olivine basalt. SEE tholeiite.

Ordovician Period. SEE Appendix A.

orogeny: the process of forming mountains, particularly by folding and faulting.

pahoehoe: lava with a ropy or billowy surface.

palagonite tuff: a brown, sandstonelike tuff containing innumerable angular, yellow or brown grains called palagonite and originally thought to be a definite mineral but now known to be devitrified basaltic glass.

Paleocene Epoch. SEE Appendix A.

Paleozoic Era. SEE Appendix A.

Pennsylvanian Period. SEE Appendix A.

period: the fundamental unit of the standard geologic time scale during which a standard system of rocks was formed.

Permian Period. SEE Appendix A.

phenocryst: a large or "evident" crystal embedded in a much finer grained (or even glassy) groundmass. Such a rock is known as a porphyry, and most lavas are porphyries. The phenocrysts develop during slow cooling in the magma chamber, while the groundmass is the result of rapid cooling when the material is poured out on the surface.

phreatic explosion: an explosion caused by the conversion of ground water to steam, resulting from the mixing of volcanic gases or magma with ground water.

pino. SEE Plinian.

pit crater: a circular, steep-walled depression sunk below the gently sloping surface of a volcano and not surrounded by a rim; commonly located along the rift zone on the flanks of shield volcanoes, such as Kilauea.

plateau basalt: term applied to those basaltic lavas which occur in essentially horizontal position over vast areas, such as the Columbia River Plateau. They are believed to be the product of fissure eruptions. They are also known as flood basalts.

plate tectonics: concept that the earth's crust is divided into a number of plates which are slowly moving with respect to one another and that many of the tectonic features, such as mountains, are formed at the juncture of the plates.

Pleistocene Epoch. SEE Appendix A.

Plinian: a term now generally applied to the phase of an eruption in which there is a tremendous uprushing of gas, producing an eruption cloud which Pliny described as resembling a *pino*, or pine tree.

Pliocene Epoch. SEE Appendix A.

pluton: a body of igneous rock formed beneath the surface by consolidation of magma.

plutonic: a general term applied to igneous rocks which have crystallized at great depth and have assumed a granitoid texture.

porphyry. SEE phenocryst.

Precambrian Era. SEE Appendix A.

pressure ridge: an elongate upbowing of the crust of a lava flow, believed to be due to the compressive force imparted by the viscous drag of slowly moving subcrustal lava. Similar features occur on glaciers.

psi: pounds per square inch.

psig: pounds per square inch gauge pressure.

pumice: a highly vesicular, frothy natural glass with a high silica content. It is normally light in color and will float on water.

pyroclastic: a general term applied to volcanic material (ash, cinders, etc.) which has been explosively ejected from a volcanic vent.

pyromagma: the liquid or vesiculate basaltic lava of surface pools and flows of shield volcanoes. It is spongy and tends to froth as gases in solution escape from it.

pyrometer: an instrument for measuring temperatures, especially those beyond the range of mercurial thermometers.

Quaternary Period. SEE Appendix A.

radioactive element: an element capable of changing spontaneously into another element by the emission of charged particles from the nuclei of its atoms; e.g., uranium.

radioactive heat: the heat formed in rocks by the active disintegration of natural radioactive elements.

Recent Epoch. SEE Appendix A.

remanent magnetism: the magnetism remaining in rock particles, which causes a magnetic field to persist.

resurgent caldera: one in which a renewal of activity results in an uplift or up-arching of the caldera floor.

rhyolite: a fine-grained rock, normally a lava, having the composition of granite.

rift zones: fissures along which repeated eruptions occur. They usually radiate from the summit of a volcano.

ring dikes: circular dikes which dip steeply outward, probably formed by the intrusion of magma along concentric fractures formed by the subsidence of a roughly circular mass of roof rock into a magma chamber.

ropy lava: same as pahoehoe lava.

S: the element sulphur.

saturated steam: the maximum amount of steam for a given temperature and pressure.

scoria: a basaltic type of volcanic ejecta, characterized by its vesicular nature; a volcanic slag.

sea-floor spreading: hypothesis that new oceanic crust rises from the mantle along mid-oceanic ridges and spreads laterally across the sea floor.

sector graben: a depressed section on the side of a volcanic cone.

seismic: pertaining to earthquakes or earth vibrations.

shear plane: the plane along which one part of a body, such as a lava flow, moves with respect to the other part.

shield volcano: a broad, gently sloping volcanic cone composed chiefly of overlapping flows of basaltic lava; e.g., Mauna Loa.

Si: the element silicon.

sial: a layer of rock underlying the continents, largely granitic in composition. The thickness varies from 30 to 35 km.

Silurian Period. SEE Appendix A.

sima: one of the layers of the crustal zone of the earth, largely basaltic in composition. In the continental areas it underlies the sial.

SiO₂: silicon dioxide (silica).

SO₂: sulphur dioxide.

SO₃: sulphur trioxide.

solfatara: a volcanic vent from which only gases are emitted.

somma: a ridge or rim representing the remnant of an ancient caldera wall.

soufrière: in French-speaking regions, a common name for volcanoes giving off sulphurous gases; solfatara.

spatter cone: a mound or cone formed by lava fragments (spatters) accumulating around a vent.

squeeze-up: a small bulbous, linear, or irregular-shaped accumulation of lava formed by the extrusion of viscous lava through an opening in the solidified crust.

stratosphere: the layer of the atmosphere above the troposphere. The height of the base of the stratosphere varies from about 9 km. at the poles to 16 km. at the equator.

strato-volcano: a volcanic cone, usually of large size, built of alternating layers of lava and pyroclastic material; also known as a composite cone.

subduction zone: the zone, according to the sea-floor-spreading hypothesis, where the crustal layer descends into the mantle.

superheated: said of a liquid heated above its boiling point without converting into vapor or of steam that has an excess of heat over that required to maintain its state as a dry gas.

syncline: a fold in the rocks in which strata dip inward from both sides toward the axis.

tectogene: a large downfold of the granitic crust (sial) beneath a mountain belt.

tectonics: study of the broader structural features of the earth and their causes.

tephra: a collective term for all clastic volcanic material, including ash, cinders, bombs, etc.

Tertiary Period. SEE Appendix A.

tholeiite: one of the two types of flood basalts, the other being olivine basalt. They are distinguished on the basis of their mineralogical content, primarily the amount of olivine and the type of ferro-magnesium minerals.

tholoid: a volcanic dome, usually composed of viscous lava filling a crater.

tilt meter: an instrument used to measure the displacement of the ground from the horizontal; used in volcanology to measure the doming-up of a volcano by magmatic pressure.

trachyte: an extrusive rock composed of alkalic feldspar and minor amounts of biotite, hornblende, or pyroxene. It is the extrusive equivalent of a syenite.

trachytic: a textural term applied to the groundmass of volcanic rocks in which the feldspars are arranged in parallel or sub-parallel fashion around the phenocrysts and corresponding to the flow lines of the lava.

transform fault: a type of fault associated with sea-floor spreading along mid-oceanic ridges.

trap rock: a term applied to dark-colored rocks of dikes, sills, and lava flows.

Triassic Period. SEE Appendix A.

troposphere: that portion of the atmosphere next to the earth's surface. SEE stratosphere.

tsunami: a sea wave produced by a submarine earthquake or a volcanic eruption. Often improperly called a tidal wave.

tuff: a rock composed of compacted volcanic fragments, generally smaller than 4 mm. in diameter.

tumescence: in volcanology, the swelling of a volcano during periods of rising magma preceding an eruption.

tumulus (pl., tumuli): a small, dome-shaped feature on the surface of a congealed lava flow. Tumuli result from a buckling of the flow crust, aided by pressure of the underlying liquid lava.

volcanic dome: a steep-sided mass of viscous lava forming a more or less dome-shaped mass over the volcanic vent.

welded tuff: a fine-grained volcanic rock in which the particles were so hot when deposited that they fused together.

xenolith: a rock fragment that is foreign to the igneous rock in which it occurs; an inclusion.

Bibliography

Abbe, Cleveland. 1906. Benjamin Franklin as a meteorologist. *Proceedings of the American Philosophical Society* 45:117–128.

Abbot, C. G., and F. E. Fowle. 1913. *Volcanoes and climate*. Smithsonian Miscellaneous Collection, vol. 60, no. 29. Washington, D.C.

Adams, F. D. 1938. *The birth and development of the geological sciences*. Baltimore: Williams and Wilkins Co.

Agostinho, J. 1931 [published in 1936]. The volcanoes of the Azores Islands. *Bulletin Volcanologique*, nos. 27–30, pp. 123–138.

Alfano, G. B., and I. Friedlander. 1928. *La storia del Vesuvio*. Naples: K. Holm.

Allen, E. T., and A. L. Day. 1927 *Steam wells and other thermal activity at The Geysers, California*. Carnegie Institution of Washington Publication 378. Washington, D.C.

———. 1935. *Hot springs of the Yellowstone National Park*. Carnegie Institution of Washington Publication 466. Washington, D.C.

Anderson, J. H. 1973. Vapor-turbine cycle for geothermal power generation. In *Geothermal energy*, edited by Paul Kruger and Carel Otte, pp. 163–175. Stanford: Stanford University Press.

Anderson, Tempest. 1903. *Volcanic studies in many lands*. London: John Murray.

Anderson, Tempest, and J. S. Flett. 1902. Preliminary report on the recent eruptions of the Soufrière in St. Vincent and of a visit to Mont Pelée, in Martinique. *Proceedings of the Royal Society of London* 70:423–445.

———. 1903–1908. Report on the eruption of the Soufrière, in St. Vincent, in 1902, and on a visit to Montagne Pelée in Martinique. *Philosophical Transactions of the Royal Society of London*, ser. A, 200:353–553; 208:275–332.

Arduino, Giovanni. 1759. Fisico-mineralogico di Lythogomia e orognosia. *Atti dell'Accademia delle Scienze di Siena*, vol. 5.

Arsandaux, H. 1934. L'éruption de la Montagne Pelée en 1929. *Revue Scientifique* 72(8):248–251.

Atwater, T. 1970. Implications of plate-tectonics for Cenozoic evolution of Western United States. *Geological Society of America Bulletin* 81:3513–3536.

Atwood, W. W., Jr. 1935. The glacial history of an extinct volcano, Crater Lake National Park. *Journal of Geology* 43:142–168.

Bailey, Roy A., G. Brent Dalrymple, and Marvin A. Lanphere. 1976. Volcanism, structure, and geochronology of Long Valley Caldera, Mono County, California. *Journal of Geophysical Research* 81(5):725–744.

Baker, Howard B. 1912. The origin of continental forms. In *Michigan Academy of Science Annual Report 1911–1912*, pt. 2, pp. 116–141; pt. 3, pp. 107–113.

Banco di Roma. 1954. *Review of economic conditions in Italy for 1954* 8:21. Rome.

Barth, Tom F. W. 1950. *Volcanic geology, hot springs and geysers of Iceland*. Carnegie Institution of Washington Publication 587. Washington, D.C.

———. 1952. *Theoretical petrology*. New York: John Wiley and Sons.

Bemmelen, R. W. van. 1929. *Het caldera probleem*. De Mijningenieur, no. 4.

———. 1939. The volcanic-tectonic origin of Lake Toba (north Sumatra). *De Ingenieur Nederlandsch-Indie* 6:126–140.

Bodvärsson, Gunnar. 1960. Hot springs and the exploration of natural heat resources. In *Guide Book to Excursion A-2*, pp. 46–55. Copenhagen: International Geological Congress, XXI Session.

Bosanquet, F. C. T., ed. 1903. *Pliny's letters*. London: George Bell and Sons.

Bowen, N. L. 1928. *The evolution of igneous rocks*. Princeton: Princeton University Press.

Brooks, C. E. P. 1949. *Climate through the ages*. Rev. ed. New York: McGraw-Hill.

Bruce, J. A., and F. B. Shorland. 1932–1933. Utilization of natural heat resources in thermal regions. *New Zealand Journal of Agriculture* 45:272–279; 47:29–33.

Brun, A. 1911. *Recherches sur l'exhalaison volcanique*. Geneva: Kündig.

Brunhes, Bernard. 1906. Recherches sur la direction d'aimantation des roches volcaniques. *Journal de Physique*, 4th ser. 5:705–724.

Budd, Chester F., Jr. 1973. Steam production at The Geysers geothermal field. In *Geothermal energy*, edited by Paul Kruger and Carel Otte. Stanford: Stanford University Press.

Bullard, Fred M. 1947*a*. Studies on Parícutin Volcano. *Geological Society of America Bulletin* 58:433–449.

———. 1947*b*. The story of Parícutin. *Scientific Monthly* 65:357–371.

———. 1954*a*. Volcanic activity in Costa Rica and Nicaragua in 1954. *Transactions of the American Geophysical Union* 37:75–82.

———. 1954*b*. A volcanic cycle as exhibited by Italian volcanoes. *Tulsa Geological Society Digest* 22:101–110.

———. 1954*c*. Activity of Stromboli in June and December, 1952. *Bulletin Volcanologíque*, ser. 2, 15:91–98.

———. 1954*d*. Stromboli, lighthouse of the Mediterranean. *Alcalde* (University of Texas) 42:284–289.

———. 1956. Resumen de la historia del Volcán Parícutin, Michoacán, México. *Twentieth International Geologic Congress Guide Book*, Excursion A-15, pp. 61–74. Mexico City.

———. 1971. Volcanic history of the Great Rift, Craters of the Moon National Monument, south-central Idaho. *Geological Society of America Abstracts with Programs* 3(3):234.

Bullard, Fred M., and Don Rylander. 1970. Holocene volcanism in Craters of the Moon National Monument and adjacent areas, south-central Idaho. *Geological Society of America Abstracts with Programs* 3(3):234.

Bullard, Sir Edward, and H. Gellman. 1954. Homogeneous dynamos and terrestrial magnetism. *Philosophical Transactions of the Royal Society of London*, ser. A, 247:213–277.

Bulletin of Volcanic Eruptions. 1964. No. 4. Naples: International Association of Volcanology.

———. 1969. No. 9. Tokyo: Volcanological Association of Japan; Naples: International Association of Volcanology.

———. 1970. No. 10. Tokyo: Volcanological Association of Japan; Naples: International Association of Volcanology.

Bunsen, R. 1847. Physikalische Beobachtungen über die hauptsachlichsten Gisire Islands. *Poggendorf's Annalen der Physik und Chemie* 72:159–170.

Burnett, Thomas. 1681–1689. *Telluris theoria sacra*. London: R. N. Impensis Gault, Kettilby. Translated in 1734 as *Sacred history of the earth*. London: H. Lintot.

Butler, Samuel. 1897. *Authoress of the Odyssey*. London: A. C. Fifield.

Capps, S. R. 1915. An ancient volcanic eruption in the upper Yukon Basin. *U.S. Geological Survey Professional Paper* 95D:59–64.

Cassius, Dio Cocceianus. 1914. *Dio's Roman history; with English translation by E. Carey on the basis of the version of Herbert Baldwin Foster*. 9 vols. London: W. Heinemann.

Catalogue of the active volcanoes of the world, including solfatara fields. 1951–1967. Pts. 1–21. Naples: International Volcanological Association; Rome: International Association of Volcanology.

Center for Short-Lived Phenomena. 1969–1973. *Annual report*. Cambridge, Mass.: Smithsonian Institution.

Ceram, C. W. 1951. *Gods, graves and scholars*. Translated by E. B. Garside. New York: Alfred A. Knopf.

Christiansen, Robert L. 1974. Volcanology. *Geotimes* 19(1):33.

———. 1980. Mount St. Helens eruption. *Nature* 285(5766):531–533.

Christiansen, Robert L., and P. W. Lipman. 1972. Cenozoic volcanism and plate-tectonic evolution of the Western United States, Pt. II, pp. 249–284. In A discussion of volcanism and structure of the earth, organized by J. Sutton et al. *Philosophical Transactions of the Royal Society of London*, ser. A, *Mathematical and Physical Sciences*, 271(1213): 101–323.

Christiansen, Robert L., and C. Dan Miller. 1976. Volcanic evolution of Mt. Shasta, California. *Geological Society of America Abstracts with Programs* 8(3): 360–361.

Church, Alfred, and W. J. Brodribb, trans. 1872. *Pliny's letters*. Ancient Classics for English Readers. London: William Blackwood and Sons.

Coats, R. R. 1950. *Volcanic activity in the Aleutian arc. U.S. Geological Survey Bulletin* 974B.

———. 1962. Magma type and crustal structure in the Aleutian arc. In *Crust of the Pacific basin*, edited by Gordon A. Macdonald and H. Kuno, pp. 92–109. American Geophysical Union Monograph 6. Washington, D.C.

Combs, J., and J. P. Muffler. 1973. Exploration for geothermal resources. In *Geothermal energy*, edited by Paul Kruger and Carel Otte, pp. 95–128. Stanford: Stanford University Press.

Coombs, H. A. 1939. Mt. Baker, a Cascade volcano. *Geological Society of America Bulletin* 50:1493–1510.

———. 1960. *Catalogue of active volcanoes of the world*, Pt. 9, *United States of America*. With Arthur D. Howard. Naples: International Volcanological Association.

Corti, E. C. C. 1951. *The destruction and resurrection of Pompeii and Herculaneum*. Translated by K. and R. Gregor Smith. London: Routledge and Kegan Paul.

Cotton, C. A. 1944. *Volcanoes as landscape forms*. Christchurch, New Zealand: Whitcombe and Tombs.

Cox, A., G. B. Dalrymple, and R. R. Doell. 1967. Reversals of the earth's magnetic field. *Scientific American* 216(2):44–54.

Cox, Alan, and G. B. Dalrymple. 1967. Statistical analysis of geomagnetic reversal data and the precision of potassium-argon dating. *Jouranl of Geophysical Research* 72:2603–2614.

Crandell, Dwight R. 1969. *The geologic story of Mount Rainier. U.S. Geological Survey Bulletin* 1292.

———. 1972. Glaciation near Lassen Peak, Northern California. *U.S. Geological Survey Professional Paper* 800-C, pp. 179–188.

Crandell, Dwight R., and Donal R. Mullineaux. 1967. *Volcanic hazards at Mount Rainier, Washington. U.S. Geological Survey Bulletin* 1238.

———. 1978. Potential hazards from future eruptions of Mount St. Helens Volcano, Washington. *U.S. Geological Survey Bulletin* 1383-C.

Crandell, Dwight R., Donal R. Mullineaux, and C. Dan Miller. 1979. Volcanic hazard studies in the Cascade Range of the Western United States. In *Volcanic activity and human ecology*, edited by Payson D. Sheets and Donald K. Grayson, pp. 195–219. New York: Academic Press.

Crandell, Dwight R., Donal R. Mullineaux, and Meyer Rubin. 1975. Mount St. Helens Volcano—recent and future behavior. *Science* 187(4175):438–441.

Crandell, Dwight R., Donal R. Mullineaux, Robert S. Sigafoos, and Meyer Rubin. 1974. Chaos Craigs eruptions and rock-avalanches, Lassen Volcanic National Park, California. *U.S. Geological Survey Journal of Research* 2(1):49–59.

Crandell, Dwight R., and Meyer Rubin. 1977. Late glacial and post-glacial eruptions at Mt. Hood, Oregon. *Geological Society of America, Abstracts with Programs* 9:406.

Curie, Pierre. 1895. Propriétés magnétiques des corps à diverses températures. *Journal de Physique, Chimie et Histoire Naturelle Elémentaires* 4:197–212; 263–272.

Curtis, G. H. 1968. The stratigraphy of the ejecta of the 1912 eruption of Mt. Katmai and Novarupta, Alaska. In *Studies in volcanology*, pp. 153–211. *Geological Society of America Memoirs* 116.

Daly, R. A. 1933. *Igneous rocks and the depths of the earth.* New York: McGraw-Hill.

———. 1940. *Strength and structure of the earth.* New York: Prentice-Hall.

Dana, J. D. 1891. *Characteristics of volcanoes.* New York: Dodd, Mead and Co.

Daubeny, Charles. 1827. *A description of active and extinct volcanoes.* 1st ed. London: W. Phillips.

———. 1848. *A description of active and extinct volcanoes, of earthquakes and thermal springs.* 2d ed. London: Richard and John E. Taylor.

Davidson, George. 1885. Recent volcanic activity in the U.S.: Eruption of Mount Baker. *Science* 6(138):262.

Day, Arthur L., and E. T. Allen. 1925. *Volcanic activity and hot springs of Lassen Peak. Carnegie Institution of Washington Publication* 360.

Day, Arthur L., and E. S. Shepherd. 1913. Water and volcanic activity. *Geological Society of America Bulletin* 24:573–606.

Decker, Robert. 1959. *Renewed activity of Anak Krakatoa.* Bandung: Institute of Technology, Contributions of the Department of Geology, no. 34, pp. 1–5.

Decker, Robert, and Barbara Decker. 1981. The eruption of Mount St. Helens. *Scientific American* 244(3):68–80.

De Fiore, O. 1922. *Vulcano. Revista Vulcanologica,* supp. 3, pt. 1. 380 pp.

Deitz, R. S. 1961. Continent and ocean basin evolution by spreading of the sea floor. *Nature* 190:845–857.

———. 1962. Ocean basin evolution by sea-floor spreading. In *Crust of the Pacific basin,* edited by Gordon A. Macdonald and H. Kuno. American Geophysical Union Monograph 6. Washington, D.C.

De Lorenzo, G. 1906. The eruption of Vesuvius in April, 1906. *Quarterly Journal of the Geological Society of London* 62:476–483.

Dewey, F., and J. M. Bird. 1970. Mountain belts and the new global tectonics. *Journal of Geophysical Research* 75(14):2625–2647.

Dickinson, W. R., and T. Hatherton. 1967. Andesitic volcanism and seismicity around the Pacific. *Science* 157:801–803.

Diller, J. S., and H. B. Patton. 1902. *The geology and petrography of Crater Lake National Park. U.S. Geological Survey Professional Paper* 3.

Diodorus Siculus. 1913. *Diodorus of Sicily; with an English translation by C. H. Oldfather.* London: W. Heinemann.

Dott, R. H., Jr., and R. L. Batten. 1971. *Evolution of the earth.* New York: McGraw-Hill.

DuToit, A. L. 1937. *Our wandering continents.* Edinburgh: Oliver and Boyd.

Easterbrook, D. J., and D. A. Rahn. 1970. *Landforms of Washington–the geologic environment.* Bellingham: Western Washington State College.

Eaton, J. P., and K. J. Murata. 1960. How volcanoes grow. *Science* 132:925–938.

Eichorn, Arthur F. 1957. *The Mount Shasta story.* Rev. ed. Mount Shasta, Calif.: The Mount Shasta Herald.

Elsasser, W. M. 1956. Background of geomagnetic dynamo theory (summary). *Journal of Geophysical Research* 61(2, pt. 2):340–347.

———. 1958. The earth as a dynamo. *Scientific American* 198(5):44–48.

Elskens, I., H. Tazieff, and F. Tonani. 1964. A new method for volcanic gas analysis in the field. *Bulletin Volcanologique,* ser. 2, 27:347–350.

Escher, B. G. 1919. De Krakatau groep als vulkaan. *Handelingen, Nederlandsch-Indisch Natuurwetenschappelijk Congres,* pp. 28–35. Weltevreden.

Fenner, C. N. 1920. The Katmai region, Alaska, and the great eruption of 1912. *Journal of Geology* 28:569–606.

———. 1923. *The origin and mode of emplacement of the great tuff deposit of the Valley of Ten Thousand Smokes. National Geographic Society Contributed Technical Papers,* Katmai Series, no. 1. Washington, D.C. 74 pp.

———. 1936. Bore hole investigations in Yellowstone Park. *Journal of Geology* 44:225–315.

———. 1950. The chemical kinetics of the Katmai eruption. *American Journal of Science* 248(9):593–627; 248(10):697–725.

Finch, R. H. 1930. Mud flow of Lassen Volcano. *Hawaiian Volcano Observatory, Volcano Letter* 266:1–3. January 30, 1930.

———. 1937. A tree ring calendar for dating volcanic events. *American Journal of Science* 33:140–146.

Finch, R. H., and C. A. Anderson. 1930. The quartz basalt eruption of Cinder Cone, Lassen Volcanic National Park, California. *University of California at Berkeley Publications, Bulletin of the Department of Geological Sciences* 19:245–273.

Fiorelli, G. 1861–1865. *Giornale delgi scavi de Pompei.* Naples.

Fisher, N. H. 1957. *Catalogue of the active volcanoes of the world, including solfatara fields.* Pt. 5, *Melanesia.* Naples: International Volcanological Association.

Fisher, Richard V., and Aaron C. Waters. 1970. Base surge bed forms in maar volcanoes. *American Journal of Science* 266:157–180.

Fiske, R. S., C. A. Hopson, and A. C. Waters. 1963. *Geology of Mount Rainier National Park, Washington. U.S. Geological Survey Professional Paper* 444.

Fiske, R. S., and W. T. Kinoshita. 1969. Inflation of Kilauea volcano prior to its 1967–68 eruption. *Science* 165:341–349.

Fiske, R. S., and R. Y. Koyanagi. 1968. *The December 1965 eruption of Kilauea Volcano, Hawaii. U.S. Geological Survey Professional Paper* 607.

Forbes, H. B. 1967–1968. A note on volcanic activity. In *Annual report of the Geophysical Institute, University of Alaska.* College, Alaska.

Forbes, James D. 1829. Physical notices of the Bay of Naples, no. 5: On the Temple of Jupiter Serapis at Pozzuoli and the phenomena which it exhibits. *Edinburgh Journal of Science* 1:260–261.

Fouqué, Ferdinand André. 1879. *Santorin et ses éruptions.* Paris: G. Masson.

Fournier, R. O., and J. J. Rowe. 1966. Estimation of underground temperatures from the silica content of water from hot springs and wet-steam wells. *American Journal of Science* 264:685–697.

Foxworthy, Bruce L., and Mary Hill. 1982. *Volcanic eruptions of 1980 at Mount St. Helens: The First 100 Days. U.S. Geological Survey Professional Paper* 1249.

Frank, David, Mark F. Meier, and Donald A. Swanson. 1977. *Assessment of increased thermal activity at Mount Baker, Washington, March 1975–March 1976. U.S. Geological Survey Professional Paper* 1022-A.

Frazer, James B. 1930. *Myths of the origin of fire.* London: Macmillan Co.

Fries, C., Jr. 1953. Volumes and weights of pyroclastic material, lava, and water erupted by Parícutin Volcano, Michoacán, Mexico. *Transactions of the American Geophysical Union* 34:603–616.

Fries, C., Jr., and C. Gutiérrez. 1950a. Activity of Parícutin Volcano from August 1, 1948, to June 30, 1949. *Transactions of the American Geophysical Union* 31:406–418.

———. 1950b. Activity of Parícutin Volcano from July 1 to December 31, 1949. *Transactions of the American Geophysical Union* 31:732–740.

———. 1951a. Activity of Parícutin Volcano from January 1 to June 30, 1950. *Transactions of the American Geophysical Union* 32:212–221.

———. 1951b. Activity of Parícutin Volcano from July 1 to December 31, 1950. *Transactions of the American Geophysical Union* 32:572–581.

———. 1952a. Activity of Parícutin Volcano from January 1 to June 30, 1951.

Transactions of the American Geophysical Union 33:91–100.

———. 1952*b*. Activity of Parícutin Volcano from July 1 to December 31, 1951. *Transactions of the American Geophysical Union* 33:725–733.

———. 1954. Activity of Parícutin Volcano in 1952. *Transactions of the American Geophysical Union* 35:486–494.

Frost, K. Y. 1939. The Critias and Minoan Crete. *Journal of Hellenic Studies* 33:189–206.

Gadow, Hans, 1930. *Jorullo*. Cambridge: The University Press.

Galanopoulos, George A. 1960. Tsunami observed on the coast of Greece from antiquity to present time. *Annali Geofisica* 13:369–386.

Galanopoulos, George A., and Edward Bacon. 1969. *Atlantis: The truth behind the legend*. New York: Bobbs-Merrill.

Gardner, J. Starkie. 1885. Can underground heat be utilized? *Geological Magazine*, ns., decade 3, 2:397–406.

Gautier, A. 1906. The genesis of thermal waters and their connection with volcanism. *Economic Geology* 1:687–697. Lancaster, Pa.

Gayley, Charles M. 1911. *Classic myths in English literature and art*. Boston: Ginn and Co.

Gealey, W. K. 1951. *Geology of the Healdsburg quadrangle. California Division of Mines Bulletin* 161.

Gedney, L., C. Matteson, and R. B. Forbes. 1970. Seismic refraction profiles of the ash flow in the Valley of Ten Thousand Smokes, Katmai National Monument, Alaska. *Journal of Geophysical Research* 75:2619–2624.

Geikie, Sir Archibald, 1903. *Textbook of geology*, vol. 1. 4th ed. London: Macmillan.

———. 1905. *The founders of geology*. 2d ed. London: Macmillan.

Georgalas, G. C. 1962. *Catalogue of the active volcanoes of the world, including solfatara fields*. Pt. 12. *Greece*. Naples: International Volcanological Association.

Gibbs, George. 1874. Physical geography of the northwest boundary of the United States. *American Geographic Society Journal* 4:298–392.

Giggenbach, Werner F., Philip R. Kyle, and Graeme L. Lyon. 1973. Present volcanic activity on Mount Erebus, Ross Island, Antarctica. *Geology* 1:135–137. Boulder Colo.: Geological Society of America.

Gilbert, Sir William. 1600. *De Magnete* (in Latin). London. An English translation with notes by S. P. Thompson was issued by the Gilbert Club of London in 1900.

Gilluly, James. 1971. Plate tectonics and magmatic evolution. *Geological Society of America Bulletin* 82:2383–2396.

Gilluly, James, A. C. Waters, and A. O. Woodford. 1959. *Principles of geology*. 2d ed. San Francisco: W. H. Freeman and Co.

———. 1968. *Principles of geology*. 3d ed. San Francisco: W. H. Freeman and Co.

Glasstone, Samuel, ed. 1950. *The effect of atomic weapons*. Los Alamos, N.M.: Los Alamos Science Laboratory, U.S. Atomic Energy Commission.

González Reyna, Jenaro, and William F. Foshag. 1947. The birth of Parícutin. In *Smithsonian Institution Annual Report for 1946*, pp. 223–234. Washington, D.C.

Goranson, R. W. 1931. The solubility of water in granitic magmas. *American Journal of Science*, 5th ser. 22:483–502.

———. 1938*a*. Phase equilibria in the $NaAlSi_2O_5-H_2O$ and $KAlSi_3O_8-H_2O$ systems. *American Journal of Science* 235A:71–91.

———. 1938*b*. High temperature and pressure phase-equilibria in albite-water and orthoclase-water systems. *Transactions of the American Geophysical Union* 19:271–273.

Gorshkov, G. S. 1959. Gigantic eruption of volcano Bezymianny. *Bulletin Volcanologique*, ser. 2, 20:77–109.

————. 1960. Determination of the explosion energy in some volcanoes according to barograms. *Bulletin Volcanologique*, ser. 2, 23:141–144.

————. 1970. *Volcanism and the upper mantle: Investigations in the Kurile Island arc.* New York: Plenum Publishing Corp.

Grange, L. I. 1955. *Geothermal steam for power in New Zealand. New Zealand Department of Scientific and Industrial Research Bulletin* 117.

Great Britain. Naval Intelligence Division. 1945. *Italy*, vol. 4. Geographical Handbook Series. London.

Greeley, Ronald, ed. 1974. Field guide to summit area and upper rift zone, Kilauea Volcano, Hawaii, by staff of Hawaiian Volcano Observatory. In *Planetology Conference*, edited by Ronald Greeley, pp. 199–216. Moffet Field, Calif.: NASA–Ames Research Center.

Greeley, Ronald, and R. Baer. 1971. Hambone, California and its magnificent lava tubes—preliminary report. *Geological Society of America Abstracts with Programs* 3(2):128.

Greeley, Ronald, and J. H. Hyde. 1972. Lava tubes of the Cave Basalt, Mount St. Helens, Washington. *Geological Society of America Bulletin* 83:2397—2418.

Gregg, D. R. 1960. *The geology of Tongariro subdivision. New Zealand Geological Survey Bulletin* 40.

Griggs, D. 1939. A theory of mountain building. *American Journal of Science* 237: 611–650.

Griggs, Robert F. 1917. The Valley of Ten Thousand Smokes. *National Geographic Magazine* 31:13–68.

————. 1918. The Valley of Ten Thousand Smokes. *National Geographic Magazine* 33:115–169.

————. 1922. *The Valley of Ten Thousand Smokes (Alaska).* Washington, D.C.: National Geographic Society.

Griggs, Robert F., J. W. Shipley, Jasper D. Sayre, Paul R. Hagelburger, and James S. Hine. 1920. *Scientific results of the Katmai expeditions. Bulletin of Ohio State University* 24(15).

Grindley, G. W. 1965. *The geology, structure and exploitation of the Wairakei geothermal field, Taupo, New Zealand. New Zealand Geological Survey Bulletin*, n.s. 75.

Gutenberg, B. 1959. *Physics of the earth's interior.* International Geophysics Series, vol. 1. New York: Academic Press.

Gutenberg, B., and C. F. Richter. 1938. Depth and geographic distribution of deep-focus earthquakes. *Geological Society of America Bulletin* 49:249–288.

————. 1941. *Seismicity of the earth.* Geological Society of America Special Paper 34.

Hamilton, W. M. 1954. *Geothermal energy.* Cawthorn Lecture Series, no. 27. New Zealand: Cawthorn Institute.

Hamilton, Wayne L. 1973. Tidal cycles of volcanic eruptions: Fortnightly to 19 yearly periods. *Journal of Geophysical Research* 78:3363–3375.

Hamilton, William. 1774. *Observations on Mt. Vesuvius, Mt. Etna, and other volcanoes.* London: T. Cadell.

————. 1776. *Campi Phlegraei: Observations on the volcanoes of the two Sicilies as they have been communicated to the Royal Society of London.* Naples.

————. 1779. *Supplement to Campi Phlegraei, being an account of the great eruption of Vesuvius in the month of August, 1779.* Naples.

Harris, Stephen L. 1976. *Fire and ice: The Cascade volcanoes.* Seattle: Mountaineers–Pacific Search Books.

Hatherton, T., and W. R. Dickinson. 1969. Relationship between andesitic volcanism and seismicity in Indonesia, the Lesser Antilles, and other island arcs. *Journal of Geophysical Research* 74:5301–5310.

Hay, R. L. 1960. Rate of clay formation and mineral alteration in a 4,000-year-old volcanic ash soil on St. Vincent, B.W.I. *American Journal of Science* 258:354–368.

Hazen, Henry A. 1884. Sun glows. *American Journal of Science* 27:201–212.

Healy, J. 1964. Volcanic mechanism in the Taupo Volcanic Zone, New Zealand. *New Zealand Journal of Geology and Geophysics* 7(1):6–23.

———. 1965. Geological notes on volcanoes. In *New Zealand volcanology: Central volcanic region*, edited by B. N. Thompson, L. O. Kermode, and A. Ewart. Department of Scientific and Industrial Research, Information Series 50. Wellington.

Hedervari, P. 1963. On the energy and magnitude of volcanic eruptions. *Bulletin Volcanologique*, ser. 2, 25:372.

Heilprin, A. 1903. *Mount Pelée and the tragedy of Martinique*. Philadelphia: J. B. Lippincott.

———. 1904. *The Tower of Pelé*. Philadelphia: J. B. Lippincott.

Heirtzler, J. R., G. O. Dickson, E. M. Herron, W. C. Pitman, and X. Le Pichon. 1968. Marine magnetic anomalies, geomagnetic field reversals, and motions on the ocean floor and continents. *Journal of Geophysical Research* 73:2119–2136.

Hess, H. H. 1962. History of ocean basins. In *Petrologic studies: A volume in honor of A. F. Buddington*, edited by A. E. J. Engel et al., pp. 599–620. Boulder: Geological Society of America.

Hickel, W. J., et al. 1972. *Geothermal energy: A national proposal for geothermal resources research*. Fairbanks: University of Alaska.

Hill, David P. 1976. Structure of Long Valley Caldera, California, from a seismic refraction experiment. *Journal of Geophysical Research* 81(5):745—753.

Hill, R. T. 1902. Report by Robert T. Hill on the volcanic disturbances in the West Indies. *National Geographic Magazine* 13:223–267.

Hoblitt, Richard, Dwight R. Crandell, and Donal R. Mullineaux. 1980. Mount St. Helens eruptive behavior during the past 1500 years. *Geology* 8:555–559.

Holmes, Arthur. 1928. Radioactivity and earth movements. *Transactions of the Geological Society of Glasgow* 18:559–606.

———. 1945. *Principles of physical geology*. 1st ed. New York: Ronald Press.

———. 1950. Petrogenesis of katungite. *American Mineralogist* 35:772–792.

———. 1959. A revised geologic time-scale. *Transactions of the Edinburgh Geological Society* 17(pt. 3):183–216.

———. 1965. *Principles of physical geology*. 2d ed. New York: Ronald Press.

Horner, Leonard. 1847. On the origin of Monte Nuovo, in a letter from an eyewitness of the eruption of 1538. *Quarterly Journal of the Geological Society of London* 3(pt. 2):19–22.

Hovey, E. O. 1902a. Martinique and St. Vincent: A preliminary report upon the eruption of 1902. *Bulletin of the American Museum of Natural History* 16:333–373.

———. 1902b. The eruption of La Soufrière, St. Vincent, in May, 1902. *National Geographic Magazine* 13:444—459.

Hoyt, J. B. 1958. The cold summer of 1816. *Annals of the Association of American Geographers* (Minneapolis) 48:118—131.

Hughes, John M., R. E. Stoiber, and Michael J. Carr. 1980. Segmentation of the Cascade volcanic chain. *Geology* 8:15–17.

Humboldt, Alexander von. 1811. *Essai politique sur le royaume de la Nouvelle-Espagne*. Paris: F. Schoell.

———. 1823. *Essai géognostique sur le gisement des roches dans les deux hemispheres*. Paris: F. G. Levrault.

———. 1845–1862. *Kosmos: Entwurf einer physischen Weltbeschreibung von Alexander von Humboldt*. 5 vols. Stuttgart and Tübingen: Cotta.

———. 1866. *The cosmos.* translated by E. C. Otté. New York: Harper and Brothers.

Humphreys, W. J. 1940. *Physics of the air.* New York: McGraw-Hill.

Hutton, James. 1788. Theory of the earth. *Transactions of the Royal Society of Edinburgh* 1:209–304.

———. 1795. *Theory of the earth with proofs and illustrations.* 2 vols. London: Cadell, Junior, and Davies.

Hyde, H. 1975. *Upper Pleistocene pyroclastic flow deposits south of Mount St. Helens, Washington. U.S. Geological Survey Bulletin* 1383-B.

Hyde, Jack H., and Dwight R. Crandell. 1978. *Postglacial volcanic deposits at Mount Baker, Washington, and potential hazards from future eruptions. U.S. Geological Survey Professional Paper* 1022-C.

Illingworth, Frank. 1949. Iceland's municipal water system. *Water and Water Engineering* 52:437–444.

Imbo, G. 1928. Variazioni cicliche nella successione di periodi di riposo etnei. *Bulletin of Volcanology,* nos. 15–18, pp. 80–88.

———. 1951. L'attività eruttiva vesuviana e relative osservazioni nel corso dell'intervallo intereuttivo 1906–1944 ed in particolare del parossimo del marzo, 1944. *Annali dell'Osservatorio Vesuviano,* 5th ser. 1(pt. 1).

———. 1965*a*. Eruptive energies. *Annali dell'Osservatorio Vesuviano* 7:106–160.

———. 1965*b*. *Catalogue of the active volcanoes of the world, including solfatara fields.* Pt. 18, *Italy.* Naples: International Volcanological Association.

———. 1970. Pozzuoli uplift. Center for Short-Lived Phenomena, Event Card 878 (March 5). Cambridge, Mass.: Smithsonian Institution.

Isacks, Bryan, Jack Oliver, and Lynn R. Sykes. 1968. Seismology and the new global tectonics. *Journal of Geophysical Research* 73:5855–5899.

Jackson, E. D., E. A. Silver, and G. B. Dalrymple. 1972. Hawaiian-Emperor Chain and its relation to Cenozoic circumpacific tectonics. *Geological Society of America Bulletin* 83:610–618.

Jaggar, Thomas A. 1902. Field notes of a geologist in Martinique and St. Vincent. *Popular Science Monthly* 61:352–368.

———. 1931. Volcanic cycles and sunspots. *Volcano Letter,* no. 326.

———. 1940. Magmatic gases. *American Journal of Science* 238:313–353.

———. 1945. *Volcanoes declare war.* Honolulu: Paradise of the Pacific.

———. 1949. *Steam blast volcanic eruptions.* Hawaiian Volcano Observatory, 4th Special Report.

Jeffreys, Harold. 1928. The times of transmission and focal depths of large earthquakes. *Royal Astronomical Society Monthly Notices: Geophysical Supplement* 1:500–521.

Johnston, M. J. S., and F. J. Mauk. 1972. Earth tides and the triggering of eruptions from Mount Stromboli, Italy. *Nature* 239:266–267.

———. 1973. On the triggering of volcanic eruptions by earth tides. *Journal of Geophysical Research* 78:3356–3362.

Johnston-Lavis, H. J. 1888–1890. Recent eruptions of Vulcano. *Nature* 39:109–111, 173; 42:78–79.

———. 1918. *Bibliography of the geology and eruptive phenomena of the more important volcanoes of southern Italy.* 2d ed. London: University of London Press.

Judd, John W. 1875. Contributions to the Study of Volcanoes. *Geological Magazine for 1875,* pp. 1–16, 56–70, 99–115, 145–152, 206–214.

———. 1881. *Volcanoes: What they are and what they teach.* New York: D. Appleton and Co.

Kay, Marshall. 1951. *North American geosynclines. Geological Society of America Memoirs* 48.

Keller, W. D., and A. Valduga. 1946. The natural steam of Larderello, Italy. *Journal of Geology* 54: 327–334.

Kennan, George. 1902. The tragedy of Pelée, pt. 5. *Outlook* 71:769–777.

Kennedy, George C. 1955. Some aspects of the role of water in rock melts. In *Crust of the earth*, edited by A. Poldervaat, pp. 489–504. Geological Society of America Special Paper 62.

Kinoshita, W. T., R. Y. Koyanagi, T. L. Wright, and R. S. Fiske. 1969. Kilauea Volcano: The 1967–68 summit eruption. *Science* 166:459–468.

Kjartansson, G. 1967. Volcanic forms at the sea bottom in Iceland and mid-oceanic ridges: Report of a symposium. *Societas Scientiarum Islandica* (Reykjavik) 38:53–64.

Koenig, James B. 1969. The Geysers geothermal field. *California Division of Mines and Geology Mineral Information Service* 22(8):123–128.

———. 1973. Worldwide status of geothermal resources development. In *Geothermal energy*, edited by Paul Kruger and Carel Otte, pp. 15–67. Stanford: Stanford University Press.

Koyanagi, Robert Y., Elliot T. Endo, and Jennifer S. Ebisu. In press. Reawakening of Mauna Loa Volcano, Hawaii: A preliminary evaluation of seismic evidence. *Geophysical Research Letters* (American Geophysical Union, Washington, D.C.).

Krauskopf, Konrad B. 1974. *The third planet: An invitation to geology*. San Francisco: Freeman, Cooper, and Co.

Kuno, H. 1966. Lateral variations of basaltic magma across continental margins and island arcs. In *Continental margins and island arcs*, edited by W. H. Poole, pp. 317–336. Canadian Geological Survey Paper 66–15. Ottawa.

Lacroix, A. 1904. *La Montagne Pelée et ses éruptions*. Ouvrage publié par l'Académie des sciences sous les auspices des Ministères de l'Instruction publique et des Colonies. Paris: Masson et Cie.

———. 1908. *La Montagne Pelée après ses éruptions, avec observations sur les éruptions du Vésuve en 79 et en 1906*. Paris: Masson.

Lamb, H. H. 1970. Volcanic dust in the atmosphere; with a chronology and assessment of its meteorological significance. *Philosophical Transactions of the Royal Society of London*, ser. A, 266:425–533.

Latham, G., et al. 1971. Moonquakes. *Science* 174:687.

Leet, L. Don. 1948. *Causes of catastrophe*. New York: Whittlesey House.

Leet, L. Don, and S. Judson. 1954. *Physical geology*. Englewood Cliffs, N.J.: Prentice-Hall.

Le Pichon, X. 1968. Sea-floor spreading and continental drift. *Journal of Geophysical Research* 73:3661–3697.

Lipman, P. E., and T. A. Stevens. 1969. Petrologic evolution of the San Juan volcanic field, southwestern Colorado, U.S.A. (Abstract). In *Abstracts of the International Association of Volcanology and the Chemistry of the Earth's Interior Symposium on Volcanoes and Their Roots*, p. 254. Oxford University.

Lipman, P. W., and Donal R. Mullineaux, eds. 1981. *The 1980 eruption of Mt. St. Helens. U.S. Geological Survey Professional Paper* 1250.

Lliboutry, L. 1969. Sea-floor spreading, continental drift and lithosphere sinking with the asthenosphere at melting point. *Journal of Geophysical Research* 74:6525–6540.

Lobeck, A. K. 1939. *Geomorphology*. New York: McGraw-Hill.

Lobley, J. L. 1889. *Mount Vesuvius*. London: Roper and Drowley.

Long, Leon. 1974. *Geology*. New York: McGraw-Hill.

Longwell, Chester R., Richard F. Flint, and John E. Saunders. 1969. *Physical geology*. New York: John Wiley and Sons.

Loomis, Benjamin Franklin. 1926. *Pictorial history of Lassen Volcano*. Rev. ed. by P. E. Schultz, 1948. Mineral, Calif.: Loomis Museum Association.

Luce, J. V. 1969. *Lost Atlantis*. New York: McGraw-Hill.

Lyell, Charles. 1830. *Principles of geology*. 1st ed. London: John Murray.

———. 1875. *Principles of geology*. 2 vols. 12th ed. London: John Murray.

McBirney, A. R. 1955. Chemical aspects of the fumarolic activity in Nicaragua and El Salvador. *Communicaciones del Instituto Tropical de Investigaciones Científicas, Universidad de El Salvador* 5:95–101.

———. 1956. An appraisal of the fumarolic activity near Ahuachapán, El Salvador. *Anales del Servicio Geológico de El Salvador*, bol. 2, pp. 19–32.

———. 1968. Petrochemistry of Cascade andesite volcanoes. In *Andesite Conference guidebook. Oregon Department of Geological and Mineral Industries Bulletin* 62:101–107.

Macdonald, Gordon A. 1952. The 1952 eruption of Kilauea. *Volcano Letter*, no. 518.

———. 1962. The 1959 and 1960 eruption of Kilauea Volcano, Hawaii, and the construction of walls to restrict the spread of the lava flow. *Bulletin Volcanologique*, ser. 2, 24:249–294.

———. 1972. *Volcanoes*. Englewood Cliffs, N.J.: Prentice-Hall.

Macdonald, Gordon A., and A. T. Abbott. 1970. *Volcanoes in the sea: The geology of Hawaii*. Honolulu: Hawaii University Press.

Macdonald, Gordon A., and Arturo Alcaraz. 1954. Philippine volcanoes during 1953 and early 1954. *Volcano Letter*, no. 523.

Macdonald, Gordon A., and J. R. Eaton. 1954. The eruption of Kilauea Volcano in May 1954. *Volcano Letter*, no. 524.

———. 1955. The 1955 eruption of Kilauea Volcano. *Volcano Letter*, nos. 529–530.

Macdonald, Gordon A., and R. H. Finch. 1949. The Mauna Loa eruption of January, 1949. *Volcano Letter*, no. 503.

———. 1950. The June 1950 eruption of Mauna Loa. *Volcano Letter*, no. 509.

Macdonald, Gordon A., and T. E. Gay. 1969. Geology of the Cascade Range. *Mineral Information Service, California Division of Mines and Geology* 21(7)108–111.

Macdonald, Gordon A., and D. H. Hubbard. 1970. *Volcanoes of the national parks in Hawaii*. 5th ed. Hawaii National Park: Hawaii National History Association.

Macdonald, Gordon A., and T. Katsura. 1965. Eruption of Lassen Peak in 1915. *Geological Society of America Bulletin* 76:474–882.

McDougall, Ian. 1964. Potassium-argon ages of lavas of the Hawaiian Islands. *Geological Society of America Bulletin* 75:107–128.

MacGregor, A. G. 1939. The Royal Society expedition to Montserrat, B.W.I.: The volcanic history and petrology of Montserrat with observations on Mt. Pelée in Martinique. *Philosophical Transactions of the Royal Society of London*, ser. B, 229:1–90.

———. 1951. Eruptive mechanisms: Mt. Pelée, the Soufrière of St. Vincent and the Valley of Ten Thousand Smokes. *Bulletin Volcanologique*, ser. 2, 12:49–74.

Mackin, J. H. 1960. Structural significance of Tertiary volcanic rocks in southwestern Utah. *American Journal of Science* 258:81–131.

McNitt, James R. 1960. Geothermal power. *California Division of Mines and Geology Mineral Information Series* 3(2):1–9.

———. 1968. *Geology of the Kelseyville quadrangle, California*. Map. Sheet 9. California Division of Mines and Geology.

Macrini, Giusèppe. 1699. *De Vesuvio*. Naples.

Maiuri, Amedeo. 1945. *Herculaneum*. Translated by V. Priestley. Guide-Books to Museums and Monuments in Italy, no. 53. 3d ed. Rome: Minister of Public Instruction.

———. 1951. *Pompeii*. Translated by V. Priestley. Guide-books to Museums and Monuments in Italy, no. 3. 5th ed. Rome: Minister of Public Instruction.

Malone, Stephen D., and David Frank. 1975. Increased heat emissions from Mount

Baker, Washington. *EOS: Transactions of the American Geophysical Union* 56:679–685.

Manelli, G. n.d. The soffioni of Larderello. Mimeographed report. Florence: Istituto di Chimica, University of Florence. 4 pp.

Marinatos, S. 1939. The volcanic destruction of Minoan Crete. *Antiquity* 13:425–439.

Marshall, P. 1935. Acid rocks of the Taupo-Rotorua district. *Royal Society of New Zealand Transactions* 64:323–366.

Martin, George C. 1913. The Katmai eruption. *National Geographic Magazine* 24:131–181.

Mason, Arnold C., and Helen L. Foster. 1953. Diversion of lava flows at O'Shima, Japan. *American Journal of Science* 251:249–258.

Matuyama, M. 1929. On the direction of magnetization of basalt in Japan, Tyôsen and Manchuria. *Proceedings of the Japan Imperial Academy* 5:203–225.

Mavor, James W. 1969. *Voyage to Atlantis.* New York: Putnam's.

Melmoth, William, ed. and trans. 1763. *The letters of Pliny the consul.* 5th ed. London: R. and J. Dodsley.

Menard, H. W. 1960. The East Pacific Rise. *Science* 132:1737–1746.

Mercalli, G. 1907. *I vulcani attivi della terra.* Milan: Hoepli.

Mercalli, G., O. Silvestri, G. Grablovitz, and V. Clerici. 1891. *La eruzione dell'Isola di Vulcano. Annali dell'Ufficio centrale del metèorologicae geodinamica,* pt. 4, vol. 10. A review and summary of the conclusions is given in English by G. M. Butler, Eruption of Vulcano, August 3, 1888, to March 22, 1890, *Nature* 46:117–119 (1892).

Miller, C. Dan. 1978. Holocene pyroclastic-flow deposits from Shastina and Black Butte, west of Mount Shasta, California. *U.S. Geological Survey Journal of Research* 6(5):611–624.

Miller, C. Dan, Donal R. Mullineaux, Dwight R. Crandell, and Roy A. Bailey. 1982. *Potential hazards from volcanic eruptions in the Long Valley–Mono Lakes area, east-central California and southwest Nevada. U.S. Geological Survey Circular 877.*

Minakami, Takeshi. 1956. Report on volcanic activities and volcanological studies in Japan for the period from 1951 to 1954. *Bulletin Volcanologique,* ser. 2, 18:39–55.

Mitchell, J. Murray, Jr. 1961. Recent secular changes of global temperature. *Annals of the New York Academy of Science* 95:235–250.

———. 1965. Theoretical paleoclimatology. In *Quaternary of the United States,* edited by H. E. Wright, Jr., and D. G. Frey. Princeton: Princeton University Press.

———. 1970. A preliminary evaluation of atmospheric pollution as a cause of global temperature fluctuations of the past century. In *Global effects of environmental pollution,* edited by S. Fred Singer. New York: Springer-Verlag; Holland: D. Reidel.

Mohorovičić, A. 1910. Das Beben vom 8-X-1909. In *Jahrbuch des meteorologischen Observatorium in Zagreb (Agram) für das Jahr 1909* 9(pt. 4): 1–63.

Mohr, E. C. J. 1945a. Climate and soil in the Netherlands Indies. In *Science and scientists in the Netherlands Indies,* edited by P. Hong and F. Verdoon, pp. 250–254. New York: Board of Netherlands Indies.

———. 1945b. The relation between soil and population density in the Netherlands Indies. In *Science and scientists in the Netherlands Indies,* edited by P. Hong and F. Verdoon, pp. 254–262. New York: Board of Netherlands Indies.

Moore, James G. 1967. Base surge in recent volcanic eruptions. *Bulletin Volcanologique,* ser. 2, 30:337–363.

Moore, James G., and W. G. Melson. 1969. *Nuées ardentes* of the 1968 eruption of Mayon Volcano, Philippines. *Bulletin Volcanologique,* ser. 2, 33(pt. 2):600–620.

Morgan, W. J. 1968. Rises, trenches, great faults and crustal blocks. *Journal of*

Geophysical Research 73:1959–1982.

Muffler, L. J. P., and D. E. White. 1972. Geothermal energy. *Science Teacher* 39(3): 413–452.

Mullerried, F. K. G. 1932. Der Chichon, ein bisher unbekannter taetiger Vulkan in noerdlichen Chiapas, Mexico. *Zeitschrift für Vulkanologie* 14(3):191–209.

Mullineaux, Donal R., Robert S. Sigafoos, and Elroy L. Hendricks. 1969. A historic eruption of Mount Rainier, Washington. In *Geological Survey Research, 1969. U.S. Geological Survey Professional Paper* 650-B.

Murray, Harold W. 1945. Profiles of the Aleutian Trench. *Geological Society of America Bulletin* 56:757–781.

Ninkovich, D., and Bruce C. Heezin. 1965. Santorini Tephra. In *Submarine geology and geophysics*. Colston Papers, no. 17. London: Butterworths.

Ollier, C. D., and M. C. Brown. 1965. Lava caves of Victoria. *Bulletin Volcanologique*, ser. 2, 28:215–229.

Ordóñez, Ezequiel. 1906. *Excursion du Jorullo*. Guide des excursions du X Congrès Géologique International, no. 11. Mexico City.

———. 1943. The new volcano of Parícutin. In *Inter American Intellectual Exchange*, pp. 62–78. Austin: Institute of Latin American Studies of the University of Texas.

———. 1947. *El volcán de Parícutin*. Mexico City: Editorial Fantasia, Juan M. Aguirre A.

Palmieri, L. 1873. *Incendio Vesuviano del di 26 Aprile del 1872*. *Reale Academia delle scienze* (Naples) 5(7).

Papadakis, J. 1968. Crystal Ice Caves. *Speleologist* 2(2):5–19.

Parks, James. 1910. *Geology of New Zealand*. London: Whitcombe and Tombs.

Parsons, Willard H. 1960. Kilauea speaks. *Inside Wayne* 21 (April 6).

Parsons, Willard H., and John W. Mulford. 1958. Capelinhos Volcano, Fayal Island, Azores. *Cranbrook Institute of Science Newsletter* 28(2):10–22.

Peck, D. L., et al. 1964. *Geology of the central and northern parts of the Western Cascade Range in Oregon. U.S. Geological Survey Professional Paper* 449.

Peck, D. L., J. G. Moore, and G. Kojima. 1964. Temperature in the crust and melt of the Alae lava lake, Hawaii, after the August 1963 eruption of Kilauea Volcano—a preliminary report. *U.S. Geological Survey Professional Paper* 501D:1–7.

Peck, D. L., T. L. Wright, and J. G. Moore. 1966. Crystallization of tholeiitic basalt in Alae lava lake, Hawaii. *Bulletin Volcanologique*, ser. 2, 29:629–655.

Perret, Frank A. 1907. Eruption of Stromboli, April, May and June 1907. *Brooklyn Institute Museum of Science Bulletin* 1:313–323.

———. 1924. *The Vesuvius eruption of 1906*. Carnegie Institution of Washington Publication 339. Washington, D.C.

———. 1935. *Eruption of Mt. Pelée 1929–32*. Carnegie Institution of Washington Publication 458. Washington, D.C.

———. 1950. *Volcanological observations*. Foreword by L. H. Adams. Carnegie Institution of Washington Publication 549. Washington D.C.

Peterson, Donald W. 1973. Kilauea Volcano in fifth year of eruption. U.S. Department of Interior, Geological Survey news release, July, 1973.

Peterson, Donald W., et al. In press. Recent activity of Kilauea Volcano, Hawaii. *Bulletin Volcanologique*.

Phillips, John. 1869. *Vesuvius*, Oxford: Clarendon Press.

Pirsson, L. V. 1914. Geology of Bermuda Island: The igneous platform. *American Journal of Science*, 4th ser. 38:189–206.

Playfair, John. 1822. *Collected works of John Playfair, Esq., with a memoir of the author*, 4 vols. Edinburgh: Arnold Constable.

Plinius Secundus, G. 1942. *Natural history*. With an English translation by H.

Rackham. Bk. 3, sec. 9. Loeb Classical Library. Cambridge: Harvard University Press.

Pliny the Elder. SEE Plinius Secundus, G.

Pliny the Younger. SEE Bosanquet, F. C. T., ed.; Church, Alfred, and W. J. Brodribb, trans.; Melmoth, William, ed. and trans.

Plutarchus. 1910. *Plutarch's Lives*. Translated by John Dryden; revised by Arthur H. Clough. New York: E. P. Dutton and Co.

Pocock, L. G. 1955. *The landfalls of Odysseus*. Christchurch, New Zealand: Whitcombe and Tombs. 15 pp.

———. 1957. *The Sicilian origin of the Odyssey*. Wellington: New Zealand University Press.

———. 1959. *Reality and allegory in the Odyssey*. Amsterdam: Adolph M. Hakkert.

Ponte, G. 1952. *Stromboli*. Catania: Associazione Internazionale di Vulcanologia. 14 pp.

Powers, H. A. 1960. A distinctive chemical characteristic of Snake River basalts of Idaho. *U.S. Geological Survey Professional Paper* 400B, p. 298.

Preller, C. S. DuRiche. 1924. *Italian mountain geology: Northern Italy and Tuscany*. London: Wheldon and Wesley.

Quantin, P. 1971. On the nature and fertility of volcanic ash soils derived from recent volcanic eruptions in the New Hebrides Archipelago. In *Abstracts of the 12th Pacific Scientific Congress*, vol. 1. Canberra: Australian Academy of Science.

Reck, Hans, ed. 1936. *Santorin, der Werdegang eines Inselvulkans und sein Ausbruch 1925–1928*. 3 vols. Berlin: D. Reimer, Andrews und Steiner.

Reclus, E. 1891. La terre et les hommes: Indes occidentales, Mexique, etc. In *Nouvelle géographie universelle* 17:488–489. Paris.

Reynolds, Doris L. 1954. Fluidization as a geological process, and its bearing on the problem of intrusive granites. *American Journal of Science* 252:577–614.

———. 1956. Calderas and ring-complexes. In *Verhandelingen, Geologisch-Mijnbouwkundig Genootschap*, pp. 355–379. Geologische Serie, vol. 16 (Brouwer Jubilee Volume). The Hague.

Riaño, Antonio de. 1789. Superficial y nada facultativa descripción del estado en que hallaba el volcán de Jorullo la mañana del día de 10 de marzo de 1789. *Gazeta de México* 3(30):293–297. English translation of excerpt by Hans Gadow, *Jorullo*, pp. 86–88. Cambridge: The University Press, 1930.

Riccò, A. 1907. *Sulla attività dello Stromboli dal 1891 in poi. Bollettino della Società Sismologia d'Italia*. Modena.

Richey, J. E. 1957. Birth of volcanoes: Recent eruption in the Azores. *Times Science Review* (London), Winter 1957.

Richter, C. F. 1935. An instrumental earthquake magnitude scale. *Bulletin of the Seismological Society of America* 25:1–32.

Richter, D. H., J. P. Eaton, K. J. Murata, W. U. Ault, and H. L. Krivoy. 1970. *Chronological narrative of the 1959–60 eruption of Kilauea Volcano, Hawaii. U.S. Geological Survey Professional Paper* 536E.

Riddihough, Robin P. 1978. The Juan de Fuca plate. *EOS: Transactions of the American Geophysical Union* 59:836–842.

Rittmann, A. 1929. Der Atna und seine Laven. *Naturwissenschaften* 17:94–100.

———. 1933. Die geologische bedingte Evolution und Differentiation des Somma-Vesuvmagmas. *Zeitschrift für Vulkanologie* 15:8–95.

———. 1939. Threngslaborgir-line isländische Eruptions-Spalte am Myvatn. *Natur und Volk* 69:275–289.

———. 1944. *Vulcani attività e genesi*. Naples: Editrice Politècnica.

———. 1969. Mount Etna volcanic activity. Center for Short-Lived Phenomena,

Event Card 777 (October 6). Cambridge, Mass.: Smithsonian Institution.

Rittmann, A., R. Romano, and C. Sturiale. 1971. *L'eruzione etnea dell'aprile-giugno 1971*. Istituto Internazionale di Vulcanologia, pub. 37. Cantania.

Robson, G. R., and J. F. Tomblin. 1966. *Catalogue of the active volcanoes of the world, including solfatara fields*. Pt. 20, *West Indies*. Rome: International Association of Volcanology.

Rogers, H. D., and W. B. Rogers. 1842. On the physical structure of the Appalachian chain as exemplifying the laws which have regulated the elevation of great mountain chains generally. *British Association for the Advancement of Science Report: Notices and Abstracts of Communications*, pp. 40–42. Abstract in *American Journal of Science* 43(1842):177–178.

Ross, C. S., and R. L. Smith. 1961. *Ash-flow tuffs: Their origin, geologic relations, and identification*. U.S. Geological Survey Professional Paper 366.

Rubey, William. 1951. Geologic history of the sea. *Bulletin of the Geological Society of America* 62:1111–1148.

Russell, I. C. 1902a. *Geology and water resources of the Snake River Plains of Idaho*. U.S. Geological Survey Bulletin 199.

———. 1902b. The recent volcanic eruptions in the West Indies. *National Geographic Magazine* 13:267–285.

Sapper, Karl. 1925. *Los volcanes de la América Central*. Halle (Saale): M. Niemeyer.

———. 1927. *Vulkankunde*. Stuttgart: Englehorn.

———. 1931. *Volcanology, physics of the earth*. National Research Council Bulletin 77.

Schuchert, C. 1935. *Historical geology of the Antillean-Caribbean region*. New York: John Wiley and Sons.

Scofield, John. 1958. A new volcano bursts from the Atlantic. *National Geographic Magazine* 63:735–757.

Scrope, G. Paulett. 1825. *Considerations on volcanoes*. 1st ed. London: W. Phillips.

———. 1872. *Volcanoes, the character of their phenomena, their share in the structure and composition of the surface of the globe, and their relation to its internal forces with a descriptive catalogue of all known volcanoes and volcanic formations*. 2d ed. London: Longmans, Green, Reader, and Dyer.

Segerstrom, Kenneth. 1950. Erosion studies at Parícutin, State of Michoacán, Mexico. U.S. Geological Survey Bulletin 965A:1–164.

Shand, S. J. 1938. *Earth lore*. New York: E. P. Dutton and Co.

Shapley, Harlow. 1945. On astronomical dating of the earth's crust. *American Journal of Science* 243A (Daly Volume):508–522.

Shepherd, E. S. 1938. The gases in rocks and some related problems. *American Journal of Science*, 5th ser. 35A:311–351.

Shoemaker, E. M. 1960. Penetration mechanics of high velocity meteorites, illustrated by Meteor Crater, Arizona. In *Report of the 21st International Geologic Congress*, pt. 18, pp. 418–434. Copenhagen.

Sicardi, L. 1940. Il recente ciclo dell'attività fumarolica dell'isola di Vulcano. *Bulletin Volcanologique*, ser. 2, 7:86–140.

Signore, F. 1937. La deficienza gravimetrica nella zona di Boscoreale. *Bulletin Volcanologique*, ser. 2, 2:173–182.

Sigurdsson, H., J. B. Shepherd, J. F. Tomblin, et al. 1971–1972. *The Soufrière volcanic eruption, St. Vincent Island, Caribbean Sea*. Cambridge, Mass.: Center for Short-Lived Phenomena, Smithsonian Institution.

Sigvaldason, G. E., and G. Elisson. 1968. Collection and analysis of volcanic gases at Surtsey, Iceland. *Geochimica et Cosmochimica Acta* 32:797–805.

Silvestri, S. C. 1964. Etna. *Bulletin of Volcanic Eruptions*, no. 4, pp. 7–10.

Smith, R. L. 1960. Ash flows. *Bulletin of the Geological Society of America* 71:795–842.

Smith, R. L., and R. A. Bailey. 1962. Resurgent cauldrons: Their relation to granitic ring complexes and large volume rhyolite ash flows. In *Abstracts of the International Symposium on Volcanology*, pp. 67–68. Tokyo: Science Council of Japan.

———. 1966. The Bandelier Tuff: A study of ash flow eruption cycles from zoned magma chambers. *Bulletin Volcanologique*, ser. 2, 29:83–104.

———. 1968. Resurgent cauldrons. *Geological Society of America Memoirs* 116:613–662.

Smith, William. 1816. *Strata identified by organized fossils*. London.

Snyder, G. L. 1954. *Eruption of Trident Volcano, Katmai National Monument, Alaska, February–June 1953. U.S. Geological Survey Circular 318*.

Sonder, R. A. 1937. Zur Theorie und Klassifikation der eruptiven vulkanischen Vorgange. *Geologische Rundschau* 28:499–549.

Spallanzani, Lazzaro. 1798. *Travels in the two Sicilies and some parts of the Apennines*. Translated from the original Italian. 4 vols. London: G. G. and J. Robinson.

Squier, E. G. 1850. On the volcanoes of Central America. *Proceedings of the American Association for the Advancement of Science*, New Haven meeting.

———. 1852. *Nicaragua: Its people, scenery, monuments*. New York: D. Appleton and Co.

———. 1859. Volcanoes of Central America. *Harper's New Monthly Magazine* 19: 739–763.

Stearns, Harold T. 1946. *Geology of the Hawaiian Islands*. Division of Hydrography, Territory of Hawaii, Bulletin 8. Honolulu.

———. 1963. *Geology of the Craters of the Moon National Monument, Idaho*. Craters of the Moon Natural History Association, no. 34. Arco, Idaho.

Stearns, Harold T., and Gordon A. Macdonald. 1946. *Geology and ground water resources of the Island of Hawaii*. Division of Hydrography, Territory of Hawaii, Bulletin 9. Honolulu.

Stebbins, A. K. 1960. *A special report on high altitude sampling program*. Washington, D.C.: Defense Atomic Support Agency.

Stehn, O. E. 1929. The geology and volcanism of the Krakatoa group. In *4th Pacific Science Congress guidebook*. Batavia.

Stoffel, Keith L. 1980. The May 18, 1980, eruption of Mt. St. Helens: A view from the top. *Washington State Department of Natural Resources, Division of Geology and Earth Resources, Information Circular* 71:9–11. Olympia, Washington.

Stokes, W. L. 1960. *Essentials of earth history*. Englewood Cliffs, N.J.: Prentice-Hall.

Stoppani, A. 1871–1873. *Corso di geologia*. 3 vols. Milan: G. Bernardoni e G. Brigola.

Strabo. 1854–1857. *The Geography of Strabo; literally translated with notes*. Books 1–6 translated by H. C. Hamilton, remainder by W. Falconer. London: H. G. Bohn.

Strutt, R. J. 1906. On the distribution of radium in the earth's crust, and on the earth's internal heat. *Proceedings of the Royal Society of London*, ser. A, 77:472–485.

Suess, Eduard. 1904. *The face of the earth*. Translated by H. B. C. Solas. Oxford: Clarendon Press.

Suwa, Akira. 1970. Submarine volcano Myozin-syo erupted after 10 years' repose. *Bulletin of Volcanic Eruptions*, no. 10, p. 10. Tokyo.

Swanson, D. A. 1973. Volcanology. *Geotimes* 18(1):32.

Tanner, William F. 1973. Deep-sea trenches and the compression assumption. *Bulletin of the American Association of Petroleum Geologists* 57:2195–2206.

Taylor, Frank B. 1910. Bearing of the Tertiary mountain belt in the origin of the earth's plan. *Geological Society of America Bulletin* 21:197–226.

Taylor, G. A. 1958. *The 1951 eruption of Mt. Lamington, Papua. Bulletin of the Bureau of Mineral Resources: Geology and Geophysics* (Australia), no. 38.

Tazieff, H. 1969*a*. Investigation of eruptive gases. In *Abstracts of the International Association of Volcanology and the Chemistry of the Earth's Interior Symposium on Volcanoes and Their Roots*, addendum. Oxford University.

———. 1969*b*. Mt. Etna volcanic activity. Center for Short-Lived Phenomena, Event Card 656 (July 10). Cambridge, Mass.: Smithsonian Institution.

———. 1970. Pozzuoli uplift. Center for Short-Lived Phenomena, Event Cards 915–916 (April 22); 939 (May 14). Cambridge, Mass.: Smithsonian Institution.

Thorarinsson, S. 1950. The eruption of Mt. Hekla, 1947–1948. *Bulletin Volcanologique*, ser. 2, 10:157–168.

———. 1956. *Hekla on fire*. Munich: Hanns Reich Verlag.

———. 1976*a*. *Surtsey*. New York: Viking Press.

———. 1967*b*. Iceland, Surtsey. *Bulletin of Volcanic Eruptions*, no. 7, pp. 9–10. Tokyo.

———. 1967*c*. *The eruption of Hekla, 1947–1948*. Pt. 1, *The eruption of Hekla in historic times*. Reykjavík: Societas Scientiarum Islandica.

———. 1970*a*. The Lakagigar eruption of 1783. *Bulletin Volcanologique*, ser. 2, 33:910–929.

———. 1970*b*. *Hekla: a notorious volcano*. Translated by Johann Hanesson and Pétur Karlsson. Reykjavík: Almenna Bókafélagid.

———. 1971. Hekla volcanic eruption. Center for Short-Lived Phenomena, Event Cards 1093–1094 (January 19). Cambridge, Mass.: Smithsonian Institution.

———. 1973. Helgafell volcanic eruption. Center for Short-Lived Phenomena, Event Cards 1547 (January 24); 1549 (January 26); 1551 (January 26); 1552 (January 29); 1556 (January 30); 1567 (February 13); 1569 (February 23); 1582 (March 12); 1591 (March 26). Cambridge, Mass.: Smithsonian Institution.

Thorarinsson, S., Th. Einarsson, G. Sigvaldason, and G. Elisson. 1964. The submarine eruption off the Vestmann Islands, 1963–1964. *Bulletin Volcanologique*, ser. 2, 27:435–445.

Thorkelsson, Th. 1940. *On thermal activity in Iceland and geyser action*. Reykjavík: Isafoldarprentsmidja.

Tilling, Robert I., et al. 1975. Recent eruptions of Hawaiian volcanoes and the evolution of basaltic landforms. Paper given at International Colloquium of Planetary Geology, Rome, September 22–30. To be published as an extended abstract in program.

Trask, Parker. 1943. The Mexican volcano Parícutin. *Science* 98:501–505.

Tsuya, H. 1955. Geological and petrological studies of Volcano Fuji. Pt. 5. On the 1707 eruption of Volcano Fuji. *Bulletin of the Earthquake Research Institute, University of Tokyo* 33(pt. 3): 341–393.

Umbgrove, J. H. F. 1947. *The pulse of the earth*. The Hague: Martinus Nijhoff.

———. 1950. *Symphony of the earth*. The Hague: Martinus Nijhoff.

Utilization of volcanic steam in Italy. 1924. *Nature* 113:54–55. Reprinted in *Smithsonian annual report for 1923*, pp. 519–521 (published in 1925).

Van Padang, Maur Neumann. 1951. *Catalogue of the active volcanoes of the world, including solfatara fields*. Pt. 1, *Indonesia*. Naples: International Volcanological Association.

———. 1953. *Catalogue of the active volcanoes of the world, including solfatara fields*. Pt. 11, *Philippine Islands and Cochin China*. Naples: International Volcanological Association.

Vening-Meinesz, F. A., J. H. F. Umbgrove, and P. H. Kuenen. 1934. *Gravity expeditions at sea, 1923–1932*, vol. 2. Delft: Netherlands Geodetic Commission.

Verbeek, R. D. M. 1886. *Krakatau*. Batavía: Imprimerie de l'Etat.

Verhoogen, Jean. 1937. Mount St. Helens, a recent Cascade volcano. *California University Department of Geological Sciences Bulletin* 24(9):263–302.

Verhoogen, John, Francis J. Turner, Lionel E. Weiss, Clyde Wahrhaftig, and William S. Fyfe. 1970. *The earth*. New York: Holt, Rinehart and Winston.

Vine, F. J. 1969. Sea-floor spreading—new evidence. *Journal of Geological Education* 17(1):6–16.

Vine, F. J., and D. H. Mathews. 1963. Magnetic anomalies over oceanic ridges. *Nature* 199:947–949.

Vonsen, M. 1946. Minerals at The Geysers, Sonoma County, California. *California Journal of Mines and Geology* 42(3):287–293.

Wadati, K. 1928. On shallow and deep earthquakes. *Geophysical Magazine* 1:162–202. Tokyo.

Washington, H. S. 1917. Persistence of vents at Stromboli. *Geological Society of America Bulletin* 28:249–278.

Wegener, Alfred. 1966. *The origin of continents and oceans*. Translated by John Biram from the German 4th ed. (1929). New York: Dover.

Wexler, Harry. 1952. Volcanoes and world climate. *Scientific American* 186(4):74–80.

White, D. E. 1965. *Geothermal energy*. U.S. Geological Survey Circular 519.

———. 1973. Characteristics of geothermal resources. In *Geothermal energy*, edited by Paul Kruger and Carel Otte, pp. 69–94. Stanford: Stanford University Press.

Wilcox, Ray E. 1947. Activity of Parícutin Volcano from December 1, 1946, to March 31, 1947. *Transactions of the American Geophysical Union* 28:725–731.

———. 1954. Petrology of Parícutin Volcano, Mexico. *U.S. Geological Survey Bulletin* 965C:281–349.

Williams, Howel. 1932a. The history and character of volcanic domes. *University of California at Berkeley Publications, Bulletin of the Department of Geological Science* 21:51–146.

———. 1932b. Mount Shasta, a Cascade volcano. *Journal of Geology* 40:417–429.

———. 1932c. Geology of the Lassen Volcanic National Park, California. *University of California Publications in Geological Sciences* 21(8):195–385.

———. 1941a. Calderas and their origin. *University of California Publications, Bulletin of the Department of Geological Science* 25:239–346.

———. 1941b. Volcanology. In *Geology, 1888–1938*, pp. 367–390. Geological Society of America, 50th Anniversary Volume. New York.

———. 1945. Geologic setting of Parícutin Volcano. *Transactions of the American Geophysical Union* 26:255–256.

———. 1950. Volcanoes of the Parícutin region, Mexico. *U.S. Geological Survey Bulletin* 965B:165–279.

———. 1952. The great eruption of Coseguina, Nicaragua, in 1835. *University of California Publications in Geological Science* 29(2):21–46.

Williams, Howel, G. W. Curtis, and R. W. Juhle. 1956. Mt. Katmai and the Valley of Ten Thousand Smokes (a new interpretation of the great eruption of 1912). In *Proceedings of the Eighth Pacific Science Congress, Philippines, 1953* 2:129.

Williams, Richard S., Jr., and James G. Moore. 1973. Iceland chills a lava flow. *Geotimes* 18(8):14–17.

Wilson, J. T. 1963a. A possible origin of the Hawaiian Islands. *Canadian Journal of Physics* 41:863–870.

———. 1963b. Continental drift. *Scientific American* 208(4):86–100.

———. 1965. A new class of faults and their bearing on continental drift. *Nature* 207:343–347.

Wise, William S. 1968. Geology of the Mount Hood Volcano. In *Andesite Conference guidebook. Oregon Department of Geological and Mineral Industries Bulletin* 62:81–98.

———. 1969. Geology and petrology of the Mt. Hood area: A study of High Cascade volcanism. *Geological Society of America Bulletin* 80:969–1006.

Wolff, F. von. 1914–1931. *Der Vulkanismus*. Stuttgart: Von Ferdinand Enke.

Wyllie, P. 1972. Earthquakes and continental drift. *University of Chicago Magazine* 64:12–27.

Yokoyama, I. 1956. Energetics in active volcanoes, 1st paper. *Bulletin of the Earthquake Research Institute, University of Tokyo* 34:185–195.

————. 1957. Energetics in active volcanoes, 2d and 3d papers. *Bulletin of the Earthquake Research Institute, University of Tokyo* 35:75–106.

Zen, M. T., and D. Hadikusumo. 1965. The future danger of Mt. Kelut (eastern Java, Indonesia). *Bulletin Volcanologique*, ser. 2, 28:275–282.

Zies, E. G. 1924. The fumarolic incrustations in the Valley of Ten Thousand Smokes. *National Geographic Society Contributed Technical Papers*, Katmai Series 1(3): 157–179.

————. 1929. The Valley of Ten Thousand Smokes. *National Geographic Society Contributed Technical Papers*, Katmai Series 1(4):1–79.

Zittel, Karl F. von. 1901. *History of geology and paleontology*. Translated by Marie M. Ogilvie-Gordon. London: Walter Scott.

Index